FRÉMONT

Pathmarker of the West

JOHN CHARLES FRÉMONT, THE FIRST UNITED STATES SENATOR
FROM CALIFORNIA, 1850

FREMONT

Pathmarker of the West

By ALLAN NEVINS

"Down the edges, through the passes, up the mountains steep"

University of Nebraska Press
Lincoln and London

First Bison Book printing: 1992
Most recent printing indicated by the last digit below:
10   9   8   7   6   5   4   3   2   1

Library of Congress Cataloging-in-Publication Data
Nevins, Allan, 1890–1971.
Fremont, pathmarker of the West / by Allan Nevins.
p.   cm.
Includes bibliographical references and index.
ISBN 0-8032-8364-4
1. Frémont, John Charles, 1813–1890.   2. Explorers—United
States—Biography.   3. Generals—United States—Biography.   4.
Presidential candidates—United States—Biography.   I. Title.
E415.9.F8N46   1992
973.6092—dc20
[B]
91-40734   CIP

⊗

Preface

IN 1926, when a young newspaperman on the editorial staff of the New York *World*, I met Major Frank P. Frémont, who possessed a fragmentary collection of his parents' papers, the larger part of which had been destroyed in the burning of a warehouse. As a friendship with William *.* Ghent had aroused my interest in Trans-Mississippi history, *I* gladly embraced the opportunity of using these papers for a long overdue life (no biography having appeared since 1856) of John C. Frémont.

This was published in 1928 under the title of *Frémont, the West's Greatest Adventurer*. It emphasized the romantic aspects of Frémont's career; probably overemphasized them, though no less a person than Willa Cather wrote me that the color and adventure of the story had delighted her. Eleven years later, the book, chastened in style and much enlarged in content, was reissued as *Frémont: Pathmarker of the West*. I am now happy in the opportunity of a third edition. Needless to say, if I were to write the biography completely anew, it would be with a marked difference of approach. A careful restudy of the edition of 1939, however, has revealed remarkably little which demands change. With a number of corrections, which I have duly made, and a few textual alterations, it can well stand. I have added a long final chapter containing such additional information on Frémont as I could gain over the years, and a bibliography of his writings.

Frémont, as I hope this book shows, is a singularly interesting subject; he had a personality brilliant, versatile, and adventurous, and his career abounded in almost melodramatic alternations of good and bad fortune. Topographer, explorer, writer, political leader, general, railroad planner, he touched history at many points; controversy sprang up all along his path; he aroused enthusiastic loyalty and violent antagonism.

An illegitimate child, reared by an impoverished widow, he began life under many disadvantages. But his personal charm, quickness of mind, and courage won him the friendship of Joel R. Poinsett and other influential men, and after he gained the hand of Thomas Hart Benton's gifted daughter his advancement was rapid. His traits of impulsiveness, intrepidity, endurance, and rashness were the source both of striking successes and dismaying failures. Such a career can be understood only when studied in terms of environment, historical forces, and psychology. This fact, I believe, justifies the detail of the biography.

The picturesqueness of Frémont's history should not obscure the fact that it abounds in difficulties. To tell even a plain story of his travels, as I wrote in an earlier preface, is not easy. The narrator has to do justice to Frémont's exploration of the Great Basin without injustice to Jedediah Smith, who crossed it north and south, east and west; has to avoid getting lost in that tangled mountainous area of southern Colorado in which Frémont himself once got lost; has to make it plain that the same stream could be successively Mary's River, Ogden's River, and Humboldt River; has to find what Frémont meant by Tulare Lake Fork when the lake does not fork; has to distinguish Las Vegas, Nevada, from Las Vegas, Utah; has to choose between different spellings in Pit River and Pitt River, Cochetopa Pass and Chocetopa Pass; has to know that the Moapa and Digger Indians were the same; and has to learn that Frémont's "opal" arrowheads were probably obsidian. Beyond all this lie the great controversies: that over the Gillespie message and Frémont's course in California in 1846; that over the Kearny quarrel; that over the Missouri campaign in 1861; and that over Frémont's withdrawal from the presidential race in 1864. In these I have made an effort to state the facts with impartiality and fullness.

The impetuous Frémont was often his own worst enemy; he tried, moreover, to shine in too many fields, and by undertaking tasks for which he was ill-equipped courted not only failure, but a charge of false pretensions. He should have kept mainly in the field of geography and exploration. But his reputation suffered also from circumstances not his own fault. He was caught in 1846 in a cruel dilemma: whether he took his well-armed force back home from the Pacific, or kept it in California to watch and assist the movement toward war, he was sure to be harshly censured. In the Civil War he suffered heavily from the enmity of West Pointers. They were jealous of all non-professional generals; they had disliked him ever since the Kearny quarrel; and two West Point subordinates, Sturgis and Pope, were more anxious to see Frémont fail than to hasten Confederate defeat. Lincoln's biographers Nicolay and Hay, too, gave a biased version of the Lincoln-Frémont differences which has been too uncritically followed by later writers. As W. T. Sherman said, those commanders were lucky who did not get high posts too soon; and Frémont, sharing the fate of McDowell, McClellan, and Buell, has had less justice than they. Operating in a most difficult theater both politically and militarily, neglected by the Eastern command, and suffering from the selfish demands of the Blair clan, he made a record of positive achievement which the *Official Records*, the news-papers, and the statements of many fair observers fully estab-lish, and which must be studied alongside his fatal mistakes.

Once more, it is necessary to thank a few of the many people who have aided me in this book. At the head of the list must stand two members of the Frémont family, the late Major Frank P. Frémont and Mrs. Henry Hull, son and grand-daughter of the explorer; and two eminent authorities in West-ern history, now dead, W. J. Ghent and Frederick S. Dellen-baugh. I owe much also to Mr. R. L. Underhill of California; Mr. Leroy R. Hafen of Colorado; Professors Herbert E. Bolton and Herbert I. Priestley of the University of California; Mr. H. J. Eckenrode and Mrs. Mary Newton Stanard of Virginia; Dr. J. H. Easterby of South Carolina; Dr. W. E. Smith of Miami University; and the staffs of the Huntington Library and the Library of Congress.

ALLAN NEVINS

Columbia University, November 1, 1954

Contents

Illustrations

I

Charleston Boyhood

ABOUT John Charles Frémont's cradle hung as dark clouds as have surrounded the infancy of any notable American—the clouds of illegitimacy, poverty, and total uncertainty of the future. In his veins ran the blood of a strange and far from auspicious union; the union of an impulsive, warm-hearted, and wilful Virginia girl, and of a roving, adventurous, erratic French émigré. His earliest years were spent in wanderings from state to state, town to town, with his parents; from Georgia to Tennessee, from Virginia to South Carolina.

All this was a fitting overture to one of the stormiest, the most erratic, and the most adventurous of American careers. There are two great elements of interest in Frémont's biography. One lies simply in the unfailing drama of his life; a life romantically wrought out of the fiercest tempests and most radiant bursts of sunshine. From birth to death fortune gave him one sustained adventure. His fate carried him along our wildest frontiers, into the clash of national ambitions in the Far West, up to the higher reaches of party politics, through the thick of the Civil War, and into the thorniest jungles of post-bellum finance. It was no mean destiny. To explore more of the West than any other single man, to be a leading figure in the conquest of California, to be the first candidate of a great party for the Presidency, to pen a book that helped in molding now-populous communities, to rise from poverty to millions and sink to poverty again, to leave a name written across the geography of one-third of the continent—this constitutes an absorbing story. It tells us much of the United

States as well as of Frémont. The conditions which made so flamboyant a career possible were as remarkable as the man, and are well worth pondering. And merely as a spectacle, we can rejoice in the scope and color of the story; for be assured, no spectacle of *that* kind will Americans ever see again. Whether we dislike or like the man, whether we applaud or condemn his acts (and it has been as difficult to remain neutral about him as about Mary Queen of Scots or Alexander Hamilton or Andrew Jackson), his life will always touch our imagination.

The other interest in Frémont's career is provided by its element of psychological mystery. How could the man who sometimes succeeded so dazzlingly at other times fail so abysmally? How can we account for his dizzy alternations of triumph and disaster? Sometimes he snatched victory from the direst perils; sometimes Fortune came bearing her amplest gifts on a golden platter, and as he touched them they turned to apples of Sodom. How can we explain the love of Kit Carson and the hatred of Stephen W. Kearny? How explain that Horace Greeley thought him fitter than Lincoln to be President in 1864, while others thought him unfit to be governor of Arizona Territory? Part of this psychological problem is undoubtedly to be solved by reference to his ancestry: to his inheritance of impulsiveness as well as brilliancy from emotional and ill-balanced parents. Part of the explanation is to be sought in his early training. His upbringing was singularly adapted to heighten the venturesome, heedless, self-reliant traits which the precocious boy inherited, and singularly wanting in the discipline which his ardent spirit and quick mind most needed.

On his parentage, as we have said, falls a dark shadow. Our history begins with an intrigue and elopement which in 1811 produced a furor of excitement in Richmond, Virginia. The Virginia capital was at this time, on the eve of the War of 1812, a vigorous, attractive town of six or seven thousand people, one-third of them Negroes, another third artisans, shop-keepers, and truck-gardeners, and the remainder people of means living in handsome brick houses on the well-shaded hills overlooking the James. It was a commercial and industrial center of importance, exporting tobacco, milling flour, and importing goods for distribution through the Upper South. On Shockoe Hill stood the homes of Chief Justice Marshall, Bishop Moore, Colonel Edward Carrington, Thomas Ritchie the editor of the *Enquirer,* and Judge Philip N. Nicholas; on Gamble Hill stood the homes of William Wirt, later Attorney-General, and William H. Cabell. Such great figures as Jefferson and Madison sometimes appeared; while Monroe was now governor. The embargo and Napoleonic Wars had diminished Richmond's prosperity. But it was still an aristocratic town, a Federalist stronghold, with much wealth and conservatism; the life of its patrician society was enlivened by balls, theatrical performances, receptions, and hunt-meetings. Legislative sessions brought land-speculators and canal-promoters flocking in, and were marked by angry battles of sections and parties —Feds, Republicans, and Quids. Though the time and town were strait-laced, Virginia blood ran hotly enough to furnish passionate courtships, deadly rivalries, intrigues, and duels; and from an illicit and tempestuous love affair sprang John C. Frémont.

Between Byrd and Arch Streets, overlooking the falls of the James, lived old Major John Pryor and his young wife. Mrs. Pryor, according to records of the time, was a spirited and beautiful young woman, the picture of animation and energy. Her family was well known in Tidewater Virginia. She had been Anne Beverley Whiting, youngest daughter among the twelve children of Colonel Thomas Whiting, a large landowner of Gloucester County, and at one time a leading member of the House of Burgesses.[1] He had died in Anne's early childhood, and her mother had married a man named Carey, who soon ran through most of the widow's estate. Anne

---

[1] *Virginia Magazine of History and Biography,* XXII, p. 131; XXXIII, p. 203.

had been brought up by a married sister, and apparently knew
the bitterness of the bread of charity. In 1796, when she was
seventeen, her charms attracted the Revolutionary veteran
John Pryor. Evidently her sister was anxious to be rid of her,
while other relatives brought pressure to bear; and to escape
her poverty she married a man certainly old enough to be her
father.[2] It could hardly have been a marriage of love, for her
husband was past middle life, gouty, and—according to family
tradition—of decaying physical powers. It is significant that
they had no children.

Yet John Pryor was a man of character and force, who had
made himself well known throughout the state. He had fought
under Washington, had been a very energetic Commissary-
General of Military Stores for Virginia in the last critical years
of the Revolution, and had become vice-president of the Virginia
Society of the Cincinnati when that post held a certain distinction.[3] Every Virginian knew his livery-stable, the largest in the
capital, where travelers could have their horses "elegantly
nicked for a guinea each," with "cropping and foxing in the
latest styles," and "all manner of farriery."[4] Horse-racing was
one of the most passionately followed of southern sports. Pryor
had been a leader in organizing it—a secretary of the Jockey
Club, a familiar figure at races, and a shrewd judge of horse-
flesh. He had also the reputation of a town wit. To augment his
income, he owned the principal recreation park of the town,
some two acres bounded by Arch, Byrd, Seventh, and Eighth
Streets, called the Haymarket Garden; an attractive green spot
where citizens could escape the dust, indulge in ices, punch, and
cake, and sometimes listen to music while watching the rapids
of the James. Mrs. Pryor doubtless helped to supervise it. The
Major's house was a modest structure built in a common
Southern style, with living quarters in the center, and two long

---

[2] *Journal,* House of Delegates, 1811-12, p. 29.

[3] For various state services performed by Pryor see *Virginia Calendar of
State Papers,* II, III, *passim;* V, p. 128; VII, p. 503; VIII, p. 320*ff.;* IX,
p. 88*ff.*

[4] Mary N. Stanard, *Richmond, Its People and Its Story,* p. 55.

narrow wings which connected it with kitchen and pantry at one extremity, and with servants' quarters at the other.[5] The Pryors held a respected place in the middle stratum of Richmond society.

Unfortunately for the Major, about 1810 his wife, doubtless long since rather tired of her fast-ageing husband, became acquainted with a handsome French émigré named Charles Frémon, lately arrived in the capital. We are told that he was a dark, slender man, with fine features and much distinction of manner. His life had been packed with adventure. Born in a village near Lyons, he had identified himself with the Royalists during the French Revolution and had been compelled to take passage on a French ship to Santo Domingo. Here he hoped to find refuge with an aunt. On the Atlantic his vessel was captured by an English cruiser and taken into one of the British West Indies, where Frémon and other prisoners were interned. A protracted captivity followed. But being allowed the freedom of the island, he supplemented his prisoner's allowance by making basketware, doing cabinet work and upholstery, and painting frescoes upon the ceilings of the better houses. Evidently he had some artistic capacity, and a manual dexterity which his son later inherited. In time he was released, and arrived in Norfolk, Virginia, penniless and friendless, but undaunted. French refugees were then numerous in the United States, and the Francophile Republicans of the southern and middle states held them in high favor. Frémon was promptly taken into the best circles in Tidewater Virginia. He gave lessons in French, and perhaps continued his frescoing. Finding Virginia agreeable and seeing Europe scourged by war, he gradually surrendered his original design of returning to France. William and Mary College employed him for a time, but he left it to join the staff of a Richmond school kept by the well-known scholar, Jefferson's friend, Louis Girardin.[6]

---

[5] Richmond *Dispatch*, July 8, 1856.

[6] John Bigelow, *Life and Public Services of John Charles Frémont*, p. 12. Family tradition holds that the name was always Frémont. But the patronymic

In 1809, Frémon was teaching in Girardin's academy, one of the best-known in the South, as chief assistant to Girardin and his partner, David Doyle. It speaks well for him that he was employed by so reputable an establishment. But he was of irregular habits and wilful, impulsive nature. He was soon known to be living in a house "on the Hill" with a woman not his wife, and when he defied his superiors, Doyle had him summarily dismissed.[7] However, he remained popular in the town. When John Wood soon afterward became Girardin's partner, he was reëmployed, Wood remarking that "Richmond people do not care much about these things." No doubt he was still received in the best houses. After the break-up of his old ménage he went to live in a cottage of Major Pryor's at the Haymarket; he began, according to one story, to teach Mrs. Pryor French, and their friendship quickly ripened into intimacy.

Mrs. Pryor, now past thirty, saw her youth slipping away; her husband was growing old, but he was sufficiently vigorous later to take an active part in the War of 1812, and he might live long. The attachment between her and the ardent young Frémon was watched with sympathetic interest by several friends. Mrs. Pryor had with her a niece, Kitty Cowne, who disliked the rather vulgar, horsey old livery-stable keeper, and encouraged the love affair. Frémon had a fellow-refugee named John Lataste, who had lived with him at the Haymarket for a time, and whom he made a confidant. He often discussed his intrigue with Mrs. Pryor with Lataste, and told him they had agreed to wait for Pryor's death and then be married.[8] But their conduct was so indiscreet that it soon aroused Pryor's suspicions.

Early in July, 1811, the inevitable explosion occurred. In the presence of Frémon and Kitty Cowne, the enraged husband

---

Frémon is not uncommon in France; and his friend Lataste spells the name Frémon in a sworn deposition, as Girardin does in repeated newspaper advertisements. For his service with William and Mary College, see R. B. Osborne, "The Professional Biography of Moncure Robinson," *William and Mary College Quarterly*, Second Series, Vol. I (1921), pp. 237-260.

[7] Letter by Doyle in Virginia *Patriot*, August 23, 1811.

[8] MS deposition by Lataste, December 3, 1811, Virginia State Library.

taxed Mrs. Pryor with flagrant misconduct and even threatened to erase the blot on his honor by killing her. She drew herself up, blazing with anger, and told him: "You may spare yourself the crime. I shall leave your house to-morrow morning forever!" [9] Frémon was with difficulty restrained from assaulting the Major. He told Lataste that he would kill Pryor or anybody else who tried to interfere with their immediate elopement, or to maltreat Mrs. Pryor on his account. On the morning of July 10th the pair left Richmond in the stage for Williamsburg, Mrs. Pryor taking her personal belongings and two slaves. Kitty Cowne's father came to remove her from the Haymarket; the Major was left alone, while Richmond rang with the scandal. It almost disrupted the school of poor Girardin, who had to make profuse explanations that he had been unaware of Frémon's misconduct.

The intrigue and elopement constituted an offense far too grave for the Virginia society of those days to forget or forgive. Mrs. Pryor and Frémon had no wish to tarry in Williamsburg or Norfolk longer than was necessary to gather together what property she possessed there. At the earliest possible moment they set out southward. A family tradition, given to John Bigelow almost fifty years later, stated that their joint capital was sufficient to gratify Frémon's wish to tour the South and learn something of the habits of the Indians, in which he felt a keen interest; that they took their own horses, carriage, and servants, and began a quasi-scientific tour. This may be true, for Mrs. Pryor had inherited just a year previously from her father's estate, long involved in litigation, slaves valued at $2,400, and possibly other means; [10] while Frémon was an improvident man. But the story seems a dubious bit of gilding. It is probable that Frémon moved from town to town finding work as teacher of French, fresco-painter, upholsterer, or dancing-master, and it is certain that their means were soon straitened.

[9] Statement by Mrs. Mary Mead Burrill, John Bigelow MSS.
[10] MS Records, Richmond Superior Court of Chancery, June 13, 1810.

Family tradition, as recorded by Bigelow, also asserts that the Virginia legislature promptly passed an act divorcing Major Pryor and his wife—for the legislature alone could grant divorces—and that the two soon remarried, the Major with his housekeeper, and Mrs. Pryor with Frémon. But this tradition is plainly inaccurate. When Major Pryor made petition for a divorce, the legislature refused it December 11, 1811. No reasons appear on the record, but the refusal makes it seem probable that the Major also had been guilty of misconduct, or had grossly maltreated his wife. A search of subsequent legislative proceedings fails to reveal any record of favorable action. Certainly no divorce had been granted when on January 21, 1813, the boy John Charles Frémon (t) was born in Savannah, whither Frémon and Mrs. Pryor had traveled by way of Charleston. He was of illegitimate birth—as illegitimate as Erasmus, or Alexander Hamilton, or many another man whose parents had united in a permanent union without benefit of clergy.

If Mrs. Pryor actually had $2,400 when they left Williamsburg in midsummer of 1811, most of that sum had been dissipated before they reached Savannah in early October. For Frémon immediately began advertising in the *Columbian Museum* of Savannah for pupils in French, while Mrs. Pryor was eager for boarders at the house they occupied "in the rear of the residence of Charles Howard," then one of Savannah's most prominent citizens. Evidently few cared for private French lessons; for several weeks later Frémon is found as teacher and dancing-master in the service of J. B. LeRoy, who announced the reopening of his Savannah academy with the émigré as his assistant. For the next two years, as advertisements in the city papers show, the pair depended upon his teaching and her labors as boarding-house mistress. After a time they took up their home in a two-story-and-basement building of warm red brick in what was then the Yamacraw section (now 563-565 West Bay Street); a house that, with heavy basement pillars, a door and four front windows on the first floor, and five large windows on the second, still stands. It was the property of the Gibbons family, to whom the land had been granted by George II in 1760. To-day Yamacraw has deteriorated and is largely given over to Negroes; but at this time it was the home of families of good social position, and Frémon was in convenient access to those who could afford lessons in French and dancing. In this Gibbons house John C. Frémont first saw the light. In fancy we can picture the baby boy in the arms of a Negro nurse, sunning on West Bay or the neighboring West Broad—wide, sandy, sleepy streets, lined with comfortable residences and large gardens, where life passed drowsily.[11]

In 1813 the family again took up its travels. Perhaps Savannah failed to offer sufficient pupils; perhaps the parents merely wished to take their baby away from the summer heat of Georgia. At any rate, another family tradition declares that this summer the orbit of the infant Frémont impinged momentarily upon that of a statesman with whose later career his own was to be so closely bound, Thomas Hart Benton. The Frémons (the "t" was not yet added) were staying at the huge rambling City Hotel at Nashville, Tennessee, when on September 4, 1813, they witnessed a memorable episode. Among other guests were Benton, then a fiery young frontier colonel, lawyer, and legislator of Tennessee, and his brother Jesse. Suddenly there arrived at the Nashville Inn just across the square no less a personage than General Andrew Jackson, with the laurels of his march from Natchez to Nashville to meet the Creeks still upon him, the laurels of New Orleans still to be won; making the building ring with his commands, and receiving the cheers of the townsfolk. A feud had been smoldering between Jackson and the two Bentons. It had originated in a trifle: Jackson had served as second to an opponent of Jesse Benton's in a duel, and when Thomas Hart had heard of this he had angrily assailed Jackson for conducting the affair in a "savage" and "base" manner. The Indian-fighter had then sworn to horse-

[11] Contemporaneous Savannah newspapers; see also article by Thomas Gamble, Savannah *Press,* March 20, 1928.

whip Benton on sight. The quarrel was an opera bouffe episode, all the more ironically ludicrous because in later years Benton became one of Jackson's stanchest supporters. But an encounter now occurred at the City Hotel which might have been tragic. Blows and shots were exchanged; Jackson was carried away with his left shoulder shattered by a ball from Jesse Benton's pistol, so that he soaked two mattresses with blood and for a time seemed near death; Thomas Hart Benton pitched headlong down a flight of stairs, and other combatants—for the mêlée became extensive—were slightly injured.[12] The parents of little John Charles heard the uproar, and it is said that a bullet passed through their room. In the turbulent South of that day they were doubtless used to such affrays.

The Frémons tarried in Nashville until a second child, a daughter, was born. Soon thereafter they removed to Norfolk, Virginia. Apparently by this time Pryor was dead, they could and doubtless did legally marry, and the scandal was laid to rest. Mrs. Frémon had relatives near-by, and her husband had a brother named Francis. We know nothing of their life during the next few years. Another son was born, of whom we shall hear but little. Then, in or about 1818, the émigré himself passed away.[13] He had lived but seven years after his union with Mrs. Pryor, and given her little but poverty and hardship. Francis Frémon was on the point of returning to his native land with his family, and proposed that Mrs. Pryor accompany him. But she would hear nothing of such an exile, for she was resolved to remain an American. She lived for a time at Dinwiddie Courthouse, where young John Charles—called "Charley"—received his first instruction. Then, with an income too pinched to make life among her old neighbors comfortable, she removed to Charleston. Here after the passage of a few years the daughter died, leaving only the two sons.

Our first real glimpse of John Charles Frémont is thus caught

---

[12] Marquis James, *Andrew Jackson,* pp. 152-154; Theodore Roosevelt, *Thomas Hart Benton,* p. 28; John Bigelow, *Frémont,* p. 22.
[13] Bigelow, *Frémont,* p. 23.

when he was a school-boy in the old city on the banks of the Ashley and Cooper; a city which, though counting fewer than twenty thousand people, boasted no little wealth, culture, and social gaiety. It was an ideal place for a lad of Frémont's lively, adventurous temperament. The French Huguenots made him feel his paternal blood an advantage, not a liability. The placid, genial life offered much to enjoy. Stately residences stretched away from the outskirts of the town—Drayton Hall, Middleton Place, Greenfield, Hampton, the Elms, and others; a bustling trade in cotton, rice, indigo, and other staples, largely in the hands of foreigners, kept the business district active. Every May the more affluent planters of the lowlands, fleeing the pestilential heat of their inland estates, came to town to enjoy its sea-breezes. They returned home when the first frosts fell in November, killing the malaria, but many of them were back in town shortly after Christmas—by the end of January. This was the "gay season" beloved by young people. It included the concerts and ball of the St. Cecilia Society, the dancing assemblies, the Philharmonic concerts, the Jockey Ball, and the races. Race week was a carnival period; planters then thronged to town, the traders stopped their business, and all the men talked horses and laid bets over their juleps. Negroes abounded, for it was a poor planter or merchant who did not keep a half dozen servants in attendance upon his stables, table, and household; their merry chatter filled the streets, and their songs echoed from the wharves, covered with imported luxuries and West Indian products—barrels of molasses, bags of coffee, cocoanuts, and bananas—as well as Carolina staples. Those who wished to drink and gamble had ample opportunity; but accredited persons who sought a refined society could find really intellectual circles, for the old families—the Rutledges, Haynes, Pinckneys, Pringles, Hugers, Middletons, and others—prided themselves upon their books and ideas as well as plate, furniture, and Madeira.

Young Frémont was the son of a poor widow, who probably still took boarders for her support; and in this city of sharply drawn class lines he could not have moved in the best circles until his brilliancy of mind attracted attention. South Carolinians doubtless knew the claims of the Whitings and Beverleys of Virginia to social distinction—they knew that Mrs. Frémont's line had been allied with Washington's. Charleston was never harshly puritanical, and many of its people would have sympathized with her tragic elopment. The Revolution had made only too many of the best Charleston families poverty-stricken themselves. Nevertheless, the moral canons of the Episcopalian city would have caused many who heard Mrs. Frémont's story to look at her askance. She soon became a member of St. Philip's Church, for she was a pious woman,[14] and at sixteen, in 1829, Frémont himself was confirmed in this church. Indeed, we are told that until he was fourteen he was educated in the expectation that he would become an Episcopal minister. At St. Philip's and elsewhere it is probable that the Frémont family saw some of the most interesting people of Charleston without being part of their group.

But the boy soon began to make friends. He grew up wonderfully agile and hardy of body, active of mind and, with his dark hair, olive skin, penetrating blue eyes, and chiseled features, a very handsome lad. Charleston had no more attractive youngster than "Charley" Frémont. Every one befriended him. When he finished his early schooling, his mother, hoping that he could master a profession and earn a living at the same time, accepted John W. Mitchell's offer to give him a clerkship in his law office. But Mitchell was struck by the boy's quick mind, ardent temperament, taste for good literature, and instinctive refinement. The original plan to fit him for the pulpit was better, he decided, than training for the bar. Frémont then had, and kept throughout life, a decided religious conviction, which of course contributed to the decision. In pursuance of the idea, Mitchell met the cost of sending John Charles at fourteen—that is, in 1827—to a preparatory school kept by Dr. Charles Robertson, a Scot who had been educated at the University of

14 Henry Ward Beecher, New York *Tribune*, July 4, 1856.

Edinburgh, and who specialized in preparing boys for Charleston College. Years later Robertson recalled the impression that Frémont had made upon him when he entered. He was a youth of "middle size, graceful in manners, rather slender, but well formed, and upon the whole what I should call handsome; of a keen piercing eye and a noble forehead, seemingly the very seat of genius." [15] It was a stroke of fortune for Frémont's intellectual growth that he was thrown into early association with so learned and sympathetic a man.

In this school the boy first exhibited his quickness of apprehension, the rapidity of his progress astonishing his masters. Upon entrance, he knew only the rudiments of Latin; Robertson undertook to instruct him in that tongue, in Greek, and in mathematics, so that he could quickly matriculate at the college. He seemed, as Robertson said later, to master the ancient languages by intuition. In no time he was at the head of the class in Cæsar, and showed an equal excellence in Greek. Within a year he had read Cæsar, Nepos, Sallust, Horace, half of Virgil, two books of Livy, and four books of the *Iliad*. "Whatsoever he read," writes Robertson, "he retained." The retention was certainly not permanent, for there is little evidence in Frémont's writings of classical culture, and none at all of a taste in his busy later life for classical studies. But it is clear that the richness and novelty of the ancient writers, and the keen interest which Robertson showed in his progress, stimulated his mind. Robertson even found a "genius for poetic composition" in the boy— and we shall note later how some truly poetic phrases by Frémont have embedded themselves in the history of the West.

Such was his precocity that at the end of about two years' study, when only sixteen, he was able to enter Charleston College in the junior class. His work began on or about May 1, 1829, that marking the commencement of the college term. The institution was just being lifted to true collegiate grade by its new head, the Reverend Jasper Adams, formerly of Brown University; its curriculum emphasized mathematics, the classics,

and religion—one out of every four of the early graduates went
into the ministry.[16] In 1830 Frémont was one of the sixty-two
students enrolled in the college classes. He showed a particular
aptitude for mathematics—and this knowledge he always did
retain. Dr. Robertson tells us he liked to pore over his volumes
of the Greek dramatists in their beautiful Edinburgh print.[17]
Applying himself hard, he seemed for a time the pattern of an
enthusiastic scholar. But he had more enthusiasm than scholar-
liness. His devotion to study displayed the zest and curiosity
of the future explorer, not the application of a future savant.
Greek especially, he wrote later, "had a mysterious charm, as if
behind the strange characters belonging to an ancient world I
was to find things of wonderful interest." Robertson suspected
that it was love of novelty and intellectual inquisitiveness, not
sober devotion to learning, which inspired the lad. "When I
contemplated his bold, fearless disposition," he writes, "his
powerful inventive genius, his admiration of warlike exploits,
and his love of heroic and adventurous deeds, I did not think
it likely he would be a minister of the gospel." His classmates
noted that he was taciturn and reserved, but of brilliant mind; [18]
and they soon perceived also that qualities of restlessness, in-
stability, and rashness, were allied with his brilliancy.

For about nine months Frémont's diligent application to his
college studies continued. Then early in 1830 he was given
leave of absence to go to the country and teach, probably as
tutor in the household of some wealthy planter. He returned
at the beginning of April, and after some delay—his books not
having arrived with him—resumed his studies.[19] For a time
following this interruption all continued well. In the "Scientific
Department" (for now all thought of the pulpit or law had
ended) he held a high place among his classmates, who included
such scions of leading Charleston families as C. C. Pinckney,

[16] J. H. Easterby, *A History of the College of Charleston, passim;* David
D. Wallace, *History of South Carolina,* III, pp. 24, 41.

[17] John Charles Frémont, *Memoirs of My Life,* I, p. 19.

[18] Charleston *News and Courier,* July 15, 1890.

[19] MS. Faculty Journal, weekly record.

Theodore Grimké, Josiah Huger, and Nelson Mitchell. But Frémont had become a little spoiled. He learned too easily; he yielded too readily to his love of novelty and excitement. We must always remember the strange mixture of blood which flowed in his veins—his descent from an impulsive, high-spirited Virginia girl and from a Frenchman who had roved restlessly till the end of his days. We must remember that he had come into the world in a boarding-house, had been suckled in a carriage traversing endless dusty southern roads, had been surrounded in infancy by the changing panorama of the frontier, and had known no settled home till well past school age. His weeks of tutoring on some up-country plantation had now aroused his innate love of outdoor life, always fierce in intensity. Doubtless his mother, burdened with the cares of a poor widow trying to keep her home and children, was unable to control the impetuous lad.

It is remarkable how closely the fragments of young Frémont's personal history which have survived in his *Memoirs* or the recollections of others fit the pattern of his personality and tastes as exhibited in later years. At sixteen his salient traits —ardor, imagination, ambition, quickness, endurance, and reckless impetuosity—were well established. It was sheer impulsiveness, the heedlessness of a boy immersed in a calf-love affair, which made him suddenly drop his books and higher aims. He was mastering subjects that proved of great value to him in later years: mathematics, botany, and the elements of chemistry. He had won the regard not only of lawyers like Mitchell, but of the rector of St. Philip's, the Reverend Christopher Gadsden, later bishop, who had given him material assistance. But though the strict rules of Charleston College required all students to be on the "premises" seven hours daily except Saturday and Sunday, he began to cut classes, and when he did attend was ill-prepared. He was passionately in love—so he fancied.

For three years he had been intimate with a Creole family which had escaped the massacres in Santo Domingo following the uprising under Toussaint L'Ouverture and Dessalines, and had taken refuge in Charleston. Like himself, they spoke French. Of the five children, three girls and two boys, the eldest daughter was named Cecilia; a handsome girl, with clear ruddy skin, large dark eyes, and flowing blue-black hair. With the two boys, young Frémont ranged the woods behind Charleston, still wild and tangled, or sailed a boat down the bay to the historic islands, where they hunted or fished—sometimes going far out to sea. Occasionally, when the breeze failed and they drifted near the breakers pounding on the bar, they had the exhilaration —always keen to him—of physical peril. "I remember, as in a picture," he wrote nearly a half a century afterward,[20] "seeing the beads of perspiration on the forehead of my friend Henry as he tugged frantically at the oar when we found ourselves one day on Drunken Dick, a huge breaker that to our eyes appeared monstrous as he flung his spray close to the boat. For us it was really pull Dick, pull Devil. Those were the splendid outside days." But soon he was preoccupied with Cecilia. To be with her on some outdoor excursion was the acme of happiness. College was forgotten. In after years he sighed over this "bit of sunshine that made the glory of my youth"—over these "days of unreflecting life when I lived in the glow of a passion that now I know extended its refining influence over my whole life."

It was characteristic of Frémont that he took the consequence of his rashness with gay insouciance. He received formal warning from Dr. Adams, who had declared that he would make the college "a fountain of intelligence and virtue." But he persisted in staying away whole days until on February 5, 1831, within three months of his graduation he was dismissed for what the faculty journal calls "habitual irregularity and incorrigible negligence."[21] Under the spell of his love affair, he cared naught for this supposed disgrace. The punishment itself he thought "sweet as a perfumed breeze," for it meant liberty. "I smiled to myself while I listened to words about the disappointment of

[20] Frémont, *Memoirs*, p. 20.
[21] MS. Faculty Journal, February 5, 1831.

friends and the broken career. I was living in a charmed atmosphere and their edict only gave me complete freedom." With no thought of the harvest expected from him, he "gathered the cornflowers from the upspringing grain." For some time he carelessly enjoyed his days in the open and his evenings with Cecilia and her brothers, often prolonged to so late an hour as to arouse the ire of her tall, stern, gray-haired grandmother, who would break out in a torrent of French rebuke. But after a time Cecilia began to pall upon him. The continued reproaches of his elders made an impression, and his ambition reasserted itself.

It was sternly necessary, moreover, that he earn his bread and contribute to the family support. Fortunately, his reputation for brilliance and the fact that he been so near graduation helped him escape the worst consequences of his expulsion. His services as teacher were still in demand. For a time he served in John A. Wooten's private school, and in the "Apprentices' Library," a collection of books with some instructional facilities added. While teaching, he read in desultory but profitable fashion, and long afterward recalled gratefully two books, one contrasting certain men who had distinguished themselves by noble deeds with others who had made themselves infamous by base acts, and the other a Dutch work upon practical astronomy. The beautiful maps of constellations and the lucid tables of astronomical calculations fascinated him, and laid the foundation of his subsequent familiarity with the heavens.[22]

Thus closed the first phase of Frémont's preparation for life; a preparation that possessed some fortunate aspects, but which would have been far better had it embodied a sterner discipline, a greater emphasis upon labor and planning. The second phase, now about to begin, was to be notable in two respects. It was to throw him into association with distinguished men, who would lend him powerful assistance; and it was to give him a

---

[22] Charleston *Courier,* October 27, 1856; Frémont, *Memoirs,* p. 21. By special action the college authorities gave Frémont the degree of B.A. on March 19, 1836, Minutes of the Board of Trustees, p. 263.

scientific training which, united with his nomadic tendencies, did much to equip him for eminence as an explorer. He had been unfortunate in his illegitimacy, his poverty, and his unruly youth; now he was to be fortunate in his patrons and in a solid grounding for scientific work.

II

An Explorer's Training

THE first important gift of fortune in Frémont's life—
and he was to enjoy a long and spectacular series of
such gifts—was the friendship of one of Charleston's
most eminent citizens, Joel Roberts Poinsett. In the summer of
1830 Poinsett, then forty-nine, returned to Charleston after
four and a half years as the first American Minister to Mexico.
A member of St. Philip's and a friend of struggling Charleston
College, he soon became acquainted with Frémont. He liked to
give aid and advice to young men of promise, and singled out
Edward McCrady, later known as general and historian, C. G.
Memminger, who in time served in the Confederate Cabinet,
and Frémont for special attention. All Frémont's distinction was
destined to be won in government service, and it was Poinsett
who obtained his first opening for him.

Perhaps Poinsett is best remembered to-day as introducer of
the flamboyant poinsettia into the United States from Mexico.
But actually he had many more valid titles to distinction.[1] He
was one of the best-educated and most widely traveled Americans of his day. The son of a cultivated and moderately wealthy
physician of Charleston, he had been schooled partly in Charleston, partly in Timothy Dwight's academy in Connecticut, and
partly in England. He had then studied medicine in Edinburgh,
but had turned from it first for military training at Woolwich,
and then for legal study in Charleston. His health had been
permanently injured by his first application to books, but not
to an extent which impaired his energies; in old age he used

[1] See J. Fred Rippy's excellent biography, *Joel R. Poinsett, Versatile American.*

to say that despite the doctors, he had lived strenuously for sixty years. A period of travel early in the century took him over most of Western Europe, where he saw some of the best society of Paris, Vienna, and other capitals; into Russia, where he received marks of favor from Czar Alexander I and was invited to enter the imperial service; and as far to the east as the Caucasus and the Caspian Sea. These extensive travels were an excellent training for his diplomatic years. When he returned home, Madison sent him in 1810 as commercial agent to South America, where he did much to promote the Chilean movement for independence from Spain. Then came service in Congress and the ministry to Mexico. His career in Mexico City was stormy, for the country with filled with disorder. He labored vigorously to sustain American rights and when he left, his old friend Commodore David Porter welcomed his "escape from that den of devils."

Frémont could have found no more useful friend than this influential gentleman. Living on the outskirts of Charleston in a white two-storied house, adorned with portico and columns, Poinsett made his weekly breakfasts a feature of the city's social life. Once a week he collected at his table the most charming women and intelligent men he could find; distinguished visitors always made their way there, and President Monroe was a guest when he visited Charleston in 1819. Though a man of short stature and plain, modest manners, Poinsett was an accomplished conversationalist and story-teller. The imagination of young Frémont, sitting at his board, was kindled by the recital of his wanderings and adventures. Poinsett, attracted by the vivacious manners and handsome person of the lad, learned that he was eager to see the world, and would like a naval or military appointment.

To this friendship with Poinsett we may largely trace one important fact in Frémont's career: the fact that, born a Southerner, bred and schooled a Southerner, throughout life he remained warmly attached to the Union and free from any sectional views. Poinsett was the principal leader of the Union men of South Carolina in the Nullification controversy of 1830-32, the most trusted lieutenant of President Jackson in his contest with Calhoun, Hayne, and the other Nullifiers. When leaving Washington for Charleston in the spring of 1830, he had told Jackson that he would oppose "the strange and pernicious doctrine advanced by some of the leading men of our State." Frémont was a witness of the excited meetings held by the two parties in Charleston during 1831, ending in a Nullification victory in the city elections. He witnessed the still stormier events of 1832, when in the canvass for a new legislature Poinsett and the Unionists again went down in defeat. The entire state government was now in control of the Nullifiers, who had determined upon a defiance of the Federal Government. While Frémont was quietly teaching school in November, 1832, a state convention passed an ordinance declaring the Tariffs of 1828 and 1832 null and void, and authorizing the legislature to take steps to prevent their enforcement. President Jackson answered in December with a proclamation warning South Carolina that disunion by armed force was treason. He immediately sent the sloop of war *Natchez* to Charleston, and in January, 1833, ordered General Winfield Scott to the city to halt by armed force any attempt to seize the forts.

For some months intense excitement reigned in the proud little capital. Early in 1833, when Jackson wrote Poinsett that if necessary he could throw from ten to fifteen thousands troops into Charleston within two weeks, an outbreak of war between the state and Federal governments seemed possible. The *Natchez* was expected to sustain the national authority even if it had to bombard the town. Fortunately Henry Clay and others who counseled a compromise prevailed, and in March, when the Nullification ordinance was rescinded in return for a Federal law reducing the tariff, the storm blew over.[2] The visit of the *Natchez*, which had shotted its guns and taken precautions against fire-ships, ended in a round of balls and other social

[2] Claude G. Bowers, *Party Battles of the Jackson Period*, pp. 254ff.; 268ff.; 285.

courtesies. In April, the vessel returned to Hampton Roads, and in May, it sailed on a cruise to South America. With it went Frémont, just twenty years old, in the capacity of teacher of mathematics. No naval academy as yet existing, such teachers were required for the 450 midshipmen, who were assigned to cruising ships, navy yards, or schools ashore.[3] He had obtained his appointment through Poinsett, who disapproved of his entry into the navy, but was glad to help him seek a larger sphere than he could find in Charleston.

His only hesitation was in parting from his mother, who had to be left entirely alone. Warmth of heart is reflected in the lines he wrote long afterward: [4]

We were only two, my mother and I. We had lost my sister. My brother was away, making his own career, and I had to concern myself for mine. I was unwilling to leave my mother. Circumstances had more than usually endeared us to each other, and I knew that her life would be solitary without me. I was accustomed to be much at home and our separations had been slight. But now it was likely to be for long and the hard part would be for the one left alone. With me it was very different. Going out into the excitement of strange scenes and occurrences I would be forced out of myself.... But my mother had an experience of sacrifice which with her true womanly nature it had been hard to learn. Realizing that now the time had come for another, she, but not cheerfully, sent me forward on my way.

Though this naval interlude responded to Frémont's innate love of wandering, later in life he looked back upon it as dull and without bearing on his future. The routine of ship life was tedious. The captain, Zantzinger, made no impression on him. But he did extract a few advantages from the monotonous cruise. One was association with David Farragut, lieutenant or executive officer of the ship;[5] a vigorous, able man still in his early thirties, though a veteran of the War of 1812, in which

[3] Register of Debates in Congress, 22d Congress, 2d Session, IX, 1666-75.
[4] Frémont, Memoirs, pp. 21, 22.
[5] Alfred T. Mahan, Life of Admiral Farragut, p. 75.

he had served as midshipman. Another advantage was the opportunity of exploring some of the principal ports of South America, of which Frémont writes that he saw more than a traveler usually does. They touched at Buenos Aires, whence the tyrant Rosas was ruling the best part of the Argentine with a steel grip. At Rio de Janeiro, Frémont and another youth were instrumental in preventing bloodshed in a senseless duel. Two young officers of the ship, a South Carolinian and a New Englander, had quarreled, exchanged challenges, and selected Frémont and this other youth as seconds. Only a short time before two midshipmen had fought a duel, and one had been killed. The seconds now held a conference and agreed that they would charge the pistols with powder only; but that if another shot was insisted upon, they would then load with ball. The officers were rowed ashore, took their stand at twelve paces, and fired pointblank. Both looked astonished and relieved when they found themselves unscathed. Thereupon the seconds hurried up, and asserting that the quarrel was not sufficiently grave to justify another shot, declared the affair closed. "Hurst and I," writes Frémont, "greatly enjoyed our little *ruse de guerre*."

Before long he was back in Charleston; and here, fortunately, circumstances gave him a better opportunity ashore than any available at sea. But for a time he was genuinely tempted to remain afloat. Congress had provided for several professorships of mathematics in the navy at $1,200 a year; [6] Frémont applied for a commission, and being ordered before an examining board at Norfolk, spent a month at home in preparation. "The strong motive I had now added to the pleasure I always found in study. All day long I was at my books, and the earliest dawn found me at an upper window against which stood a tall poplar, where the rustling of the glossy leaves made a soothing accompaniment." He successfully passed the examination, but the appointment was no sooner in his hands than he declined it. He had been offered an opportunity to help Captain W. S. Williams of

[6] Act of March 3, 1835; compare J. R. Soley, *History of the Naval Academy*, p. 27.

the United States Topographical Corps survey the route of the projected Louisville, Cincinnati & Charleston Railroad. Once more Poinsett was his good angel, for the statesman, long interested in internal improvements, was leader of a committee to promote this railroad in South Carolina. He believed that Charleston might be made an outlet for the commerce of the West and Northwest, and that this link between the two sections would strengthen the Union—perhaps even bring a large immigration of free whites into the South, and thus weaken slavery. Frémont, accepting employment as a surveyor, moved a step nearer the field in which he was to achieve his fame.

It is not difficult to imagine the zest with which the youth, always passionately fond of wild natural scenery, exchanged the tedium of a warship for the forest and mountain range. His immediate superior was Lieutenant Richard M. White, a South Carolinian graduated from West Point and now in civil life,[7] who made the hard work of their party, one of several running trial lines, agreeable. Spending the day in surveys, they would return to a farm-house or inn for a hearty supper, and sometimes be up till midnight plotting their notes. The weather in the Carolina and Tennessee mountains was fine, water abundant, and the scenery delightful. Fifty years later, Frémont, recalling the beauty and fragrance of the white azaleas, wrote: "The survey was a kind of picnic, with work enough to give it zest, and we were all sorry when it was over."[8]

If we may believe some ill-natured gossip collected (and doubtless expanded) by political opponents in 1856, scenery and outdoor exertion were not the sole attractions of the summer. He spent part of it boarding at the Mansion House in Greenville, South Carolina. Citizens of the town found him a lighthearted, active and strikingly handsome youth with a taste for society. "He became acquainted with a very pretty girl, in moderate circumstances," one of them wrote twenty years

[7] G. W. Cullum, *Biographical Register of the U. S. Military Academy, I,* p. 160.

[8] Frémont, *Memoirs,* p. 24.

later,[9] "and, as she lived in front of the house I occupied, I had every opportunity of seeing the *love* exhibited by the couple, on very many occasions. He was engaged to her, and deserted her without a cause, and the family were very much distressed about the matter. I have witnessed the intimacy myself, and the facts are notorious in our town at this time." The writer adds that Frémont's mother, who had remarried and was known as Mrs. Hale, subsequently spent a summer in Greenville and was deeply disturbed by the way in which her son had treated the girl. The editor of the Greenville *Patriot and Mountaineer* made the corroborative statement in 1856 that Frémont "became engaged to a young lady here, and we understand that the time was appointed for their wedding, and he proved false to his plighted faith." The girl's heart was not broken, for in time she married. The episode harmonizes with what Frémont tells us of his love affair with Cecilia in Charleston, and with what we know of his ardent courtship with Jessie Benton in Washington later. It is not to his credit, but the only safe inference is that he was impetuous in matters of the heart as in everything else.

The autumn of 1836 found him once more unemployed; and again an unexpected chance took him a step nearer his true vocation of explorer. The government, in pursuance of its policy of removing the principal Indian tribes from the Eastern States to areas beyond the Mississippi, was about to transfer the Cherokees. Having established prosperous homes in the land ceded them by Georgia in 1783, and in neighboring strips of North Carolina and Tennessee, the Cherokees desperately opposed the step. Georgia authorities were insistent, and hostilities threatened. For military purposes if war broke out, and for facilitating the distribution of land among white settlers if it did not, the government needed a rough survey of the region. Captain Williams was ordered to make a military reconnaissance of this thinly settled, half-wild country, and chose Frémont as an assistant. Here, on a rawer frontier than he had yet

[9] Charleston *Courier*, October 27, 1856.

seen, the young man began his principal life-work—as he says in his *Memoirs,* found the path in which he was to walk. "The occupation of my prime of life was to be among Indians and in waste places. There were to be no more years wasted in tentative efforts to find a way for myself. The work was laid out and it began here with a remarkable continuity of purpose." [10]

This winter survey, 1836-37, had to be carried out with haste, and the mountain country of the Cherokees presented numerous obstacles and hardships. A young man with sedentary tastes or a soft streak would have found it intolerable. To Frémont the novelty, adventure, and strenuous effort were fascinating. Williams's party was split into a number of squads assigned to separate tasks. Sometimes Frémont would be sent out with a single guide to make a sketch of some lonely stream or mountain spur; sometimes he would accompany a half-dozen men, with pack-mules carrying tents and food, sent to map a better-inhabited district. It was a heavily forested region, with Indian farms thinly scattered along the broad, fertile valleys. If lucky, the rangers could halt at night at some Indian cabin; if they were deep in the woods they set up their half-faced tents, built great fires of hickory logs, and roasted the choicest parts of one of the many wild hogs fattening on acorns. Frémont learned to make the most of the services of a frontier guide—he had one named Loudermilk, intimately acquainted with the region. He learned to pack a motley assortment of provisions, tools, cooking utensils, and bedding on mule-back so tightly as to resist steep trails and brushing boughs; to make an appetizing meal from a little flour, water, and raw meat; to pitch a tent in a snowdrift, with an icy wind blinding him with sleet. He mastered a hundred lessons of woodcraft. The joy of lonely hills and glowing sunsets; of sinking to sleep by glowing coals, the wind singing in the pines and the whippoorwills making the hills echo, entered his blood.

Another element of instruction lay in the opportunity of studying the semicivilized Indians of the country. Some of them,

[10] Frémont, *Memoirs,* p. 25.

living on farms as good as those of white men, exhibited a considerable degree of culture. Making a reconnaissance of the Hiwassee River, he stopped at an Indian's house which, built on a high bluff with carefully planed logs and glazed windows, was a handsome example of forest architecture. The Cherokee villages were clean, orderly, and comfortable. But a small element among the tribe, as Frémont noted, had been corrupted by the proximity of rough whites. He sometimes attended Indian feasts which broke up, when the Cherokees became maddened with liquor, in bloody affrays, the braves slashing each other with knives. Reaching one Cherokee village while the men were having a carouse and dangerously drunk, he and his companions were hidden for the night by squaws in a rat-infested corn-crib. Next morning they bathed in the Nantaheyle River: "There was ice along the banks, and the water in my hair froze into fretful quills."

In this survey Frémont reached the conclusion, afterward more strongly impressed upon him, that the Indians were capable of being civilized, that their culture depended upon their physical and social surroundings, and that the Washington authorities were too changeable, lax, and political-minded to be trustworthy agents for their care. He was later to find that their development varied from the high level of John Ross and his Cherokee followers to the degradation of the Digger Indians of the Great Basin. He also concluded that the Christianization of the Indians by missionaries was of the utmost importance, and that here again stability and continuity of effort were required. While he speaks with admiration of the courage and indifference to pain shown by the Cherokees, he seems to have made no friendships among them. And it is noteworthy that he refers to their expulsion, in its circumstances one of the cruellest acts in our national history, as a measure beneficial both to Indians and whites.[11]

---

[11] Frémont, *Memoirs,* pp. 24, 25; for the real character of the removal see Grant Foreman, *Indian Removal: The Emigration of the Five Civilized Tribes,* p. 229*ff.*

All too soon the Cherokee reconnaissance ended. Frémont returned to Charleston to stay with his mother and renew old friendships. Now twenty-four, he was in the full vigor of young manhood, tanned, lithe, and hardy. He had evidently acquitted himself well in all his employments, for Poinsett continued to think highly of him. Various parts of his training—his solid grounding in mathematics, his experience as a surveyor, his partial knowledge of navigation, of which he had gained a smattering on shipboard, his recent intimacy with frontier conditions, his wood-lore—constituted a valuable preparation for the career now about to open before him. Though he had never received the hard discipline which his character most needed, he had been given more of it than ever before. Poinsett had become Secretary of War under Van Buren. He was as keenly interested in science as ever, and his department was especially concerned with trans-Mississippi exploration. These facts were to mean much to the young man.

III

First View of the Great West

SECRETARY POINSETT, knowing what Frémont most wanted, brought him to Washington early in 1838 and took steps to have him commissioned second lieutenant in the Topographical Corps. The young man arrived in the capital at an auspicious moment. The War Department had determined upon a new western survey—an examination of the wide plateau country between the upper Mississippi and upper Missouri rivers; and a distinguished foreign scientist, Joseph Nicolas Nicollet, had been chosen to conduct it. Poinsett planned to include his protégé in the expedition. When Frémont heard of his assignment, he was exuberantly elated. The flat, frowsy little capital had at first seemed a distasteful place to him. He possessed no friends outside Poinsett's family; there were no amusements beyond watching the alternate reigns of mud and dust along the single important street, Pennsylvania Avenue; and the ugliness of the surroundings weighed upon his spirits. He missed such spots as the Battery in Charleston, where both eye and mind could feel their freedom; space, he moralized later,[1] "reacts on the mind, which unconsciously expands to larger limits and freer range of thought." His body was so inured to constant exercise that a routine of streets, offices, and boarding-houses affected him with physical malaise. To be sent to the romantic West, the land of Indians, buffalo, and stupendous natural wonders, was an incredible bit of luck. He went forward with little delay to St. Louis, making the trip by stage over the Alleghenies and steamboat down the Ohio and up the Mississippi.

[1] Frémont, *Memoirs*, p. 30.

Nicollet, who thus at Poinsett's request took Frémont as chief assistant, was a commanding figure, certain to make a strong impression on the young man. Fifty-two years old, he was in the prime of life. A member of the Legion of Honor, a man who had missed election to the Academy of Sciences by only one vote, a mathematician who had stood high in the circle of Laplace and Arago, one-time secretary of the Observatory in Paris and professor at the Collège Louis-le-Grand, he had come to America only when ruined by disastrous speculations on the Bourse.[2] His imagination had been touched by the exploits of La Salle and Champlain, and he hoped to make some worthy addition to the record of French explorations in the West. With his Parisian background, his friendships with eminent Europeans, his skill in music, his natural urbanity and polish, he became a social favorite wherever he went. Reaching New Orleans in 1832, he soon made friends in its hospitable Franco-American society, which was touched by the spectacle of a once-wealthy man who had fled from the painful scenes of his ruin. He first used what little funds he had in exploring the southern Appalachians and ascending the Red River and Arkansas River, labors which brought him to the notice of army officers. Then, going to St. Louis, he won the support of the rich fur-trading house of Chouteau & Company. It shared his view as to the desirability of more information regarding parts of the Indian country; and in 1836 he set out for a tour of the upper Mississippi, intending to determine its sources with astronomical accuracy. He encountered various adventures among the Chippewa—for he gave much time to the customs, manners, and languages of Indian tribes—and spent the winter with the officers of Fort Snelling. The War Department had furnished him letters to them and to Indian agents on the frontier, and had lent him instruments, but did no more.[3]

In 1837, with funds exhausted and health seriously impaired,

---

[2] See articles on Nicollet in *La Grande Encyclopedie; Dictionary of American Biography.*

[3] *Minnesota Historical Collections,* I (1872), p. 183*ff.*

Nicollet was back in civilization, recuperating among his Catholic friends at St. Mary's College in Baltimore. He had accomplished a notable feat of exploration. Visiting Lake Itasca, he had traced its principal affluent, now known as Nicollet's Infant Mississippi, several miles to the southwest; and it is agreed by historians that he divides with Schoolcraft the honor of discovering the real source of the river, and indeed accomplished more than Schoolcraft. Poinsett heard of him and sent what Nicollet calls a "flattering invitation" to repair to Washington. There they talked in detail of further plans for exploring the upper Northwest. Nicollet wished to make a geographical and topographical map of the whole country, and the Secretary of War approved. Such a work was much needed. Pike had made a march in the winter of 1806 to the headwaters of the Mississippi, and a few others had followed in his path. Lewis and Clark had explored the Missouri to its supposed sources. But the vast fan-shaped area between the heads of the two rivers was as yet little known to any save fur-traders. In 1823 Major Stephen H. Long, accompanied by a mineralogist from the University of Pennsylvania, had made a rapid trip up the Minnesota River, down the Red River to the Canadian line, and thence along the boundary to Lake Superior. His work proved the fertility of the great valleys of the Minnesota and Red rivers, later the richest wheat lands on the continent, but it was too hurried to show much else. In 1835 George H. Featherstonhaugh, an Englishman who had entered the Federal service, made a "geological reconnaissance" for the government to the Coteau des Prairies in southwestern Minnesota and northeastern South Dakota. He published a report, but his expedition also was too hasty to furnish any important contribution to knowledge.[4] A wide field lay open to Nicollet.

For Frémont to become associated with such a scientist was a triple piece of luck. He soon learned from him ten times as much about scientific exploration, mapping, and description as he could have obtained at any American school. Indeed, Nicollet

[4] W. J. Ghent, *The Early Far West*, pp. 178, 179.

trained him in mathematics, surveying, botanical and geological observation, and topographical mapwork until he had become thoroughly proficient, and within five years Frémont was able to step boldly into Nicollet's shoes. Nicollet also brought Frémont into touch with some of the best society of Baltimore, Washington, St. Louis, and other cities. Finally, Frémont's name was at once prominently associated with an expedition which engaged the interest of every one concerned with western development; and Nicollet never scanted the credit given him.

In St. Louis, Frémont enjoyed a pleasant interval of leisure while the party was outfitting. Not only did he make friends among military men—among them Robert E. Lee, a captain of engineers, just then busy with Mississippi improvements, whose polite manners and helpfulness made an enduring impression upon him—but he was taken by Nicollet among the old French residents. These circles, proud of their distinguished countryman, offered a profuse hospitality. Invitation to dinners, receptions, or dances, were showered upon the two men, while Frémont frequently accompanied Nicollet, who was intimate with the clergy, to agreeable suppers in the refectory of the Catholic cathedral. Meanwhile, the house of Chouteau was equipping the expedition, its officers selecting both stores and men; the latter for the most part practised voyageurs in the fur company's employ. At his own expense, Nicollet employed Charles Geyer, a German botanist, to accompany the expedition. The lieutenant was intensely interested in the strange new scenes—in the turbid, yellow flood of the Mississippi, rolling past the town, with flatboats, rafts, and keel-boats dotting the waters, and an occasional steamboat pouring smoke from two high pipes above its gingerbread hull; the lazy, grunting Indians, hugging the shade on hot spring afternoons; the buckskin-garbed, long-haired trappers, ready to pour their tales of adventure into his ears in rough French. This elation and curiosity accompanied him through the summer expedition of 1838, which surveyed a long strip westward from the headwaters of the Mississippi.[5]

[5] See Nicollet's MS Journals and Reports, Library of Congress.

Their steamboat made a rapid trip up the river to the mouth of the St. Peter's or Minnesota River, where Henry Sibley commanded a whole province of the American Fur Company, in which he was a partner. His district, in fact, extended from the upper Mississippi westward to the heads of the Missouri tributaries, and northwest to Pembina on the Canadian line, embracing most of what is now Minnesota, the Dakotas, and southern Manitoba. A large number of fur posts, with traders, clerks, and voyageurs, were under his charge; the chief being at Lac Traverse, Lac qui Parle (both fortified), Traverse des Sioux, Little Rapids, and Coteau des Prairies. The French-Canadian voyageurs, enlisted for three years at Montreal and paid in livres, were supplied with provisions and goods, visited Indian camps, and returned laden with beaver and other pelts. Sibley maintained discipline with an iron hand. His headquarters were at the hamlet of St. Peter's (now Mendota), where stood a large fur depot; near at hand was a small white settlement in log houses, a Sioux village, and, on the high bluff between the Minnesota and Mississippi, the heavy stone walls of Fort Snelling.[6]

With Sibley, a tall, handsome young man of about Frémont's own years, the lieutenant spent many profitable hours. Born and educated in Detroit, the son of a politically influential lawyer, Sibley had abandoned his legal studies at eighteen to become a sutler's clerk on the Sault-Ste. Marie, and within a year joined the American Fur Company at Mackinac. Serving here for five years, he fell in love with the picturesque, dangerous, profitable business of fur trading. For two winters he was purchasing-agent of supplies in Ohio, riding thousands of miles on horseback to buy corn, flour, tobacco, pork, and other commodities. Then, when John Jacob Astor sold out his holdings in 1834 and the company was reorganized, Sibley became part owner, and went at once to St. Peter's. Now, his remarkable career as lawmaker and administrator all before him, he was living the life of a bachelor frontiersman, engrossed in trade and adventure. His house was a hunting-lodge, filled with Irish

[6] W. P. Shortridge, *Transition of a Typical Frontier*, p. 15ff.

wolfhounds, guns, and saddles, and he was fond of long hunting excursions.[7] His influence over the Indians, who admired his prowess with arms, his powerful frame, and his decision of character, was remarkable, and Frémont learned much from it. While the expedition spent several weeks in completing its outfit and making astronomical observations, the young explorer fraternized with Sibley; wandered about the fort; admired the charms of a Sioux girl whose name, "Beautiful Day," he never forgot; and absorbed the atmosphere of this borderland between civilization and savagery.

Their ensuing expedition, made with one-horse carts driven by voyageurs, took them first up the Minnesota some hundred and fifteen miles to the fur-trading post at Traverse des Sioux, where the river makes an abrupt bend toward the northwest; and thence westward over the high plains to the Red Pipestone Quarry, an abrupt bluff about three miles in length composed of red rocks of different shades. It was devoid of any peril or special excitement. Near the Traverse lay the summer encampment of the Sisseton Sioux, and as the expedition halted beside their principal village, Frémont found another opportunity to study Indian life. The excitability of the savages impressed him:

We were occupied quietly among the Indians, Mr. Nicollet, as usual, surrounded by them, with the aid of the interpreter getting them to lay out the form of the lake and the course of the streams entering the river near by...; Geyer, followed by some Indians, curiously watching him while digging up plants; and I, more numerously attended, pouring out the quicksilver for the artificial horizon, each in his way busy at work; when suddenly everything started into motion, the Indians running tumultuously to a little rise which commanded a view of the prairie, all clamor and excitement. The commotion was caused by the appearance of two or three elk on the prairie horizon.[8]

---

[7] W. W. Folwell, *History of Minnesota*, I, p. 161*ff.; Nathaniel West, Life of H. H. Sibley, passim;* Theodore C. Blagen, *Building Minnesota*, p. 112*ff.*

[8] Frémont, *Memoirs*, pp. 34, 35.

In marching to the Red Pipestone Quarry, they crossed the plateau (Coteau des Prairies) which divides the Mississippi and Missouri valleys. Here Nicollet explored one chain of lakes, Frémont another. As they approached the Quarry a thunderstorm broke, delighting the Sioux as confirmation of their legend that the Spirit of the Red Pipestone spoke in thunder and lightning whenever the bluff was visited. Then as the sun burst forth, under its rays the distant cliff loomed up like some ruined city of marble and porphyry.[9]

They carefully examined the Quarry, a place of resort for all the neighboring tribes. The pipestone lay in a stratum about eighteen inches thick, overlaid by perhaps twenty-six feet of hard reddish sandstone. The water in the little valley below had caused the buffalo to pour through it in their annual migrations, and tradition related that the tread of these countless herds had exposed the pipestone. Spending three days here in company with a party of friendly Sioux, Nicollet's men helped the Indians by blasting the vein free with gunpowder. The explorers then resumed their march, this time northward over the plateau to the Lac qui Parle. They found the air of the high plains, 1,500 feet above sea-level and studded with lakes, sparkling and invigorating. Reaching Lac qui Parle, they camped at the trading-post maintained under the American Fur Company by the Renville family, where Frémont found another valuable mentor. Joseph Renville was a half-breed born in this region, who had been a captain in the British forces in the War of 1812, had accompanied the expeditions of Zebulon Pike and Major S. H. Long as guide, and had become one of the shrewdest fur-traders of the Northwest.[10] Near Lac qui Parle he maintained for the company a stockaded post, Fort Renville, the base for a large force of voyageurs, half-breed hunters, and hangers-on, whom he dominated in an easy baronial fashion. He needed their protection for his herds of horses, cattle, and sheep; they needed

---

[9] Nicollet, *Report Intended to Illustrate a Map of the Hydrographical Basin of the Upper Mississippi River*, pp. 15, 16.

[10] Rev. E. D. Neill, "A Sketch of Joseph Renville," *Minnesota Historical Collections*, I, p. 196ff.

the employment and bounty which he and the company gave them. Once more the lieutenant had an opportunity to observe how a man of energy, decision, and tact exercised a sway over large bodies of Indians, for Renville and his son were regarded with admiring deference by the savages who roamed the regions westward and northward for hundreds of miles. Frémont aptly calls him a border chief.

They stayed for some time at Fort Renville, enjoying the fresh meat, milk, and vegetables; watching the Indians play lacrosse; and exploring the country. Homeward bound, Nicollet surveyed the Le Sueur, while Frémont was sent to examine the Mankato, a deep stream walled by high narrow banks or cliffs, its stone escarpments frequently of great beauty. Then they returned to the protection of Fort Snelling and the comforts of Sibley's lodge. Nicollet spoke in high praise of Frémont. He was convinced, writes Sibley, "that the modest and unassuming youth, if his life should be spared, would, in due time, carve out for himself a distinguished position among the *savans* of the age." [11]

Frémont concluded this first season of the Nicollet expedition by a glorious hunting trip, undertaken with Sibley and an experienced officer of the fur company, Jean Baptiste Faribault, head of the post at Little Rapids.[12] The three took with them a whole Sioux village under the chief Red Dog, an excitable, clamorous crowd, and set off in the crisp November weather. After some days they reached the Iowa hunting grounds, stretches of prairie intersected with well-watered woods, and gave themselves up to killing deer and elk. It was a royal hunt, Frémont records. To the end of his life he recalled the pleasures of camping at night along the woods, with "bright fires, where fat venison was roasting on stocks before them, or stewing with

[11] H. H. Sibley, "Memoir of Nicollet," *Minnesota Historical Collections, I,* p. 190.

[12] Frémont, *Memoirs,* pp. 37, 38. Sibley in his "Reminiscences," *Minnesota Historical Collections,* III, pp. 254-256, describes a hunting-party with Frémont and Faribault, but assigns it to 1840, when Frémont was not in the West. Frémont's date of 1838 must therefore be accepted, though the year may have been 1839.

corn or wild rice in pots hanging from tripods; squaws busy over the cooking, and children rolling about over the ground. No sleep is better or more restoring than follows such a dinner, earned by such a day." [13] They met some ordinary hardships and risks, including a prairie fire whose roar and glare aroused them in the dead of night from a sound sleep, and gave them just time to set a counter fire and transfer their beasts and belongings to cleared ground before it swept past in a sheet of flame. They had an intimate view of Indian life. Each family owned one or more ponies, who dragged the household articles on poles. At streams the squaws were expected to carry the baggage across on their shoulders. Frémont remarks that one day on the march a squaw dropped behind, but trudged into camp a little after the others carrying a baby a few hours old.

December, 1838, found the Nicollet party in St. Louis, preparing for the work of the next year, which was to carry them to the upper Missouri. Just after Christmas Frémont was sent on to Washington with official despatches, letters to Nicollet's friends, and a verbal report for Poinsett.[14] A few weeks later his chief followed him. Returning to Missouri in the spring, they hired five men as the nucleus of their new party, including Louis Zindel, a Prussian artilleryman skilled in making rockets, and a famous frontiersman and trapper, Etienne Provôt. One of the best of the "mountain men," hardly excelled in his knowledge of the wild West by even Kit Carson and Jim Bridger, his name is commemorated by the city of Provo, Utah.

The little party left St. Louis as soon as the annual rise of the Missouri followed the melting of the Rocky Mountain snows; that is, on April 4, 1839, on the steamer *Antelope* of the American Fur Company. It required nearly two and a half months to struggle northward against the turbid, rushing current. Their little vessel, traveling only by day, and carrying

[13] Frémont, *Memoirs*, p. 37.
[14] Nicollet to F. R. Hassler, from St. Louis, December 25, 1838, introducing Frémont; Hassler Papers, New York Public Library. In this letter Nicollet speaks of Frémont as "my special friend, very anxious to make your acquaintance. and very capable of appreciating your achievements."

sixty or seventy French or half-breed employees of the fur company, rasped against snags and ground over sand-bars; at times the current was so swift that the boat would hang perfectly motionless, seeming to rally her strength till, with a roar of the exhaust pipes, she would fight her way into smoother waters. Torn branches, uprooted shrubs, and other debris sailed past them in the yellow water. Wicked-looking snags lifted their heads above the current. Moreover, it was almost impossible at times to find the channel, for the Missouri continually changed its course, wearing away ragged islands and cutting across peninsulas. For the steamboat to lose her way in the shallows was to thrust herself into a thick chevaux-de-frise of trees and limbs brought down by the flood, embedded like a military abattis in the sand. Nicollet sketched the stream from daybreak until nine o'clock, Frémont from nine to two, and Geyer from two until nightfall. They were totally unable to recognize many of the bends and bluffs described by Lewis and Clark.[15]

As they pushed on the river grew lonelier and lonelier, and the intense stillness, broken only by the echo from the exhaust pipes, the washing of the waves, and the sudden splash of a distant bank caving into the water, impressed their imaginations. At first the country was monotonous, but the shore-line became steadily more attractive. Sometimes they found themselves running between high perpendicular cliffs of gray and yellow rock, with shrubbery and trees nodding over their brows; sometimes the river opened out into a flat expanse over which it wandered in several channels, like a delta breaking into the sea. When hilly country came into view on the west bank, Nicollet and Frémont went ashore to examine the geological character of several bluffs. Finally, on the seventieth day they reached Fort Pierre, 1,271 miles above St. Louis, named for Pierre Chouteau—the principal post of the American Fur Company on the upper Missouri. This was near the center of present-day South Dakota, surrounded on all sides by the wild

[15] Frémont, *Memoirs*, p. 38; Nicollet, *Report*, pp. 29-42.

country of the Indian and buffalo. A large village of Yankton
Sioux stood several miles distant, and Nicollet at once gave
their chiefs, a noble-looking set of men, gifts to ratify their
promises of good-will and free passage.

This time Frémont participated in the equipment of a fairly
large expedition, for they hired a number of new men, including Louison Frenière, a half-breed guide from Fort Pierre who
had a local fame as hunter and scout; one Dorion, son of the
post interpreter; and William Dixon, another well-known guide.
When Provôt announced on July 1st that all was ready, the
party was ordered to the east bank. Its crossing took most of
two days, for heavy rains had swollen the river to a width of
a mile and a half. On calling the roll, they found that in all
they were nineteen strong. This seemed a small force if the
Sioux proved hostile, but relying on their arms, on Zindel's
rockets, and on the hope of reinforcements from Lac qui Parle,
they joined in a lusty huzza, and set forth.[16]

Their path lay northeast toward the rising sun, over the
plateau termed by the half-breeds the Coteau de Missouri,
nearly two thousand feet above sea-level. The bed of the Missouri lay nearly five hundred feet below this plateau. Frémont's
days, as they pushed outward by astronomical reckoning, were
at first full of leisure, for the level plain required little sketching or description. He spent them chiefly with Frenière, as
hunter. The two rode far ahead to spy out the country and kill
buffalo; game was abundant, and their only anxiety was to
find sufficient water and wood. For a young man of twenty-six,
this employment as vidette was exhilarating. The grand simplicity of the prairie, its grass thrown into waves by the wind,
the broad cloud-shadows chasing each other across its sunny
bosom, held an impressive beauty. On hot afternoons they saw
the giant thunderheads mount like blue snow-capped peaks in
the West. The long rolling slopes were gay with puccoon, red
Indian-pipe, mullen flower, and wild rose; as they reached
more broken country, silver streams laced the green prairie at

16 Nicollet, *Report*, pp. 43, 44.

intervals, and sometimes they came upon pretty lakelets, bordered with rocks, aspens, and grasses growing into the water.[17] The lieutenant took an eager interest in the moving shapes glimpsed on the horizon, and in Frenière's skill in determining, at astonishing distances, whether they were antelope, buffalo, or Indians. Where another man would have distinguished nothing, his practised eye told him which was enemy and which friend. Finally, toward the eastern limits of the plateau, Dixon led them through dark ravines and over steep hills till he suddenly brought them out on the precise point he desired—a headland with a magnificent view over the immense basin of the James River. As they gazed in admiration, he exclaimed: "You wanted geography; look—there's geography for you!" [18]

It was an exciting moment for the young explorer when, in the district between the James and Sheyenne rivers (now North Dakota), they came into touch with illimitable buffalo herds moving slowly southwest toward the plains bordering the upper Missouri. Here were ponderous old bulls, enormous in size and weight, their eyes gleaming from matted forelocks, their manes hanging shaggily down their necks, and patches of last year's hair standing like tattered islands on their backs; lean and restless cows; and, under their anxious eyes, calves playing antics through the herd. The face of the wide prairie, far as the eye could reach, was dotted with them. They trooped along in columns beside the expedition, or gathered in grazing knots; farther beyond, they were seen scrambling, tails erect, over sudden hillocks; and in the remote distance the pale blue swells were peppered with groups and individuals. For three days Frémont and Nicollet were in the midst of this concourse of bison, threading their way through the herds by day and so closely pressed by them at night that it was necessary to picket all the horses and mules, and to hobble the more restive. It was a memorable experience, and the spirits of the party, depressed

---

[17] Frémont, *Memoirs,* p. 40; Nicollet, *Report,* p. 43.
[18] Nicollet, *Report,* p. 45.

MINNESOTA-DAKOTA, SHOWING PLACES VISITED BY FRÉMONT

Courtesy of the Nicollet-Frémont Explorations

by some days of ninety-three degree heat, flies, and fatigue, at once rose.

The expedition had just pushed through the buffalo to a branch of the Sheyenne when Frémont brought in three Indians, who announced that encampments of about two thousand Sioux were hard by, slaughtering game and preparing for a grand "surround" of buffalo. It would have been dangerous to interfere with the maneuver, and Nicollet wisely sent Frenière to request the chiefs to point out the best time and route for the whites to continue their march. With characteristic hospitality, the Sioux invited Nicollet's party to visit their camp. Received with talks, dances, songs, and other ceremonials, the explorers distributed presents, after which they were bidden to the lodges of the chiefs to dine. In return Nicollet gave a feast at his own camp, which Frémont engagingly describes: [19]

The chiefs sat around in a large circle on buffalo robes or blankets, each provided with a deep soup plate and a spoon of tin. The first dish was a generous pot-au-feu, principally of fat buffalo meat and rice. No one would begin until all the plates were filled. When all was ready the feast began. With the first mouthful each Indian silently laid down his spoon, and each looked at the other. After a pause of bewilderment the interpreter succeeded in having the situation understood. Mr. Nicollet had put among our provisions some Swiss cheese, and to give flavor to the soup a liberal portion of this had been put into the kettles. Until this strange flavor was accounted for the Indians thought they were being poisoned; but, the cheese being shown to them and explanations made, confidence was restored; and by the aid of several kettles of water well sweetened with molasses, and such other tempting delicatessen as could be provided from our stores, the dinner party went on and terminated in great good humor and general satisfaction.

Frémont was an alert observer of the Indian "surround" the following day. This was a grand slaughter of fat buffalo cows, whose meat was cut into long strips and draped over low scaffolds all about the encampment to be dried in the sun. Feasting

[19] Frémont, *Memoirs*, p. 48.

and dancing were prolonged throughout the night. A few days later he was equally interested in observing at Devil's Lake traces of a large hunting-camp of the Bois Brulés or half-breeds of the Red River of the North. The ashes of camp-fires, the deeply trodden ground and trails, and the ruts cut by heavily laden carts, showed that the great annual hunt had been successful. These métis, descendants of French, English, and Scotch, crossed with Chippewa, Sioux, and other tribes, now numbering six to eight hundred people, came down twice a year from Canada, where the buffalo were steadily growing scarcer. Each family had its yoke of oxen and a cart made to hold the meat of ten buffalo; each hunter had a fleet horse. By turns half of the hunters watched the camp, the other half pursued the game, and the spoils were divided communally. Most of the meat was made into pemmican; that is, dried by sun or fire, pounded into a coarse fibrous mass, mixed with melted fat, and packed into skin sacks. It was of two grades, the coarse pemmican of commerce, and a finer compound consisting of the choicest steaks carefully kneaded up with the marrow. The *gens libres,* as the half-breeds called themselves, were a picturesque race, living on the sale of pelts, buffalo-tongues, and pemmican, and so formidable with their rifles that the Indians were eager to make them allies.

After a nine-day survey about most of Devil's Lake, the expedition, tormented by mosquitoes, turned southeast across the Dakota plateau toward the basin of the Red River. On August 11th they crossed the dividing line between the Sheyenne and the Red at a height of about fifteen hundred feet; and soon afterward they came out on a small knoll commanding a magnificent view. Before them lay the far-stretching valley of the latter river, the green woods along its margin extending north toward the Canadian line and losing themselves southward in the summer haze. Even the scout Dixon was ecstatic over this landscape. Moving south, they explored the headwaters of several tributaries, Frémont making sketches and helping determine positions. Then they descended again to the valley of the Sheyenne; traversed the beautiful lake region of western Minnesota; and coming down to the lower prairies, pursued their march to the trading-post at Lac qui Parle, where the Renvilles once more greeted them with open arms. Here they lingered, examining Big Stone and other lakes, making observations for Nicollet's map, and going on short excursions with the Renvilles, until the fall was far advanced.

Forever afterward, Frémont remembered the rare beauty of the prairies as the gradual northern autumn came on, turning the aspen leaves to gold and the cottonwoods to silver, and brightening the far-spreading plain with clumps of sere buffalo grass and vari-colored flowers. The lowlands near the Renville post were sprinkled with purple asters and ablaze with golden-rod, for that year the prairie flowers were exceptionally luxuriant. On clear days the azure sky merged imperceptibly with the remote horizon, and distant objects trembled and loomed till their size could hardly be judged; in the warmth of Indian Summer smoke veiled the far-off swells, and gossamer drove before the breeze. Finally the expedition, still making observations,[20] descended the Minnesota and Mississippi; and early in November Frémont, paddling down the latter stream with a detachment of the party, landed at Prairie du Chien. Here he received an important lesson upon the necessity, in exploration or any other enterprise, of seizing time by the forelock:

A steamboat at the landing was firing up and just about starting for St. Louis, but we thought it would be pleasant to rest a day or two and enjoy comfortable quarters while waiting for the next boat. But the next boat was in the spring, for next morning it was snowing hard, and the river was frozen from bank to bank. I had time enough while there to learn two things: one, how to skate; the other, the value of a day.[21]

[20] Nicollet was the first to use the barometer in obtaining altitudes of the interior, and he was tireless in making his skilful observations for latitude and longitude; F. S. Dellenbaugh, *Frémont and '49*, p. 14.

[21] Frémont, *Memoirs*, pp. 53, 54.

A second phase of Frémont's apprenticeship to exploration had now been completed. He had become acquainted with a great region of the ill-known Northwest; he had learned comradeship with scouts, voyageurs, fur-traders, frontier soldiers, and Indians; he had mastered the art of camp-management; he had been taught woodcraft and prairie-craft by Sibley, Renville, Provôt, Dixon, and Frenière. He knew how to find water and firewood where both were scarce, to conciliate Indians, to deal with buffalo, prairie fires, and camp emergencies. Above all, Nicollet and Preuss had taught him how to make an expedition into a new country scientifically profitable—to take accurate astronomical observations at every halt, record topography, observe botany, soils, and minerals, and draught careful sketch-maps. Possessed by his passion for science, Nicollet tasked himself to exhaustion, as Sibley noted, and at times made the lieutenant work equally hard. Frémont still lacked discipline and still showed his abiding defects of judgment. He delighted in reckless feats of hardihood. In his *Memoirs* he relates how at Red Pipestone Quarry he leaped from the bluff to the top of a detached pedestal about twenty-five feet high— "quite a feat . . . as the top was barely a foot square and uneven, and it required a sure foot not to go farther"; how soon after leaving Fort Pierre he got completely lost on the prairies while pursuing a buffalo—a position of considerable peril, from which Frenière's good judgment in pursuit saved him. These weaknesses he was never to conquer. But he had been drilled in the best possible school for exploration, and his quick mind, ardent temperament, and zest for outdoor life had made the most of his tuition. Above all, he had found himself; he had embraced a calling in which he took, as he wrote later,[22] "the true Greek joy in existence, in the gladness of living," and which was to make him famous.

[22] *Ibid.*, p. 602.

IV

Washington Courtship

FRÉMONT returned to Washington the possessor of a certain dignity, even a certain reputation; to less fortunate officers he could talk with a casual air of what he had seen beyond the Mississippi, while he knew that the engineering branch of the army regarded him as a young man of promise. As we have noted, scientific information upon the wide region which they had crossed had been almost totally lacking. Nicollet now brought back a mass of careful data which far transcended in value the notes of Major Long's rapid exploration of the Minnesota and Red rivers, and Featherstonhaugh's superficial reconnaissance of the Coteau des Prairies; and he wished Frémont's aid in working it up. He took the lieutenant to call on the President and Secretary Poinsett. We can easily imagine the young explorer, erect, tanned, with his sharp, intense eyes, clear-cut features, and quick movements, shaking hands with the genial Van Buren, and interjecting an occasional word as Nicollet described their work. The President was appreciative. Nicollet took pains to impress upon Poinsett the fact that his aide had acquitted himself brilliantly; and, writes Frémont, "his kind reception and approval were to me the culminating pleasure" of the expedition.[1]

Physically exhausted, Nicollet required some time to recuperate, and took Frémont to Baltimore for a pleasant vacation. Friends there, particularly the higher officers of the Catholic hierarchy, gave them a cordial welcome, and they were deluged with invitations. Their quarters were at the Sulpician seminary, St. Mary's College, where comfortable rooms were always ready

[1] Frémont, *Memoirs*, p. 55.

46

for Nicollet, and where the president, J. M. J. Chanché, made them at home. Nicollet showed his assistant, who for months had seen him in rough frontier garb, a wardrobe full of fine linen and other sartorial luxuries. They had long talks with Chanché, a fine-looking, courtly, cultivated man, soon to become Bishop of Natchez, and with other churchmen; men of elevated, secluded lives, obviously marked by learning and generous aims. The two dined at some of the best Baltimore homes, and thoroughly enjoyed their return to civilization. Frémont's vacation was cut short by the death of his brother in South Carolina, and he obtained leave to visit Charleston to comfort his aged mother. "I was happy for her sake," he writes, "in the unusual brightness my presence brought with it; for awhile it was almost the old time again." Then he rejoined Nicollet in Washington.

He now had an opportunity to observe the capital and its society under pleasanter conditions than before. Washington was still far more of a southern country town than a national center. Only one of the broad streets, Pennsylvania Avenue between the White House and Capitol, had been paved; the others were deep with mud in winter, and poured out choking clouds of dust in hot weather. Houses and shops were scattered at wide intervals over the open lots, "like the teeth of some superannuated crone." [2] Many streets, avenues, and circles were defined by one or two dwellings standing alone in a waste of clay. Hills and valleys had not been touched, and their irregular levels were to remain until a generation later Boss Shepherd smoothed them away. Harriet Martineau had recently written that the town showed nothing but "a few mean houses dotted about, the sheds of the navy yard on one bank of the Potomac, and three or four villas on the other." [3] A few really fine mansions clustered about Capitol Hill; the section about the White House—"the Co't End"—boasted a considerable group of others. But west of the White House little was to be

[2] Nathan Sargent, *Public Men and Events,* I, p. 54.
[3] *Retrospect of Western Travel,* I, p. 160.

seen but pastures and ill-fenced fields, while east of the Capitol lay a series of quagmires, sending up miasmatic fogs at
night; and all efforts to build a respectable city between the
two had thus far failed.

Frémont and Nicollet were able to make fortunate arrangements for living and working. For years a close friendship had
subsisted between Nicollet and the head of the Coast Survey,
Ferdinand R. Hassler, a scientist of Swiss birth now seventy
years of age. Since Hassler's duties took him into the field much
of the time, and his children were grown, he was glad to open
his house to the two men. It was conveniently placed on the
slopes of Capitol Hill overlooking the Potomac, not far from
the Coast Survey building. Partly in a large room here, partly
in the Survey building itself, the map-work for the years of exploration was done. For considerable periods Hassler, a remarkable personality, would be with the two men. Coming to the
United States in 1805 with a thorough mathematical training
and large library, he had soon lost much of his money in an ill-
managed land-colonization scheme, but had made influential
friends. One was Jefferson, "whose kind expressions towards
me, and interest for me," he wrote in 1828, "have until his death
been my greatest satisfaction in this country." [4] After teaching
mathematics at West Point and in Union College, he had been
sent abroad to procure instruments for the recently authorized
Coast Survey, and after the War of 1812 became its head for
two years. Jackson made him Superintendent of Weights and
Measures, and on the revival of the Coast Survey in 1832 he
was made its chief again. The country had no riper scientist,
and there was no better geodetic surveyor in the world.

It was still another stroke of fortune for Frémont that he
was brought into such close association with Hassler. He had
much to learn from him in scientific method, and all his later
work bore the impress of this training. Whenever Nicollet and
Hassler debated some question of mathematics, topography, or
mensuration, and this was often, the lieutenant was an eager

4 Hassler Papers, New York Public Library.

listener. Both were steeped in scientific lore and thoroughly congenial, but so different in temperament—Hassler abrupt, intolerant of pretence, impatient of obstruction, and sharp-tongued, and Nicollet urbane but intense—that clashes were frequent; "the one flint and the other steel, fire flashing out in every argument," writes Frémont. Hassler had many peculiarities. It was not without cause that his wife, after bearing nine children, had deserted him. Thin, tall, and intellectual looking, dressing in summer in white flannels, he used to drive through the streets in what he called his "ark." This was a huge comfortable carriage which he used in his field surveys, packing it with bedding, choice foods, and the best Rhine wines. Nicollet was tactful in his devotion to science, Hassler headlong and imperious. He did what he thought was scientifically right in the shortest way, and paid no attention to outside criticism. To a Congressman who reproached him for tardiness with a report, remarking that when he had such a paper to write he did it overnight, Hassler retorted: "That is time enough for such reports, but before you could write one of mine your days would be numbered." Yet at heart, as Frémont soon found, he was a kindly man.[5]

Nicollet built an observatory on top of Hassler's house, where the three made frequent night observations. Sometimes they were aided by J. J. Abert, head of the Topographical Corps, who liked to drop in. The work was confining, and at moments Nicollet and Frémont longed heartily for the open. The former wrote Sibley in the spring of 1840 that all their regards were perpetually turned toward the west, that all their conversations were on frontier scenes and friends.[6] "If we take a promenade our recollections haunt us—the sight of a fine hunting dog, a double-barrelled gun, the sound of the wild cry of the geese which emigrate from North to South, all this for us seems to come from Sibley! ... Frémont says to me every now and then,

'Let us go and see Sibley. When will we go and see Sibley?' "
But they made steady progress, save when Nicollet's growing
weakness interrupted them. He wrote Hassler on September
20, 1840: [7] "Nothing new in your establishment, where everything proceeds with the same order, tranquillity, and exactitude
as under your direction. . . . Frémont and I have had eleven
good series of astronomical observations this week. I am applying myself completely to my map, having finished the calculations which it demands. In eight or ten days there will be
nothing more to introduce but the topographical details." A
little later, unfortunately, he sent Hassler disquieting news:
"That languor which troubled me sometimes during the summer
seems to resolve itself now into an affection of the chest." And
on New Year's Day, 1841, he wrote sadly that he had been
confined to his room for more than a month, spending half of
that period in bed, and that he was deeply depressed.

When Hassler was at home and Nicollet was well, the three
led a pleasant social life. Hassler had a competent French chef,
a mark of distinction; his cuisine was excellent, the house was
admirably furnished, and he did a good deal of entertaining.
In this city of thirty thousand people, every one of importance
soon knew everybody else, and Frémont, introduced by two
eminent scientists, had the entrée to the best homes. He saw
or cared little for the purely political circles. Many Congressmen, living in hotels or boarding-houses, formed "messes," each
group having a table to itself and making its own arrangement
with a landlord or landlady for food. But he became a familiar
figure at receptions and balls, some of which were rather glittering affairs with distinguished visitors from other cities and
Europe. Among the more imposing mansions were John Tay-
loe's exquisite "octagon house," designed by Thornton, and
John Van Ness's house, which Latrobe had erected at a cost of
$60,000. On Lafayette Square just across from the White House
the venerable Dolly Madison, conspicuous for her old-fashioned
gowns, snowy turban, and dignified manners, held court. Poin-

[7] Hassler Papers, New York Public Library.

sett had a hospitable ménage, where Frémont was always welcome, and the wives of other Secretaries entertained frequently.
At the dances, lasting until three in the morning and drawing
rather more elderly people than young men, Frémont was in
demand for his vivacity, his handsome if dapper figure, and his
ability to talk about South American ports and western wigwams. Doubtless he liked these diversions. They broke in agreeably upon the long days spent in careful calculations, the long
night watches in the observatory. He was a light-hearted young
fellow, and in his *Memoirs* tells some stories of pranks that half-
pleased, half-irritated Nicollet.

Inevitably the introductions which Poinsett and Nicollet gave
him, the social round into which he was drawn, brought him
friends who were to prove of lasting importance. Two in particular were to exert a powerful influence on his behalf. Though
the summer and fall of 1840 found the country in the throes
of the log-cabin campaign, some men were interested in larger
issues than Whig or Democratic victory. With population fast
spreading into the West, many had their eyes upon Texas, the
Mexican possessions north and west of it, and Oregon. The
junior Senator from Missouri, Lewis F. Linn, was one. Born of
Kentucky pioneer stock, and long a frontier physician at Ste.
Genevieve, Missouri, he had entered the Senate seven years
earlier as a devoted Jacksonian and an enthusiastic believer
in manifest destiny. During Van Buren's Administration he
became a leader in the revival of sentiment at Washington for
"saving" Oregon from the British—it then being held jointly
by the two powers. After introducing in 1838 a bill to "re-
occupy" the territory and establish a government there under
military protection, he continued to urge legislation for its
occupation and settlement. Not at all a fire-eater, indeed a mild,
amiable, and much-beloved man, he believed that Americans
must press rapidly to the Pacific. Far more influential than Linn
was the senior Senator from Missouri, Thomas Hart Benton.
He, too, supported by the economic interests of his state, believed whole-heartedly in western expansion. Though he held

that the Texas question had been settled by the treaty of 1819 and that our absorption of that area was unwarranted, though his views on British rights in Oregon were so mild that he became a strong adherent of the compromise line of 49°, he wished to see the American flag carried all the way from San Juan to Lower California.[8] His dynamic personality, persistence, and reputation as Democratic floor-leader in the Senate, made him a powerful figure.

Frémont made speedy acquaintance with these men. Benton lived on C Street amid an interesting circle of friends.[9] He and Poinsett had long been acquainted—Poinsett had in fact urged his appointment as Minister to Mexico before taking the place himself; and of late years Poinsett as head of the War Department had transacted much business with Benton as chairman of the Senate Military Affairs Committee. Soon after Frémont came back from the Northwest he met Benton at the Secretary's home, and the two immediately found much in common. Benton's belief in the rich possibilities of the West, and his earnest desire to see all the country to the Oregon coast explored, protected, and colonized as promptly as possible, led him to call frequently at the Coast Survey to study Nicollet's map. While Nicollet dilated on the fertility of the Minnesota-Dakota country, Frémont described the topographical details. He found Benton somewhat disappointed by the slowness of the map-making, and had to explain that it was an exacting process. First observations had to be taken in the field; then with astronomical aids they had to be reduced to latitude and longitude; then the map had to be projected and the positions as fixed by observation laid down upon it; then from the sketch-books the lines of the rivers, forms of lakes, and contours had to be inserted.[10] As Benton watched the map grow he asked many questions.

---

[8] William M. Meigs, *Life of Thomas Hart Benton*, pp. 276ff., 339ff.

[9] *Memoirs of John A. Dix*, I, p. 249.

[10] Frémont prints in his *Memoirs*, pp. 45, 46, a letter by an engineer of the Chicago & Northwestern Railroad, C. W. Irish, who in 1879-80 made observations for altitude along much of Frémont's route in Minnesota and Dakota, and found his records accurate within a few feet.

In return for Frémont's information the Senator, always ready to expound his vision of western development, dwelt upon the opportunities for exploration beyond the Missouri. This wild region, known only by the disjointed reports of a few travelers, offered much the same challenge to scientific exploration as Central Africa a few decades later. It should be traversed, mapped, and made known to the American people, declared Benton. Moreover, roads should be opened through it and settlement encouraged. He wished to see the Columbia River Valley occupied by emigrants, and the American title to its rich lands fully established.

Benton had to be taken seriously, for he was the principal floor-leader of the Van Buren Administration in the Senate, and despite his eccentricities, a respected statesman who represented much of American opinion. Those observers did him wrong who regarded him as an opinionated, tiresome, humorless crank on western expansion and other questions. He was thoroughly sincere, courageous, capable of great intellectual detachment, and on many points surprisingly moderate—on slavery, for example, as well as the boundary issues. To be sure, when he rose the Senate chamber emptied and gallery visitors filed out to avoid his interminable speech. To be sure, he was pompous, vain, and in some ways arrogant, and extraordinary stories could be told to illustrate his self-esteem. When Appletons inquired what sale his *Thirty Years' View* might be expected to have, he replied with crushing dignity: "Sir, I believe that the census states how many families there are in the United States." Complimented upon the striking impression he had made by a stump speech, he answered: "Always the fact, sir—always the fact." He once assured the Senate that small boys playing in the remoter parts of the republic learned year by year the story of his achievements, and found in them an irresistible incitement to ambition and public service. But unlike some other humorless and vain leaders, such as Charles Sumner, he had a sense of proportion and was essentially likeable.

It was a stormy age; he carried some of his political convictions into personal intercourse, and repeatedly was hardly on speaking terms with such Whig opponents as Webster and Clay. Stiff-necked and self-confident, he never surrendered one of his deliberate positions. He had proved his staying-power in his long fight to expunge from the journals of the Senate Clay's resolution censuring President Jackson. Yet the dogmatic, imperious Senator possessed qualities that his foes admired. He had assiduous scholarship, breadth of view, and a high sense of civic responsibility. A Southerner and slaveholder, he held Jefferson's conviction that slavery was a pernicious institution and always opposed its spread to new lands. Though a devoted expansionist he adhered strictly to principle; the annexation of Texas offended him, as did the warlike cry of "Fifty-four forty or fight" in the Oregon controversy. He was a true democrat in favoring the grant of free homesteads of 160 acres to all bona fide settlers. As his biographer, Roosevelt, has said, he was morally as far superior to Webster as intellectually he was inferior. His public career and personal life was alike unsullied. Austere, of imposing dignity, loyal to his friends but never encouraging intimacy, he showed a dignity and polish that were refreshing in this era of Jacksonian informality and conviviality.

Frémont quickly recognized the statesmanlike vision of Benton, and soon realized also that the Senator was remarkably well versed in geography and travel. Though he had never been far beyond the Mississippi, he devoured every book and article upon western exploration, and took pains to talk with every man who penetrated into unknown regions. Upon these subjects he was pronounced a better authority than any reference library.[11] Frémont's imagination was profoundly stirred by his very first interview with the Senator. Up to this moment the lieutenant had fixed all his ambitions upon engineering, and tells us that he had made the lives of great engineers his "treasured exemplars." Now he saw opening before him the possibility of extending to the remoter West the type of work which he and Nicollet had been performing in the Minnesota-Dakota coun-

[11] Theodore Roosevelt, *Life of Thomas Hart Benton,* p. 36.

try; of pinning his name to the western map, and grasping fame as the pathmarker of the great plains and the mountains. In this undertaking there would be adventure, activity, scope for all his energies and ambitions, and perhaps fortune. "This interview with Mr. Benton," he exclaimed later of their first long talk, "was pregnant with results and decisive of my life."

Fired by his new aims, he began spending more and more time at Benton's house, until his acquaintancy grew into intimacy. Here, Congress being in session, he met many western members, whose talk fell often upon exploration and expansion. Among them was Augustus C. Dodge, at this time Delegate and later Senator from Iowa. Dodge was a tall man, powerfully built, with an imperious manner; he was a half-brother of Senator Linn. Senator Robinson of Illinois was often present, with others keenly interested in opening the Far West. Nicollet's health continued poor, and the energy and vivacity of the younger officer brought him into the foreground of attention at the very time that Benton and his colleagues began to make definite plans for an exploring expedition beyond the Missouri.[12]

The Benton family at this time consisted of four daughters and one son, and Frémont caught glimpses of an affectionate but disciplined home life which seemed very attractive to him. He learned of the Senator's rigorous habits of work: every morning Benton rose before six o'clock, curried himself, as he put it, with some stiff brushes, and sat down in his dressing-gown of white flannel to his writing. For light, he depended upon an ingenious candelabrum of his own invention, with four spermaceti candles fastened in front of a large square of white blotting paper as reflector.[13] Mrs. Benton and he were devoted to one another. They insisted that the children should be carefully dressed for dinner, should be in the drawing-room before it was served at five, and should make the meal cheery and amusing. If any one brought a disagreeable topic to the table, the punish-

---

[12] Frémont, *Memoirs,* p. 66.
[13] Jessie Benton Frémont MSS, Bancroft Library.

ment was exclusion from the circle next day. When Frémont became familiar with the household, only three children, the two youngest daughters and the son Randolph, were at home, for Sarah (the oldest) and Jessie were at Miss English's boarding-school in Georgetown, three miles away. This was the most fashionable school anywhere near Washington, with a Danish lady for principal, more than a score of teachers, a hundred boarding pupils, and many day scholars. The roster included Fitzhughs, Calverts, and even a Washington. But the Benton daughters, reared in a simple, wholesome fashion, were not sent to it because it was fashionable. Sarah, in ailing health, needed a special regimen; both required good tuition; and the blooming Jessie was kept in the school partly to avoid suitors—for she had already received two direct proposals of marriage.

Frémont and Jessie first met at a school concert in George-town, to which he escorted the eldest sister. The result was love at first sight, or almost that. She was like a rose, like a beautiful picture, he exclaimed many years later. Jessie was not quite sixteen, but in the full bloom of girlish beauty, her perfect health effervescing in bright talk. Frémont, who had not seen many pretty girls since his long stay on the frontier, was in a susceptible mood. He was carried away by Jessie's brown hair and bright brown eyes, her lovely oval face and rich high-colored complexion, her sparkle and vivacity, which more than matched his own; her grasp of mind, her tenacious memory, and her quick perceptions, all inherited from her father. He perceived also in her a quality of imagination which the Senator never possessed. Indeed, Jessie was already known in the capital as a girl of rare character and brilliancy, who gave promise of a still rarer womanhood. For her part, she responded as quickly to Frémont's dash, energy, and impetuosity. Years later people recalled him as "the handsomest young man who ever walked the streets of Washington." She was naturally emotional and warm-hearted. Each perceived the other's feelings, and neither had the temperament for much restraint. "There

JESSIE BENTON FRÉMONT

(From the portrait by T. Buchanan Read)

KIT CARSON

THOMAS H. BENTON

(From Frémont's *Memoirs*)

came a glow into my heart," Frémont wrote decades later,[14] "which changed the current and color of daily life, and gave beauty to common things."

Months passed before Jessie, coming home for a vacation, was able to see the ardent lieutenant with any frequency. When she did return, his visits to the Benton home became more frequent than ever, and their object was not long in doubt. She was so transparent, her soul (as Frémont expressed it) was so white, that she was unable to conceal her girlish emotions. "At that time of awakening mind the qualities that made hers could only be seen in flitting shadows across her face, or in the expressions of incipient thought and unused and untried feeling." The Senator and Mrs. Benton became alarmed.

It was difficult to exclude an irreproachable and brilliant officer from the Benton home. By fixed custom friends and neighbors were always welcome to the evening circle in the drawing-room upstairs. Here, if the weather were chilly, a bright fire snapped on the hearth. On one side of the fireplace the Senator had a large table with his evening mail and the book he was then reading, its pages illuminated by his ingenious candelabrum or an astral lamp. On the other side Mrs. Benton sat placidly at a smaller table, her hands busy with knitting or embroidery. The four sisters had a great heavy square desk with shaded lamp, work-baskets, and portfolio; and as they were good musicians, if any guest requested it one would play, and Jessie and another, who had a beautiful contralto voice, would sing. In these surroundings the courtship was carried on, and it progressed so rapidly that the parents finally intervened. While they liked and admired Frémont, he was very poor, his salary was meager, and army promotion was slow. As yet his future seemed far from bright. Jessie's parents lectured her, while the Senator intimated to the lieutenant that she was far too young to think of marriage, and that when she did, they hoped she would not be subjected to the unsettled existence of an army

[14] Frémont, *Memoirs,* p. 67.

officer's wife. By the winter of 1840-41, it was understood that Frémont was not to see Jessie except on rare occasions.

But the attachment was too ardent to be halted, and within a short time ripened into a definite engagement. By a strange contrast of scenes, this bright event in the young people's lives occurred on President Harrison's funeral day, just a month after his festal inauguration. Since the Benton windows did not command a view of the funeral assemblage, Frémont asked Jessie, her grandmother, and a few friends to watch it from Hassler's house, which stood at the foot of Capitol Hill and offered a complete view of the procession as it defiled up to the east front of the Capitol. The large workroom was selected for the party, the desks were removed to another floor, and the place was made attractive by potted flowers and nosegays. A cheerful fire which had been kindled on the hearth, for it was a chill gray day outside, threw its gleam over a pretty tea-table, laden with cakes, French sweets, and ices. The grandmother was the guest of honor, and ostensibly all the flowers and delicacies were for her. While the elders of the group were troubled by the expense to which this "poor army man" had gone in entertaining them, Frémont, exalted and happy, was everywhere ministering to his guests' comfort. Without regard for his best uniform, he brought in logs and kept the fire blazing; he served the tea and ices with his own hands. Outside echoed the tramp of a great and mournful crowd in the raw cold of early April and the wailing of dirges as the plumed hearse carried Harrison's body, drawn by six white horses, to the Congressional Cemetery. Inside, as Jessie later wrote, was "our friendly group excited and amused (and two entirely content.)" [15] While the others were intent upon the funeral procession, these two had decisively plighted their troth.

The happiness of the pair was all too evident, and when next day Frémont sent all the geraniums and roses to Jessie's mother with a graceful message, she and the Senator decided that the situation had become perilous. They laid a shrewd plan. Mrs.

[15] Jessie Benton Frémont, *Souvenirs of My Time*, pp. 37, 38.

Benton knew Mrs. Poinsett well, and going to her, frankly stated the case: Jessie's extreme youth, Frémont's poverty, and the need for a separation. The Poinsetts agreed, and Frémont was astonished by orders suddenly detaching him from his duty of map-making, and directing him to proceed at once to make a survey of the Des Moines River in Iowa Territory, the stream along which the Sauk and Fox dwelt. The ailing Nicollet protested that he could ill spare his most efficient and experienced aide, but in vain. *"Il y a quelque diablerie lá-dedans,"* the French scientist ejaculated, shaking his head, and Frémont hurriedly set off by stage-coach. To be given charge of this reconnaissance was a promotion, but he went reluctantly. Jessie mourned his departure for a few days, and then she too was caught up and taken south to Lexington, Virginia, where a great wedding in her mother's family, the McDowells, with thirty-five house-guests, was about to occur.[16] The lovers were not left without hopes. There had been an agreement, at least informal and tacit, between them and Jessie's parents, that their engagement was to have a year's probation, and that at the end of that period they might, if their minds were unchanged, be married.

[16] See *Ibid.*, p. 40*ff.*, for an animated description of this wedding.

V

A Runaway Marriage

RÉMONT'S survey of the Des Moines River was by no means unimportant. Nicollet and he during their northern expedition had covered part of its headwaters; and now Secretary Poinsett declared that its course should be carefully plotted to its mouth in order to make their map of the Mississippi-Missouri system more nearly complete. Ordinarily Nicollet would not have been reluctant, but he was in bad health, and needed Frémont's daily help. Another assistant had to be found, and in his report he indicates how indispensable was the aid of both: [1]

The elements of the celestial bodies observed, as they were needed for the calculation, were taken from the *Nautical Almanac:* and the calculation of this considerable mass of astronomical observations has been executed by Lieut. Frémont and myself, aided for three months by Lieut. E. P. Scammon, corps of topographical engineers, whose zeal and intelligence on this occasion, as well as the talent with which he had assisted Lieut. Frémont in the construction of the map, insures my gratitude.

The map dragged badly after Frémont left. The young man, however, enjoyed at twenty-eight an opportunity to shoulder an independent responsibility of importance.

Since settlement was pressing rapidly into the Des Moines region, an accurate topographical survey and map would be of material value. Already Iowa Territory, which included that part of Minnesota lying west of the Mississippi, had about 45,000 people. For the most part they clung rather closely to the Mississippi. The Des Moines, flowing into the larger stream

[1] Nicollet, *Report,* p. 106.

near Keokuk, and draining a great part of central and southern Iowa, was still almost wholly wild. But within about two years Ottumwa was to be established on its banks, and Fort Des Moines, on the site of the city of that name, was to be built to protect the Sauk and Fox from white encroachments.

Frémont was expected to complete his task within six months. Proceeding to St. Louis, he enlisted the aid of Pierre Chouteau, hired his old companion the botanist Geyer at $1,500 a year to accompany him, and set off up the river. The party included several voyageurs who had been with the Nicollet expedition. Though their exploration was confined to the immediate valley of the river, they frequently ranged back into the woods, abounding with deer and wild turkey. It was an enjoyable and health-giving summer, but as Frémont drily records, it did not cure his special ailment.

A letter of Nicollet's, which illustrates the affection between them, shows plainly what was uppermost in Frémont's mind—what questions Nicollet was expected to answer.[2] Dated in Washington July 11, 1841, it answered a note which Frémont had sent from St. Louis on June 23rd, just as he was setting out northward. "I assure you," wrote Nicollet, "that our separation gives me as much pain here as it did to you in St. Louis." He was pleased to learn that all Frémont's preparations had gone smoothly and that Geyer was with him. "You had hardly left Baltimore when the idea occurred to me, and I should have written to St. Louis to suggest it had I not believed that M. Geyer was probably otherwise engaged and would not be able to accept your offer." Estimating the date of Frémont's arrival at the forks of the Raccoon and Des Moines, Nicollet found that he would not have the aid of the moon, at least before midnight, in making his calculations; but, he added, he could base them partly on the sun. To aid poor Geyer in some money difficulties with his St. Louis landlord, he had sent $100 through Pierre Chouteau, with instructions to keep the identity of the donor secret.

[2] Frémont MSS, Bancroft Library.

Everything in the Washington office, Nicollet went on, was going well; they were working hard, and were in harmonious relations with their superiors. After spending almost a month carefully revising the map, they had written all the notes which accompanied it: "there remains only your work upon the Des Moines, and to finish the topography." He had been pleased to find that there was nothing to change "in your admirable Missouri"—that is, in Frémont's map of the stream. Only two small errors in plotting, and two in calculations, had been found. Nicollet included various messages to friends in St. Louis, and asked that Geyer be reminded to make a search for fossils in the vicinity of the city. "I shall await you," he concluded, "with open arms to embrace you and congratulate you." All this we can imagine Frémont reading with interest; but the passage which he must have devoured again and again occurred in the middle of the letter:

Everyone here and in Baltimore inquires after you; even the Benton household, every time I go there. The young girls returned home evening before last, ten days later than they were expected, on account of the grandmother, who died at the moment when they were about to set out on their journey to Washington. *Everything is going well; she is quite happy, and she is impatient to see you.*

If Jessie's parents had expected her to change her mind during Frémont's six months' absence, they knew less about their daughter than they should have done. Strength of will and constancy of purpose, a tenacity like her own father's, were among her salient characteristics. Benton had waited seven years after his first rejection to marry her mother. As a young girl, Elizabeth McDowell, who sprang from a proud Virginia family—a brother became governor of the State—had said that she would never marry a redhaired man, a Democrat, or an army man, but her redhaired, Democratic, and military suitor would not take a refusal. Now Jessie's purpose was equally fixed, her will equally firm.[3]

[3] Jessie's traits are well described in Catherine Coffin Phillips, *Jessie Benton Frémont,* Chs. 3 and 4.

Nor, though still less than seventeen and a half years old, was she unfit for the duties of wifehood. Maturing early, she was gifted with womanly qualities and abounding energy. The oldest Benton daughter was delicate; but I, she writes, "was a perfectly healthy child. I don't remember a headache until I was twenty-three; gay-hearted, affectionate, with a keen delight in life, and that *besoin d'aimer* that made loving and being loved necessary to me." Her education had been remarkably complete and wholesome. From her earliest years she had been a companion, and from young girlhood an aide, to her father. She wrote long afterward: "I think I came into my father's life like a breath of his own compelling nature; strong, resolute, but open to all tender and gracious influences." She recalled how once, when she was three, the Senator found her sprawled on the floor of the library, covering the sheets of his latest speech with red and blue chalk marks. He asked angrily, "Who did this?" Jessie instantly planted herself in front of him, and with a disarming smile found the weakest joint of his armor by saying: "It's a little girl that cries, 'Hurrah for Jackson!'" From the time she learned to read she profited by Benton's earnest mind and wealth of learning. The family had a large collection of books, and her taste matured early. She was attracted at once to Shakespeare, and "to the British state trials; huge folios I came to know well through the full-page illustrations before I could read." [4]

She had the advantage also, one of great importance to the future wife of an explorer, of acquaintance with widely different scenes and circles; from her earliest years she was accustomed to the movement, life, and variety that she loved to the end. During her girlhood the Bentons possessed three homes. That in Washington was the official residence. That in St. Louis, which the difficulties of travel made it impossible to reach except in the alternate years of the short Congressional session, boasted wide grounds, handsome trees and shrubbery,

---

[4] Jessie Benton Frémont, *Souvenirs of My Time, passim;* see also her biographical sketch of Benton in Frémont's *Memoirs,* I, pp. 1-17.

and a gay social life among the Americans and Franco-Americans of the city. But the home which Jessie loved best was her Grandfather McDowell's extensive estate at Lexington in the beautiful Shenandoah. She had connections with some of the best families of the Old Dominion. Her father was descended from one of the colonial governors, Sir William Gooch, her mother from the Prestons; and when as a child she traveled down from Washington, to be met at Fredericksburg by her grandfather's carriage, she stopped every night from there to Lexington at some friendly mansion of importance.

She associated this ancestral estate with picnics in its large park, with hunting, with gay masquerade parties, with Negro mammies and uncles, and with a joyous outdoor life. Here she would follow her father up some ravine as he shot quail, and eat lunch with him under a tree. Resting against his shoulder in the southern sun, the wind stirring her hair, she would listen while he read aloud an English poet, a French translation of Homer, or the *Arabian Nights*. On the long western trips by stage and steamboat, she delighted in the scenery of the National Road or the Ohio; and St. Louis, a genial half-southern, half-western town, with the teeming activity of the mighty river rolling past, was always dear to her. In spring the town, full of blossoming locusts and catalpas, seemed en fête, every one happy and gay; and her father, freed from official routine, gave himself up to outdoor life. Settee, table, and a colony of chairs were taken to the long gallery on the ground floor, where all his friends were welcome to an early breakfast of fruit, hot-breads, and coffee.

This varied training fed Jessie's natural vivacity and interest in all kinds of people, and deepened the social charm which made her so captivating. Her ancestry was purely British. Her visits to the Virginia estate, her father's tastes in literature and law, made her familiar with the best Anglo-American tradition. Yet from infancy she was also imbued (and this was an essential contribution to the perfect understanding between her and Frémont) with the spirit of Franco-American life in the Southwest. Even in Washington she was given French as well as English governesses. In St. Louis, the family had many French neighbors who called informally and took a warm interest in the children. One of the Senator's closest friends was a Spanish gentleman who had served with Wellington in Spain, and another a Colonel Garnier who had fought under Napoleon and talked of his experiences at great length.

Benton always insisted that his children assimilate knowledge, not acquire it parrot-wise. To Jessie's delight, therefore, in St. Louis she was first sent to an undisciplined but effective school for practise in French with other children. Her mother's stiff, taciturn maid Sara conducted her and her sisters for the pleasant walk of a mile, drilling them in their "manners." When they passed Mme. Desirée, the clear-starcher, Sara instructed them to speak with special politeness, for she was a poor workingwoman and brusqueness might hurt her feelings. The house-doors of various ladies, Mme. Auguste, Mme. Pierre, Mme. Jean, would be open, and they would call the children into their large inner courtyards, pet them, and give them some fruit or other gift. When at last the promenade ended, the youngsters would be put not at formal lessons, but to whipping ruffles or hemming handkerchiefs in the garden of Mme. Savary's school, overlooking the wide tawny river below the bluff; practising their French all the while. Later came a more rigorous tuition in the convent of the Sacré Cœur. It was no ordinary convent school. It had a staff of accomplished teachers, models of French breeding and refinement, who taught Jessie not merely history and literature but a *savoir faire* which she could never have acquired so well elsewhere.

Yet *savoir faire* came naturally to the daughter of Senator Benton, who saw so much of the best society of the country in Washington. She was frequently at the White House, for as a little girl she became a favorite of President Jackson's. She remembered sitting on his knee as he and the Senator chatted. She recalled such experiences as a tour of the White House a few minutes before a state dinner: the long silent rooms bright with candles, the enormous table gleaming with silver, linen, and banked smilax, and at each end of its oval expanse a great salmon, half-buried in rippling waves of meat-jelly. She was a bridesmaid at the famous wedding of the Russian Minister, Count Bodisco, to one of her schoolmates at Georgetown, a wedding extraordinary for the disparity of age—the ugly, kindly count being sixty-one and the blooming bride sixteen —and for the distinction of the guests. President Van Buren was there: Henry Clay, tall and slender in his black coat, gave the bride away; and the groomsman paired with Jessie was the handsome Senator, James Buchanan, who sixteen years later was to contest the presidency with her husband.[5] In spite of all predictions, it proved a happy marriage. At her father's house, Jessie became familiar with all the Democratic leaders of the day. But society, however interesting, never quite won her away from books: [6]

The supreme delight for me was to be found in Washington only, for there was the Congressional library. While reading was still a little difficult, the books of glorious pictures were mine to pasture in: Audubon's birds, the Louvre Gallery, fine French engravings of many others. Many a noble collection of sculptures and paintings were all freely laid before me on their broad, low rests, where I, sitting entranced, took in visions of art and beauty that must have moulded my thought and life. My father would take me when he walked to the Senate at ten, leave me to the care of kind Mr. Meehan, the librarian, and at twelve our nurse came for me, often finding me on the broad recessed gallery opening from the center of the library, where I would find in the noble view of the Potomac and its opposite hills, historical Arlington chief, as lovely a picture as any in the books—plus color and life. This was a growing happiness. Year after year that hushed scholarly atmosphere entered into me. As a young girl I was (ex officio) on the purchasing committee of the Senate. My judgment would be asked, and often taken, for French works. Books costing hundreds were in this way open to me—and many others of little cost but great value.

[5] Helen Nicolay, *Our Capital on the Potomac,* pp. 221-224.
[6] Jessie Benton Frémont MSS, Bancroft Library.

We must think of Jessie at seventeen as a young woman already mature, with a training which had made the best of her naturally decisive character and strong mind. Far from being an unripe and wavering school-girl, whose romantic fancy for a young officer would leave her as quickly as it had come, she had a will of her own. She had seen much of the world, and knew men, cities, politics, and literature. Vivacious, keenly interested in life, quick to measure others, strong in her dislikes and still stronger in her likes, with a delightful combination of poise and animation, she felt that her choice had been fixed. The engagement made in the spring was not to be broken in the summer; it was to become marriage in the fall.

Frémont's work on the Des Moines was accomplished as quickly as impatience could desire. He established the course of the river upward from its mouth to the Raccoon Forks, about two hundred miles in all; taking his astronomical observations with great care, giving Geyer time to make a botanical survey. He felt strongly the responsibility of the expedition, and its successful completion marked another stage in his development.[7] We may be sure that he was proud to return to Washington with his data, supplementing Nicollet's own survey of the upper portions of the Des Moines, complete and in order.

Just when he was back in the capital we do not know—probably early in September. Nor do we know under just what circumstances he and Jessie met again. For a time he was busy completing the maps, for Nicollet's health was now at a low ebb. The map-making was the chief crown and goal of these expeditions, and had to be done with the greatest care. Altitudes had been determined by barometer; latitudes by deduction from a long series of astronomical observations of stars to the north and south of the zenith; longitudes by telescopic observation of the eclipses of the satellites of Jupiter, eclipses of the sun, occultations of the planets and fixed stars by the moon, and transits of the inferior planets over the sun's disc. All these calculations were difficult, and some of them exceedingly intri-

[7] Frémont, *Memoirs,* uncorrected proof sheets, Bancroft Library.

cate.[8] The reconnaissance or survey of the country traversed had been made by taking the magnetic bearing of every point, estimating its distance, and then making a sketch or bird's-eye view of the whole; this operation being constantly repeated as they moved forward. Even in Nicollet's first summer the sketching had been left to Frémont. The scientist reported to the government that

his coöperation during 1838 and 1839, while it left me more time to spend upon other duties, as the chief of the expedition, proved also otherwise advantageous, by the talents which he displayed for the branch of the service, and the activity and accuracy which have always characterized what he has had occasion to perform under my direction.

In the Des Moines expedition, Frémont was, of course, compelled to do all the work of ascertaining altitudes, latitudes, and longitudes as well as the lighter labor of sketching. It was always fascinating to him to see his maps approaching final form—to place on paper the results of laborious travel through the uncharted wilderness as a guide for future wayfarers.

The Bentons were still adamant in their opposition to the match. Sometimes Frémont saw Jessie at her parents' home, sometimes clandestinely. It was the dull season in Washington; as dull, wrote James Gordon Bennett,[9] "as the last season philippics. Pennsylvania Avenue reminds one of the prophet Ezekiel's valley of dry bones. Hardly so much as a dun stirring." The two discussed their position carefully. If they waited for parental approval they might have to wait ten years, and they were far too impetuous, far too much in love, to face such a prospect. A runaway marriage, they decided, was the only means of securing their happiness. Frémont, with Jessie eagerly awaiting the result, went to several Protestant clergymen of Washington and asked them to perform the ceremony. By now

[8] Nicollet, who had worked out carefully the best technics of determining altitudes, latitudes, and longitudes, and had taught them to Frémont, describes the processes in his *Report*, pp. 95-142.

[9] New York *Herald*, November 10, 1841.

it was well known that Senator Benton was wrathfully opposed to the match, and the ministers answered that while they would be glad to marry the two openly, they would not officiate at a secret wedding. For one reason, Jessie was only seventeen years and five months old. We can imagine how her eyes flashed over this news. Frémont's Catholic friends in Baltimore would have been glad to come to his aid, but this was unnecessary. A friend of Jessie's, Mrs. J. J. Crittenden, wife of the Senator from Kentucky, who had watched the romance with warm interest, interceded for them with Father Van Horseigh of a Washington parish and he promised to perform the ceremony. On October 19, 1841, with the Crittenden family as witnesses, they were married in a parlor of Gadsby's Hotel, the two immediately parting.[10] For some time they kept their secret from the Benton family, and we have a curious letter from one of Frémont's frontier associates, F. W. Gody, dated in Washington on November 7th, urging him to make a public announcement. Gody wrote Frémont: [11]

Your letter dated Baltimore I have received in due time, and would not have delayed my answer on this particular occasion for an hour if it had not been for breaking up my camp and leaving for Washington. I have arrived here on Friday morning, and now I hasten to offer you my best congratulations, and beg you to accept my most sincere wishes for your future happiness. Perhaps you have noticed, Mr. Frémont, that I am not very fond of much and big talk, but so much I can assure you, that none of your friends (you have permitted me to class myself amongst them) feel a warmer interest for you than I do, that no one wishes more truly and more cordially that those expectations of a blessed domestic happiness, which you naturally must have formed, may soon and continually be realized. I hope you will not think it too great a liberty, when I repeat the word "soon." Although, my dear Frémont, I cannot judge in this particular case clearly, yet I would venture to say,

[10] New York *Tribune*, June 23, 1856. Another account states the ceremony was performed at the Crittenden home; C. C. Phillips, *Jessie Benton Frémont*, p. 57.

[11] Frémont MSS, Bancroft Library.

that any delay of an open declaration, which some time or another must follow, makes your excuse, as well as this declaration itself, much more difficult. Besides, the possibility of an accidental discovery is very strong— Why don't you go, manly and open as you are, forward and put things by a single step to right—never mind in what this step consists—only act now and you will soon get over little disturbances which might arise at first. Nothing very serious can happen now more to you—the prize is secured and the rest will soon be smoothed by help of time and mutual affection and love.

If I am mistaken in my suggestion it is for want of information, and then I beg to forgive me. It is friendship that makes me write so. Anyhow, I sympathize with you—and entertain no fears for a fortunate conclusion.

I arrived here on Friday morning, and am perfectly happy in the society of my lovely girl. I don't like it much you beat me so decidedly, but I hope now to follow soon, and then if I should go out in spring again, I will not have to leave her behind me. I had no time in Baltimore to call on you, besides I did not know your residence altho supposing it to be Bainims.

Mrs. Cummings and Mary desire to be remembered to you and I conclude with the assurance of friendship and personal esteem.

P.S. When walking last night with my Mary and Mrs. Cummings we met Mrs. Frémont. I had a glimpse at her, and thought she looked very well and happy.

Excuse all the blots, neither pen nor ink are good for anything.

Frémont had said that he did not care who performed the wedding ceremony, so long as it was performed quickly and surely. Early in November, visiting Nicollet in Baltimore, he was urged by his superior to disclose the marriage at once, but replied that Mrs. Frémont must decide the time. He in turn urged Jessie, and received a characteristic answer: "We will explain together. Come to the house tomorrow morning before ten o'clock. I shall ask for an early interview." Next morning the two entered the library together to tell their news to the grim-faced Senator. Frémont alternately paled and flushed, but Jessie defiantly placed her hand in his as he asked for a hearing. Years afterward she delighted to tell the story of the sequel to her grandchildren. It was a story of the lieutenant stammering, embarrassed, but determined; of Benton blazing with anger; of his sharp commands—"Get out of the house and never cross my door again! Jessie shall stay here!"; and of her own dramatic and defiant intervention, as she clutched Frémont's arm tighter and silenced the Senator by the words of Ruth: "Whither thou goest, I will go; and where thou lodgest, I will lodge; thy people shall be my people, and thy God my God!" [12] Benton knew that she would be as good as her word, and he was not the man to drive his daughter from her home. In the end she stayed, and Frémont, leaving his boarding-house forever, came to stay with her.

[12] Mrs. Henry Hull (a granddaughter) gave me this information.

VI

The Stakes of the West

FRÉMONT, unfortunate (as we may have said) in his illegitimate birth, his poverty, and his undisciplined early schooling, had been fortunate in his later scientific training; and now he was fortunate most of all in the time and circumstances in which he began his greatest work. He had completed his apprenticeship to exploration, and had obtained by marriage the support of the American statesman most interested in mapping and colonizing the West, at the opening of the forties. The decade which followed was to be preëminently the decade of American expansion; the decade in which Texas and the Southwest, California and Oregon, were all added to the Union, and in which a flood of emigrants swept to the coast. For this expansion and emigration Frémont was to do spectacular service.

Before the western wilderness lying beyond the Missouri could be opened to the broad American advance—a land of mountain, plain, cañon, and forest regarding which the eastern public possessed little accurate knowledge—various preparatory labors had to be performed therein. The different types of men who accomplished them each deserve no small meed of gratitude. First the paths of this wilderness had to be found; the trails by which men could ford rivers, thread the mountains, traverse parched deserts, without needless danger. Indians and buffalo knew most of these paths, and the first white hunters and trappers absorbed and added to their lore: men like John Colter, who was with Lewis and Clark, who served the fur-trader Manuel Lisa, and who made a famous journey southwest from the Yellowstone and back again to

Lisa's Fort Raymond as early as 1807; like Jedediah Smith and Thomas Fitzpatrick, who marched westward through South Pass in 1824; like Etienne Provôt, Kit Carson, Jim Bridger, and Old Bill Williams.[1] These "mountain men" spied out the natural highways of the West before the pulse of emigration began to throb along the Missouri.

But not one, not even Kit Carson, knew the paths and trails completely for more than a limited region. Nor was any member of this rude, daring, semi-illiterate group capable, even in the areas he most frequently ranged, of mapping trail, pass, and waterway with precision. Though they were the true pathfinders, their knowledge was relatively useless, for it could not be diffused. An expedition which hired one or several as guides might find its way expertly through the Far West, but their physical presence was required, and they were elusive men. At any moment, a tomahawk might wipe out all the knowledge that one of them had laboriously gained. Indeed, early in the forties arrow and bullet did extinguish much of their lore. This stern breed of mountain-men has had prose celebrators like Stanley Vestal and minstrels like John G. Neihardt, and it deserves them. But the group could not do the sustained work requisite for linking the local trails and natural highways into three great sets of transcontinental routes for colonists—the southern, the central, and northern routes. Even had they been able to do this, they would have been helpless to diagram accurately, to capitulate, and to advertise the highways of the West. They could furnish many of the raw materials of geographical knowledge; Carson, Bridger, and Fitzpatrick in particular were gifted with the photographic mind, and could give *orally* a clear and definite picture of any district they had visited; but they could hardly do more.

A second, more varied, and equally heroic group was made

[1] Excellent biographies have been written of most of these men: E. L. Sabin, *Kit Carson Days;* J. Cecil Alter, *Jim Bridger, Trapper, Frontiersman, Scout, and Guide;* W. J. Ghent and Leroy Hafen, *Broken Hand (Thomas Fitzpatrick);* A. H. Favour, *Old Bill Williams, Mountain Man.*

up of government experts and regular army officers specially detached for exploration; but perhaps the most remarkable feature of their work up to 1840 was its unevenness and incompleteness. Lewis and Clark were sent into the Louisiana Purchase in 1803 not merely to explore the possibility of a northern transcontinental route, but to survey one. Admirably as these great explorers did their work, their path lay too far to the north to be usable as a whole by large parties of settlers. Its eastern section was valuable for the fur-trade branching out from the Upper Missouri, and for little else. Early in the century the government sent additional expeditions to explore the Red River of the South, and other territory between the lower Mississippi and the Spanish domains. But only Zebulon M. Pike accomplished any substantial result, and here again its benefits to colonization were limited. His explorations succeeded in establishing the road to Santa Fé, but the Santa Fé trail was used almost wholly for trading—for that commerce of the prairies upon which Gregg later wrote his classic book. Moreover, the continuation trails to the Pacific remained so generally unknown to any save mountain men and daring traders that when Kearny marched his Army of the West from New Mexico to California in 1846, he had to kidnap Kit Carson and impress him into service as guide. When in 1820 the government sent Major Stephen H. Long west to explore, he penetrated only as far as Long's Peak in eastern Colorado, then visiting the Royal Gorge of the Colorado and returning homeward by way of the valley of the Canadian.

During the next twenty years, 1822-42, the face of the West was but slowly and imperfectly unveiled—very imperfectly indeed to those at a distance. Particularly did the great central area, which time was to prove the most important of all to settlers, remain ill-mapped. Long's expedition had opened the Platte River route to the Rockies. But Long performed no service to settlers when, publishing two volumes of his *Travels in the Interior of North America* in 1828, he grossly overemphasized the arid and inhospitable character of the plains around the upper Platte and upper Arkansas; for already men made too much of the Great American Desert. We have seen what Long and Featherstonhaugh accomplished, or rather how little they accomplished, in the Minnesota-Dakota country: Nicollet had done far more there for both science and settlement, and his map was extremely useful to emigrants of this area for many years.[2]

The third group was made up of leaders and heads of fur companies; daring men who possessed more education than trappers like Kit Carson and Jim Bridger, who had commercial motives for wishing to see the West explored, and who found means of diffusing the news of discoveries. The forerunner of the Rocky Mountain Fur Company, General William H. Ashley, equipped a party under Jedediah Smith and Thomas Fitzpatrick which in 1824 traversed the famous South Pass of the middle Rockies, some eighty miles southwest of the center of Wyoming, and thus opened a long section of what a decade later became known as the Oregon Trail. Ashley himself made in 1824-26 two long journeys (one of them to Great Salt Lake) in which he was the first to follow the Platte in winter, to cross the Rockies by Bridger's Pass, and to navigate the Green River. His chief successor in this trapping group, the intrepid Jedediah Smith, in 1826 led a party from Great Salt Lake to explore the country to the southwest, then quite unknown. Descending first the Virgen River and then the Colorado, he finally struck west across the Mojave Desert and other barren wastes of southern California, reaching San Gabriel Mission, near Los Angeles, in November. Thence he followed the San Joaquin Valley northward for about three hundred miles, spent the winter trapping, and crossed the Sierras and the Nevada plains, reaching Great Salt Lake again. The Rocky Mountain Company had other bold employees—the Sublettes, James Bridger, the before-mentioned Provôt and Fitzpatrick —who made still other discoveries. Before its affairs were

[2] See E. W. Gilbert's study in historical geography, *The Exploration of Western America, 1800-1850*, Part II; W. J. Ghent, *The Early Far West*.

wound up in 1836, its men had become familiar with the whole region to the westward of South Pass. They had explored the Green River, the Colorado, the Utah, Sevier, and Great Salt Lake; they had crossed and recrossed the Rockies, the Sierras, and the intervening plains of the Great Basin. Smith had traveled by land up the Pacific Coast from California to the Columbia.[3] The employees, who sent $500,000 worth of beaver pelts to St. Louis and lost about a hundred lives in doing it, had familiarized themselves with a central transcontinental route to the Pacific.

But while these men explored, they did not survey, map, or describe the country. Smith's note-books were lost, and unfortunately no great part of his information found its way to cartographers. When Albert Gallatin in 1836 published in his work on the Indian tribes the best map of the West yet seen, he gathered many of his geographical facts from Smith's and Ashley's statements. But Gallatin's map must to-day excite our wonder chiefly for its inadequacy. Small, ill-proportioned, and lacking in detail, it can be published without essential loss on a duodecimo page. It showed Great Salt Lake, but indicated no mountains between it and the Sierras. It failed to mark the Ogden (later Humboldt) River, or even the San Joaquin. Jedediah Smith's route from the Sierras eastward to Great Salt Lake in 1827 was roughly indicated, and the Nevada-Utah country which he traversed was labeled the "Great Sandy Desert," but no detail whatever was presented upon this area, or upon California. Even less satisfactory in some respects was the map which Captain B. L. E. Bonneville published in

[3] Cardinal Goodwin, *The Trans-Mississippi West*, p. 126*ff.*, p. 428*ff.* The Astor expedition of 1811 went up the Missouri River as far as the Arikaras, near the present North Dakota-South Dakota boundary, and then struck off westward through Wyoming for the Columbia River. But Astor did not attempt the penetration of Wyoming until 1832. For the Smith-Fitzpatrick expedition through the South Pass, see Charles L. Camp, "James Clyman, His Diaries and Reminiscences," in the *Quarterly of the California Historical Society*, June, 1925; Alter's *Bridger*, p. 38. The journal of Robert Stuart, as recently edited by P. A. Rollins in *The Discovery of the Oregon Trail*, shows that a party led by this employee of Astor was the first known to have traversed South Pass (1812).

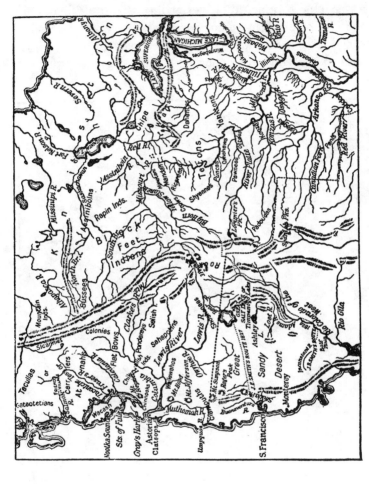

WESTERN AMERICA, BY ALBERT GALLATIN

FROM *American Antiquarian Society Transactions*, II (1836)

1837.[4] This was the result of his long expedition in the West in
1832-35, when the fur trade was at the height of its prosperity,
with the object primarily of extending the trade and only
secondarily of exploring unknown areas. His work, ostensibly
unofficial though perhaps secretly encouraged by the Jackson
Administration, gave the country a captivating book when he

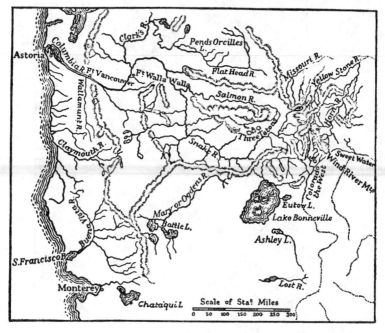

WESTERN AMERICA, BY B. L. E. BONNEVILLE (1837)

turned his manuscripts over to Washington Irving. But his
map could be published on a duodecimo half-page, and at
points was actually misleading. It showed a bay at Monterey
five times the size of San Francisco Bay, and a lake between

---

[4] These maps are reproduced in Gilbert, *Exploration of Western America,
1800-1850*, pp. 199, 200. It should be said that parts of Smith's journals were
discovered by M. S. Sullivan; see Sullivan's books, *The Travels of Jedediah
Smith* (1934) and *Jedediah Smith, Trade and Trail Breaker* (1936).

Monterey and the Sierras half as large as Great Salt Lake. The main respect in which it surpassed Gallatin's was in its clear delineation of Ogden's (later the Humboldt) River. American knowledge of the trans-Missouri West in 1840, weighed in the scales of the scientific geographer, was far from creditable to the nation; and by 1842 a host of Americans were eager to pour westward for settlement.

The crying need of would-be colonists in that year was for a detailed survey and accurate map of the central routes to the Pacific Northwest and California; a survey and map of day-by-day utility to emigrants. The Gallatin and Bonneville maps were not even rudimentary. The Lewis and Clark route, comparatively well mapped, lay in the main too far north. The Santa Fé route, well known and much traveled, led but half-way to the coast. Upon much of the central belt from South Pass to the Pacific the piecemeal information of Indians, trappers and traders had never been gathered together, and could not be utilized. The fast-gathering forces of emigration needed some really complete summary of both scientific and popular information upon the Oregon Trail, leading through South Pass, the Bear River Valley, the Snake Valley, and on across the Blue Mountains to the Columbia River. They needed a similarly comprehensive body of topographical information upon the shortest paths from the Great Salt Lake to the northern Sierras and down into California; and together with this, a survey of possible routes southward from the Columbia and Willamette Rivers into northern Nevada and California. The nation also needed both exploration and mapping of the huge barren area west and south of Great Salt Lake, which Gallatin had vaguely marked as the Great Sandy Desert, and Bonneville had not marked at all.

But the public felt the need for still another body of materials upon the wilder West; for a full, accurate and readable *description* of its main highways. A scientific map is at best a limited and difficult representation of a country, which few men can read properly, and still fewer have the patience to study.

While American pioneers, from the days of the Wilderness Road, have seldom been extensive map-users, they had always shown themselves hungry for graphic descriptions of the West. This fact accounts for the considerable wealth and variety of those early western travels which Reuben Gold Thwaites later collected, and for the eagerness with which even the pedestrian journals of the Lewis and Clark Expedition (apart from the captains', only those by John Ordway and Patrick Gass offered any detail), had been seized upon in their early editions. Henry R. Schoolcraft's narratives of his tour to the Ozark district and of his subsequent travels to the source of the Mississippi had attracted much attention. The practical quality of the general curiosity was demonstrated by the response to Zebulon M. Pike's two-volume account of his explorations and captivity in the Spanish Southwest. Since the jealous policy of Madrid had thrown a veil about all her Mexican territories, which many Americans supposed to be full of wealth, his book was eagerly seized upon in the Mississippi Valley. As Gregg says in his *Commerce of the Prairies,* Pike's descriptions "spread like wildfire through the western country," and gave a strong impulse alike to development of the Santa Fé trade and to emigration into Texas. Just so, a multitude of Americans at the close of the thirties were stirred to eager interest in the Rocky Mountain and Oregon country by Irving's brilliant *Adventures of Captain Bonneville* and *Astoria.*[5]

It was at this opportune moment that Frémont came forward to play his part in the West. If we read the next three years of his career aright, we must banish from our minds the legend of a brilliant Lochinvar, a dashing knight-errant of adventure. Frémont was still the product of the training imposed upon him by Poinsett, Nicollet, and Hassler; the training of Charleston College's "scientific department," of mathematics classes on a Federal warship, of officers of the Topographical

[5] F. L. Paxson, *History of the American Frontier,* p. 333. Irving himself had traveled in 1832 from the Mississippi across the Arkansas Valley to a point within a day's journey of the Texas boundary, and had written charmingly of the trip in *A Tour on the Prairies.*

Survey, of Nicollet's two campaigns. Erase the legend, and we see in him far less a scientific novice than Lewis, Clark, or Zebulon M. Pike, a far more thoroughly trained expert in geographical field-work. The brilliant amateur disappears; there emerges instead an expert, laborious topographer, a careful observer of scientific fact, the director of a hardworking and meticulously accurate survey. The members of the Lewis and Clark expedition had all been simply soldiers and frontiersmen. Encouraged to keep a record of the trip, each had been provided with note-books in a waterproof cover, and several took pains to write down their experiences. But none save William Clark knew how to map the country with even general accuracy; Lewis had picked up his astronomy rather hurriedly, and in turn had given Clark a hurried tuition in the fixing of latitude and longitude; and no member of the party could set down even elementary facts regarding botany and geology, or converse with the Indians.[6] Pike's notes of his southwestern expedition had been somewhat more valuable than the Lewis and Clark *Journals*, but were seized by the jealous Spaniards and hence unavailable when he wrote of his experiences. Captain Bonneville took some casual and infrequent astronomical observations to establish his position, but the principal value of his memoranda lay in the materials they supplied for Irving's graceful pen. Compared with these men, Frémont was a scientist. There is much in his life which his friends could wish blotted from it; but the five years 1842-46 were a strenuously busy period in which he honestly and laboriously earned his fame as explorer, and performed services of lasting importance to the nation.

Benton, Linn, Dodge, and other believers in national expansion to the Pacific had good reason in 1841 to urge Nicollet

[6] R. G. Thwaites, *Brief History of Rocky Mountain Exploration*, p. 92*ff*. As the facsimiles published by Thwaites (not by any means complete) indicate, Clark made some really excellent maps of the country traversed. For materials supplementing the main journals of the Lewis and Clark Expedition, those by the two leaders, by Ordway, and by Gass, see O. D. Wheeler, *The Trail of Lewis and Clark*.

to press forward with his report and map so that he might soon take the field again. The time was ripening for action. As the thirties closed and the forties opened, public attention was more and more directed to the Oregon Trail and Santa Fé Trail, and the possibilities of American settlement and trade in Oregon, California, and the Far Southwest. The press, led by the enterprising New York *Herald*, printed special correspondence from the frontier. Events in Texas, which was in the full tide of revolt in 1835 and declared its independence in 1836, kindled eastern interest in trans-Mississippi affairs. The Alamo was captured and its garrison slaughtered in March, 1836; the following month, Sam Houston crushed Santa Anna's army at San Jacinto. Thereafter, Texas was seldom out of the news or absent from the minds of political-minded Americans. Simultaneously, the Oregon country began to press upon the American consciousness. Before the thirties it had been a region as far distant as Outer Mongolia is to-day, where hardy post-traders exchanged blankets and ironware with the Indians for furs. But in 1832 Nathaniel J. Wyeth, with not a little beating of tom-toms, recruited a company in Boston, and led it across the continent to Fort Vancouver. His ambition was to establish a permanent seat of trade with an overland line of supply, and though the Hudson's Bay Company proved too strong for him, he did advertise the commercial possibilities of the region. Methodists and Presbyterians, burning to convert the Indians whom Lewis and Clark had described as possessing such fine traits of character, sent missionaries to the Oregon country in 1834-35, while a year later Dr. Marcus Whitman and his bride crossed the mountains by wagon to set up their mission near the point where the Walla Walla flows into the Columbia.[7]

[7] J. C. Bell, *Opening a Highway to the Pacific, 1838-1846*, Chs. 3, 4. The Methodists sent four missionaries to the Pacific Northwest in 1834. The Presbyterians sent Marcus Whitman and an associate, Samuel Parker, in 1835; and Whitman, returning east after going only as far as the Green River rendezvous, in the following year went back to the Columbia with four other workers. See W. A. Mowry, *Marcus Whitman*.

At the beginning of the forties the whole border was alive X
with activity, and the tide of American emigration was ready
to roll westward. The panic of 1837 and the lean years following had paralyzed the expansive energies of the country, and
compelled men to give their attention to recovery. But now the
depression was being succeeded by prosperity. The election of
a Westerner as President in 1840, a border hero, a believer
like Benton in cheap lands and plenty of them, encouraged the
expansionists.

Benton's interest in the West was primarily political and only
secondarily scientific; for the Oregon question was plainly approaching a crisis, and he and other western members were resolved that the Northwest must be American up to at least
the 49th parallel. For more than twenty years, ever since the
treaty of 1818 had established joint Anglo-American sovereignty over the Oregon country, this object had been near to
his heart. As we have seen, he had long advocated systematic
occupation of the Columbia River Valley under Federal protection. His bill of 1825 had authorized the President to employ
the army and navy to establish a port to shelter American
trading ships and whalers, to foster the fur trade, and to create
a safe overland highway to Oregon. Senator Dickerson of New
Jersey, who believed that the region would never be good for
anything but an Indian reserve, vehemently objected that "all
the sea-otters we shall ever take upon the coast of Oregon
Territory would not pay the expense of marching a single company across the Rocky Mountains." Though many shared this
incredibly myopic view, Benton persisted year after year in
offering his legislation.

It was clear by 1841 that the country was fast being converted by pressure of facts to his stand; only three years later,
one of the northern rally-cries in the Polk campaign was "fifty-
four forty or fight." The establishment of mission posts in
1835-36 was followed by the immediate emigration of farmers
to the new country. This rill of settlement, though at first tiny,
demonstrated that the treaty for a condominium with Great

Britain would soon have to be altered, and the bounds of American ownership fixed once for all. An inhabited country would need a single government and courts. The moment the issue of eventual American possession was squarely presented it became important to send settlers westward, and in 1842 Washington gave official encouragement to emigration by appointing Dr. Elijah White as Indian sub-agent in Oregon. Early that year White set off for the Northwest with about one hundred ten persons and eighteen wagons, while other parties, eager for free land in a mild climate, followed him.

The Oregon Trail, as the one well-established route to the beautiful Columbia Valley was known, ran northwest from the town of Independence on the Missouri to near Grand Island on the Platte, and thence turned westward up the Platte Valley to the Rockies, the road being level all the way to a point near the present-day Julesburg, Colorado.[8] As the trail left the forks of the Platte, the country grew hilly; and after emigrants reached the junction of the Laramie and North Platte, they found it sufficiently mountainous to offer many obstacles to loaded wagons. Their ordinary procedure was to follow the Platte and the Sweetwater River, in a general westward line, to South Pass, in what is now southwestern Wyoming. After crossing this broad, easy divide, they found themselves in the valley of the Green River, down which they moved to the trapping post called Fort Bridger, thence continuing northwest to the Bear and the Snake at Fort Hall. The tortuous course of the Snake was followed to a point beyond Fort Boisé (like Fort Hall, a post of the Hudson's Bay Company), whence the trail cut across the Blue Mountains to Walla Walla, the Columbia Valley, and the goal of the emigrants. Here and there were variations from the established route, like the Sublette cut-off beyond South Pass, which bolder travelers might take. The whole journey from the Missouri to the Willamette was about two thousand miles; and of this one thousand was a rocky,

[8] See W. J. Ghent, *The Road to Oregon,* and its companion volume, R. L. Duffus, *The Santa Fé Trail.*

steep, Indian-infested trail, with fierce alternations of heat and cold, which rigorously tested the courage of the emigrants. The Idaho country beyond South Pass was especially harsh and dangerous, with rapid torrents, an ill-marked trail which might easily be lost, and brackish or alkaline streams whose water was repugnant to both men and animals. By 1843, the wayfarer met at every difficult point tokens of the hardships which others had suffered; roughly marked gravestones, bones of horses and mules, and the discarded furniture of emigrants who had lightened their wagons. The rocky, sandy route wore out the animals and smashed the wheels. The heavy dust, the burning sun, the thirst, and the long hours exhausted the women and children. It was a land of sagebrush, hunger, Indian peril, fever, and utter fatigue and discouragement. But every student of the West knew that in 1843 and the years following emigrants would pour along the trail by thousands. In fact, within three years after 1842 some five or five and a half thousand Americans had settled in the Oregon country.

This Oregon Trail did not need exploration in the strict sense of the word; many a "pathfinder" had followed it before Frémont, and its course was well known. But it was important to have the route scientifically mapped, to examine the character of South Pass and other salient points, to fix latitudes and longitudes with care, and to report upon the fertility of the soil, navigability of streams, the best positions for forts, and the nature of the mountains beyond the crest of the Rockies in Wyoming. Senators Benton and Linn, with their fellow "Westerners," wished an expedition to do for at least the first section of the long trail what Nicollet had done for the Dakota-Minnesota country. Such exploration would give emigrants assurance of the government's interest, and advertise the importance of Oregon to the eastern public. Indeed, at a later date it was acknowledged that the expedition was "auxiliary to and in aid to emigration to the lower Columbia," though such a statement at the time would have been diplomatically impolitic. Frémont took part in these discussions, and found that they "gave shape and solidity to my own crude ideas." [9] His Gallic enthusiasm was aroused by the vision of western empire. "I felt," he wrote later, "I was being drawn into the current of important political events; the object of this expedition was not merely a survey; beyond that was its bearing on the holding of our territory on the Pacific; and the contingencies it involved were large."

There could be little question who would head this expedition. When Frémont and Jessie decided upon their sudden marriage, Nicollet was ill in his old quarters in St. Mary's College in Baltimore, carefully attended by the clergy. These men of secluded lives had welcomed him as the friars of La Rabida welcomed Columbus, for they enjoyed his reports of adventure in the wilderness as much as he enjoyed the security, peace, and comfort of the college. While Frémont worked hard to complete the map, Nicollet was laboring from his sickbed upon the report, to be printed as a Senate document. He wished to make this, like the map, a model to be followed by all other scientific explorers in government service. But now he was not only weak but thoroughly dispirited, suffering from complete nervous exhaustion. He could not muster sufficient energy to prosecute his work steadily, and his composition seemed to him feeble compared with his ideal of a scientific document. He lay abed late every morning, and sometimes did not rise all day, doing a little discouraged writing on a pad. Immediately after their wedding, Frémont and Jessie slipped away on a train to visit him, and the sight of their fresh, glowing happiness momentarily revived his spirits. But he soon relapsed into his former gloom, and though in intervals of exceptional energy and animation he came to Washington and visited the young couple, whom he fondly called *mes enfants,* he was plainly near the end of his career. He conjured up imaginary discouragements and obstacles in everything he undertook. Every discussion of the plan for mapping the Oregon Trail, an under-

[9] Frémont, *Memoirs,* pp. 65, 66.

taking which he knew to be totally beyond his strength, aroused in him a spirit of melancholy.[10]

Frémont, hoping to succeed Nicollet as head of the proposed expedition, for a time was uncertain of the post. Then on New Year's Day the plans of the group of expansionists were fully matured, and he was assured of their support. That holiday season had been one of great happiness to the newly married couple. On New Year's afternoon Frémont and Jessie went to call on President Tyler, and accepted Hassler's offer of his large foreign-built carriage, the "ark." In this lumbering vehicle they arrived at the White House and alighted, Jessie in full dress, Frémont in uniform, amid the pleased smiles of the crowd. It was a balmy, sunny day, like May; the Executive Mansion had been thrown open to the public at noon, and every street leading to it was crowded with carriages and hacks. While the Marine Band discoursed music in the vestibule, Tyler shook hands in the East Room with a crush of visitors eminent and obscure. The crowd was said to be the greatest the White House had seen since President Jackson had exhibited Colonel Meacham's gigantic cheese. Calhoun was there, Winfield Scott blazing with the insignia of his rank, the Hon. Cost Johnson with Lady Blanc on his arm, Webster, looking rugged and cheerful, and a large group of Democratic Senators —among them Benton.[11]

After the call, Jessie returned early to her father's house to assist in receiving guests; a family dinner followed; the charming Senator Linn and other "Westerners" came in; and the men withdrew to talk over their plans. Benton was emphatic in saying that Nicollet could never recover sufficiently to serve, that they must not wait, and that Frémont must at once make preparations to take charge. An allotment of $30,000 had

[10] J. H. Alexander wrote Hassler from Baltimore September 1, 1842: "Poor M. Nicollet, whom I went to see today for the first time for a fortnight, has been quite sick. He has been in a very bad way." Hassler MSS, New York Public Library. Nicollet's *Report* was printed as *Senate Doc.* 237, 26th Cong., 2d Sess.

[11] Jessie Benton Frémont MSS, Bancroft Library; New York *Herald*, January 4, 1842.

already been arranged for the expedition in the money budgeted for the Topographical Corps. The appropriation of this sum had to be handled diplomatically; President Tyler, much more intent upon the annexation of Texas than upon the acquisition of Oregon, was cautiously averse to measures which might lead to a clash with England. His Secretary of War, John C. Spencer of New York, was opposed to hasty expansion anywhere in the West. But such experienced parliamentarians as Benton and Linn had little difficulty in obtaining the appropriation. "With the New Year," writes Frémont, "began my joint work with Mr. Benton in behalf of our western territories. The months immediately following were occupied in preparation."

Lieutenant-Colonel J. J. Abert, head of the Topographical Corps, issued orders for the expedition which Frémont thought inadequate. Carrying them back for alteration, he persuaded Abert to fix the Rocky Mountains as the object of exploration and the South Pass the chief point to be examined and mapped. Benton tells us [12] that "the design was conceived by the young lieutenant," and that President Tyler knew nothing about it.

[12] Thomas Hart Benton, *Thirty Years' View*, II, 478.

VII

The First Expedition

PROBABLY there was no happier young man in the country on May 2, 1842, than John C. Frémont. We can imagine him taking leave of his wife of six months in the Benton home; kissing Mrs. Benton; receiving some pompous, fatherly admonitions from the Senator; and, spruce in his blue and gold uniform, running down the steps in the warm spring sunshine to the carriage that was to take him to the railway station. He was but twenty-nine years old. Yet he was at last in full command of his own expedition, with a long summer of outdoor life and adventure ahead of him, and an opportunity to achieve new distinction as an explorer. The poor half-orphan of the Charleston streets, the youth brought into the backdoor of the Army by Poinsett's influence, had achieved a position that any West Pointer might envy: the son-in-law of Senator Benton, the husband of the most charming girl in the capital, the successor of the famous Nicollet.

Could he have foreseen what a pleasant and profitable expedition lay before him, his feeling of elation would have been heightened. Frémont within the next decade was to pass through harrowing physical hardship, but this first expedition included few days that he could not remember with pleasure. It was a summer's tour in the kindliest of weather. It was not too ambitious; going only as far as the South Pass and Wind River Mountains, he penetrated no dangerous country. Yet it was sufficiently full of contacts with Indians, buffalo, and frontiersmen, of adventures on plain, mountain precipice, and river rapids. At the end he was to receive not only the congratulations of Lieutenant-Colonel Abert and Senator Benton, but a public interest and recognition which surpassed his best hopes.

It took twenty days for the lieutenant, accompanied by Jessie's brother Randolph, to reach the Missouri. Those curious as to his mode of travel may find a full description in the works of a man not much older than Frémont himself, who followed substantially the same route that spring—Charles Dickens. Both went from Washington to St. Louis, and there can be no doubt that in essentials, if not details, they used the same means. First there were the "cars" to Baltimore, then a steamboat to Philadelphia. The Harrisburg mail-coach, huge, lumbering, and crowded, with Frémont's carefully watched baggage on top, took him up the valley of the Susquehanna, and into Harrisburg. Here a canal-boat was waiting, where Frémont, like Dickens, could have "sat down to tea, coffee, bread, butter, salmon, shad, liver, steak, potatoes, pickles, ham, chops, black puddings, and sausages." As they crossed the Alleghenies they began to meet rough western types like the frontiersman Dickens heard protesting against a crowded boat-cabin: "This may suit you, it may, but it don't suit me . . . I'm a brown forester, I am. I ain't a Johnny Cake. There are no smooth skins where I live. We're rough men there. Rather. If Down Easters and men of Boston raising like this, I'm glad of it, but I'm none of that raising nor of that breed. No. This company wants a little fixing, it does."

From Pittsburgh to Cincinnati the travelers had their choice of a number of high-pressure steamboats, where tiny staterooms gave some privacy, and where they could sit in a narrow gallery outside and gaze upon the changing green shores of the Ohio. They were crude affairs, these steamboats, with high iron chimneys and a glassed steering-cabin atop, a mass of ill-built staterooms, two cabins, one for men and one for women, between decks, and underneath everything the hickory-fed furnace and the machinery, open to every wind. Dickens, seeing the furnace "that rages and roars beneath the frail pile of painted wood," the machinery working away amidst a crowd of idlers, emigrants, and children, and the management of the boat entrusted to reckless, inexperienced men, concluded that the wonder was, not that there should be so many fatal accidents, but so many safe journeys.[1]

Where the Ohio began to broaden into a noble river, Frémont could feel that he was again entering the wilderness; for while they passed an occasional town or hamlet, the banks were for the most part a leafy solitude, with no clearings, no thread of smoke from a log cabin, no life but the flash of the blue jay or tanager. Only here and there could he see wheat coming up green amid the stumps of a new farm, and the lank settler leaning on his ax and gazing curiously as the steamboat throbbed past. Here and there, too, the steamer landed a little group—a roughly dressed man, a woman in calico, a few children, and some old chairs and cooking utensils—to begin their pioneering venture. Sometimes at night, after gliding for hours through the silent darkness, they came suddenly to a spot where men were "burning off," and the tall trees stood sharply defined in the red glow of the fires of brush and logs. Cincinnati they found a beautiful city with well-paved streets, clean, fresh-painted houses, shops that would do credit to New York, and a suburb, Mount Auburn, on the high bluffs, where pretty villas stood in well-kept gardens. Here Frémont, like Dickens, probably took a larger and better steamboat, and once more the wilderness closed around him.

Men who made such a journey in 1842 found the tide of western travel mounting to a torrent. The boats were crowded with land-speculators, talking of fortunes in the new Illinois and Iowa townships; surveyors; Louisville and Cincinnati drummers; an occasional hunter and trapper, conspicuous in leather garments and coonskin cap; frontiersmen who found their old homes too crowded and were seeking new; and above all, a motley throng, mechanics from the East, Englishmen with capital, Irishmen without, and guttural Germans, hunting cheap land and free opportunities. Their talk was of the great new Mor-

---

[1] Charles Dickens, *American Notes for General Circulation*, Ch. XI.

mon community growing up at Nauvoo, Illinois; of the money
which Kentuckians made by taking droves of mules and horses
to market through Cumberland Gap; of the latest lynching in
Arkansas or Missouri; of the work the government was doing
for the Chicago harbor, and the huge lake trade; of new river
cities like Hannibal, Quincy, and Keokuk; and of the trade
the Magoffin brothers were carrying on with caravans of goods
to Santa Fé. Some were talking of the Missouri trading posts
and the Oregon country. The curiosity of the emigrants when
the Ohio boat reached the Mississippi was intense. The enormous stream, a mile wide, sometimes two or three, pouring its
muddy flood lazily southward, rolling whole forest trees along
in its frothy current, their tangled roots sometimes dangerously
grazing the steamboat's sides; dotted with lumber rafts, old-
fashioned arks, hay-boats, keel-boats filled with flour and
bacon, and skiffs; the steaming marshes; the far-away vistas of
forest opened up by an occasional creek—all this produced an
irresistible impression of power and wildness.

Frémont's imagination must have responded to it. He knew
that every turnpike, every canal and lake route from East to
West, was adding its share to the volume of emigrant travel.
He recalled Benton's prediction that within a century the population west of the Rockies would exceed the whole population
of the nation in 1820.[2] And here he was, avant-courier and
pathmarker for this human stream so rapidly remaking
America!

Reaching St. Louis, Frémont was received at one of its finest
mansions—the home of Mrs. Sarah Benton Brant, Mrs. Benton's favorite niece and the wife of an old friend and army
officer.[3] Here he had not only a room, but an introduction to
the best St. Louis society, curious to see Colonel Benton's son-
in-law. Yet he tarried only a few days. He or Benton had doubtless written ahead to the Chouteaus in St. Louis to assemble
men and material, which they could easily do; and Cyprian

[2] *Register of Debates in Congress*, I, p. 712.
[3] Frémont, *Memoirs*, uncorrected proof sheets, Bancroft Library.

Chouteau now gave his entire time to Frémont's needs. Preparations were quickly completed. Frémont records an observation of latitude and longitude at the Brant house on May 27th, and certainly within a few days thereafter he was on his way up the river.

The personnel and equipment of this party were to a considerable extent typical of his later ventures. One man had been hired before leaving Washington—Charles Preuss, a skilled German topographer. He had called one evening on Frémont with a note from Hassler, his face so red, his voice so incoherent from nervousness, that they had at first thought him drunk. A failure of appropriations had thrown him out of employment, and Frémont saw to it that his family, then in need, were provided with a Christmas dinner. He did more; he found a job for Preuss in reducing astronomical observations, and since Preuss knew nothing of such tasks, himself performed the work at night. Thus he kept the man on a payroll until the expedition started. This service Preuss repaid by years of devoted and much-enduring service as topographer. In St. Louis Frémont hired as hunter the frontiersman Lucien B. Maxwell, son-in-law of a wealthy New Mexican merchant, and himself in later years owner of the vast Maxwell grant. Henry Brant, young son of Frémont's host, was taken along as general aide. In addition to these and the boy Randolph, there were nineteen voyageurs, most of them French Creoles of long experience in the fur trade; the most notable being Basil Lajeunesse, of the Santa Fé Trail, Taos, and Bent's Fort, who later lost his life in Frémont's service. All were well armed, and all but eight mounted on good horses. These eight drove as many mule-carts, packed with baggage, instruments, and food. Some loose horses and four oxen for slaughtering completed the train.[4]

What the party at first lacked was a frontiersman of

---

[4] J. C. Frémont, *A Report on an Exploration of the Country Lying Between the Missouri River and the Rocky Mountains on the Line of the Kansas and Great Platte Rivers.* This report, published in various forms, is a general authority for this chapter and will not be cited again.

thorough acquaintance with the plains and mountains to serve as guide. For a time Frémont had thought of employing an old experienced "mountain-man," Major Andrew Drips, who had trapped through much of the Rockies for the American Fur Company, and Pierre Chouteau wrote to Drips in Frémont's behalf; but a much better man unexpectedly became available.[5] A rare stroke of luck threw Frémont into contact with one of the most efficient, and certainly the most picturesque, of western scouts, Kit Carson. In his autobiography Carson says simply that he met with Frémont, informed him that he had spent some time in the mountains and believed that he could guide the party to any point it wished to go, and after some inquiry, was employed. Frémont's story is fuller. He writes that as his party was ascending the Missouri by steamboat from St. Louis to Chouteau's Post, or Kansas Landing, near the present site of Kansas City, his attention was drawn to a man of medium height, broad-shouldered, deep-chested, of clear, steady eye and frank, modest speech. It was Carson, and the lieutenant was so much pleased with his personality and qualifications that he was glad to accept his services. Perhaps the fact that Carson and Lucien Maxwell were old companions and close friends had something to do with the arrangement.

The attraction between Carson and Frémont, which gave birth to a deep and life-long attachment, was largely the magnetism of opposites. Carson showed his Scotch-Irish ancestry as clearly as Frémont did his French blood; he was cool, quiet, observant, and determined, while Frémont was quick, sensitive, passionate, and impetuous. His rugged honesty, his transparent sincerity, his gentleness and kindliness (save to Indians and Mexicans, whom he regarded as most frontiersmen did), his loyalty and reliability, made him unusual among mountainmen. Possessing no high intellectual qualities, probably inferior in mental grasp to such a frontiersman as Thomas Fitzpatrick ("Broken Hand"), and no better acquainted with western wilds than Jim Bridger, Fitzpatrick, or several other contempo-

[5] Pierre Chouteau, Mafitt MSS, Missouri Historical Society, Collection D.

raries, he owed his preëminence chiefly to the solidity and wholesomeness of his character. It was precisely in solidity and balance that Frémont was most deficient. Both were young men, Carson being thirty-three; but Carson, who was a widower and father—he had visited St. Louis to place his young daughter with relatives or in a Catholic school—was much the more mature. Both might be called well educated, but in very different senses. Frémont's education was almost all scientific, Carson's was almost all the practical education of that frontier to which he had been an apprentice since the age of fifteen. He possessed no book-knowledge, he was as yet unable to read and write, and he spoke an ungrammatical lingo of the Southwest, something like the "Pike" dialect that later found its way into print. But his mind was broader, and more thorough, if less superficially brilliant, than Frémont's, and he had made the utmost of his opportunities for learning what is not in books. He had a serviceable command of French, Spanish, and several Indian tongues, could carry on a conversation with unfamiliar tribes by signs, and had fully mastered the lore of plains and mountains.

Since Frémont was to see much not only of Carson but of other mountain-men, we may pause briefly to examine the ways of this picturesque and useful breed of men.[6] Many of the principal figures led lives that were stamped by a remarkable similarity, for as a group they passed through three well-defined phases. The mountain-men appeared early in the century as trappers, threading the snow-crowned ranges and following the rushing streams through dark fir-clad valleys or cañons of red rock for beaver pelts. By 1842 the beaver, forerunners of the buffalo, were so nearly exterminated that trapping became unprofitable, while the tides of conquest and settlement were about to flow over the Far West. Some mountain-men, therefore, as masters of topography, veritable walking maps, turned aside to guide exploring expeditions like Frémont's, parties of emigrants, and military columns; others turned to supplying emigrant trains with meat and other necessities. But that phase

6 Compare Stanley Vestal, *Mountain Men.*

proved even more transient than the day of the trapper. Within
another fifteen years the West had become so well mapped and
so largely settled that guides lagged superfluous on the stage.
Some adventurous frontiersmen, like Hawkeye in *The Prairie*,
turned at last into prosaic farmers, some to trade, and some to
government appointments as Indian agents.

Nothing better demonstrates the general similarity of their
careers than the striking parallelism in the lives of Carson,
Fitzpatrick, and James Bridger; men representing three different blood-strains, hailing from three widely separated points,
and wholly unlike in character and gifts. Carson, of Scottish
blood, was born in Kentucky, Fitzpatrick, of Irish, in County
Cavan, and Bridger, of English, in Virginia. Yet their lives
were molded by social and geographical forces into much the
same pattern. All three, carried by the westward movement to
Missouri, began their careers from that state within a half
dozen years of its admission into the Union. Bridger at St.
Louis in 1822 joined General William Ashley's first expedition
up the Missouri to trap furs—that famous undertaking in which
the general advertised for "one hundred enterprising young
men." A year later Fitzpatrick, having drifted westward from
his emigrant ship, joined Ashley's second expedition up the
Missouri. In 1826 Kit Carson, his father dead, apprenticed to
a harsh Missouri saddler, ran away to join an expedition to
Santa Fé, and was soon trapping with Ewing Young's party in
the Southwest. All three spent fewer than twenty years as
trappers and hunters, when the depletion of the beaver colonies
brought their calling to an end. Fitzpatrick quit the mountains
in 1841 to guide the first emigrant train, the Bidwell-Bartleson
party, from the Missouri to Fort Hall. Carson quit in 1842 to
join Frémont. Bridger quit in 1842 to establish the first important supply-station on the Oregon Trail, Fort Bridger. The
days of the old-time trapper were gone forever. Then, after a
few years, the curtain rose on the third and quietest phase in
the lives of the three men. They must perforce adjust themselves to an increasingly settled and workaday West. The gov-

ernment in 1846 appointed Fitzpatrick as Indian agent for the
Cheyenne, Arapahoe, and part of the Sioux on the upper Platte
and Arkansas. In 1853 it appointed Carson as Indian agent at
Taos in charge of two tribes of Utes. Bridger, driven out of his
way-station business in 1853 by the Mormons, thereafter divided his time between farming and government positions, repeatedly acting as official interpreter and intermediary with the
Indians, and as an army guide.

Naturally it is the first phase in the lives of these rovers
which has chiefly appealed to students of the West. They were
as distinct a group, these mountain-men, as the cowboys who
came later; a hard, practical race, who dealt in the unknown,
and without compass, often without companion, wrested a
living from its perils. The French *coureurs,* a daring set of
adventurers, had been the first to penetrate the West, but the
cooler, longer-headed, deadly shooting Missourians, born
woodsmen all, easily surpassed them. The trappers were of
course rude and ignorant, with frontier manners; so wild that,
like Kit, they were glad to marry Indian women; many of them
with records as killers. A streak of pride, a wild vanity often
entered into their composition, and they liked to be called
"white Injuns," but off of the trail and away from the rendezvous they were essentially modest. After all, the pride was
chiefly in their stoic endurance of exertions, toils, and privations, their prowess with trap, knife, and ax, their deadliness
with their trusted guns—Old Bullthrower; Knock-Him-Stiff;
Old Straightener. A trapper might take many wives, but he was
monogamous in his devotion to his rifle. They were hard workers, hard players, hard fighters, hard drinkers—even Kit, in his
early days; they were inured to excess. Leading lives of perfect
liberty in the wilderness, in society they often turned to perfect license; and in his autobiography even the quiet Kit speaks
of his wild early courses when fresh in Taos from the lonely
trail with money burning in his pocket and the barroom and
fandango to allure him.

Their roving mountain life, for all its hardships, grime, and peril, was sweet at the bottom of the cup; its wild intoxication, like that of the sea, gradually entering the veins. Ashley said after he entered Congress that his best days had been his mountain days, his best friends his trapper friends. That adventurous Briton, Lieutenant George F. Ruxton, on his last trip to the Far West wrote his New York publisher that he was "half froze for buffler meat and mountain doin's," and died seeking his favorite spot beyond the Park Range, "my solitary camp in the Bayou Salade." Kit Carson, for twenty years a tireless wanderer, ever courting new adventures, felt this fascination as much as the others. He even more than others was absolutely fearless, for death rode close by each trapper as by Dürer's knight. It was death in a dozen forms—by famine; by sudden blizzard in the savage mountains; from wild beasts; from still wilder savages; "anything possible and nothing permanent except death." Three great preoccupations ever filled the trapper's mind—beaver, buffalo, and Indians; fur, meat, and peril; money, food, and war. Carson knew as well as any one how to set his line of Newhouse beaver-traps, to bait them with the medicine of pungent oils used by the mountain-men, to skin, grain, and stretch the pelts for dry-curing in the sun, to pack them into bales for carriage to market. He was as expert as the best in detecting beaver-sign on apparently deserted streams and in reaping a rich harvest up solitary valleys. Sometimes hundreds of pelts, worth eight dollars or more apiece, would be taken on a single small river. Like other mountain-men, he became a remarkable horseman. He was "the most daring and reckless of riders," avers his Taos friend Oliver Wiggins, adding that he could "with ease pick up a silver dollar from the ground, when going at full speed, mounted on the swiftest pony." At one time he delighted to take a heavy American horse and "dash down steep hills at full gallop." Hardihood, nerve, perfect health, and a delight in reckless feats, made trapping and guiding an ideal occupation for half his lifetime.[7]

[7] E. L. Sabin, *Kit Carson Days*, *passim*.

As the years passed, Carson had extended his activities until few men knew the great West so well, or could be trusted to meet every wilderness contingency so expertly. He had won his first spurs as member of a singularly daring expedition. With Ewing Young's trapping party, he had crossed upper Arizona and the Mojave, gone west to Los Angeles, and then, turning north, had traversed California to the Sacramento River, there lingering for some time. This acquaintance with interior California was later to serve Frémont well. Then entering the service of the Rocky Mountain Fur Company, a number of years before he met Frémont he carried a zigzag line through the Rockies north from Taos almost to the Canadian boundary. He and his companions on this remarkable trip first struck into the interior of Colorado, then crossed the continental divide at South Pass, and continuing through western Wyoming, finally reached the Salmon River in northern Idaho, where they spent the winter with the friendly Nez Percé. Thereafter, in one employ or another, Carson was found in successive years at widely scattered points in the West, his trails making an intricate network. He was in the Three Forks country, part of the sources of the Missouri; along the valley of the Green; with an expedition which went down the Humboldt in northern Nevada; at Fort Hall on the Snake; and with James Bridger on the Yellowstone. Incessantly moving, incessantly observant, he was accumulating an unsurpassed fund of information upon all parts of the West, from the Gila to the Columbia, from the Sacramento to the Platte.

By the time Carson met Frémont, no one was better skilled in Indian customs, ways, and mental habits, and no one knew more of the craft of mountains and plains. His sagacity, caution, and quick intuition had become famous. Place him in a situation of imminent danger from Indians, wild beasts, or prairie fire, and he would instantly devise the best means of extricating himself. Once in 1833, while his party were trapping on the Arkansas, some Crow Indians stole nine horses from them, and Carson and others went in pursuit. Creeping

at night upon the Indian encampment, they succeeded in leading the horses off while the Indians slept. Most of the party
favored immediate flight with their recovered property, for
they would have a start of several hours. But Carson demurred
because he desired revenge. Moreover, he grasped the dangerous elements in the situation: the horses were exhausted; they
would assuredly be followed; the Indians outnumbered them
three to one and could surround them at pleasure, when they
would certainly be shot from ambush without mercy. Their
proper course, he thought, was to attack the savages. In the
battle which followed Carson's men, profiting by surprise, won
an easy and bloody victory. One of his undoubted faults at this
period was his implacable harshness toward Indians. But we
must remember that throughout much of the West hostilities
were almost incessant. Lieutenant G. Douglas Brewerton in his
fine narrative of a ride with Kit Carson has described his in-
grained caution whenever in hostile country: [8]

During this journey I have often watched Carson's preparation
for the night. A braver man than Kit perhaps never lived. In fact,
I doubt if he ever knew what fear was. But with all this he exercised great caution. While arranging his bed his saddle, which he
always used as a pillow, was disposed in such a manner as to form
a barricade for his head. His pistols, half-cocked, were placed above
it, and his trusty rifle reposed beneath the blanket by his side,
where it was not only ready for instant use, but perfectly protected
from the damp. Except now and then to light his pipe, you never
caught Kit at night exposing himself to the full glare of the camp-
fire.

Though Carson had been doing fairly well as one of the
best trappers alive, as trader, and as hunter for Bent's Fort, he
knew that the days of profitable beaver-taking in the West
were numbered, and was glad to accept a fixed salary. Frémont
offered him $100 a month. Moreover, Carson's visit to Mis-
souri had left him restless and in the mood for a roving summer

---

[8] Lieutenant George Douglas Brewerton, *A Ride With Kit Carson,* first published in *Harper's Magazine,* 1853-54, since issued in book form.

trip. He had spent only ten days in St. Louis, for though he was curious as to the sights of the town, the noise, crowds, and heat wearied him; "for many consecutive years," he said later, "I never slept under the roof of a house, or gazed upon the face of a white woman." He longed for new scenes in the open. The friendship begun on the little Missouri steamboat struggling upstream in the June sunshine of 1842 was to last until Carson's death in 1868, and throughout two expeditions was to be the happiest of partnerships. Carson could truthfully inform a Senate committee six years later that he was "under more obligations to Frémont than to any other man alive." Until now, his name had seldom if ever appeared in print, and he was totally unknown outside his own trapper circles; but Frémont was to give him a generous publicity which would make him famous throughout the land. This service he was to repay by unremitting loyalty and unselfish effort. "With me," testified Frémont in a letter of 1847, "Carson and Truth mean the same thing. He is always the same—gallant and disinterested."

At the Cyprian Chouteau post, about ten miles up from the mouth of the Kansas, Carson hurried two Delaware runners off down the Santa Fé Trail to Taos, with instructions for about fifteen of his own men to meet him, with equipment, at Fort Laramie. The final parcels were placed in the carts. On Friday, June 10th, the column lengthened out from the belt of woods bordering the Kansas, past several well-kept Indian farms, and on to the open prairie. The routine of the march was at once established, and, as it was typical of later expeditions, we may glance at it in some detail.

Frémont and Carson planned their discipline, like that of all emigrant trains, freight caravans, and trapping bands, in a way to give them constant protection against a surprise attack. They did not wait until dusk to camp, but chose a suitable spot a good hour or two before nightfall. By sunset they had the carts wheeled into a compact circle. Within this effective barricade the tents were pitched, with a merry din of stake-driving; saddles, blankets, and eating utensils were thrown down; four fires were kindled and kettles slung for as many different messes; and a homelike scene soon presented itself. Meanwhile, the horses and mules had been hobbled and turned loose, under a guard, to graze. While it was yet broad daylight, the men ate supper, and the fires were allowed to die down so that they would throw no dangerous illumination over the camp. When darkness fell, the animals were driven close to the wagons, and picketed by a twenty or thirty-foot halter, which permitted them to get a little grass. Camp guard was mounted at eight, and the three sentries were relieved every two hours, the last or morning watch constituting the horse guard for the day.

By nine o'clock, the tired men were usually wrapped in slumber; by half past four, they were aroused. The horses and mules were again turned loose with hobbles, breakfast was eaten, and by six-thirty they were on the march again. At noon, they would halt for one, or sometimes two, hours, rather to rest the animals than the men. Such was the regular daily procedure, disturbed only by accident or unexpected physical obstacles. A stormy night was at first their chief hardship, for it meant sleeping in muddy puddles. Twenty-eight miles over the open prairie seems to have been regarded as "a hard day's march," and twenty-four miles was more usual.

The provisions of the camp were substantial and not altogether Spartanly simple. The party carried sugar, and great were the lamentations of one of the messes when, in crossing the swollen Kansas at the usual ford, it lost its supply in the muddy waters. Greater still was the regret of the whole expedition when, at the same crossing, almost all its coffee disappeared under the swirling current.[9] They purchased some twenty pounds from a half-breed, but this did not go far. Later they fell back upon a tea brewed from the roots of the wild cherry. In the early stages they were able to buy from the Indians vegetables—pumpkins, onions, beans, and lettuce. Later, when they came up with the herds of buffalo, the men

[9] Frémont, *Memoirs*, p. 75.

were jubilant over the supply of tender meat. Shouts and songs resounded from every part of the line, and the evening camp-fires signaled a feast which ended only with the break-up of the encampment the following morning; at any time of the night, men might be seen roasting the choicest bits—the hump, the tenderloin, the tongue, the sirloin steaks—*en appolas* (that is, on sticks) over the fire. There was no scarcity of tobacco, and at first enough bread, though later it became a coveted luxury. Of course the garb of the men, as the journey lengthened, grew steadily more ragged. A dozen days out they met a party of trappers coming from a long sojourn in the interior; "we laughed then at their forlorn and vagabond appearance," says Frémont, "and in our turn, a month or two afterward, furnished the same occasion for merriment to others."

Frémont was busy from morning to midnight. He maintained discipline with an iron hand under a glove of unvarying tact. He occupied himself evening and noon, when the weather permitted, in taking astronomical observations; he carefully observed botanical and geological features of the country, and wrote a detailed daily journal. The map of the expedition was kept complete from day to day, and Preuss was assigned the task of sketching any scene or position of unusual importance. At various halts, the men were trained in firing at a mark and in repelling attacks.[10]

[10] *Ibid.*, p. 78*ff.*

VIII

South Pass and Frémont's Peak

THIS first expedition, thus led by Frémont and guided by Carson, was absent from June 15, 1842, the date when they left the ford of the Kansas, until October 1st, when, marching down the Missouri, the men at daybreak heard the cowbells on the first border farms. In three and a half months it accomplished all the objects expected by the government, and still others expected only by Benton and his fellow-expansionists. Nominally, the expedition was intended to acquaint the government with the nature of the "rivers and country between the frontiers of Missouri and the base of the Rocky Mountains; and especially to examine the character, and ascertain the latitude and longitude of the South Pass, the great crossing-place to these mountains on the way to Oregon." Actually, as Benton's before-quoted statement upon the government's ignorance of its main conception indicates, it had far larger objects in view. Senator Linn intended to bring into the next session of Congress (1842-43) another bill for the occupation of Oregon; and Frémont's expedition was a preparatory measure. As he himself writes, it was "auxiliary to and in aid to the emigration to the Lower Columbia," already in full swing; and it was intended not only to advertise the easiness of the Platte River–South Pass route, but to "indicate and describe the line of travel, and the best positions for military posts."

The party first proceeded up the Kansas to observe the general character of its valley, and then crossed to the Platte, which it followed to the foothills of the Rockies. It was a great moment when, on July 9th, they caught their first glimpse of the snowy summit of Long's Peak. Next day they halted at St. Vrain's Fort, a trading-post about forty miles north of present-day Denver, where the courtly Ceran St. Vrain, of the St. Louis trading-firm of Bent, St. Vrain & Co., himself welcomed them. Struggling up the Sweetwater Valley, the party on August 8th reached South Pass. This was not, as Frémont in spite of all that Carson had told him, was surprised to find, an abrupt break in the mountain wall, but a broad opening reached by such a gradual ascent that he had difficulty in fixing the precise point of the Continental Divide, where the waters flowing east parted from those flowing to the Pacific. There was no gorge, like the Allegheny gaps or Alpine passes. Instead, a wide sandy road lifted by a slow and regular grade to the summit, about 7,000 feet above the sea.

The party, now 950 miles from the mouth of the Kansas, continued its march to the headwaters of the Green River, which flows into the Colorado. This reached, Frémont set out to explore the Wind River chain, a magnificent group of snow-capped mountains, the highest in Wyoming, which rose before them, pile upon pile, their icy caps glittering in the bright light of the August day.

The spectacular feat of the expedition, whose leader always delighted in the spectacular, was the ascent of what Frémont mistakenly considered the highest peak of the Central Rockies, Frémont's Peak, which is 13,730 feet high. One other summit in the Wind River chain, Gannett Peak, five miles north, is actually some fifty or sixty feet higher, while Colorado has almost thirty peaks of 14,000 feet or more. Nor is Frémont's Peak difficult of access or dangerous to the climber. Frémont and five companions set out early on the morning of August 15th; they found themselves, after some rough ascents, riding beneath a nearly perpendicular wall of granite, terminating from two to three thousand feet above their heads in a serrated line of broken, jagged cones. At what seemed the best point, they undertook to mount this wall, climbing leisurely. Three little lakes of dark emerald, apparently deep, lay in a chasm below.

Above the snow line, they had to use thin moccasins of buffalo skin, and at one point Frémont worked his way across a vertical precipice by clinging to the crevices; but from the ledge thus gained it was an easy matter to reach the crest.

"I sprung upon the summit," writes Frémont, "and another step would have precipitated me into an immense snow field five hundred feet below. To the edge of this field was a sheer icy precipice; and then, with a gradual fall, the field sloped off for about a mile until it struck the foot of another ridge." Though the day was sunny and bright, a slight shining mist obscured the view over the surrounding country. Nevertheless, the prospect was inspiring. To the west, they descried a vast shining network of lakes and streams, the waters from which fed the Colorado; and on the other side, the deep-forested trough of the Wind River Valley, with the faint gleam of streams which flowed into the Yellowstone and down to the Missouri. Far northwestward, bright in the haze, they could pick out the snowy peaks of the Three Tetons, which marked the sources of the Snake and the Columbia. Frémont's breast expanded as he surveyed this immense landscape. Fixing a ramrod in the gneiss, he unfurled a special flag, carrying the regulation thirteen stripes, but bearing in the corner a white field with a blue eagle perched upon an Indian pipe of peace, and blue stars.[1] They lingered till mid-afternoon, when they returned to their cache of dried coffee and meat at the foot of the peak, and slept that night on the rocks.

The principal adventure of the party occurred on its return. Frémont's orders were to survey the Platte, and he wished to save time by making as much use of waterways as possible. While still on the Sweetwater, he had his men inflate the collapsible rubber boat which he had brought from the East, and load it with the instruments and equipment he carried. The shallowness of the stream made progress impossible, and they took to the land again. But when the Platte was reached, they found it flowing broad and deep, swollen beyond its usual size.

[1] Frémont, *Memoirs*, pp. 151, 152.

Frémont therefore divided his party. The larger group he directed to proceed across country on foot to a point named Goat Island, an unmistakable mark; while he, Preuss, and five others provisioned the rubber boat for a dozen days, and began the descent by water. After a few hours, a hollow roar announced that a series of falls was before them. Frémont reconnoitered, and then, thinking of the heavy labor of unloading his apparatus and other baggage, recklessly determined to run the rapids. He did not know until afterward that some eighteen years earlier Fitzpatrick had lost a valuable cargo of beaver pelts at this point.

One series of little cataracts was traversed successfully, the elastic boat bending to every shock. A steeper and fiercer channel lay just ahead, shut in by high rocky walls; but emboldened by their previous success they decided to risk its descent also. Everything was tied securely; the men threw off most of their clothing, and pushed into the stream. To save the valuable chronometer, Preuss took it and attempted to walk along the stream on rocks which were piled up on either side, but shortly found that the shore disappeared and the walls fell vertically into the torrent. He therefore clambered back into the boat, which moved more and more swiftly.

At once it became plain that their position was perilous. They had attached a rope about fifty feet long to the stern of the boat, and three men had been left to clamber along the rocks with it, trying to lessen its speed. All in vain; after a few hundred feet they realized that their Bucephalus was too much for them: "To go back was impossible; the torrent before us was a sheet of foam; and, shut up in the chasm by the rocks, which in some places seemed almost to meet overhead, the roar of the waters was deafening." The force of the torrent became too great for the men on shore to withstand. Two of them loosed their hold, but Basil Lajeunesse hung on an instant too long, and was jerked head foremost from a twelve-foot ledge into the boiling water. The boat shot downstream like an arrow, Lajeunesse being carried down after it in the rapid waters and needing all his strength as a swimmer to keep from being dashed against the rocky shore. His head could be seen at momentary intervals as a black spot bobbing in the foam. Fortunately, the boat was soon brought into an eddy below and held stationary long enough to allow the half-drowned man to be dragged over its gunwale, cursing. Then, after catching breath, they went on, and in another moment met disaster: [2]

We cleared rock after rock, and shot past fall after fall, our little boat seeming to play with the cataract. We became flushed with success and familiar with the danger; and, yielding to the excitement of the occasion, broke forth together into a Canadian boat-song. Singing, or rather shouting, we dashed along; and were, I believe, in the midst of a chorus when the boat struck a concealed rock immediately at the foot of the fall, which whirled her over in an instant. Three of my men could not swim, and my first feeling was to assist them, and save some of our effects; but a sharp concussion or two convinced me that I had not yet saved myself. A few strokes brought me into an eddy, and I landed on a pile of rocks on the left side. Looking around, I saw that Preuss had gained the same shore on the same side, about twenty yards below; and a little climbing and swimming soon brought him to my side. On the opposite side, against the wall, lay the boat, bottom up; and Lambert was in the act of saving Descoteaux, whom he had grasped by the hair, and who could not swim.... For a hundred yards below, the current was covered with floating books and boxes, bales of blankets, and scattered articles of clothing; and so strong and boiling was the stream that even our heavy instruments, which were all in cases, kept on the surface, and the sextant, circle, and the long black box of the telescope were in view at once.

Yet the party extricated itself better than it might have expected. The boat was righted and taken downstream a mile and a half, where a broad expanse of rock offered a resting place. For this distance, the banks and shallows were searched, and much of the baggage was recovered. One of the men had

[2] *Ibid.*, p. 157.

clung to Frémont's double-barreled gun. All the registers were found with the exception of one of Frémont's journals, containing his notes upon incidents of travel, topographical descriptions, some scattered astronomical observations, and the barometrical register west of Laramie. Happily, duplicates of his most important barometrical observations were preserved in the other journals. The circle was saved, and a number of blankets. But all the heavier articles—the sextant, telescope, and remaining guns—had sunk beyond recovery; the party was left stripped of every morsel of food, ammunition, and arms, at the mercy oı savages and in danger of starvation. It was necessary to push on at once to the men who had gone by land to Goat Island.

The battered boat had to be left behind, for the rocky pass was too narrow to allow egress from the cañon; while the recovered baggage was deposited in a safe spot and left. Climbing slowly to the top of the cañon, the half-naked explorers hurried forward over the rocky ground. Frémont hobbled along on one moccasin, his unprotected foot cut by sharp rocks. The party had to cross the winding river repeatedly, sometimes fording it and sometimes swimming, and to climb the ridges of two more cañons before, late in the evening, they came within sight of Goat Island. They were soon sitting about a hot fire, eating pieces of buffalo steak roasted at the coals, and telling the story of their adventures.

This catastrophe was a forcible lesson upon the folly of Frémont's precipitancy. The cautious Nicollet would never have permitted him to take such a risk. His impetuosity might have destroyed completely the records of his expedition and given a disastrous check to his career; it might have cost several lives, and, if his group had failed to join the other members of the expedition, would certainly have done so. This instance of rashness was all too characteristic of the man; but fortunately his character had another side, which was amply demonstrated in these three months.

On the whole, Frémont in this expedition showed coolness,

sagacity, and more than once a really remarkable resourcefui·
ness in meeting emergencies. A test of his ingenuity occurred
as they were just entering the Wind River Range. In crossing
a broad stream, pouring rapidly over a slippery bed of boul-
ders and quartz slabs, where the pack animals fell repeatedly,
the horse bearing the barometer struck it against a rock and
broke it. It was the only barometer the expedition owned. Since
it was indispensable for an accurate measurement of altitudes,
its loss seemed a heavy blow. They had brought it a thousand
miles, watching over it with anxious solicitude day and night,
and now, just as they reached the high Rockies, it was smashed.
The men were as dejected as Frémont himself. But they no
sooner made camp than he set about trying to repair the
catastrophe.

He discovered that while the glass cistern had been broken
about midway, no air had found its way into the tube. He had
a number of vials of rather thick glass, some of them of the
same diameter as the cistern, and, with a rough file from the
tool chest, he spent the day slowly endeavoring to cut them to
the requisite length. Unfortunately, they all broke. Next morning, having placed the barometer at night out of harm's way in
a groove in one of the trees, he began to work upon a different
device. Taking a powderhorn which happened to be remarkably
translucent, he boiled it, stretched it on a piece of wood to
the requisite diameter, and scraped it very thin, until it was
almost as clear as glass. Then using some strong glue made from
a buffalo's tendons, he fastened the horn firmly in its place
on the instrument, and filled it with mercury, properly heated.
A piece of skin, secured with thread and glue, furnished a suitable pocket, and the brass cover was screwed into place. After
the instrument had been left some hours to dry, Frémont and
his companions anxiously tested it. When it was reversed, they
had the joy of finding it in perfect order, its indications being almost identical with those it had marked before it was
broken. The day was saved.[3]

[3] Frémont, *Memoirs*, p. 141.

Frémont also proved his ability to secure a firm hold upon the confidence of his men. On its outward march the party had divided at the forks of the Platte, the main body under Clement Lambert and Carson going by the regular Oregon Trail route to Fort Laramie, while Frémont with four others proceeded toward the same point by the before-mentioned Fort St. Vrain. When the two detachments joined hands at Fort Laramie they were met by alarming news. This fort, strongly built of adobe and wooden palisades, was maintained by the American Fur Company for its traders and the protection of emigrants along the Oregon Trail. The famous frontiersman, Jim Bridger, had just come down the North Platte trail with a company of traders. He brought word that the Sioux, Blackfeet, and Cheyenne had combined and were on the warpath, and that the route from Laramie to South Pass was very perilous. This news was received with alarm by the voyageurs, and even Carson was so much affected that he made an oral will, which trappers seldom did save in extremity.[4] Less than a year earlier the Sioux and Cheyenne had fallen upon a party of about sixty whites on the Little Snake, and in the ensuing encounter had killed five, including the leader. These tribes had recently let a party of emigrants led by Fitzpatrick through their country, but had served notice that the path was no longer open, and that any new group found upon it would be destroyed. From all that Frémont could learn, the country ahead was swarming with scattered groups of warriors.

Yet the lieutenant, though Carson believed that the party would almost certainly have a clash if they pushed forward, did not hesitate. Both traders and Indians advised him to wait until the war parties had completed their raids and returned home; but he knew that to stop was in fact almost impossible. It was he who had insisted that the orders for the expedition include South Pass, and he felt he had to go thither. A main purpose of the reconnaissance was to determine the best points

[4] Compare F. S. Dellenbaugh, *Frémont and '49*, p. 71.

at which to plant forts for protection against Indians, and it would hardly do to refuse to face the Indians in the field. There was an Oregon caravan not far ahead of Frémont, and if it was in trouble his duty was to follow at once. Moreover, Frémont well knew with what sneers he would be greeted in the East by West Point men if he returned confessing that an Indian scare had forced him to abbreviate his plans. He was a newcomer in the Army, and very decidedly upon his mettle. If he flinched, the regular officers would never cease reminding him that he had allowed a trail—a settler's trail at that—to be closed in his face.

As a measure of precaution, Frémont engaged an interpreter, one of the fur traders of the region, named Joseph Bissonette, who, if they came in contact with the Indians, would be able to explain that the purposes of the expedition were purely scientific. Bissonette told him that the chief danger would lie in being attacked before the savages knew who they really were. Then, the equipment repaired and everything ready for a start, the lieutenant called his men about him at evening and told them he was determined to push forward at dawn the next day; that they were well armed and accustomed to the country; and that they had known on the Missouri that the Indians were restless, and ought not to object now to the peril. However, he wanted no undependable followers, and those who were apprehensive might drop out. A few days before, the voyageurs had been complaining of the lack of excitement: *"Il n'y aura pas de vie pour nous."* Now only one man had the effrontery to come forward and accept the permission to retreat, and Frémont, after asking some questions to expose him to the ridicule of the others, let him go.

The two youths, Randolph Benton and Henry Brant, were reluctantly left at the fort—Randolph's high spirits had made him a general favorite—for it was unjustifiable to risk their lives. As it turned out, the party sighted few Indians on the Sweetwater Trail, and none hostile enough to contest their passage. The episode gave Frémont added prestige. Carson's biographer has aptly characterized him as he must have appeared at this time to the mountain-men: [5]

A states-bred man but a man who showed trail experience; something of the dandy but nothing of the popinjay; a captain in command but prompt to fall to with the best of them; a captain and a comrade in one—a leader with the enthusiasm of a greenhorn, but without the greenhorn's blatant ignorance.

Kit Carson's task as guide was finished when the expedition turned back from the Wind River Range, and he did not complete the circuit with Frémont. The party of trappers and hunters for which he had sent to Taos did not actually join the explorers. They were never engaged as part of Frémont's company; they had to hunt and trap somewhere, and Carson simply wished to have them near him in the event of trouble with the Indians. Leaving Taos late in June with laden packhorses, they pushed northeast up the Indian trail to Fort Laramie; their road running through Pueblo, a Mexican village of a few adobe houses, past the site of the present city of Colorado Springs, over the site of Denver, then a virgin wilderness without even a hut or a tent, and on to their destination. Keeping near Frémont on the Sweetwater, they crossed to the western side of the Rockies, and were there joined by Kit Carson at a spot thirty miles from the Atlantic and Pacific Springs. With Carson as leader, they then returned to Taos with their pelts for the winter. But before the separation took place, Frémont and Carson had agreed that the latter was, if possible, to act as guide for a second expedition the next year, 1843.

The final stages of Frémont's return trip exhibited his tenacity and his skilful use of the experience gained with Nicollet and Sibley. Even after the wreck of the rubber boat he did not give up his wish to descend the Platte by water. There was little wood, but he did not need it. Several buffalo bulls were killed and skinned; the four best hides were sewn together

[5] E. L. Sabin, *Kit Carson Days,* pp. 331, 332.

with buffalo sinews, and this tough fabric was stretched over a framework of river willows. Then the seams were caulked with a glue made of ashes and tallow, and the vessel was left in the hot sun till the drying skins drew taut. The result was a broad shallow "bull boat," such as trappers often used, eight feet long and almost wide enough for a man to lie down in. It drew, when Frémont, Preuss, and two others took up the paddles, only four inches. Unfortunately, the Platte did not offer four inches. For three or four miles the men tugged and pushed their ungainly craft over sandy shallows, and finally in discouragement left it on a sandbar. They continued afoot, and on September 18th reached the Grand Island; four days later, they bought some green vegetables from friendly Pawnees engaged in harvesting their gardens. On September 30th, they sighted the yellow Missouri; and on October 1st, Frémont, rising long before daybreak, heard with a feeling of inexpressible pleasure the mellow tinkle of cowbells from farms on the opposite side of the river. He was back on the edge of civilization.

What Frémont had accomplished was best summarized by his friend Linn a little later in a speech to the Senate. After describing how he had followed the Platte and Sweetwater, the Missourian remarked: [6]

He reached the [South] Pass on the 8th of August, and describes it as a low and wide depression of the mountains, where the ascent is as easy as the hill on which this Capitol stands, and where a plainly beaten wagon road leads to the Oregon through the valley of Lewis's River, a fork of the Columbia. He went through the Pass, and saw the headwaters of the Colorado, of the Gulf of California....

Linn, accepting the story of the "loftiest peak" of the Rockies, briefly dilated on it, and then proceeded:

From that ultimate point he returned by the valley of the Great Platte, following the stream in its whole course, and solving all

[6] Benton, *Thirty Years' View*, II, 478; *Cong. Globe*, 2d Sess., 27th Cong.

questions in relation to its navigability, and the character of the country through which it flows.

He added that the use of the eight mule-drawn carts proved the facility of traveling in this region; that herds of buffalo had given food to the men, the short-grass to the horses and mules; and that the fact that two boys, one only twelve, accompanied the expedition, proved that whole families could traverse the country without risk. The expedition had done something to encourage Oregon migration; it would do still more when Frémont's report was published.

IX

The First Report

TARRYING briefly in St. Louis to sell what remained of his equipment, Frémont left by steamboat on the eighteenth, and reported to Colonel Abert in Washington on the twenty-ninth. He had special reason for haste. A few days after he arrived Jessie gave birth to a daughter. Spreading over her bed a ragged, wind-whipped flag, he told her proudly: "This flag was raised over the highest peak of the Rocky Mountains; I have brought it to you." [1]

He found the Benton household under a cloud which even the advent of the new baby, and Jessie's happiness in his return tanned and rugged, could not dispel. Mrs. Benton shortly after Frémont's departure had suffered a stroke of paralysis. Jessie believed that it had been caused by her mother's insistence upon old-fashioned medical practice, for even when she had nothing worse than a sick-headache, Mrs. Benton would insist, despite the Senator's opposition, upon being bled. Repeated use of the lance had converted this once-vigorous woman, after only twenty years of marriage, into an emaciated wreck, who talked but slowly and imperfectly, and whose mind had obviously been impaired. The Senator, Jessie wrote later, would come in buoyantly every day, impressed by the doctor's command that he remain cheerful, would keep up appearances for a time, and then would steal away to his room to give way to overpowering grief. His incessant care of the invalid, destined to live a dozen years longer, was touching to watch. Family loyalty and affection were one of the strongest elements in his character, and his display of them recalls McKinley's

[1] Jessie Benton Frémont MSS, Bancroft Library.

devotion to his invalid wife. Once the Senator was talking with important political visitors when Mrs. Benton appeared at the door, her dress disordered and her faculties plainly wandering. Without hesitation, he hastened to her with all his characteristic dignity, brought her to his guests, and introduced her with an air of pride.

For Frémont the immediate task was his report, and he had no time for a vacation. A plan for a second and longer expedition was probably being discussed by Benton and the other expansionists soon after his return; and if he were to set out in the spring, he must make haste. It is evident that both he and Benton envisaged a document that could be widely circulated and read. No doubt both remembered the interest excited by Irving's *Captain Bonneville* and *Astoria*. At any rate, during the fall and winter of 1842-43 Frémont and his wife achieved what had never been done before in a government report upon the West. We have said that it was necessary not only to explore the trans-Missouri areas, not only to survey and map the main westward routes, but to describe the country. A contribution to that task had been made, with considerable authority but no literary skill whatever, by the men who kept journals under Lewis and Clark. The volumes by Pike, the record of Long's explorations (Edwin James's *Expedition from Pittsburgh to the Rocky Mountains, 1823*), and Featherstonhaugh's report were of mediocre quality. Irving's books showed great literary talent but possessed little scientific accuracy. It was now Frémont's aim to combine a high degree of authority with a high degree of literary finish—an aim in which he perfectly succeeded. This was only part of his winter's work. He and Preuss had to prepare a map of their route, and at Benton's suggestion determined to make it a guide-book in atlas form; that is, a series of detailed maps representing each a day's journey toward the Oregon country. Such a guide-book, with the camp-sites affording water, wood, and grass clearly indicated, would be invaluable to emigrants. Many hundreds of specimens in botany and zoölogy had to be classified, but most of this task Frémont was able to assign to the botanist, John Torrey, who had done the same service for Nicollet.

An unnecessary mystery has been made of the division of credit for this report between Frémont and his wife. Some writers give much of the praise for its literary sparkle to Jessie, who later proved herself in many volumes a finished and vivid writer. But while her collaboration was invaluable, no one who reads the document carefully can doubt that it is nine-tenths his. It is close-packed with factual information which he alone could supply, and which determines its whole form and flavor. What she did for him was simple. He had a natural command of graphic English, and even documents which he later produced under unfavorable conditions, such as his long letter from Taos after the wreck of his fourth expedition, show force and lucidity. But writing alone, he found that he lacked facility and grace. In beginning his report he spent some days of mental anguish, which Jessie had tactfully described: [2] "The horseback life, the sleep in the open air, had unfitted Mr. Frémont for the indoor work of writing—and second lieutenants cannot indulge in secretaries. After a series of hemorrhages from the nose and head had convinced him that he must give up trying to write his report, I was let to try and thus slid into my most happy life-work." His own statement is significant: "I write more easily by dictation. Writing myself I have too much time to think and dwell upon words as well as ideas." What Jessie taught her husband was simply this—that many a man who is awkward and dull when he writes is expressive and interesting when he dictates. Frémont dictated, Jessie copied, and all went well. Beyond question she added elegant touches and gave variety to his vocabulary, but the reports are close-knit transcripts of his own ideas and experience, and resemble nothing that Jessie ever wrote.

The work, carried forward every morning in the Benton home on C Street, was done under sustained pressure. Jessie took her desk daily at nine, and never left it till one, writing

<hr>

[2] Jessie Benton Frémont MSS, Bancroft Library.

madly to follow her husband's dictation. He paced the room, notes in hand, as he talked. "I soon learned that I could not make a restless motion," writes Jessie; "it was hard, but that was lost in the great joy of being useful to him, and so, swiftly, the report of the first expedition was written." No doubt her eager questioning, her insistence upon concrete detail touched his poetic vein, and enabled him to give perspective and coloring to his picture; no doubt also her acquaintance with English literature often suggested a superior phrasing. It was a true collaboration of two quick and sympathetic minds, but the content is wholly Frémont's. When Jessie wrote the last sentence she exclaimed with joyous emotion: "I have not put to paper one half the beauty and truth you have shown me, but I have done the best I could, my darling." Then followed the proof correction, which she mastered, "and behold! Mr. Frémont's first book!" A compact brochure, it had a value and interest which made his reputation.[3]

Three qualities in this and Frémont's later reports, taken in combination, give them distinction. The first is the fullness and precision of their information on every matter important to emigrants. They answered satisfactorily the essential questions as to topography, terrain, water, soils, vegetation, wild life, temperature, and weather. The second is the skill with which, while doing this, they also responded to the curiosity of Americans upon more general sights and experiences in the West. An army engineer or closet scientist, after furnishing precise but dull information on roads, plants, and climate, would have stopped. Frémont does much more. Take a few pages from the report on this first expedition after it reached Fort Laramie on July 13, 1842. We find a description of this heavy adobe fort, with tower and bastions; of the mode of trading with Indians for pelts; of the superiority of Indian buffalo-skin lodges to American tents; of the impediments of

[3] Frémont's *Report* was first issued (Washington, 1843) in a volume of 207 pages, but was reprinted by George H. Derby & Co. in 1849 in 122 pages; other publishers also brought it out. Citations hereafter made will be from the Derby edition as that preserved in the Frémont papers.

the artemisia bushes (sage-brush) to travel; of the method of making a cache; of the fondness of grizzlies for wild cherries; of the Indian use of bread-root (*Psoralea esculenta*); of the straits of the Oglallah Sioux, their horses starved to death by drought; of the habits and palatability of mountain sheep; of the appearance of Rock Independence—an isolated granite mass, two-fifths of a mile long and forty feet high, on which numerous travelers had carved their names; of the cañons of the Sweetwater. So the narrative runs on, giving that miscellaneous as well as utilitarian information which Americans then desired.

All this informational breadth would have been far less effective but for the third quality of the reports, the warm subjective feeling which charged them. The first document was a young man's work, written in the first person, and filled with zest and enthusiasm, with Frémont's glowing love of novelty and adventure. Having Jessie's curiosity to spur him on, he felt no false inhibitions in showing that the romance, peril, and novelty of the trip had been the very wine of life to him. Where a professional soldier would have been flat and pedantic, he was eloquent. He recalled the party's thrill of alarm when some distant elk were taken for Indians: "Mounted on a fine horse, without a saddle, and scouring bareheaded over the prairie, Kit was one of the finest pictures of a horseman I have ever seen." He put contagious excitement into his description of the chase: "My horse was a trained hunter, famous in the West under the name of Proveau; and, with his eyes flashing and the foam flying from his mouth, sprang on after the cow like a tiger." He found something glorious in the first view of buffalo: [4]

In the sight of such a mass of life, the traveller feels a strange emotion of grandeur. We had heard from the distance a dull and confused murmuring, and, when we came in view of their dark masses, there was not one among us who did not feel his heart beat quicker. It was the early part of the day, when the herds were feeding; and everywhere they were in motion. Here and there a

[4] Frémont, *Report*, p. 21.

huge old bull was rolling in the grass, and clouds of dust rose in the air from various parts of the bands, each the scene of some obstinate fight. Indians and buffalo were the poetry and life of the prairie, and our camp was full of their exhilaration.

Parkman later might have been proud of this imaginative last sentence, a sentence such as had never before appeared in an official report. But numerous other passages showed the same poetic ardor; for example, his description of an Indian buffalo-hunt:

The clouds of dust soon covered the whole scene, preventing us from having any but an occasional view.... We were too far to hear the report of the guns, or any sound; and at every instant, through the clouds of dust, which the sun made luminous, we could see for a moment two or three buffalo dashing along, and close behind them an Indian with his long spear, or other weapon, and instantly again they disappeared. The apparent silence, and the dimly seen figures flitting by with such rapidity, gave it a kind of dreamy effect, and seemed more like a picture than a scene of real life.

Another and even better extract offers us a glimpse of the knightly quality of Frémont as he rode on his westward quest. He had reached a village of the Cheyenne and Arapahoe:

As we rode along, I remarked near some of the lodges a kind of tripod frame, formed of three slender poles of birch, scraped very clean, to which were affixed the shield and spear, with some other weapons of a chief. All were scrupulously clean, the spearhead was burnished bright, and the shield white and stainless. It reminded me of the days of feudal chivalry; and when, as I rode by, I yielded to the passing impulse, and touched one of the spotless shields with the muzzle of my gun, I almost expected a grim warrior to start from the lodge and resent my challenge.

His quick sense of natural beauty, which remained with him through life, lends constant charm to these pages. He was pleased by the sunflowers which yellowed the Kansas prairies, and the carpets of smaller blossoms in the river bottoms farther west. The Platte where it issues from the Black Hills (the Laramie Mountains), with overhanging precipices of red sandstone, crowned by green woods three or four hundred feet above the stream, seemed to him of a striking beauty. But it was over the Alpine magnificence of the Wind River chain that he waxed most enthusiastic. The morning of August 10th had found the party encamped on a little tributary of the Green River, which ran swiftly over a bed of granite, milky quartz, and sand. Just in front rose a mountain wall two thousand feet in height, the bottom wrapped in morning fog, and the top gilded by the first rays of the sun. Farther in the distance loomed the dim forms of high peaks. Then as the sun rose above the wall, it brought a magical change. The whole valley, with its green pines, foaming stream, and many-colored rocks burst into color, while the crests brightened above it like domes and pinnacles of silver. They took up their march, traversing long ridges of granite-strewn ground, and after winding up a long gorge, came upon a delightful lake set like a jewel in the mountains. "Here," writes Frémont, "a view of the utmost magnificence and grandeur burst upon our eyes. With nothing between us and their feet to lessen the effect of the whole height, a grand bed of snow-capped mountains rose before us, pile upon pile, glowing in the bright light of the August day. Immediately below them lay the lake, between two ridges, covered with dark pines which swept down from the main chain to the spot where we stood. Here, where the lake glittered in the open sunlight, its banks of yellow sand and the light foliage of aspen groves contrasted well with the gloomy pines."

The human element bulked large in this first report, and was offered with the same frank informality. No enlivening touch was omitted. Thus Frémont mentioned some Yankee trappers on the Platte: "All had their squaws with them, and I was really surprised at the number of little fat, buffalo-fed Indian boys that were tumbling about the camp, all apparently of the same age, about three or four years old." He spoke of "tobacco, that sine qua non of a voyageur." He described a supper of dog meat in an Indian village:

The dog was in a large pot over the fire, in the middle of the lodge, and immediately on arrival was dished up in large wooden bowls, one of which was handed to each. The flesh appeared very glutinous, with something of the flavor and appearance of mutton. Feeling something move behind me, I looked around, and found that I had taken my seat among a litter of fat young puppies. Had I been nice in such matters, the prejudices of civilization might have interfered with my tranquillity; but fortunately, I am not of delicate nerves, and continued quietly to enjoy and empty my platter.

Forts St. Vrain and Laramie were succinctly described; the operations of the fur trade were analyzed, with some real sympathy for the Indians ruined by the liquor traffic. At Fort Laramie, Frémont found that the traders of the American Fur Company annually received great piles of buffalo robes which they stacked up like cordwood, giving the savages in exchange blankets, calico, guns, ammunition, tobacco, cheap gew-gaws, and drink. The general policy of the Company was firmly opposed to the introduction of spirits. But at a time when the country was well supplied with alcohol, when a keg of it would purchase from an Indian his furs, his lodge, his horses, and even his wife, and when any vagabond who owned a mule could go to an Indian village and out-trade the company, it was impossible for the Company wholly to avoid the use of liquor. Unlicensed traders sold their spirits at $36 a gallon:

The difference between the regular trader and the *coureur des bois* (as the French call the itinerant or peddling trader) with respect to the sale of spirits, is here, as it has always been, fixed and permanent, and growing out of the nature of their trade. The regular trader looks ahead and has an interest in the preservation of the Indians...; the *coureur des bois* has no permanent interest, and gets what he can, and for what he can.

Frémont mentions a plague of locusts which had destroyed the grass west of Laramie; he describes the Indian process of

jerking buffalo meat. Even in speaking of the top of Frémont
Peak he added a humanizing touch:

> Here, on the summit, where the stillness was absolute, unbroken
> by any sound, and solitude complete, we thought ourselves beyond
> the region of animated life; but while we were sitting on the rock,
> a solitary bee (*bromus,* the humble-bee) came winging his flight from
> the eastern valley, and lit on the knee of one of the men. It was a
> strange place, the icy rock and the highest peak of the Rocky
> Mountains, for a lover of warm sunshine and flowers; and we
> pleased ourselves with the idea that he was the first of his species
> to cross the mountain barrier—a solitary pioneer to foretell the
> advance of civilization.

Unquestionably the most important lesson taught by the report was its demonstration that the plains between the Missouri and the foothills of the Rockies were not arid but fertile—
that the Great American Desert had no existence in this region. Frémont showed that they afforded nutritious grass for
horses and other live stock; that for some hundreds of miles
the country was highly attractive in its alternations of woodland and prairie; and that the soil of the Platte Valley was
rich. There had been no scientific report upon this strip since
Major Stephen Long's army expedition in 1820, and Long's
observations had been superficial and unfavorable. Writing of
the country he traversed in a circuit of the Platte, the Rocky
Mountain foothills, and the Arkansas, Long had said, "I do not
hesitate in giving the opinion, that it is almost wholly unfit for
cultivation, and of course uninhabitable by a people depending
on agriculture for their subsistence." This of what are now
the great farming siates of Nebraska, Kansas, and Oklahoma!
Frémont's report was the first sharp thrust at the popular
delusion that an American Sahara lay in regions which are now
the very granary of the United States—a delusion, however,
that persisted till the gold rush of '49 finally slew it.

His favorable report was of immediate importance to the

expansionist Senators. During 1842, Elijah White's party of about one hundred and twenty emigrants (the exact number is still unsettled), perhaps spurred on by newspaper accounts of Oregon, had made the long pilgrimage from Missouri to the Columbia Valley. The great migration of 1843, which included the Burnett and Applegate families of Missouri, both well-known to Benton, was shortly to set out. Yet President Polk continued to favor a policy of delay, though to the anxious western congressmen this seemed merely playing into the hands of Great Britain. The President's annual message of December, 1842, suggested that it would be improper to grant any titles of land to Oregon emigrants until "the respective claims of the two governments should be settled." At the same time the Administration, preparing for debate upon the Ashburton Treaty regarding the northeast boundary, sounded out the Missouri Senators upon a suggestion, emanating from the negotiators of the Treaty, for a "conventional division line," to run along the north bank of the Columbia; thus surrendering most of what is now the state of Washington to the British. The resentment of the western group in Congress was instant. Senator Linn, taking the lead against the President, introduced a bill which he and Benton believed would promote settlement. It provided that the President should erect a series of forts along the Oregon route to the Rockies, and one at the mouth of the Columbia; that every adult settler should be given 640 acres of Oregon land, with an additional quarter section for his wife and every child; and that American courts should be set up in the Oregon country, leaving British offenders to British jurisdiction. Calhoun and McDuffie of South Carolina led the opposition to the bill, which after passing the Senate twenty-four to twenty-two, was stifled in the House. But the effect that Benton and Linn intended was fully accomplished. The impression was established that a large and growing element in Congress stood ready to support those who entered Oregon, and that colonization of the far-off region was a patriotic duty. Benton declared that he looked forward to the day when we should

have "thirty or forty thousand rifles beyond the Rocky Mountains" as our "negotiators."

While the Senate debate on Oregon was proceeding, Frémont
put the finishing touches to his report and filed it with the War
Department. As we have seen, Senator Linn was waiting to
give it due advertisement. A motion was passed calling upon
the Secretary of War to transmit it to the Senate, and Linn
then offered a resolution that it be printed for Congress, with
a thousand extra copies for public distribution. The printing
was ordered and the report was no sooner in type than the
newspapers seized upon it.

X

The Second Expedition: Outward Bound

BENTON informs us that Frémont's first expedition was "barely finished" before he "sought and obtained orders for a second one"; the initiative coming from Benton, Linn, and the young explorer, not from the Administration.[1] These orders were from the War Department through Colonel Abert, chief of the Topographical Engineers. They instructed him to carry his explorations westward into the Anglo-American territory of Oregon; or, to be precise, "to connect the reconnaissance of 1842 with the surveys of Commander Wilkes on the coast of the Pacific Ocean, so as to give a connected survey of the interior of our continent." Lieutenant Charles Wilkes in his famous exploring expedition of 1838-42 (which ended in his court-martial), had surveyed much of the west coast of the United States, including San Francisco Bay, the Sacramento, and the Columbia. The main object of Frémont's tour was to do for the whole of the Oregon Trail what he had already done for the stretch to South Pass. As a matter of fact, he was destined to accomplish more than even the sanguine western expansionists could have expected. His exploration finally embraced not only Oregon, but parts of Utah, Nevada, and California; it resulted in advertising the fertility of the Great Salt Lake region as well as the Columbia Valley; it dispelled some of the mystery still clinging about the Great Basin between the Rockies and Sierras; and it culminated in a memorable passage across snow-choked ranges into the smiling lap of springtime California.

---

[1] Thomas Hart Benton, *Thirty Years View*, II, p. 477.

Already, as we have seen, the tide of westward colonization was flowing strongly. This was the year of the "great migration" to Oregon, when nearly nine hundred men, women, and children, assembling at Independence, Missouri, crossed the plains in a body to settle in the Columbia Valley. The stream was to rise steadily, about fourteen hundred crossing in 1844, and about three thousand in 1845. Though Frémont's expeditions strongly encouraged the movement, it would have taken place with not greatly diminished volume had he never made a start. Yet his work was to be of memorable utility none the less. He was expected to approach the South Pass by a different route, push on west, and examine the broad region south of the Columbia, lying between the Rockies, the Pacific, and California. His tour, it was hoped, would furnish a connected scientific description of much of the Pacific Northwest, dispel any idea that the Oregon journey was terrifyingly difficult, and emphasize the attractions of the Columbia. Actually, as we have said, it did much else. It brought California more vividly into the American consciousness than ever before, so that its attractions caught the imagination of tens of thousands. The first expedition had exploded the legend of a Great American Desert; the second disclosed to multitudes a shining new land of flowers, sunshine, and wealth.

Congress broke up at the beginning of March, 1843, and the Benton-Frémont household broke up with it. The Senator hurried west to St. Louis alone. Frémont, accompanied by Preuss, went to New York to buy his instruments, and then traveled by rail and steamboat to St. Louis. For Jessie, her ailing mother, and the baby, a private stage or "accommodation" was provided and packed with comforts. These three set out over the National Road, moving slowly with many stops for rest; and taking the boat at Wheeling, reached St. Louis in about a fortnight. All were reunited at the Brant mansion, but only briefly, Benton then ranging the state to mend his political fences, and Frémont, after hiring men and buying mules, proceeding to the Kaw or Kansas (Westport) Landing, the site of present-day Kansas City, to make his final preparations. He was at this point by the middle of May, 1843.

Never had an American exploring expedition, private or governmental, been better fitted out than this second body. His force comprised thirty-nine men, not counting supernumeraries, most of them being French-Canadians and Creoles, though a number of American names (White, Campbell, Lee, and so on) occur.[2] Half a dozen of them, including Basil Lajeunesse, always gay, energetic, and a great favorite, were voyageurs who had been with the first expedition. A free Negro of eighteen, Jacob Dodson, who was devoted to the Benton family, went along—his black visage destined to excite great curiosity among the Indians. Agreeably to Abert's instructions, Theodore Talbot of Washington was taken with them for training, and kept a journal which offers an informal record of some value. Another interesting figure attached to the expedition was the twenty-year-old William Gilpin of St. Louis, a brilliant young man who had already passed through many adventures. He had been page to Andrew Jackson, cadet at West Point, second lieutenant of dragoons in the Seminole War, and editor of the St. Louis *Argus,* a Benton paper of extreme expansionist views.[3] For guide, since Carson did not join him until he reached what is now Pueblo, Colorado, Frémont engaged Thomas Fitzpatrick or "Broken-Hand," not only one of the most experienced trappers of the Rockies, but a man of exceptional intellect and character. He also hired his old friend Louis Zindel, the Prussian veteran who had been with Nicollet and knew so much about explosives and rockets. Two stalwart Delaware Indians, father and son, were taken as hunters.

The party, rather crippled at the outset by a shortage of animals, had a dozen large carts, each drawn by two mules, and a light covered wagon for the scientific instruments. These instruments were Frémont's pride. They included a fine re-

[2] For the full list of names see Frémont, *Memoirs,* I, p. 169.
[3] Sabin, *Kit Carson Days,* I, p. 352. For a fervent tribute to Gilpin see W. E. Connolley, *Kansas Historical Society Collections,* Vol. X, p. 113.

fracting telescope, two pocket chronometers, two sextants, a
reflecting circle, a syphon barometer and cistern barometer, half
a dozen thermometers, and an assortment of compasses. Packed
with the tents were a large supply of gifts for Indians, and a
rubber boat, not so well made as the one taken on the first
expedition. Their provisions included an abundance of flour,
rice, sugar, and coffee, while for meat they depended upon
game. The party was armed with a really superior weapon, the
Hall breech-loading rifled carbine, a piece fired by flintlock,
but using ready-fixed ball-and-powder cartridges, and susceptible of rapid reloading. We shall meet the Hall carbine again
in Frémont's Civil War days.

But the most interesting part of the equipment was a howitzer cannon firing a twelve-pound ball. Frémont had applied
to Colonel Stephen Watts Kearny, commanding the Third
Military Division, for this piece from the St. Louis arsenal.
Perhaps Zindel had suggested taking it, perhaps Benton. Cannon were not unknown as weapons against Indians, for General
William H. Ashley had fitted out a supply-train with a four-
pounder, while Jedediah Smith had taken one on the last trip
of his life. The general feeling of frontiersmen was that they
were worse than useless, but Frémont doubtless believed that
one of them might strike terror to an overwhelming war-party
of Indians.

Kaw Landing in these May days of 1843 was a busy place.
Crowds of men, including many hundreds of emigrants to
Oregon or California, fur traders, trappers, and freighters down
the Santa Fé Trail, were there, and hundreds more were coming. The facilities of the little settlement were taxed to the
utmost. Long lines of horses and mules, switching their tails
against the flies, stood eating grain out of rough troughs made
by tying sacking to lines of stakes. The swearing of teamsters,
the shouts of roustabouts, the bellowing of oxen, made the steep
sides of the bluff echo.[4] Baggage was piled high on the shore.

---

[4] The scene is vividly described in the MS Journal of Theodore Talbot,
Library of Congress.

Every few days a steamboat pulled in with a hoarse musical roar, or dropped downstream. Amid the bustle, Frémont's men scurried about, seeking the aid of a blacksmith here, loading goods into the carts there, making purchases in the stores which, crude and small, were doing a business that pretentious eastern shops might envy. We can imagine the bristly blond head of Preuss bobbing everywhere, the white locks of Fitzpatrick—whose hair had suddenly turned gray when, beset by Blackfeet in the mountains, he had lost every companion and had been closely hunted among the rocks for days—streaming in the wind. While they were thus busy, suddenly Frémont received from his wife a letter which urged him to set out immediately. Giving no reason, but declaring that haste was imperative, it commanded him to go on to Bent's Fort instantly.

Frémont knew that there must be good reason for this urgency. It was only eleven days since he had reached Kaw Landing, but he gave the word, and next morning the teamsters cracked their whips over the straining mules, while he galloped ahead with Fitzpatrick and Preuss. They proceeded only four miles over the rolling prairie, for a nasty rain was falling, and some of the green animals were balky; but they camped safely out of sight of the village.

The sending of this peremptory message by Jessie is an incident which reveals much as to her character. She was so much his aide that he had asked her to open all mail and forward only what related to the expedition. One day there came a long official envelop marked "Topographical Corps," and reading it, she dropped it to her lap in consternation. It was an order directing Frémont to return at once to Washington and explain why he had taken a cannon. His was a peaceful scientific survey, wrote Colonel Abert, and not a trip requiring a howitzer. Meanwhile, another officer would be sent west to take charge of his men. Jessie's temper instantly blazed up. She writes: [5]

---

[5] Jessie Benton Frémont MSS, Bancroft Library.

Fancy his fine picked men, "every man a captain in himself," as Carson once said to me, under the line-and-rule control of an ordinary officer. But here intuition came to my aid. Behind the chief of that Bureau (Colonel Abert), who was a placid, indolent man, I saw his son-in-law who was an envious, discontented person. I ought to say here that the Report had given immediate fame to Mr. Frémont—then why not the same to another officer?

I felt the whole situation in a flash, and met it—as I saw right. I had been too much a part of the whole plan for the expeditions to put them in peril now—and I alone could act. Fortunately my father was off in the State attending to his political affairs. I did what I have always since been glad to remember. First I told no one. I knew that one of the men engaged, a French Canadian named De Rosier, had been permitted to remain in St. Louis on account of his wife's health, gaining for her the month the party were at Kaw Landing with Mr. Frémont. Now I sent for De Rosier.

Mrs. Frémont was doubtless mistaken in attributing the order to jealousy. The Washington authorities rightly objected to giving a scientific expedition the appearance of a military reconnaissance. Our relations with Great Britain and Mexico were so delicate that it was improper to march with a cannon into debatable or foreign territory. That weapon, in the hands of the impulsive Frémont, might cause an international incident. But the determined Jessie gave De Rosier his orders: [6]

I told him an important letter had come for the Captain, and I wanted it delivered without loss of time. I had to send him, for I thought he would not return. "How long will you need to get ready?" "The time to get my horse." "Say nothing of this, De Rosier," I said, "but you going up by land know how to cut off the bends in the river, and can save the time the mail boat will have to lose lying at anchor by night on account of the river fogs." He suggested taking a brother along—"two horses travel together better, and he will bring back a letter from the Captain." You see I was afraid the order had been sent in duplicate, and might, even

[6] *Ibid.*, but in her article "The Origin of the Frémont Explorations," *Century Magazine*, Vol. XIX, New Series (1890-91), p. 768ff., Jessie says that she sent the message by Basil Lajeunesse, "who was to join him with the last things."

with the detentions from fogs and snags, yet overtake Mr. Frémont. It was in the blessed day before telegrams, and character counted for something then, and I was only eighteen, an age when one takes risks willingly. It was about 400 miles to Kaw Landing as the crow flies. So I wrote urging him not to lose a day but start at once on my letter....

In a marvelously short time De Rosier's brother was back with the letter. "Good-bye," said my captain, "I trust, and *go*." Nothing was asked.

As soon as she received Frémont's announcement of his start, Jessie wrote Colonel Abert informing him of her action. She declared that he had sent his order without fully understanding the situation, that Frémont's party needed to be well-armed to pass through the hostile Blackfeet and other tribes, and that she had therefore suppressed his despatch. When Benton returned from his fence-mending, he sent Abert a letter accepting full responsibility for Jessie's step. Indeed, he did more than this, for he tells us that he felt outraged when he heard of the attempt to recall Frémont. He wrote the War Department, as he says, "condemning the recall, repulsing the reprimand which had been lavished upon Frémont, and demanding a court-martial for him when he should return." No doubt it was a characteristically fiery, pompous letter, for he shared Jessie's suspicion that an attempt had been made to set the lieutenant aside in favor of some West Pointer. Dislike of West Point, belief that the graduates were jealous of any one who came into the service by other channels, was strongly fixed in the chairman of the Senate Military Committee, himself an old soldier. The good-natured Abert probably felt no resentment, and at any rate seems never to have replied to Jessie or her father. Doubtless he thought it best, since Frémont was beyond recall, to accept the situation and not arouse the antagonism of men so powerful as Benton and Linn.

The cannon was really of small importance, though such good authority as E. L. Sabin concludes that "it paid for itself in lending morale." It never fired a shot; at one point it apparently helped avert a threatened Indian attack, though the attack could probably have been beaten off without it; and at last it was abandoned on the foothills southeast of Lake Tahoe, on the Nevada-California border.[7] To her dying day, Mrs. Frémont took pride in her quick, decisive action. Unquestionably it was justified if, as she believed, the Washington authorities meant to make Frémont's recall final and turn his expedition over to another officer. His taking the cannon did not justify such drastic action; no other officer was so well fitted to head an exploring expedition; and he was, of course, better trusted by the expansionists than any one else. Jessie, it must be remembered, had been the confidante of Benton and Frémont, had listened to their discussions with such Westerners as Linn, Dodge of Iowa, Smith of Indiana, and Young of Illinois, and understood perfectly the belief of this group that manifest destiny would soon make Oregon and California part of the United States. She knew what hopes her father pinned to the expedition as a means of furthering the acquisition of the Pacific Slope; she doubtless knew that Frémont meant to enter California as well as Oregon. As she wrote long afterward, she feared that his recall "would make delays which would involve the overthrow of great plans."

The one unhappy consequence of the affair became visible four years later. It lent strength to the view among professional army men that Frémont, a political favorite, headstrong and impulsive, failed to appreciate the value of discipline and obedience. It placed a blemish of insubordination upon his conduct. When later he came into conflict with other officers upon an issue of obedience to his superiors, the episode was remembered to his discredit; and nobody remembered it more clearly than the commander in St. Louis in 1843, Colonel S. W. Kearny.

---

[7] The expert judgment of F. S. Dellenbaugh in *Frémont and '49*, p. 110, is that the same weight in dried beans would have been more valuable to the party.

Thus started prematurely, the expedition waited on the prairies one day, May 30th, while some members rode back to the settlement for the missing parts of their equipment; then, on the thirty-first, the journey was resumed in company with several emigrant wagons. These wagons, under the direction of J. B. Chiles of Missouri, were bound to the Sacramento, and were filled with provisions, furniture, and farm implements, including the complete machinery for a sawmill which he intended to erect in Napa Valley. There was no question now of the scope and vigor of the westward movement. As the expedition moved out along the Santa Fé Trail, Frémont saw trains of wagons far to the front and others stretching irregularly to the rear, giving the road an animated and populous appearance. Most of these belonged to the "great migration" of this year to Oregon. On the fourth night out, the missionary Dr. Marcus Whitman camped with the party.[8] The majority of the season's emigrants had already reached or passed the point where the Santa Fé Trail intersected the Kansas River, but still the stream of late-comers for Oregon and California showed no slackening. The clouds of dust, the gleam of the canvas-topped wagons, were evidence to Frémont that his services were needed immediately.

The labors and adventures of the second expedition between the Missouri and the Dalles of the Columbia, occupying the period between June 1st and November 5, 1843, may be briefly summarized. Frémont at once deviated southward from the route of his first trip, hoping thereby to find a new road to the coast through a country of more genial climate. His plan was, instead of following the Platte to the South Pass in southern Wyoming, to go up the Kansas to the head of the Arkansas River, in what is now central Colorado, and try to discover a new pass through the mountains, far to the south of the gateway most emigrants were using. If he could have found such a corridor as that which railway builders later utilized up the Gunnison Valley into Utah, and proved it suitable for emigrant

[8] Theodore Talbot, MS Journal, Library of Congress.

use, he would have greatly benefited the country.[9] He was not destined to succeed in this attempt. He was, however, to bring his party through many new scenes to Oregon and California.

Following the northernmost fork of the Kansas westward, the expedition found itself at first in an arid, unproductive country, where the broad shallow stream, some six hundred yards wide and only a few inches deep, seemed to struggle for its life among yellowish-white quicksands. Crossing this fork, the Republican, toward the northwest, they pushed on over a terrain more and more broken and elevated. Suffering greatly from thirst, they had to drink the half-putrid water of buffalo wallows, an experience that Theodore Talbot describes with amusing disgust:

About eight o'clock we found some ponds in which the water was not quite so nauseous and there we camped. These ponds or wallows are formed by the buffaloes wallowing, an amusement they are very fond of. When any rain falls, it is collected in these places, and here the buffalo come to drink and stand during the heat of the day; adding their own excrements to the already putrescent waters. This compound, warmed for weeks in a blazing sun and alive with animalcules, makes a drink palatable to one suffering from intense thirst. Oh, that some over-dainty connoisseur might taste of it!

A cold rain was welcomed eagerly. On the afternoon of July 1st, when already four thousand feet above sea level, they caught a far glimpse of a faint blue mass penciled against the glowing sky, a mass behind which the sun disappeared. In the clear morning air next day, they could see Long's Peak and the high neighboring mountains, still covered to their bases with gleaming snow. On July 4th, they arrived at St. Vrain's Fort, and joined the veteran fur trader in a feast in honor of the day. Even this wild country was beginning to be thinly settled, for only ten miles away they reached the post of another trader, Mr. Lupton. This post was called Fort Lancaster.

[9] "In later days the Overland Stage from Denver to Salt Lake, by way of Fort Collins, the Medicine Bow Mountains, and Bridger's Pass, approximated the route that Frémont sought to open"; Sabin, *Kit Carson Days,* I, p. 355.

It was coming to look like a well-stocked farm, with hogs, cattle, chickens, and turkeys foraging on the prairie, and a large vegetable garden. Thence the explorers continued southwest, moving parallel with the Rockies, till, on July 9th, they had a momentary glimpse through the clouds of Pike's Peak.

At the point where the Boiling Spring River [10] enters the Arkansas, Frémont, "accidentally" met and reëngaged his old comrade, Kit Carson. There was a village here, where a number of mountaineers, principally Americans, had taken up farming. They had a fine stock of cattle, and obtained what ready money they needed by a desultory Indian trade. Formerly, they had also traded with New Mexico, and had married Spanish women in the Taos Valley, but Mexican decrees had stopped all commercial intercourse. These decrees were a heavy blow to Frémont. He had expected to obtain California mules from Taos to replace the exhausted animals which had dragged his heavy carts for many hundred miles, and to buy new supplies of sugar, flour, and other necessaries. Both the mules and provisions were indispensable if he were to continue west over the mountains.

With the advice of Carson, he decided to retrace his steps. Kit was despatched forthwith to Bent's Fort, some seventy-five miles downstream on the Arkansas, with instructions to lay before Charles Bent the imperative needs of the expedition. Fortunately, Bent was able to spare ten good mules, some pack animals, and a quantity of foodstuffs; and taking these with him, Kit traveled to St. Vrain's Fort, where he met Frémont. The explorer now found himself at the foot of the central chain of the Rockies, with the supplies he needed. He knew that he must go almost straight west, for the usual ford of the Green River beyond the mountains lay in that direction. Unfortunately, he could obtain no information upon the character of the passes, and no guide. Thus handicapped, he separated his

[10] This Boiling Spring River is the Fontaine Qui Bouille or Bouit of all early travelers, and the village at its mouth is the Pueblo so frequently mentioned. Preuss found the springs to resemble the Seltzer springs of Germany.

party, for greater speed and safety, into two parties. Fitz-patrick, with the heavy baggage and the majority of the men, was to take the usual emigrant road by way of the mouth of the Laramie River to Fort Hall, the Hudson's Bay Company post on the Snake. With him went Alexander Godey, a hunter esteemed by experts to be "in courage and professional skill a formidable rival to Carson"; a man of whom we shall hear more.

Frémont meanwhile took charge of the other body, a picked group of men, including Kit Carson, Preuss, and Zindel, and set out to cut through the mountains to South Pass by way of the valley of the Cache de la Poudre River. He shortly found himself in one of the wildest and most beautiful parts of the Rockies:[11] "Towering mountains rose round about; their sides sometimes dark with forests of pine, and sometimes with lofty precipices, washed by the river; while below, the green river bottom was covered with a wilderness of flowers, their tall spikes rising about our heads as we rode among them."

From this point, their way, even in its smoother portions made "terribly rough" by the dense sage-brush, four to six feet in height, became more and more difficult. They counted them-selves lucky in killing many buffalo, and stopped for two days, some two hundred miles from St. Vrain's Fort, to dry large quantities of the meat for future use. But after struggling for-ward till August 7th, with the terrain growing worse and threatening to make progress with the light carriages wholly impossible, Frémont gave up. From an eminence that after-noon, he tells us, a mountain range became visible in the north, in which he recognized some rocky peaks of the Sweetwater Valley Range; and "determining to abandon any further effort to struggle through this almost impracticable country," he turned back. The party proceeded north-northwest along the east side of the Medicine Bow Range till it reached its northern extremity, then moved west parallel with the present-day line of the Union Pacific, crossed the North Platte, moved up the

[11] Frémont, *Memoirs,* pp. 189, 190.

Sweetwater Valley, and traversed South Pass ahead of Fitz-patrick's division of the expedition. His efforts to find a more southerly route to Oregon and northern California had failed.

After Frémont's party reached the well-marked Oregon Trail on the· banks of the Sweetwater River, it found the broad smooth highway, where the constant passage of emigrant wagons had beaten the sage-brush out of existence, a happy exchange for the sharp rocks and tough shrubs through which their horses had been toiling.[12] From this point onward their path was easy and, despite dust and heat, their progress was rapid. They saw many evidences of the stream of travel. Twice within nine days they passed the new-made grave of an emi-grant; once they fell in with a stray ox wandering slowly toward his eastern home. When they reached the fertile valley of the Bear River they overtook a single emigrant family, traveling courageously alone with three or four span of fine oxen. Frémont concluded that they were the rear guard of a larger party just ahead, and this proved to be the fact. The next afternoon, crossing a narrow spur, they descended into a lovely valley tributary to the Bear, and came upon a striking scene:

The edge of the wood, for several miles along the river, was dotted with the white covers of emigrant wagons, collected in groups at different camps, where the smokes were rising lazily from the fires, around which the women were occupied in preparing the eve-ning meal, and the children playing in the grass; and herds of cattle, grazing about in the bottom, had an air of quiet security and civilized comfort that made a rare sight to the traveller in such a remote wilderness. In common with all the emigration, they had been reposing for several days in this delightful valley, in order to recruit their animals on its luxuriant pasturage after their long journey, and prepare them for the hard travel along the compara-tively sterile banks of the upper Columbia.

[12] *Ibid.*, p. 198; *Report, Second Exploring Expedition* (Derby ed., 1849), p. 161.

The Oregon Trail was now a great American highway, as busy as the Cumberland Road a generation earlier.[13] Frémont did not halt but, driving directly on, left the emigrants in the rear. But next morning, on breaking camp, he found just ahead of him another large party of emigrants leisurely resting, while still farther along the road there was a third. These groups were all parts of the great train of this year, but partly for convenience in travel and partly through factionalism they kept apart. As each camp received him with cheers and eager greetings, again he could feel that America was on the march.

They were now near the Great Salt Lake, and with this as an objective, Frémont accelerated his pace. Some Shoshone Indians supplied him with fresh horses, vegetables, and berries. Despite this, his men were so hard pressed for food that they were glad to make a supper of stewed skunk. Frémont saw, and later described, some natural curiosities—hot springs, red and white hills, an extinct volcano, and so on; but he gave little time to them. On September 6th, he reached the lake, and looking down upon it from a high peninsular butte, experienced one of the memorable moments of his exploring career: [14]

The waters of the inland sea stretched in still and solitary grandeur far beyond the limit of our vision. It was one of the great points of the exploration; and as we looked eagerly over the lake in the first emotions of excited pleasure, I am doubtful if the followers of Balboa felt more enthusiasm when, from the heights of the Andes, they saw for the first time the great Western Ocean. It was certainly a magnificent object, and a noble terminus to this part of our expedition; and to travellers so long shut up among mountain ranges a sudden view over the expanse of silent waters had in it something sublime. Several large islands raised their high rocky heads out of the waves; but whether or not they were timbered was still left to our imagination, as the distance was too great

[13] Compare J. R. Schafer, *History of the Pacific Northwest*, p. 127ff.
[14] Frémont, *Memoirs*, I, p. 228. The Oregon Trail is separated from the Great Salt Lake district by the Wasatch Range. Frémont went up the trail to the end of the range and to Bear Lake, then turning southward to Great Salt Lake.

to determine if the dark hues upon them were woodland or naked rock.

The expectations of the party had been whetted by remarkable tales related of the lake in camp and fort, for old hunters familiar with the region made it the theme of exaggerated stories. Hitherto it had been visited only by them and by trappers searching for beaver streams. Possibly Etienne Provôt was one of the earliest in the vicinity; but its discovery seems to have been made by Jim Bridger in the autumn of 1824. It was Bridger who, stooping for a drink, was astonished to find the water salt, and exclaimed, as he spat it out: "Hell, we are on the shores of the Pacific!" James Clyman and three others are credited with having completely circumnavigated the lake in 1826. But as yet no scientist or any one really interested in geography had visited it; its islands had not been trodden; and no instrumental observations or geographical survey had ever been made in the vicinity. Most men supposed that it had no outlet; but some of Frémont's own voyageurs believed that it contained a terrible whirlpool, through which its waters found a subterreanean way to the Pacific. He tells us that hearing various men talk, "my own mind had become tolerably well filled with their indefinite pictures, and insensibly colored with their romantic descriptions, which, in the pleasure of excitement, I . . . half expected to realize." But he resolved to give the lake its first scientific examination.

Nearly a week of the bracing September weather was devoted to this task. Frémont made a voyage in his india-rubber boat, taking Carson with him, and enjoying the sensation of paddling over water "almost transparently clear, of an extremely beautiful bright-green color." The frail and badly-pasted boat, unfortunately, was kept afloat with great difficulty, and when two of the air cylinders gave way, almost wrecked them in the middle of the lake. They landed on one of the islands, ascended its hills to a rocky eminence eight hundred feet above the water, and spent the windy night hearing the waves break on the shore like "the roar of an ocean surf." Next day, paddling back, a sudden storm almost cost them their lives. In the course of his wanderings, he made a careful chemical analysis of the water—boiling down a five gallon pail of it, he obtained fourteen pints of fine white salt—and took observations upon the botany and animal life.[15]

One of his conclusions was that the region about the lake, and especially to the north of it, in the Bear River Valley, was suitable for a military post and a flourishing civilized settlement, which would be of great strategic value. The bottom lands of the Bear River and the creeks, he pointed out, already formed a natural camping ground for emigrants. Nutritious bunch grass for live stock was abundant; service berries flourished; timber and water were plentiful, and the soil was adapted to grain. As a result of Frémont's description of the Great Salt Lake and Valley, Brigham Young determined four years later to lead the Mormons into this far-off region to set up the State of Deseret. Young did not read Frémont's report with full comprehension; for with reference to comments on Utah Lake, he later charged him with representing the Great Salt Lake as in part salt, and in part fresh, which Frémont had not done at all. He also declared that Frémont had described as a fertile country what was in reality a desert. But despite Young's misconceptions, the Mormons had reason to be grateful to the explorer whose accounts had led them across the Rockies.[16]

[15] Carson tells us in his autobiography that Frémont and he ascended the mountain and cut a large cross under a shelving rock. "Next morning started back. Had not left the island more than a league when the clouds commenced gathering for a storm. Our boat leaking wind kept one man continually employed at the bellows. Frémont directed us to pull for our lives, if we did not arrive on shore before the storm commenced we will surely all perish. We done our best and arrived in time to save ourselves. We had not more than landed when the storm commenced and in an hour the waters had risen eight or ten feet." Carson, *Own Story*.

[16] On this point see Frémont, *Memoirs*, pp. 415, 416. It is to be noted that Frémont did say in his *Report* (Derby ed., p. 209) and in his *Memoirs* (p. 388) that "the Utah is the southern limb of the Great Salt Lake; and thus we had seen that remarkable sheet of water both at its northern and southern extremity." The Utah, a fresh-water sheet, is really connected with the Salt Lake.

Setting out northward from the lake on September 12, 1843, Frémont and his party rode forward so steadily that they reached Fort Hall on the Snake River at sunset of the eighteenth. They were tormented by hunger; on their first night, they supped upon some sea-gulls which Carson shot near the lake, and on their third Frémont gave the men permission to kill a fat young horse which he had purchased from the Snake Indians. The horse-meat soon restored the forlorn group "to gayety and good humor," but neither Frémont nor Preuss could eat of it. They had too much of civilized prejudice, wrote Frémont: "feeling as much saddened as if a crime had been committed." Later still, they bought an antelope from an Indian for a little powder and lead.

At Fort Hall, where they joined forces again with Fitzpatrick and his party, a thorough refitting and reorganization of the expedition took place. The officer in charge of this southeastern outpost of the Hudson's Bay Company, a Briton named Richard Grant, sold them several poor horses and five fat oxen. This meat was much needed, though Fitzpatrick had rigidly husbanded his share of the stock of flour and light provisions. Already the weather warned them that winter was approaching. On September 19, 1843, it snowed thickly all day; on the night of the twenty-first, standing water froze fairly hard. The lieutenant therefore called his men together, and amid a cold drizzle told them that he thought it best to cut off from his expedition all who were not ready to face the rigors of steady midwinter exploration with scanty food and other supplies. He described the hardships they would probably suffer. Eleven men, including the trusty Basil Lajeunesse (who was needed at home), decided to return east, and set out at once. Frémont and the others on the same day, September 23rd, resumed their

But Frémont made it clear that he thought the connection between the two very slender, and he never said, as Brigham Young stated, that "the south end of the lake was fresh and the north salt." On this point see his letter to the New York *Times,* June, 1877, reprinted in the *Memoirs,* pp. 415, 416. As for the fertility of the region that Brigham Young called a desert, Dellenbaugh (p. 154) pithily remarks that the best answer to Young is the character of the Salt Lake Valley to-day, a rich garden in the midst of the mountains.

journey down the Snake Valley toward the Pacific, the wind driving the chill drizzle in their faces in sharp gusts. He had made up his mind that at or near Fort Hall there ought to be a strong American military post, keeping guard over a farming settlement in this part of the valley, and protecting the Oregon emigrants from Indians. It was deplorable, he wrote later, that these emigrants, exhausted by the long journey of 1,320 miles from Missouri, should have no assistance save the aid furnished by a none-too-friendly British fur post.

At the end of the first week in October, the expedition reached Fort Boisé, another Hudson's Bay Company post, at the point where the Boisé River flows through high basalt precipices into the Snake. A fortnight later, the weather steadily growing colder, they found themselves approaching the district where the Snake, the Columbia proper, the Yakima, and the Walla Walla all merge to form that magnificent stream, the lower Columbia. Frémont was impressed by the scenery. Far to the west, one hundred and eighty miles away, they saw the snowy cone of Mount Hood standing high above the surrounding country, majestic in its isolation. Here was the mission establishment of Dr. Marcus Whitman, consisting at this time of a single adobe house. Frémont felt that he was again approaching civilization: [17]

I found Dr. Whitman absent on a visit to the Dalles of the Columbia; but had the pleasure of seeing a fine-looking family of emigrants, men, women, and children, in robust health, all indemnifying themselves for previous scanty fare in a hearty consumption of potatoes, which are produced here of a remarkable good quality. We were disappointed in our expectation of obtaining cornmeal or flour at this station, the mill belonging to the mission having been lately burned down; but an abundant supply of excellent potatoes banished regrets, and furnished a grateful substitute for bread. A small town of Nez Percé Indians gave an inhabited and even a populous appearance to the station; and, after remaining about an hour, we continued our route and encamped on the river about four miles below, passing on the way an emigrant encampment.

[17] Frémont, *Report, Second Expedition* (Derby ed.), p. 249.

From Whitman's mission to the Dalles—that is, the trough where the Columbia is squeezed into a narrow basalt gash, only fifty yards across at the narrowest point—was a difficult journey along the shores of the Columbia, taking till November 5th. Here the bulk of the expedition was left to make repairs and prepare for the homeward journey, while Frémont, Preuss, and two others went on by canoe to Fort Vancouver, far down the Columbia River. The trip was necessary to connect Frémont's operations with those of Captain Wilkes, and was quickly and easily made. On November 18, 1843, the explorer was back in the general camp at the Dalles, bringing with him a three months' supply of flour, peas, and tallow. At the Dalles, the expedition had also obtained some cattle to be driven along and slaughtered, and enough horses and mules to bring the number of pack animals up to one hundred four. Then, abandoning the carts and preparing a large number of pack-saddles for the supplies, the party set out on its return to the United States.

Had Frémont been an explorer who chose the safe and easy path, had he been intent upon getting back to St. Louis quickly with his observations upon the Oregon Trail and the Columbia River country, he would simply have retraced his steps. But to back-track in this way would have been a waste of time, and his intention was very different. He had planned, in his talks with Benton and Linn, to return by a sweeping southward journey which would reveal some of the secrets of the Great Basin, the desert valley which includes so much of Utah, Nevada, and New Mexico. This huge region, more than seven hundred miles square, offered a challenge which he could not resist. Already crossed from east to west by Jedediah Smith, Joseph Walker, and others, it had never been fully traversed from north to south. Frémont meant to attempt just this. His main geographical objectives were to find and describe a supposed Klamath Lake, a "Mary's Lake" which lay oasis-like in the midst of the desert, and—if it existed—the Buenaventura River, which various men (including Benton) believed might flow from the Great Basin to the Pacific. He meant also to give the Great Basin, or as Gallatin's map, borrowing from Jedediah Smith, had called it, the Great Sandy Desert, a more scientific inspection than it had yet received. In all this he was encouraged by Dr. John McLoughlin of the Hudson's Bay Company at headquarters at Fort Vancouver, who even drew for him a rough sketch-map of the interior showing this mythical Buenaventura.[18]

No one knew better than the lieutenant that this was a serious and dangerous undertaking. Winter was just commencing; he had only twenty-five men; the country before him was wild and strange, and he did not possess even the imperfect maps of the latest travelers. Weird and almost incredible tales were told of the disappearing rivers, wind-parched deserts, high mountains, and treacherous savages of the region. As Frémont later recalled, no man of his party blenched, or failed to exhibit entire courage and cheerfulness; "nor did any extremity of peril and privation, to which we were afterwards exposed, even belie, or derogate from, the fine spirit of this brave and generous commencement." But as yet they little understood how grave these perils would be.

[18] McLoughlin was director-in-chief of all the posts of the Hudson's Bay Company west of the Rockies. A kindly man, he was very helpful to American settlers, and eventually became an American citizen. Fort Vancouver stood just opposite the present city of Portland.

XI

Over the Winter Sierras

A S Frémont must have guessed, the most significant portion of his second expedition lay just before him when he turned south from the Columbia. What he had done thus far was simply to complete a scientific survey of a much-traveled trail. He was now to make a journey through a region largely unknown, and to execute a peaceful invasion of a foreign country. On November 25, 1843, the party set out on its long journey; twenty-five men in all, besides some Indian guides hired to go part way, and more than a hundred horses and mules. Frémont generously left his instrument wagon as a gift to the mission. They pushed steadily south along the eastern slopes of the Cascade Mountains, the commander making his usual assiduous notes on topography, botany, zoölogy, geology, and soil-fertility. The scenery was magnificent. But the nights were frigid, the marches laborious; and they soon entered country where the Indians were reputed highly dangerous.

Klamath Marsh in lower Oregon was reached in zero weather, and the lieutenant, in order to explore its banks and give his animals pasturage, lingered there two days. Whether he saw Klamath Lake, which lies thirty miles to the southward, is uncertain. Over the greater part of what he calls the "extensive meadow or lake of grass," at the time of his December visit, the water, or rather the ice, was scattered in shallow pools. The marsh was little more than a wide irregular depression, twenty miles in diameter, which for a short time after the spring melting of the winter snows filled up with water; this subsequently drained away through the Klamath River, leaving

most of the bed in summer a waving green savannah. The
explorer fell in with the fish-eating Indians of the marsh region,
who had adapted their life with remarkable skill to the locality.
Living in large round huts, perhaps twenty feet in diameter,
they had learned to make expert use of the grass and rushes.
Their grass shoes were well suited to the snowy country; the
women had woven large close-textured caps of basket shape;
and they also made handsome varicolored mats, some of which
the expedition bought for table-cloths and mattresses. On his
last morning here Frémont's camp was thronged with these
Klamaths, armed with heavy bows and arrows; and knowing
their treacherous habits, he kept a vigilant guard.[1]

The marsh was left behind them on December 13th, and
they pushed farther east, with the sun shining brightly but the
cold intense, and the snow from four to twelve inches deep.
The mules pulling the howitzer floundered heavily along the
uncertain way, and the men found walking laborious. Farther
southeast they went, always farther southeast, toward what is
now the southern boundary of Oregon. On December 14th,
amid a thick snowstorm, they crossed what Frémont mistakenly
believed to be the headwaters of the Sacramento, the stream
actually being the Klamath River.[2] He was misled by Indian
information, and by the John McLoughlin map, which Benton
later called "disastrously erroneous." Next day they killed the
cow they had brought from the Columbia, which could find no
grass above the snow and was getting thinner and thinner.
When they broke camp on December 16th, they found the
snow three feet deep, and so crusted that the pack animals

---

[1] "I was not unmindful of the disasters which Smith, and other travelers, had
met with in this country, and therefore was equally vigilant in guarding against
treachery and violence"; Frémont, *Report, Second Expedition* (Derby ed.),
pp. 286, 287. Jedediah Smith had lost fifteen men in 1828 at the hands of the
Umpqua tribe. This sentence of Frémont's is evidence that he knew of Smith's
journey through northern California, and should therefore have known of his
traverse of the Great Basin in 1827.

[2] According to Dellenbaugh, *Frémont and '49*, pp. 191, 192, the Sycan River,
a branch of the Klamath.

FRÉMONT'S PARTY ATTACKED BY KLAMATH INDIANS

(From Frémont's *Memoirs*)

AMONG THE BUFFALO

(From Frémont's *Memoirs*)

constantly cut their legs in breaking through it. Their path lay through a dense pine forest, the green branches bowed with snow, and the air dark with the falling flakes. The depths of the somber woodland were profoundly still, and Frémont felt a wonderful impressiveness and beauty in the quiet, broken only by some sudden breath of wind whirling the snow through the upper branches. One direction looked like another; they seemed to be going through some detached and enchanted wilderness, and it required an exertion of the will to preserve a constant course. Thus struggling forward, they came out at noon on the verge of a vertical rocky cliff. They were traversing an upland ridge which overlooked one of the valleys of the Great Basin, and south and southeast their eyes fell upon an entrancing scene: [3]

At our feet—more than a thousand feet below—we looked into a green prairie country, in which a beautiful lake, some twenty miles in length, was spread along the foot of the mountains, its shores bordered with green grass. Just then the sun broke out among the clouds, and illuminated the country below, while around us the storm raged fiercely. Not a particle of ice was to be seen on the lake, or snow on its borders, and all was like summer or spring. The glow of the sun in the valley below brightened up our hearts with sudden pleasure; and we made the woods ring with joyful shouts to those behind; and gradually, as each came up, he stopped to enjoy the unexpected scene. Shivering in snow three feet deep, and stiffening in a cold north wind, we exclaimed at once that the names of Summer Lake and Winter Ridge should be applied to these two proximate places of such sudden and violent contrast.

Descending to this central valley, the expedition found travel for the next few days much easier, and the weather milder. They celebrated Christmas Day on the banks of Warner Lake in lower Oregon by a discharge of the howitzer and their small arms, and by serving a ration of brandy, sugar, and coffee. The next night they made camp nearly on the present Nevada

[3] Frémont, *Report, Second Expedition* (Derby ed.), pp. 289, 290.

boundary line, and the following morning pressed on into northwestern Nevada. Their march carried them at first through a district of lakes and streams, the drainage of the great Sierra Range, dominated by Mount Shasta, which rose to their right; then into a forbidding country of gullies, arid hills, sage-brush flats, and sandy stretches sown with black volcanic rock. Frémont began to grow worried, for his twenty-five men were tired and his equipment was failing, while they had met no evidence whatever of Mary's Lake or the Buenaventura River. He was simply verifying the accuracy of the Bonneville and Gallatin maps, which had omitted any such waterway. The party had lost fifteen pack-animals, dead, abandoned, or stolen by skulking savages since they left the Dalles; water and grass were scarce; and early in the new year (1844) they killed the last of the beeves they had brought from the Columbia for meat.

They were genuinely hungry when, January 10th, they reached a large lake, thirty-five miles long, full of salmon trout on which they feasted. By this time they were in a region populous with Indians, and as they advanced saw signal smokes in every direction. Frémont named the water, after an extraordinary rock rising from its midst, Pyramid Lake, and the fresh stream flowing into it, to-day known as the Truckee, the Salmon Trout River. Still moving south, the expedition camped some twenty-five miles from the site of Reno, and on January 18th reached the Carson River. By this date the men were again tired and hungry, and the pack animals all footsore; moreover, the country ahead seemed to be barren, rocky, and difficult.

Under these circumstances, Frémont felt justified in announcing to the men a determination which he was only too glad to reach; a resolution which had perhaps been half-formed when he left the Missouri, and had then taken more definite shape with every mile. This was the crossing of the Sierras into California. It is barely possible that the expansionist senators, and Benton and Linn in particular, had reached an understanding with Frémont that he was to enter California and spy out the land. They knew that it was like a great ripe fruit, ready to fall into the first hand that touched it; they knew that some Britons were casting envious eyes upon it. They felt that if there was to be war with Mexico over Texas, the United States should possess authentic information upon the feasible mountain passes for an invasion of California; upon the resources of its fertile valleys; upon the attitude of the Californians toward the United States; and upon the strength and position of the Mexican forces under Governor Alvarado. Who could collect this information so well as Frémont, whose journey would carry him to the very gates of California anyway?

Very possibly, Frémont had cherished a faint hope that the mythical Buenaventura might be found, and would lead him down to San Francisco Bay, which the expansionists were so eager to prevent from falling into British possession. When this hope disappeared, he made up his mind to cross the great Sierra Range anyway, just as an American army might have to cross it if war broke out. The exhausted state of his expedition and the difficulty of pressing on by the southwestern route to the Arkansas without recuperation and refitting were a sufficient excuse for this bold move. Actually, there was no necessity for entering California. He could have spent the remainder of the winter comfortably in the Truckee Valley, his men living on antelope, small game, salmon, and pine nuts, his mules growing fat on the good pasturage, and the best homeward route established by a reconnaissance. The only risks were that the loss of animals, which the Indians would continue stealing day by day, might leave his party helpless and stranded; and that the discipline of the men would deteriorate. But to remain would in any event have been a waste of good opportunities. A Mexican decree had prohibited Americans from entering California anywhere, under any pretext, but that did not daunt Frémont, any more than it did numerous American settlers. E. L. Sabin justly comments: [4]

[4] *Kit Carson Days*, I, p. 361.

Life would possibly have flowed more smoothly for Frémont had he been more of a routine officer, and he would have been spared resentment and humiliation. But, he would have been less of a man. For political ends he was styled the Pathfinder. The paths that he actually found were of scant public utility and were bettered by other paths. He was however a Pathseeker, and there can be no quibbles as to the inspirational values, to the common mind, of his gallant initiative. For Frémont testified to the fact that things could be done.

As a physical venture, the attempt to cross the high Sierras in midwinter was appallingly foolhardy. This mighty range, in places 14,000 feet high, rises precipitously from the east, steep on steep, to a point where, in January, all is a silent, frozen waste of snow and rock, as bleak, empty, and bitter as the Himalayas themselves, with no life or movement save the terrific storms which sweep across the peaks and valleys. The pine forests which lead up to these heights are choked with snow. Paths and trails are hidden beneath the drifts, and the sub-zero temperature means death for those who lose themselves in the mountain corridors. If an unusual series of blizzards had overtaken Frémont's party, it could not have avoided the fate of the Donner emigrants, overwhelmed and unable to move either forward or back.[5] There are few passes in the high Sierras, and in the year 1844 they were virtually unknown. No maps were available, no scientist had ever examined the range, and no white man had ever crossed it in winter.

Yet Frémont embarked upon this perilous undertaking in a characteristically headlong way. Though he might profitably have spent a week or two on the Truckee gaining strength and by brief expeditions searching for the best pass, he plunged immediately and blindly into the maze of foothills which led

[5] The Donner party of about eighty men, women, and children, caught by the mountain snows near what is now Truckee, California, in the winter of 1846-47, suffered a terrible disaster. Thirty-nine died. When Sutter sent two Indians with mule-loads of beef to them, they ate both the beef and the Indians. A child of the party, Eliza P. Donner Houghton, wrote in old age *Expedition of the Donner Party and its Tragic Fate* (1911).

to the formidable icy rampart beyond. As F. S. Dellenbaugh says, a delay of a fortnight would have cost nothing and would have benefited him materially; but delay was never congenial to Frémont. Setting out January 19, 1844, on the second day he camped in the Pine Nut Mountains near the present site of Virginia City. He little thought that within a few miles was a stupendously rich vein of gold and silver, the Comstock Lode, which twenty years later was to bring into existence one of the roaring cities of the West. On January 24th, he met an old Indian of the Washoe tribe, who volunteered to lead the expedition to a good pass, and not only accompanied them for two days, but introduced some friendly tribesmen who sold them pine nuts. The road grew constantly rougher as they approached the main chain of the Sierras, and on January 29th they were compelled to a step which Frémont deeply regretted; they abandoned their little howitzer, which had been dragged so many miles and had never proved more than a useless encumbrance. A young Washoe was hired as guide and on January 30th he led them into the head of Antelope Valley, but becoming cold and discouraged, shortly left.

The Indians whom they met at this point all advised Frémont against continuing farther. They could communicate with him only by signs, but in their earnestness they spoke rapidly and vehemently, emphasizing the folly of his intentions. The word *tahve*, signifying snow, occurred often in their discourse. They plainly thought the Sierras impassable. Already, in the foothills, the thermometer was below zero at night, and the snow three or four feet deep in places. Frémont, however, assured the savages that his horses were strong and would force a passage through the drifts. On January 31st, they perceived clearly what was before them. That afternoon, with the snow falling heavily and the weather so frigid that one man had a foot frozen, they descended a pass which gave them a long view westward. They saw embanked before them a great continuous range, its foot defined by the Carson River Valley, its lower parts steep and darkly clothed with pines, its magnificent crests hidden in gloomy snowclouds. This forbidding rampart was the central chain of the Sierras.

Just what Frémont's men thought of the enterprise we do not know. The young commander served an occasional ration of brandy to heighten their spirits; he exhorted them like Napoleon before the Pyramids. He reminded them of the beautiful valley of the Sacramento, so often described by Kit Carson, who had delighted the expedition by speaking of its rich pastures and abundant game. He drew a contrast between its summer climate, less than a hundred miles distant, and the bitter cold they now suffered. He informed them that his instruments, in which long experience had given them complete confidence, showed that seventy miles directly west was Captain Sutter's great ranch; and that from the heights just before them they would be able with one effort to place themselves in the midst of plenty. Frémont had at times a ready French eloquence, but it is not certain that his sanguine confidence carried the men with him. He tells us that some of them remained "unusually silent." [6]

They started upward on the morning of February 2, 1844, a clear and frosty dawn, in a deeply serious mood. From this point, an old chief told them, it took six or seven days to cross the mountains in fair summer weather. Their Indian guide—for they had procured another—shook his head ominously as he pointed to the icy pinnacles of the Sierras thrusting high into the sky. They knew that the issue of their adventure was doubtful. They now had sixty-seven animals with them, but their provisions were falling low. They possessed no tallow or grease, no salt, and had been so long without meat that one mess received permission to eat a fat dog which they had with them. The snow deepened immediately, and it was necessary to begin systematic path-breaking. This was done by forming a party of ten, mounted on the strongest horses; each man took turns in breaking a way, and as he became tired, the next one took his place. So well did this plan work that

---

[6] Frémont, *Report, Second Expedition* (Derby ed.), p. 324*ff.*

on the first day they traveled sixteen miles, and mounted to an altitude of 6,760 feet, camping in four feet of snow, but near a meadow of bunch grass partly cleared by the wind.

Thus they pushed on. On February 3rd they made less progress, only seven miles; on February 4th they were brought almost to a stop. In the afternoon they attempted to force a road toward a pass which the guide indicated ahead, but their horses, after laboriously plunging two or three hundred yards, became exhausted and refused to make any further effort. The guide regarded their position as hopeless, telling them they were just beginning to enter the deep snow. Most of the animals had been pushed thus far only by leaving their packs behind, so that the trail was strewn with stores and equipage. The party had no choice but to camp where they were, on the heavily wooded mountainside, without shelter, in a freezing wind. They built fires, covered the snow with large boughs, and soon had a degree of comfort. But many of the men were ready to give up. There ensued a striking scene, of which Frémont has left us a vivid picture: [7]

Two Indians joined our party here; and one of them, an old man, immediately began to harangue us, saying that ourselves and animals would perish in the snow, and that if we would go back, he would show us another and a better way across the mountain. He spoke in a very loud voice and there was a singular repetition of phrases and arrangements of words which rendered his speech striking and not unmusical.

We had now begun to understand some words, and with the aid of signs, easily comprehended the old man's simple ideas. "Rock upon rock—rock upon rock—snow upon snow—snow upon snow," said he; "even if you get over the snow you will not be able to get down from the mountains." He made us the sign of precipices, and showed us how the feet of the horses would slip, and throw them off from the narrow trails which led along their sides.

Our Chinook [guide], who comprehended even more readily than ourselves, and believed our situation hopeless, covered his head with

[7] Frémont, *Memoirs*, I, p. 332.

his blanket and began to weep and lament. "I wanted to see the whites," he said; "I came away from my own people to see the whites, and I wouldn't care to die among them; but here"...and he looked around into the cold night and gloomy forest, and, drawing his blanket over his head, began again to lament.

Seated around the tree, the fire illuminating the rocks and the tall bolls of the pines round about, and the old Indian haranguing, we presented a group of very serious faces.

A man with less force of will, less buoyancy of temperament, would have turned back, but Frémont was not daunted. At dawn next morning their faint-hearted Indian guide deserted. Frémont, who found the night too cold to sleep, had seen him standing by the fire with all his finery on, and, observing him shiver, had kindly thrown his blanket over his shoulders; a few minutes afterward the treacherous fellow decamped. The lieutenant's mind had been busy overnight, and he had resolved to set the majority of his party to making sledges and bringing up the scattered baggage while he and a few others undertook a reconnaissance on foot of the heights ahead.

This reconnaissance, in the face of terrifying obstacles, was effected on February 6th. The snow lay in an average depth of five feet, and not infrequently, as they judged by the treetops emerging from it, was twenty feet deep. On steep slopes it was covered with an icy crust of great slipperiness, down which the horses would sometimes slide, helpless till some tree or rock arrested them. At this elevation of 7,500 feet the cold was intense the moment the sun passed behind a peak or cloud, and the party had to keep moving briskly even at midday. They made a weaving, circuitous path, for the depth of snow in the hollows compelled them to follow the hillsides and cross the jutting spurs where wind and sun had in part cleared away the drifts. The men, wearing snow-shoes, marched in a single file, trampling down the snow heavily, so that after freezing hard at night it would bear the weight of the horses the following day.

The ground first ascended sharply to the top of a fairly high ridge; beyond this lay a broad timbered basin, some ten miles across; and at its extremity rose the high crest of the Sierras, a gloomy wall of volcanic rock. The summit presented a line of naked peaks, the harsh rock glowing in the morning sun, bare of either snow or vegetation; but leading up to the timber-line, the slopes were covered with pines and other trees of extraordinary size.

After much effort, the party reached the crest of the range, slightly to the left of a pass which had been pointed out by their guide. A welcome sight met their eyes. The mountain slopes, in part densely wooded, descended steeply below them. Far in the distance at their base, lying half defined in a warm haze, stretched a great, smiling valley, its greens and browns untouched by any sign of snow. Straining their eyes, they could descry far to the west, not less than a hundred miles away, another and smaller line of mountains—the low Coast Range. Frémont gazed in delight, while the men shouted for joy. It was the fertile Sacramento basin. "There," exclaimed Kit Carson, pointing toward the coast, "is the little mountain —it is fifteen years ago since I saw it; but I am just as sure as if I had seen it yesterday." [8] They could pick out spots of prairie in the valley, and with the telescope could vaguely follow the dark line of the Sacramento. Then they turned hur-riedly back toward camp, for the sun was sinking.

It proved a difficult struggle to bring up the animals and to carry the whole outfit over the summits. Snow-glare rendered many of the party almost blind, and only by tying black hand-kerchiefs over their eyes could they keep on. The trail that had been beaten on the sixth was filled with driving snow on Febru-ary 9th and 10th, when Frémont and a few others advanced only about five and a half miles, leaving the animals at the base camp. For a time, it seemed almost impossible to get the horses and mules over the pass at all. Fitzpatrick, who had been left behind to make the attempt, reported that his efforts were futile. When he led them out on the half-hidden trail,

[8] Frémont, *Memoirs*, I, p. 333; the little mountain was Monte Diablo.

the packed snow beneath would not support them, and they broke through; some plunged about in the drifts, and some lay buried in the white mass. The poor beasts, which Carson tells us had been driven by hunger to eat one another's tails and the leather of the pack-saddles, possessed little strength. But Frémont refused to be defeated. He had the entire force turn to with mauls and shovels, set them to scooping and packing down a road, and made them strengthen it with pine boughs. It was exhausting work, and the food on which they did it was none too substantial. On the thirteenth the cook killed their little pet dog Klamath, and that night they supped on mule meat, dog meat, and pea soup.

Final victory was won on February 20, 1844. On that day, the expedition camped with all its animals and equipment on the summit of the pass, one thousand miles by their tortuous road from the Dalles of the Columbia. (This pass, to-day called Carson Pass and marked for tourists by a granite boulder and inscription, lies west of the present-day town of Woodfords, California.) They had conquered the Sierras in midwinter. By boiling water on the pass, they computed its elevation at 9,338 feet. Only the descent lay before them, and this seemed easy. The weather became delightfully clear, and as they went downward they had the benefit of wide views of the country below, with light and shadow playing across it. On the afternoon of the twenty-third, they heard the roll of thunder, and looking down saw the broad breast of the valley wrapped in the darkness of a storm, the jagged lightning playing in and out of the clouds. They watched the thunderstorm till sunset, when the clearing skies revealed another magnificent scene: a long shining line of water which led westward toward another gleaming expanse, a broader and larger sheet. They knew that this could be nothing but the Sacramento River and San Francisco Bay. That night, as they made their camp-fires, they saw blazes lit in the valley below, as if in answer. They were actually the fires of Indians in the *tulares* of the bay, eighty miles distant.

On March 6th, after many further trials, the ragged, hungry expedition, a woeful procession of weak and emaciated men each with a horse or mule as emaciated as himself, was approaching such civilization as that part of California afforded. They had found the Sacramento Valley, as they advanced, an enchantingly beautiful country, which seemed unequaled anywhere in the West for stock growing. Its reaches were gay with flowers, and in places were a mass of gold with the California poppy. Much of the valley was beautifully wooded with evergreen and white oak, and as there was no underbrush, it all had the appearance of a carefully tended park. Here and there were traces of horses and cattle, and once they had passed a small village of Indians. In mid-afternoon, cantering forward, Frémont and a little body of men in advance [9] gave a sudden shout. They had come in sight of a little bluff, topped by a neatly built house with glass windows! It was occupied only by a few Indians, but they rode forward more eagerly than ever. A large stream, sometimes one hundred yards wide, flowed on their right, and swept around a broad bend; the hills grew lower, until they entirely ceased; and entering a wide valley, the men rode unexpectedly into a populous Indian village. The inhabitants wore clean cotton shirts and other civilized apparel. Frémont's men were overjoyed when a well-dressed Indian came up, and saluting them in courteous Spanish, told them they were upon the Rio de los Americanos, which flowed into the Sacramento ten miles below them. The weary party was near its goal.

Carson continued questioning the Indian and joyously translated his replies to Frémont. The native told them that he was a vaquero, or cowboy; that all the other Indians about were employees of the same ranch; and that it belonged to Captain Sutter, upon whose riches and power he expatiated. The men had heard the name; in fact, it was known all the way from

[9] Frémont, Kit Carson, and a squad of others had pushed ahead of Thomas Fitzpatrick, who brought on the cripples and the baggage; Frémont's *Report, Second Expedition* (Derby ed.), p. 352. Frémont makes it clear that he depended upon Fitzpatrick for many responsible duties.

the Pacific to the Mississippi. Frémont asked to be directed to his house, and was told that it lay just over the hill, whither the Indian would conduct them. They rode forward, splashed through the river, and after a few miles came within sight of a large, low, powerful-looking structure of whitish adobe, with several buildings rising over its enormously thick walls. This post, its chief angles bastioned by little blockhouses, was the fort built by Sutter as a defense against savages, marauding bands, and the guerrillas whom the frequent outbreaks of civil war in California set loose upon the country. It was an edifice of manifest strength. They were upon the site of the future city of Sacramento.

XII

Sutter's Fort and California

IT was a tattered, exhausted, woebegone caravan which wound its way up to the gates of Sutter's Fort. Of the sixty-three horses and mules which had begun the ascent of the Sierras, only thirty-three survived. Frémont and a few others who led the way had good mounts, but the rest made a pathetic procession, crawling along single file, skeleton men leading skeleton horses. They needed all of Sutter's generosity.

Johann August Sutter, as his short, stout figure, the blond hair fringing his bald head, his large blue eyes, and his air of cherubic kindness all testified, was of German blood. He had been born in Kandern, Baden, forty-one years earlier, had spent much of his early life in Switzerland, according to some accounts had attended the military academy at Neuchatel, and had certainly married, begotten children, and served in various mercantile employments. He always spoke of himself as a Swiss. A dreamer, enterprising and adventurous, he had slipped all his home responsibilities and arrived in New York, almost penniless, in the summer of 1834. His imaginative French biographer tells us that, leaving a trail of creditors behind him, he signalized his landing in New York by a wild gesture. "He leaped upon the quay, dodged past the police guard placed there, threw a single rapid glance along the whole water front, uncorked and emptied at a draught a bottle of Rhine wine, threw the empty bottle into a West Indian lugger, and with an exultant burst of laughter launched himself into the passing crowd." [1] For some weeks he picked up a living in the East by

---

[1] Blaise Cendrars, *L'Or,* p. 31. This wildly inaccurate book deserves some credit for helping recreate interest in Sutter. A somewhat too favorable but otherwise useful life of Sutter has been published since by Julian Dana; while

turning his hand to anything he could find, from bookkeeping to taxidermy, and then set out restlessly for the West. He brought up at St. Louis, and presently settled for a time at St. Charles, Missouri. In 1835 he accompanied a trading party to Santa Fé, and repeated the trip in 1836. He seemed a born rover.

In the spring of 1838, Sutter joined the Eels-Walker missionary party, and followed the Oregon Trail to the Dalles. Arriving at Fort Vancouver in October, he was told that the snow in the mountains and the hostile Indians made it impossible for him to continue on to California, and was urged to accept employment with the Hudson's Bay Company. But his imagination had been set on fire by what he had been told of California—its incomparable wealth, its scanty population, and the feeble Mexican grasp upon its allegiance. He took a vessel to Honolulu, and thence to Sitka, where he waited until he found a ship which brought him into San Francisco Bay on July 1, 1839. During this Hawaiian stay, he was struck by an ingenious and profitable idea: since labor was scarce in California, and he would need many hands for the ranch he planned, why not employ a company of the sturdy Kanakas whom he saw all about him? Some associates in Honolulu gave him material encouragement in the project, and it was arranged that the first Kanakas should arrive at New Helvetia—for this was the name Sutter bestowed upon his future domain—within a year and a half.[2]

Once landed in California, Sutter hastened to present himself before Governor Alvarado at Monterey. With the Governor's permission, he declared, he would take up a ranch in the country, bring in Kanakas to till the ground, and establish a post, well-armed, that would serve as a protecting barrier to settlements between it and the coast. Alvarado was favorably impressed by the energetic, enthusiastic young man, and by his

more thorough studies of some phases of Sutter's career have been printed in the *California Historical Society Quarterly* by James Peter Zollinger.

[2] See *Sutter's Own Story*, edited by Erwin G. Gudde (1936).

apparently well-matured plans. The Swiss pointed out that his undertaking might be made of far-reaching benefit to the civilized Indians, thousands of whom had been thrown back into savagery and misery by the confiscation in 1834 of the religious establishments by the Mexican Government; that as his ranch developed, he could bring many of these Indians together, and assign them land to be worked under his direction. He wished to plant the ranch in the Sacramento Valley. If all went well, he would strike a telling blow for the rehabilitation of upper California, so depressed since the birth of an independent Mexico.

The result was that Alvarado authorized him to select a tract, promising him that within a year a grant would be made; and the indomitable Swiss, chartering at San Francisco Bay a schooner and yacht and buying a pinnace, voyaged inland to the mouth of the American River. Here, about August 16, 1839, he discharged his possessions, and with fifteen men mounted guns, posted sentries, and began placing his colony on a solid footing. Before winter closed in, he drove to his ranch about 500 head of cattle and 75 horses, purchased at low cost from native Californians. Apparently he had in his employ a motley crew—sailors, Kanakas, Mexican cowboys, and friendly Indians. The energy with which they labored soon transformed the place. Wells were dug; water was brought from the river in wooden pipes; fields were laid out, bridges thrown across streams, roads constructed, and trails marked. On a spot of rising ground overlooking the Sacramento and the American, they set to work upon a ranch house and other structures: stables, granaries, storehouses, kitchens, and workshops. These and the surrounding walls were built of the most substantial materials and planned to last a lifetime. A village for the Kanakas was constructed in a neighboring ravine, and constant supervision kept them as busy as the rest. The colony soon took sturdy root. In June, 1841, Sutter paid another visit to Alvarado, and having already become a Mexican citizen, he received a grant of eleven square leagues of land, or a little less than

49,000 acres. He at once began the work of fortifying his New Helvetia. His stronghold, with high walls, loopholed bastions, and frowning cannon, was completed before the end of 1843.

For a time the Indians proved a grim menace; once Sutter's life was saved by a mastiff which sprang upon a would-be assassin who had entered his bedroom, and repeatedly, he later told American visitors, he was so hemmed in by hostile savages that he had to subsist upon the seeds of wild grass. They watched his encroachments upon their ancient hunting-ground indignantly, and were ready at the first opportunity to fall upon him, murder his employees, and burn his grain and buildings.[3] Moreover, the region was overrun by bands of brigands, some of them formidable. But the ranch grew steadily in strength and importance. For military aid Governor Michel-torena in 1845 made him a new grant of twenty-two square leagues of land; and more and more land was brought under cultivation. Additional Kanakas arrived from the Pacific Islands. Sutter sent recruiting agents among the friendly Indian villages, and within a short time some two hundred and fifty natives, partly civilized by mission contacts, were busy on his estate. In 1841 he was joined by several American immigrants who had come overland, and whom he was glad to use as over-seers. Other Americans straggled in, and even those who did not take up land under his grant, or hire themselves out to him, grew accustomed to use his fort as a rendezvous. The Sacramento Valley, in fact, by the winter of Frémont's sudden arrival, was the seat of an extensive American settlement, upon which the Mexican authorities looked with increasing suspicion.

Frémont, observing all that he could in California, was impressed by Sutter's establishment. He found that this grand seigneur was making arrangements for extensive irrigation along the American River. The waving green of his wheat fields, all sowed by the thin, ragged, sun-darkened Indians, represented about six hundred bushels of seed. His herds were increasing, his fields expanding, and he was surrounded by a

---

[3] Edwin Bryant, *What I Saw in California*, p. 265ff.

peaceable, industrious population. The Indians labored stolidly at all the operations of the huge ranch—ditch digging, plowing, harrowing, seeding, brick making, and building and Frémont saw those about the fort feeding like animals upon the poorer meat of slaughtered oxen, and the bran sifted from Sutter's horse-mill. This bran was boiled into a mush in large wooden kettles and then placed in wooden troughs, in the courtyard, from which the messes scooped out what they wanted in their hands. The fort contained a blacksmith shop, distillery, cannery, flour-mill, and room for other industries. For their work, the Indians were paid in goods from Sutter's large store, and tin coins, each stamped with a certain number representing the days labored, were issued by Sutter for circulation. The rancher needed only to apply to a friendly chief to receive an ample supply of Indian boys and girls for training. At the moment he had a large company of girls at the fort, whom he hoped to employ as operatives in a woolen factory.

It was plain to Frémont that Sutter thoroughly enjoyed his position as margrave of the upper Sacramento, the ruler of a domain equal to several cantons of Switzerland. He allowed the story to become current that he was a former courtier of Charles X of France.[4] He had an appetite for popularity, applause, and even gross flattery, which his dependents gave him in generous quantity. But Frémont saw that he was shrewd enough to preserve a position of comparative independence in a country torn by conflicting forces and a fierce factional strife. Some of the American settlers were plotting to detach the province from its loose allegiance to Mexico, and throw it into the hands of the United States; and the Californians were well aware that an uprising might occur at any moment. Between the two sides, Sutter maintained a position of safe neutrality. He assumed an appearance of fidelity to the Mexican Government, yet gave Americans of the region to understand that if the test came at the right time they might count on his sup-

---

[4] Josiah Royce, *California from the Conquest in 1846 to the Second Vigilance Committee in San Francisco*, p. 41.

port; and by courier service he kept himself and them in communication with St. Louis. The result was that the Mexican authorities paid him every outward mark of respect and gave him the title of Guardian of the Northern Frontier, with the rank of captain, while at the same time the Americans regarded him as a potential ally.

The skilled workmen of the little settlement were invaluable to Frémont's exhausted expedition. The forge of the blacksmith's shop roared day and night while the horses and mules were shod; bridles and pack-saddles were brought from the store-rooms; one shift followed another at the horse-mill, grinding flour for the party; all was bustle and movement. Fresh horses and cattle were delivered and paid for. Sutter, insisting that Frémont and his men get as much repose as they could, seemed the soul of hospitality. "In manners, dress, and general deportment," later wrote one American, "he approaches so near what we call the 'old school gentleman' as to present a gulfy contrast with the rude society by which he is surrounded." The dining-room at the fort was plainly furnished with an ordinary pine table and benches, and its dishes were very ordinary china. But Sutter's Indian girls were able to serve what seemed to Frémont a sumptuous feast. They brought in salmon and trout fresh from the river; roast ham, venison, bear meat, smoked tongue, and fresh steaks; green peas, salads, and many fruits; and good Rhine wine—a refreshing change from the piñon nuts and dog-stew upon which Frémont and his fellow explorers had been faring.

Most important of all for the future of Frémont and California was his intercourse with the American settlers of the Sacramento Valley. By 1840 the foreign population settled in California, chiefly American and British, exceeded four hundred souls. Sutter had in his employ some thirty white men, of whom part were Europeans, but a majority Americans. A few miles distant on the American River lay the ranch of an American named Sinclair, while just across the Sacramento was that of the new-comer Joseph B. Chiles. The explorer was told that the previous summer a party of Easterners had entered the valley from Oregon, while in the fall a second company had arrived after an arduous journey by way of Fort Boisé and the Pit River Valley.[5] He learned that trappers tired of the mountainside and sailors tired of the sea were constantly settling in California. Sutter, as a California official, was accustomed to issue permits to new-comers allowing them to remain in the country, though as aliens they were disqualified from holding land. It was evident that American immigration was swelling to a considerable stream. Only two years later, the consul of the United States in Monterey was able to report that there were almost twelve hundred foreigners in California, and to describe the mounting flow from the East: [6]

The first arrival of American settlers on the Sacramento has been since 1840; three-fourths of the full number of foreigners in this country are Americans, of the remaining fourth, the subjects of Great Britain predominate. Of this fourth, the majority are in expectation of being under the government of the United States; probably all are willing, in preference to remaining as they now are; for the last five years, the larger proportion of the emigrants have arrived at New Helvetia (Captain Sutter's establishment) excepting a few of them from Oregon; they leave Independence, Mo., which is the starting point, every April or May, arriving on the Pacific in September or October. Soon after their arrival at New Helvetia they [are] scattered over the River Sacramento and the Bay of San Francisco, asking for farms from the government, or settling on private grants by the owners' consent; some have arrived at the Pueblo de los Angeles (Town of the Angels), near San Pedro, via Santa Fé, some of whom had married at the latter place; a few arrived from Valparaiso, Callao, and the Sandwich Islands; a person traveling from San Diego to San Francisco, or Bodega,

---

[5] The Oregon party had come under the leadership of an Ohio lawyer, Lansford Hastings; the other company was the Chiles-Walker party, which gave Sutter some valued employees.

[6] Thomas Larkin, *Reports,* State Department Archives; evidently written 1846, but dated May 1, 1847. The Larkin Papers, including letterbooks, are in the Bancroft Library, and have been made the basis of R. L. Underhill's thorough biography of Larkin.

can stop at a foreigners' farmhouse almost every few hours, and travel without any knowledge of the Spanish language.

...The emigration in 1845 amounted to from four to five hundred; from the United States newspaper reports to 1845, from one to two thousand are expected to arrive this August to October 6 [1845].

The economic rewards of settlement in California, as a glance at Sutter's rich possession showed, were tempting. Wheat made an average yield of 25 bushels to the acre, and, transported easily down the Sacramento River to San Francisco Bay in launches of 50 tons' burden, sold there for $2.50 a *fanega,* or about $1.20 a bushel. Land was incredibly cheap, and $200 would buy a square league (4,438 acres) of excellent quality and situation; labor cost little but food and clothing, and no expensive buildings or fences were needed. Frémont also heard that there were numerous American trading ships constantly on the coast. He learned that in 1842 Monterey had been suddenly seized by a Yankee commodore, Thomas Jones, who had heard an unfounded rumor that the United States and Mexico were at war, raced from South America with what he supposed to be English warships, took the fort, and ran up the American flag. Next day he had learned that there was no war and that he had not even raced English ships! The Mexican Government had taken umbrage at this aggression, but native Californians were little disturbed by it.[7] Not a few would have welcomed American sovereignty, as relieving them from atrocious customs burdens and increasing the value of their lands.

Before Frémont left the Sacramento Valley, he had gained a clear impression of the anomalous state of affairs in this wealthy Mexican province. The white population amounted to not more than eleven thousand people, "descendants," as Consul Larkin said, "of Spanish and Mexican fathers, mostly from native mothers." These Californians were proud to think them-

---

[7] According to *Life in California,* by an American (Alfred Robinson), many wealthy Californians apparently shared the pleasure of American settlers in Jones's act.

selves a distinct and superior element in the loose Mexican federation. Devoted almost wholly to ranching, they lived in rude but comfortable adobe houses, surrounded by the ordinary farm buildings and corrals. The family was usually large; its head an affable and hospitable man, its sons handsome, high-spirited young blades, finely skilled in horsemanship, and its daughters comely, buxom, virtuous girls. Vaqueros or cowboys and Indian servants of both sexes abounded, making the life of the land-holder rather indolent. The cattle were branded or ear-marked, and the annual *matanzas,* or round-ups, occurred in August. Though agriculture was so little practised that now and then the people almost starved, in general they lived well on beef, mutton, tortillas, vegetables, and the magnificent fruits of the region. They had, however, few luxuries, for the extortionate duties made them unattainable. Roads were bad, or rather non-existent; the houses crude; and conveniences few and simple. Carts, for example, used the cross-section of a tree for wheels. The trade of the country was largely in the hands of a few Boston houses, which sent out cargoes of textiles, shoes, hats, hardware, and "notions," and, keeping their ships two years at a time in California ports, brought back hides and tallow at an enormous profit.[8]

The Spanish or part-Spanish population held closely to the coast all the way from San Diego to the bay of San Francisco; a narrow, much broken ribbon of settlement. The fertile interior valleys were left to the wild Indians, to trappers, and in the north to the American ranchers who were becoming so numerous. Four coastal towns were "fortified"—San Diego, Santa Barbara, Monterey, and Yerba Buena; but the fortifications were ruinous and worthless. Indeed, since the seizure of the missions old California had been sinking into decay; but the cheap, fruitful, and pleasant land was happy in its decline.

Lazy, gay, uneducated, the people of California might have led an idyllic life, had it not been that for more than a decade

[8] Bryant, *What I Saw in California,* Chs. 21, 22; Walter Colton, *Three Years in California,* p. 27*ff.*; Alfred Robinson, *Life in California, passim.*

now they had been tormented by opera bouffe wars and petty convulsions, in part springing from, and in part merely accompanied by, a growth of republican sentiment. The Californians, who surpassed the Mexicans in stature, activity, and mental grasp, or at least believed that they did, resented any interference by officers *"de la otra banda."* They had repeatedly shown themselves capable of driving Mexican governors out of the province; in 1836, they had thus revolted against and deposed Governor Nicolas Gutierrez; and under his revolutionary successor, Juan Alvarado, had insisted that California was a free and sovereign state. But for the quarrels between rival families, and the marked jealousy between the northern and southern sections of California, this freedom might have been made absolute. It is a noteworthy fact that American residents had been prominent in the incidents of this little revolution of 1836, the foreigners in the country siding with and even leading the native Californians in their opposition to Mexico. But Alvarado, whose strength lay in the northern region about Monterey, San José, and San Francisco Bay, had difficulty at first in obtaining the support of the southern district about Los Angeles and San Diego. The Mexicans, striving to maintain some vestige of their authority, were always able to play upon this ill-feeling between the northern and southern parties. Yet even so, by 1840 their grasp upon the province or department was weak and precarious.[9]

When Frémont met the settlers and native Californians of the upper Sacramento, under Sutter's hospitable roof-tree or in excursions through the country, the tide of resentment against the Mexican connection was fast rising toward a new revolt. Some recalled with indignation that Alvarado had arrested a large body of Americans, notably a group captained by Isaac Graham, a trapper, and had exiled forty to a Mexican prison, where they spent months under charges of plotting a revolt before being allowed to return. In 1841 the central authorities had made a final effort to place a

[9] Theodore H. Hittell, *History of California*, II, p. 234ff.

Mexican governor in power, the before-mentioned Manuel Micheltorena. He was personally disliked, and the Mexican soldiers whom he brought with him, some of them former convicts, were bitterly hated. Talk of independence was becoming steadily more earnest. Every one felt that the hour was near when California would be launched into freedom like a ship from the stocks. Would it set up as an independent nation, as Texas had done? Would it fall into the hands of the British, who had many traders along the coast, whose Hudson's Bay Company was well established in northern California, and who were believed ready to exchange their Mexican bonds for the possession of the province? Or would it come under the control of the Americans?

There can be little doubt that Frémont discussed these questions with Sutter, Chiles, Sinclair, and others; above all, with Sutter. The "Governor of the Fortress of New Helvetia," as he liked to be called, had long considered the possibility of himself heading a movement for independence. He had drawn up, to be sent to Washington, a plan for the conquest of the province, under which he was to be given command of the troops and half of the territory conquered.[10] Knowing that the Mexican authorities regarded him with suspicion and hostility, he had taken pains to strengthen his fort by mounting twelve good Russian cannon on his walls, which were six feet thick, and had acquired muskets, rifles, and ammunition for eighty men. When Frémont arrived, there was a garrison of forty uniformed Indians, one always on duty at the gate. Commodore Wilkes had reported that Sutter was "using all his energies to render himself impregnable," and that only his success in doing so prevented the Mexicans from trying to eject him; Larkin had reported that they would like to buy him out. All Americans who took up land in the Sacramento Valley looked upon his fort as a rallying point in the event of trouble.

Nor was Sutter averse to making occasional threats against

[10] John Bidwell, *Out West Magazine*, XX, p. 183ff.; Frémont, *Report, Second Expedition* (Derby ed.), p. 354.

the Mexican officials. Resentful when Governor Alvarado authorized the Hudson's Bay Company to send trappers along the Sacramento, he wrote an angry letter in which he spoke of his military strength:

> The people don't know me yet, but soon they will find out what I am able to do. It is too late now to drive me out of the country; the first step they do against me is that I will make a Declaration of Independence and proclaim California for a Republique independent from Mexico.

He had breathed defiance in this letter against José Castro, a resident of Monterey and partisan of Alvarado's who became military commander of the province. If they leave me alone, he wrote, I will be quiet; "but when this Rascle of Castro should come here, a very warm and hearty welcome is prepared for him." [11] Castro had been prominent in the arrest of the Isaac Graham party. The feelings of many Americans were precisely the same as Sutter's. Most of them had a horror just now of Micheltorena's vicious and ill-controlled soldiery and were eager to see them—fortunately poorly armed and few in numbers—expelled from the country.[12]

Doubtless it was a somewhat one-sided view of California life and conditions which Frémont obtained. The American settlers probably spoke somewhat contemptuously of their California-born neighbors. Had Frémont come into contact with such leaders as Alvarado and his relative, General Vallejo, who lived just north of San Francisco Bay, he would have found them men of cultivation, intellectual power, and high character. Had he stayed longer and penetrated toward the coast, he would have admired the peaceful and attractive existence which the

---

[11] Irving Berdine Richman, *California Under Spain and Mexico*, p. 271.

[12] Royce, *California*, p. 29; compare Charles E. Chapman's *History of California: The Spanish Period*, pp. 478, 479. Alfred Robinson wrote of Micheltorena's *cholos* that they presented a state of unequaled wretchedness and misery, not one of them possessing a jacket or pantaloons. "They appeared like convicts, and indeed the greater part of them had been charged with the crime either of murder or theft. And these were the *soldiers* sent to subdue this happy country."

rancheros led. They were jovial and friendly; their family life was remarkably pure, and the women were possessed of great innate refinement; into all their works, acts, and speech there entered an element of beauty and artistry. They loved their horses and were perfect Arabs in managing them. They worked in moderation; rode from ranch to ranch a great deal; dressed in gay colors; held pleasant dances and serenaded the belles with old Spanish songs; raced a little, drank more, and gambled a great deal. In fact, with some gaming at monte was a passion, and, when excited, the young men would not only stake all they possessed upon a deal of cards, but would give a note upon some *tio* or uncle, some *primo* or cousin, the payment of which family honor made obligatory.[13] Their chief faults were their indolence, pride, quarrelsomeness, and an occasional tendency toward cruelty. Their life as a whole was genial, interesting, and charming, but not such a life as appealed to strenuous American frontiersmen.

It would have been better for all California two years later had Frémont obtained a more sympathetic impression of the Californians, but his time was limited. Two days after he reached Fort Sutter, on March 8, 1844, he pitched his camp at the junction of the American and the Sacramento. On March 22nd, when he had finished re-equipping his party, he ordered camp broken; and as the first stage of his journey southward, moved to a point near Sinclair's ranch. On the twenty-fourth, he resumed his progress in earnest. Five of his expedition, including the blacksmith Samuel Neal, had been left behind by their own wish. But he drove off with him a huge cavalcade of animals, numbering one hundred and thirty horses and mules and about thirty head of cattle, including five milch cows. Sutter, who accepted in payment drafts upon the Topographical Bureau which he had to cash at 20 per cent discount, furnished an Indian lad to help manage the half-wild beasts.[14] He also presented Frémont with a saddle-horse named Sacramento,

---

[13] J. W. Revere, *A Tour of Duty in California*, Ch. 13.
[14] Sabin, *Kit Carson Days*, I, p. 369.

an iron-gray of the best California stock. The kindly, exuberant Swiss accompanied them for some miles, and as they disappeared in a cloud of dust down the valley waved them a cordial farewell. He little thought that when Frémont returned it would be to make him prisoner in his own fort.

XIII

Homeward Over the Rockies

FRÉMONT had so planned his homeward journey that he might see the greatest possible amount of new country. He intended to travel five hundred miles south, skirting the western base of the Sierras, to a pass which had been discovered far below the San Joaquin, near the upper course of the South Fork of the Kern River, by Joseph Walker, the famous Santa Fé trapper who had served under Bonneville and had broken the trail from Great Salt Lake west across the Great Basin to Monterey.[1] Having crossed the Sierras by this pass, Frémont meant to strike southeast toward Santa Fé. This town could be reached by the ancient "Spanish Trail" running across from Los Angeles; but his design was to halt before actually arriving at the capital of New Mexico, and turn off into Colorado, where he could make for the headwaters of the Arkansas.

Simple as the route seemed, it involved two thousand miles of heavy travel, much of it through a rough and semi-desert country. There was not a settlement anywhere, and the names of the points and rivers on the way—Indian and Spanish names —showed that few Americans had ever traversed it. But this was precisely the reason why it appealed to Frémont's imagination. It would enable him to trace the Sierra Nevada southward, identify the streams flowing from it to the coast, explore the boundaries of the Great Basin between the Sierras and Rockies, ascertain whether any great rivers other than the Colorado flowed southwest from the Rockies—thus making absolutely certain there was no Buenaventura—and examine

[1] W. J. Ghent, *The Early Far West*, p. 256.

the southern end of the Great Salt Lake. This program was all carried out.

It was not executed without hardship and some adventures of peculiar interest. The first of these occurred in the closing days of April, 1844, soon after they had reached the Spanish Trail, which was still a virgin road with sufficient grass, though the thousands of horses and mules belonging to the annual Los Angeles caravans would soon be on their tracks. High noon of April 24, 1844, saw them following the arid bed of the Mohave River, with water to be found only in scattered pools. The country about, save for occasional damp spots overgrown with cottonwood, willow, and acacia, was desert and forbidding. Some Mohave Indians whom they met carried large gourds of water, an eloquent fact. The explorers knew that on the route before them they would have to make many a *jornada* of forty to sixty miles without finding water between their stopping places, and that the trail would be dotted with the bones of wild animals.[2] In preparation for the test before them, they had killed three of their cattle and dried the beef.

On the afternoon of the twenty-fourth they were surprised to see two Mexicans, a grizzled man and a handsome boy of eleven, burst into camp. Wild, disheveled, and exhausted, they gasped out a terrible story. Their party of six, traveling from Los Angeles, had been overwhelmed by a hundred hostile Indians, who descended upon them with the yells of fiends and a storm of arrows. These two, out guarding the horses, alone escaped, and driving what animals they could through the very line of the Indians, rode at top speed for sixty miles. Leaving their exhausted horses at Tomaso Spring, they had continued on foot, hoping to find succor. They were overjoyed when Frémont promised every possible assistance. Early the next day he and his party swung abruptly away from the Mohave River and soon reached Tomaso Spring. They found, as they expected, that the horses were gone; driven away, a swift examination of the ground showed, by the Indians. Frémont felt

---

[2] Frémont, *Memoirs*, I, p. 368.

that he had no right to divert his entire expedition to follow
the savages, but he did not object when Kit Carson and the
almost equally experienced scout Alexis Godey volunteered
to ride on with the older Mexican in pursuit.

The horse which the Mexican, Fuentes, was riding, soon
failed—or perhaps his courage did so—and he turned back;
but Carson and Godey pressed on alone. Toward nightfall, the
trail entered the gloomy mountains and became rougher, but
they followed it by moonshine till late at night, when, in a dark
and narrow gorge, it became too indistinct to trace. Afraid of
losing it, they tied their horses to trees and lay down to sleep
in the still, inky darkness, not striking a light. At the first
glimmer they were astir and took the trail again. They had not
gone far, and the sun was just beginning to rise, when they
discovered horses ahead of them. Halting at once, and leading
their own mounts back to a hidden point, they crept up cautiously to a little eminence commanding the Indian encampment. Here they saw four large skin lodges pitched among
the trees, fires blazing, pots boiling, and the savages gathered
about breakfast. At this moment, a young horse became frightened at the two creeping men, snorted, and betrayed them to
the Indians.

Carson and Godey, never hesitating, gave a war-whoop and
charged into the camp, firing point-blank from their rifles. Two
Indians fell mortally wounded, and the others, fearing that the
boldness of two men who thus attacked thirty meant a trap,
took to their heels. An arrow passed through Godey's shirt
collar, grazing his neck. With a final volley, the scouts turned
to the savages writhing on the ground. Thinking them dead
or dying, they stripped off their scalps, when one of the men,
though he had received two balls through the body, sprang
to his feet with a howl of agony. With the blood streaming from
his gory head, he was a horrifying sight. An old squaw, possibly
his mother, looked back from the mountain side up which she
was hurriedly clambering, and pausing hysterically to fling a
handful of gravel at the white men, loosed a volley of threats

and lamentations. Momentarily appalled by the frightful spectacle, Carson and Godey despatched the Indian. Then they turned on their trail and soon aroused Frémont's camp, Carson shouting and Godey waving the two scalps tied to his gun.

It is evident that when Frémont heard of the scalping he felt pained and regretful, but his compunction was dissipated by subsequent events. Carson's biographer surmises that Kit and Godey were actuated less by a desire to avenge the wretched Mexicans than by a shrewd impulse to throw a proper fear into these murderous desert Indians, and thus clear the trail ahead.[3] One outrage, if not decisively punished, would soon lead to others.

The expedition continued northeastward, across the dismal, waterless plain that constitutes the semi-desert region of California and Nevada; a land hot, rocky, and brown, with no vegetation except prickly cacti, sage-brush, and yucca trees. The desolate region was walled in with forbidding mountain ranges. To escape the pitiless glare of the sun, Frémont adopted the plan of starting late each evening and traveling all night. It was an unhappy-looking procession that wound through the dusty darkness. Scouts were sent ahead and on the flanks, the armed men were divided into front and rear divisions, and the baggage animals and cattle were driven in the middle, making a cavalcade a quarter mile in length. On April 28th they were tormented by a heavy gale, which flung the sharp sand in their faces so violently that it was almost impossible to continue, but they camped that night in a green valley, with good grass and clear water. Next day they soon covered the seven miles of desert which lay between them and the Archilette, or campground of the Spanish Trail where the Mexican party had been ambushed. Frémont describes what met their eyes as they rode to the grassy spot, with its springs and willows: [4]

The dead silence of the place was ominous; and, galloping rapidly up, we found only the corpses of two men: everything else was

[3] E. L. Sabin, *Kit Carson Days,* I, p. 380.
[4] Frémont, *Memoirs,* I, pp. 375, 376.

gone. They were naked, mutilated, and pierced with arrows. Hernandez had evidently fought, and with desperation. He lay in advance of the willow half-faced tent which sheltered his family, as if he had come out to meet danger, and to repulse it from that asylum. One of his hands and both his legs had been cut off. Giacomo, who was a large and strong-looking man, was lying in one of the willow shelters, pierced with arrows. Of the women no trace could be found, and it was evident they had been carried off captive. A little lap dog, which had belonged to Pablo's mother, remained with the dead bodies, and was frantic with joy at seeing Pablo; he, poor child, was frantic with grief, and filled the air with his incessant lamentations for his father and mother. *Mi padre!* —*mi madre!*—was his incessant cry. When we beheld this pitiable sight, and pictured to ourselves the fate of the two women carried off by savages so brutal and so loathsome, all compunction for the scalped-alive Indian ceased; and we rejoiced that Carson and Godey had been able to give so useful a lesson to these American Arabs, who lie in wait to murder and plunder the innocent traveler.

They soon learned that they were on the border of an exceedingly hostile Indian country. On May 3, 1844, after following the general line of the present Los Angeles-Salt Lake City Railroad, they reached Las Vegas in Nevada, a marshy basin where two springs, warm but pure, gushed up with great force. The horses and mules were becoming exhausted from want of water and grass, while the continuous flinty rocks were cutting their hoofs to pieces.[5] One by one, they dropped and had to be abandoned; the men clipping off their tails and manes to make saddle girths. On May 4, 1844, the expedition made its hardest day's journey since leaving the Sierras. They had started early, for the skeletons of horses along the trail soon proved that they had a long, parched *jornada* before them— between fifty and sixty miles without a drop of water. Their thirst became almost unsupportable. The sun glared down and the hot yellow sand reflected it like a burning glass; waves of sultry heat shimmered across the desert. Occasionally they halted to chop into a cactus of the variety called bisnaga, the

[5] Frémont, *Report, Second Expedition* (Derby ed.), p. 386.

pulp of which has a slightly acid juice, or moistened their mouths by chewing some leaves of sour dock. Hour after hour they toiled on, expecting to find water just ahead, and always disappointed. The sun dropped low, the stars came out, and still they plodded forward, fatigue and thirst making every step a burden. Finally, near midnight, when they had been on the march sixteen hours, the mules suddenly kicked up their heels and began running impetuously ahead. They had scented water. Another mile or two, and the party reached a rushing stream, the Rio de los Angeles, or Muddy River.

Here, after they had made camp and settled down for a day's rest, they were surrounded by Indians who threatened an attack. At dawn the savages, jabbering a Ute dialect, began emerging from the wild country about and crowding toward the camp. Frémont told the guards to warn them off, kept his men under arms, and had the horses driven back to camp. Repeatedly the Indians made insulting demonstrations, which he felt it best to ignore. His position was badly exposed, for though it had the river and some willow thickets on one side, on the other it was commanded by a rocky bluff. The savages were a treacherous-looking crew. They were naked save for breech-clouts; their fashion of gathering their hair into a tight knot at the crown of their heads lent an unnatural and fiendish aspect to their faces; the restless, furtive glare of their eyes, their ill-controlled movements, their evident tendency to act upon impulse instead of reason, made them resemble fierce beasts of prey. Each carried a powerful bow and a quiver of thirty or forty arrows, tipped with a clear, translucent stone, a kind of obsidian, which was nearly as hard as a diamond; and Frémont knew well that at close range these were as effective as a rifle. They would pierce a man's body almost through, and leave him lifeless in an instant.

Once hostilities seemed likely to begin. In spite of Frémont's strict orders, an old chief forced his way full-armed into camp. His mien was threatening and provocative. "Why, there are none of you," he said tauntingly. Counting the men about the camp, he tallied twenty-two on his fingers insultingly. "Only that many," he said, "and we—we are innumerable!" With this, he waved to the hills and mountains about. When the white men pointed to their rifles, he thrust his fingers into his ears and pretended he could not hear. "If you have your arms," he said a moment later, twanging his heavy bow, "we have ours, too." This was as much as the hot-tempered Carson could endure. "Don't say that, old man," he exploded; "don't say that —your life's in danger." Probably, as Frémont commented, the old chief was nearer his end than he would be till he actually met it.

They left without mishap, and two days later camped at a point nearly fifty miles distant, on the Rio Virgen, which Frémont describes as the dreariest river he had ever seen: a deep, rapid, turbid stream, running swiftly through a desert country. By this time they had killed their last steers. The wretched Moapa Indians of the country hung constantly about the expedition, but refused to come into camp. They seemed little better than wild beasts. Living upon the lizards and other small animals of the rocks, using long hooked sticks to draw them out of their holes, they were cowards, thieves, and in all the most degraded human beings Frémont had ever seen. As the expedition pushed up the Rio Virgen, an increasing pack, like so many wolves, stealthily followed the white men; and whenever Frémont had occasion to double momentarily upon his trail, he found the sandy soil of the river bottom thickly covered with their footprints. It was impossible to let a tired horse or mule drop behind for even an hour. The half-starved Indians would pounce upon it and leave nothing but hair and bones. Under these circumstances, they made camp for a day's rest on May 9, 1844, at a spot on the river where there was a considerable patch of grass; and here the expedition met its first fatality.

Frémont, worn out with his responsibilities, the heat, and some recent extra labor in arranging botanical specimens, lay down for an afternoon nap. Before he sought his tent one of his men, Tabeau, had gone back on the trail to seek a lame mule. When he awoke, the worried Carson reported that Tabeau should have been back long before. A moment later they perceived a smoke rise suddenly from a cottonwood grove below. It was an unmistakable token that he was dead, for such signal fires were kindled to tell the Indians roundabout that a blow had been struck. Carson and several others were instantly sent down the river on good horses, and soon returned with sad news. They had come upon the mule lying in a thicket, mortally wounded, while not far distant they had found a little puddle of blood. The next morning all their apprehensions were confirmed: [6]

...As soon as there was light enough to follow tracks, I set out myself with Mr. Fitzpatrick and several men in search of Tabeau. We went to the spot where the appearance of puddled blood had been seen; and this, we saw at once, had been the place where he fell and died. Blood upon the leaves and beaten-down bushes showed that he had got his wound about twenty paces from where he fell, and that he had struggled for his life. He had probably been shot through the lungs with an arrow. From the place where he lay and bled, it could be seen that he had been dragged to the bank of the river and thrown into it. No vestige of what had belonged to him could be found except a fragment of his horse equipment. Horse, gun, clothes—all became the prey of these Arabs of the New World.

The men under Frémont were now a family of brothers, and they sent up a general cry of grief and anger. They would willingly have stopped to avenge Tabeau's death, but the exhaustion of their horses forbade any plunge into the unexplored mountains about. The tribe which had committed the murder was the same which had been hanging upon the skirts of the expedition. But after this day they disappeared like ghosts, melting into the wilds; they knew they deserved punishment, and instead of the numbers visible before, not one appeared for more than a fleeting glimpse.

Yet this loss marked almost the end of their hardships. They

[6] Frémont, *Memoirs*, I, p. 381.

were then camping just west of a mountain gap through which the Spanish Trail wound. As they approached it by a rocky defile, they saw that the nature of the country was swiftly changing. It had been arid, bare of all but the roughest vegetation, and inhospitable; now it became forested with cedar, nut-pine, and cottonwood, with heavy underbrush; and they perceived many birds in the trees. They were entering a country which furnished grass, game, and water; they were emerging from the arid regions. On May 11, 1844, the transformation was signalized by a brisk shower, while in the evening, with heavy clouds covering the sky, a cold wind sprang up and made overcoats desirable. They were now well within the future state of Utah, following the Santa Clara River. On May 12th, they arrived at the great camping ground, Las Vegas de Santa Clara (the Spaniards used *vegas* to signify fertile, well-watered meadows, as distinguished from *llanos* or dry and barren flats), where the annual caravan from Los Angeles always halted and recruited for some weeks before pushing on to Santa Fé.

This point, regarded as the terminus of the desert journey from the West, was later named Mountain Meadows, and was the spot rendered infamous by the murder thirteen years later of nearly all of a party of western emigrants by some Mormon fanatics and Indians. Subsequent travelers have found it a dismal place under the shadow of that crime, but to Frémont's men it was wonderfully fresh and attractive. They were now on a dividing ridge between the waters of the Rio Virgen, flowing south to the Colorado, and those of the Sevier River, flowing north into the Great Basin. Having remained one day for rest, they descended into a broad valley, its streams tributary to Sevier Lake, and the next morning, moving northward, came within sight of the high peaks of the Wasatch Range, which sweeps toward Wyoming and looks down, in its northern portion, upon the expanse of Great Salt Lake.[7]

[7] Dellenbaugh correctly comments (*Frémont and '49*, p. 270): "He had now seen more of this Great Basin than any other white man with the exception,

The events of the remainder of their journey were in part commonplace. They were shortly joined by the noted hunter Joseph Walker, who had been traveling from Los Angeles with the great California caravan just behind them on the Spanish Trail, and who, seeing their fresh camp-fires, had guessed their identity. Walker possessed a fuller knowledge of this region than any other man living, and Frémont was glad to hire him as guide. They met also the famous Ute chief called Walker, with a powerful band armed with good rifles, journeying slowly toward the Spanish Trail to exact his annual tax from the Los Angeles caravan. A little later they lost one of their men, Badeau, by an accident with a gun. On May 24th, they approached Utah Lake, and Frémont took time for a cursory examination of this sheet of water. It was unfortunate that he did not make a more thorough investigation, for in his report he later stated, as we have seen, that it is connected with Great Salt Lake as "the southern limb"; though a brief reconnaissance would have made it clear that the Jordan River flows northward into Great Salt Lake, and that a wide belt of land, thirty miles or more across, intervenes between Utah Lake and the larger sheet.[8]

From Utah Lake, Frémont might easily have returned by the well-traveled Oregon Trail, but he was too tireless an explorer for that. Instead, he penetrated the Wasatch and the Uinta Mountains, crossed the Continental Divide through what is now termed Muddy Pass, which he called "one of the most beautiful we had ever seen," and turning south through the beautiful park region of Colorado, then moved southeast to Pueblo, Colorado, which he reached June 28, 1844. On July 1st, they were at Bent's Fort, and here Carson and Walker, feeling that their work was done, remained. George Bent treated the party with his usual warm hospitality. On the last

perhaps, of Walker; but Walker had no knowledge by experience with that portion lying north of Pyramid Lake along the flank of the Sierra. Frémont's estimates and deductions concerning the immense interior country were remarkably accurate even to its approximate area."

[8] Compare Dellenbaugh, *Frémont and '49*, p. 271.

day of July they were again at Kaw Landing on the banks of the Missouri River. After fourteen months' absence from civilization, they were exultant to revisit the familiar scene. They lost no time in resting, but the day following their arrival took a steamboat and were gliding down the Missouri. Frémont, with his usual humanity, refused to sell his travel-worn animals, to be scattered over the West for fresh toils and starvation, but placed them in good pasturage on the frontier—to be used in still a third expedition, if he could arrange one.

The fourteen months following Frémont's departure had been a period of anxious waiting for Jessie. She had spent them, summer and winter, in the roomy Benton mansion, in St. Louis, whither the family had soon removed from the Brant house. She could not possibly have heard from him after he reached Fort Hall on the Snake River in late September, 1843; it does not appear that she heard from him at all. Aware of his intention to skirt the Sierras and visit California, she guessed that midwinter might find him in an unexplored and dangerous mountain country. Nevertheless, she hoped that he would be able to return quickly and safely by some warm southern route. As early as January, 1844, she cajoled herself into believing that he might arrive any day, and hopes and fears struggled together in her mind. Each evening a place was set for his supper, and a bed made ready for his arrival; each night a lamp was trimmed and placed near the window, to burn through the darkness. Jessie would lie awake worrying and listening for his quick, firm tread on the flagging. Then in the morning she would look ruefully upon her preparations, and take away the little supper table she had kept ready.[9]

The household watched Jessie's increasing anxiety with concern. During the summer, when Senator Benton had been in Missouri, she had been entirely cheerful. For one thing, Benton insisted that she keep occupied—he had on a previous occasion of the kind set her to work translating Bernal Diaz;

[9] Jessie Benton Frémont, *Souvenirs of My Time*, p. 162.

for another, he kept the house lively with society. He loved to sit in the long gallery looking out on the inner courtyard, shaded by large acacias, with their clusters of vanilla-scented blooms; and here he would hold a morning levee attended by politicians, prominent St. Louis citizens, army officers, and old family friends. In the evening, others would call. St. Louis was growing fast, and its population of thirty thousand gives an utterly inadequate impression of its importance as the chief port of the upper Mississippi, the doorway to the West. The old French town was being shouldered to one side by hustling American "additions"; business streets toward the river were taking on a Broadway aspect; the water-front was lined in summer with scores of steamers and alive with roustabouts; the flood of emigrants, traders, trappers, and ranchers pouring westward grew heavier and heavier; Jefferson Barracks had become the chief military post beyond the Alleghenies. All the currents of the city's life were represented in the wide Benton circle.

But Benton had to return to Washington in November, 1843, for the opening of Congress, and thereafter Jessie saw less society. She had two families of relatives, the Brants and Pottses; she knew the Chouteaus, "Colonel" Dent, whose future son-in-law, Ulysses S. Grant, was a second lieutenant fresh from West Point at Jefferson Barracks, and many other of the old residents. Two young men of whom she had seen a good deal in Washington were much at her house: Montgomery Blair, an attorney of thirty who had just become mayor of the city, and his brother, Frank P. Blair, a hot-tempered but able young man who had graduated from Princeton two years earlier, and was now practising law. Her father and their father—Francis P. Blair, the great Jacksonian editor of the Washington *Globe* —had long been intimate. Jessie had also her baby and her invalid mother. But these distractions did not really occupy her. Nor was the news, in March, 1844, that a great explosion had occurred on the warship *Princeton* on the Potomac, and that the bursting of a 225-pounder gun which slew Secretary Upshur and Secretary Gilmer had narrowly missed killing her father, who escaped with only an injured eardrum, more than a momentary interruption of her anxiety.

Toward spring, as trappers and traders came down the Missouri for their annual supplies, a rumor reached Jessie's friends that Frémont had gone up into the high Sierras after winter closed in, had suffered from severe storms and starvation, and had pushed on and disappeared. This rumor purported to come from Indian sources. Naturally, her friends kept it from Jessie's ears, but she was aware that something was held in reserve under the increasing expressions of tenderness which her family threw about her.[10]

Spring reminded her that time was passing; on May 29th, with a sinking heart, she realized that Frémont had been absent precisely a year. June—July—the first of August all passed, while her apprehension mounted, and she even felt moments of despair.

Frémont, journeying impatiently down the bar-choked, snag-filled river, reached the junction of the Missouri and the Mississippi about sunset on August 6, 1844, and remained awake as the boat chugged toward the town. It was after midnight when the levee, marked in the darkness by scattered lights and the lanterns of moored steamboats and scows, came into sight. Some yawning Negroes emerged under the August stars upon the wharves; ropes were thrown and missed with a splash; there was an uproar of screaming escape valves and the plunge of wheels backing water; the gang-plank went down with a rumble, and Frémont was one of the first men ashore. No carriages were available at two o'clock in the morning, and he walked uptown. He passed through sleeping business streets, entered the French quarter, and was soon under the windows of the Benton mansion. Old Gabriel, the coachman, slept on the second floor of the carriage-house, and by throwing pebbles at the open window Frémont roused him. His first question was

[10] Jessie Benton Frémont, *Souvenirs*, p. 163.

whether the family were all well. "Yes, dey's all well," came Gabriel's raucous whisper. "Can you let me in without waking anybody?" asked Frémont. "Is dat really you, and not a ghost?" demanded Gabriel. Frémont repeated his question. "Yes, I can let you in," said Gabriel; "but Mrs. Frémont, she's at Miss Anne's, for Mr. Potts is very sick."

Frémont turned and hastened downtown at a brisk walk. Miss Anne was Jessie's cousin; the Rev. Mr. Potts was her husband, living in the parsonage next the Presbyterian Church. The lieutenant's first thought was to awaken the family and see Jessie. But he recalled that Potts suffered from tuberculosis, and that an alarm in the middle of the night might bring on another hemorrhage. Already there was a faint tinge of rose in the east. The best spot to while away the hours till servants in the parsonage began to stir was the lawn in front of Barnum's Hotel, and here he sat down on a bench, watching the stars begin to pale. An employee, seeing his uniform, came out to offer him a room, and at once recognized the worn explorer.[11] The hotel clerk was insistent that he come up to a bedroom and rest, and Frémont had little inclination to refuse. He knew that the Bentons were well; all his responsibilities and anxieties had rolled from his shoulders like Christian's load; and stretching himself upon his first bed in eighteen months, in a few minutes he was asleep.

Meanwhile, the coachman Gabriel had risen at dawn and carried his strange news to the Benton family. He was heard with incredulity. A messenger was hastily despatched to the Potts house to make inquiries, and awakened Jessie. The incredulity increased. Nobody had seen Frémont except Gabriel, and Gabriel was not certain that the visitor had not been an apparition. The nurse for the baby promptly accepted the ghost theory, and raised a weird lament. At this moment came a ring at the door, and in walked the tired and emaciated explorer. He had slept long past daybreak at the hotel, and in hurrying to the parsonage had met one St. Louisian after an-

[11] Jessie Benton Frémont, *Souvenirs*, pp. 164, 165.

other who stopped to welcome him. Even now, he and Jessie were not left alone. The parsonage was soon thronged with friends, the Blairs and other prominent citizens came in, and Frémont had to hold an impromptu reception before he could breakfast with his family.

Frémont had in his direct charge several members of the expedition—the Mexican orphan Pablo, rescued on the Los Angeles trail, a Chinook Indian, and two California Indian boys, Juan and Gregorio, of whom he had to make some disposition. Juan and Gregorio were sent to a farm of Benton's near Lexington, Kentucky, and took with them Frémont's saddle-horse Sacramento. The Chinook Indian, whose devouring wish was to see some of the great eastern cities of the white man, accompanied the lieutenant to Washington, and was educated by the Indian Bureau. As for Pablo, his bright, cheerful ways won the heart of everybody in the Benton household; and as he seemed to become attached to the Senator and his family, he was kept with them. The Mexican minister, General Almonte, offered him transportation home to Mexico, but he wished an American education, and for a time showed ambition and aptitude. Unfortunately, as he grew up he drifted away from the Bentons, fell into evil ways, and was finally heard from—or so Frémont avers—as the famous robber Murietta in the San Joaquin Valley.

XIV

Washington Expansionists and the Far West

AFTER a brief rest in St. Louis, Frémont hurried on to Washington with Jessie, for he was eager to make his report and lay plans for a third expedition. He found that his old circle in the capital had been largely destroyed by death. Nicollet and Hassler had died within a few weeks of each other in the autumn of 1843, the former, after a complete mental breakdown, having passed away alone at a Washington hotel. "After all," wrote Frémont feelingly,[1] "it would have been a fitter end for him to have died under the open sky, and been buried rolled up in a blanket, by the side of some stream in the mountains, than to have had life close in the night and alone at a hotel." Senator Benton's enthusiastic colleague, the lively, winning Lewis Linn, who came so naturally by his zeal for western development—his grandfather had been one of the first to navigate the Mississippi from Pittsburgh to New Orleans—had also died in the fall of 1843, a grievous loss to the expansionist group.[2] Frémont reported upon reaching Washington to General Scott, and made an official call on the Secretary of War, Wilkins, who was astonished by his youth. Then he settled down to a short interlude of home life.

There ensued a happy period of social ease, domesticity, and congenial work. The young couple lived with the Bentons, whose house gave them ample room. The family dined sometimes alone, sometimes with guests of importance. The evening was spent about the fireplace, the Senator reading or writing, Mrs. Benton, whose health had much improved, though her

[1] Frémont, *Memoirs*, I, p. 412.
[2] Benton, *Thirty Years' View*, II, p. 485.

speech was impaired, sewing, and Frémont studying his notes. At first, much occupied with mathematical computations, he was vexed by the numerous visitors who came to talk to him about Oregon and California, and by the stream of questioning letters. His work, in fact, for a time almost stopped. To escape interruptions, he rented as workshop a little wooden cottage of two stories, set well back in enclosed grounds not far from the Benton home. Here he and his assistant, a young man proficient in astronomy and mathematics, rapidly reduced the calculations of the expedition to order. Then came his report, a much more interesting employment, upon which, as before, Jessie gave him invaluable assistance.

They made a delightful partnership of the undertaking. Frémont would marshal his data the evening before; he was up at dawn for a breakfast of coffee and rolls; and punctually at nine Jessie would join him in the workshop. There they labored uninterruptedly till one o'clock, he dictating and she writing. As before, the method was congenial to his rapid, enthusiastic mind, and favorable to the style of the report. He would plunge ahead, without the interruption of using a pen; the necessity of making everything clear to Jessie enhanced the lucidity of his exposition; and her questions upon details, her instinct for the significant, her sense of literary form, were indispensable. She liked the work. "Talking incidents over," testifies Frémont, "made her familiar with the minuter details of the journey, outside of those we had recorded, and gave her a realizing sense of the uncertainties and precarious chances that attend such travel, and which day and night lie in wait; and it gave her for every day an object unusual in the life of a woman."

At one o'clock the baby was brought in; Jessie rose from her cramped position; the colored mammy gave them their luncheon of cold chicken, beaten biscuit, and fruit; and off they went for a walk to the Potomac. On some nights, Frémont had observations to verify. One or two o'clock in the morning would find him with his assistant Hubbard and a Negro servant, stretched on his back on the flagstone of a neighboring church, watching for the emersion of a particular star. Sometimes he and Hubbard, both young, were noisy. A deacon who lived opposite the church thought it his duty to come to Benton and to tell him that Frémont and two boon companions often returned late from a revel so drunk that Frémont lay down on the church steps and could hardly be roused. Jessie tells us what followed: [3]

Just then we came in from our after-lunch walk, all fresh and animated. Calling us into the library, my father said in his most dangerously polite way, "There are Mr. and Mrs. Frémont, and I wish you to repeat to them what you have been telling me."

The deacon hemmed and hawed, but my father's stern command, "Repeat it, sir," could not be evaded.

The explosions of laughter which followed from us might have enlightened him—but when the simple fact was told him, he had to stand a lecture from my father on his looking for the worst motive, and his want of Christian charity.

Frémont's second report, which was shown to Benton and in part to Benton's friends as it progressed, was nearly three times as long as the first (more than 300 duodecimo pages) and even more interesting. With as much scientific exactness as before, with the same clear data upon topography, climate, soils, vegetation, and wild animals, it again contained that wealth of general information upon western life for which Americans were eager. Turning to a few pages upon the work of the expedition after it reached the upper Platte at the beginning of July, 1843, for example, we find matter that would interest everybody. He offers a description of Long's Peak, as first glimpsed, "a faint blue mass," on the horizon; notes on the number of the Oglallah Sioux, who had lost all their beasts the previous winter; comments on the growing scarcity of game in the Platte Valley; an account of the trading-post, Fort Lancaster, and the Arapahoe villages near by; a narrative of an encounter with a bear which charged the party; a long discussion of the fertility of the soil between the Platte and Arkansas; a description of the

[3] Jessie Benton Frémont MSS, Bancroft Library.

gas-charged waters of Boiling-Spring River; a sketch of a settlement of "mountain-men" married to Spanish women from Taos; a discussion of the passes of the Rockies and the general ignorance of them since the Indians had slain so many mountain-men; a brief comparison of Kit Carson and Alexis Godey as scouts; a note on the food value of the yampa plant; and a summary of the available information on the Grand Canyon of the Colorado as he pieced it together from vague tales by trappers and Indians. So the report proceeds. Frémont included frequent descriptions of natural scenes, recommendations for military posts and settlements, thumb-nail sketches of everything from geysers to grizzlies, and random remarks on such subjects as the effect of brandy taken on a cold night after a hard day's march.

He even inserted entertaining bits of frontier gossip. Writing of the Great Salt Lake, he paused to describe a little insect larva which was washed up in great numbers on the shore:

Alluding to this subject some months afterwards, when travelling through a more southern portion of this region, in company with Mr. Joseph Walker, an old hunter, I was informed by him that, wandering with a party of men in a mountain country east of the great California range, he surprised a party of several Indian families encamped near a small salt lake, who abandoned their lodges at his approach, leaving everything behind them. Being in a starving condition, they were delighted to find in the abandoned lodges a number of skin bags, containing a quantity of what appeared to be fish, dried and pounded. On this they made a hearty supper, and were gathering round an abundant breakfast the next morning, when Mr. Walker discovered that it was with these, or a similar worm, that the bags had been filled. The stomachs of the stout trappers were not proof against their prejudices, and the repulsive food was suddenly rejected.

The appreciation of natural beauty which had marked the first report was again prominent. On the far-widened Platte during the outward journey, "when at night the broad expanse of water grew indistinct, it almost seemed that we had pitched our tents on the shore of the sea." A little later he exulted in the morning beauty of the massive peaks Rainier and St. Helen's, "the snow being entirely covered with a hue of rosy gold." He wrote poetically of the hopes attached to the mythical Buenaventura, "where in the softer climate of a more southern latitude our horses might find grass to sustain them, and ourselves be sheltered from the rigors of winter and from the inhospitable desert." The high Sierras (after he had gotten safe over them) excited his admiration: "Immediately above the eastern mountains was repeated a cloud-formed mass of purple ranges, bordered with bright yellow gold; the peaks shot up into a narrow line of crimson cloud, above which the air was filled with a greenish orange; and over all was the singular beauty of the blue sky." Even more was he pleased with the descent into California, with its towering trees, green grass, clouds of brilliant butterflies, and blooming shrubs, among which the high blue lupin was prominent: "A lover of natural beauty can imagine with what pleasure we rode among these flowering groves, which filled the air with a light and delicate fragrance." He wrote later of the forests, "the summer green of their beautiful foliage, with the singing birds, and the sweet summer wind which was whirling about the dry oak-leaves, nearly intoxicated us with delight."

Again his pages were rich in human touches. When his party met the large red ox wandering back on the Oregon Trail, they gathered about him "with all their domestic feelings as much aroused as if we had come in sight of an old farmhouse"; and Frémont would not have him touched, "for I would rather have gone through a starving-time of three days than let him be killed after he had successfully run the gauntlet so far among the Indians." He and his men, encountering a Shoshone village, wished to exchange cloth, vermilion, and trinkets for food, but found the savages miserably poor. "Several of the Indians drew aside their blankets, showing me their lean and bony figures; and I would not any longer tempt them with a display of our merchandise to part with their wretched subsistence." He could look at himself humorously. Take his half-rueful description of the aspect of the second expedition as it turned back from California:

Our cavalcade made a strange and grotesque appearance; and it was impossible to avoid reflecting upon our position and composition in this remote solitude. Within two degrees of the Pacific Ocean —already far south of the latitude of Monterey—and still forced on south by a desert on one hand, and a mountain range on the other—guided by a civilized Indian, attended by two wild ones from the Sierra—a Chinook from the Columbia, and our mixture of American, French, German—all armed—four or five languages heard at once—above a hundred horses and mules, half wild—American, Spanish, and Indian dresses and equipment intermingled—such was our composition. Our march was a sort of procession. Scouts ahead and on the flanks; a front and rear division; the pack-animals, baggage, and horned cattle in the centre; and the whole stretching a quarter of a mile along our dreary path. In this form we journeyed, looking more as if we belonged to Asia than to the United States of America.

Frémont was glad to emphasize the practicability of the Oregon Trail, though he did not gloss over the difficulties of many stretches—shortage of grass and water; rough and rocky roads; difficult fords; numerous short, steep ascents, exhausting the worn-out animals. He was glad also to dissipate the impression, fostered in some quarters by publications of the day, that the Pacific Northwest was a harsh, repellent country. A book published in London in 1844 by an officer of the Hudson's Bay Company, John Dunn, called *History of the Oregon Territory and North American Fur Trade,* had contained many misrepresentations. It declared that no route existed from the Eastern States to Oregon which could ever furnish facilities for a large overland flow of emigrants; that for hundreds of miles the trails wound over barren ground, where scorching heat alternated with bitter cold; and that west of the Rockies, the country was broken by towering cliffs, deep ravines, and rapid streams, while the travelers had to toil through deep sand or over sharp basaltic rocks. The ornithologist J. K. Townsend, who had accompanied Nathaniel Wyeth's second expedition to Oregon, and had published a *Narrative* of it in Philadelphia in 1839, had much exaggerated the difficulties of the Trail—the craggy mountains, burning sun, and parching winds. Frémont told the truth about the trail. He also reported that his friend Gilpin came back from the Willamette settlements with invigorated health, "highly pleased with the country." [4]

A dry government report would have done little to dispel the vague terrors many connected with the Oregon Trail, to advertise the value of the Columbia River country, and to call attention to the attractions of California. But this narrative, always readable, frequently engrossing, and published at the most propitious moment, carried its message home. Frémont completed it late in February, 1845; on March 1st he formally presented it to the War Department; and on March 3rd a Senate resolution called for printing five thousand extra copies. Buchanan, who was shortly to become Secretary of State, told the Senate that he had watched Frémont's progress with interest, "and was satisfied that he was a young gentleman of extraordinary merit, great energy, and ability to serve the country. He deserved encouragement." He (Buchanan) would therefore move to increase the number of copies to be printed from five thousand to ten thousand. The motion carried.[5] Various commercial publishers in America and England took up the report and in the next half dozen years printed

---

[4] It is to be noted that he also contributed greatly to general knowledge of the Great Basin. This term, forever afterward fixed upon the region, he invented; and he gave an accurate description of that part of the Basin which he had seen: "It is called a desert, and from what I saw of it, sterility may be its prominent characteristic; but where there is so much water there must be some oasis...; where there is so much snow there must be streams; and where there is no outlet there must be lakes to hold the accumulated waters, or sands to swallow them up." For warm tributes to Frémont's scientific work upon the Great Basin, see Dellenbaugh, *Frémont and '49*, pp. 270, 271; Gilbert, *The Exploration of Western America, 1800-1850*, p. 175. The latter truly states that "The expeditions of Frémont between the years 1842 and 1853 explained the real nature of the Great Basin."

[5] *Congressional Globe*, March 3, 1845.

large editions, some running into thousands of copies. From that day to this no one in the United States has ever had any difficulty in procuring it at little cost. The newspapers seized upon it and printed copious extracts. Frémont found himself one of the heroes of the hour, holding such a place in the popular imagination as Hobson, Admiral Byrd, and Colonel Lindbergh later gained.

He was especially gratified to receive from President Tyler, at the instance of General Winfield Scott, a double-brevet as first lieutenant and captain "for gallant and highly meritorious services in two expeditions commanded by himself." He was pleased also by an invitation to dinner from Daniel Webster, who was deeply interested in California. Webster believed that San Francisco Bay and other Pacific ports should by all means be made American—they were "twenty times as valuable to us as all Texas"—but despite Frémont's protests, he thought the interior of California almost valueless.

Misapprehensions as to the West, in fact, died hard. Soon after Polk's inauguration, Benton took his son-in-law to the White House to meet the narrow, precise, hardworking President, and to lend support to Benton's views on the value of the Far West. Frémont gave Polk a brief account of his observations in Oregon and California, dilating upon the value of these areas. To illustrate the prevailing ignorance of the western slope, he remarked that he had recently drawn from the mapstand in the Library of Congress a map which represented the Great Salt Lake as connected with the Pacific by three large rivers; one emptying into the Columbia, one into the Gulf of California, and one flowing west through the Sierra Nevada into San Francisco Bay! He explained that trappers had given the geographers inexact and conflicting information, which, combined with some known facts and such fables as that regarding the Buenaventura (which dated back to Father Escalante), resulted in such ridiculous maps. His remarks were intended to illustrate the propriety of giving the West still more of such scientific examination as he had been furnishing. But the conservative Polk was not impressed. He evidently held the map-makers in high respect. "Like the Secretary [of the Navy]," writes Frémont,[6] "he found me 'young,' and said something of the 'impulsiveness of young men,' and was not at all satisfied in his own mind that these three rivers were not running there as laid down." The explorer came away somewhat glum.

Political events had meanwhile been moving with great rapidity. When Frémont reached St. Louis from the West, the presidential campaign of 1844, with Polk pitted against Clay, was in full swing. Neither the little-known Democratic candidate nor the Democratic plank for the acquisition of Texas appealed to Benton. He believed that Van Buren had been entitled to the nomination, and was convinced that the annexation of Texas meant an unjust war for the benefit of the slaveholders. The Democratic plank for the "reoccupation" of Oregon met his wishes, though he was always ready to see the boundary drawn on the forty-ninth parallel, and to give vigorous opposition in the Senate to the blatant "Fifty-four Forties," led by Cass, Allen, and Hannegan. That fall the election of Polk gave the country an expansionist President, and the opening of Congress in December, 1844, showed that sentiment for new territorial acquisitions ran high. Before the session ended Texas had been annexed by joint resolution, Benton casting a silent vote in its favor. It was generally believed that war in Mexico would soon result. But Polk hoped for the best; his diary reveals that a few months later the Cabinet decided to negotiate with Mexico in an effort to settle the Texan boundary question, and in addition "to procure the cession of New Mexico and California and if possible all north of latitude 32 from the Passo on the Del Norte (El Paso) and west to the Pacific or (if that failed) then the next best boundary which might be practicable, so as at all events to include all the country east of the Del Norte, and the Bay of San Francisco."

Benton, of course, strongly approved of this decision. He be-

[6] Frémont, *Memoirs*, I, pp. 412, 418.

lieved with all his usual fervor of conviction that the United States and Mexico ought to be close friends, and that America should act as aid and protector to the weak Hispanic-American nations. It would be shameful, he held, to assail Mexico with predatory aims. But he was convinced that California, New Mexico, and a satisfactory Texan boundary could and should be obtained by treaty and purchase. Although he never admired Polk and his Cabinet, his relations with them were close and his advice was frequently sought. Secretary of State Buchanan frequently conferred with the Senator, and Frémont was sometimes included in their conversations. Buchanan was ignorant of Spanish, and his wavering nature found encouragement in Benton's positive character. Often he brought papers from a confidential Mexican agent for translation, and Jessie tells us a bit of "secret history." The Mrs. Greenhow whom she mentions was undoubtedly a versatile spy, who was destined in Civil War days to do good work for the Confederates: [7]

My sister and myself would make the translations. General Dix (of New York) was on the Military Committee and knew Spanish. He was a near neighbor and congenial friend, and he [Benton] and General Dix would read out a translation to Mr. Buchanan, and afterwards, we (who knew Spanish well) made out the written papers.

The librarian and translator at the State Department Mr. Greenhow of course knew Spanish. But his wife was in the pay of the English legation as a spy, and our private information reached them through her. Mr. Buchanan when he knew this thought best to cut off opportunities but did not betray knowledge of being watched. This is only one of many corroborating bits of circumstantial evidence of constant rivalry and counteraction by England regarding Mexico.

As the Polk Administration thus took over the foreign problems of Tyler, and as Frémont supervised the printing of his report, war clouds thickened.

As soon as Texas was annexed the Mexican Minister, Señor

[7] Undated Memorandum, Huntington Library.

J. N. Almonte, immediately protested in terms which carried a threat of resistance; and his government broke off diplomatic relations. When the Mexican press learned early in July that Texas had accepted the American terms of annexation, a burst of passion shook the higher circles of the republic. "Union or war!" was the watchword enunciated by various newspapers. Public indignation compelled the Executive to lay the question of war before Congress. An army was mobilized, money was appropriated, and steps were taken to raise fifteen million dollars. Fresh guns were mounted at Vera Cruz and the fortress prepared for an attack; munitions and provisions were accumulated at Matamoras on the northern border; from many points came news of the mustering of troops. Before midsummer Mexico notified her ministers in London and Paris that she intended to appeal to arms. In Washington, that well-informed observer Baron Gerolt, who had long been Prussian minister in Mexico City, believed that war was imminent and so informed Secretary Bancroft. But still for a time the apparently inevitable outbreak was postponed. The United States, with Polk grimly hoping for peace, took a passive attitude, waiting for Mexico to provoke the first clash. In Mexico City a short-lived government arose under General Herrera, and—apparently anxious for peace at any price—hinted to Polk that a minister would be received.

In short, throughout the spring of 1845, while Frémont was preparing for his third expedition, and talking with Benton of the situation, American leaders were highly uncertain of the future. At any moment the Mexican army, acting on the theory that Texas was merely a rebellious Mexican province, might cross the border and begin hostilities. Polk had despatched a confidential agent, William S. Parrott, to Mexico City to attempt to smooth over the difficulties, and had authorized him to promise liberal payments for a satisfactory boundary. How far the Administration would have gone in this direction is shown by the fact that when it sent John Slidell to Mexico in the autumn as the new minister, he was instructed to offer forty millions for a good settlement./But Parrott was received abusively by the Mexican press and accomplished nothing. Rumors of conflict persisted; news of preparations by the Mexican Government continued to flow north. Various European powers manifested their concern over the possibility of war, which they knew would result in American aggrandizement, and in no unselfish spirit made it known that they would be glad to use their friendly offices. There was talk—which our diplomatic representative in London in March, 1845, took very seriously —of setting up a monarchy in Mexico under some European prince.

It is important, in view of Frémont's later actions, to note that this fear of early hostilities with Mexico was accompanied by widespread apprehensions of unfriendly action by Great Britain. In these years men like Calhoun were almost hypnotized by a belief that England would at any favorable moment turn aggressor in the western hemisphere. Into the intricate mesh of foreign relations involving England, France, the United States, Mexico, Texas, and Oregon we cannot possibly go. It is sufficient to say that in 1844 great numbers of Americans believed that war with England over Oregon and other issues was unescapable; and that even when Polk took office, he felt that "no compromise [upon Oregon] to which Great Britain would accede, could pass the Senate," and that a conflict was at hand. It should also be said that during 1844-45 a persistent rumor was current that Great Britain intended to seize California. We know now that this rumor was quite unfounded, but a multitude of Americans took the supposed British threat in that quarter as a grim reality. Polk was one, and he made his fears of British occupation of California a foundation-stone of his foreign policy. Benton was another, for his attitude toward the British Government had always been stiff and suspicious. All informed men knew that California was a derelict craft, ready to be picked up by any captain who would take it into the port of a strong and stable government. Frémont had described to Benton how this beautiful and fertile region was hanging like a ripe fruit, ready to break from its stem at a touch. Its forests, fields, and harbors, and teeming fisheries were almost unused; the greatest part of it was lying waste, a mere Indian country, receiving not even a dribble of Mexican colonization. Of its white population, hardly yet sufficient to fill a thriving township, the native Californians were disloyal and discontented, while the fast-growing American group was only biding its time until it should rebel. Plots and intrigues swept the scattered settlements as eddies of wind sweep an exposed pond.

This fear of British action explains much that occurred in Washington in 1845-46. When Slidell went to Mexico City he was told to say that the United States could not allow California to fall into other hands, and to offer twenty-five millions for Upper California and New Mexico. George Bancroft, the new Secretary of the Navy, was as eager as his chief to obtain the whole Southwest, and indeed, his zeal for the acquisition of California was older than Polk's. Jessie's words about that lifelong spy Mrs. Greenhow indicate the suspicions that were rife in the Benton circle. Long afterwards Frémont wrote: [8]

As affairs resolved themselves, California stood out as the chief subject in the impending war; and with Mr. Benton and other governing men at Washington it became a firm resolve to hold it for the United States.... This was talked over fully during the time of preparation for the third expedition, and the contingencies anticipated and weighed.

Supported by Benton's powerful influence as chairman of the Senate Military committee, by Secretary Bancroft, and by his own prestige, Frémont found no difficulty in obtaining the approval of the War Department for a third expedition. Apparently Benton and Bancroft were responsible for the de-

---

[8] Frémont, *Memoirs*, pp. 423, 424. Frémont also writes: "Mexico, at war with the United States, would inevitably favor English protection for California. English citizens were claiming indemnity for loans and indemnity for losses." He states that to Benton, Bancroft, and others "it seemed reasonably sure that California would eventually fall to England or the United States, and that the eventuality was near."

cision that it should carry him far into Mexican territory. He was instructed to explore

that section of the Rocky Mountains which gives rise to the Arkansas River, the Rio Grande del Norte of the Gulf of Mexico, and the Rio Colorado of the Gulf of California; to complete the examination of the Great Salt Lake and its interesting region; and to extend the survey west and southwest to the examination of the Cascade Mountains and the Sierra Nevada.

All this pointed straight toward California. His explorations in the Great Salt Lake region and Sierra Nevada were expected to open a shorter southern route for travel to California; the examination of the Cascades was expected to show an easy means of travel between Oregon and the interior of northern California. Such roads, useful in peace, would be equally useful in hostilities. And "in arranging this expedition," Frémont subsequently wrote, "the eventualities of war were taken into consideration." He meant that his trails were expected to be useful to armed forces; perhaps he also meant that Benton and Bancroft envisaged the possibility that when he reached California, his exploring band might be transformed into a hard-fighting company.

In his *Memoirs* Frémont unfortunately treats this aspect of his third expedition without detail or corroborative documents. He asserts that Bancroft took a leading part in the plan for combining scientific and military objects:

Imbued with the philosophy of history, his mind was alive to the bearing of the actual conditions, and he knew how sometimes skill and sometimes bold action determine the advantages of a political situation; and in this his great desire was to secure for the United States the important one that hung in the balance. In the government at Washington he was the active principle, having the activity of brain and keen perception that the occasion demanded. With him Mr. Benton had friendly personal relations of long standing.

Certainly Bancroft later claimed for himself the rôle of "active principle" of the government in plans relating to California, a region which he made his special charge. The Secretary, now almost forty-six and nationally known by his historical writings, was a man of enormous energy and a sincere believer in expansion. Throwing himself into the administration of the navy, though it was an uncongenial post, he had resolved to use his Cabinet influence to gain fresh territory and to improve sectional relations. California seemed to fall within his province as a possible bone of contention between the British and American navies.

Frémont states that his associates believed that if Mexico went to war with the United States, she would ask for British protection of California; that "our relations with England were already clouded, and in the event of war with Mexico, if not anticipated by us, an English fleet would certainly take possession of San Francisco Bay." Though we now know that no such danger existed, it is doubtless true that Polk, Benton, Bancroft, and others strongly feared it. Frémont adds: "My private instructions were, if needed, to foil England by carrying the war now imminent with Mexico into the territory of California." Unfortunately, he does not say under just what circumstances or in just what words Secretary Bancroft gave him these "private instructions"; nor does he mention the fact that Bancroft was not his official superior. Later, we shall record Bancroft's own statements endorsing those of Frémont. But we must note that Secretary of War Marcy, in his annual report at the close of 1846, declared that the objects of the captain's third expedition "were, as those of his previous explorations had been, of a scientific character, without any view whatever to military operations." It is difficult to avoid the view that Frémont served two masters: the War Department, which thought of the purposes of his work as purely scientific, and Senator Benton and Secretary Bancroft, who had ulterior political objects for it.

Once more Frémont set off westward in May to recruit his

company in St. Louis, obtain stores, and begin his march before spring ended. This time his corps was larger than before —sixty-two men; better armed; and more mobile, for it dispensed with carts. War was to overtake it. As war did so, it was destined to play a more dramatic and controversial rôle than any other expedition of the kind in American annals; a rôle which seemed at the time to change history, and which is even yet wrapped in partial mystery, and the subject of vigorous dispute.

XV

The Third Expedition

IN St. Louis, Frémont met some amusing difficulties in selecting his company from the crowd of applicants. The St. Louis *Weekly Reveille* of June 9, 1845, remarks:

Yesterday we found ourselves, with others, near the enclosure opposite the Planters' Warehouse, endeavoring to hear what Capt. Frémont's ideas were in relation to his contemplated mountain expedition. He was, at the time, attempting to address a motley crowd of French, Irish, Dutch, and Mountain men, to the number of several hundred, who had surrounded and were importuning him to obtain the much desired "diamond gudgeon" of this government affair. The Captain was disposed to gratify them, and accordingly mounted the most convenient rostrum—which was near—the old rickety fence which bounds the enclosure. He had commenced and was going on with his remarks, which could not be heard, however, excepting by those who were immediately crowding round him, when a sudden pressure of the crowd broke down the fence and over went the crowd, Captain, and all embracing their mother earth. About this time, a well-meaning Irishman, who had been standing on the corner of Second Street, not knowing what all the fuss was about, rushed up with the idea that it was a "big fight," shouting at the top of his lungs, "Fair play! Fair play! and be d——d to yez; don't you see the man's down?"

Later, the reporter heard fragmentary sentences of Frémont's speech. "Those who desire to go—fifty men—good riflemen and packers—been to the mountains before—are not such —discharge them before I get up." He says that Frémont's description of the hardships "took the starch out of many a good fellow."

Frémont had purchased a dozen of the finest rifles on the market, and offered them to his corps as prizes for the best markmanship.[1] Obviously, sixty men were an excessive force for a mere topographical party, and sharpshooting is not a topographical necessity. The party included many of Frémont's old comrades, among them the two distinguished frontiersmen, Joseph Walker and Alexis Godey; the Captain's favorite French voyageur and aide, Basil Lajeunesse; the hunter Lucien Maxwell, and Theodore Talbot of Washington. This time twelve Delaware Indians, good hunters, and brave men, were taken along. Lieutenant Abert of the Topographical Corps, a relative of its head, and James McDowell, a nephew of Jessie's, were members. Frémont found that the horses and mules which he had left pasturing near the site of the future Kansas City were in fine condition, fat and rested.

One man was conspicuous by his absence: Preuss, whose wife had persuaded him to buy a comfortable home in Washington and insisted that he remain there, though he ardently longed to rejoin Frémont.[2] His place was taken by Edward M. Kern, of Philadelphia, who had eagerly applied for the post; a gay, headstrong young artist whose skill in sketching from nature, and in drawing and coloring birds and plants, made him a valuable addition to the party. Kern was to play a rôle in California far more important than any one dreamed. As for Carson, Frémont had no sooner reached Bent's Fort on August 3rd than he sent a messenger post-haste from it to the scout's new ranch on the Cimarron, east across the mountains from Taos, where Carson and Richard Owens were launching into stock-raising on a large scale. Kit was tilling, planting, and building with the zeal of a man who, now tired of roving, happily married, and with children in prospect, hoped to settle down to a life of quiet industry. But though he had resolved to change his mode of life, the message from Frémont instantly caused him to abandon his plans. His ranching enterprise had

[1] Frémont, *Memoirs*, I, p. 424.
[2] Jessie Benton Frémont MSS, Bancroft Library.

been contingent upon a promise to Frémont that he would come at any call. He gave up much—"This was like Carson, prompt, self-sacrificing, and true," writes Frémont. But he loved adventure and activity, the government pay was sure while ranching was precarious, and without delay, he disposed of his ranch, placing his young wife Josefa with friends. The willing Owens accompanied him to Fort Bent.[3]

It was sufficient recommendation for Owens that he was Carson's friend. "Cool, brave, and of good judgment," says Frémont in his *Memoirs;* "a good hunter and good shot; experienced in mountain life, he was an acquisition, and proved valuable throughout the campaign." Indeed, upon three men, Carson, Owens, and Godey, Frémont in the anxious days just ahead placed his chief reliance. They were shrewd, quick, and resolute. Under Napoleon, said the young leader, they might have become marshals. Within a year, Owens was to be captain of the first company of Colonel Frémont's First California Battalion, and in that capacity to distinguish himself by valiant and loyal service.

August was drawing to a close when the explorer, with his sixty men, two hundred horses, and a few cattle for food, rode westward from Bent's Fort in a heavy cloud of dust. Abert was no longer with him, having led a smaller detachment on a reconnaissance into northern Texas, whence he was to turn east to the lower Arkansas River, and then return up the Mississippi to St. Louis. The young Brevet Captain was in absolute command of what was to all effects a little army. His order to march marked the beginning of two crowded years whose adventures, perils, triumphs, and humiliations were to make him one of the most famous figures of his generation.

Until the expedition reached the eastern foothills of the Sierras, its journey was uneventful and prosperous. The first marches were up the Arkansas Valley into the heart of Colorado. The party crossed the plains in the delightful weather of late summer, and the men found them beautiful, with the coun-

<hr>

[3] Sabin, *Kit Carson Days,* I, p. 384.

try fresh and green, broken by aspen groves, pine woods, and clear, cool streams rushing over rocky beds. Early in September, they were on the shores of the Great Salt Lake, where Frémont spent almost a fortnight sketching the geographical features of the country, taking astronomical observations, and making careful explorations. He found great beds of mineral or rock salt; traversed the environs of the lake on horseback; and at Antelope Island, near its southern extremity, had an interesting encounter with a grizzled old Ute chief, who declared himself the owner of the game thereabouts, and required Frémont to pay him in red cloth, tobacco, and hardware for the meat he had taken.[4]

West of Salt Lake, the course seemed to lie over a flat, arid plain, concerning which neither Walker nor Carson knew anything whatever, and which no white man save the ubiquitous Jedediah Smith had ever crossed. The Indians declared that they knew of no one who had traversed it, and that parties had ventured far out without finding a drop of water anywhere. But Frémont thought of a shrewd expedient. At the far edge of the desert, sixty miles away, faintly loomed a high-peaked mountain, which looked verdurous, and which he thought he could safely reach. He arranged that Carson, Lucien Maxwell, and two others should set out in the coolness of the night, taking a pack mule with water, and make the mountain by a single forced march. On the following day, Frémont and his companions should follow more leisurely, try to reach a halfway point, and wait for a smoke signal in the event that Carson discovered a spring or stream. Two days later the whole expedition was at the foot of the peak, where it found water, grass, and wood abundant, and where the animals could be turned loose.[5] Frémont called the friendly mountain Pilot Peak. Be-

---

[4] Frémont, *Memoirs*, I, p. 431.

[5] Carson writes in his *Own Story* of this desert: "It had never before been crossed by white men. I was often here. Old trappers would speak of the impossibility of crossing, that water could not be found, grass for the animals, there was none. Frémont was bound to cross. Nothing was impossible for him to perform if required in his explorations."

ginning the next year, it was used as guide-mark by a number of emigrant parties. This briefer route west of Great Salt Lake was called the Hastings Cut-off, after its discoverer, Lansford W. Hastings, who in 1845 had published *The Emigrants' Guide to Oregon and California*. But after 1846 emigration over it was rare. Frémont's horses had now become what the voyageurs called *resté*, having reached a point at which they were easily overfatigued; but the mules, however tired at night, needed only plenty of good grass and water to be as fresh as ever in the morning.

At the beginning of November the expedition, finding easy passes from valley to valley, continued its journey westward across Nevada. It was an arid region, but they spread scouts out over the country on every day's march, and seldom had difficulty in finding a comfortable camping place by some stream or spring. When Frémont reached the picturesque river which had theretofore been called the Ogden, after the famous fur trader Peter Skene Ogden, but which he renamed the Humboldt in honor of the great geographer, he divided his party. One body, under Kern, was to follow the Humboldt to its termination in the Carson Sink, was to go on to the eastern foot of the Sierras, and was then to follow the mountains southward till it reached a body of water which Frémont called Walker's Lake. Frémont had appointed Joseph Walker as guide to the party and felt secure as to its safety, for in following the river and the Sierras it could not go astray, while it would have ample grass and water to keep the animals in good condition throughout its journey.

For himself, the Captain took ten picked men, including several Delawares, Dick Owens, Lucien Maxwell, and Basil Lajeunesse, and set out from the Humboldt River directly across the bed of the Great Basin, westward with a slight inclination to the south. Carson, of course, guided him. By splitting the expedition into two parts, Frémont doubled the information obtained. Since "the winter was now approaching, and I had good reason to know what the snow would be in the Great Sierra,"

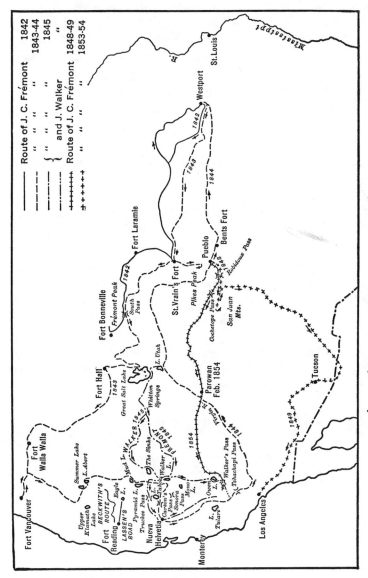

FRÉMONT'S FIVE EXPLORING TRIPS, 1842–54

he thought it imprudent to linger longer in examining the Great Basin. But, as Dellenbaugh suggests, if this had been purely an explorative party, it would have been much better for it to spend the winter mapping the almost unknown regions east of the Sierras than to hurry on to the well-known coastal belt of California. Why did he not stay, find a suitable base, and study all the problems of the Great Basin at leisure? The obvious answer is that it was not a mere explorative party. One of its objects was to carry out a military reconnaissance in California, be at hand in that desirable territory if hostilities broke out, and give the American settlers on the Sacramento assurances of aid.[6]

The passage of the Great Basin was dull and eventless, though it added not a little to our geographic knowledge of one of the most obscure parts of America. Once they chanced upon a naked Indian, cooking a stew of sage-brush marmots, pierced with his obsidian arrows, over a sage-brush fire; and though the Delawares would have killed him, Frémont sent him away with a small present. On another occasion they encamped for the night at a spring, supped upon antelope, and were lying about the fire smoking when they were startled by an unexpected apparition. Frémont's record is a good illustration of his eye for the picturesque:[7]

---

[6] For the political background of the third expedition, see W. J. Ghent and Leroy Hafen, *Broken Hand* (*Thomas Fitzpatrick*), p. 163ff. As they point out, with war apparently imminent in the Southwest, the Government despatched three expeditions, one of them military, the other two semi-military. "Frémont with sixty well-armed men was to put himself where he could watch developments in California and be ready to act should action seem warranted." Lieutenant James William Abert, with thirty-two men, was to make a reconnaissance through no-man's land. Colonel Stephen W. Kearny, with a force of dragoons, was to march to South Pass and back, warning the Indians on the way that any violence would be punished with promptness and severity. It should be noted that a question of policy was involved in the work of the Kearny expedition: Would the safety of the emigrants be better assured by establishing a chain of forts from the Missouri to the Columbia, or by sending out an occasional force of troops as evidence of the government's power to punish? Frémont favored the line of forts, Kearny the occasional despatch of expeditionary forces; thus early the two officers were at odds.

[7] Frémont, *Memoirs*, I, pp. 436, 437.

Carson, who was lying on his back with his pipe in his mouth, his hands under his head, and his feet to the fire, suddenly exclaimed, half rising and pointing to the other side of the fire: "Good God! Look there!" In the blaze of the fire, peering over her skinny, crooked hands, which shaded her eyes from the glare, was standing an old woman apparently eighty years of age, her grizzled hair hanging down over her face and shoulders. She had thought it a camp of her people, and had already begun to talk and gesticulate, when her open mouth was paralyzed with fright, as she saw the faces of the whites. She turned to escape, but the men had gathered about her and brought her around to the fire. Hunger and cold soon dispelled fear, and she made us understand that she had been left by her people at the spring to die, because she was very old and was no longer good for anything. She told us she had nothing to eat and was very hungry. We gave her immediately about a quarter of the antelope, thinking she would roast it by our fire, but no sooner did she get it in her hand than she darted off into the darkness. Some one ran after her with a brand of fire, but calling after her brought no answer.

Frémont's route led through the central portion of Nevada. Striking southwest from Franklin Lake, he skirted what is now known as the Alkali Desert, penetrated Nye County, and proceeded west through Esmeralda County to Walker's Lake, which lies near the western boundary of Nevada, its southern tip just opposite Sacramento. In making this trip, he blazed the most feasible trail of the time across Nevada. Theretofore, maps and geographic texts had represented the whole Great Basin, from the Salt Lake to the Sierras, as a sandy, barren plain, without water or grass. Frémont proved, as he wrote Jessie, that instead of being a plain, it was "traversed by parallel ranges of mountains, their summits white with snow (October); while below, the valleys had none. Instead of a barren country, the mountains were covered wth grasses of the best quality, wooded with several varieties of trees, and containing more deer and mountain sheep than we had seen in any previous part of our voyage." Had later events not obscured Frémont's exploratory labors in 1845, these facts would have attracted wide attention.

On November 24th, after this unexciting passage, Frémont found himself at the rendezvous on Walker's Lake, where three days later the main party joined him. The weather was still open and beautiful, but the temperature was growing sharply chill; even during the journey across the Basin the thermometer had stood below the freezing point at sunrise, and now the cold of the grim Sierras, looming above them to the west, was in the air. The members of the expedition were in overflowing spirits and health. But game was becoming scarce as the wild animals denned themselves up or migrated southward for the winter, and their store of provisions was falling low. A brief storm, whitening the lower hills and valleys of the range with a few inches of snow, had warned them of the difficulties if they delayed. Frémont was not far from the point where he had forced a crossing of the Sierras the previous winter, and meant to conquer them again at once. He knew that heavy snows might be expected at any moment to block the passages; and that if they came, he could not possibly extricate his baggage. He therefore resolved again to divide his party, sending the main body and impedimenta under Kern south along the Sierras until, opposite southern California, they could pass through open valleys, known to Walker, where snow was rarely or never seen. He himself would go directly over the mountains, and the two companies would reunite at the Lake Fort of the Tulare Lake.

Leaving behind him the Great Basin, which he had branded with "the Frémont irons"—Humboldt River and Mountains, Basil Creek, Sagundai Spring, Walker's River and Lake, Owens Lake—he successfully carried out this program. With fifteen selected men, at the beginning of December he reached the Salmon Trout River flowing into Pyramid Lake, and four days later was standing on the east side of a feasible pass in the Sierras. This may have been Truckee or Donner's Pass; the pass he had used in 1844 lay on his left. He had succeeded in his effort to reach the divide before the first heavy fall of snow. Nervous even yet lest the party be overtaken by a blizzard, he kept a close watch all night on December 4th, so that at the first swirl of snowflakes they might hurry over the crest before it was too late. Happily the sky continued clear, and when they gained the summit the only snow visible was that shining on the high peaks above. Reaching the middle of the divide, they found the temperature surprisingly mild—only 22 degrees—and began the descent into the warm California plains.

It was again a delightful experience, after the scorched, broken plateau of the Great Basin, to come out into the lovely rolling country just west of the Sierra pinnacles. First they passed through great pine forests, the columns high overtopping any pines of the East or of Europe; then they descended into a region wooded with varieties of oak, bearing an abundance of acorns which the Indians used for food. The long-acorn oak rose to a hight of eighty feet, and was frequently six feet in diameter. In the foothills, where rain fell frequently, everything bore a green, well-watered aspect. Small Indian villages were scattered through the oak glades, and Frémont noted their little mills, or rather mortar-holes, for pounding acorns; idyllic spots, where the clean, smooth granite rocks stood out amid the fresh green grass, and the running water pleased the ear and eye. So attractive was the whole region, with its flowers, game, and other temptations to man and beast, that they camped early every afternoon to enjoy it, and so consumed four days in coming down to the Sacramento bottoms.

On December 9, 1845, Frémont was once more approaching the thick adobe walls of Sutter's Fort on the American River, and was being welcomed by the waving hands of the ranch employees, clustered in the gateway. He made camp that night just above the fort. Just behind him lay some of his most important geographical achievements. Circumstances prevented him from ever writing such a report of this third expedition as had followed the first and second, and the world has therefore been inclined to ignore his really important accomplishments. Previously a Pathmarker, in this trip across the Nevada desert from east to west, and this passage of the Sierras, he had really been a Pathfinder. As E. L. Sabin succinctly puts it: [8]

Another joint (the first being the Mary's River) had been found in the armor of the Great Basin. The map submitted by Frémont in 1848, based upon his explorations of 1845, was very different from his map of the Great Basin of 1844. Where much had been white, save for the arching legend "Unknown," now much was etched with physical symbols and place names. And although the Frémont southern route was improved upon and shortened by later explorations, although, in consequence of the California troubles, his feat of 1845 received less notice by the world and was less exploited by himself than his previous feats, he really pioneered a permanent feasible trail between the Salt Lake and Northern California. Moreover, he and his stalwarts were the first white men, as he rightfully asserts, to make a survey of this, the prospector's end of Nevada, long thereafter to be terra incognita save to the emigrant, the stage, the pack animals, the Mormon station-keepers, the treasure delver, and the wandering Indian.

With the long westward march completed, with his camp pitched not far from Sutter's Fort, there opened one of the most eventful chapters of his history. He little realized then that, as he wrote later, "my way of life had led out from among the grand and lovely features of Nature, and its pure and wholesome air, into the poisoned atmosphere and jarring circumstances of conflict among men, made subtle and malignant by clashing interests."

[8] *Kit Carson Days,* I, pp. 396, 397.

XVI

A Clash with Californians

O N December 10, 1845, Frémont rode down from his camp to Sutter's Fort, where he found the robust Swiss proprietor absent, and John Bidwell (who had reached California with the Bartleson-Bidwell party in 1841) in charge. To the Captain, requesting various supplies, rough-spoken Bidwell seemed unfriendly. He offered to find some horses, but said that he could not furnish the sixteen mules which Frémont needed; he would lend him the blacksmith shop, but declared there was no coal for the forge. Frémont errone-ously concluded that since the Mexican and American govern-ments were drifting toward war, and Sutter was an officer of the former and he of the latter, the men at Sutter's Fort had received orders to do as little as possible for him. Indeed, the Captain had just learned that his previous visit to California had created, as he writes, "some excitement among the Mexi-can authorities." Americans on the Sacramento informed him that soon after he left Sutter's Fort in the spring of 1844, a Mexican officer and twenty-four men had ridden up from the coast to inquire in Governor Micheltorena's name the meaning of this sudden armed entry into the country. Made uneasy by the news, the Captain now feared trouble.[1] But he soon learned that Sutter was as friendly and hospitable as ever. On his return next day the good Swiss set to work; he promptly found four-teen mules, and furnished cattle, horses, and other supplies; while at the same time he sent word to the commander in

[1] Frémont's *Memoirs*, I, p. 441, indicate clearly that he had just now heard of the alarm of 1844 among the Mexican authorities. But he might have learned of it in Washington; Consul Larkin had reported it by a despatch of April 12, 1844, to the State Department (State Department Archives).

northern California, General Mariano Guadalupe Vallejo, that
the American party had arrived and wished to rest and refit in a
mild climate.

Much had occurred in California since Frémont left it in
the spring of 1844. A revolt against Micheltorena, led by Juan
B. Alvarado and José Castro, had broken out in the autumn
of that year, and though a number of Americans under Sutter
and Isaac Graham had given listless aid to the governor, he
had been compelled to surrender in February, 1845. He agreed
to depart with his disorderly retainers, and next month did so.
With him went the last effective traces of Mexican rule, and
even the shadow of allegiance endured but a few months longer.
California was now in all practical respects a little independent
republic. The government was divided between a civil and a
military chief, Pio Pico holding sway as governor from Los
Angeles, and José Castro as military commandant from Monterey.[2] The old antagonisms between north and south, accentuated by personal rivalries, naturally reappeared; difficulties
arose over revenues, and while Pico had legislation drafted
favorable to his aims, Castro controlled the treasury and custom-house at Monterey in a way promoting his own. Renewed
civil war was sooner or later a certainty unless the lowering
conflict between Mexico and the United States supervened.
Sutter and the other Americans in California were watching
the situation uneasily, fearing that they might be disastrously
involved—some of them fearing also that Great Britain might
be invited by one party or the other to intervene.[3]

Delaying only a few days at the Fort, Frémont on December
14th marched south, driving his cattle and horses with him,

[2] T. H. Hittell, *History of California*, II, p. 346*ff*. Sutter joined Micheltorena
with a hundred riflemen, including such Americans as O'Farrell, Hensley, and
Bidwell, and a considerable force of armed Indians.

[3] The Americans had still other fears. By orders from Mexico dated June
10th, and published in California September 12th, the immigration of foreigners without passports was to be halted; Castro had soon afterward warned
Americans that unless they obtained regular license to hold lands as Mexican
citizens, they would have to leave. Frémont must have been told of all this as
soon as he arrived. Sabin *Kit Carson Days*, I, p. 398.

to find the main body under Kern, Talbot, and Joseph Walker from which he had separated on the shores of Walker's Lake. Though he had but sixteen men, he gained confidence from the fact that when the parties reunited he would possess sixty, all well mounted and each armed with "three to six guns, rifles, and pistols." He was not afraid of the Californians, still less of the Indians. Indeed, as he rode southward along the San Joaquin Valley he undertook to teach a lesson to the thievish savages who had so troubled his march in 1844. A desultory warfare was constantly being waged between these Indians on one side, and all Californians—native *rancheros,* Mexican officers, American settlers—on the other. Frémont in his *Memoirs* aptly describes the situation:

The Horsethief tribes had been "Christian Indians" of the Missions, and when these were broken up by Mexico the Indians took to the mountains. Knowing well the coast country, and the exact situation of the missions where they had lived and the ranchos and the range which their horses were accustomed to, they found it easy to drive off the animals into the mountains, partly to use as saddle-horses, but principally to eat.

In time they became a scourge to the settlements. The great ranges which belonged with the ranchos not only supported many thousands of cattle, but also many hundreds of horses which were divided into bands, *"manadas."* The Indians were the vaqueros or herdsmen who attended to both; herding the cattle and breaking in the colts. The Californians had great pleasure in their horses. On some ranchos there would be several hundred saddle-horses, in bands of eighty or a hundred of different colors; *Alazan* (sorrel) always the favorite color. Deprived of their favorite food, the Indians took to the mountains and began to drive off horses. Cattle would not drive fast enough to avoid the first pursuit. In their early condition they had learned to eat wild horsemeat and liked it. Familiarity with the whites and the success of their predatory excursions made the Horsethief Indians far more daring and braver than those who remained in fixed villages....

Carson had fought these raiding Indians in the San Joaquin Valley in 1830, and Sutter had led an expedition against them in 1844. Now Frémont's little band had a series of encounters with them; as he wrote his wife, "we ... got among the Horse-thieves (Indians who lay waste the California frontier) ... and fought our way down into the plain again and back to Sutter's. Tell your father that I have something handsome to tell him of some exploits of Carson and Dick Owens, and others." In the first clash the Indians, as he tells the story, were the aggressors, and nearly cut off Owens, Maxwell, and two Delawares; in the second Maxwell fought a successful duel with an Indian before Frémont could gallop up. Perhaps this fighting was unavoidable, but it suggests that Frémont felt a more aggressive temper than in 1844, and was not unwilling to take up a quarrel of the American settlers.

The main object of this trip southward was unsuccessful; his search along the San Joaquin Valley as far as the headwaters of Tulare Lake Fork failed to reveal the Talbot-Kern detachment. Frémont was disconcerted but not alarmed, for he knew that the party was too strong to have met with any disaster, and concluded that they had loitered along the way to hunt the abundant game. Thus reassuring himself, he turned northward again to Sutter's Fort, a convenient headquarters until Kern could rejoin him, reaching it January 14, 1846.

His plan was to take the expedition, as soon as it was reunited, up the eastern branch of the Sacramento, past Klamath Lake, and on into the lovely Willamette Valley. He would thus have blazed a new, shorter, and as he believed far superior road from the Missouri River into Oregon. He wrote Jessie on January 24th that he could travel from the Fontaine qui Bouit River to the Sacramento in thirty-five days or less, over a road materially better for wagons than any then in use—a road which made use of the grass, wood, and abundant deer and mountain sheep he had found in parts of the Great Basin; while from Sutter's Fort he could push on north by an admirable natural highway, instead of the rocky, mountainous path which emigrants on the Oregon Trail took down the Snake and the Columbia. His letter bubbled over with pride in his new road; with pride also in his discovery that much of the supposedly desert Great Basin was green and fertile; and with hopes of the future. He spoke only of errands of peace, and of his happiness in having accomplished so much of his task. "So soon as the proper season comes, and my animals are rested, we turn our faces homeward, and be sure that grass will not grow under our feet. All our people are well...and I hope to be able to bring back with me all that I carried out. Many months of hardship, close trials, and anxieties have tried me severely, and my hair is turning gray before its time. But all this passes, *et le bon temps viendra.*" [4] He seemed to cherish only the prospect of another triumphant report, and quiet fireside pleasures.

Actually, he could not have failed to give close attention to the uneasy political situation in California, and to ponder the possibility that it might complicate his program. Nor could he have failed to wonder what was occurring beyond the mountains in Washington, beyond the desert in Mexico City. What had actually happened was as momentous to him as to others. The mission of John Slidell to Herrera's government had ended in total failure, and Herrera himself was overthrown by a military politician, Paredes, who took a more belligerent attitude toward the United States. In August, 1845, while Frémont was on his way westward, Zachary Taylor had been ordered to the Nueces River, beyond which lay a strip of land debated by the United States and Mexico. When it became plain that Slidell had failed, Polk on January 13th, as Frémont reapproached Sutter's Fort, directed Taylor to advance to the Rio Grande, thus taking possession of all the debatable area. The intervening territory had never yet been surrendered by Mexico, or effectively occupied by Texas. That step, of course, led directly to war.

Had he wished, Frémont might have waited quietly near Sutter's Fort for the arrival of the Talbot-Kern party, supplied himself with what animals and stores he could obtain there

---

[4] This letter is printed in *Memoirs*, I, pp. 452, 453.

and on San Francisco Bay, and pushed on north. The road was easy, game was obtainable, and when spring opened he would be at the Oregon posts, where he could further refit. But his course was different, and it seems plain that he was delaying for news of the Mexican-American situation. He might hear of war; he might receive instructions from Washington for some decisive act. Though he did not know it, a lieutenant of the Marine Corps—Archibald H. Gillespie—was actually on his way through Mexico to California with messages for Sloat and the American consul in Monterey, Thomas O. Larkin, and for Frémont. Speaking Spanish, Gillespie had ample opportunity on his trip through Mexico to learn of the rising sentiment for hostilities and to observe the demonstrations which placed Paredes in power.[5] While Frémont was not aware Gillespie was coming, he may have anticipated messages from some quarter. Declaring that he needed more camp equipment, he decided to visit some of the principal California settlements. Leaving his men at the Fort, on January 19th he took Sutter's launch down the Sacramento to Yerba Buena (San Francisco), where he spent a few days with the genial American vice-consul, William A. Leidesdorff. Then, equipped with a passport from Sutter, he proceeded southward on horseback to Monterey.

Here, ninety miles below San Francisco,[6] was the liveliest and most important town in California. Though the seat of civil government had recently been transferred by Pio Pico to the rival town of Los Angeles, the treasury, custom-house, and military headquarters remained here; here, too, stood the ruinous San Carlos Mission, founded by Father Junípero Serra before the American Revolution. It was the strategic center of the

[5] Gillespie's reports or rather letters to the Secretary of the Navy, February 11, 1846—July 8, 1848, are published by George Walcott Ames, Jr., in "Gillespie and the Conquest of California," *California Historical Society Quarterly*, XVII (1938), p. 123ff., p. 271ff.

[6] For clarity we shall hereafter call Yerba Buena, still the merest hamlet, San Francisco. Here, as Bret Harte wrote later, "through the great central valley the Sacramento poured an unstained current into a majestic bay, ruffled by no keels and fretted by no wharves."

territory, and no officer who thought of the possibility of an American conquest would lose an opportunity to familiarize himself with it. The explorer was accompanied by Leidesdorff as he rode down the Santa Clara Valley, a beautiful pastoral region wooded with oak; and his heart must have leaped as, a little after noon on a clear January day, he caught his first glimpse of the town between two low green hills. On the right lay the blue waters of the Bay, with several vessels at anchor; on the left were the scattered one-story buildings, tile-roofed, with a wavering outline of pine-clad hills behind; over all was the sunshine of central California, tempered by a snapping breeze.

Monterey consisted of two or three irregular streets, unlighted, paved only with the deep sea sand, which in the rainy season was better than clay, and bordered by houses of sunbaked adobe. Some of the Spanish homes were elegant in their symmetry and spaciousness, and their low-ceiled, wide, comfortable rooms, built about large patios, were pleasant refuges from the summer heat. All were substantially erected, and looked as if no gale could shake them.[7] On the bluff above the town stood the fort, with the Mexican flag floating gaily above it; there was a neat and spacious presidio of yellow stone; and a road led over the hills to the former mission of Carmel, four miles distant. As Tamalpais furnished a landmark for the inhabitants of San Francisco, so a high rocky ridge called Toro Mountain, east of the town, made a landmark for the people of Monterey. The atmosphere of the place, cosily ensconced on its spacious bay, was quiet, mellow, and almost purely Spanish. Its natural surroundings were enchanting. It lay at the extremity of a curving fishhook peninsula, facing across its Bay, with the Pacific Ocean, hidden by the pine hills, booming faintly in the distance at its rear. In front, the waves lapped idly about the few wooden wharves; but any one who pushed through the deep green woods behind would come out upon a

[7] Bayard Taylor, *Eldorado* (Household ed.), p. 133; Walter Colton, *Three Years in California,* pp. 19, 20.

sea which might be very stormy, with the breakers leaping high
along its beach. Everywhere in the town the haunting presence
of the ocean was felt, its low, distant, thrilling roar hanging
over the coast and the inland regions near-by like smoke above
a battle-field.[8]

Frémont's first business was to hunt up the American consul,
Thomas Larkin, a shrewd, energetic, patriotic Yankee of slender education, whose firm-set jaw impressed the explorer. Larkin, like his compatriots, Abel J. Stearns in Los Angeles and
Jacob Leese in Sonoma, had come out to trade, and was well
on the way to being the first California millionaire.[9] He was a
confidential agent of the State Department, and a good one.
He told Frémont that Governor Pio Pico exercised very little
power in the north from his distant capital in Los Angeles. He
also told him much more about the troubled, discontented
state of the country, with Pio Pico's own seat none too sure;
and he took the Captain to pay a formal call upon the commanding General, Don José Castro, upon ex-Governor Alvarado, and upon the Prefect and Alcalde.

Toward these officials, Frémont assumed a deferential and
conciliatory attitude. When queried in a formal note by the
Prefect, he responded that he was actually not a soldier but
an engineer, employed by the Topographical Bureau in making
a survey of the briefest route from the eastern states to the
Pacific. He came in the interests of science and trade, and his
party, whom he had left upon the frontier, were civilians as
peaceable as himself. All they asked was what the scientific
workers of one nation might justly request of the courtesy of
another. Their camp equipment, clothes, tents, and horse-trap-
pings were almost destroyed; they wished merely to replace
them and lay in a decent store of provisions. He also suggested
that he might like to do a little exploring in the direction of
the Colorado River.

---

[8] Compare Robert Louis Stevenson's essay on "The Old and New Pacific
Capitals."

[9] Bryant, *What I Saw in California*, p. 337; I have also used R. L. Underhill's scholarly life of Larkin.

To these requests, the Mexicans, polite but plainly suspicious, acceded—at least by tacit consent, for no written reply was made. For a few days Frémont stayed in Monterey with the hospitable Larkin, buying there and in the neighboring country horses, leather goods, food, tents, and some small luxuries for his comrades. He had by this time heard of the whereabouts of his lost party. They had mistaken the place of meeting, which Walker wrongly supposed to be a certain pair of lakes some eighty miles south of the Tulare Lake Fork. For some time he waited there, and then marched northward down the San Joaquin toward Sutter's Fort, till (having heard that Frémont was at San José pueblo, and turned thither), he was found on February 11th by Carson and Dick Owens. The result was that by the middle of the month the whole expedition was reunited on the ranch of the American settler William Fisher some thirteen miles southeast of San José, between San Francisco and Monterey.[10] The men were in good health and spirits, for game had been plentiful, and the animals were fast recuperating. California officials might well have been a little alarmed by this formidable troop of sixty well-armed men now in their very midst; but Pio Pico on February 18th instructed the Prefect, Don Manuel Castro, to content himself with vigilant waiting.

The spot which Frémont had selected for rest and refitting was the Laguna, a vacant ranch owned by the before-mentioned Fisher near the public road through the Santa Clara Valley, only a few miles from the present site of the Lick Observatory. The gentle slopes of the mountains about, the Calaveras and Santa Cruz Ranges, were covered with wild oats, which later in the season rolled in waves of gold, while the soft spring weather had brought a wealth of flowers. Frémont's one objection was that the place was too pleasant and indolent, without "the invigorating salt breezes." Many hard-riding Cali-

[10] Details of this reunion are given in E. M. Kern's *Journal,* printed as an appendix to J. H. Simpson's *Report of Explorations Across the Great Basin of the Territory of Utah.*

fornians visited the ranch, and his men became friendly with the polite, hospitable, shiftless people. Americans from the region also came in, among them Dr. John Marsh, Harvard man, physician, and owner of a large ranch. A good deal of rough play enlivened the days, and the men shot at marks, hunted, and tramped the country while Frémont bought more supplies, botanized, and made scientific observations upon the redwoods, madrona, and other trees. He was killing time.

Finally, near the end of February, the expedition broke camp and set out—but not northeast toward the San Joaquin for Oregon or any other northern point, and not southeast toward the Colorado. Instead, they moved to the southwest, on a line which would take the sixty well-armed men through the best-settled parts of California. Santa Cruz and Monterey lay just ahead, but Frémont passed the latter town on the east, camping March 3, 1846, on the Hartnell ranch (owned by an Englishman who had come to the country by way of South America about 1830), some twenty-five miles distant, near the present-day town of Salinas.

Here, as they were resting in the long still afternoon, their camp was thrown into turmoil by the sudden appearance of a Mexican cavalry officer, in tight blue jacket, bright serape, red sash, and buckskin leggings, who, with two men, reined up abruptly before Frémont's tent. He introduced himself as Lieutenant José Antonio Chavez, and the Captain found him rude and curt in speech. Chavez brought two letters, one from General Don José Castro and one from the Prefect, ordering the party instantly to leave California, under penalty of arrest and forcible expulsion. Frémont, irritated by the Lieutenant's manner and offended by the phrasing of the letters, blazed up angrily. He replied that he was equally astonished by the fact that, after solemnly promising his protection to the expedition, Castro should have withdrawn it, and by Castro's use of such rude and peremptory language. He told Chavez that he defied the officials; that he would refuse to obey an order so insulting to his country and himself, and would leave when he got ready—not before.

In this attitude, Frémont was unquestionably in the wrong, while the Mexican authorities were thoroughly correct. They had a perfect right to dismiss him from California, and possessed good grounds for doing so. Frémont's movement toward the southwest and the coast settlements had no connection with his objects as explorer, was totally unexplained, and was certain to arouse suspicion and fear. He had at least by implication promised not to approach the settlements with his party. In his *Memoirs* he offers the feeble explanation that he desired to inspect the coastal slope with a view to making his home there some time in the future; and that he intended to march to a pass in the coast range, by which he would cross into the interior valley. But if he wished a site for a ranch he might have searched for it alone—better still, have commissioned Larkin to find it. As for crossing the coast range into the San Joaquin Valley, why? Oregon lay in the opposite direction, and one of the main objects of the expedition was to find a better road into Oregon. Frémont was obviously playing for time—obviously waiting for the expected news of war; and the California authorities could simply not tolerate his action.

Moreover, complaints were being made against his men. We may overlook the fact that Don Sebastian Peralta, a ranch-owner near Santa Clara, declared that some of his horses had been taken without payment by the Americans; this was probably a trumped-up charge. But it was a more serious matter when another rancher, an uncle of General Don José Castro himself, reported that three of Frémont's men had burst into his house and frightened the women, one of them even insulting the rancher's daughter.[11] The demand now made upon Frémont was stiffly but not insultingly worded. José Castro wrote that he

[11] Hittell states that "there does not appear to have been any truth in the report about stolen horses, nor was there any truth in the report of violence offered to the daughters of Angel Castro." *History of California*, II, p. 418. Castro himself later admitted that Frémont had *returned* some valueless animals which wandered into his camp.

had invaded the settlements—"and this being prohibited by our laws, I find myself obliged to notify you that on the receipt of this you must immediately retire beyond the limits of the department, such being the orders of the supreme government, which the undersigned is under the obligation of enforcing."

But, however much in the wrong, Frémont did not even explain himself—as courtesy required—by a written reply to the Prefect and military commander. Instead, he hastily prepared to give Castro battle. Doubtless he knew that if he yielded to the California demands, if he turned about and left the country without even a show of resistance, he would lose all prestige with his own men, and all credit with the American settlers in the region. Having provoked the challenge, he must meet it. He marched his men to a small wooded flat at the top of a neighboring eminence, Hawk's Peak in the Gabilan Mountains, where wood, water, and grass were all available. Here he could fight off a large force of assailants; he commanded a view of the surrounding Santa Clara Valley and Salinas plain; and if a retreat were necessary, he could easily escape to the San Joaquin on the east. While his party was building a rough but strong fort of logs, a tall sapling was cut and stripped, and when all was ready the American flag was raised to its top amid the cheers of the men.

For three days Frémont remained, holding his fort, his flag flying defiantly the while. He received messages from Larkin, the American consul, which gave him news of the Mexican movements,[12] and some settlers in the region also brought him word of what was going on. He wrote Larkin on March 9th that "I am very busy in making myself as strong as possible, and if attacked we will fight to extremity, and refuse quarter, trusting to our country to avenge our deaths. As yet no one has come to our camp from the Californians. But from our heights where we are encamped with a glass we can see troops collecting at St. John's and preparing cannon." With his glass, he perceived horsemen galloping and a body of two hundred

[12] Larkin Papers, Bancroft Library, No. 80.

men gathering at the San Juan Bautista Mission. Some vaqueros told him that Indians were being enticed into the camp and worked up to the fighting point with drink. The Americans awaited the event with a determination to die before surrendering. As evening approached on the second day, they espied a body of cavalry approaching, and Frémont, descending with forty men to a point where a thicket offered an excellent ambush, prepared to repel them. Happily the courage of the Mexicans failed, and when within a few hundred yards they stopped, consulted with each other, and turned back. Meanwhile, their commander had issued a proclamation: [13]

The citizen José Castro, Lieutenant-Colonel of the Mexican army and commander-in-chief of the Department of California:

Fellow Citizens: A band of robbers commanded by a captain of the United States army, J. C. Frémont, have, without respect to the laws and authorities of the department, daringly introduced themselves into the country and disobeyed the orders both of your commander-in-chief and of the prefect of the district, by which he was required to march forthwith out of the limits of our territory; and without answering our letters he remains encamped at the farm "Natividad," from which he sallies forth committing depredations, and making scandalous skirmishes.

In the name of our native country I invite you to place yourselves under my immediate orders at headquarters, where we will prepare to lance the ulcer which (would it not be done) would destroy our liberties and independence, for which you ought always to sacrifice yourselves, as will your friend and fellow citizen.

Headquarters at "San Juan."

8th March, 1846.

This proclamation was dated, it may be interjected, on the very day that Zachary Taylor's first troops crossed the Nueces into disputed territory, and so brought war within sight. Minister Slidell was about to be given his passports and return home; Archibald Gillespie was about to reach Honolulu on the last stage of his journey to California.

[13] Fort Sutter Papers (Huntington Library), Vol. III.

Having shown the Mexican officials what he thought of their insulting conduct, having, as he supposed, maintained his own and the American dignity, Frémont decided to retire. Larkin was insistent that hostilities ought to be avoided, while other American residents were nervous regarding the consequences.[14] Moreover, though Frémont had written Larkin that "we have in no wise done wrong to the people or the authorities of the country," he had come to realize that after all his conduct was rash; he might begin a war which Washington did not want, and if President Polk still hoped to obtain California peaceably, his belligerent acts might make such an acquisition impossible. Finally, Castro's force seemed to be growing uncomfortably large; he had three pieces of artillery, and Larkin sent word that an attack was about to begin. At this juncture, the pole bearing the flag fell down, and Frémont, as he wrote later, "took advantage of the accident to say to the men that this was an indication for us to move camp." But, setting off on the evening of March 9th, under cover of darkness, toward the San Joaquin at his rear, the Captain moved with defiant slowness. His men, and the American settlers in the area, thought that he retired with the honors of his encounter. Kit Carson, reflecting this view, writes in his autobiography that Castro had failed to frighten them by the thunders of his big guns:[15]

We had in our party about forty men armed with rifles, Castro had several hundred soldiers of artillery, cavalry and infantry. Frémont received expresses from Monterey from Americans advising him to leave, that the Mexicans were strong and would surely attack us. He sent them word that he had done nothing to raise the wrath of the Mexican commander, that he was in performance of a duty, that let the consequences be what they may, execute a retreat he would not.

We remained in our position on the mountain for three days, had become tired of waiting for the attack of the valiant Mexican general. We then started for the Sacramento River.

[14] *Memoirs*, I, pp. 462-464.
[15] Quoted in Sabin, *Kit Carson Days*, I, pp. 418, 419.

Turning north toward the Sacramento, Frémont for the better part of a week covered only four or six miles a day. Then he accelerated his pace, and leaving Sutter's Fort again on March 24th, passed rapidly up the Sacramento Valley and across the Oregon line.

He left behind him the Mexican officials breathing threats and boasts, although they seemed to have been impressed by Frémont's spirited conduct, and Castro is authentically reported to have said, "He has conducted himself as a worthy gentleman and an honorable officer." He left the American settlers in the Sacramento buzzing with excitement, and Consul Larkin writing feverish letters to Washington to explain the affair and to ask that a warship be sent up from Mazatlan. Rumors flew wildly about the country. Larkin wrote to Leidesdorff on March 21st:

We have had an excitement of late respecting the natives going to San Juan to drive away Capt. Frémont which deed they say they done, tho' I suppose he has gone to Santa Barbara as I presume he will go where he intends to go. They give him a hard name in their great Banda, a copy of which I have wrote to the General with the intention of answering it.

Up in the Napa Valley an American settler, James Clyman, heard the rumors. Men said, as he wrote March 17th, that Frémont had raised the American flag near Monterey, and that all loyal Californians had been summoned to rally with arms at Sonoma under General Vallejo to defend the rights of Mexican citizens. Unquestionably the affair had increased the suspicion and dislike that considerable bodies of Americans and native Californians felt for one another. Many of the rough Anglo-Saxons in the region thought any one of Mexican blood treacherous, shiftless, and dishonest; many Californians looked upon every American as potentially a lawless filibuster. Americans had heard a good deal of a supposed plan of Castro's to drive them out and keep them out, and some of them now looked to Frémont as a champion.

Castro, exultant at getting rid of his enemy, posted a flaring proclamation (the one referred to by Larkin) in which he informed the people that a band of freebooters—*bandoleros*—had come into the country to sack and slay, but that with two hundred courageous patriots he had driven the cowards off to the Tulares. Meanwhile, Captain William D. Phelps of an American merchant ship at Monterey, the *Moscow*, sent Frémont word that he would pick up the command at any point on the coast if it were hard-pressed. The before-mentioned James Clyman also wrote a note promising him the instant aid of a company of frontiersmen if he needed them. To this Frémont presently replied, somewhere on his northward march (the date is uncertain) that his position was perplexing; that the California authorities threatened "to overwhelm me"; that he thought "a declaration of war between our government and Mexico is probable," but did not have authoritative news. If peace continued, he wrote, "I have no right or business here," while if war began, "I shall be outnumbered ten to one," and compelled to "retreat, pressed by a pursuing enemy." In either event he did not want Clyman's reinforcements.

The whole episode was in one light a bouffe affair. It had given an impetuous captain of the American Topographical Corps and a fiery, unstable lieutenant-colonel of the Mexican Army an opportunity to thumb their noses at each other. It had furnished a week of tense excitement for the native Californians and the English and American settlers. Nobody had been hurt, and neither side could take any pride in the affair. But in the main consequence above noted it was by no means to be taken lightly. Frémont and his men had succeeded in antagonizing many native Californians, who charged them with insolence, horse-thievery, and a desire for looting and guerrilla warfare.[16] The restiveness of the Anglo-Saxon settlers had been greatly increased. Some of them had hastily gathered and sent off word to Frémont that they would ride to his rescue at once. Consul Larkin, writing to Secretary Buchanan, was explicit in

[16] Fort Sutter Papers (Huntington Library), Vol. III.

saying that they were ready at any instant to join just such a standard of revolt as the explorer had raised. He also declared that Castro was not eager to try conclusions with Frémont. In fact, with all California behind him, Castro would not have dared to attack the explorer "even had he been sure of destroying the whole party, as five times their number could have taken their places before the expected battle. Captain Frémont received verbal applications from English and Americans to join his party, and could have mustered as many men as the natives." [17]

At Fort Sutter, the American settlers gathered around Frémont with loud expressions of approbation and encouragement. Many of them deplored his departure. The Captain must have taken north with him the knowledge that he could raise an army almost equal in numbers, and superior in tenacity and strength, to any the Mexicans in California would be likely to bring against him. It was a rather dangerous idea to implant in the mind of an impressionable, headstrong, and ambitious young man. As he left, Lieutenant Gillespie was upon the high seas between Hawaii and California with his instructions for Larkin and papers for Frémont; and Zachary Taylor had penetrated to within thirty miles of the Rio Grande despite a written warning from the Mexican forces that this advance would be deemed equivalent to a declaration of war.

[17] Larkin despatches, State Department, April 2, 1846.

XVII

The Message from Gillespie

IT is difficult to determine just how seriously Frémont turned his mind toward exploration again after leaving Sutter's Fort for the North. His letters and memoirs would indicate that his old zest in the blazing of fresh wilderness trails had reawakened; and to some extent, it undoubtedly did. But in the main his eyes were still fixed upon California; his purpose to remain within easy marching distance of it was apparently unaltered, and it is significant that he made no energetic effort to reach the posts upon the Columbia. His movements before he was so dramatically recalled to the California stage may be briefly dismissed.

The close of March, 1846, found his expedition at the well-known ranch of Peter Lassen on Deer Creek, a tributary of the upper Sacramento, about two hundred miles from Sutter's Fort. Frémont formed a liking for Lassen, a Dane whose history was only less romantic than Sutter's, and who was a man of practical sense and courage. His wheat was yielding large returns, he was experimenting with cotton, and a vineyard had lately been set out. For almost a month, as if he were intent upon merely killing time, Frémont kept at or near the ranch. First his party rested and outfitted for six days; then they set off north up the Sacramento Valley, passing what Carson calls "Shasta Butte"; [1] then, finding the weather stormy, they turned back south, reaching Lassen's Ranch again on April 11th; and here they delayed for almost two weeks more. Why this marching and counter-marching? Perhaps Fré-

[1] It was on April 6th, that Frémont first saw the snowy peak of Shasta on the northern horizon. At this time he was following almost the same route as. Jedediah Smith in 1827–28. Dellenbaugh, *Frémont and '49*, p. 313.

234

mont was waiting for two of his men, Godey and Martin, who had been left behind to bring up some horses from the Indian herds in the lower San Joaquin Valley; perhaps he was waiting for Theodore Talbot, left behind to bring some special supplies from San Francisco. But it seems more probable that he was delaying week after week for news of Mexican-American developments. He named a high peak of the coast range Mount Linn, after his friend the dead Senator; he made various geographical observations; and he wrote notes on plant life, especially that picturesque shrub the manzanita.

Finally, on April 24th, he actually took his departure. The day he left was, though he did not know it, an eventful one in American history, for it marked the first clash between Mexican and American troops on the Rio Grande. General Taylor reported this engagement with the ominous words: "Hostilities may now be considered as commenced." Pushing northward again, on May 6th Frémont reached Klamath Lake, and could, of course, easily have taken up his old trail to the Columbia River. But this did not suit his plans, and he decided instead to turn west and explore the almost untouched Cascade Range. He writes: [2]

As I have said, except for the few trappers who had searched the streams leading to the ocean, I felt sure that these mountains were absolutely unknown. No one had penetrated their recesses to know what they contained, and no one had climbed to their summits; and there remained the great attraction of mystery in going into unknown places—the unknown lands of which I had dreamed when I began this life of frontier travel. And possibly, I thought, when I should descend their western flanks some safe harbor might yet be found by careful search along the coast, where harbors were so few; and perhaps good passages from the interior through these mountains to the sea. I thought that till the snow should go off the lower part of the mountains I might occupy what remained of the spring by a survey of the Klamath River to its heads, and make a good map of the country along the base of the mountains. And if

[2] *Memoirs*, I, p. 486.

we could not find game enough to live upon, we could employ the
Indians to get supplies of salmon and other fish.

The scenery of the North, he adds, had taken hold upon his
imagination:

I had not forgotten how fascinated I had been with the winter
beauty of the snowy range farther north, when at sunrise and at
sunset their rose-colored peaks stood up out of the dark pine forests
into the clear light of the sky. And my thoughts took the same
color when I remembered that Mr. Kern, who had his colors with
him, could hold these lovely views in all their delicate coloring.

But we may doubt if Frémont really had any earnest desire
to traverse the Cascade Range, and it is certain that he was
soon ready to turn back. Snow was falling heavily and con-
tinuously in the mountains which rose across his path. The
ground was discouragingly difficult. Fallen timber, the debris
washed down by rain and melting snow, and the rocky ridges
made a march of a few miles exhausting. Their way led between Klamath Lake and the foot of the Cascades; and after
rising early, plunging all day through the marshy coves and
toiling over the rocky spurs of the hills, they would sometimes
find at nightfall that they had hardly advanced at all. Their
provisions were almost exhausted; their horses were enfeebled,
for the early season offered little forage. They saw nothing
of the Indians except now and then a canoe glancing rapidly
across the gloomy waters, but they knew that hostile forces
were not far distant. Although Frémont records in his narrative
for May 6th that "Animals and men all fared well here [on
Klamath Lake]," and was certain next day that he could obtain enough lake fish if game grew scarce, there is evidence
that he found his force uneasy and depressed, and that he himself began to feel serious misgivings. At this moment, on the
evening of May 8th, a voice came out of the dark forest behind him, and he was recalled to that ambitious dream of Californian conquest which, beyond doubt, had seized upon his
imagination long months before.

The voice was that of the farmer and blacksmith Samuel Neal, who had a ranch on Butte Creek, another branch of the Sacramento, well to the south of Lassen's.[3] While Frémont sat beside his camp-fire, he heard a trample of hoofs in the silent woods; the noise grew steadily louder; and then Neal suddenly shouted from the gloom toward the camp, and rode into the firelight with a companion. As the men stiffly dismounted, it was plain that they and their horses were almost spent. They had ridden nearly a hundred miles in the two preceding days. Why? From their first sentences, Frémont gathered that a United States officer was on his trail with despatches from Washington. When the men had refreshed themselves with coffee at the fire, they told a fuller story. The officer was Lieutenant A. H. Gillespie of the Marine Corps, who had letters for Frémont. He had come up the Sacramento in a small boat, made inquiries at Sutter's Fort, and hurried on. Reaching Neal's ranch in the upper Sacramento Valley, he had been warned that hostile Indians were about, and that it would be dangerous for an inexperienced man with tired horses to follow Frémont. He had therefore despatched Neal and one of his employees to overtake the expedition and bring it back. These two couriers had ridden ahead, at one point charging pistol in hand through a party of hostile savages.

As always, Frémont acted without hesitation. They must make up a party to set off at daybreak, he decided; and he chose ten men, including Carson, Godey, Dick Owens, Maxwell, and Basil Lajeunesse, to accompany him. Doubtless a thrill of excitement ran through the whole camp; doubtless conjecture rose high upon the possibility that war had begun and that their little force was needed for immediate action in California. At dawn the party was ready to march; and having covered thirty or forty miles of rough ground by a herculean

[3] Neal had been with Frémont on his earlier expedition into California, and had remained behind at Sutter's Fort; since then he had stocked a prosperous ranch on the Feather River, which Frémont had visited on his way up to Lassen's.

effort,[4] at sunset they met Gillespie and his three companions in a glade which formed a natural camp-site near the southern end of Klamath Lake. That meeting, with its physical background of wild forest and water in the virgin Northwest, its political background of territorial ambition and war, was one of the most dramatic in the history of the Pacific Coast.

It was not only one of the most dramatic, but in its implications one of the most mysterious; for here we are confronted by the most baffling problem of Frémont's career. What were the instructions brought by Gillespie which caused Frémont to cut short his explorations, turn south, invade California, and help begin in earnest the war which he had threatened a few weeks earlier? He knew that mere re-entrance upon California soil, from which he had been expelled with a warning to keep off, would be construed as a hostile act. Did he have genuine warrant for his course? Or did he, with characteristic precipitancy, base a bold and stubborn policy upon inadequate authority?

Gillespie, an energetic, ambitious, egotistical, and rather excitable young officer, who had left Washington early in November, 1845, had reached Monterey on April 17, 1846, by way of Vera Cruz, Mexico City, Mazatlan, and Honolulu. He brought Frémont a copy of an official despatch from Secretary of State Buchanan, some American newspapers, family missives from Benton and Jessie, and some verbal explanations, as well as much news picked up en route. Whether he brought secret instructions remains a burning question, for even the belated publication of his reports to the Secretary of the Navy, furnishing phrases which may be construed to support both views of the matter, has not settled the issue. The family letters of course had no official weight. Frémont knew how powerful was the Senator's influence with the Administration; he knew that

---

[4] Dellenbaugh says forty-five miles; *Frémont and '49*, p. 317. In this he follows Frémont's *Memoirs*, I, p. 488. Sabin says thirty miles; *Kit Carson Days*, I, p. 427. Gillespie in his letter to the Navy Department says fifty!

Benton would stand by him loyally in any reasonable action. But as an army officer Frémont also knew that nothing the Senator wrote could be used as warrant for any military step, and that to launch his force upon a warlike course he required some direct official authority—unless he took the risk of disavowal and punishment. Apparently the only really official document brought by Gillespie was Buchanan's despatch. What policy did it suggest?

The answer appears simple. The despatch dated October 17th, was directed not to Frémont but to the consul, Larkin, though Gillespie had been ordered to take a copy to Frémont. It contained nothing that the explorer could construe as a suggestion for the use of armed force against the Californians.[5] Instead, it instructed Larkin to carry on a peaceful intrigue for the secession of California from Mexico by the voluntary act of its inhabitants. He was requested to be discreet, cautious, and sleepless. He was to approach the California authorities, assure them of American goodwill in their disputes with Mexico, and encourage them to break loose with a promise of our "kind offices as a sister republic." Once they became such a separate nation as Texas had been, they might look forward to annexation. "If the people should desire to unite their destiny with ours," wrote Buchanan, "they would be received as brethren." One other injunction was laid upon Larkin with special emphasis; he was told that Washington had reason to fear British or French aggression in California. He must counteract these foreign machinations by friendly appeals: "On all proper occasions you should not fail prudently to warn the government and people of California of the danger of such an interference to their peace and happiness; to inspire them with a jealousy of European dominion; and to arouse in their bosoms that love of liberty and independence so natural to the American continent." Obviously, in all this Frémont not only

[5] The text is published in the *Century Magazine*, April, 1891; compare Ernest A. Wiltsee, *The Truth About Frémont: An Enquiry*, p. 9ff. Gillespie before reaching Vera Cruz had committed the instructions to memory and destroyed the written copy.

found no authority for hostile action against the Californians, but was given a direct warning against it.

The desire of the Polk Administration to conciliate the Californians might be attested by many other facts and documents. A despatch from Secretary Bancroft was sent to Commodore Sloat, commander of the Pacific squadron at Mazatlan, under almost the same date as Buchanan's despatch to Larkin, October 14, 1845. Sloat was ordered to keep in constant touch with Larkin, and to ascertain the attitude of the Californians toward the United States and Mexico City. "You will do everything," he was directed, "that is proper to conciliate towards our country the most friendly regard of the people of California." If hostilities with Mexico did not occur, he was to detach part of his squadron to display the American flag in the Columbia River. This despatch, like that to Larkin, breathed friendliness to the Californians, and a hope for peace.[6]

So much for the official documents; but there remain the private letters and Gillespie's verbal information, upon which Frémont, as he stated later, unquestionably based his actions. Gillespie brought exciting news. He told Frémont that Sloat had heard of his encounter with Castro through the brig *Hannah,* and to protect the Americans had promptly sent the *Portsmouth* to San Francisco. Since Gillespie had left Mazatlan February 22nd, when he had news from Mexico City of about February 10th, he could tell Frémont that Mexico and the United States had then stood on the very brink of war. Actually Taylor on March 28 reached the Rio Grande, where fighting was expected at any time. He doubtless also had much to say about the revolution in Mexico City which had ousted Herrera and elevated Paredes, head of the war party, to leadership; for Gillespie, who spoke Spanish well, had seen the excitement accompanying this overturn. He could tell Frémont of the proclamation issued at Monterey on April 17th that unnaturalized foreigners in California could not hold land and were subject to expulsion.

[6] Compare H. H. Bancroft, *History of California,* V, pp. 85-90.

Finally, he may have shown Frémont a letter which Larkin had written him on April 23rd and sent to San Francisco, just as he was starting north to find the explorer; and if he did not show the letter, he probably conveyed its contents.[7] It contained news that at last reports the Mexican authorities at Mazatlan had expected Sloat to blockade the port, and had fled to Rosario with the archives. It also declared that Captain Montgomery had expressed the opinion "that Commodore Sloat may by the next mail (6 or 8 days) have a declaration on the part of the United States against Mexico, in which case we shall see him in a few days to take the country." Consul Larkin added that the Californians were much disturbed by the *Portsmouth's* arrival:

I have (as my opinion) said to Generals Castro, Carrillo, and Vallejo, that our flag may fly here in thirty days. The first says, for his own plans, war is preferable to peace, as by war affairs will at once be brought to a close, and each one will know his doom.... I have had many of the leaders at my house to inquire into the news, and believe they are fast preparing themselves for the coming events.

As a matter of history, on the very days that Neal and Gillespie reached Frémont, May 8 and 9, 1846, the first sharp battles of the Mexican War occurred. The sun that went down upon Gillespie and the Captain shaking hands in that Klamath glade sank also upon the bloody and smoking field of Resaca de la Palma. Frémont might well have felt almost certain that fighting was already under way. In the light of Gillespie's news of the imminence of war, in the light of what Frémont knew of the stormy situation in California, the peaceful injunctions in the despatch to Larkin might well have struck him as unreal and out of date. They would probably so have impressed even a cautious and conservative officer, and Frémont

---

[7] It is not certain that the letter reached Gillespie before he left San Francisco, but it does seem fairly certain that at least the same information reached Leidesdorff in time for the latter to give it to Gillespie; Sabin, *Kit Carson Days*, I, p. 436.

was never cautious. In his *Memoirs* he frankly states that he believed the instructions inadequate. "This idea [of annexation by conciliation] was no longer practicable as actual war was inevitable and immediate," he writes, "moreover, it was in conflict with our own instructions. We dropped this idea from our minds, but falling on others less informed [i.e., Sloat], it came near losing us California." He adds that "the rapid progress of affairs had already rendered" conciliation impossible, and made it necessary to "carry out the ultimate purpose of the government."

That Gillespie was full of his impression that hostilities on the Rio Grande might be announced at any moment, may be gathered from a letter which vice-consul Leidesdorff wrote Larkin from San Francisco on April 25th, just after seeing Gillespie. He was sure that Frémont would be jubilant over what the messenger told him: [8]

> According to your request, I have done everything in my power for Mr. Archibald H. Gillespie, he leaves this place in a few hours for the Sacramento, as I do not know exactly what funds he will require previous to his leaving this, I cannot inform you by this opertunity however in my next I shall forward you my private account; Glorious news for Capt. Frémont. I think I see him smile. by your letter it appears that this news was not generally known. however here they must have some as the Sub Prefecto was busy dispatching couriers in the different part of the country. and Capt. Hinckley had been heard to say, that Guierera [Guererro] had received a courier yesterday, advising him of the expected war with Mexico. how he got his news I cannot say. If Mr. Swasey has no employ yet, send him to me for I am all alone, and have a great deal to do....

Altogether, there was much in both the circumstances of Larkin's errand and the news he bore to impress Frémont—quite willing to be impressed—with a belief that he ought to turn back to California. Here was an officer who had come all the way from Washington with letters and intelligence for him;

[8] Wiltsee, *The Truth About Frémont: An Enquiry*, pp. 9, 10.

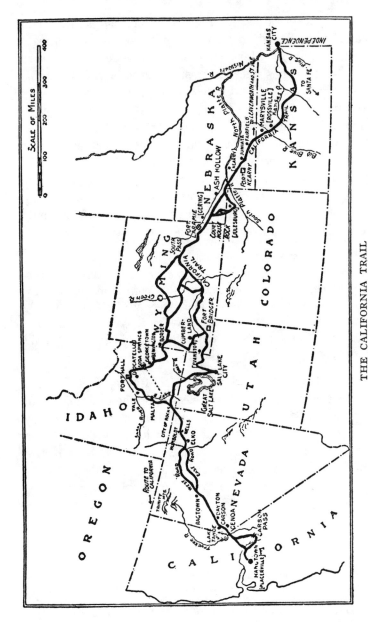

THE CALIFORNIA TRAIL

(FROM ARCHER BUTLER HULBERT, *Forty-niners*; BY COURTESY OF LITTLE, BROWN & COMPANY.)

who had been forwarded to him with eager haste and at great expense, by the American consul and vice-consul; who brought word that war with Mexico was imminent. He brought word also that the Oregon question was still unsettled, Polk having rejected the latest British proposals—that the tension between the two nations on that issue was still great. Doubtless Gillespie saw that his "glorious news" lost nothing in the telling.[9]

But Gillespie also bore family letters, and verbal instructions from Secretary Bancroft. Upon these family letters we have explicit statements from both Frémont and Jessie, who agree that they warned Frémont to be ready to take a militant stand. Mrs. Frémont asserts that they might be said to be in a family cipher, and Frémont declares this more emphatically. Benton's letter, he writes,

while apparently of friendship and family detail, contained passages and suggestions which, read by the light of many conversations and discussions with himself and others at Washington, clearly indicated to me that I was required by the government to find out any foreign schemes in relation to California, and so far as it might be in my power, to counteract them.

Conversing long afterward with Josiah Royce, Frémont said that the letters were particularly clear upon the desirability "of taking and holding possession of California in the event of any occurrence that would justify it, leaving it to my discretion to decide upon such an occurrence." He was warned of the British designs and told that Polk desired that he "should not let the English get possession of California, but should use any means in his power, or any occasion that offered, to prevent such a thing."[10]

Frémont's recollection of the affair might well be regarded as

---

[9] Larkin wrote Leidesdorff that "Mr. Packingham has the second or third time made Oregon propositions to Mr. Buchannan," that "Mr. Polk will have none of it," and that Polk "is for our own territory...without arbitration." This information, relayed to Frémont, might well have increased his fears of a British stroke on the coast. Wiltsee, *op. cit.*, pp. 12, 13.

[10] Jessie Benton Frémont, *Century Magazine*, Vol. XIX, New Series, p. 922; Frémont, *Memoirs*, I, p. 489; Royce, *California*, p. 116.

confused, or colored by a desire for self-justification; but it is measurably corroborated by a letter, inaccurate in a few particulars but nevertheless illuminating, which Secretary Bancroft wrote him in old age, when Royce's book had made the subject controversial. Bancroft speaks of verbal instructions: [11]

You as an officer of the army were made thoroughly acquainted with the state of things in California.

My motive in sending so promptly the order to take possession was not from any fear that England would resist, but from the apprehension that an English man of war in San Francisco harbor would have a certain degree of inconvenience, and that it was much better for us to be masters there before the ship should arrive; and my orders reached there very long before any English vessel was off California. The shameful delay of Sloat made a danger, but still he took possession of San Francisco before a British ship arrived.

Not having my papers here, all I can say is, that after your interview with Gillespie, you were absolved from any orders as an explorer, and became an officer of the American army, warned by your government of your new danger against which you became bound to defend yourself; and it was made known to you, on the authority of the Secretary of the Navy, that a great object of the President was to obtain possession of California. If I had been in your place, I should have considered myself bound to do what I could to promote the purpose of the President. You were alone, no Secretary of War to appeal to, he was thousands of miles off; and yet it was officially made known to you that your country was at war; [12] and it was so made known expressly to guide your conduct. It was further made known to you, that the acquisition of California was become a chief object of the President. If you had letters to that effect from the Secretary of War, you had your warrant. If you were left without orders from the War Department, certainly you learned through the Secretary of the Navy that the President's plan of war included the taking possession of California.

[11] Original letter in Frémont MSS, Bancroft Library, dated Newport, Rhode Island, September 3, 1886.
[12] This was of course not true.

The truth is, that no officer of the government had anything to do with California but the Secretary of the Navy, so long as I was in the Cabinet. It had been my desire to acquire California by all honorable means much before that time.

As to the President, if you see fit to state what I have stated to you, that President Polk entered on his office with a fixed determination to acquire California, if he could acquire it in an honorable and just manner; if you see fit to make that statement, and anyone disputes it, I give you full leave to cite me as your authority. I held and the President held, that it was impossible for Mexico, situated as things then were, to have retained possession of California; and therefore it was right to negotiate with Mexico for the acquisition of California by ourselves as the decisive point in the perfect establishment of the Union on a foundation that cannot be moved. Up to that time the division was between North and South. From that moment all division, if there was to be one, was between the North, Centre, and West against the South.

Bancroft's memorandum, enclosed with this letter, declares:

Very soon after March 4, 1845, Mr. Polk, one day when I was alone with him, in the clearest manner and with the utmost energy declared to me what were to be the four great measures of his administration. He succeeded in all the four, and one of the four was the acquisition of California for the United States. This it was hoped to accomplish by peaceful negotiation; but if Mexico, in resenting our acceptance of the offer of Texas to join us, should begin a war with us, then by taking possession of the province. As we had a squadron in the North Pacific, but no army, the measures for carrying out this design fell to the Navy Department. The Secretary of the Navy, who had good means of gaining news as to the intentions of Mexico, and had reason to believe that its government intended to make war on us, directed timely preparation for it. In less than four months after the inauguration, on the 24th day of June, 1845, he sent orders to the commanding officer of the United States naval forces on the Pacific that "if he should ascertain that Mexico had declared war against the United States, he should at once possess himself of the port of San Francisco and such other ports as his forces might permit." At the same time he was instructed to encourage the inhabitants of California "to adopt a course of neutrality." The Secretary of the Navy repeated these orders in August and in October, 1845, and in February, 1846. On one of these occasions he sent the orders by the hands of an accomplished and thoroughly trustworthy officer of the navy as a messenger, well instructed in the designs of the Department and with the purposes of the administration, so far as they related to California. Captain Frémont having been sent originally on a peaceful mission to the west by way of the Rocky Mountains, it had become necessary to give him warning of the new state of affairs and the designs of the President. The officer who had charge of the dispatches from the Secretary of the Navy to Commodore Sloat, and who had purposely been made acquainted with their import, accordingly made his way to Captain Frémont, who thus became acquainted with the state of affairs and the purposes of the government. Being absolved from any duty as an explorer, Captain Frémont was left to his duty as an officer in the service of the United States, with the further authoritative knowledge that the government intended to take possession of California.

Bancroft adds in this memorandum that while the United States had no reason to fear a conflict in California with any European nation, some Power might take a position which would be "inconvenient" and that the Administration wished for "due celerity" in the movement of its forces. As we have said, Great Britain actually had no designs upon California. But this the Polk Administration did not know; it believed the opposite. Bancroft was aware that the British squadron at Mazatlan was much stronger than the American, and that a state of tension existed between the two. The British Government had shown a wavering attitude toward American annexation; while sometimes it seemed acquiescent, early in 1845 it had informed its vice-consul at Monterey that it "would view with much dissatisfaction the establishment of a protectoral power over California by any other foreign state." Uneasiness in Washington was by no means incomprehensible. Moreover, we know now that Gillespie had been much impressed by news that the British sloop *Modeste* had been lingering in the Columbia River. He wrote the Secretary of the Navy just before he reached Monterey: "The settlers shew much feeling upon her entrance, and most heartily wished that they could seize their rifles and rake her decks as she passed. They look with great anxiety and hope for the arrival of an Agent of our government, if not to take immediate jurisdiction, at least to have an eye upon the movements of British agents." [13]

Altogether, Frémont might be excused for feeling more disturbed than ever after receiving Gillespie's messages. The instructions to Larkin, as repeated to him, enjoined a peaceful policy toward the Californians, an effort to foster an independent California republic. But what was California? Divided between a northern government and a southern government; between men loyal to Mexico and men disloyal; between native Californians and Anglo-American settlers—no republic could be set up without initial turmoil. The instructions seemed to contemplate another Texas, but the independence of Texas had been achieved by American residents, not by its Mexican population, and after much hard fighting. Could California's independence be achieved otherwise? Buchanan knew little of affairs on the coast; moreover, instructions written in the fall of 1845, with war still distant, hardly fitted the spring of 1846, with war about to break. And then Benton, who opposed war with Mexico, was fearful of British intervention on the coast. Any officer in Frémont's shoes would have hesitated. With the knowledge that war was almost certainly at hand, that fighting could hardly be avoided in California, that a large British naval force was not far distant, which was he to do: push on homeward by the Oregon Trail with his well-armed men, a force obviously equipped with an eye to possible military service, or turn back toward California?

[13] President Polk himself may have given Gillespie verbal warnings of importance. He writes: "I held a confidential conversation with Lieut. Gillespie of the Marine Corps, about 8 o'clock p.m., on the subject of the secret mission on which he was to go to California. His secret instructions and the letter to Mr. Larkin . . . will explain the object of his mission." *Diary*, Octber 30, 1845. Gillespie's remarks on the British warship *Modeste* may be found in George Walcott Ames, Jr., *op. cit., California Historical Society Quarterly*, XVII, p. 135.

Theoretically, he should have held himself strictly bound by the official instructions to Larkin; he should have known that the government would not permit an army officer to do what it had forbidden its consul. Its orders forbade open interference with California affairs unless Mexico "should commence hostilities against the United States." But Frémont, still only thirty-four, believed in action and disbelieved in binding orders. At his back stood a group of rugged frontiersmen, Carson, Owens, and others, who believed still more strongly in daring initiative. It was impossible to stand still; beyond doubt it seemed to him a spiritless and craven act to turn his back on California. Perhaps his later career would have been happier had he regarded himself purely as an explorer, and moved east to report in Washington. But after all, he had never been purely an explorer; he had been partly an agent of that militant expansionist Senator Benton, of the other Westerners in Congress, and of Secretary Bancroft. If he were purely an explorer, why did he have sixty armed men at his back? And what would be said of him when he arrived tamely in St. Louis, his sixty men having gained nothing but a pocketful of data on deserts and mountains, while the press resounded with reports of battle and conquest in the Southwest?

We can easily imagine the thoughts that passed through his mind that May night in the forest opening of southwestern Oregon, beside the creek rippling toward the lake. He paced back and forth by the fire, interrogating Gillespie. In his excitement he failed, for the second time in his life in Indian country (the men being exhausted by their thirty- or forty-mile march) to post sentries.[14] Long after his party had wrapped themselves in their blankets he remained by the fire, going over the home letters. Every line in them, he wrote years later, seemed to say: *"The time has come. England must not get a foothold. We must be first. Act: discreetly but positively."* If

---

[14] Gillespie, writes Frémont, had told him that there were no Indians on his trail. The other night when he failed to post a guard was the night spent on the island in the midst of Great Salt Lake. *Memoirs,* I, p. 490.

war came, abrogating the instructions to Larkin, an opportunity lay before him to help realize in their fullest extent all the dreams of Senator Benton, all the plans which the Western group in Congress had based upon the principle of manifest destiny. The Pacific would at once be made the western boundary of the republic, and he would bear a hand in performing the feat. But he must be in a position to act before the Mexican Government could organize its defense in California, or a British captain interfere at Monterey. Full of these thoughts, he crept to his bed under some low cedars growing along the margin of the woods, their boughs almost touching the ground, and drowsed off.

The story of the remainder of that tragic night, the one night on which Frémont permitted a surprise, has been retold by Western historians a hundred times. Only seventeen or eighteen men (Carson mistakenly says fourteen) lay about the dying fire. Toward dawn, Carson was awakened by the noise of an Indian driving his ax through the head of one of the sleepers, Basil Lajeunesse. He called out in alarm, and heard the groan of another man killed in the same way. The camp instantly roused itself as the Klamaths charged into it. As they leaped into the open, one of the Delawares fought them with a clubbed gun until he was riddled with arrows; Frémont, Carson, Godey, and two other white men rushed to the rescue, shouting and firing point-blank. The Klamath chief fell and his followers, disheartened, dodged back into the woods. Then ensued a desultory warfare in the dark, the white men replying with lead to every volley of arrows.

When at dawn the savages slunk away, the light revealed a tragic scene. Lajeunesse, the Delaware named Crane, and the half-breed lay dead in their blood, while another Delaware was wounded. On the ground also lay the Klamath chief, and, Carson vengefully seized an English half-ax which hung at the Indian's waist and knocked his head to pieces. His quiver contained forty of the finest and most deadly arrows the party had ever seen, tipped with steel heads of lancet sharpness, obtained probably from the Hudson's Bay Company, and poisoned for six inches. The disaster sealed Frémont's determination to turn south, for his party was too much shaken and demoralized to push on into the wild Cascade Range.

Angered by their loss, the survivors, after reuniting the next day with the main party, determined that before they left they would wreak vengeance upon the treacherous Indians. They made a complete circuit of Klamath Lake, Carson being sent ahead to find a village for attack. He set upon the largest one within reach, and while Frémont galloped up with reinforcements, completely routed the braves and slew fourteen men. Then they fired the rush huts and the scaffolds upon which the Indians were drying their annual supply of fish; the flames "a beautiful sight," writes Carson. This retaliatory expedition offered few dangers for frontiersmen armed with the best rifles of the day, and facing only bows and arrows, though at one point an ambushing Indian would assuredly have killed Carson had not Frémont bravely ridden him down with his steed Sacramento. The raid gave Frémont profound satisfaction. "I had kept the promise I had made to myself, and had punished these people well for their treachery," he writes, "and now I turned my thoughts to the work they had delayed."

On May 24th, the expedition arrived again at Lassen's Ranch on the upper waters of the Sacramento, well within the borders of California. Here, as Gillespie wrote the Secretary of the Navy, they met the alarming report that Don José Castro, by a proclamation of April 17th, had ordered all non-citizens to be ready to leave the province, and that he was determined to prevent the entrance of the new American immigrants expected during the summer. The party received this intelligence with anger. Frémont increasingly felt that he could no longer regard himself as head merely of an exploring expedition; that he was rather the leader of a body of armed Americans who must observe the situation, protect American settlers, and stand ready to strike in the event of war. His position on Mexican soil was more than anomalous; strictly speaking, it was lawless.

Yet to abandon the settlers, leave a coast on which British warships were stationed, and march meekly homeward—would not that be cowardice and folly? To protect himself and to cast a thin mantle of legality about his acts, he still posed as an explorer, who intended in good time to push back to St. Louis by a southern route; but he and his men stood ready for more decisive action.[15]

---

[15] Sabin bids us remember the influence of Frémont's men on his course, and especially in the light of the rankling insult which they all believed that Castro had given them. Such hardy adventurers as Kern, Talbot, Kit Carson, Maxwell, Owens, and Alexis Godey resented the acts of the insolent don; they would have voted heartily in favor of waiting near or in California to learn if war had not begun, and for taking an energetic hand in hostilities. *Kit Carson Days*, I, p. 442. A clear indication that Gillespie also urged him is found in Gillespie's statement to the Navy Department under date of July 8, 1848: ". . . But for my perilous journey into the mountains of Oregon, in pursuit of Col. Frémont to perform faithfully the duty entrusted to me by the Government, the early movements which frustrated British intrigue in California could not have been made." *California Historical Society Quarterly*, XVII, No. 4.

XVIII

The Bear Flag Outbreak

MEANWHILE, storm clouds were rapidly gathering over all the fair province of California.

While Frémont's party had been moving north from Sutter's Fort to Peter Lassen's and there marking time as its leader waited for news, Castro had been taking steps for the defense of the northern areas. Late in March he brought a junta of military men together at Monterey to discuss the situation and advise him as to the best policy. This body immediately recognized Paredes as the new President *ad interim* of the Mexican nation. It then on April 11th reached a series of decisions which had the effect of taking all practical power out of the hands of Governor Pio Pico at Los Angeles, and placing it in that of Don José Castro. These decisions were that the northern towns must be fortified and defended; that Castro's presence in charge of this work was indispensable; that Pico should be invited to Monterey to take part in the defensive activities, but that if he declined Castro should assume full powers with headquarters at Santa Clara; and that he should exercise these powers until the assistance promised by Mexico arrived. Pio Pico violently protested against all this, and the upshot was an embittered division between the two chiefs. When Pico appealed to General Vallejo at Sonoma for support, the latter took Castro's side. He declared that the danger of foreign invasion from the north was real and urgent, that immediate defensive steps were imperative, and that in an emergency Castro could not possibly consult a governor two hundred leagues away.[1]

[1] Hittell, *History of California*, II, p. 395ff.

But Pio Pico stood his ground, and took every measure within his power to oppose Castro. He deemed the acts of the Monterey junta illegal and treasonable, and equivalent to a virtual declaration of war by the north against the south. That danger of a foreign invasion existed he refused to believe. Castro's real intention, he suspected, was to raise troops on the pretext that Frémont was approaching, and then use them to overthrow the Los Angeles government. He and his friends resolved to fight fire with fire. They would recruit a military force ostensibly to resist American invasion, march north with it in response to Castro's invitation, and then fall upon that officer and remove him from command. They also summoned a general council to meet at Santa Barbara on June 15th, with delegates from both north and south, to determine upon measures "to avoid the fatal events impending at home and abroad." The real purposes of this council (which never sat) were a mystery. But many believed that an effort would be made to declare the independence of California from Mexico, while it was suspected that some leaders would go so far as to urge an English or French protectorate. This suspicion, as H. H. Bancroft tells us, was not without foundation; indeed, we now know that before the end of June, Governor Pio Pico formally applied to the British vice-consul in California for the protection of British naval forces "to stop the progress of the ambitions of the Americans." [2]

Thus as Frémont turned back toward San Francisco Bay, civil war was threatening between the northern and southern parts of the province, a movement for independence was developing fast, and certain groups were urging a European protectorate. Castro during May and June was ranging the northern country from Monterey to Sonoma to raise troops to meet invasion, and his efforts were creating the greatest alarm among the weak and undefended American settlers. Every one

---

[2] Bancroft, *History of California*, V, p. 47. For Pio Pico's application see Ernest A. Wiltsee, "The British Vice-Consul in California and the events of 1846," *California Historical Society Quarterly*, X (1931), p. 99ff.

knew that the Mexican Government could not protect California, that a revolution in its status was now certain, and that it would result either in a republic or in annexation to some foreign power. Every one who was aware of the intrigues in Monterey and Los Angeles feared that civil strife would accompany these changes. It was a gloomy, confused land toward which Frémont moved. As he threaded the thinly-wooded valley to the Buttes of the lower Sacramento, a position some sixty miles north of Sutter's Fort, well fitted to command the river and to threaten Sonoma, and as he and Gillespie talked with the first settlers they met, his purposes rapidly clarified. First, he was almost certain from his talks with Gillespie that the next few weeks would bring decisive news of war; second, whether he had secret instructions through Gillespie to do so or not, he felt it his duty to wait near the scene of war; third, he believed that in the meantime he must place himself where he could extend moral protection to the American settlers; and fourth, when and if war began he was resolved to play an active part in it. All this seems clear from his actions.

It is not difficult to follow the development of his purposes. On May 25th, the day after arriving at Lassen's Ranch, he sent post-haste to Captain Montgomery of the *Portsmouth* in San Francisco Bay for 8,000 percussion caps, 300 pounds of rifle-lead, and a keg of powder, as well as food, medicine, soap, and tobacco. His command, he wrote, was "at present almost destitute," and it was true that the northern march had stripped it of supplies; but he was thinking of more than provisions—he was plainly thinking of possible fighting. At Lassen's Ranch he also paused to write Benton a letter which, since it had to go home by sea from a California port and might be opened, was in most respects studiously non-committal. Much of it was devoted to affairs in Oregon. He called attention to the fact that the British had a fur-trading post on the Umpqua River, directly west of Klamath Lake, in the heart of the Klamath tribe. They had planted it, he believed, as an outpost in the event of war with the United States, so that Indians might be recruited there and supplied with firearms. These Indians were brave men, deadly shots, and much attached to the British. "If there is to be a war with England," urged Frémont, "it is of great importance that they [the English] should instantly be driven from this and similar posts. . . . These things may be worthy of Mr. Buchanan's attention." After expressing regret that he had heard nothing directly from Buchanan, he added: "I shall now proceed directly homewards, by the Colorado, but cannot arrive at the frontier until late in September." Gillespie sent a note by the same courier to Consul Larkin, describing his experiences, and making an excuse for Frémont's return southward: "There was too much snow upon the mountains to cross. He now goes home from here." [3] Actually, with summer at hand, the snow upon the mountains was a very thin pretext.

Frémont's real intentions became evident—and were confirmed—as soon as he arrived on May 30th among the American settlers who were scattered about and below the Buttes. He halted briefly here to rearm his party, collect provisions, and observe the situation. Kit Carson writes significantly in his autobiography that "camp was made to await positive orders in regard to the war, to hunt." Positive orders in regard to the war!—for Frémont now regarded his party rather as a military force than as an exploring expedition. As he states in his *Memoirs:* "I clearly saw that my proper course was to observe quietly the progress of affairs, and take advantage of any contingency which I could turn in favor of the United States, and, where uncertainties arose, to give my country the benefit of my doubts by taking decided action." As the correspondence of Captain Montgomery indicates, he canvassed plans for perhaps going as far southward as the Santa Barbara area, Pio Pico's seat, and having the *Portsmouth* proceed to that town. [4]

[3] Frémont, *Memoirs,* I, pp. 449, 500, 504, 505. Frémont's letter was dated May 24, 1846; he stated that he would probably reach Benton before the letter, subject to long sea delays, could do so.

[4] *Ibid.,* I, p. 508. Ernest A. Wiltsee, *ut supra,* gives Montgomery's letters with shrewd comment. On June 10th, Montgomery wrote Frémont that if, as a message brought by Gillespie indicated, he wished the *Portsmouth* to meet him at

For he was powerfully moved by what he heard from the settlers. His sudden reappearance within forbidden bounds naturally created a commotion among the American residents, many of whom rode forthwith into Frémont's camp. During 1845 a large number of new emigrants had arrived, so that the province now counted fully eight hundred Americans, nearly all able-bodied men. Some were legal landowners, but the greater number had simply squatted on the land, or picked up a living by a combination of work as ranch-hands with hunting and trapping. In general, they were a heterogeneous lot, alike only in being rugged and hard-hitting. The majority were farmers and ranchers of sterling character, good material for a new state. Mingled with them, however, were reckless sailors, ignorant and drifting backwoodsmen, and buckskin-clad trappers of erratic ways. With the Anglo-Saxon's instinctive feeling of superiority to other races, most of them looked condescendingly upon the gay, inefficient Californians, who loved gambling, guitars, and fandangos, and made so little use of the beautiful country. They felt that California ought to be in the hands of their own virile, energetic race, and that it was only a question of time and opportunity until they should take over its control. Some malcontents and adventurers who longed for a conflict with Mexico now saw opportunity in the crisis. But the peaceable majority were genuinely frightened by the drift of affairs.

These settlers brought Frémont a wild variety of rumors—that war between the United States and Mexico was about to begin; that Castro and others were plotting to separate California from Mexico, but were unwilling to place it under American protection; that the British were scheming to annex California forthwith. Most of them agreed upon one circumstantial report—that Castro and his merciless crew were planning to raise the Indians and fall upon all foreign settlers to scatter

Santa Barbara, the ship would be there. Why should a naval captain obey the hinted command of a Captain of the topographical corps if he did not have reason to believe that Washington desired close coöperation?

them to the winds. "On our road down the valley," wrote Gillespie to the Navy Department,[5]

we found that General Castro was fast hurrying the crisis, which time would soon have brought about. The Indians of the valley, formerly so peaceful, had become hostile and had deserted their *rancherias* or wigwams for the mountains, and killed some servants of the settlers, and had threatened the lives of many whites. Arriving within sixty miles of New Helvetia (Sutter's), we were informed that the Indians threatened to burn the wheat then advancing towards the harvest. . . . The Department can readily imagine the state of feeling among the people. It would have given pain to the hardest heart, to have witnessed the applications of the hardy settler and his wife, when begging aid and protection of Captain Frémont on his road down the valley; who, true to his position and the strict neutrality required by the delicate situation which he occupied under the existing state of affairs, could only give them advice, and begged them to wait a positive demonstration on the part of General Castro.

Samuel Hensley and Neal, with whom Frémont talked at length, agreed that American residents would either have to leave the country, or fight for the homes they had made.[6] The

[5] Ames, "Gillespie and the Conquest of California," *California Historical Society Quarterly*, XVII (1938), p. 271ff.

[6] In corroboration, see the William Hargrave MS, Bancroft Library. Hargrave, a Napa Valley settler, declared in 1878: "Disputes about land and personal property were the first causes of bad feeling, but the appearance of Frémont west of the Rocky Mountains and the dispatch of United States vessels of war to the Pacific Coast made the 'foreigners' bolder and the Californians suspicious. In 1845 the Mexican authorities at Monterey sent an officer of the government over all the settlements north of San Francisco Bay to count the foreigners able to bear arms, evidently for the purpose of making an estimate of the number of men to overcome in the event of hostilities. We all knew perfectly well the object of his mission. At the same time the Spaniards became very threatening, especially when reports reached the valley of a large force being organized to capture Frémont and his command or drive them from the country. When in the winter of 1845-46 it became known that Frémont was preparing to return to the States in spite of the near prospect of war between the United States and Mexico, many offers of assistance were made to Frémont, but the offers were generally refused pointblank. In the meantime the excitement increased on both sides and the feeling among the English and Americans became general that in bold and united action lay the only prospect of retaining a hold of the country and laying the foundation for future prosperity."

explorer and his men lent an attentive ear to the reports of an imminent and murderous attack on the settlers. Their own clash with Castro had prepared them to believe anything of Mexican treachery and aggression. It must have seemed imperative to Frémont that he keep himself at hand to help protect his countrymen.

Indeed, for some time both official threats against Americans and private outrages upon them had been numerous, and had been resented by quiet, substantial American residents as well as by the rougher immigrants. Only the previous October Captain Elliot Libbey, of the bark *Tasso*, had been set upon in the main street of San Francisco, stabbed, beaten, and left senseless—and nobody had been punished. American residents near San Francisco, together with ship-captains, merchants, and the American and British vice-consuls, had petitioned the commander of the *U.S.S. Levant* for the presence of a man-of-war in the Bay; for they believed the sub-prefect hostile to them, and declared that "the situation of all foreign residents at this place is extremely insecure and precarious." Farther inland, the settlers had long feared that hostile Californians would inflame the Indians against them. The previous year an attack by the Mexican authorities upon Sutter's Fort had been so imminent, in the opinion of various Americans, that the clerk Bidwell had ridden day and night to warn Sutter. Bidwell tells us that the "Californians were always talking of expelling Americans."

Most ominous of all, while Frémont was still proceeding northward into Oregon, Castro had made public his beforementioned proclamation of April 17th warning the Americans once more that they had no right whatever to hold land unless they became Mexican citizens. A copy was displayed at Sutter's Fort. In this paper he instructed all magistrates that they could not legally permit any sale or other transfer of realty to foreigners; while he gave brusque notice to Yankee squatters that not only would they forfeit any purchase they had made, but they would "be subject, unless they retire voluntarily from the country, to be expelled from it whenever the government may find it convenient." [7] Castro, who loved to strut and bluster, talked loudly of bringing armed forces to harry the gringos from the land; and it is no wonder that reports of his threats flew rapidly to the upper Sacramento. [8]

That there already existed a deep suspicion and a fast-mounting antagonism between the majority of the American settlers and the native Californians is unquestionable. Josiah Royce writes in his brief history of California as if Frémont's share in precipitating the so-called Bear Flag War had been the origin of that sullen hostility between the two peoples which was a painful though not very important sequel of the annexation of the province. Actually the tension between the races was already grave. While Americans looked upon most Californians as dissolute and treacherous idlers, while the Californians regarded most Americans as overbearing and brutal fellows intent only on gain, mutual understanding was difficult. Anglo-Saxon against Latin, Protestant against Catholic, strenuous pioneer against loiterer, they were sundered by instinctive antipathies. The part which Americans had played in various California revolts had excited animosity and distrust. Moreover, the native-born had resented the American annexation of Texas, and were well aware that the Spanish-speaking residents there had fared badly. While a small body of liberal and well-informed Californians really desired American rule, and some others were tempted by the rise in land-values which would follow annexation, the predominant Latin view was bitterly opposed to it. [9]

Frémont was impressed not only by Castro's threatening attitude, but by the reports that Mexican officials were trying

[7] For the effect of this proclamation, see Wm. F. Swasey MS, Bancroft Library, p. 8. Swasey also lays emphasis upon the belief of settlers that the meeting of California leaders at Monterey intended to place the country under the British flag. They "would undoubtedly have succeeded in carrying that project into effect," he writes, but for the influence of General Vallejo, who favored American sovereignty.

[8] Larkin Dispatches, State Department Archives, April 17, 1846.

[9] Compare Smith, *War with Mexico*, I, p. 327.

to incite the savages to an uprising. Settlers who came to his camp at Neal's post declared that the fact that the semi-civilized Indians on the ranches were leaving their work and taking to the mountains pointed to imminent hostilities. Sutter also sent Frémont word that he believed that an Indian on-slaught was being fomented by the wily Castro. On May 29th Gillespie left camp and rode forward to Yerba Buena:

> On reaching Sutter's Fort [he later wrote the Navy Department], I was informed that Castro was already organizing his force, had engaged the Indians to burn the wheat when dry and ready for the sickle, had given a musket to an Indian of some note to shoot Mr. Sutter, and was preparing every measure and making every effort to cut off the emigration, and to leave the wayworn traveller, as also the settlers, without one morsel of bread.

At this time or a little later he also heard that Castro had promised his "miserable soldiery the ravishing of the women, and the destruction of the children."

The Indian threat was not to be taken lightly. Between Lassen's Ranch and San Diego, California contained perhaps twenty thousand aborigines, of whom half had a smattering of civilization; but current reports exaggerated their numbers to forty thousand or more.[10] Both physically and mentally, this lazy, treacherous, and thievish race were greatly inferior to the best plains Indians, like the Sioux or Cheyenne; but when aroused and collected in numbers, they were a real menace. Frémont shared the almost universal frontier dislike of the savages, whom he regarded as untrustworthy, vindictive, and cruel. Once he had seen a party of immigrants after an Indian band had wreaked its worst upon it, the men mutilated and flayed alive, the women impaled on sharp stakes, and he had never forgotten the sight; like Theodore Roosevelt, he writes that some Indian cruelties were literally too horrible to be de-

---

[10] Walter Colton, *Three Years in California*, p. 19ff.; Revere, *A Tour of Duty in California*, Ch. 12; of course some of the Indians long exposed to the civilizing work of the missions were, as Helen Hunt Jackson's *Ramona* indicates, of fine character.

scribed. He still felt intense resentment over the murder of faithful Basil Lajeunesse. Telling the settlers that he would take precautions to protect them and their families, he kept a close surveillance over such Indians as he could, and made ready for active operations.

The Buttes of Sacramento, where Frémont camped at the end of May, constitute an isolated mountain ridge, a half-dozen miles in length, which runs up at the summit nearly two thousand seven hundred feet above the sea. He had chosen a point at the southeastern base with strong natural defenses and good water. As the days passed settlers brought him still more alarming reports. One rumor was that Castro was advancing against Frémont with two or three hundred armed men; another that Castro was planning to build a fort near the Bear River Pass to drive back the heavy concourse of American immigrants expected that summer.[11] In fact, Castro had been instructed the previous December by the Mexican Government to "redouble his precautions to avoid the introduction of these strangers." [12] But most disturbing of all were the more and more circumstantial reports of an impending Indian attack. The wheat throughout the valley was now like tinder, and Castro was said to be inciting the savages to set fire to it. This step would have been quite consonant with Mexican methods, and Hensley and Neal, still with Frémont, believed the story. So also did Sutter, farther down the river. He writes in his diary that he had rallied "most all of the men in my employ, for a campaign with the Mukelumney, which has been engaged by Castro and his officers to revolutionize all the Indians against me, to kill all the foreigners, burn their houses, and wheatfields." [13] Frémont decided that "the time for me too had come." He resolved to forestall the Indians and strike a blow which would thoroughly intimidate them. Thus he would insure the safety of the settlers, and at the same time protect his communications to the rear,

[11] Monterey *Californian,* August 29, 1846.
[12] Edward Channing, *History of the United States,* V, Ch. 17.
[13] Sutter, MS Diary, June 3, 1846.

making sure that if he moved south upon Monterey no formidable Indian force would be left behind him to cut off supplies and recruits from the American ranches.[14]

Sallying out at daybreak, Frémont and about fifty men rode rapidly down the west bank of the Sacramento. The dry season had turned the countryside brown; the wild oats were shaking sere in the wind, and the trees drooped dustily over the half-empty creeks. Along the river, where fish and acorns were plentiful, lay the largest Indian villages. No warning was given, and the savages were taken utterly by surprise. Riding into the first *rancheria* as the sun dispersed the river mist, Frémont's men raised a wild chorus of yells and opened fire, killing several Indians, and driving the rest, including several wounded, helter-skelter into the woods and the water. Then without delay the party hurried along the river to other villages, only to find that the news was traveling faster than themselves. The moment they came in sight of the rude wooden shelters, the smoking camp-fires, the assemblage of barking dogs and half-wild, flea-bitten ponies, they could see the Indians scurrying for shelter. Before sunset nearly all the villages had thus been emptied. As they rode down a hill toward the last one they could see the Indians in wild flight, and when they reached its huts the Sacramento was dotted with painted heads hastily making for the other shore. It was a "rude but necessary measure," says Frémont of the foray. No doubt he sincerely thought so, but in spite of the fact that his scouts reported many of the Indians in war paint and conducting war ceremonies, the necessity is doubtful.[15]

Meanwhile, the more impetuous American settlers had made up their minds to take rapid defensive measures against Castro and his Californians. They did not have Frémont's direct incitement, and the Bear Flag outbreak would doubtless have occurred without his presence; but they did have his indirect encouragement. This is the conclusion which must be drawn

[14] Frémont, *Memoirs*, I, p. 516.
[15] This is the judgment of Dellenbaugh; *Frémont and '49*, p. 330.

from a confusing and largely contradictory mass of evidence on the subject. Apparently to one settler he made one statement, and to another said something else—or they thought so; but on the whole he stimulated them to take active steps, while save for the Indian raid he kept his own party standing by as mere observers. He was still waiting on events, still gambling uneasily on that news of war which had not yet come. But the rougher frontiersmen did not wish to wait, and he was doubtless glad to see them act defensively.[16] One contemporaneous story states that he even suggested offensive operations to William B. Ide, a leading settler, but this seems improbable. The more trustworthy account is that which certain immigrant leaders gave to a correspondent of *Niles's Register,* saying that he wished them to act, although cautiously declining to do so himself: [17]

Information was received by Mr. William B. Ide, living on the Sacramento, on the eighth of June, by letter brought up by Indian runner, that 200 mounted Mexicans were on their march up the Sacramento River, with the design of destroying the crops, burning the houses, and driving off the cattle belonging to the foreigners. [This was a baseless rumor.] Mr. Ide immediately visited the settlements on the Sacramento, and finding most of the men of the valley with Capt. Frémont, repaired to his camp. He then conversed with Capt. Frémont on the subject of the revolution, who advised immediate organization and resistance on the part of the foreigners, but declined any action on his part, or that of the men under his command.

Many settlers had reached the conclusion that, no matter what Frémont did, the time had come for them to strike. William Hargrave, who had settled in the Napa Valley two years earlier, tells us that his American neighbors considered the outlook "very gloomy"; that they feared the Mexicans would try to eject them; and that "we foreigners were ready

[16] For evidence of the intensity of the settlers' resentment against the authorities, see B. F. Bonney, *Across the Plains by Prairie Schooner,* p. 12ff.

[17] Vol. 73, p. 110ff.; for the story of the suggestion to Ide, see Hittell, *History of California,* II, p. 419ff.

to fight for our new homes." We have a similar account by William F. Swasey, for a time Sutter's bookkeeper. The settlers had heard, he states, that a large number of native Californians had met at Monterey to discuss a plan for declaring the territory free and placing it under the protection of a foreign flag, and that a majority were in favor of a British protectorate. The arrival of the *Collingwood* made English annexation seem a distinct danger, and Swasey writes that a spontaneous American revolt was on the point of breaking out when Frémont returned. Hargrave tells us that he was one of a party of nine or ten men who went to Frémont's camp to seek assistance:

Kelsey acted as spokesman [he says], and I do not recollect the language used, but my impression was at the time that Frémont, though very cautious and evidently averse to precipitate action, was willing enough to resume active operations, but he preferred to see for himself in how far the settlers of Napa and Sonoma Valley were ready to shake off the Mexican yoke. At any rate, he peremptorily refused to take any responsibility for sudden action on our part and endeavored to delay or frustrate our efforts. Whether Frémont expressed himself differently when he spoke to Kelsey alone, later in the day, I cannot say.[18]

Frémont was playing a waiting game; and though in retrospect it seems neither very heroic nor very scrupulous, what else could he do? He knew that the settlers were almost ready to act, he gave them encouragement, and he bided his time. Hargrave writes of the settlers that they "made no secret of our intentions to keep up the agitation till the opportunity arrived for a bold stroke. On our return to the Napa Valley we found that the revolutionary movement had gained more ground, and steps were taken at once to organize a force sufficient for our first enterprise—the capture of Sonoma." He adds that a majority of the men north of San Francisco Bay did not feel friendly toward Frémont at the beginning of the Bear Flag War, but became cordial later. John Fowler corroborates Hargrave's account. He declares that the fear of Mexican

[18] Hargrave MS, pp. 3, 4; Swasey MS, pp. 8, 9; Bancroft Library.

attack was such that many settlers had been preparing to leave California for the States or for Oregon. Others wished to fight, and "I was in favor of acting at once, independent of Col. Frémont and without consulting him." Swasey says simply that "the Americans and foreigners generally were called together in Sacramento, Napa, and Sonoma Valleys for the purpose of resistance." [19] It would seem that Swasey, who was close to Larkin, thought he knew what were the confidential instructions which Gillespie had brought to Frémont. "Their substance was," he writes, "that the Colonel should be governed by circumstances, and, if a movement appeared among the Americans to bring about an annexation to the United States, or to defeat the designs of another government (the object of the *Collingwood* being well understood), he should identify himself therewith, keeping near to California to be prepared for such emergency." This testimony, while worth little as regards the supposed instructions, is worth a good deal as to what was in Frémont's mind.

Frémont's waiting tactics were obviously if unescapably the game of an opportunist, and irritated even contemporary observers. But we should note that although later writers have criticized him for being too aggressive and precipitate, the American settlers at the time criticized him for being hesitant and overcautious. "We left him," says Hargrave, "most of us somewhat disgusted with the result of our interview." While he waited, having some difficulty in holding his own men in restraint, the first blow was struck. It was a blow for which, despite his Fabian tactics, he must take partial responsibility.[20]

Early in June the fiery Castro had sent a Lieutenant Arcé to the north shore of San Francisco Bay to collect scattered horses bearing the government brand. This officer rounded up about one hundred and fifty animals, and was taking them southward by way of Sutter's Fort and the San Joaquin Valley. According to one account, the horses were to be used against

[19] John Fowler, MS Narrative, Bancroft Library; Swasey MS, p. 26.
[20] Royce, *California*, p. 59; compare *Congressional Globe*, August 9, 1856.

Governor Pio Pico at Los Angeles in the civil war now impending; according to boastful statements of Arcé himself, they were to be used against American settlers in the Sacramento Valley. Necessarily, the whole countryside knew of the movement: Arcé, in the bright Mexican uniform of blue, red, and silver effects, supervising a dozen men, with their serapes, high Mexican saddles, and lassoes, as they herded the mounts at a trot toward the fords of the Sacramento, the cavalcade raising a thick cloud of dust under the June sky. They reached Sutter's Fort, stayed overnight as Sutter's guests, and went south the next day to the Cosumnes River, sixteen or eighteen miles distant, where they camped for the night. Here they were surprised by a party of a dozen or more settlers under Ezekiel Merritt, who disarmed them, took away their horses, and insultingly told them to carry the news to Castro.[21] It was the first clear blow for American independence and control in California. Merritt was a tall, raw-boned frontiersman, fearless, simple, and fond of risks—a natural chieftain for the rougher immigrants. He regarded Frémont with enormous respect, and later Frémont called him his field lieutenant.

These two strokes, the raid against the Indians and the capture of Arcé's horses, raised in northern California the standard of Mars. No one in this remote Mexican province yet knew that a month earlier (May 12, 1846) Congress had declared war; that in the battles of Palo Alto and Resaca de la Palma, Taylor had driven the Mexicans across the Rio Grande. The acts of Frémont and Merritt produced a feeling of consternation among some peace-loving Americans and all friendly Californians. When Sutter heard that Arcé had been attacked by a group of settlers, he expressed astonishment and indignation.[22] But other Americans were immensely pleased. At last, they felt, California was about to be brought under the American flag. They saw in aggressive action their only defense from

[21] W. B. Ide, letter to Commodore Stockton; one story says twenty-five settlers.
[22] Sutter, *Diary;* Bidwell, *Century Magazine,* XIX, New Series, p. 519*ff.*

expulsion, their sole hope for a secure prosperity. Long afterward an observer asked an estimable pioneer who had four sons
under Frémont if he felt any compunction in attacking the
Californians. "He said he had Scripture example for it. The
Israelites took the promised land of the East by arms, and the
Americans must take the promised land of the West in the same
way." [23]

Frémont now saw that forces had been aroused which could
not easily be suppressed; that events had set in motion men of
headlong temper, and made it certain that the Mexican authorities would strike back. The result was his decision, still keeping in the background, to instigate an attack upon the little
military post of Sonoma, fifteen miles north of San Francisco
Bay.[24] Here were cannon, small arms, munitions, and horses,
which Frémont needed; here lived General Mariano G. Vallejo,
once military commandant of the province, who had supplied
the cavalcade of horses to Arcé, and who (though by no means
unfriendly to American annexation) had stood firmly behind
Castro in preparing to resist invasion. Vallejo, a man of high
principles, broad cultivation, and great wealth, stood almost
the equal of Sutter as a powerful baron of northern California.
He held vast estates of land, and huge herds of cattle, and at
one time had built up a large armed force to defend California
against the Russian menace from the north. At Sonoma, Castro
had been busily engaged in obtaining more war supplies. Frémont evidently believed that a quick stroke, with the raising
of the American flag, would do much to paralyze his activities,
and would once for all end the danger that English naval forces
might land in California. The explorer states that he sent Merritt, his field lieutenant, into the town "instructed to surprise"
it.[25] It is clear that he had planned all the steps beforehand,
and anticipated little or no resistance.

[23] Colton, *Three Years in California,* Ch. 10.
[24] Thomas S. Martin, MS Narrative, Bancroft Library, pp. 23, 24.
[25] *Memoirs,* I, p. 523. Compare the excellent series of articles by George Tays,
"Mariano Guadalupe Vallejo and Sonoma—A Biography and a History," *California Historical Society Quarterly,* XVI and XVII (1937-38).

The feat was quickly accomplished. Sonoma was an old mission establishment and military post, now a dull and shabby-looking place, infested by countless fleas. Its chief buildings—the mission, the barracks, the residences of Vallejo, his brother, and his brother-in-law, Jacob Leese, and a few others—looked upon a large plaza, disfigured after the careless California fashion by the skulls and skeletons of slaughtered beeves.[26] No soldiers were posted there. At break of day on June 14th some thirty-three or thirty-four armed settlers under Ezekiel Merritt rode into the unsuspecting hamlet, or as they grandiloquently called it, fortress, routed the astonished Californians out of bed, and took possession of the military equipment. This included nine brass cannon, two hundred and fifty muskets, and almost a hundredweight of powder. Vallejo, protesting, was taken with the rest to Frémont's camp on the American River, arriving late on the afternoon of the 15th. Here, while several of the prisoners sat on canvas bags filled with silver coins from Frémont's camp-chest, a council of war decided that they should be sent on to Sutter's Fort and imprisoned there.

They had not consulted the owner; and within the heavy adobe walls on this morning of June 16, 1846, occurred a dramatic clash between Frémont and Sutter. No one overheard it. But it seems certain that Sutter reproached Frémont for his harsh and arbitrary course, and that Frémont told him he had better support the uprising or keep his mouth shut. When the interview ended, Sutter came to Bidwell "greatly agitated, with tears in his eyes," and said that he had been informed that "if he did not like what he [Frémont] was doing, he would set him across the San Joaquin River, and he could go and join the Mexicans." [27] In other words, Frémont threatened to eject him (as a Mexican citizen and official, which he was) from the Fort, and take possession. The flurry over, the two men outwardly resumed their former attitude toward each

<hr>

26 Bryant, *What I Saw in California*, p. 333ff.
27 Bidwell, *Century Magazine*, XIX, New Series, p. 520.

other. Actually, the episode marked the end of Sutter's control over his own post.

Frémont, declaring that Sutter would be severely punished if the prisoners there escaped, placed his assistant Kern in charge of them, and thereafter in the explorer's absence Kern virtually commanded Sutter's Fort. In short, the Captain had executed a double stroke: he had taken not merely Sonoma, but also the stronghold of the redoubtable Swiss. Both the barons of Northern California were now under his control, and he possessed two good bases for controlling all northern California. His treatment of the dignified and high-minded Vallejo, always a good friend to the American settlers, was harsh— Vallejo's biographer terms it "a contemptible and inexcusable outrage"—but he doubtless thought it necessary.[28] As for Sutter, he was shortly asked by Commander Montgomery to enter the service of the United States, acting as Kern's adjutant; and he did so, becoming a lieutenant of dragoons at fifty dollars a month!

Events now moved rapidly. The settlers who had captured Sonoma held ideas of their own as to how a revolt should be conducted. Such figures as William B. Ide, a shrewd, fussy, dogmatic Jack-of-all-trades, who had wandered west from Vermont, successively a farmer, school-teacher, carpenter, and rancher, or Dr. Robert Semple, an unbelievably long and lanky Kentuckian, who was quick on the trigger and loved an illiterate kind of rhetoric, are more amusing than impressive. But they tried hard to be dignified, and their efforts to organize their little uprising with some care, to give it orderly forms, and to justify it to the world in the best Jeffersonian manner, have an appealing quality. Sonoma was held by the settlers as a combination of fort and headquarters, and the little garrison rapidly increased from fifteen or eighteen to forty men. On

---

[28] Bidwell, *California in 1841-48*, pp. 164-167; Revere, *Tour of Duty*, p. 74ff.; Tays, "Vallejo," *California Historical Society Quarterly*, XVII, p. 225. Poor Vallejo was kept prisoner until August 3rd, when by order of Commodore Stockton he was released. He had vainly tried to obtain an interview with Frémont.

the very first day, June 14th, 1846, the captors tried to redeem themselves from the charge of being a loose mob of marauders by declaring the "Republic of California." This scheme of an independent republic had been in the minds of Americans for years. One recruit, William L. Todd, a nephew of Mrs. Abraham Lincoln, took a piece of whitish brown cloth a yard and a half in length, and with either some paint or pokeberry juice (the accounts are conflicting) placed upon it a large star in the upper right-hand corner, and facing this at the top the figure of a grizzly bear. Native Californians gazing contemptuously at this design were heard later to call it "the shoat." Across the middle of the flag were painted the words, "California Republic." When it was hoisted on the empty Mexican staff, the Bear Flag Party and Bear Flag War had found an imperishable name. This standard was a symbol to which the settlers attached the utmost importance. It meant order. Only one unruly fellow dared to suggest that Sonoma be sacked, and "an unanimous indignant frown made him shrink from the presence of honest men." It meant liberty, for Dr. Semple was voluble in preaching the abstract principles of republicanism. It meant the eternal substitution of American rule for Mexican rule, as Ide formally asserted.[29]

A proclamation which Ide, with the consent of the garrison, had written in hot haste between the hours of one and four in the morning was published June 18th, 1846, setting forth the principles of the revolt. It guaranteed peace and security to all persons not found under arms. The purpose of the uprising, it stated, was to overthrow a selfish, incompetent government, which had confiscated property, and shamefully oppressed the people of California by its enormous exactions on imported goods.[30]

Frémont unquestionably looked upon all this with undiluted pleasure, for it suited his rather equivocal purposes precisely.

[29] Bidwell, *Century Magazine*, XIX, New Series, p. 521*ff.*; Bryant, *op. cit.*, p. 289.

[30] Monterey *Californian*, August 22, 1846.

He heard within a few days from Commander Montgomery of the *Portsmouth* at Sausalito, who was equally delighted; a "master stroke," said Montgomery, but it should have been "followed up by a rush upon Santa Clara, where Castro might have been taken by thirty men." [31] Montgomery, like Frémont, was playing a double part. At the very time that he sent these hearty congratulations he was informing a messenger from Vallejo that neither the United States nor himself nor Frémont had any connection with the attack, and that he greatly sympathized with the Californian! For their part, the Bear Flag leaders were now eager to draw Frémont from his nominal neutrality. The shrewd William Ide in especial thought that the explorer was playing somewhat too Machiavellian a game. His scheme, as Ide said, was to keep in the background and avoid military action as an American officer, but at the same time to egg on the American settlers in steps which would provoke Castro to some punitive measure, when Frémont could openly take a hand. The Captain could thereupon allege that his interference had been necessary to save the Americans from brutal maltreatment, and that the revolt had advertised to the world the settlers' eagerness to be rescued from Mexican tyranny. Ide disliked this plan of "neutral conquest" as timid, selfish, and unnecessary. He believed that Frémont should cut boldly through the mesh of Mexican bluster and threats, and should have used Castro's proclamation against the American squatters as a signal for war.

Both the acts and entreaties of the Bear Flag fighters were now designed to draw Frémont into the open, and within a few days they succeeded. They were, of course, aided by events in other spheres. As early as June 7th Commodore Sloat at Mazatlan had become convinced by information from the interior that war was under way on the Rio Grande, and had sailed northward to seize the port of Monterey. He feared that the British admiral Sir George Seymour, now lying at San Blas with the powerful frigate *Collingwood* of eighty guns, might

[31] Frémont, *Memoirs*, I, p. 334.

intervene and forestall American seizure by proclaiming a British protectorate; that is, he held precisely the apprehension that Frémont later confessed was one of his own governing motives. (The historian Hittell tells us that "as a matter of fact the British vice-consul had for a length of time been endeavoring to bring about British intervention.") Sloat did not reach Monterey until July 2nd, and even then hesitated. But meanwhile the same reports of hostilities which had sent him northward must have been leaking by other channels into California. On June 16th, Frémont, still uncertain but more and more convinced that news of war would soon come, wrote Montgomery in curiously equivocal terms. He began cautiously. It was his intention "to abandon the further prosecution of our exploration and proceed immediately across the mountainous country . . . to the eastward and thence to the frontier of Missouri." He added that the nature of his instructions and operations "do not contemplate any active hostility on my part in the event of war between the two countries; and therefore, although I am resolved to take such active and precautionary measures as I shall judge necessary for our safety, I am not authorized to ask from you any other than such assistance as, without incurring yourself unusual responsibility, you would feel at liberty to afford me." But he closed on a firmer note. The most significant part of his letter declared that he meant to stay where he was until about July 1st, and contemplated possible fighting: [32]

In the meantime, should anything be attempted against me, I cannot, consistently with my own feelings and respect for the national character of the duty in which I am engaged, permit a repetition of the recent insults we have received from General Castro. . . . Between Indians on the one hand and a hostile people on the other, I trust that our government will not severely censure any efforts to which we may be driven in defence of our lives and character. In this condition of things I can only then urgently request that you

[32] Josiah Royce, "Montgomery and Frémont," *Century Magazine*, XIX, New Series.

will remain with the *Portsmouth* in the Bay of San Francisco, where your presence will operate strongly to check proceedings against us; and I would feel much more security in my position should you judge it advisable to keep open a communication with me by means of your boats. In this way you would receive the earliest information, and you might possibly spare us the aid of one of your surgeons in case of accident here.

The raising of the Bear Flag, the circulation of Ide's proclamation of the republic, and the news of the occupation of Sonoma aroused the immediate anger of the Mexican officials. Castro replied with a rhetorical proclamation on June 17th, denouncing the Bear Flag "adventurers." He had no forces beyond San Francisco Bay, but he promptly collected what troops he could farther south, and despatched them under an officer named Joaquin de la Torre to the relief of Sonoma. Their approach became known on June 23rd; the Bear Flag forces sent couriers to ask Frémont's help, and marched out under Lieutenant Ford to repulse the Californians. The result was a brisk engagement about a dozen miles from San Rafael, in which the Bear Flag men killed two Californians, wounded several more, and put the whole body to helter-skelter flight. While this happened, Frémont was casting off all disguise and taking the field, glad to be called to arms. He made up his mind that the crisis had arrived, and that it was "unsafe to leave events to mature under unfriendly, or mistaken, direction." [33]

Frémont and his rescue party reached Sonoma on June 25, 1846, and with an augmented force of one hundred and sixty men at once took up the pursuit of de la Torre's retreating troops. He was at last acting with genuine resolution. He believed that his open entry into the struggle would prevent the Bear Flag settlers from being ultimately crushed by the stronger forces of Castro, and would deter any British agents from proclaiming a protectorate of California. If war had begun between the United States and Mexico, all would be well. Or

[33] *Memoirs,* I, p. 520.

the other hand, if peace were maintained between the two nations he would take his punishment with a good face. Part of that punishment would certainly be dismissal from the service in disgrace, and Frémont took steps to anticipate this by drafting his resignation and laying it aside in an envelop to be sent to Senator Benton, who could transmit it to the War Department at his discretion.

It was only by good luck and an adroit ruse that de la Torre's crippled force escaped south of San Francisco Bay to a point of safety. The Californians had better horses than the Americans. De la Torre, having thus gained the head start, put a false message into the hands of an Indian, announcing an imminent attack upon Sonoma by Castro himself; and when the Indian was captured, Frémont hastily turned back from his pursuit to protect the threatened town. De la Torre was then fortunate enough to find a large boat at Sausalito on the north shore of the Bay, and made his way across. The chagrin of the Americans at failing to crush their antagonists was extreme. They had as yet lost no men in open battle, but when Lieutenant Ford was marching to repulse de la Torre near San Rafael on the Bay, the settlers had come upon the bodies of two American immigrants, Tom Cowan, or Cowie, and a man named Fowler, murdered by the roadside. It was later asserted that they had been tortured to death, and that their disemboweled and mutilated corpses presented a shocking spectacle. Gillespie sent gory details to the Navy Department. Since Cowan had been widely known and greatly liked, the episode excited a desire for vengeance. A little later (June 28th), when the Americans held possession of San Rafael, three Californians were landed from a boat under the very eyes of Frémont's party on the shore of Point San Pedro. Frémont ordered Carson to take two men and cut them off. Carson, after coming back for further instructions, then galloped down to the shore and with his companions halted and shot the strangers, one of whom was an old man. This at least seems the most probable version of what occurred, for many conflicting stories have been told. Frémont later wrote that the men were killed by "my scouts, mainly Delawares" in retaliation for the murder of Fowler and Cowan; Alexis Godey declared they had been shot by Carson, then on patrol duty, when they resisted; John Fowler declared that Carson and a companion were drunk and so shot them; James O'Farrell, an Irish resident of San Rafael, who apparently did not see the affair, later deposed (in the heat of the Presidential campaign of 1856) that Frémont ordered no quarter given the men; William Swasey writes that Carson alone was responsible and "the firing was perfectly justifiable under the circumstances." [34] Justifiable this cold-blooded murder certainly was not; but the question of the responsibility is one that cannot now be decided with any certainty. The weight of evidence is stronger against Carson, who repeatedly showed himself heedless of human life, than against Frémont, who was always most careful of it.

Meanwhile Frémont, after finding Sonoma perfectly safe, had followed de la Torre's cold trail to Sausalito. Here he made camp, and we have a good picture of him as the Yankee skipper of the trading-ship *Moscow* found him at rest: [35]

As yet I had not seen the captain, but my imagination had pictured him out somehow as I thought he ought to look. Of course a knowledge of his exploits and renown led me to suppose that I should see a full-whiskered military-looking man, towering in size above all his command, stiff with uniforms and straps, looking blood,

[34] Swasey writes that the men were killed trying to escape. "The order to fire upon them was given by Kit Carson, and although Frémont has been frequently accused of having given the said order, he was not personally present at the time." MS Narrative, Bancroft Library, p. 10. Godey's narrative exculpating Frémont is in the New York *Evening Post*, October 30, 1856. Two of the men killed were twin sons, nineteen years old, of Francisco de Haro, after whom a street in San Francisco is named.

[35] Narrative of William D. Phelps, New York *Tribune*, August 14, 1856. Phelps in 1871 under the pseudonym "Webfoot" published *Fore and Aft, or Leaves from the Life of an Old Sailor*. For his services to Frémont, Captain Phelps later tried (with Frémont's endorsement) to collect $10,000 from the United States Government; but when Gillespie certified that $50 would be ample, received that sum! *California Historical Society Quarterly*, XV (1936), pp. 62, 63.

bullets, and grizzly bears. But I saw nothing of the kind. After a survey of the different groups about the camp, I could discover no one that bore resemblance to my picture, and going up to a tall, lank-looking specimen of a Kentuckian, dressed in a greasy deerskin shirt and trousers to match, and a coonskin cap on his head, with the tail in front, I asked if the captain was in the camp. The individual (the long doctor) replied in the affirmative, and pointed out to me as Capt. Frémont a slender and well-proportioned man, of sedate but pleasing countenance, sitting in front of a tent. His dress, as near as I remember, was a blue flannel shirt, after the naval style, open at the collar, which was turned over; over this a deerskin hunting shirt, figured and trimmed in hunter's style, blue cloth pantaloons and neat moccasins, all of which had very evidently seen hard service. His head was not cumbered by hat or cap of any shape, but a light cotton handkerchief, bound tightly round his head, surmounted a suit which might not appear very fashionable at the White House or be presentable at the Queen's levee; but to my eye it was an admirable rig to scud under or fight in.

A few minutes' conversation convinced me that I stood in the presence of the King of the Rocky Mountains. He said "his operations were against the military force of the country; that his government had been outrageously insulted in his person, and he would compel from Castro a public apology or hunt him from the country." Capt. Frémont now determined on spiking and disabling the guns of the fort on the opposite side of the passage, as this place, if garrisoned by the enemy, would much obstruct the passage of ships and consequently endanger the safety of supplies which might arrive by sea.

Frémont's designs, with the whole area north and west of San Francisco in his hands, were by this time of a most ambitious character. He meant to rally the settlers into an army sufficient to defeat Castro and capture Monterey and Santa Barbara. Arcé's horses and those at Sonoma had given him an adequate supply of mounts; at Sonoma he had taken guns and munitions which supplemented the powder, lead, and caps sent him by Captain Montgomery of the *Portsmouth*. Now on

July 2nd, crossing San Francisco Bay to Fort Point, he seized
the little fort of El Castillo de San Joaquin there, ruinous and
quite ungarrisoned, spiked its ten old Spanish brass guns, and
captured some additional supplies. The spiking party consisted,
besides Frémont, of Kit Carson, Gillespie, and Captain Phelps
of the *Moscow,* with some of Frémont's and Phelps's men.
Amid all his anxieties, the explorer's poetic vein prompted
him to bestow upon the entrance of San Francisco Bay the
name of the Golden Gate, an appellation that has become im-
mortal. Settlers were flocking in to reinforce the American
camps at both Sutter's Fort and Sonoma in steadily increasing
numbers. Reports of the successes of Frémont, Merritt, and
Ide, of the brutal murder of Cowan and Fowler, and of the
proclamation of a California republic, had aroused much excitement and enthusiasm. Native Californians of the region,
threatened with severe punishment if they took up arms, were
making haste to declare their peaceful intentions. The road
was open for a triumphant march southward.[36]

From these new designs of Frémont was born the California Battalion, the little army which he was to use in his "conquest." On July 4, 1846, he was back again in Sonoma, and participated in a celebration which included much firing of salutes,
speeches, and a ball. During that day and the next, the settlers
were organized with Frémont's men into the Battalion, comprising four companies of 234 men in all, grim and formidable-
looking soldiers. Frémont took over the command from Ide,
and calling the men before him, made a brief address, dwell-
ing on their joint responsibilities, enjoining them to do nothing
to discredit their cause, and promising energetic action until
Castro was subdued. Ide replied in behalf of the settlers. At
once a firm discipline was given to the force, Frémont bringing
it under rigid control and requiring long hours of drill. Simultaneously, he sent out foraging parties which requisitioned

---

[36] Compare the letter of one Grigsby, Sen. Exec. Doc. No. 1, 29th Cong., 2d.
Sess., p. 665.

horses and drove in cattle to be butchered for food.[37] For the nonce, this looked a good deal like robbery to the Californians, but the government later paid them and reimbursed Sutter for the use of his Fort.

The California Battalion, a motley array of voyageurs, trappers, scouts, former sailors, frontier farmers, and ranchmen, was a body unlike any other that has ever fought on American soil, and yet with close affinities to our pioneer fighters in all generations. Miles Standish, Robert Rogers, Daniel Boone, and Davy Crockett would have recognized the breed at once. Most of the men wore broad-brimmed hats pulled low over the eyes, shirts of buckskin or blue flannel, and buckskin trousers and moccasins, all much the worse for wear and smeared with dirt, blood, and gunpowder. From a leather girdle about every man's waist hung an ugly-looking bowie or hunter's knife, and sometimes a brace of pistols. Most of the recruits were bearded and long-haired; all were sunburnt and fierce of visage. A single sorry-looking bugle sounded the calls. One member of Frémont's original force, a tall, manly Illinoisan named Risdon Moore (whom Frémont likened to one of Cromwell's men), had hung back, feeling that these military operations against the peaceful Californians were unjustifiable; but Frémont had quickly converted him by clapping him overnight in a hot, ill-ventilated dungeon of Sutter's Fort, swarming with fleas. The others were athirst for the fray. Gillespie, who had continued a close adviser of Frémont, was made a major of the Battalion, and the roster of members who then or a little later received officers' commissions—Owens, Ford, Swift, Sears, Grigsby, Hastings, Thompson, Jacobs, McLean, Hensley, Gibson—showed the predominance of the old Anglo-Saxon stock.

At this moment, with the advance about to begin, came news which Frémont must have received with a sigh of relief; news that war between the United States and Mexico had opened, and

---

[37] Frémont, *Memoirs*, I, p. 526; *Congressional Globe*, August 9, 1856; Fort Sutter Papers, Huntington Library, Vol. V; *Niles's Register*.

that powerful American warships were in California waters.
His gamble had succeeded; his position was now regularized.
Commodore Sloat of the Pacific squadron, anchored at Mazatlan, had received information on May 31st of the battles of
Palo Alto and Resaca de la Palma. With inexcusable timidity,
he had refused to act, though he held explicit instructions from
Washington that the moment he received certain news of war
he was to occupy San Francisco and such other California ports
as he could reach. Sailing north after more than a week's delay,
on July 2nd he was in Monterey, with the town under his guns.
Here he again hesitated, and in fact even made the usual call
of courtesy on the authorities.[38] But learning of Frémont's
operations, and still fearful that Sir George Seymour of the
British fleet on the coast might raise the British flag, he took
his preposterously belated action. On July 7th, he demanded the
surrender of the town, and landed two hundred and fifty sailors
and marines to hoist the American colors. He also sent orders to
the *Portsmouth* in San Francisco Bay to seize Yerba Buena or
San Francisco, and on July 9th despatched a courier to Frémont informing him of all that had occurred.

The Bear Flag War was now over, and the Mexican-American
conflict in California had taken its place. Frémont, receiving
from Montgomery on the evening of July 10th the news that
Sloat's flag was flying over Monterey, spent a few days preparing his force and making certain that the Sacramento Valley was secure, and then set out from Sutter's Fort with one
hundred and sixty picked men for that town. He could now
feel that events had justified him. He had played his cards one
after the other in the firm belief, shared by Gillespie, that the
renewed rupture of American and Mexican relations was a prelude to certain war. He had so played his hand that when the
vacillating Sloat came upon the scene all California beyond San
Francisco Bay was in American hands and a large and well-
equipped land force was ready to coöperate with the navy.

[38] Smith, *War with Mexico*, I, p. 334.

His course had been illegal, and to the last degree opportunistic, but it had succeeded.

Yet had Frémont foreseen how harshly a group of historians would later criticize his course in turning back from his explorations, helping foment the Bear Flag uprising, and finally assuming its open leadership, he would have been far less complacent than he doubtless felt when Commodore Stockton congratulated him in Monterey harbor. This criticism has been stated by such writers as H. H. Bancroft, Josiah Royce, and Theodore H. Hittell in terms varying from mild severity to extreme condemnation. Frémont is accused of acting without specific authority and, of course, that charge is true. He was six months' travel by a dangerous and difficult route from Washington; through Gillespie he had received news and letters which made him feel it was his duty to assume a certain independent responsibility. He did just what a long line of officers of the English-speaking race have always done in emergencies. The British Empire owes half its territory to subalterns, generals, ship-captains, and merchants who have acted without authority and been applauded later. Andrew Jackson had no authority in 1818 to invade the Spanish territory of Florida and seize Pensacola, but he did it. Commodore T. A. C. Jones had had no authority in 1842 for the occupation of Monterey, but he occupied it. Frémont doubtless believed that an officer who will not go beyond out-of-date and insufficient orders in an emergency, who will not use his own discretion, is not worth his salt. Admiral Sloat was just such an officer, and the Administration in Washington regarded Sloat's timidity and vacillation on the Pacific Coast as a national misfortune, making that fact quite clear to everybody.

Frémont has been accused, again, of taking action which, orders or no orders, was not justified by the facts of the California situation, or his knowledge of the general wishes of the Federal Government. But to this he could have answered that the position of the American settlers in the Sacramento Valley, as he found it on his return to that region, warranted him in the "precautionary" measures of which he wrote to Montgomery on June 16th. And so far as it went, this would have been a good answer. It is useless to deny that the fear of an Indian attack was general; Sutter himself feared it. It cannot be denied, moreover, that Castro was acting in a way which filled the American settlers with apprehension for their property and personal safety—his own orders and proclamations prove that —or that Frémont had some reason for fearing a sudden British proclamation of some form of protectorate. Royce is especially caustic in his treatment of the panic of the Bear Flag leaders regarding Castro. But of this one of the ablest historians of the period, Justin H. Smith, with much fuller and more recent knowledge than Royce, has written: [39]

First, many of the settlers had ample reasons to feel alarmed: the illegality of their presence; Castro's sudden and cruel seizure of Americans in 1840; his attack upon Frémont in violation (the Americans believed) of a promise; official notices, issued about May 1, to the effect that a majority of the Americans were liable to be expelled at the convenience of the authorities; Castro's warlike preparations; his talk of moving against the immigrants with armed forces; and reports, more or less authentic, and reliable, from various persons regarding what he said, or intended. Secondly, the contemporary testimony of Frémont, Gillespie, and other Americans —some of it given under oath—that alarm was actually felt is too strong to be rejected. Much has been made [by Royce] of Bidwell, a clerk of Sutter's, who tells us that alarm was not felt. But (1) his statement was made thirty years after the events; (2) he admits that he was not on good terms with Frémont, and his statement aims to show that Frémont invented the story of alarm as an excuse for his conduct; (3) his statement is in other respects clearly inaccurate; (4) it assumes that he knew the sentiment of all the persons on the Sacramento, yet proves that an important fact may have been known to but few; (5) it shows that at the critical time he was absent in the mountains; (6) it says, "Californians were always talking of expelling Americans," and therefore were talking of it in April, 1846; (7) his book mentions that in 1845 an attack

[39] *Ibid.*, I, p. 529.

upon New Helvetia was so confidently expected that he rode night and day to warn Sutter....

Almost equally violent is Royce's attack upon the "legend" that the British had designs upon California; but the point is not that this legend was exaggerated, as it was, but that all kinds of Americans in responsible posts—Polk, Buchanan, Bancroft, Benton, and others—believed it, and that California settlers believed it. This being so, Frémont may be excused for believing it. The apprehension that England would forestall us was dwelt upon in the Senate early in 1846; it was widely voiced by the American press. "The expansive course of Great Britain," says the historian just quoted, "remarks dropped by English writers, repeated warnings dropped from our diplomatic and consular agents at Mexico, and the consensus of opinion in California, Mexico, France, and the United States were quite enough to warrant suspicions of England." [40] Sloat, Stockton, and Larkin all feared Rear Admiral Sir George Seymour's intentions. British policy during the last century has usually been extremely considerate of American susceptibilities, and it was really so in this instance. But under all the circumstances Sloat and Frémont had some reason to fear that the strong British naval force on the Pacific Coast might be used to proclaim a protectorate, or at least to gain a diplomatic foothold there for use in the Oregon controversy. Sloat swung northward in that belief, Frémont swung southward. They believed that they had to guard against a contingency. Had such a contingency actually existed, Frémont's activities along the coast, and his return at a critical juncture from the north, might well have accentuated the feeling of the British officers that the United States was determined to obtain California,

[40] *Ibid.*, I, p. 324; compare T. G. Cary, *Conquest of Alta California* (MS; Boston Athenaeum); London *Times*, September 28, 1846. Governor Pio Pico wrote the British vice-consul, J. A. Forbes, on June 29, 1846: "The undersigned is satisfied that Great Britain, being an ally of the Republic of Mexico, and both nations having great consideration for each other, will doubtless give her protection." *California Historical Society Quarterly*, X (1931), p. 114.

and that it would be impossible to act without coming into sharp collision with American aims and agents.

Above all, Frémont has been assailed as a mischief-maker who spilt innocent blood, aroused a resentment among the native Californians which quadrupled the difficulties of the subsequent American occupation, and laid the foundations for a lasting animosity between these Californians and the Americans. Unquestionably he acted in flat violation of the instructions to Larkin, as relayed to him. If he had not so acted, it is barely conceivable that a quiet, peaceable annexation of California might have occurred. But it must be remembered that the Bear Flag uprising did not cost a dozen lives all told. A more nearly bloodless conquest or revolution it would be hard to find. The probabilities are that, in view of the outbreak of the Mexican War, and in view also of Castro's vigorous defensive efforts, an armed clash was inevitable, and that northern California could not have been secured with a shorter casualty list. As for the ill-feeling aroused by the Bear Flag uprising, much of it appears quickly to have evaporated. The American settlers, after Frémont took full control, bore themselves for the most part in an exemplary manner. There were no outrages, no depredations, and few aberrations from the rule of strict obedience and orderliness; Alexis Godey tells us, truthfully,[41] that Frémont's operations "were eminently characterized by a regard for the rights and interest of the inhabitants of the country through which his forces marched, which secured to him the kindest feelings of regard and respect of the entire California population." It is true that there was a sudden angry flare-up of the Californians against the Americans after Sloat raised his flag, and much semi-guerrilla warfare. But where did it occur? Not in northern California where Frémont had acted, but in southern California. What little permanent ill-feeling the events of 1846 left was largely inevitable. Any historian who supposes that two races so alien in blood, religion, habits, temper, and aims as the Americans and the

[41] New York *Evening Post*, October 30, 1846.

Mexican-Californians could have reversed the positions of governed and governing without sharp friction is somewhat naïve.

At bottom, what seems most irritating in Frémont's course is its lack of candor and directness, its consistent opportunism, and its frequent descent into what can only be termed equivocation. He headed an exploring expedition which he also made a military expedition; he lingered in California under pretense of refitting his men and searching for an estate when his real purpose was otherwise; he turned back into California under still other pretexts quite divorced from his true aim; he spoke in two voices to the California leaders, to the settlers, to Montgomery, and even to Benton; he turned two faces to the world. He seemed to lack straightforwardness and rugged strength of character, and bore himself with less resolution and direct honesty than befitted an American leader in such a situation. Andrew Jackson in West Florida had behaved even more lawlessly than Frémont in California, and in his treatment of Ambrister and Arbuthnot came close to the line of murder; but he was never inconstant or evasive. His conduct was marked by a firmness and grim strength that do not appear in Frémont's. And yet it must be said that Frémont's position was difficult. A certain duplicity was stamped upon the expedition from the outset, for the government, or at least Secretary Bancroft, Senator Benton, and others had anticipated that it might serve two purposes. Moreover, the murky atmosphere in which he moved during May and June, knowing little, suspecting much, fearing and hoping more, made it difficult to act with firm candor. After all, the important object in studying these events of 1846 is not to condemn or commend but to understand. Frémont's motives were patriotic. His temperament being so adventurous; his understanding of the ambitions of Bancroft and Benton being so clear; the situation in California offering so many hazards; the fact that Gillespie traveled six hundred miles into the wilderness beyond Monterey to find him being so remarkable; Gillespie's story of the rapid drift of Mexico to war chiming so precisely with Frémont's own expectations; the pleas of the settlers for protection being so fervent—when we realize all this, we can understand why he acted as he did. No "secret instructions" are necessary to explain it.

He meant to be useful to his government and compatriots, and beyond doubt he was. Of course, it is impossible to-day to believe that he decisively affected the course of events on the Pacific. California would have fallen under American sovereignty almost as easily, though not as soon, as it did, had he turned back on the Oregon Trail to Missouri in the spring of 1846. But his exploits nevertheless laid the basis of a popular legend that was to carry him far—in 1856, even within sight of the Presidency.

XIX

The California Battalion

O N July 19, 1846, the approach of Frémont's California
Battalion to Monterey was heralded by a heavy cloud
of dust under a burning sun, from which emerged the
men in a long and wild-looking file. Frémont rode first, a thin,
wiry, energetic young man, with flowing hair, a bearded sun-
bronzed face, and eyes that seemed to burn with a consuming
fire—"such an eye!" wrote a British naval officer. He was
dressed much as the Yankee skipper had seen him at Sausalito,
in buckskin trousers, blouse, and moccasins, a blue shirt thrown
open at the neck, and a felt hat on his head. Behind him
came five swarthy Delaware Indians who served as his bodyguard. After them, on sturdy ponies, rode the men, two and
two, their long, heavy Hawkins rifles thrown across their
saddle-pommels. With heavy knives slung at their hips, with
the sun glinting on their polished rifles and revolvers, and with
their gaunt, steel-muscled, determined look, they seemed a
force which few would care to meet. Many were even blacker
than the Indians, and their long untrimmed hair, the heavy
dark beards through which their white teeth gleamed, gave
them a savage aspect. The women stared timidly but admir-
ingly at them through the grated windows. They camped that
night just outside the town, among the firs and pines near the
sea, and their watch-fires threw a quivering light into the forest
glades and far along the waves.[1]

Frémont, as usual, had an eye to the beauty of his camp.[2]

[1] See descriptions in Walter Colton, *Deck and Port;* Lieutenant Fred Wal-
pole, R.N., *Four Years in the Pacific in Her Majesty's Ship Collingwood* (2
vols.).

[2] Frémont, *Memoirs,* I, p. 534.

"Before us, to the right, was the town of Monterey, with its red-tiled roofs and large gardens enclosed by high adobe walls, capped with red tiles; to the left the view was over the ships in the bay and on over the ocean, where the July sun made the sea-breeze and the shade of the pine trees grateful." In the harbor still rode not merely Sloat's flagship the *Savannah,* but for a brief time the powerful eighty-gun flagship *Collingwood* of the British admiral, Sir George Seymour. According to Sloat's purser, an able, careful young man named Rodman M. Price, later governor of New Jersey, who had fumed angrily at his chief's indecision and delays, Seymour had said when he arrived three days earlier: "Sloat, if your flag was not flying on shore, I should have hoisted mine there." Down at Santa Barbara, as Price later recalled, was the English frigate *Juno.*[3]

When Frémont went aboard the *Savannah* to call on Sloat, he found an aged, sallow, nervous little man, not at all certain of himself and much concerned over the legality of everything done in California. Secretary Bancroft was shortly to write him, very truly, that "your anxiety not to do wrong has led you into a most unfortunate and unwarranted inactivity." He timidly asked Frémont under what authority, what instructions, he had taken up arms against the Mexican officials in California? "I informed him," Frémont tells us, "that I had acted solely on my own responsibility, and without any expressed authority from the government to justify hostilities." The wavering, overcautious little Commodore was evidently shocked and puzzled. He had hoped to learn that Frémont had received orders through Gillespie that would serve to justify his own action in taking Monterey and Yerba Buena. Indeed, he remarked that Frémont's operations in the Sacramento Valley had been one reason for his decision to occupy the coast. Now he was left in an unhappy frame of mind, uncertain that he had not gone too far. He made it clear that he disapproved

---

[3] See Price's long statement in Frémont, *Memoirs,* I, pp. 539-542. Price, whose later career showed him a man of judgment and insight, believed that Sloat's timidity had almost lost California to the British, as Frémont's decision had helped to save it; another bit of evidence on American psychology of the time.

of Frémont; made it clear also that he would sit tight and undertake no aggressive plan of action. Frémont, who had looked forward to a campaign against Castro and the capture of Santa Barbara and Los Angeles, returned to shore somewhat discouraged.[4]

American history was being made rapidly in those days. Zachary Taylor, having driven the Mexicans across the Rio Grande, was advancing from Matamoras into the northern part of the Republic. General Kearny was concentrating an army at Bent's Fort to invade New Mexico and California. On June 15, 1846, Secretary Buchanan and the British minister had signed at Washington the treaty partitioning Oregon at the forty-ninth parallel, and thus adding to our country the territory of three states, Oregon, Washington, and Idaho. The great Mormon invasion of the West, sixteen thousand strong, had crossed the Mississippi, and its advance guard, using Frémont's early reports as guide, was at Council Bluffs on the Missouri preparing for the passage of the plains. A new and greater flood of emigration was embarking on the California and Oregon Trail. Among the California trains was the company of J. T. Reed and the Donners, destined the ensuing winter to be caught in the Sierras by heavy blizzards, and to furnish the Far West with one of its most horrible tragedies; among them was also Edwin Bryant, who was to become alcalde of San Francisco and to write a book from which we have already quoted. In New England, the war was unpopular; in the West, it had been received with enthusiasm, fifty thousand volunteers had flocked to the colors, and U. S. Grant and Robert E. Lee were about to win their first laurels. Every-

---

[4] When Sloat left Mazatlan for Monterey on June 8th he had received word by an express from Mexico City that the battles of Resaca de la Palma and Palo Alto had been fought. He nevertheless wrote the Secretary of the Navy on June 6th that since he had not been apprised of a formal declaration of war, he would take no aggressive action in California! He added that he found it humiliating to refrain from action "while it appears to the world that we are actually at war on the other coast." Many of his officers naturally felt outraged by his course. Bancroft's sharp letter of rebuke, dated August 13, 1846, is printed in Frémont's *Memoirs*, I, p. 537.

where, east and west alike, the country's eyes were fixed upon
Taylor and the Rio Grande, upon the Santa Fé objective of
Kearny, and upon far-off California.

Commodore Sloat, worried lest he had exceeded his authority
in belatedly seizing Monterey, and perplexed over the problem of carrying out his orders to conciliate the Californians
when the Bear Flag men and Frémont were already in arms
against them, soon found an escape. He sailed away from the
coast in the ship *Levant,* leaving the command of the *Congress*
and *Cyane* to his ambitious, smart, and headstrong second,
Commodore R. F. Stockton; commissioning him to use these
warships "to restore peace and good order to this territory,"
as Stockton wished to do. This officer had Frémont's energy,
together with a flamboyancy all his own; and like Frémont, he
believed in handling the Californians with a firm hand. Between the new Commodore and the Captain there sprang up
a warm and enduring friendship. They were much together,
and the result was the issuance on July 29th over Stockton's
name of a bombastic proclamation, abusing Castro for his "repeated hostilities and outrages," declaring that daily reports
came from the interior of "scenes of rapine, blood, and murder," and asserting that after protecting the lives and property
of American settlers and restoring order, Stockton would "leave
the people to manage their own affairs in their own way." At
the same time, Stockton and Frémont planned an energetic
land campaign, which should either take Castro prisoner or
drive him, Pico, and other dangerous officials into Mexico.

Their plan of operations for this purpose was simple and
promised to be effective. Castro was supposedly waiting near
Los Angeles with about five hundred men and seven or eight
pieces of artillery, a little army that was slowly increasing.
Frémont's battalion was taken into the naval service, and he
was made major in command, with Gillespie as captain; the
men were allowed the regulation ten dollars a month pay
(which they considered too little), and were reinforced by 80
marines. This body of 220 hardy fighters was carried by sea

in the sloop *Cyane* to San Diego, a trip which made Kit Carson and others ingloriously seasick. Landed here to cut off Castro from the rear, they sent out men to scour the country and press horses into service. Much to their surprise, Frémont's battalion were received with cordiality by the principal inhabitants and given every aid in obtaining supplies; they fared admirably.

In fact, for the week or ten days that they were outfitting, Frémont and his men enjoyed a beguiling mixture of picnicking and foraging in the beautiful countryside about San Diego. Irrigation was widely practised here, and repeatedly they came upon a ranch that was a veritable Garden of Eden, blooming with vivid flowers and crowded with pear trees, peach trees, olive trees, fig trees, and vines on which the grapes were already purple. The days were bright and hot, the skies a dome of cloudless light, and the nights cool and star-spangled. Forty years later Frémont remembered the most enchanting of these excursions. The noonday heat forced a halt in a pretty garden near a farmhouse. Here the water from a little stream flowed into a basin some fifteen feet across, kept pure and clear by a cement coping. Pomegranates and other fruit trees hung over the water, and they lounged under the branches as they roasted a portion of lamb on skewers at a fire, and ate it with bread, fruit, and wine. At the end of the refitting period, on August 8th, about one hundred and twenty of the battalion (the rest having been left to garrison San Diego) took up their march for Los Angeles, still through a country whose luxuriant fertility, with the golden wheat in shock, impressed the volunteers.

Their victory was won more easily than Frémont, who learned that Castro and Pico had effected a juncture and were encamped upon a mesa in front of the town, had expected. Beyond San Pedro, he joined Commodore Stockton with a force of 360 men and several pieces of artillery. To face this formidable little body Castro and Pico had only about two hundred and fifty men, ill-armed and divided between partisans of the north and the south. On the northward march no hostile figures were seen except a few scattered horsemen who vanished

on the horizon. On the afternoon of August 13, 1846, the little
American army entered Los Angeles unopposed, and with a
brass band in front marched through streets lined with curious
and not unfriendly people, more like "a parade of home guards
than an enemy taking possession of a conquered town." [5]
Castro's force, frightened by the American advance, had buried
part of its powderless guns, and scattered to the four winds.
Its commander was reported hidden in the cloudy-penciled
mountains overlooking the San Gabriel plain.

The results of this occupation of the official capital of California, and of a series of proclamations which Stockton in
his usual histrionic fashion immediately issued, were at first
gratifying. Stockton declared that while California was now a
possession of the United States, under martial law, the people
would be unmolested in their ordinary business, would be considered citizens of the territory, and in due time would be
given a regular governor, secretary, and legislative council. A
reign of justice and amity seemed about to begin. Many prominent native Californians surrendered, and were released on
parole. Sentiment rallied to the American side as manifestly
certain of victory. The first California newspaper, of course in
English, appeared—the *Californian,* established at Monterey,
on August 15, 1846; the first public school was opened. In
September, some successful municipal elections were held.
Chaplain Colton was appointed alcalde of Monterey, and his
administration proved immediately popular. The Mexican inhabitants were delighted when a large number of horses, driven
off by the Indians, were restored to them, while Stockton
evinced a gratifying tact in settling some civil disputes brought
before him. His intention was, after creating a legislative council, to make himself governor, but he did not wish to hold that
office long. He was revolving an absurd dream of a spectacular
attempt upon Mexico City from the west, landing his troops at
Acapulco and marching them overland.

Frémont was sent northward by Stockton to his old positions

[5] Frémont, *Memoirs,* I, pp. 566, 567.

in the Sacramento Valley, with instructions to muster as large a force as he could, and with the promise that as soon as Stockton began the invasion of Mexico, he would be made governor of the province. Meanwhile, California was divided into three military districts of which Stockton took charge of that in the middle, Frémont the one at the north, and Gillespie the one at the south. Frémont's labors were especially easy. Surrounded by his friends and associates of the Bear Flag War, and fearing no enemies, for the native Californians were cut off from Mexico and were overawed by the large population of American settlers, he could begin recruiting his California Battalion to full strength without worries. But Gillespie's task was very difficult. Southern California was closely in touch with Mexico, the native Californians were restless and numerous, and the country held few Americans and few other residents who sympathized with American aims. His force was pitifully small, for despite Larkin's warnings, Stockton could supply him with only about fifty volunteers. When Gillespie's rigid military rule aroused discontent, such a corporal's guard was merely a temptation to an outbreak.

While Frémont was busiest recruiting his forces, the inevitable flare-up set southern California in sudden flame. An attack on the Los Angeles garrison occurred on the night of September 22, 1846; four hundred Californians were shortly in arms; and when they cut off an American detachment of twenty-five men at the Chino farm near the town, the movement gained powerful headway.[6] Gillespie was overborne with a rush. Having no fortifications and few arms, he was compelled on September 29th to surrender Los Angeles on favorable terms, being allowed to embark his troops upon a mer-

[6] H. H. Bancroft deals thoroughly with the causes of this revolt in his *History of California*, V, p. 305ff. As he writes, a large element in the Los Angeles population had always been turbulent, lawless, and uncontrollable; the inexperienced Gillespie promulgated some needlessly oppressive measures; and a wild young fellow named Varela gathered other wild spirits about him and began the fighting. Within a short time nearly all the male inhabitants of southern California were in a sense engaged in the revolt; but the rebel leaders could not arm even two hundred of them.

chant ship at San Pedro. When a few days later Stockton, who was at San Francisco, heard of this, he was filled with anger and mortification, and forthwith despatched a strong force against the rebels.

With the guerrilla fighting at the south, the marching and countermarching of petty forces which occupied the period from October 1 to December 15, 1846, we have nothing to do. It is sufficient to say that, in these seventy-five days, Stockton's operations against Los Angeles accomplished nothing, and that early in October, Captain William Mervine, moving against the town, was thrown back in disorder with somewhat serious losses.

Meanwhile, Frémont was acting with a degree of caution highly unusual and on the whole justified by the disastrous consequences of Stockton's more precipitate moves. In October, he did indeed make a brief gesture toward intervening in the conflict. Receiving orders from Stockton to hasten south from the Sacramento, he proceeded as far as Santa Barbara with some one hundred and seventy well-armed men. Here he learned of Mervine's defeat and was informed that the enemy had denuded the country of horses and cattle, so that he would be left without transportation or meat. He concluded that further preparations were necessary, and using, as he wrote Stockton,[7] "the discretionary authority you have given me," returned to the vicinity of Monterey. Stockton condemned his return in vigorous terms, and censured Frémont in letters to the Secretary of the Navy, a fact which later excited the indignation of the explorer. "I have sometimes wondered," he wrote, "if it never occurred to Stockton that the same difficulties which blocked his march upon Los Angeles were also in the way of my command, which was expected to operate as a mounted force in the interior." He learned at Monterey that he had been made lieutenant-colonel in the army July 10, so he was not strictly subordinate to the Commodore. Certain that he was taking the right course, he continued, with headquarters first

[7] Frémont, *Memoirs*, I, p. 580.

in Monterey, and later in San Juan, his work of finding good
mounts and laying in a store of beeves and other supplies. Re-
ceipts were given to friendly inhabitants, while hostile ranchers
lost their property without recourse; for this H. H. Bancroft
concludes that "the commander cannot be blamed," but some
bitter feeling was aroused. Very shortly Frémont had at his
back, according to Bryant, 428 "splendid fighters," Kern having sent down the garrison at Sutter's Fort and enlisted Indians
in their places, and Grigsby having brought in the Sonoma men.

At the end of November Frémont and this laboriously collected army, with two pieces of artillery, moved out from San
Juan, advancing by way of the San Benito River and Salinas
Valley toward San Luis Obispo. It was an inclement season.
The weather was chilly, and for whole days the men struggled
forward through a frigid drizzle; the roads and trails were
fetlock deep in mud; the horses found little pasturage, and became so weak for want of nourishment that many fell out by
the way. Many of the *caballada* of some five hundred horses and
mules which they drove along with them soon had to be left
behind. The provisions consisted of necessary foodstuffs carried
on pack mules, and a herd of cattle which as fast as they were
slaughtered were replaced by others picked up, sometimes a
hundred at a swoop, from ranches along the way. Edwin Bryant
tells us that thirteen or fourteen large cattle were slaughtered
every afternoon, and that the men ate amazing quantities of
beef; the average ration seemed to him ten pounds a day, and
some consumed much more, rising at two o'clock in the morning to roast fresh slabs of juicy, tender steak. Yet the health
of the men continued remarkably good.[8]

At San Luis Obispo, where Frémont posted a strong guard
over the mission property to save it from depredation, he was
lucky enough to capture Don Jesus Pico, a man of wide influence. After a court-martial had tried him for breaking his
parole, and sentenced him to death, Frémont wisely pardoned
him—amid the weeping entreaties of his wife and other rela-

[8] Bryant, *What I Saw in California*, p. 365ff.

tives. Then the march was resumed under continued hardships from wind, cold, and rain. With excessive precaution against an insurgent ambush along the road, Frémont took a rough mountain path far from the sea. Christmas Day found the little army on a high ridge behind Santa Barbara, breasting a bitter southeasterly storm which swept with torrents of water the precipitous slopes of sandstone and clay that they must descend. Undaunted, they set forward, drawing their hats over their eyes and shouting to their beasts. They would have done better to make camp and wait. The wind continued blowing like a tornado, the water falling in sheets, until two o'clock that night. The trail was obliterated and the pack animals, stiffened by the cold and blinded by the rain, constantly lost their footing. Many fell into the deep ravines, where foaming torrents swept over them and drowned them; others slipped over the steep precipice which lay at one side. Before the descent ended more than a hundred horses were lost. The advance guard did not reach the foot of the mountain and find a camping ground till impenetrable darkness had shut down. Then the men dropped exhausted in a sea of mud, and those who tried to light camp-fires found them almost immediately extinguished. Some, left on the mountainside, crept under shelving rocks and stayed there all night.[9]

After a week's rest at Santa Barbara, where they found most of the houses closed and the streets deserted, the march was resumed, the Battalion now keeping near the shore of the ocean. At times their path was so close that the surf washed their feet, and they could see scores of grampus whales spouting in the offing. On January 5, 1847, in warm, springlike weather, they reached San Buenaventura, and entered a fertile ranching country where provisions were easy to obtain. Six days later, on January 11th, the advance party met two Californians riding bareheaded and in great haste. They brought Frémont news that the California insurgents had met an American army jointly commanded by Kearny and Stockton, and had been

[9] For a vivid description see Bryant, *op. cit.*, p. 380*ff*.

defeated after hard fighting, the American soldiers then—on the previous day—marching into Los Angeles.

The situation had in fact changed with amazing rapidity. General Stephen W. Kearny had led his Army of the West, comprising some two thousand men, to Santa Fé, had taken possession of that town soon after the middle of August, 1846, and had spent about a month reducing the country to order. He had then set out on September 25th with an expeditionary force of three hundred dragoons for California. On the way he met Kit Carson, hurrying East with official despatches from Stockton and private letters from Frémont, and there ensued an historic interview. Carson told Kearny that the conquest of California was virtually completed. The General thereupon decided to send back all but one hundred of his dragoons, and ordered Carson to turn about and serve as guide for his diminished party. Naturally, Carson protested; he had pledged himself to Commodore Stockton, he said, to go to Washington; moreover, he had already covered eight hundred of the nine hundred and fifty miles from Los Angeles to Santa Fé, and was eager to see his family, from whom he had been so long parted. But Kearny insisted, the scout reluctantly acquiesced, and the despatches were sent on by another hand.

With his hundred dragoons and two mountain howitzers, Kearny reached the frontier of California at the beginning of December, 1846, and at once learned that an insurrection was raging. Commodore Stockton, pent up in San Diego, had sent out Captain Gillespie with a small force of mounted riflemen and a fieldpiece to meet the General. Thus reinforced, on December 6th Kearny with his hundred and sixty officers and men came in contact with a smaller mounted force of the enemy at San Pasqual, about forty miles from San Diego, and in a sharp skirmish was decidedly worsted, with a loss of twenty-one killed or fatally wounded. Kearny's tactics were bad, for he regarded the Californians contemptuously, and failed to move his men forward in a compact, well ordered body; with the result that an advance guard was simply cut to pieces by a furious charge of the insurgent lancers. The loss of the Californians was trivial. Kearny's shaken and worried force staggered forward next day nine or ten miles to the *rancho* San Bernardo, threatened all the way by the enemy; and here on a hill were brought to bay, the Californians holding the trail in front. The Americans had to subsist on mule-meat and a little muddy water, the wounded suffering intensely. During the night Carson, Edward F. Beale, and an Indian boy heroically slipped through the enemy lines to carry a plea for help to Stockton in San Diego. A relief force was instantly despatched and on the night of December 10th this little body of one hundred and eighty sailors and marines under Lieutenant Gray reached Kearny's hard-pressed detachment, where it frightened the beleaguering Californians from the field.[10]

At San Diego, Kearny joined hands with Commodore Stockton, and a joint force was organized. It comprised about fifty-seven of Kearny's original dragoons, sixty of Gillespie's riflemen, some four hundred and thirty of Stockton's sailors and marines, and a number of Indians, California teamsters, and others—about six hundred in all, grouped in four battalions. Stockton had also prepared a battery of six pieces. It is obvious that this little army, designed to coöperate with Frémont, defeat or frighten away General José M. Flores, and capture Los Angeles, was made up chiefly of Stockton's men. It was led jointly by Stockton and Kearny, but Stockton (who thought with much justice that he had saved Kearny's force) took pains to make it clear that he maintained his rank of commander-in-chief and civil governor. Unfortunately, later events showed that Kearny failed to concede the rank. Not far outside Los Angeles occurred the final decisive engagements with the in-

---

[10] Various descendants and admirers of Kearny have wasted much ink in trying to convert his defeat into a victory; for accurate and impartial accounts of his worsting, see Smith, *War With Mexico*, I, p. 342; Sabin, *Kit Carson Days*, II, p. 526*ff*. Sabin's judgment may be accepted as final; "Ethically, it was a victory for the Californians, who had achieved much more than reason could have warranted. The tactics of General Kearny were a blunder."

surgents, on January 8 and 9, 1847, the Americans winning with the loss of only one man killed, and throwing the Californians back to the site of the present city of Pasadena. On the tenth the troops marched into Los Angeles, and Gillespie, commanding one of the battalions, had the satisfaction of raising with his own hands over the government house the flag he had lowered four months earlier. Kearny and Stockton at once took up their headquarters in the town.

There was still some danger of sporadic fighting by the Californians, but Frémont now proved the instrument to avert it. Camping on the afternoon of the twelfth near the mission of San Fernando, he received a message from the commander of the Californians, Don Andres Pico, who intimated that the insurgents were ready to surrender. It would seem that Frémont, who knew that Stockton was at hand and had just defeated the Californian army, should have left his superior to arrange the terms of capitulation. He might have been severely censured by Stockton for arrogating the authority to make a treaty of peace, but it does not appear that the Commodore ever protested. The terms which Frémont granted in this hasty capitulation of Couenga were exceedingly generous. He guaranteed to the insurgents protection in person and property, equal rights with the Americans in the territory, exemption from armed service or from any oath of allegience during the War, and liberty to leave the country at will; he required only that they lay down their arms, disperse to their homes, and promise to assist in restoring tranquillity and submissiveness among the people. In short, he virtually allowed men who were defeated, hopelessly at bay, and subject even to execution for breaking their parole, to dictate the terms of surrender. It was a characteristically impulsive action, taken probably because Frémont believed the Californians much stronger and bolder than they were.

Yet the terms thus precipitately granted were, on the whole, thoroughly wise; they did much to conciliate the southern Californians and to secure their friendship for American rule.[11]

It is not difficult to imagine the sensations which filled Frémont's mind as on the morning of January 14, 1847, with the capitulation of Couenga in his pocket, he prepared to march into Los Angeles. A heavy rain began falling, amid which the California troops brought in and surrendered to him a brass howitzer which they had captured from Kearny at San Pasqual. Camp was broken, and the men, urging their jaded animals over slippery hills, entered the beautifully verdant plain surrounding the town. At three in the afternoon, the rain still pouring, they were marching down the muddy principal street. A more ragged, ill-provided, unprepossessing battalion it would have been difficult to imagine; they might have been taken, as one of them remarked, for a tribe of Tartar nomads. Their garments tattered, drenched, and plastered with mud; some of them without shoes or hats; their horses dispirited and exhausted—only their military order and arms made them seem soldiers. Yet Frémont had the proud consciousness that California was conquered, that he had played one of the most important rôles in the conquest, and that it was to him that the last hostile force had surrendered. He had the promise of Commodore Stockton that he would be appointed governor, and would thus shortly rule over the territory from which only a few months earlier Castro had ignominiously expelled him.

All seemed well in California; all was well at home. While still in camp at San Juan, the explorer had received through Consul Larkin at Monterey a letter from Jessie. It is worth quoting entire, for it not only provides a budget of news upon events in the Benton household and in Washington generally, but offers an appealing glimpse of Jessie's whole-souled devo-

[11] See article by Don Romulo Pico, Los Angeles *Times,* January 3, 1914. Frémont's whole course in California had been extremely considerate of the natives. At Santa Barbara, Bryant writes (p. 383): "Strict orders were issued by Col. Frémont that the property and the persons of Californians, not found in arms, should be sacredly respected. To prevent all collisions, no soldier was allowed to pass the lines of the camp without special permission, or orders from his officers."

tion. It was dated Washington, June 16, 1846, and began "My Dearest Husband": [12]

A Mr. Magoffin says he will be at Bent's Fort a month from tomorrow, and that he will leave a letter for you, so I write, dearest husband, to tell you how happy I have been made by hearing of you up to the 31st of March, through Mr. O'Larkin. Only the day before, I had received the Mexican account of your being besieged by Gen. Castro, and I was much relieved by what Mr. O'Larkin says—that you could present yourself in Monterey, alone, if you wished, and not be harmed. But I hope that as I write you are rapidly nearing home, and that early in September there will be an end to our anxieties. In your dear letter you tell me that *le bon temps viendra,* and my faith in you is such that I believe it will come: and it will come to all you love, for during your long absence God has been good to us and kept in health your mother and all you love best. This opportunity of writing only presented itself last night, so that there is not time for a letter from your mother herself, but I had one from her two days ago in which she tells me that during the warm weather she will remain at a place about ten miles from the city called Mount Pleasant. Her stay in the country did her health much good last fall and indeed it has been good generally throughout the winter. Her heart has been made glad by your brilliant success, and your late promotion, although it distressed her to anticipate more separations, could not but be most gratifying in many respects. You must let me make you my heartiest congratulations. I am sorry that I could not be the first to call you Colonel. It will please you the more as it was entirely a free will offering of the President's, neither father nor I nor anyone for us having asked or said we would like it.

So your merit has advanced you in eight years from an unknown second lieutenant, to the most talked of and admired lieutenant-colonel in the army. Almost all of the old officers called to congratulate me upon it, the Aberts among them, and I have heard of no envy except from some of the lower order of Whig papers who only see you as Colonel Benton's son-in-law. As for your Report, its popularity astonished even me, your most confirmed and oldest worshipper. Lilly has it read to her (the stories, of course) as a

[12] Frémont MSS, Bancroft Library.

reward for good behavior. She asked Preuss the other day if it was true that he caught ants on his hands and eat them—he was so amazed that he could not answer her, and she said, "I read it in papa's lepote; it was when you were lost in California." Father absolutely idolizes Lilly; she is so good and intelligent that I do not wonder at it. And then you should see his pride in you!

Mother's health has been worse than ever during the winter, but the force of the disease seems now to have expended itself, and she is quite well again. That gave me a reason for staying at home quietly as I wished, and I have read so much that is improving that you will be very pleased with me. Your mother was kind enough to send me your daguerreotype, and it hangs over the head of my bed and is my guardian angel, for I could not waste time or do anything you did not like with that beloved face looking so kindly and earnestly at me. I opened a new history of Louisiana, a week or two ago, and it commenced with the Spanish discoveries on the southern part of the continent. I was by myself, Lilly asleep, and reading by our lamp. When I came to De Soto's search for the fountain of youth, I stopped, for it seemed as if pleasant old days had returned; and then I remembered so well what you once wrote to me that I could not help bursting into tears. Do you remember, darling?

It was soon after we were married, and you wrote me, "Fear not for our happiness; if the hope for it is not something wilder than the Spaniards' search for the fountain in Florida, we will find it yet." I remembered it word for word, although it was so long since I read it. Dear, dear husband, you do not know how proud and grateful I am that you love me. We have found the fountain of perpetual youth for love, and I believe there are few others who can say so. I try very hard to be worthy of your love.

I had meant to tell you of many things which might interest, but it would take a day to choose out from the year's accumulation. The road you have discovered is spoken of as giving you more distinction than anything you have yet done. I had to publish almost all your letter, and like everything you write it has been reprinted all over the country. I have some beautiful poetry to show you on our motto *le bon temps viendra*. Editors have written to me for your biography and likeness, but I had no orders from you and then you know it would look odd to leave out your age, and you never told me how old you were yet.

How old are you? You might tell me now I am a colonel's wife—won't you, old papa? Poor papa, it made tears come to find you had begun to turn gray. You must have suffered much and been very anxious, "but all that must pass." I am very sorry you did not get our letters.[13] Yours gave so much happiness that I grieved you could not have had as much from ours. You will of course come on here as soon as you get back. I wanted to go to St. Louis to meet you, but father says I had better not, as it will be very uncomfortable and even dangerous to go out in the worst of the season, and I don't want to be sick, for I am not going to let you write anything but your name when you get home. And then we will probably have to be at Jefferson Barracks during the winter and until the new regiment is ready for the field. Father says you are to accept the appointment as it was given, with the understanding that you were to be kept on scientific duty under the direction of the Senate. Mr. Webster says it would be too great a loss to the science of the country if you were stopped in your onward course. If I begin telling you the sincere compliments from people whose names are known in Europe as well as America I would need a day.

You must have a few to think of, however. Edward Everett, Mr. Gallatin, Stevens (Central America), Davis, the author of "Jack Downing," a Dr. Barrett of Connecticut, a botanist who sent me his herbarium of American grasses (for which he wants the buffalo and bunch grasses) are among the Northern men. The South Carolinians claim you bodily, and Dr. Grayson of Charleston wrote one of the most beautiful of all the notices I saw. Your early and steady friends, Mr. McCrady and Mr. Poinsett, were the first to whom I sent well-bound copies of your book. You are ranked with DeFoe. They say that as *Robinson Crusoe* is the most natural and interteresting fiction of travel, so Frémont's report is the most romantically truthful. I have a letter from the President of the Royal Geographical Society, Lord Chichester, who says he could not help preparing a paper on your travels to be read at their meeting—and more and more and many more of the same.

Mr. Magoffin has come for the letter and I must stop. I have not

---

[13] That is, up to January 24, 1846.

had so much pleasure in a very great while as today. The thought that you may hear from me and know that all are well and that I can tell you again how dearly I love you makes me as happy as I can be while you are away.

All Jacob's relations [the negro servant Jacob Dodson] are well. I see Mrs. Talbot and her daughter constantly. They are so grateful to you for your mention of Theodore.

Farewell, dear, dear husband. In a few months we shall not know what sorrow means. At least, I humbly hope and pray so.

Your own affectionate and devoted wife,

Jessie B. Frémont.

So every one knew that Frémont was now a lieutenant-colonel, and his report had carried his fame throughout the country; Daniel Webster and Lord Chichester had praised him, and the President himself was interested in his promotion. These were facts which, with the knowledge that he would soon be hailed as one of the conquerors of California, must have filled his cup to overflowing.

XX

The Quarrel with Kearny

FRÉMONT was never to drink the cup of triumph or prosperity long, and his life was to prove a dizzy alternation of successes and humiliations. But seldom were the alternations so abrupt and pronounced as in the early months of 1847. From the surrender at Couenga and the exultant entry into Los Angeles it was but a single step to isolation, arrest, and attempted degradation. The civil governor of California was converted within a few weeks into a cashiered officer, facing trial on grave charges; the man who had expected to return east a popular hero was dragged thither by his military superior as a prisoner.

That Frémont was himself in part responsible for this sorry change of fortune is undeniable; but circumstances were also to blame, the mistakes of friends like Stockton were to count, and above all the malice of Stockton's and Frémont's enemy, General Stephen Watts Kearny, was at fault. It was a dark day for the young explorer when this last-named soldier, a life-long army man, a veteran of the War of 1812, a grim martinet, a fighter without any mild or ingratiating qualities whatever, entered California with the rank of brigadier-general in command of the Army of the West.[1] He was a leader of courage, energy, and a certain ability, who had seen thirty years of service on the frontier after his part in the second war with England. Having won his promotion only with plodding slowness, he was not the man to feel sympathetic toward an officer

---

[1] Thomas Kearny devotes the sixth chapter of his *General Philip Kearny* to an account of the services and exploits of Stephen Watts Kearny, treating him as the just man rendered perfect.

of brilliant parts and swift, spectacular advancement to fame, such as Frémont. His conquest of New Mexico had been one of the more remarkable exploits of the Mexican War. Outfitting 1,660 men at Fort Leavenworth, he had taken barely enough food to reach Santa Fé, confident that he could live on the country—and had done so. In New Mexico he had capably organized a civil government. But he was a stern-tempered soldier who made few friends and many enemies—who has been justly characterized by the most careful historian of the period, Justin H. Smith, as "grasping, jealous, domineering, and harsh." [2] Possessing these traits, feeling his pride stung by his defeat at San Pasqual, and anxious to assert his authority, he was no sooner in Los Angeles than he quarreled bitterly with Stockton; and Frémont was not only at once involved in this quarrel, but inherited the whole burden of it as soon as Stockton left the country.

In its essentials, the original dispute was whether Kearny or Stockton should have the chief command in California. The two had hardly met in San Diego, after Kearny was brought into that city by Stockton's relief force, when this dispute broke out. Stockton later testified that he had made preparations for the march of the joint forces to Los Angeles under the impression that Kearny would go thither as his aide-de-camp, and this was confirmed by a note from Kearny. "It seems however that I was either mistaken in my views, or that General Kearny suddenly altered his mind"; for on the day they left San Diego, December 29th, Kearny gave him to understand that he would like to command the troops in place of Lieutenant Rowan of the *Cyane,* who had been appointed to that post. "I immediately sent for Lieutenant Rowan," deposed Stockton, "and assembled the officers that were near at hand, and stated to them that General Kearny had volunteered to take command of the troops; that I had appointed him to the command of the troops; but that I retained my own po-

2 Smith, *The War with Mexico,* II, p. 264.

sition as commander-in-chief." Stockton continued in his subsequent testimony: [3]

> I directed my aide-de-camp and the commissary to make a note of what I said on the occasion; the impression made upon my mind was that General Kearny had, for the time being, laid aside his commission of brigadier-general, and had volunteered to serve under my command, and to perform the duties which had been assigned to Lieutenant Rowan as commander of the troops. When the force was paraded, the dragoons were among the troops. With these impressions and views, and considering that I, and I alone, was responsible for the result of the expedition, we commenced our march for the City of the Angels, during which march I performed all the duties which I supposed devolved upon the commander-in-chief of the forces, and, as I supposed, with the hearty acquiescence of General Kearny. General Kearny had repeatedly said he would aid me.... A few days after we commenced the march, I went in advance when the troops arrived at San Bernardo; I made my headquarters a mile and a half or two miles in advance of the camp, and I sent General Kearny to send me the marines and a piece of artillery, which was immediately done. I was in the habit of sending my aide-de-camp to General Kearny to inform him what time I wished to move in the morning, and I always decided upon the route we should take, and where we should camp.

Stockton instanced not only numerous occasions on which he had given orders to Kearny to which the latter submitted, but several occasions on which he had directly countermanded Kearny's orders—once during the fight before Los Angeles—and had been obeyed without the slightest question. When they marched into Los Angeles, Kearny asked him for instructions as to the road. It was Stockton who gave orders for the hoisting of the flag; who directed the quartering of the officers and men. A few days after their arrival, Kearny sent him a letter

[3] *Senate Exec. Docs., No. 33, 30th Cong., 1st Sess.,* p. 191ff. This volume of testimony in Frémont's court-martial will hereafter be cited simply as *Court-Martial Proceedings.* It runs to 447 pages.

directed to "Commodore Stockton, governor of California and commanding United States forces." Stockton also testified: [4]

As I have stated, the civil government had been already put into operation; having only been interrupted at Santa Barbara and the City of the Angels; peace having been restored, the civil government in those places went again into operation, and therefore there was nothing for me to do in relation to the establishment of a civil government, except to hand to Lieutenant-Colonel Frémont the commission as governor, which I had pledged my word to do; which I had informed the government I would do, and which would probably have been done, on the 25th day of October, if the insurrection had not broken out. Being desirous to get down on the southern coast of Mexico, I proceeded as rapidly as possible to make the necessary arrangements to leave the Ciudad de los Angeles. In the meantime, Lieutenant Colonel Frémont reported to me his arrival with the other part of the battalion. The position of the parties, and my own position at this time, was, in my judgment and opinion, this: General Kearny had laid aside, for the time being, his commission as brigadier general, and was serving as a volunteer under my command. The troops which were placed, by my orders, under the command of General Kearny, were the dragoons, sailors and marines, and Captain Gillespie's two companies of the California battalion, and no other. On the arrival of Lieutenant Colonel Frémont, he reported to me; and I did not give, nor did I intend to give, General Kearny any control or command over that part of the California Battalion. It was under my own immediate command. Lieutenant-Colonel Frémont at this time, was also serving under my command as a volunteer; he having likewise laid aside his commission in the army; and I was recognized in everything up to this time, as far as I know, as their mutual commander-in-chief. Having appointed Lieutenant-Colonel Frémont the governor, I appointed Captain Gillespie to be major of the battalion; and, if I understand the matter before this court, the disobedience of orders charged against the accused, whilst I was the commander-in-chief, is, that he would not obey an order which required him not to recognize my appointment of Captain Gillespie as major of the battalion.

[4] *Court-Martial Proceedings*, p. 194.

But while Stockton believed that Kearny had acquiesced in this reservation of the chief command, and while there was much evidence that he had actually done so, it shortly appeared that he entirely denied making any such concession. Instead, he held (whether after an initial change of mind or not) that he was the rightful commander-in-chief. With this quarrel smoldering between them, with an active temperamental dislike for one another—for Stockton was generous, warm-hearted, expansive, and impulsive, while Kearny was frigid, grim, and unyieldingly selfish—the two occupied their respective headquarters in Los Angeles. Here they received Frémont on the fourteenth, Stockton friendly and appreciative, Kearny doubtless acid and silent. The explorer had no sooner arrived than Kit Carson hastened to leave Kearny, whom he never liked, and join his old commander. Two days later, Stockton, as he has noted above, on January 16, 1847, issued a proclamation declaring Frémont governor and commander-in-chief in California until the President of the United States should otherwise direct. Kearny, beyond question fuming inwardly but for the moment impotent, immediately left with his dragoons for San Diego; while Stockton made ready to lead his sailors and marines at once to the coast of Mexico, where he hoped they would give a good account of themselves. He was not destined to carry out this plan, however, and soon returned overland to the East.

How was such an unhappy dispute over the chief command in California possible? It could not have arisen but for the vagueness and confusion of the orders sent to Stockton and Kearny from Washington. Each officer had not a little right to feel that the principal authority was in his hands. General Kearny had been instructed by the War Department on June 3, 1846, that "should you conquer and take possession of New Mexico and upper California, or considerable places in either, you will establish temporary civil governments therein." But Stockton had been authorized by orders of the Navy Department on March 14 and 21, May 5, June 24, and October

17, 1845, and June 13 and 15, 1846, to occupy and administer the ports of California—which in effect meant practically all of the province. An additional order of July 12, 1846, reminded him that it was his duty to take and hold all California. "This," he was instructed, "will bring with it the necessity of a civil administration. Such a government should be established under your protection." He was to communicate his instructions to General Kearny when the latter arrived, "and inform him that they have the sanction of the President." [5] It has been objected that while this order was sent, Stockton did not actually receive it before his departure from California. But the powers which it explicitly conferred had been already conferred by implication in the previous orders, and he had acted on that theory. What wonder that each commander honestly thought that he had the exclusive right to erect and control the new civil government of California?

It was the misfortune of Frémont to be caught in the collision between these two officers; it was his further misfortune to choose the side which subsequent orders from Washington failed to sustain. Little blame can attach to him for this. He might well have felt that the orders which Stockton held were superior to those in Kearny's hands; the order of July 12, 1846, to establish a civil administration "under your protection" was actually a month later in date. Moreover, Kearny's instructions were conditional. "Should you conquer and take possession of ... upper California," he was told, "you will establish a civil government there." But both Stockton and Frémont took the view, with entire justice, that the conquest of California had been substantially completed before Kearny's arrival; that they had already set up a civil government, which was interrupted but at two points, Santa Barbara and Los Angeles, and

[5] *Court-Martial Proceedings*, p. 412. Stockton deposed that "I was received at San Francisco, and acknowledged to be the governor of the territory and commander-in-chief." He offered written evidence, which the court-martial refused to accept, to show that he was so considered "at the City of the Angels, and that as I began governor, I left there as such."

then but temporarily; and that Kearny had done nothing but get defeated at San Pasqual and require rescuing.

Moreover, Frémont felt a natural and legitimate personal preference for Stockton as his superior. Both headstrong, quick, and fond of action, they were congenial in temperament; they had worked together with little friction for more than six months, and had a high personal regard for each other. Frémont's California Battalion had been organized under Stockton's direct authority, with the explicit understanding that it should act under the Commodore's orders so long as he remained on the coast and needed its services. All its officers save Frémont derived their appointments from Stockton and it was paid by his orders. It was, as Stockton himself wrote later, never in any form mustered into the army, but was exclusively a naval organization. Frémont himself, to be sure, was still in the army, having accepted a Lieutenant-Colonelcy in the "Regiment of Mounted Rifles," but he felt controlled by the fact that he commanded his battalion by authority of Stockton, and that this battalion was attached to the navy. Moreover, he had long believed that the Navy Department under Secretary Bancroft (now resigned) was more efficient, alert, and sympathetic toward him than the War Department. Then and later he suspected, not without reason, that many West Point graduates and older army officers were jealous of his rapid rise. Finally, and very importantly, he kept in mind the fact that Stockton had solemnly promised to make him governor. Kearny also wished to make him governor, and spoke to other officers of his exceptional fitness for the position; but Kearny's promises were less definite.

Altogether, Frémont's course must have seemed perfectly clear to him. Kearny, with his customary Irish assertiveness, lost no time after the three officers had taken their quarters in Los Angeles in trying to establish himself as boss. Before leaving that town for San Diego, he sent a curt note to Stockton, demanding that the Commodore cease all further proceedings relative to the organization of a civil government, and another curt missive to Frémont, ordering him to make no changes or appointments in the California Battalion without the express sanction of Kearny as his commanding officer. We can imagine Frémont and Stockton conferring in consternation. The peppery Commodore had no inteition of taking orders from the man he had rescued from Mexican hands only a few weeks before. He immediately informed the General that a civil government was already in successful operation, that he would do nothing that Kearny demanded, and that he would send the General's note to President Polk and ask for his recall. Kearny, on the next day, January 17, 1847, replied with asperity. He asserted that the credit for conquering the country belonged to the army forces under his command, and declared that it might now for the first time be considered in American possession. "As I am prepared to carry out the President's instructions to me," he added, "which you oppose, I must, for the purpose of preventing a collision between us and possibly a civil war in consequence of it, remain silent for the present, leaving with you the great responsibility of doing that for which you have no authority...." [6] Thus the rival commanders of army and navy glowered at each other during their last hours in Los Angeles.

It was in some ways a comic-opera quarrel, but its conquences to Frémont were most serious. That young officer had to make his choice on the morning of January 17th, when Kearny summoned him to the low adobe headquarters, and asked him if he had received the orders of the day before. Frémont with a touch of defiance stated that he had written a reply, which he had left with his clerk to copy. At this moment, Kit Carson entered with the document in question, which Frémont read through and, seizing a pen from Kearny's table, signed. He then seated himself, at Kearny's request, while the latter read the reply. It was a decisive though tactful refusal to obey Kearny's command. Frémont wrote that he believed Commodore Stockton to be the governor and commander-in-

[6] For these letters see Bigelow, *Frémont*, p. 194ff.

chief in California, that he had received a commission from Stockton, and that Stockton was still exercising the functions of civil and military governor. "I feel myself, therefore," he concluded, "with great deference to your professional and personal character, constrained to say that, until you and Commodore Stockton adjust between yourselves the question of rank, where I respectfully think the difficulty belongs, I shall have to report and receive orders, as heretofore, from the Commodore." In all this, Frémont was ill-advised. After all—since he was now back in the army—Kearny was his superior officer; Stockton should have counselled him to obey the General or at least try to reach an agreement with him. But Stockton's influence was evidently exerted in another direction, and Frémont was not politic enough to make terms.

The General, though a man of hot temper and iron will, gave him a full opportunity. Frémont had known something of him in St. Louis, where Kearny had been in command and where he had married a stepdaughter of General William Clark. He had heard the story of how this harsh-featured veteran of the War of 1812 once fell from his horse in front of his parading troops, and, pinned beneath the animal, had imperturbably continued his orders to the advancing men: "Fourth Company, obstacle—March!" [7] He knew how implacable Kearny could be when aroused. Nevertheless, for the moment, Kearny was patient in his irritation. He told Frémont that he was a much older man and soldier, that he had a warm regard for Senator Benton, who had done him many favors, and a real affection for Jessie, and that he would give the young explorer some honest advice. This advice was to take the letter back and destroy it. Frémont, of course, declined, saying that Stockton would support him; to which Kearny rejoined that Stockton could never support him in disobeying the orders of his superior officer, and that if Frémont persisted, he would ruin

[7] Fayette Robinson, *Organization of the Army of the United States*, II, p. 130*ff.*

himself. The two parted stiffly, and from that moment it was war to the knife.

It was on this same day that Frémont received from Stockton the commission dated January 16th, appointing him governor and commander-in-chief of California until the President should otherwise direct.[8]

For the next fortnight, Frémont was regarded almost everywhere in California as the civil governor under Stockton's appointment; and for somewhat more than two months, or until late in March, he was recognized as governor by the people in and about Los Angeles, while Kearny's authority was established farther north. The regular army officers, of course, refused to recognize Frémont, though they were in much perplexity as to who was actually at the head of affairs. A young lieutenant named William Tecumseh Sherman, who had just come out by sea around Cape Horn, tells us that the mess-room query was very frequent, "Who the devil *is* the governor of California?"[9] Making Los Angeles his capital, Frémont appointed his friend Captain Owens "secretary of state," and began issuing gubernatorial orders in due form. On January 22nd, he posted an official proclamation declaring the restoration of civil authority; and on January 25th, directed Captain S. K. Wilson of the Light Artillery to raise a company of men for "the California service," enlisting them as soon as possible. He purchased an island near the mouth of San Francisco Bay, taking title for the United States and promising a payment of five thousand dollars. His treatment of the people of southern California was conciliatory and kind, and rapidly made them his firm friends.

General Kearny, meanwhile, after a few days in San Diego, departed with a couple of officers in the sloop *Cyane* for Monterey, which he reached on February 8, 1847. Here he met Commodore Shubrick, who had arrived on January 22nd in command of the frigates *Independence* and *Lexington,* and who

[8] *Court-Martial Proceedings,* p. 38ff.; Bigelow, *Frémont,* p. 273.
[9] W. T. Sherman, *Memoirs,* I, p. 23.

now supplanted Stockton as chief naval commander. Kearny was rowed over to the *Independence*, wearing an old dragoon coat and army cap, to which he had added a broad visor cut from a full dress hat to shade his face and eyes from the glaring sun.[10] He showed Shubrick his orders; learned of the Navy Department orders dated July 12, 1846, by which the chief naval officer in California was then entrusted with the civil administration of the territory; and was promptly recognized by the Commodore "as head and commander of the troops in California." The two agreed to work together in harmony, ignoring Frémont, and to let the situation rest until further despatches came from Washington.[11] Going ashore and establishing his headquarters at Larkin's house, Kearny was pleased to find a strong company of artillery ready waiting for him. In the ensuing weeks, other important bodies of troops arrived from the East. The famous battalion of Mormons, about five hundred strong, which had been recruited in Council Bluffs after that sect had been driven from Nauvoo, reached the territory and made camp at San Luis Rey. A regiment of New York volunteers under Colonel John D. Stevenson came out by sea, and, like the Mormons, were expected in large part to remain as settlers.[12] All these soldiers supported Kearny as governor and refused to have anything to do with Frémont. When Frémont received a curt and chilly letter from Commodore Shubrick, under date of February 13th, showing that Shubrick and Kearny were working in perfect accord, he must have realized that he was left standing alone.

In fact, though he did not know it, all ground for claiming the authority of governor had now been cut from beneath the young explorer's feet by new orders from Washington. These orders, written November 5, 1846, by the Secretary of the Navy, informed both Kearny and Shubrick that the President deemed it best to invest the military commander with the direc-

[10] *Ibid.*, I, p. 24.
[11] *Court-Martial Proceedings*, p. 96ff.
[12] Smith, *War with Mexico*, II, p. 219.

tion of land operations and with the civil government, and ordered Shubrick to give General Kearny the entire control over these matters.[13] This was decisive. It made Kearny governor and commander-in-chief. If the government had only possessed wisdom enough to take this clear step six weeks earlier, it would have prevented the whole dispute. The message reached Kearny in San Francisco on February 12, 1847, and must have been read by Shubrick in Monterey before the fifteenth, or within a month after the original quarrel of Stockton and Kearny. The General had won a swift triumph.

Unfortunately, Kearny made a brutal and hectoring use of his victory. It would have been the part of a gentlemanly officer to inform Frémont at once of the new orders, and to treat him with consideration in his sudden humiliating drop from governor to subordinate. Kearny instead said nothing about them to Frémont. Long afterwards, when he was being cross-examined in Washington on the subject, the following colloquy occurred: [14]

Question: Did you communicate the instructions of the 5th of November, 1846, to Lieutenant-Colonel Frémont?

Answer: I did not. I am not in the habit of communicating to my juniors the instructions I receive from my seniors, unless required to do so in those instructions.

Question: Do you know whether the said instructions were communicated to him by Commodore Shubrick or Commodore Biddle?

Answer: I do not believe that they were; but I know not.

This statement of Kearny's that he was not in the habit of communicating instructions to juniors unless required to do so is a very lame excuse for a base act. Frémont always spoke of the concealment with justified resentment, and believed that it was dictated by a wish to plunge him deeper in seeming disobedience to the government. Nor was Kearny less domineering in other regards.

---

[13] *Court-Martial Proceedings*, p. 55.
[14] *Ibid.*, p. 102.

The painful events which followed and led up to Frémont's departure for the East as a virtual prisoner of General Kearny's make an unhappy chronicle. Kearny and Shubrick, at the beginning of March, issued a joint announcement of the President's orders; and the same day Kearny published a proclamation in which he formally assumed the governorship. According to Kearny, a copy of the joint announcement was sent to Frémont, but there is no evidence that he received it. What is certain is that Kearny transmitted to him a curt order to bring to Monterey, as the territorial capital, all archives and public documents pertaining to the government, and to surrender them. Kearny added that he had directions from General Winfield Scott, which he enclosed, not to detain the explorer in California against his wishes a moment longer than the necessities of the service might require. Once he had complied with Kearny's instructions regarding the papers, and had obeyed the General's further orders that he muster his men into the United States service, so that they might be discharged and paid, he could depart. Naturally, but very unwisely, Frémont refused to obey this demand for the papers. He declared later that he knew nothing of the government orders of November 5th, and believed that Kearny was trying by bluster and threats to depose him from the governorship.[15]

Kearny simultaneously placed Lieutenant-Colonel Philip St. George Cooke, with the Mormon Battalion, at San Luis Rey, in command of the southern half of California. When Cooke sent a courier to Los Angeles to inquire of Frémont how many of the California Battalion had entered the United States service, he received little satisfaction:[16] "The answer was by a 'governor,' through his 'secretary of state,' that none had consented to enter the public service; but as rumors of insurrection were rife, it was not deemed safe to disband them."

If Kearny's object were to entrap Frémont into defiance of duly constituted authority, he had now succeeded. And cer-

[15] Bigelow, *Frémont*, p. 288.
[16] Cooke, *The Conquest of New Mexico and California*, pp. 286, 287.

tainly the General's tactics were as arrogant and hostile as possible. In his proclamation, he included a direct slap at Frémont
by saying that "there is no doubt that some excesses, some
unauthorized acts, were committed by persons in the service
of the United States." He cast public contempt upon the certifi-
cates which Stockton and Frémont had given in payment for
property and services, saying they were almost worthless. Once
when a merchant showed him Frémont's certificate for a considerable sum, inquiring as to its value, Kearny looked at it,
and asked a bystander for a quarter of a dollar. When the man
gave him half a dollar, Kearny replied: "That's too much; a
quarter-dollar is its value." [17] Rumors arose that Kearny considered Frémont a mutineer and was preparing a condign
punishment for the young explorer; and old-line army men
who had resented Frémont's rapid advancement gave the rumors general currency. Some of them loudly declared that the
mutinous officer deserved the death penalty!

All this unquestionably threw Frémont into intense anxiety;
and at the same time, he became worried by the growing unrest of the Californians about Los Angeles. It is difficult to determine just how great this unrest was. We can hardly believe
that even the febrile young bloods and irresponsible loafers of
the region, only two months after being soundly thrashed, with
overwhelming American forces on the scene, would think of
a revolt. They would simply be putting their necks inside a
halter. But Frémont was excited; he was full of resentment
against Kearny, and all too ready to believe that Kearny's
displacement of him would cause all kinds of trouble. He had
plumed himself upon the tranquillity and good-will of the citizens of southern California under his sway. "I lived in the
midst of the people in their ancient capital," he later boasted,
"administering the government, as a governor lives in the capital of any of our States." The security of life, limb and property seemed as complete as in New England; travelers on lonely
trails, dwellers on isolated ranches, were perfectly safe; and

17 *Congressional Globe, 30th Cong., 1st Sess., Appendix*, p. 995.

Frémont himself, sending his Battalion out to the San Gabriel Mission only nine miles away, lived almost without guard. Now, in his overwrought frame of mind, he thought that the popular temper was rapidly changing.

No doubt it really was. Little bands of armed Mexicans were galloping about the country, and news came in of men armed to the teeth patrolling the roads. Most of the Californians seemed uneasy, and rumors flew about that a bloody uprising was at hand. Frémont was at no loss to lay the blame directly upon Kearny. The discontent arose—he thought—because the Mormon troops under Cooke had been marched from San Diego toward Los Angeles, and the Californians hated and feared the Mormons; because Kearny's proclamation had annulled some of the mild and wise provisions of the Capitulation of Couenga; and because of rumors that after Frémont had been forcibly deposed, a much harsher officer would be installed in his place. Still more important was the money consideration involved in the reports that Kearny's policy opposed any payment for the cattle, horses, and goods taken, and the property destroyed, in the conquest. The antagonism of many native Californians had suddenly been re-aroused, and the explorer thought it greater than it was.[18]

Money considerations were indeed now important, for in the fifty days of his dubious governorship Frémont repeatedly borrowed large sums. He obtained a loan of $2,000 from Don Antonio José Cos on February 4, 1847, and of $1,000 more on February 20; he borrowed $2,500 from Eulogio de Celis on March 3rd; and on March 18th he obtained $15,000 from F. Huttman for drafts on the government, allowing a premium of $4,500—that is, giving Huttman drafts for $19,500 in all. Secretary Buchanan refused to honor the drafts, and they were protested, this leading ultimately (as we shall see) to Frémont's arrest in London. These loans variously bore interest at 2 or

[18] H. H. Bancroft makes light of the threatened uprising, but adds: "It is true, however, that the Missouri volunteers had succeeded in arousing some feeling against the Mormons." *History of California,* V, p. 442.

3 per cent a month. Frémont also gave Celis a certificate or receipt for the delivery of 600 beef-cattle for the army, pledging
the United States to pay $6,975 for them. These cattle never
went to the California Battalion, but were instead delivered
to Abel Stearns, to be held for breeding. Celis later declared
that Frémont, "not having time to consume said cattle on account of having received a superior order to deliver up the command and disband the force, ordered said cattle to be delivered
to Mr. Abel Stearns, as I understand, in the quality of a de-
posit, until the government should dispose of them." Frémont
himself explained that he put the cattle in private hands to
secure himself if the government should fail to acknowledge
the debt. This seems reasonable, but it does not offer a complete
explanation of his certificate of delivery for the army. It is
clear that he was getting into deep water financially, and had
reason to become apprehensive.[19]

Under these circumstances, he determined upon a characteristically rash, theatrical, and arduous enterprise—a ride night
and day to Monterey to "warn" Kearny of the danger of an
outbreak. It was not necessary for him to go in person; and
had there really been danger, his duty would have been to
stay vigilantly with his Battalion in Los Angeles. He knew
this perfectly well. The chief reason for the ride, beyond doubt,
was that he wished to find out in person his real status. Another reason very likely lay in his worry over the possibility
that Kearny would influence the government against paying
the heavy debts he had incurred.

At any rate, the effort was a feat which may well be compared with such other famous rides of history as Burnaby's to
Khiva. Accompanied only by Don Jesus Pico and the faithful
black servant, Jacob Dodson, Frémont set off at daybreak on
what was to be a round trip of eight hundred and forty miles
in eight days. They took three horses apiece, or nine in all;
the loose mounts, or six extra horses, as was customary on such

[19] On these financial claims see Bancroft, *op. cit.*, V, pp. 435, 462ff.; Cardinal
Goodwin, *Establishment of State Government in California*, pp. 35-38.

expeditions, were driven ahead, and every twenty miles or so, as a fresh steed was wanted, one was lassoed and saddled. At a sweeping gallop they covered 120 miles the first day, March 22, 1847, sleeping at a ranch beyond Santa Barbara. The following day they traversed 135 miles, reaching the old home of Don Jesus at San Luis Obispo, where they made a complete change of horses. They rode some seventy miles the third day, and slept in a cañon of the Salinas where, after midnight, they were awakened by prowling bears; at dawn they were off again, and in mid-afternoon, after traveling ninety miles, were at Kearny's headquarters in Monterey. The trip back again, after a day for a conference with the General, was made with equal rapidity. Frémont had covered a distance almost equal to that from New York to Chicago, over rough ground, in seventy-six actual riding hours, an exploit which merited the wide attention it later obtained.[20]

If he had hoped to improve his relations with Kearny by the interview, that hope was quickly dashed. He was received, he later declared, with every token of disrespect and discourtesy; and certainly a stormy scene ensued. The explorer entered alone at ten in the morning, though Larkin accompanied him to the door; he found that Kearny had with him Colonel Richard B. Mason, an able army officer, and that both men were stiff and hostile. Frémont asked if he could not be left in private with the General, and when Kearny refused to dismiss Mason, the young officer blazed up with the words: "Did you bring him to spy upon me?"[21] This ended all hope of courteous relations. From Larkin in Monterey Frémont had apparently for the first time received definite information of the orders of November 5th, though it is difficult to believe that he did not know of their nature soon after March 1st. Larkin, a shrewd, frank man, had perhaps advised him overnight to yield to Kearny. At any rate, Frémont now offered his resignation, which Kearny refused. The General instead de-

[20] Dellenbaugh, *Frémont and '49*, p. 375ff.
[21] *Congressional Globe, ut supra*, p. 1000.

manded whether Frémont would obey his orders of March 1st, and when the Lieutenant-Colonel hesitated, bade him reflect well, for his answer would be very important; if he wanted an hour for consideration, to take it; if a day, to take that. Frémont departed, and in about an hour returned and said that he would obey.[22]

The position of the deposed governor was now humiliating, and old-line officers of the regular army seem to have missed few opportunities to lacerate his feelings. His attitude was no doubt provocative. The hot-tempered accusation that Kearny was employing Mason as a spy was probably all too typical of Frémont in those days. Yet there can be no question that he was treated badly. He was sent back to Los Angeles, with orders to wind up the affairs of the California Battalion there and to surrender the public property. Colonel Mason, intensely prejudiced against Frémont, was sent after him, to have full charge over the southern district. Between these two men promptly occurred a series of clashes. Mason, experienced, practical, of stern and even harsh character, had an instinctive dislike for the impulsive, impractical explorer. Their collisions culminated in an angry scene in which Mason exclaimed, "None of your insolence, or I will put you in irons!" and in a challenge by Frémont to a duel, which Mason accepted.[23] General Kearny had to take decisive measures to prevent this encounter from occurring. It must be said that the challenge did Frémont anything but credit, and that Mason showed somewhat more cool sense and prudence than he in the matter. The explorer would have been wise to avoid any display of animosity, repress his explosive tendencies, do his work well, and conciliate his superiors. But the evidence seems clear that Mason hectored him and put needless indignities upon him in the presence of other officers.

Kearny had already made up his mind to take Frémont back East, and there place him under arrest for mutiny and insubor-

[22] *Court-Martial Proceedings*, p. 104.
[23] *Ibid.*, p. 142*ff*.

dination. For this reason, he brusquely refused Frémont's request, made in Los Angeles on May 10, 1847, that he be allowed to take sixty men and 129 horses which he had in readiness, and join his regiment under General Winfield Scott in Mexico. Later the young officer counted this refusal a gross injustice, for it contravened orders given by Scott himself. An equally peremptory "no" was given to Frémont's suggestion that he be allowed to return direct to the United States with his own original exploring party, at his own expense, instead of with Kearny's command. He was, in fact, now virtually a prisoner. How far Kearny's attitude fell short of the generosity and consideration which the War Department expected him to display will be evident from a reading of the instructions which Secretary of War Marcy had transmitted him under date of June 11, 1847:

When the dispatch from this department was sent out in November last, there was reason to believe that Lieutenant-Colonel Frémont would desire to return to the United States, and you were then directed to conform to his wishes in that respect. It is not now proposed to change that direction. But since that time it has become known here that he bore a conspicuous part in the conquest of California; that his services have been very valuable in that country, and doubtless will continue to be so should he remain there.

Impressed, as all engaged in the public service must be, with the great importance of harmony and cordial coöperation in carrying on military operations in a country so distant from the seat of authority, the President is persuaded that, when his definite instructions were received, all questions of difficulty were settled, and all feelings which have been elicited by the agitation of them have subsided.

Should Lieutenant-Colonel Frémont, who has the option to return or remain, adopt the latter alternative, the President does not doubt you will employ him in such a manner as will render his services most available to the public interest, having reference to his extensive acquaintance with the inhabitants of California, and his knowledge of their language, qualifications, independent of others, which it is supposed may be very useful in the present and prospective state of our affairs in that country.

But Kearny, far from acting in any such spirit, chose to push his charges against the explorer to the bitter end. The volunteers of the California Battalion, refusing to be mustered into service with poor pay, were discharged in a bitter frame of mind with no pay at all.[24] Left with a fragment of the loyal company which had entered California with him, only nineteen men in all, Frémont was compelled to trail eastward at the chariot-wheels of the General. All this, as he later put it, was "aggravated by a succession of indignities, commencing with a public exhibition and public insults before the assembled inhabitants and officers of the navy, at Monterey, on the Pacific, and receiving their crowning accumulation of affronts at Fort Leavenworth, on the Missouri."

In fact, the gossip of army circles and the settlers' camp-fires at the time was that Kearny intended the severest penalties for Frémont. Young W. T. Sherman heard some officers declare that the explorer would be shot; others, that he would be carried back home in irons. It may be mentioned that Sherman rode out to his tent to see him near Monterey, and took tea "without being much impressed by him." Kearny plainly told Frémont that many of the claims he had incurred in the name of the government would not be allowed, and would have to be met from his own pocket.[25] Thus the inglorious episode drew to its end. In June, the explorer joined Kearny in camp near the Sacramento, and about the middle of that month they set out on the long transcontinental journey by way of Fort Hall. Frémont was compelled by the General to leave behind him at San Francisco all his geological and botanical specimens; he had also to abandon his much-used scientific instruments; and he was not allowed to bring back with him Kern, the artist of the expedition, with his sketches and outline maps.[26]

Throughout the trip home the two parties, animated by

[24] Smith, *op. cit.*, II, p. 218.
[25] W. T. Sherman, *Memoirs*, I, p. 27; Captain Aram's story, New York *Herald*, October 1, 1856.
[26] Compare John T. Hughes, *Doniphan's Expedition*, Ch. 15.

mutual antagonism, had nothing but a formal intercourse; Kearny instructing Frémont to keep his men at a specified distance in the rear of his own Mormon escort. Once or twice, he roughly ordered Frémont to change his place of encampment. They passed on their way the camp of the Donner party, where so many had tragically perished, and Frémont paused to destroy all traces which might operate to the discouragement of emigrants, burning the broken wagons, ox-yokes, and other sad relics. On the Big Sandy River the two parties met a body of Western emigrants. Kearny with characteristic haughtiness stood on his dignity, merely inviting the settlers to come and see him—none of them doing so. But Frémont visited the emigrants' camp and spent the evening, giving them much valuable advice upon what they should do to cross the Sierras safely before winter set in. He urged them to press on without delay. Some seventy years later one of these emigrants recalled how offish and insolent they considered Kearny, and how much they liked Frémont.[27] On the day that the two military parties reached Fort Leavenworth, late in August, Kearny sent for the young Lieutenant-Colonel to come to him at the office of the commandant. There he was seated and a lieutenant read an order, directing him to give up his command, arrange his accounts, consider himself under arrest, and proceed to Washington to report.

The long ordeal was ended, and Frémont, free at last from the daily humiliation of Kearny's direct control, turned his face toward St. Louis with relief. Considering himself one of the chief figures in the conquest of California, the victim in recent months of adverse circumstances and military jealousy, he felt sure of vindication. As he and his friends reached Kansas Landing, the wide muddy river stretching away in the August haze below them, they saw a boat putting in at the

[27] Charles L. Camp, "William Alexander Trubody and the Overland Pioneers of 1847," *California Historical Society Quarterly*, XVI (1937), pp. 122-143. One emigrant, James Eastin, was a southern Democrat who liked Frémont so much that in 1856 he had difficulty in deciding whether or not to vote for him on the Republican ticket.

log wharf. Pushing through the crowd of roustabouts, loafers, and half-bewildered emigrants toward the gangplank, Frémont heard a choking cry—and Jessie ran into his arms.[28] She had come up from St. Louis to meet him. The joy of the reunion, after more than two years, may be imagined; and it was but the beginning of a reception which quickly became something of an ovation. Kearny, grim and taciturn, preceded Frémont down the river, and extended and exaggerated reports of their dispute had flown in advance of both. But public sympathy naturally inclined toward the young officer who had made so dashing a record in the West, and with whose family St. Louis had so many and such close ties. The river towns cheered him. St. Louis received him with acclamations; the leading citizens hastened to call upon him, and tendered him an invitation to a great public dinner, which he, of course, felt it necessary to decline. He did, however, make a brief speech to the crowd which surged about him on his arrival, reviewing and defending his course in California.

To his friends, who did not wait to hear the adverse evidence, the case was already clear. Frémont, like Columbus, they said, had returned from the discovery and conquest of a New World beyond the Rockies a prisoner and in disgrace.

[28] St. Louis correspondence, New York *Herald*, September 6, 1847.

XXI

A Famous Court-Martial

THE Benton family had been ready to take up arms the moment it had first heard of the clash between Frémont and Kearny. On June 7, 1847, the precise, methodical President Polk, having finished his morning's work at his desk and risen from his lunch, told the secretaries at one o'clock to open the doors of his public office. Among the first callers, richly dressed, was Jessie Frémont, and with her the short, sturdy figure of Kit Carson, weather-beaten, swarthy from the southwestern sun, and awkward in his soot-black new broadcloth. The famous scout had made the overland trip from the Pacific Coast in a little more than three months, and brought the Los Angeles news of February 25th with him. He was enjoying the hospitality of the Benton home in Washington, where his modesty and gentleness had already won him the warmest regard. Polk greeted the pair cordially.

Kit Carson, Jessie told the President, had been waiting several days for an opportunity to talk with him and tender his services as despatch-bearer to California. Carson then came forward and delivered Polk a long letter from Frémont, which had been addressed originally to Benton, and which Benton had sent on from St. Louis. It related in part to the quarrel over the governorship:

Mrs. Frémont seemed anxious [wrote the tactful Polk in his diary] to elicit from me some expression óf approbation for her husband's conduct, but I evaded [making any]. In truth, I consider that Colonel Frémont was greatly in the wrong when he refused to obey the orders issued to him by General Kearny. I think General Kearny was right also in his controversy with Commodore Stockton.

327

It was unnecessary, however, that I should say so to Colonel Frémont's wife, and I evaded giving her an answer.

At the Cabinet meeting next day the members agreed that Kearny had been in the right, Stockton and Frémont in the wrong. But Polk hoped the quarrel would blow over. Just a week later, Jessie called again with Kit Carson. This time she expressed a wish that her husband might be kept in California. The President told her that Carson would be given orders to Kearny leaving it to Frémont's option to stay on the Pacific Coast, or to return east and join his regiment, the Mounted Rifles, then in Mexico.

All this was a prelude to a much more serious attempt to enlist Polk against General Kearny. On August 17, 1847, as the hour for a Cabinet meeting approached, Senator Benton was ushered in at the White House. He was just back from the West, and Polk gladly took time to talk to him: [1]

He remarked that he had some time ago addressed a letter to the adjutant-general [relates Polk in his diary] demanding that Colonel Frémont should be recalled and a court of inquiry organized in his case, as due to the Colonel's honor and military character. I replied that I had read his communication, but that it had not been deemed necessary to take any action upon it. I told him that there had been some difficulty between the officers in California, which I much regretted, and that I had hoped it might not be necessary to institute any trial by court-martial. I also made a general remark to the effect that I had not deemed it necessary to do so. General Benton to this remarked in substance, I am glad to hear from you, sir, as President of the United States, that there has been nothing in Colonel Frémont's conduct which requires a court-martial in his case. I instantly said to him that he must not understand me as expressing any opinion in reference to the difficulty which had arisen between Colonel Frémont, General Kearny, and Commodore Stockton in California; but what I meant to say was that I hoped that the difficulty upon the arrival of the instructions of the 5th of November last had been settled, and that it might not be necessary to institute proceedings by a court-

[1] M. M. Quaife, ed., *Diary of James K. Polk,* III, p. 120ff.

martial in reference to the matter, and that I desired to avoid doing so if it could be done. To this General Benton said there was of course no commitment on my part.....

Benton thereupon added that he should introduce a resolution in the Senate calling for a full investigation of California affairs; and when Polk told him with some stiffness that the Administration had nothing to fear from the most searching inquiry, he explained that he did not mean to bother the Administration, but merely wished a broader investigation for Frémont's sake than the technical and limited procedure of a court-martial would allow. "He was evidently much excited," wrote Polk, "but suppressed his feelings and talked in a calm tone."

Benton's heat in the matter sprang from something more than his native irascibility and intense family loyalty; he was prone to imagine conspiracies, and believed that Kearny's army friends had banded together to destroy Frémont by malicious newspaper stories.[2] Unquestionably, one agent of Kearny's, Lieutenant W. H. Emory, whom the General had sent to Washington by way of Panama with despatches at about the same time that Frémont had sent Kit Carson overland, had spread partisan and ill-natured reports. Emory, who seems never to have been highly accurate in his statements, shared the usual disdain of regular army officers for Frémont.[3] He had no sooner reached Panama on his way east than he wrote a long letter attacking Stockton and Frémont. This appeared in the New York *Courier and Enquirer* of April 23, 1847. He seems to have furnished the material for prejudiced and misleading articles in the New Orleans *Picayune* of April 22nd and 27th, the Louisville *Journal* of May 1st, and the St. Louis *Republican* of May 4th, 1847. Benton believed that Lieutenant-Colonel Philip St. George Cooke of the Mormon Battalion was guilty of complicity in this defamatory campaign, which he ascribed

---

[2] See Benton's statement, *Congressional Globe, 1st Sess., Appendix*, p. 1019.

[3] Compare W. H. Emory, *Notes of a Military Reconnaissance from Fort Leavenworth ... to San Diego* (1848).

to jealousy; and there is no doubt that Cooke seldom lost an opportunity to speak slightingly of the explorer.[4] The effect upon Jessie of the sudden avalanche of press attacks was later bitterly described by Benton to the Senate:

There was a wife—young and sensitive—to whom the light of heaven became hateful, and darkness terrible, and society intolerable—who fled two thousand miles, to meet in the wilderness the "mutineer in irons," as some gave it out—a young wife, tranquil in the day, when people looked upon her—convulsed and frantic in the night when left to her own agonies—the heart bursting, the brain burning, the body shivering; and I, her father, often called, not to witness, but to calm, this terrible agitation—and these publications the cause of all.

Benton swore vengeance, and his demands made the court-martial unescapable. When aroused he was a bitter, implacable foe, and he was a great national power whom even Polk had reason to conciliate. By late summer the stage was all set. Kit Carson had left Washington, and braving the difficult trip to Santa Fé, was far in the Southwest again. Frémont and Jessie, after their joyous reunion at Kansas Landing, had lingered in St. Louis at the Brants' only a few days, and then had hurried on by way of Blue Lick, Kentucky, where Mrs. Benton was staying at one of the Senator's farms to recruit her health, to Washington; every stage in their journey chronicled in the newspapers.[5] Kearny had preceded them. Alarmed by the Senator's anger and the growing storm, he stayed with his family in St. Louis only four days, and was in New York, getting ready for the trial, on September 10, 1847.[6]

Army groups and political circles felt that a *cause célèbre* was about to begin. It divided attention with even the final battles of Scott's army before Mexico City—Molino del Rey on September 8th and Chapultepec on September 13th. Its possible

---

[4] Compare Philip St. George Cooke, *The Conquest of New Mexico and California*, p. 286*ff*.

[5] St. Louis *Weekly Reveillé*, September 20, 1847.

[6] New York *Herald*, September 11, 1847.

effect on Benton's loyalty to Polk and on Democratic strength was eagerly discussed. Already it was evident that public sympathy, with its natural leaning toward a dashing, picturesque young hero and a man under heavy and ill-explained attack, inclined toward Frémont. Benton was all confidence. "We shall demolish him (Kearny) with all ease, and overwhelm him with disgrace," he wrote on October 7th. And a little later he reassured Frémont: "You may be at ease. The enemy is now in our hands, and may the Lord have mercy on them; for I feel as if I could not."

The explorer was soon busy, together with Benton and his brother-in-law, William Carey Jones, preparing his defense. On first reaching Washington he had been called south by the last illness of his mother in Aiken, South Carolina; but she died before he arrived, and he could only accompany her body to Charleston, where she was buried. Before leaving the capital he wrote the Adjutant-General, requesting that he be given a trial as soon as the necessary witnesses could be assembled in Washington. He would have preferred, he said, to wait for Stockton and for leading citizens of California who were ready to testify in his behalf; but he was so eager for a speedy vindication that he would ask only a month to bring certain witnesses from Missouri. A larger reason than his mere desire for personal justification, he added, called for the court-martial.[7] The accusations against him covered the whole field of his operations in California, both civil and military, from his first arrival in 1846. The testimony before the court would therefore be a history of the conquest of California and an explanation of the policy he had pursued there. Being a military subordinate, he could make no report, but the trial would serve as a substitute, throwing light on the conduct of all the American officers, and indicating the proper policy to be pursued toward native Californians, American settlers, and Indians.

Polk's diary shows that he and his advisers were deeply concerned, and the court-martial was the principal business

[7] Bigelow, *Frémont*, p. 217*ff.*

considered at the Cabinet meeting of September 18, 1847. It shows also that the choleric Benton was, as various newspapers asserted, really injuring his son-in-law by excess of zeal.[8] Benton called at the White House for a long chat one evening late in October, a fortnight before the court-martial, and could talk of little but Frémont's virtues and Kearny's malignity. Seated in front of the fire, he declared with vehement gestures that the deepest concern of his life was to see justice done the young explorer. If the inquiry were not full and complete, he threatened, he would have four other officers court-martialed —Kearny, and the impudent young men of Kearny's entourage, W. H. Emory, Captain H. S. Turner, and St. George Cooke. His excitement was painfully evident, and Polk, who listened attentively, was careful to say as little as possible. The President, in fact, was becoming a little sour toward the Benton family.[9]

A day or two after this call, Polk was treated with great rudeness by Benton's son Randolph, who strode in to ask for a lieutenancy at the front, grew impatient and impudent when Polk said that commissions went by merit and not by favor, and swore audibly as he flung himself out of the door. The Senator was meanwhile bombarding the Secretary of War with requests and demands regarding the trial, some of which were inadmissible; and as the month closed, it was necessary to give most of two more Cabinet meetings to their consideration. "Benton," sighed the harassed President, "is a man of violent passions." Well realizing that he was likely to make the Senator an enemy of his administration, Polk was resolved that the explorer should be tried without favor or privilege: [10]

[8] Compare St. Louis *Republican*, August 27th; St. Louis *Weekly Reveillé*, September 13, 1847.

[9] Polk, *Diary*, III, pp. 176, 177. It is interesting to note that Polk had wished to have Benton made lieutenant-general in supreme command during the Mexican War, a plan defeated in the Senate after the necessary legislation had passed the House. Benton later declined appointment as major-general to serve in Mexico. W. M. Meigs, *Life of Benton*, p. 363ff.

[10] Polk, *Diary*, III, pp. 202-205.

I know of no reason why this case should produce more interest or excitement than the trial of any other officer charged with a military offense, and yet it is manifest that Senator Benton is resolved to make it so. I think he is pursuing a mistaken policy so far as Col. Frémont is concerned, but that is an affair of which he must judge. I will do my duty in the case, without fear or affection.

Thus the trial came on. It was superb Indian summer weather. Pennsylvania Avenue was lively with carriages and fashionably dressed promenaders. The hotels were awakening from their summer sleep to welcome the first politicians arriving in preparation for Congress; Douglas of Illinois, the "little giant," was at Coleman's; Clingman of North Carolina at Brown's; Bishop Polk of Louisiana at Gadsby's. A corps of Indians who happened to be in town divided attention with the dozens of army officers who had arrived to be witnesses or spectators at the court-martial.[11] Headlines on the front pages of the Washington and New York dailies dealt with what was considered the most dramatic army trial since the court-martial of General Wilkinson thirty years before. At twelve o'clock noon on November 2, 1847, the panel of thirteen officers, carried to the arsenal in Washington by a special omnibus, was called to order by Brevet Brigadier-General G. M. Brooke, of the Fifth Infantry.

Each side had its body of retainers and witnesses who glowered at one another, while the principals surprised the reporters by sitting as cool as cucumbers. Especial notice was attracted by Frémont's "desert rangers and mountain scalers," including his veteran scout Alexis Godey, his faithful aide Dick Owens, the trapper Thomas Williams, and Risdon Moore, the Illinoisan of his party who had disagreed with him regarding his early California operations, but who after a night in jail had become a whole-hearted adherent. Kearny and his associates, among them the Captain H. S. Turner whom Benton had named as a special object of his wrath, blazed with gold lace. The General

[11] New York *Herald*, November 4, 5, 1847.

looked solemn, stern, and inflexible, while Frémont, sitting
at a side table with the Senator, "appeared as if writing at his
camp in the mountains." Benton, calmly self-possessed,
watched every step in the proceedings like a hawk.[12]

At the outset, the explorer announced that he would make
no use of technical or legal points of defense, would raise no
artificial objections, and would do all that he could do to expedite the trial. The three essential charges were of mutiny from
January 17, to May 9, 1847; disobedience of the lawful commands of a superior officer; and conduct prejudicial to good
order and discipline. Frémont declared that he considered the
whole affair to be a comedy of three errors: "first, in the faulty
order sent out from this place; next, in the unjustifiable pretensions of Gen. Kearny; thirdly, in the conduct of the government in sustaining these pretensions, and the last of these
errors I consider the greatest of the three." Kearny would have
preferred to rest his case upon the worst charge alone—
mutiny.[13] His blood was now up, and he shortly angered Frémont and Benton by making an accusation which touched the
personal honor of the former as nothing else had done.

This was the accusation that Frémont, when summoned to
acknowledge the authority of Kearny instead of Stockton, at-
tempted to drive a bargain regarding the civil governorship of
California. The effort to sell himself to the highest bidder, said
Kearny, took place in the General's headquarters at Los
Angeles on January 17th.

He asked me if I would appoint him governor. I told him I expected shortly to leave California for Missouri; that I had, previous
to leaving Santa Fé, asked for permission to do so, and was in hopes
of receiving it; that as soon as the country was quieted I should,
most probably, organize a civil government in California; and that
I, at that time, knew of no objections to my appointing him as the
governor. He then stated that he would see Commodore Stockton,

---

[12] Washington *National Intelligencer*, November 3-7, 1847; New York *Herald*,
November 6, 1847.
[13] Benton, *Thirty Years' View*, II, p. 716.

and that, unless he appointed him governor at once, he would not obey his orders, and left me.

This charge Frémont indignantly denied. It was essentially a charge that he had a corrupt motive, and he repudiated it angrily. Never in his life, he said, had he either begged or bargained for any office, though three Presidents, Jackson, Tyler, and Polk, had given him appointments.[14]

Unquestionably we may accept Frémont's denial, for while he was frequently hot-headed, he was never base. Kearny, as Frémont and Benton had no difficulty in showing, was an unreliable witness, whose memory in other particulars was highly untrustworthy. At the same time, it is almost certain that some mention of the governorship had been made in the conversation between Kearny and Frémont. Frémont actually received from Stockton a commission as governor bearing date of January 17, the day in question. A fortnight later, in a private letter to Benton, he wrote that "both [Kearny and Stockton] offered me the commission and post of governor; Commodore Stockton, to redeem his pledge to that effect, immediately, and General Kearny offering to give the commission in four or six weeks." This was unquestionably true. Kit Carson tells us that Kearny had spoken repeatedly, in his journey from Santa Fé to California, of his intention of making Frémont governor.[15] It is altogether likely that the explorer, with his usual frankness, told Kearny that he wished to be civil governor and that Stockton had promised him the place; it is altogether likely that Kearny, in reply, said that if the young man would be patient, would accept his authority, and would wait three or four weeks, he would himself make the appointment. Kearny's error lay in giving this conversation a sinister interpretation.

[14] *Court-Martial Proceedings*, pp. 380, 392ff.

[15] *Congressional Globe, 30th Cong., 1st Sess., Appendix*, p. 978. W. H. Russell told the court-martial that Kearny had expressed this intention: "I only remember distinctly that he spoke of his intention of appointing Colonel Frémont governor." *Proceedings*, p. 263.

The court-martial dragged slowly forward, in the formal, punctilious fashion of army trials. Public interest for a time remained surprisingly intense. James Gordon Bennett's New York *Herald,* which had a truly national circulation, published two columns regarding the case on November 7, 1847; one column the following day; gave it almost the entire first page on November 9th; and throughout the remainder of the month allotted it from one-eighth to two and a half columns daily. Everywhere in the West and South the press took up the trial at great length. It advertised Frémont to the American public as never before, and on the whole the testimony presented him in a favorable light. Nobody could read the evidence and blame his insubordination in very severe terms. The oldest officers of the army, as members of the court later admitted, would have been puzzled to decide the relative rank and rights of the Commodore and the General. He was the victim of a dispute between them, a dispute not of his own making. For another consideration, insubordination was not rated a grave offense by the individualistic Americans of 1847. Finally, the trial wrote indelibly into the public mind the fact that he had played an early, daring, and important part in the events which gave California to the nation.

Frémont and his counsel made it clear that his refusal to obey Kearny had been based upon the broadest possible foundation, Stockton's constructive right to set up a civil government following conquest. They needed only to quote his letter to Shubrick at the time (February 7, 1847); a letter in which he declared that Kearny had come out with instructions designed for a still unconquered country, and had instead found one fully conquered, to which these instructions clearly did not apply:

The conquest of California was undertaken and completed by the joint effort of Commodore Stockton and myself, in obedience to what we regarded paramount duties from us to our government; that done, the next necessary step was the organization of a civil government, designed to maintain the conquest by the exercise of mild and wholesome civil restraints over the people, rather than by the iron rule of military force.

The result of our labors, which were precisely what was contemplated by the instructions of General Kearny, were promptly communicated to the Executive of the Union by an express, which has not yet brought back the approval or disapproval of the government. General Kearny's instructions being, therefore, to the letter fully anticipated by others, I did not feel myself at liberty to yield a position so important to the interests of my country until, after a full understanding of all the grounds, it should be the pleasure of my government that I should do so.

Nominally on the defensive, Frémont and his counsel were actually able much of the time to take the offensive against Kearny. They accused him, quite unjustly, of entering California to steal the laurels and the material benefits which Stockton and Frémont had won by their forced marches, dangerous skirmishes, and constant hardships. They implied that the old-line officers were unjustly jealous of the exploits of the young outsider. They emphasized the fact that the brass cannon which Kearny had lost in the defeat of San Pasqual had been recaptured by Frémont, and hinted that Kearny (who never reported its recovery to the government) felt humiliated and jealous on this score. They declared that Kearny's deliberate intent had been to ruin Frémont; that with this purpose he had refused to give Frémont notice of his impending arrest; that he had forced upon the Lieutenant-Colonel the necessity of choosing between a surprise trial, or allowing ruinous charges, supported by a defamatory press campaign, to hang over his head. These statements had enough truth to give them effectiveness. Finally, they said, Kearny had taken pains to detain Frémont's friend Gillespie in California, with the evident hope of crippling his side of the case; but fortunately Gillespie had extricated himself and reached Washington.

In fine, it was an exceedingly bitter court-martial. When the day came—January 24, 1848—for Frémont to sum up his defense, the room was crowded with army officers, Congressmen,

and fashionable ladies. Before this distinguished audience, Frémont flung accusations of perjury and false testimony in
Kearny's face. His arguments, said the reporters, made a strong
impression.[16] They would have been still stronger had they
been more moderate in tone, and had he avoided unnecessary
imputations upon the acts of the brave and effective soldier
who confronted him; but he closed his plea well:

> If it was a crime in me to accept the governorship from Commo-
> dore Stockton, it was a crime in him to have bestowed it; and in
> either event, crime or not, the government which knew of his inten-
> tion to appoint me, and did not forbid it, has lost the right of prose-
> cuting either of us.
>
> My acts in California have all been with high motives and a de-
> sire for the public service. My scientific labors did something to open
> California to the knowledge of my countrymen; its geography had
> been a sealed book. My military operations were conquests without
> bloodshed; my civil administration was for the public good. I offer
> California, during my administration, for comparison with the most
> tranquil portions of the United States; I offer it in contrast to the
> condition of New Mexico at the same time. I prevented civil war
> against Governor Stockton, by refusing to join General Kearny
> against him; I arrested civil war against myself, by consenting to be
> deposed....
>
> I have been brought as a prisoner and a criminal from that
> country. I could return to it, after this trial is over, without rank or
> guards, and without molestation from the people, except to be im-
> portuned for the money which the government owes them.
>
> I am now ready to receive the sentence of the court.

This was more dignified than Benton's conduct in the closing
days of the trial. He conceived the idea that Kearny had looked
"insultingly and fiendishly" at Frémont, and that it was therefore his duty, when Kearny took the stand, to glare at him in
an angry, intimidatory way. The result was an explosion by
Kearny, a direct clash between the General and Senator, and
an angry scene in which the latter, boasting that he had out-

[16] New York *Herald*, January 27, 1848.

stared Kearny "till his eyes fell—till they fell upon the floor!" was rebuked by the presiding officer.

After three days of deliberation, the court on January 31, 1848, found Frémont guilty on all three charges, and sentenced him to dismissal from the service. Six of the thirteen members recommended him to the clemency of President Polk, mentioning the peculiar circumstances of the case, and the distinguished professional services rendered by the defendant. The verdict thereupon went to the Cabinet, which devoted the greater part of two meetings to its consideration. All the members agreed that Frémont had been guilty of disobedience, but most of them doubted whether he had committed mutiny, and they were unanimous that so valuable an officer ought not to be dismissed. In the end, Secretary of State Buchanan and Attorney-General Nathan Clifford advised that Polk disapprove the sentence as being too severe, while Secretary of War Marcy, Secretary of the Navy Mason, and Postmaster-General Cave Johnson urged him to approve it and then remit the penalty.[17] Polk decided to follow the latter course, and made formal announcement that, believing Frémont to be innocent of mutiny but guilty on the other two charges, he approved the sentence of the court-martial, but canceled the punishment. "Lieutenant-Colonel Frémont," he ordered, "will accordingly be released from arrest, will resume his sword, and report for duty."

The President might have smiled sardonically as he published his determination. It was upon the insistence of Benton that Kearny's original charge of mutiny against Frémont, which Polk found unwarranted, had been broadened into a court-martial on the other two charges as well, which he pronounced warranted. Benton's temper had led him into a serious tactical blunder.

Although the President's decision was softened by a reference to "the previous meritorious and valuable services of Lieutenant-Colonel Frémont," it was too much for the high-

[17] Polk, *Diary*, III, pp. 335-340.

spirited explorer to endure. Probably he needed no advice from the angry Benton to shape his course. Instantly he presented his resignation, declaring that he was innocent and could not, by accepting Polk's clemency, admit the justice of the verdict. A month later, on March 15th, 1848, Polk accepted the resignation. Frémont was thus, at the age of thirty-four, released to civil life. An unfortunate and totally unnecessary episode had been closed.

Technically, the verdict of the court-martial was just; but from a broader point of view it was excessively severe, and President Polk would have done well to accept the counsel of Buchanan and Clifford, and refuse it his endorsement. The real fault attached to the Administration itself for issuing such conflicting orders that Stockton and Kearny naturally disagreed as to their authority. Kearny was morally, if not technically, censurable for concealing from Frémont the directions from Washington which decisively ended this conflict. His attitude had been bullying and harsh, and even so severe a critic of Frémont as Royce admits that the younger man appears in much the better light. However rash the explorer had been at first and however quarrelsome later, a reprimand would have been an adequate punishment. When blame should have been apportioned among all the chief actors, it was unfair to concentrate it upon a devoted and energetic officer whose chief offense was that he had not been able to decide which of two quarreling superiors was in the wrong.

That the public took this view is evident from the fact that the verdict did Frémont not a whit of harm. The press gave it scanty space, for every one was tired of the affair; one journal remarked that the trial had taken longer than Scott's siege of Vera Cruz. The general opinion in Washington had been that the explorer ought to be cleared. When the verdict was handed down, many declared that it showed the usual jealousy of veteran army men for a brilliant young newcomer. This was the view of Bennett's *Herald*, which remarked that "during the progress of the assizes we saw, from time to time, evidences of

hostility on the part of members of the court against Lieutenant-Colonel Frémont, who held a higher commission, and
was a greater, though a younger man, than a majority of his
triers; and what we then suspected, has this afternoon been
presented to us as actual truth." [18] But even the Washington
newspapers evinced little interest. The talk of the day was
upon the rivalry of Harry Clay and Zachary Taylor for the
Whig nomination, the sudden death of John Quincy Adams, the
Wilmot Proviso, and the details of the treaty with Mexico.
Frémont's condemnation thus passed almost unnoticed, after
weeks during which his defense and the story of his California
exploits had been blazoned the nation over.

He actually gained in reputation by the trial. In one sense it
was no misfortune to be taken from the Army, where his rashness and dislike of restraint would have kept him chafing, but
in another he was a heavy loser, for his resignation broke off
abruptly his career as explorer in the service of the Topographical Corps. The whole outlook before him seemed changed. He
took the termination of his military ambitions bitterly to heart,
and Jessie's sorrow was even keener. But the resentment of
neither approached that of the irascible Benton. Polk wrote
later: [19]

There is every indication now that he [Benton] will join the
Whigs in the support of General Taylor, at all events until he can
get offices for his three sons-in-law. If I had failed to do my duty
in Col. Frémont's case, and given an office which he sought for his
Whig son-in-law [Jones], he would never have quarreled with me.
His course toward me and my administration for more than a year
past has been selfish and wholly unprincipled.

Benton indeed lost few opportunities to show his enmity for
Polk. He introduced a bill to reform the procedure of courts-
martial; he opposed the Administration on the treaty with

[18] New York *Herald*, January 31, February 21, 1848. H. H. Bancroft
writes (*History of California*, V, p. 457) of the explorer's adherents: "And
it cannot be denied that they won a victory; that the verdict of popular
sympathy was in Frémont's favor."

[19] *Diary*, IV, p. 330.

Mexico; he ceased to call at the White House, and for more than a twelvemonth had no intercourse whatever with the President; and he talked of publishing a letter of Polk's which would injure the Administration. When in August, 1848, Polk nominated Kearny to a brevet-major-generalship, Benton declared that he would filibuster till the end of the session to defeat the appointment. He harangued the Senate for thirteen days, in a genuinely effective philippic against Kearny combined with laudation of Frémont; but in the end the nomination was confirmed.[20]

Kearny died this same year in St. Louis. On his deathbed, he sent word to Jessie, who was in the city, that he would be grateful for a visit, but she sternly refused the proffered reconciliation. Her second baby and first son, Benton, who was born in July, had then just died from an affection of the heart which she always believed was caused by the anxieties she underwent during the trial; and she said that between her and Kearny there was a little grave that she could not forget.[21]

Yet the two names have been strangely linked in our geography. In more than one state, like Nebraska, a town or county named Frémont stands in near proximity to a town or county named Kearny; in more than one city, like San Francisco, Frémont Street and Kearny Street lie close together. When the United States entered the First World War, two National Guard camps were established on the Pacific Coast; one, in southern California, Camp Kearny, and the other, in northern California, Camp Frémont.

[20] E. I. McCormac, *James K. Polk*, p. 476*ff*.
[21] Jessie Benton Frémont MSS, Bancroft Library.

XXII

Starvation and Cannibalism

PASSENGERS on the lake steamboat *Saratoga*, bound from Buffalo westward in the early fall of 1848, saw on its shelter deck an interesting family group: Frémont, in civilian clothes, with close-cropped beard, long mustache, and heavy curling dark hair, slightly grizzled in places; his still girlish wife, carrying a baby in her arms; the little girl of six, Lilly; and a servant. They kept to themselves and invited no approaches. But to one or two fellow travelers who won their confidence they spoke freely. They were on their way to California, with the intention of making it their future home. They frankly admitted that they were poor; they had nothing but Frémont's savings from his small army salary, and they faced the possibility that, if Congress refused to pay the debts he had contracted in his California operations, he would be held responsible for them. However, they hoped quickly to gain a footing in that rich land. Frémont had placed in the hands of Larkin, before leaving to undergo his court-martial, a small sum—$3,000—for the purchase of a ranch; and friends in the East had furnished him credit to send around Cape Horn the agricultural implements and milling machinery he would need there. They had health and courage. It was plain that Frémont was depressed by the verdict of the court-martial, which he regarded as a deep injustice, but Jessie assiduously comforted him. "And it was very pleasant," later wrote a passenger,[1] "to see how he was cheered on and encouraged by the vast prospect of doing good which was opened

[1] Letter of T. C. Rogers, Buffalo *Republic*, reprinted in New York *Tribune*, July 8, 1856.

to them in that new territory. Neither had any other thought or expectation than to obtain an honorable and respected position by their own industry and economy."

They were not going out, however, as mere emigrants. Jessie was accompanying him only as far west as Westport on the Missouri, when she would turn back and take a ship to California by the Panama route. Frémont would meanwhile assume command of a new exploring expedition to cross the Rockies by a southern pass. Nothing shows better the buoyant courage of the man than the fact that, a few months after the court-martial, he had organized his own fourth expedition.

Though it was to prove the least fruitful of all his exploring trips, and though it was destined to end in utter disaster, its objects possessed real merit. Frémont had always wished to cross the continent on a central line intersecting the head of the Rio Grande, and he now intended to do so. But this was not all. Throughout the middle west men were talking of a railroad to the Pacific; some wealthy citizens of St. Louis were interested in making that city the eastern terminus, and Frémont planned to ascertain for them whether a central route was practicable. Since the chief question was whether the snow would be an insuperable obstacle, he had determined to cross the ranges in midwinter. Just how sufficient funds were obtained for the expedition is not clear. Very probably the men planning a Pacific railway subscribed a considerable sum; Senator Benton may have contributed some money; and it seems that several of Frémont's followers, notably Edward M. Kern, recently commander at Sutter's Fort, and his two brothers, furnished their services free. Kern and several of Frémont's other witnesses in Washington had eagerly urged the undertaking, and preparations had been in progress since May.[2]

Thus did Frémont cling to his career as an explorer. The renown he had won in that calling was too great to permit him to give it up. While the court-martial was still fresh in men's minds, he had received from citizens of Charleston a gold-

---

[2] St. Louis Weekly *Reveillé*, July 3, 1848.

mounted sword and engraved gold scabbard, both of beautiful workmanship, as "a memorial of their high appreciation of the gallantry and science he has displayed in his services in Oregon and California." [3] The bill to pay the various California claims which he had incurred during his military service on the Coast, seven hundred thousand dollars in all, gave a number of Senators, before its final passage, an opportunity to eulogize his work. Benton, of course, was foremost, but Senator Clark of Rhode Island paid him glowing compliments, while John A. Dix of New York declared that he had "exhibited a combination of energy, promptitude, sagacity, and prudence, which indicated the highest capacity for civil and military command," and that his decisive movements had unquestionably "kept California out of the hands of British subjects." [4]

The magazines of the day united in praising him, for nearly all the reviews had by now published appreciative articles upon his explorations. An anonymous writer for the *Southern Literary Messenger* remarked that his reports on the West must always be the basis of scientific information upon the regions he had traversed, "and the name of Frémont is immortalized among the great travelers and explorers, and will doubtless survive as long as those of the Sierra Nevada, or the Sacramento." The *Eclectic Review* gave him many pages. The *Democratic Review* thought that he had been insufficiently rewarded: [5]

The personal merits of Capt. Frémont, in these expeditions, have been great, and evince high talent for command and for enterprise. With an average of 25 men, and no officer to aid him, he has made 10,000 miles of march among tribes of savages, without ever being exposed to surprise or defeat, providing for the subsistence of men and horses, and preserving order, subordination, and cheerful obedience throughout his command. Without the aid of scientific assistants, he has so enriched his report with science as to seem to have been the work of professional savants.... The honorary reward of

---

[3] Charleston *Mercury*, September 21, 1847; Bigelow, *Frémont*, p. 222.
[4] *Congressional Globe*, *30th Cong., 1st Sess.*, Appendix, p. 175ff.
[5] *Southern Literary Messenger*, XV, pp. 528, 529; *Democratic Review*, XVII.

brevet captain has been bestowed upon him. Lewis and Clark received something more substantial—double pay, 1,600 acres of land each, promotion to generals, appointment of government commission to treat with Indians, and copyright in their Journal. Certainly, as first explorers, they were entitled to great merit; but they lack the science which Capt. Frémont carried into his expeditions.

Even abroad he was now well-known; a little later, Baron von Humboldt, on behalf of the Prussian Government, transmitted to him a gold medal for progress in the sciences, while the Royal Geographical Society awarded him the Founder's Medal for distinguished services to geography.[6] It was unfortunate that he did not write a full scientific report of the third expedition which culminated in the California fighting. Instead, he contented himself with a careful map of Oregon and California, of which the Senate ordered twenty thousand copies, and a short *Geographical Memoir* accompanying it. This *Memoir,* which was the first publication to give currency to the phrase "the Golden Gate," might have rivaled the reports of his earlier expeditions but for the court-martial, and the inability of Jessie to help him; she served for a time as amanuensis, and then her health broke down. Writing for Frémont one evening, she suddenly said, "Do not move the lamp, it makes it too dark," and went into a prolonged fainting fit, from which she emerged a temporary invalid.[7] Thereafter, Frémont spoke of his task as "the cursed memoir," and dismissed it as summarily as his conscience would permit him. He offered to furnish Congress with a much fuller record of his trip, but although a committee under Senator Breese of Illinois reported in favor of this, the work was never authorized, and a distinct gap was thus left in the literature of the West.

Nevertheless, the *Geographical Memoir* was a valuable document, which contained some of the most important of Frémont's generalizations upon western geography. He divided America beyond the Great Salt Lake into three regions, the Great Basin,

[6] Bigelow, *Frémont,* 327ff.
[7] Jessie Benton Frémont MSS, Bancroft Library.

the Sierras, and the coastal belt; emphasizing the importance of the mountain chain as a divide between the desert on the east, the garden-lands on the west:

Stretching along the coast, and at the general distance of 150 miles from it, this great mountain wall receives the warm winds, charged with vapor, which sweep across the Pacific ocean, precipitates their accumulated moisture in fertilizing rains and snows on its western flank, and leaves cold and dry winds to pass on to the east. Hence the characteristic differences of the two regions—mildness, fertility, and a superb vegetable kingdom on one side, comparative barrenness and cold on the other.

His description of the partly arid plains of the Great Basin was by far the best yet published. In this he emphasized the importance of the grassy, wooded interior mountains, giving rise to small streams which lost themselves in lakes or the dry plains; and he justly remarked that the region seemed more Asiatic than American, resembling the elevated district between the Caspian Sea and northern Persia. Another illuminating passage was his comparison of the coastal slope of California to Italy; while a very important feature was the emphasis which he laid upon the Humboldt River Valley as a great avenue of communication. As an English scholar has written, the *Memoir* "shows that Frémont was not only a great explorer, but also a geographer with a real understanding of the conception of a region as a natural unit." [8]

Other scientific fruits of the third expedition were of distinct importance. The map which Preuss drew from surveys by Frémont and others was the most accurate yet made of the Far West. More than a thousand botanical specimens had been preserved, and John Torrey's treatise upon them was shortly published by the Smithsonian Institution.[9] Geological specimens had been collected, interesting sketches made of scenery

---

[8] This *Geographical Memoir upon Upper California* was published as *House Misc. Doc., 30 Cong., 2d Sess.,* No. 5. E. W. Gilbert's comment is in his *Exploration of Western America,* 1800-1850, p. 189.

[9] *Plantæ Frémontianæ, Smithsonian Contributions* (1850).

and animals, and a large number of bird skins prepared with plumage intact. Frémont had been plunged in June, 1848, into a controversy with Captain Wilkes regarding the accuracy of his topographical work and the consequent figures for the California coast line, from which he emerged with enhanced scientific credit. He was regarded as the best American authority upon the great new lands just acquired by the Mexican War and the Oregon Treaty, and his writings were more than ever in demand. When he set out on his fourth expedition, he felt that he was continuing an invaluable national work, and with new discoveries might wipe out old humiliations.

Once more, then, the frontier; once more the free open prairies stretching before the explorer! Years later, in preparing to write the second volume of his *Memoirs,* never published, Frémont jotted down some rough notes upon the adventure which are still kept in his manuscripts:

A winter expedition—about snow obstacles and home for family—preparations at St. Louis—Campbell and Filley—journey up the river—death of the child—Mrs. Frémont at Maj. Cummins—camp on the frontier—Mrs. Frémont's visits to the camp—Scott and the quails.

Capt. Cathcart—personnel of the party (33 men)—Godey—the Kerns—King—Brackenridge—Creutzfeldt (when was he with me?) —The two Indian boys Gregorio and Juan—Proue—the three Canadians.

Route up the Southern Kansas—the Arkansas bare of timber and exposed to snowstorms—for 400 miles abundant timber, grain, and excellent grass—Valley of the Kansas the best approach to the mountains—the valley soil of superior quality, well timbered, abundant grasses, the route direct—would afford good settlement for 400 miles.

The big timber, thirty miles below Bent's Fort—Fitzpatrick and the Indians, six hundred lodges, talks and feasts, Indians report snow deeper than for many years—November 17, mountains show themselves for first time, covered with snow, the country around also—not discouraged.

Thirty-three men, with horses and pack animals, made a large expedition for an almost penniless leader, but numbers were needed, for the Indian tribes before him, the Ute, Apache, Navajo, and others, were hostile or uneasy. The Campbell and Filley here mentioned were Robert Campbell and O. D. Filley, who, with Thornton Grimsley, all three substantial St. Louis business men, furnished financial and other assistance. Campbell had been a traveler, trapper, and pioneer of the Far West; Filley, the manufacturer of a Dutch oven then widely used for baking, gave Frémont a large part of his camp equipment. The expedition included many experienced men. Alexis Godey, Frémont's old friend and companion, was again hunter; E. M. Kern was again artist; Charles Preuss once more went out as topographer. Others who had been with Frémont before were Captain Henry King, Charles Taplin, and three mountain-men, Thomas E. Brackenridge, John Scott, and Thomas S. Martin. Among the new men were three French Canadians well experienced in the West, F. Creutzfeldt, who was employed as botanist, E. M. Kern's two brothers, Richard H. Kern, an artist, and Benjamin J. Kern, a physician, and a roving Englishman, Captain A. Cathcart of the 11th Prince Albert Hussars, who hoped to enjoy some hunting and adventure. Another new recruit was Micajah McGehee, a capable young scion of a distinguished Mississippi family, who kept a diary which in its full manuscript form is an invaluable source of information. Others of the party were L. D. Vincenthaler, who is called by Frémont and others Vincent Haler, Henry Wise, and Raphael Proue. The three California Indians, Manuel, Joaquin, and Gregorio, went along.

At the outset Frémont was saddened by what his notes call the "death of the child"—his before mentioned son, Benton.[10] The little boy had always been delicate and his physicians in

[10] Jessie Benton Frémont MSS, Bancroft Library.

Washington knew that his span of life was likely to be short; but the young mother (Jessie was still only twenty-four) had no knowledge of this. The youngster died while the parents were traveling up the Missouri by steamboat to the starting-point of the fourth expedition.

The night after Frémont and his party set out from West-port Landing for the west, Jessie and her colored servant slept at the Indian Agency there. This agency, a queer, irregular string of log houses, was in the charge of a Major Cummins. Toward dawn Jessie and her servant were disturbed by the piteous cries of a mother wolf hunting some cubs which Major Cummins had just killed, and they had hardly settled to sleep again when their rest was broken by Frémont himself. In his usual impetuous way he had ridden ten miles back from camp to have a final hour with his wife, and Kitty had to get up and make a pot of tea. "And so," wrote Mrs. Frémont after-ward,[11] "with our early tea for a stirrup-cup, 'he gave his bridle rein a shake,' and we went our ways, one into the midwinter snows of untracked mountains, the other to the long sea-voyage through the tropics."

It was October 21, 1848, when Frémont's party set out, and on November 16th they reached Bent's Fort. Already they had encountered inclement weather. The Arkansas was full of ice where they crossed it; they met a blizzard smiting the plains on the fourth; and at Bent's Fort the snow was a foot deep. The trappers and Indians at the fort told them that the depth of the snow, the brilliant aurora borealis, and other signs be-tokened an early and unusually severe winter. As they went on the outlook continued gloomy. A short detour took them to the "Big Timbers" near the fort, where Frémont visited his old guide Fitzpatrick, now stationed there as Indian agent; per-haps hoping to obtain his services again. According to Fré-mont's notes, on the seventeenth they sighted the Rockies, which were heavily mantled in white. Then on November 21st, they reached Pueblo, a mere hamlet inhabited by a few old

[11] Jessie Benton Frémont, *A Year of American Travel*, p. 20.

mountain-men, some wintering there, some settled for life with their Indian squaws. Once the fur trade had made it the seat of a considerable activity, but now it was in decay.

Here again the old mountaineers warned them against the season; they pointed to the heavy snow all about, declared that the cold in the ranges was unprecedented, and asserted that the high peaks to the west could not be crossed in winter. But Frémont was determined to press on, for a bitter winter season offered just such a test of the practicability of a railroad as he desired. His plan was to march west from the headwaters of the Rio Grande along the line of the thirty-eighth parallel, or near it, for he believed that he would find a good pass over the Sierras between the points marked by Walker Pass and Mono Lake. Certain parts of this region had not then been visited even by trappers, and few men knew that the Cañon of the Colorado cut like a tremendous gash through it. Here, between the upper Rio Grande and harsh western rim of the Utah plateaus, lie some of the worst mountain fastnesses in the United States; formidable even in summer, and to men with the best maps and equipment of the present day. One of the bitterest winters in human memory was descending, and Frémont was heading straight for this forbidding country.

Until he reached Pueblo, Frémont had no guide. Neither Kit Carson nor Fitzpatrick had been available; he had found nobody else. At Pueblo he belatedly engaged the noted trapper and hunter "Old Bill" Williams, a personage rather more typical of the frontiersmen of the time and region than the honest, prudent Carson. Now almost sixty-two, William S. Williams, though spare, lean, and full of endurance, was badly worn by his toils. A tall, stooped man, of hatchet face, nutcracker jaws, small restless eyes, and querulous voice, he was as full of ludicrous eccentricities as any of Cooper's quaint characters, and yet as expert a scout as Leatherstocking himself. Though he had begun life as an itinerant backwoods preacher in Missouri and a missionary to the Osage Indians, his speech was the rough, illiterate lingo of the mountaineer of Southern extraction and Western upbringing; "varmint," "plumb," "nigh onto," "oncet," "haint gotter." His stories had a picturesqueness which has been preserved in several verbatim reports. An indefatigable walker, who could cover enormous distances, his gait was a queer, staggering waddle, which carried him first to one side and then to another of a straight trail. When he lifted his gun the onlooker had to check a smile at the "double-wabble" with which he brought it into position, but he could hit a coin unerringly at a hundred yards. He rode on his piebald Indian pony with his chest bent over the pommel, his stirrups ridiculously short, his trousers hitched up on his bare calves, and his arms flopping up and down over his arched knees. Usually he wore a buckskin hunting shirt, black with dirt and grease, and for headpiece a blanket cap, so roughly tailored that the two corners projected like wolves' ears. In all, he was a remarkable character.

Yet "Old Bill" Williams, despite his age and growing infirmities, his oddities of speech and bearing, and an erratic quality which kept him from ever gaining the reputation of Carson, Fitzpatrick, or Milton Sublette, seemed an excellent choice for Frémont's purposes. To be sure, he was personally somewhat reckless; he had been in many an Indian fight, and bore the marks of ball and arrow. Earlier in life, after selling a load of furs, he would embark on a wild spree, drinking, gambling, and tossing whole bolts of precious calico to the vociferous squaws in the streets of Taos. He had never been much troubled by scruples in his dealings with other races. He had delighted to lift Indian scalps; at one time, along with other "land-pirates," he had made excursions into California to steal herds of horses from the missions and ranches. But his great merit was that nobody, except perhaps Jim Bridger, knew the Rocky Mountains so well. Twenty-three years earlier he had been the guide of George C. Sibley, who had led the government party which in 1825 surveyed a road from the western borders of Missouri to the American boundary in the direction of Santa Fé. Since then, a man of iron nerve, he had often gone into the wilderness to live for months alone, trapping, shooting, and exploring. Like Bridger, Carson, Provôt, and others, he took an Indian wife (indeed, several squaws followed one another in rapid succession), and ingratiated himself with various tribes. With the ranges in front of Frémont he was supposed to be completely familiar. "His knowledge of that part of the country," declares the scout Antoine Leroux, "was perfect." McGehee's diary informs us that Williams shared the misgivings of experienced frontiersmen of the region regarding a winter passage of the high Rockies; but when Frémont insisted, he concluded to go, believing that the party could fight its way, though not without great suffering, through the snow-choked passes.[12]

November 24th found the expedition at a little settlement called Hardscrabble (Pueblo de San Carlos) at the foot of the Rockies. Here one the French Canadians, as McGehee reports, daunted by the prospect of the deep snow piled on the peaks, the storms they could see raging there, and the chill blasts that blew down from the cliffs, abandoned the group, predicting evil to those who went on. On the twenty-sixth the party plunged into the mountain defiles, though McGehee writes that the ranges "presented to view one continued snowstorm." One of the men, George A. Hibbard, looked up at the icy slopes and storm-wreathed precipices as they slowly picked their way through the valleys below, and apprehensively remarked: "Friends, I don't want my bones to bleach upon those mountains." He little dreamed that they would, and that to some of his comrades death would appear a welcome relief before they were through. Several others, with a premonition of disaster, climbed to a little eminence that evening to take a last look at the wintry prairies behind. "The sight was beautiful," wrote McGehee; "the snow-covered plain far beneath us, stretching eastward as far as the eye could reach, while on the

---

[12] Mr. Stark Young kindly enabled me to obtain the original of McGehee's diary, a most absorbing document, from his descendants.

opposite side frowned the almost perpendicular wall of high mountains."

Of the character of this "almost perpendicular wall" it is proper to say a word. Pueblo and Hardscrabble lie in south central Colorado, in the valley of the upper Arkansas. To the west looms up that outer escarpment of the Rockies called the Sangre de Cristo or Sierra Blanca Mountains, with an elevation of from seven to fourteen thousand feet. This mountain rampart runs northwestward from upper New Mexico into central Colorado. Beyond it to the west is the valley of the upper Rio Grande, whose headwaters in Colorado form a line which runs sharply northwest, and at times almost west. In crossing the Sangre de Cristo to the Rio Grande, three passes were used by the mountain-men: the most northerly the Williams Pass (now the Music Pass); the central and most direct route from Pueblo the Robidoux Pass; and the southernmost the Sangre de Cristo Pass. All were practicable for a party like Frémont's, but difficult. His intention was to use the central route through the Robidoux Pass, thus passing the outer wall of the Rockies. Having gotten into the Rio Grande Valley, the traveler could push up that river west by north until he found himself confronted by a new wall of mountains, the central chain of the Rockies and true continental divide, called at this point the San Juan Range. It merged toward the north into the Uncompahgre, La Garita, and Sawatch mountains, which successively carried the chain high up into Colorado. From the Rio Grande Valley, the wayfarer had the choice of two routes well known to mountain-men. He could bear northward into the Sawatch Mountains, and cross the continental divide by Cochetopa Pass; or he could bear south into lower Colorado and cross the divide by Cumbres Pass, which is almost on the present-day boundary line between New Mexico and Colorado.[13]

---

[13] Compare Alpheus H. Favour, *Old Bill Williams: Mountain Man,* pp. 155, 156. The frontispiece shows Old Bill against the background of the Cochetopa Pass.

SAN JUAN MOUNTAINS, 1848

(From Frémont's *Memoirs*)

PORTSMOUTH SQUARE, SHOWING PARKER HOUSE

The first few days of travel beyond Hardscrabble were sufficient to show that the party had embarked upon a grim undertaking. They moved forward on foot, the mules they had bought in Pueblo carrying one hundred and thirty bushels of shelled corn. As they pushed into Huerfano Valley, just below the high Sangre de Cristo peaks, their difficulties grew heavier. The cold was intense, the ground beneath the fast-deepening snow was rocky and treacherous, and the storms of sleet were so terrific that at times it was almost impossible to make the mules face them. The men suffered from frozen hands, ears, and toes. Still greater were the sufferings of the animals, which with no food but dry grain and no water but melted snow, had to be driven to the last ounce of their strength. One by one, the mules began to drop down by the trail to die. Every climb upward made the cold more intense, until the mercury sank entirely into the bulb of the thermometer and failed to register the temperature. The men's breath congealed upon their faces until their beards and eyelashes stood out stiff and white, and they could hardly speak; the snow clogged the mules' hooves until it formed balls six inches thick. In this fashion they managed to cross the Roubidoux Pass, though a hurricane had completely filled part of their road with a tangle of fallen timbers—a veritable chevaux de frise, all the more terrible for being half-concealed by snow. They came down into the valley; but still, as McGehee writes, their difficulties continued: [14]

We descended into Grand River Valley. The snow lay deep as elsewhere and there was no sign of vegetation. One broad, white, dreary-looking plain lay before us bounded by white mountains. High, precipitous, and frozen mountains were behind us, and this broad, dreary plain lay before us and the Rio Grande, fifty miles ahead of us. So we entered with the determination of getting through it as quickly as possible. We traveled late and camped in the middle of it, without any shelter from the winds, and with no fuel but some wild sage, a small shrub which grew sparsely around. The cold was

[14] MS Diary.

intense, the thermometer to-night standing at 17 degrees below zero, and it was so cold during the day that Ducatel, a young fellow, came very near freezing to death.

By collecting a quantity of the sage, we made sufficient fires to cook or rather half-cook our supper of deer meat, five of these animals having been killed this evening by two of the men, and bolting down the half-cooked meat, we quickly turned into our blankets, in order to keep somewhat warm and for protection against the driving snow, for since leaving the states we had scarcely ever stretched tents. In the night, as ill-luck would have it, our mules, poor creatures, which stood shivering in the cold with bowed backs and drooping heads, suffering from their exposed situation and half starved, being now reduced to a pint of corn a day, and having no other resources for food, broke loose from their weak fastenings of sage bushes, and started off *en masse* on the back trail in order to obtain the shelter of the mountains we had left the day before or to find some shrubbery they could eat. As soon as it was certain that they were gone, in the middle of the night, we had to rise from our beds, lifting half a foot of snow with our top blankets, and strike out in pursuit of them through the severe cold. We overtook them several miles from camp, and taking them back, made them secure. But we rested little the balance of the night.

The next day we reached the Rio Grande del Norte, which we found frozen over, and camped in the river bottom, which is thickly timbered with cottonwood and willow. We had considerable difficulty in crossing the river, the mules slipping upon the ice and falling or breaking through in places, when we would have to raise them to their feet or draw them over the ice. We found some game, deer and elk, in the river bottom, of which we killed a few. The snow was deeper along here than we had seen it anywhere previously, and our camps, pitched upon it, presented a dreary prospect.

They had reached the Rio Grande at about the site of the present town of Monte Vista, Colorado. It was now December 11th. Before them rose the main chain of the Rockies, the high San Juan Mountains to the west and southwest, the Uncompahgre, La Garita, and Sawatch to the northwest and north. The critical moment for the expedition had arrived—the moment when they must determine by which pass they would scale this mountain wall.

By all accounts, this moment found Frémont and old Bill Williams in fatal disagreement. Although the precise issue between them is not clear, Frémont certainly declared for one route while the scout called for another. According to a story told by T. E. Brackenridge, one of the mountain-men, many years later, and related at second-hand in 1896, Williams wished to go far to the south around the San Juan Mountains, where the continental divide flattens out in northern New Mexico, and then push west on what is now the Colorado-New Mexico boundary. This trail was well known and not difficult; but to have gone so far south would have defeated the whole object of the expedition. The same authority states that Frémont insisted on continuing in a westerly direction along the thirty-eighth parallel, moving up the Rio Grande and past its head. He would thus approach the 9,200-foot pass immediately north of the river-head called the Cochetopa; and if they could get through this, they would prove the thirty-eighth parallel practicable for a railway. It seems probable that Frémont did have this route in mind. But for some reason the party did not really take it; instead, it pushed toward the Wagon-Wheel Gap, whose altitude was 8,390 feet, with the real pass beyond much higher. Whose fault was this? On this point the evidence differs, and a clear decision is impossible.[15]

According to Frémont and Alexis Godey, it was Bill Williams who led them astray. He it was who took them toward the impracticable Wagon-Wheel Gap when they should have headed for Cochetopa Pass. They probably did not get as far west as the Gap before he turned them north into the mountains. "The error of our journey," wrote Frémont, "was committed in engaging this man. He proved never to have known, or entirely to have forgotten, the whole region of the country through which we were to pass." Edward M. Kern at the time believed Williams at fault. This is clearly shown by a recently

15 Dellenbaugh, *Frémont and '49*, p. 391 *ff*.

discovered letter written February 11, 1849, to Robidoux. In this he states: "We continued a couple of days on the [Rio Grande] del Norte, and then turned up what Williams called your pass on to the Compadne [Uncompahgre?]. In this he was evidently mistaken, for a worse road I never saw." Later, after a quarrel with Frémont, Kern turned about and blamed Frémont. But we also have a full letter written by Alexis Godey in 1856, contradicting Kern's later statement, and upholding Frémont. He wrote: [16]

And now as to the statement made by the Messrs. Kerns, in relation to which you wish my opinion. I will say that every man who was with Col. Frémont on that unfortunate trip to the Carnero Pass [Godey means the Wagon-Wheel] knows it to be untrue. I had the honor of being in command under Col. Frémont on that expedition, and I say now, as I have ever averred, that if there were blame to be attached to any source, on Bill Williams, our guide, and myself should its entire weight rest.

Col. Frémont was, from the time we first came in sight of the Carnero Pass, on the 8th of December, to the 17th, a period of nine days, strongly averse to taking it in our course, preferring to turn off and go through the Cochetopy, a pass some thirty miles to the right; and scarcely a night passed without a consultation took place between the Colonel, myself, Williams, and others; but Williams, who had, as he said, frequently traveled it, evinced so much confidence, and was so strenuous in his efforts to carry his point, that I was completely in his favor, and always told the Colonel that I myself was perfectly willing to trust Williams and follow him; and in this way we traveled on, Frémont unconvinced, yet without any reason to urge, until the 12th instant, when Williams and myself, being ahead, were overtaken by Frémont, who rode up and halted us, and the entire party stopped in the middle of the day. The Colonel then again expressed his fears of trouble ahead, and then it was that Williams told him, that "if he doubted his capacity to carry the party through, say so, and he could get another pilot"; he as-

---

[16] For this illuminating document see New York *Evening Post*, October 30, 1856. For the very important new letter by Kern, which utterly discredits his later attack on Frémont, see Chapter XXXVII of this book.

serted in the most positive terms that "he knew every inch of the country better than the Colonel knew his own garden." Having every confidence myself in Williams, I advised the Colonel to let him go on, that I was perfectly willing to follow him, and that everything would result favorably.

This was the last consultation on the subject. Frémont acceded to our united arguments, and, the die cast, we pushed on, with what result is well known. For the subsequent misfortunes that befell us, Frémont is not reprehensible. He trusted to his guides, in whose representations he was bound to place confidence, and that they were deceived was no fault of his.

This is strong and circumstantial evidence. Some support for it is furnished by the fact that Bill Williams took special pride in the Wagon-Wheel Pass, which he had discovered, and which many called by his name. In summer it offered a road through the San Juan Mountains to Grand River one day shorter than by the Carnero Pass, and nearly two days shorter than by the Cochetopa. Perhaps Williams did not know that in winter the snows made it quite impassable. He seems to have headed toward it for a time, and then turned blindly up Embargo Creek into the roughest mountain country. On the other hand, several witnesses besides Brackenridge are emphatic that Frémont and not Williams was to blame for going astray. Edward M. Kern's second story, so clearly prejudiced and so flatly at variance with his first, must now be set aside.[17] But Richard Wootton, who was at Taos when the survivors came in and talked to them, declared that if Frémont had taken Williams' advice "he would never have run into the death trap," and that the explorer, having "picked out the route which he wanted to travel over the mountains," stuck to it with blind stubbornness. The same view was expressed by Dr. R. H. Wirz, an army surgeon at Taos at the time. John Scott, a mountain-man with the party, testified that Frémont had insisted on taking the fatal route after Williams proposed the Cochetopa Pass. An even more expert witness, Antoine

[17] Compare Fort Sutter Papers, Huntington Library, MS No. 125.

Leroux, after gathering all the information he could find, wrote Kern that Williams' knowledge of that part of the country was excellent, and "the course which was taken by Colonel Frémont was an impracticable one in winter...." [18]

What is certain is that Frémont's party, after pushing up the Rio Grande cañon for several days, plunged directly into mountain defiles which offered only a terrible cul de sac. When they found their way blocked, they turned north into the La Garita range, forty miles wide, and without any known pass. Here they soon found themselves in perilous difficulties. The ascending track lay through deep mountain gorges, amid towering precipices and crags, and along slopes so steep that again and again, as they toiled along, a mule would lose its footing and go rolling to the bottom. They had to cross rough-bottomed and boggy streams which rushed precipitately down deep ravines, and in which the pack animals would stick tight, sometimes half a dozen in a group. Thereupon Frémont and his men would turn back, wade in up to their waists in the floating ice, and shove, haul, and belabor the animals until they scrambled, dripping, up the banks. The obstacles multipled as they went on. Every day the snowdrifts became more appalling in depth, and the cold more intense. Every night more mules succumbed and were found stark and stiff at dawn. "It seemed like fighting fate to attempt to proceed," wrote McGehee, "but we were bent on our course, and continued to advance."

Once, the men in advance returned with the hopeful news

---

[18] On this vexed question of responsibility, see Favour, *Old Bill Williams,* Chs. 14, 15, 16; Chauncey Pratt Williams, *Lone Elk, The Life Story of Bill Williams, Old West Series,* Nos. 6, 7; Dellenbaugh, *op. cit.;* the Fort Sutter Papers, especially MSS 125-130; Bigelow, *Frémont,* p. 391, which gives Frémont's letter of December 11, 1849, on the subject. I see no justification for dogmatic assertions on the immediate responsibility for losing the party in the San Juan or La Garita Mountains; the evidence is too partial and confused. Brackinridge's testimony was given so long after the event *a priori* it seems less weighty than Godey's. It must also be remembered that the Kerns had quarreled with Frémont, and their evidence was surely prejudiced. But Godey's letter was written in part for campaign purposes. The question admits of no certain answer. Frémont's larger responsibility for the disaster is of course beyond doubt.

that there was a clearer prospect ahead and that they thought they saw grass; but when the main party came up, they found that it was only the tops of trees and bushes peering from the all-extending sea of snow. Repeatedly the expedition would break camp in the morning and set off bravely, only to find the tempest of snow too fierce to face. The bitter wind, sweeping across the peaks with incredible velocity, cut like a knife. Sometimes they were mocked at nightfall by a furnace sunset, which seemed to give out cold rather than heat, but for the most part the sky was a leaden pall. On one of the marches into the teeth of a storm, Old Bill Williams was so nearly overcome that he dropped down upon his mule in a drowsy stupor, and was almost senseless when his companions dragged him back to camp.

But it was the tortures which the fierce weather and the rough trail inflicted upon the pack animals which were most heartrending. The corn was now exhausted and the beasts were crazed with hunger. They would roam about ravenously all night, and being too weak to break a new path, would usually wander back along the trail of the previous day, pawing in the snow for vegetation. They began devouring the rawhide lariats with which they were tied; they followed this by eating the blankets which were thrown over them at night, the rigging of the pack-saddles, and finally even one another's manes and tails. They were mere specters of skin and bones; the weaker mules collapsed every fifty yards, and the men, with frozen and lacerated fingers, had to unfasten their packs and lift them up.

Finally they reached the naked, treeless crest of the Great Divide. The cold here was more intense than ever, while the storms on these high rocky ridges were almost incessant. Twice Frémont, with unconquerable resolution, forced his men to attempt a passage. On the first day, they encountered a blizzard or *pouderie*, the dry snow driven so thick by the gale that it was impossible to see more than a few feet in advance, while the roar was deafening and at times it was difficult to catch breath. After a brief fight, the men were forced back into camp.

Dead mules were lying about the fires, and it continued all night to snow steadily. Next day the storm had ceased; they made mauls and, beating a road through the snow, crossed the ridge in defiance of the gale, and pitched camp just below the timber line. "The trail," Frémont wrote, "showed as if a defeated army had passed by; pack-saddles and packs, scattered articles of clothing, and dead mules strewed along." Then the blizzard returned and paralyzed the party. They were now twelve thousand feet above the sea, and in an almost hopeless position. The long rolling ranges and valleys to the westward were buried in snow. It was impossible to go on, and almost equally impossible to turn back. "We were overtaken," Frémont writes, "by sudden and irretrievable ruin."

Under the circumstances, the only hope of escape lay in an immediate retreat. Frémont determined to recross the crest, but very mistakenly decided to try to take the baggage back with him down to the Rio Grande. Along this stream he hoped to find game. On the twenty-second of December they commenced their movement, and being now reduced to man-power, required more than a week to move their camp and equipage over the top of the pass, a distance of two miles, to the head springs of a stream leading to the river. At this altitude the slightest exertion was laborious, and sometimes caused long attacks of nosebleed. The snow was from four to thirty feet in depth; and when they built their camp-fires, cavernous pits were formed, completely hiding the different messes from each other. Deep in these holes the men slept, spreading their blankets upon the snow. In the daytime some of them, half blinded by the pine smoke and the frozen glare, staggered about uncertainly. They had begun to suffer greatly from hunger, and were living in the main upon the carcasses of the frozen mules, which they supplemented by butchering the few feverish animals which remained.

Christmas Day was spent in an atmosphere of deep depression. The men were worn out and utterly discouraged; worse than that, they were grumbling at Frémont for having obsti-

nately thrust them into all this suffering and danger. Three men
of the old exploring party, Godey, King, and Taplin, continued
loyal and cheerful, but even Kern had become morose and
resentful. Reduced to an emergency reserve of macaroni, sugar,
and bacon, they did not possess provisions for twenty days. Frémont occupied the early hours of the day in despatching an
express party to the nearest settlements to bring relief. Calling for volunteers, and choosing King, Brackenridge, Creutzfeldt, and Bill Williams, he equipped them with rations and
instructed them to hurry with all speed to the nearest settlements in New Mexico, and to bring back provisions and mules
to an agreed point upon the Rio Grande. Then, after seeing the
four men disappear among the snowy pines, he turned back to
the circle cowering about his snow-pit camp-fire. He thought
of the previous Christmas in Washington, and the merry faces
and abundant luxuries of Senator Benton's home. From the
Senator's library in the Brant house in St. Louis he had fetched
some volumes of Blackstone, to be the foundation for his possible entrance upon the practice of law in California; and, his
mind "filled with gloom and anxious thoughts," he now brought
these out to read and pass the hours. Then next day the remaining party set about removing the baggage back to the
Rio Grande.

Descending along the little stream, over ground so rugged
that they averaged scarcely a mile a day, Frémont's men finally
reached the Rio Grande again. While they were thus engaged,
their last regular provisions had been divided, and they began
boiling their rawhide ropes and parfleches to make a gluey
soup. The cold seemed to redouble in the final bleak seven
miles, and one of the men, Raphael Proue, becoming exhausted,
lay down beside the trail and froze to death. The others in trans-
porting the baggage passed and repassed his body, not daring to
stop long enough to bury him. At one point Cathcart, McGehee,
and two others were imprisoned in a cave for two days by a terrific storm, with no subsistence except some rawhide shoe-
strings and old wolf-gnawed bones. When at last the expedition

made camp on the river, they found as a fresh blow that there was no game, the deer and elk having all been driven off by the deep snow.

Frémont had given the party which he sent under King to seek relief sixteen days as ample time to make the round trip, and for a while simply waited on the Rio Grande. But when the period elapsed, with the ebbing hopes of his men giving way to despair, he grew too uneasy to stay longer. Either King and his men had lost their way, he feared, or had been cut off by hostile Ute or Apache Indians. There was just one course to follow—to set out for relief himself. Taking Preuss, Godey, and two other trusted men, with enough provisions for two or three days, he started down the river. He left orders that the men were to finish bringing all the baggage into camp, and push on with it after him till they were met by the help he would send back. He also made a statement which seems to have increased the mutinous resentment in the breasts of some of his followers: that if they wished to see him they would have to hurry, for he was going on to California.

To tell in detail the horrors which attended the closing days of the ill-fated expedition, now split into three groups, would be unnecessary and repellent. Frémont made rapidly down the ice of the Rio Grande. He hoped to meet the returning party of Bill Williams; or failing that, to reach the Red River settlement one hundred and sixty miles away, and twenty-five miles north of Taos. On the sixth day, led by a friendly Ute whom they met, they discovered a little smoke in a grove of timber near the river bank, and went to investigate it. Here they found the relief party which, twenty-two days earlier, they had sent out from the main camp. Three tottering scarecrows were left, Williams, Brackenridge, and Creutzfeldt, the most miserable objects Frémont had ever seen; and they told him that King had starved to death a few days before. Later on, charges were made that they had partly eaten his body; and Frémont records in his manuscript *Memoirs* a significant remark by Kit Carson that "in starving times no man who knew him ever walked in front of Bill Williams." [19] Some think this charge of cannibalism dubious, and that if the body had been partly devoured, it was probably by animals or vultures. Placing the three men on some horses which he had obtained from the Utes, Frémont hastened on to the Red River settlement, reaching it on the tenth evening after leaving the main camp. He at once took steps to hurry a relief party under Godey, with pack animals and provisions which he obtained from Rio Hondo and Taos, back to the half-starved men left far up on the Rio Grande.

The word half-starved is a euphemism; for, by Frémont's own statement, the party was left with provisions for only two or three meals, with some five pounds of sugar additional for each man. Its position was desperate, and to stand still was simply to wait for death. Two days after Frémont had left, when they were down to their last crumb, they held a consultation and decided to start down the river at once, hunting as they went along. Each man had a handful of sugar and they divided some bits of candles and rawhide. Trembling from weakness, their feet frozen and bleeding, they marched in gloomy silence. The river was a white streak of snow-blanketed ice; the somber pines on each side were covered with long thick plumes of frost; there was not a sound of life—not the shriek of a jay, not the howl of a wolf. They had not gone far on the first day when the California Indian Manuel, whose feet were turning black, stopped, begged his mates to kill him, and then started back to the camp. A little farther on another man, exhausted and half frozen, threw away his gun and blanket, staggered on a few hundred yards, fell into the snow, and died. That night a third, Carver, raved so violently that his companions became afraid of him, and in the morning, half-crazed, he wandered off into the woods and was never seen again. Thus the survivors went on, the strongest forging ahead, the weakest straggling far behind, while death strode with them. Some of the men were fortunate enough to knock over

[19] Frémont MSS, Bancroft Library. The Red River here mentioned is a small branch of the Rio Grande, and not the well-known river of that name.

two grouse, which they ate even to the entrails, and to find part of a dead wolf along the river, which they also devoured; some filled their stomachs with dried buds from the bushes, and scooped up water bugs where the river ice had melted slightly. Frémont has feelingly described the fate of several, and the arrival of relief:

Ferguson and Beadle had remained behind. In the evening, Rohrer came up and remained with Kern's mess. Mr. Haler learned afterwards from that mess that Rohrer and Andrews wandered off the next day and died. They say they saw their bodies. In the morning Haler's party continued on. After a few hours, Hibbard gave out. They built him a fire, gathered him some wood, and left him without, as Haler says, turning their heads to look at him as they went off. About two miles further Scott . . . gave out. They did the same for him as for Hibbard, and continued on. In the afternoon the Indian boys went ahead, and before nightfall met Godey with the relief. Haler heard and knew the guns which he fired for him at night, and starting early in the morning, soon met him. I hear that they all cried together like children. Haler turned back with Godey, and went with him to where they had left Scott. He was still alive, and was saved. Hibbard was dead—still warm.

When the first far-off halloo told that relief had come, eleven in all of the thirty-three hardy frontiersmen who had set out from Pueblo into the mountains had lost their lives, and the remainder were mere wrecks of humanity.[20] They were so emaciated that they looked like walking skeletons; their hair and beards were long and tangled; their faces were waxen under a mask of smoke and grime. Some of them had to be lifted upon the mules which Godey brought. In this condition they were all taken down to Taos, and the tragic venture was ended.

While apparently a large part of the blame for the disastrous

[20] Favour in *Old Bill Williams*, p. 168, gives the names: Raphael Proue, died January 9th; Henry King, January 12th; Henry Wise, January 17th; Manuel, January 21st or thereabouts; Vincent Sorel. January 22nd; Joseph Moran, between the 22nd and 28th; E. T. Andrews and Henry Rohrer, January 22nd; Benjamin Beadle, January 26th; George A. Hibbard and Carver, January 27th. The remainder arrived in Taos destitute.

failure rests upon Bill Williams, who was unable to impress Frémont with his knowledge of the country, and upon King and Williams jointly for their strange failure later to find the right path down the Rio Grande toward Taos, Frémont himself cannot be acquitted of the principal responsibility. He insisted upon attempting the crossing of the range after he had been warned in the most solemn terms at Bent's Fort and Pueblo that it would be highly dangerous and probably impossible, and after Williams had entered an emphatic protest. It was therefore incumbent upon him, once the passage was under way, to use every precaution to insure the safety of his men. The weight of evidence indicates that instead he clung stubbornly to his plan for moving westward along the upper waters of the Rio Grande and the thirty-eighth parallel after its perils had been forcibly pointed out. But his cardinal error was committed when he turned back deliberately instead of speedily. He should have taken what food and pack animals remained, abandoned the luggage, and made all speed to the nearest settlement, keeping his party a unit. By trying to extricate the baggage, he lost eleven men. A severe critic would say that their lives were upon his head. To be sure, as Godey explained later, he had provisions at the moment for eighteen or twenty days, and felt almost sure that King and Williams would return with help within that time; but he should have taken into consideration the very real risk that they would lose their way or be slain by savages.

Edward Kern later attacked Frémont for not using the frozen mules, after the departure of King on Christmas Day, for food. But Godey is no doubt right in answering that this was impossible, inasmuch as the weather was too severe to permit the men to get the carcasses out of drifts twenty feet deep. As for the failure of King and Williams to keep on the straight path to the settlements, this now seems inexplicable. By Godey's testimony, before they started they and Frémont had fixed and determined every day's journey, and the various camping places, both going and coming; they were experienced, capable frontiersmen; and Williams supposedly knew the whole region. Yet they did not get fifty miles from their starting place.

It would have been much more in keeping with Frémont's usual gallantry of conduct had he returned up the Rio Grande with the relief party from Taos which, under Godey, did the actual work of rescue. Possibly he was too exhausted; one leg was badly frozen, and reports to the eastern press from a Taos correspondent declared that he was "very severely frosted and scarcely able to get about." Members of his party reported him almost snow-blind. But if he was at all able to travel, he should never have rested while one of his men remained in danger in the wilderness. He took shelter in Kit Carson's hospitable home, where on January 27, 1849, we find him writing Jessie:[21] "This morning a cup of chocolate was brought to me, while yet in bed. To an overworn, overworked, much fatigued, and starving traveller, these little luxuries of the world offer an interest which in your comfortable home it is not possible for you to conceive." He spoke of Kit Carson's care, "constantly occupied and constantly uneasy in endeavoring to make me comfortable." After laying the blame for the debacle upon Williams, he spoke harshly of the want of nerve among many of his party, whose courage in the crisis had "failed fast." Unquestionably, his failure to go back, and the freedom with which he criticized his associates, accentuated the bitterness with which the three Kern brothers and others of his men always spoke of his leadership of the expedition.

Frémont was never a man for useless repining; he wrote Jessie that he had an "almost invincible repugnance" for the task of describing his sufferings, and his whole attention was now centered upon proceeding overland to California. From Major Edward F. Beale, who had been in the California fight-

[21] Bigelow, *Frémont*, pp. 365-376, contains two letters from Frémont to Jessie, one dated January 27th, one February 6, 1849. In the second letter he speaks of "a persistence of misfortune which no precaution has been adequate on my part to avert." It is a pity that he did not detail some of his precautions.

ing, had been Carson's associate in the heroic crawl through the Mexican lines after the battle of San Pasqual, and was now commanding the army forces in northern New Mexico, he received the kindest assistance, including the loan of horses and the sale of provisions from the commissary's department. Almost all his clothing and money had been lost; the saddles, instruments, and baggage had been cached in the mountains. Before leaving Taos, Frémont made an effort to regain this material, but the deep snow prevented the party he sent out from getting through. Other men besides Carson and Beale came to his aid, for Taos was full of old friends—Dick Owens, Lucien Maxwell, and Francis Aubrey among them; and Aubrey lent him a thousand dollars to purchase animals to continue his journey.

Before he left Taos, Frémont told the men of his reunited party that he would be glad to mount and equip all who would accompany him to the Pacific. Most of them, including Godey, volunteered to go. The three Kern brothers, who were impatient to return to the States, Bill Williams, and a few others declined. It may be mentioned that the following spring, Williams and Dr. Kern returned to the scene of the disaster to recover the baggage, Brackenridge's twelve hundred dollars in money, and Edward Kern's collection of specimens in natural history, and that they were attacked and killed, either by Indians or by some treacherous Mexicans who accompanied them. To increase the ill-feeling among those who were left behind, they received the impression that Frémont had made an unfair division of the stores bought from the commissary, though later Godey earnestly denied that this was the fact. It was not until they reached Albuquerque, according to Godey, that Frémont was able to obtain military supplies in any quantity. The new party which the explorer outfitted here and in Santa Fé consisted of twenty-five men and sixty horses, and he planned to use them in going south of the Sierras by way of the Gila River.

The early incidents of this final stage of his trip, Frémont has jotted down in his usual crisp English in the rough notes previously referred to: [22]

With 25 men all told and outfit renewed I resume journey, following down the Del Norte and intending to reach the Rio Grande by a route south of Gila River. The snows this season too heavy to insist on a direct route through the mountains. Engage a New Mexican for guide—spring weather in the valley—fruit trees in bloom—hospitality. Leave the river—open country—snowed on again—no wood and weather cold. Retreat into the Membres Mountains. Pleasant country, well wooded, resembling the oak region of the Sierra Nevada—color of soil—grass and water abundant. Travel along foot of mountains. Apaches around the camp—watch and watch—McGehee fired on—halt and have parley with chief—make friends. The Indians go to Membres River with us. Breakfast and presents. Indians direct us to watering place in the open country—appoint to meet us there —their war parties out in Chihuahua and Sonora. I push forward and avoid them.

The Apache visitor—Santa Cruz. The Mexican and the bunch of grass. Follow down the Santa Cruz River—Tucson. Spring on the Santa Cruz—peach orchard—the ruined missions. River lost in the sand. The grass field and water at foot of the hills. Reach the Gila River. The Pimah village (see Johnson's report)—Indian faces painted with black lead.

Follow the river around the bend. Meet large party of Sonorans going to California. Their pleasure in meeting us. Their fear of Indians. They urge me to travel with them. I consent. Many presents of fruit and provisions in various forms. Reach the Gila River. Determine position of the junction with the Rio Grande. Make bullboat—ferry women and children of the Sonorans across, with my party, and leave the bullboat for the men to complete their crossing.

Frémont was not merely undaunted; he believed that his fourth expedition had succeeded in its main object. "The survey has been uninterrupted up to this point," he wrote bravely from Taos to Jessie, "and I shall carry it on consecutively." Later, he publicly declared: "The result was entirely satis-

[22] Frémont MSS, Bancroft Library.

factory. It convinced me that neither the snow of winter nor the mountain ranges were obstacles in the way of the road, and furnished me with a far better line [for a railway] than any I had previously known." He had hopes that, if the continuance of his labors as an explorer proved to have been useful, President Zachary Taylor would take him back into government service for work upon the West coast.

For the rest, he looked forward to making a new home for Jessie, whose arrival he expected in March. The immediate prospect was that he would have to wage a legal battle before he could even claim the land upon which he had set his heart. When he gave Larkin $3,000, it was to purchase a chosen property on the hills some distance back of San Francisco. Its old orchards and vines and its atmosphere of peace and rest had appealed strongly to him, while its view over the sea recalled his Charleston boyhood. But by some error Larkin bought instead from Juan Alvarado a wild tract in the Sierra foothills, more than a hundred miles from the ocean and nearly that far from any settlement—the famous Mariposas tract, seventy square miles in area. Hostile Indians of the sturdy Cauchile tribe roamed the region in such numbers that it was impossible to reside there, or to pasture cattle, which would have been quickly destroyed. The land was apparently almost worthless. Frémont had felt outraged when, just before leaving California as Kearny's prisoner, he learned of this, and had told Larkin that he would return to demand a just settlement. He had consulted Senator Benton, whose long experience in land cases arising from the Louisiana Purchase had made his advice valuable, and had laid plans to institute a lawsuit. He meant to get either the property originally selected, or his $3,000.[23]

Despite such worries, he wrote in confident vein to Jessie. "I make frequent pleasant pictures," he told her, "of the

[23] Details of the legal history of this purchase are given in Bigelow, *Frémont*, pp. 379ff. It was bought under a Mexican title after California became a territory of the United States. Alvarado executed the deed to Frémont on February 10, 1847.

happy home we are to have, and oftenest and among the pleas-
antest of all I see our library with its bright fire in the rainy
stormy days, and the large windows looking out upon the sea
in the bright weather. I have it all planned in my own mind."
But all his schemes for exploring, for a career at the bar, for
developing a ranch, were suddenly forgotten when he learned
the news which, coming from California during 1848, had electrified the civilized world.

XXIII

Golconda and the Senate

THE dramatic vicissitudes which make Frémont's life so romantic, the extraordinary alternations of disaster and good fortune which mark its course, were never better illustrated than now. Emerging from a humiliating court-martial, he had just been thrown into the jaws of death, and had escaped only after terrible suffering and loss. But already Fortune was spinning her wheel. She was about to toss into his lap a seat in the Federal Senate, and an estate of such wealth that within a few years it would be valued by cool-headed business men at ten million dollars.

The rough notes of Frémont's which we have just printed indicate the general course of his overland journey from Taos. At Santa Fé, he dined with the military governor of the territory, Colonel Washington, and at Socorro with the local commandant. Pursuing a general southwesterly line, he penetrated well into Mexico, touching Santa Cruz in that republic, and then turned northwest toward Tucson in what is now Arizona. From the point where he reached the Gila, his line of march was along its south bank. Here one blazing forenoon he descried in the distance a cloud of dust, in which vague figures drifted along the river margin. Hurrying on, he overtook a whole community on the move—Jessie Frémont says twelve hundred men, women, and children; babies crying, drivers hallooing, mules dragging lurching carts, and horses burdened with packs. Spurring up beside the rear guard, he asked, "Where are you going?" "Alta California," came the reply. "Why such a crowd of you?" demanded the puzzled Frémont. "Gold! Gold!" was the answer.

It was the first news Frémont had received of the discovery of gold on Sutter's property. Word had traveled most rapidly by sea; it had reached the ports of western Mexico—Guaymas, Mazatlan, Colima—before it penetrated to Tucson; and all Sonora was alive with the excitement which had emptied San Francisco and Monterey in a rush for the gold-fields. These Sonora Mexicans were on their way to the diggings. Frémont acted with characteristic impetuosity. Mariposa might be the best property after all. He leaped to the conclusion that gold would be found on his new lands, and promptly engaged twenty-eight Mexicans to work for him. He was to grubstake them, they were to contribute their muscle and skill, and the gold was to be equally divided.

Frémont, with his now impressive cavalcade, pressed on rapidly to Los Angeles and Monterey, where he expected Jessie to be already waiting for him. He little guessed what his wife had been through. She had crossed the Isthmus safely under the escort of her brother-in-law, Jacobs. It had been a horrible trip; she went up the Chagres River by slowly poled boats, burned by the sun, tormented by flies and mosquitoes, drinking dirty water, eating hastily cooked food, fearing the fever at every move; thence she crossed the rest of the way by mule train, sleeping at the camps of railway surveyors. Her brother-in-law marveled at her courage. "He judged, as we all do," she wrote later,[1] "by appearances. As there were no complaints or tears or visible breakdown, he gave me credit for high courage, while the fact was that the whole thing was so like a nightmare, that one took it as a bad dream—in helpless silence." When she arrived in Panama on the West coast, she was overtaken by "forty-niners" from New York, who brought word of the tragic fate of the fourth expedition; and here she also received Frémont's long letter from Taos, giving a full account of the disaster. At the same time, she learned that there was no boat to take her on north.

The vessel on which she had expected to proceed to Califor-

[1] Jessie Benton Frémont, *A Year of American Travel*, p. 56.

nia had not returned, for all its men had deserted to rush for
the mines, and the captain was fuming helplessly in San Francisco Bay. Steamer after steamer was arriving on the Atlantic
side of the Isthmus, and discharging thousands of eager gold
hunters, who hurried across to the Pacific—and then sat down
and swore. Fortunately, Jessie bore letters of introduction,
which soon rescued her from the intolerable heat, noise, and
dirt of the hotel. She went to the home of Mme. Arcé, a cultivated widow, and, worn out by anxiety for Frémont and by
hardship, promptly collapsed. A friend named Mr. Gray one
morning brought her a newspaper containing a letter of her
father's describing the Frémont expedition, and in the evening,
when he returned with further news, found her sitting exactly
as he had left her, the paper in her hand and her forehead
purple from congestion of the brain. All Mme. Arcé's tender
nursing was needed.

As she was regaining her strength after a fever which had
almost brought her to a sudden grave, one night in the stillness
she heard the signal gun of a steamer far out at sea. There
was an instant uproar in the town. By scores, by hundreds,
the Americans rushed clattering and shouting down the streets
to the ramparts, while the excitable natives filled the streets
screaming "El vapor!" When the hubbub was at its height,
there suddenly came, from another quarter, a second signal
gun. Two steamers were in the offing. Wrapped in her dressing-
gown, and watching from a balcony, Jessie saw men weeping
and hugging one another as if they were Crusoes being taken
from some desert island. One ship, the Panama, had rounded
the Horn; the other, the California, had scraped together a
crew and come down from San Francisco. The next morning
Jessie was waited upon by the captain of the Panama and by
a naval officer, who told her she was to take their vessel. Among
her fellow-passengers were William M. Gwin and the handsome
young army officer later famous as "Fighting Joe" Hooker.
She went aboard still beset by fears for Frémont's safety, but
at San Diego was greeted by news that he had arrived before

her and had hurried on to San Francisco. "I think every man on the ship," she says, "came to tell me and say a choking word for joy for me." [2]

As her daughter Lilly relates the story, when the ship ran into San Diego, Jessie locked herself into her cabin, fearful of the tidings she might hear. The first men to board the vessel knocked at her door and called out: "The colonel's safe; riding up to San Francisco to meet you there; he didn't lose a leg— was only badly frostbitten!" [3]

Carried ashore through the surf to what is now the foot of Montgomery Street in San Francisco, Jessie found that Frémont had not yet arrived. She also found the region wild with excitement. San Francisco was a half-deserted town; deserted, that is, by its original inhabitants, and peopled mainly by newcomers counting the hours until they could get away to the interior. No servants could be had except half-trained Indians and Chinese. Mrs. Frémont was told that "time was worth fifty dollars a minute." The people lived as transients would be expected to live, in tents of dirty canvas, shanties knocked together with odd pieces of wood, or ragged shelters of blankets. The one really good private house in these first roaring "days of old, and days of gold, and the days of '49," was a two-story frame structure shipped out complete by a New Yorker, with furniture to fill it, at a cost said to reach ninety thousand dollars. It had been intended for a bride, and had witnessed her death a few weeks after it was erected. The only settled residents, besides a small corps of tradesmen who realized that the retail business was surer and richer than any placer venture they were likely to find, were the military officers, who stuck courageously to their posts. As there were no warehouses for the storage of goods, consignments were auctioned off as quickly as they arrived; and these auctions, advertised sometimes by brass bands, were a feature of the place. The hotels and lodging-houses being comfortless, at night almost the

[2] Jessie Benton Frémont, *Souvenirs of My Time*, p. 188.
[3] Elizabeth Benton Frémont MSS, Bancroft Library.

whole population betook itself to the saloons and gambling-dens. Within a few months, many of these places assumed the trappings of luxury: plate-glass mirrors, fine chandeliers, gaudy oil-paintings. Public improvements were conspicuously lacking: the streets were rivers of mud, which men tried to pave sometimes with bags of flour, bales of cotton, or other goods —for wood was not to be had. Water was one of the most precious of commodities, and laundry-work cost fabulous sums. With inadequate sanitary arrangements, cholera and fever were a grim menace, and the death-rate was high.[4]

Ships were now coming into the port in a steady stream, many of them fifty or sixty days from New York, some forty days from Australia, and some direct from Europe. As they discharged their cargoes and men, San Francisco underwent a swift change in appearance. High piers were hurriedly built out into the Bay. The ragged streets of shanties and tents, with the winds blowing furious clouds of dust down them, stretched farther and farther back over the hills. Everywhere arose buildings of all shapes and sizes, in all stages of construction. Many were mere canvas-covered sheds, open in front. Masses of merchandise were piled higgledly-piggledly in the open air, sometimes under a dirty tarpaulin, sometimes exposed. They displayed rudely painted signs in every European tongue and advertising every ware; while prominent among these "stores" rose several hotels—the Frémont Family Hotel, a two-story structure, the Parker House, the City Hotel, and others—all crammed to bursting.

Along the public ways, ankle-deep in mud or dust, crowded people of every nationality and description: Yankees nasal and electric, guttural Germans, nervous Frenchmen, burly Britons, Chinese with swinging pigtails, Californians wrapped in serapes, Chileans, Kanakas, and Malays with long creeses. Far back from the water-front lay the plaza (called Portsmouth Square after the warship which Frémont had found here in

4 Stewart Edward White, *The Fortyniners*, Chs. 8, 9, and 10, picture early San Francisco.

'47), with a high flagpole marking the adobe customhouse. Military forces policed the town. The atmosphere was one of feverish activity. Everybody was talking of claims, of diggings, of town lots, of the new cities of Sacramento and Stockton; everybody hoped to get rich.[5]

The hurry, the wild new monetary standards, and the speculative spirit bewildered the newcomer. A porter who carried one's bags a few blocks demanded $2 in payment; an old New York newspaper sold at $1 a copy; and truckmen driving for merchants of the town made $15 or $20 a day. The sudden wealth had attracted an army of gamblers and saloon-keepers. At least $60,000 a year in rent was paid by the gamblers who at one time occupied most of the second story of the Parker House. A canvas tent near-by, called "Eldorado" by the faro and monte men who occupied it, only 15 by 20 feet in size, was rented for $40,000 a year. A wandering Easterner who wished to hang out his shingle as a lawyer was shown a cellar dug in the ground and told he could have it for $250 a month. All business was transacted with a rush, and men who tried to bargain were brushed impatiently aside.

If a customer entered a store, the owner eyed him with indifference, named the price he wanted for a given article, and turned away if the customer objected. Money in smaller amounts than a quarter-dollar did not pass current. The large-minded attitude toward financial affairs was seen at its best in the implicit trust which men were perforce compelled to place in one another's honesty. Loans were made without security, and repaid punctually. Yet the gambling spirit pervaded every group. Bayard Taylor, watching curiously one of the crowded "hells" where sperm-oil lamps lighted up the players' excited features, saw a boy of fifteen coolly pocket $500; one of his fellow-travelers from Panama lose $2,400; and a hard-bitten miner betting great piles of gold dust on a single throw, and finally losing his last hundred ounces at a stroke.

It was here that, ten days after Jessie landed, Frémont

[5] Bayard Taylor, *Eldorado, or Adventures in the Path of Empire*, p. 55.

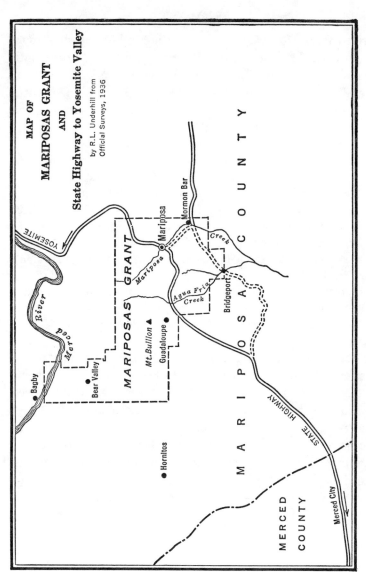

MAP OF
MARIPOSAS GRANT
AND
State Highway to Yosemite Valley

by R.L. Underhill from
Official Surveys, 1936

FRÉMONT'S MARIPOSA ESTATE AS FINALLY LAID OUT

arrived from Monterey. She was sitting in her cheerless room in the Parker House when she heard a shout from Portsmouth Square: "Your wife's inside the house, Colonel." A moment later her husband was kneeling by her chair; both of them too much overcome to utter a sound. She has described the scene with her usual feeling:

Then we both spoke at once, each wanting the other to begin at the moment we had parted over a stirrup-cup of tea that morning on the Missouri. Suddenly he looked at me closely with fear in his eyes. "You have been ill, you are ill now, my darling." I was about to deny it when Lilly came in.... She looked at her father gravely as he knelt beside me. As he rose and hugged her, then drew a chair up close, and took her on his knee, she said bluntly: "You didn't come. Mother almost died. A lady downstairs says she will die."

There was nothing to say in refutation, but I answered his stricken look: "In her innocence she is partly right. Being away from you is a kind of death. Only with you I am fully alive and well." [6]

When Frémont had exchanged with Jessie the history of the past eventful six months, the two looked earnestly for a home in this rushing beehive. The town changed with visible speed —men said that it grew daily by from fifteen to thirty houses. There was now an ebb-tide or backwash from the mines, as well as a tide setting steadily toward them. Broken-down, sick, and disheartened prospectors were returning from the diggings, and doing what they could to dampen the ardor of the new-comers. As the town leaped up to a population of six thousand its business and professional life increased in vigor. Here the Frémonts met well-known men: Major George H. Derby ("John Phoenix"), who had come on Jessie's ship and had organized theatricals to divert her; Edwin Bryant of Kentucky; the artist Osgood, who after three months in the hills had set up his easel as a portrait painter; and T. Butler King. For a time they lived in a house which had been occupied by the late vice-consul, Leidesdorff. But they could not make

[6] Catherine Coffin Phillips, *Jessie Benton Frémont*, pp. 142, 143.

themselves quite comfortable in San Francisco. The trade winds and fogs injured Jessie's lungs; moreover, it was too far from their new ranch, Mariposa. They therefore betook themselves south to Monterey, where they were only one hundred and twenty-five miles as the crow flies (about one hundred and forty miles by road) from the estate. A wing of the governor's house, the largest and best building in town, was thrown open to them, Mme. José Castro and her children occupying the other half.

For the next few months Jessie, rapidly recovering her health, enjoyed with characteristic zest her life in this long, low adobe house of red-tiled roof, with its spacious gardens and hedge of pink roses of Castile. They had Indian men for kitchen service, and she soon mastered the art of cookery with little meat, no fowls or eggs, no milk or butter, and not even potatoes—for the swarming gold-seekers had devoured all. She made friends with Mme. Castro, whose husband was still exiled in Mexico, but who felt no resentment for their lost position and fortune. Among the army officers then in Monterey, General Bennet Riley, General P. F. Smith, and young W. T. Sherman, who was thin and consumptive-looking, with a bad cough, she found congenial acquaintances. Frémont made a trip to San Francisco, and "with manlike prodigality, sent down what would have fitted up the whole large Castro House." They had bales of Chinese satins and French damasks to use for draperies and hangings, boxes of French and Chinese porcelain, bamboo couches and chairs, and wonderfully carved and inlaid Chinese furniture. Two English-china punchbowls served for wash basins. The house had a large fireplace, and Jessie threw down grizzly-bear skins to give warmth to the mat-covered floors, and to lend a cozy air to recesses between the satin-cushioned sofas and armchairs. Her Indian boys, Gregorio and Juan, shot doves and squirrels, and, broiling them upon sticks before the fire, would bring them at the most unusual hours. Jessie later wrote of the whole experience with enormous pleasure:[7]

[7] Jessie Benton Frémont MSS, Bancroft Library.

This was my first house and my first housekeeping—without any of what we consider indispensable necessities of servants, or usual supplies, but most comfortable and most charming. We had the luxuries of life, if not its necessities. Youth, health, and exultant happiness can do without commonplaces, though it is awkward to have only Indian men for kitchen service, and to study a cookery book and try to follow its directions with no staples. Whatever could be put up in glass or tins we had in quantity—and rice is a great reliance when you learn its many uses.... Again, I was in the home-keeping domestic atmosphere of Spanish women, who offered me every help, though they could not give what they themselves did not have in this locust-like sweeping away of every green thing and no replanting, for Californians too were off to the placers, and speculators had bought up all attainable cattle and sheep for San Francisco. The expenses for army people were too great up there, so headquarters were at Monterey, and there General Riley planted cabbages and sweet women grew tired but laughed over their contrivances, and were hospitable and helping in spite of all drawbacks. General, then Major Canby, was stationed there, and his most amiable gentle wife was a center of helping good will. They had an excellent cook, a Mexican who had followed the general after the war, and who did not leave them now even to go to the placers. Mrs. Canby took pity on my tinned biscuit diet, and regularly her man came with the fragrant loaf of fresh bread wrapped in its delicate napkin and set on a plate of fine green enameled Chinese china. Who could need cream with tea, to make that a breakfast of delight to mind as well as palate? Mme. Castro, true to the gentle nature of Spanish women, sent daily a cup of milk for my little girl, for she had saved a cow for her children. This was another turn of the wheel. I had the name which represented to her total loss, for her husband had not returned from Mexico after we took her country, and yet her motherly feelings were stronger than the natural resentment for lost position and fortune. She had, though, the innate Spanish pride. A birthday among her children made the opportunity for giving a coral necklace they had admired on my child. The little Modesta brought it back with her soft-voice message. "My mamma says, if it is a present, yes; if it is pay for the milk, no."

Frémont was now spending all the time he could spare at the Mariposa ranch, which he found a singularly attractive place. From high up in the central Sierras, the Mariposa River flows west to join the San Joaquin. To the northeast, some forty miles away, lies the Yosemite; below, toward the Pacific, stretches the hot central valley. Covering a large segment of the Mariposa basin, the estate comprised the high eminence which they called Mount Bullion, in honor of Senator Benton—"Old Bullion"—picturesque wooded foothills of the Sierras, and broad green flats waving with grass. To reach it in summer from Monterey, the traveler had to ride across the scorching plains of the San Joaquin Valley, where the temperature often rose high above one hundred degrees, and ford a number of rushing streams like the Tuolumne. When, through clouds of suffocating dust, he came to slopes covered with the butterfly tulips which gave the ranch its name, and caught a breath of cooler air, he was nearing his destination. Farther up, where Frémont's estate lay, the sparkling atmosphere and the freshness and elasticity it gave every breath made the sun, still very hot, quite endurable. Bear Valley, in which the Colonel soon built a pleasant two-story frame house, was a little natural paradise. Pine trees, six or eight feet in diameter, towered two hundred feet into the air; the streams were full of salmon; the ground was covered with red clover; at night in summer, blankets were required. Not many years before, this spot had been the favorite hunting ground of the Cauchile Indians. The precise boundaries of the 43,000-acre estate, according to the frequent Mexican practice, were not fixed, and the grantee, as the government decided later, had the right of locating the land on any claim within a large area.[8]

Making Monterey his headquarters, Frémont led a life of incessant activity, and Jessie was much of the time at his side. They had a six-seated surrey, the only carriage in the territory, fitted with every convenience. Lilly recalls that for a time after

[8] John R. Howard, *Remembrance of Things Past*, Ch. 9; Bigelow, *Frémont*, p. 379*ff*.

mules were obtained for this vehicle they were perfect nomads, sleeping as much in the open as under a roof. Jessie would have the cushions drawn together in the surrey to form a mattress; the little girl would go to sleep in the boot; and Frémont and the other men would bunk in the open on their blankets or in hammocks strung to the trees. In time they obtained an Englishwoman, newly landed from Australia, as their housekeeper in Monterey, and Jessie writes that "she brought English comfort and thoroughness into everything about me."

Meanwhile, fortune smiled as never before. The Sonora miners had been sent to Mariposa without delay and were busy prospecting and extracting the gold from the river gravel. Bayard Taylor, riding into San José as a correspondent for the New York *Tribune,* happened upon Frémont as the explorer was returning from his first trip to the diggings. They shook hands upon the porch of a private house. The Colonel wore California garb, with sombrero and native-style jacket. Taylor was struck by his deep-set, hawklike eyes, bold aquiline nose, and thin, weather-beaten face; above all, by the compactness of his bodily build—"I have seen in no other man the qualities of lightness, activity, strength, and physical endurance in so perfect an equilibrium." His refinement of manner and polished address, unroughened by the camp life of months, also impressed the journalist. Frémont, despite his recent disasters, was now a man of greater note than ever; for the East, its curiosity aroused by the gold rush, was reading his reports on the West with insatiable appetite.

After a brief period in the old capital the Frémonts temporarily went back to San Francisco, where they established a home on some land which the Colonel had purchased, later (Jessie says) the site of the Palace Hotel. He bought and set up a ready-made Chinese-built house, which fitted together like a puzzle, the only nails being those which fastened the shingles to the roof. Walls and floors were grooved together, and doors and windows slid into their places like some exquisite piece of cabinet-work. The family slept on grass hammocks covered with navy-blue blankets. Since the house was small, Frémont often placed his own bunk in the carriage on the sand dunes outside. Some of the most interesting men of the booming new city rode over frequently when the day's work was done and in frontier fashion ate a hearty dinner with the Colonel. A house-man whom they had luckily kept served as cook; they had all the resources of the San Francisco markets for food; and they drank choice wines which had come out from France. In good weather the dinner was served outdoors, with the tables placed on the sand dunes, the blue sky overhead, the bay at their feet, and a strong touch of color added by the flowering lupines all about. Jessie relished the deference, amounting sometimes almost to worship, which was paid her, for women were rarities and men would walk many miles merely to see one. Among her friends were Joseph Hooker, later the Civil War general, then a slim young officer; a Dr. Bowie of Maryland; Samuel Ward of epicurean fame; and adventurers who had roved in India, South America, and all parts of the world. This interlude pleased them all, but it closed when the rainy season sent Jessie and the children to Monterey again.[9]

As soon as the news spread that Frémont's Sonoran helpers were washing out gold literally by the bucketful, crowds of other prospectors rushed to the region. Before long two or three thousand were on the ground. Under the Mexican law such a grant as Frémont had obtained gave no title to mineral rights, and public opinion regarded placer deposits, no matter on whose land, as general and unrestricted property. Frémont naturally made no effort to interfere with the army of prospectors swarming over his land. But the Sonorans, as the first comers, had an advantage over others. They washed out the gold in such quantities that it was sent down to his home in Monterey, so Jessie tells us, in hundred-pound buckskin sacks,

[9] Jessie Benton Frémont MSS, Bancroft Library.
[10] Jessie Benton Frémont, *A Year of American Travel*, p. 125.

worth not far from $25,000 each.[10] The quantity sounds like an exaggeration, but unquestionably enormous sums were taken out; the Frémonts kindly sent a Negro servant named Saunders, whose family were still in slavery, but who had been offered them by the owner for $1,700, up to Mariposa to dig enough gold for the purchase, and he soon obtained it. Unfortunately, the Sonorans did not get on well with the American newcomers. They left near Christmas for home; and as the Colonel was too busy with politics at the moment to go to Monterey and divide the gold, he sent the miners the keys to his store-room there. They made the division themselves, and took not a single ounce more than their just share.

To say that Frémont was busy with politics is to say merely that as one of the prominent citizens of California he was inevitably caught into the current of public affairs. With unexampled rapidity, a new state had been built out of an almost unpeopled land. In the year 1849 more than eighty thousand emigrants, three-fourths of them Americans, reached the Coast. The population at the end of the year was well above a hundred thousand, exclusive of Indians, and still growing by tremendous leaps. Already a convention of delegates, sitting at Monterey during September, had framed an anti-slavery constitution and applied for admission to the Union. Of this convention, one of the most picturesque bodies of its kind ever seen in America, Frémont was, rather strangely, not a member. The president was none other than the seven-foot Dr. Robert Semple, familiar to us as one of the leaders and, later, the Thucydides of the Bear Flag War; he was escorted to his seat by Captain Sutter and General Vallejo; the official reporter was that rhetorical journalist and traveler, J. Ross Browne; and the members chose as the first secretary of state Henry Wager Halleck, who was later to command the armies of the North in the Civil War. Bayard Taylor was an onlooker, and attended a gay dress ball in pantaloons lent him by an officer who weighed considerably more than two hundred pounds. It was a distinguished as well as an amusing assemblage (one member objected to trial by a jury of peers on the ground that only aristocratic England had a peerage), and Frémont should have been present.[11]

But he did use his influence, so far as it was needed, on behalf of free-soil principles. There proved to be surprisingly little opposition to the clause in the bill of rights prohibiting slavery forever in California, many even of the Southerners supporting it. Men realized that the climate and the whole social order were inimical to slavery; that, as one grizzled mountaineer put it in haranguing an election-day crowd, "in a country where every white man makes a slave of himself there is no use in keeping niggers." [12] The Frémonts themselves had resolutely treated slavery as a disgrace. A Texas gold-seeker offered to sell them a strong young mulatto woman, but Jessie indignantly refused. The Colonel was told by advocates of slavery that "You will be the richest man in the world if your mines are worked by slave labor," but he rejected the idea with scorn. Jessie informs us that fifteen members of the convention came in a body to hear from Thomas Hart Benton's daughter that under no circumstances would she consent to own or use a slave. She entertained largely as long as the convention lasted— Sutter was her first guest—and argued that the land her husband had called "the Italy of America" was an ideal place for moderate holdings, well-cultivated farms and orchards, and free institutions.

From the beginning of the agitation for statehood, Frémont's name was informally before the people of California as a candidate for the Senate. He was known to be a Democrat, and to belong nationally to the free-soil wing of that party. He and Jessie, influenced by their deepest instincts and by Senator Benton's views, had long been opposed to the extension of slavery into the territories. Already the California Democracy was showing signs of a decided split upon the question, and lines were being drawn which later resulted in the protracted political

<hr>

[11] Bayard Taylor, *Eldorado*, Ch. 16; see J. Ross Browne, *Report of Debates in the Convention of California, passim.*
[12] New York *Tribune*, October 22, 1849.

duel between the slavery leader, William M. Gwin, and the free-soil leader, Broderick. To a politician who sent him a set of political questions, Frémont replied explicitly and at length. "By association, feeling, principle, and education," he wrote, "I am a Democrat." He believed in a central national railroad from the Mississippi to the Pacific, and would labor for its immediate location and construction. He defended his purchase of the Mariposa claim, and his financial transactions during his brief civil governorship in 1847.

That was in December, 1849. The same month, by a compromise between the anti-slavery and pro-slavery factions, the California legislature elected Frémont and William M. Gwin senators, and later, in drawing lots, Frémont received the short term. On the first ballot, he had received twenty-nine votes, Gwin twenty-two, Halleck twelve, and others scattering votes. Of course, the election had no validity until California was actually admitted to the Union. But Congress had already met; the question of bringing California and New Mexico in was the paramount issue before it, and it was believed that the famous explorer, with the influence of Benton to assist him, might prove a useful lobbyist in the national capital. He was expected to start for the East at once. It was further believed that, with his unequaled knowledge of the West, and his conviction that by his last exploring trip he had found the ideal route, he could do more than any one else to hasten the building of the Pacific railroad. Jessie tells us how characteristically Frémont responded to the new challenge:[13]

One evening of tremendous rain, when we were, as usual, around the fire, Mrs. McEvoy, with her table and lights, sewing at one side, myself by the other, explaining pictures from the *Illustrated Times* to my little girl, while the baby rolled about on the bearskin in front of the fire, suddenly Mr. Frémont came in upon us, dripping wet, as well he might be, for he had come through from San José— seventy miles on horseback through the heavy rain. He was so wet that we could hardly make him cross the pretty room; but...the

[13] *A Year of American Travel*, p. 159.

footmarks were all welcome, for they pointed home. He came to tell me that he had been elected Senator, and that it was necessary we should go to Washington on the steamer of the first of January.

At daybreak the next morning he was off again, having to be back in San José. A young sorrel horse, of which Mr. Frémont was very fond, brought him down and carried him back this 140 miles within 36 hours, without fatigue to either.

On New Year's night of 1850, with the rain pouring torrents and every street in Monterey a stream, Frémont bore Jessie in his arms down to the wharf and they embarked on the steamer *Oregon* for New York via the Panama route. Among those aboard were Gwin, Sam Ward, and T. Butler King; and the vessel was estimated to be carrying three million dollars in gold dust. The sudden return East meant an abandonment by the Frémonts of many plans. Mariposa had to be left under the oversight of California friends. Their hopes for a quiet life, a cessation of struggle, had to be given up. They had meant to stay seven years, "the world forgetting, by the world forgot, our first object to live our lives in independence," but the gold rush and statehood had made that impossible. It cost them both a pang to leave the free outdoor life of the West. Jessie had brought all her natural vivacity and gusto to the camping excursions, when in some mountain glade they would eat venison, drink claret, and afterward enjoy the camp-fire talk of old Knight, the hunter, or the naval lieutenant, Edward F. Beale; she had delighted in the gay, hospitable Californians, with their families of twelve or fifteen children, their profuse hospitality, their folk songs and serenades, their *guisada* and other dishes, their three-day marriage feasts, their incomparable horsemanship, and their picturesque dress—the velvet jackets, gold embroidery, slashed trousers, and jingling bells of the men making them look like figures out of an opera. She had enjoyed playing the hostess herself, and during the progress of the constitutional convention, when Frémont was fearful lest the slavery element might prove strong, and when many of his old friends and opponents, from Sutter to Castro, were in town, she had kept open house and laden her table with dainties.

Yet Frémont would have been more than human had he not felt a certain exultation in the changed circumstances of his return East. A year and a half earlier he had been traveling west on the Great Lakes, an impoverished young man of bleak prospects, just resigned under attack from the army. Now he was coming back a Senator-elect, his trunk full of buckskin bags of gold dust, with the title to one of the richest tracts on the Coast in his possession. What a transformation! An English man-of-war, at anchor off Mazatlan, fired a salute in his honor and that of Senator-elect Gwin, and lowered the captain's gig to put Frémont and Jessie ashore. He had even been gratified by an expression of Zachary Taylor's confidence in him. The President, no doubt partly to please Benton, had in June, 1849, appointed him a commissioner to run the boundary line with Mexico, and Frémont had accepted the place, resigning it, however, immediately afterward. No one in Washington would be able to sneer at him. Jessie, too, who was still ailing in health and had grown homesick, was glad to return with her small daughter to her father and invalid mother.

Before Frémont and his wife had reached Panama both were ill, Jessie with some unnamed malady which she says put her in danger of dying, and the Colonel with an attack of rheumatic fever in the leg which had been so badly frostbitten in the San Juan Mountains. They were taken to Mme. Arcé's home and nursed back to sufficient health to enable them to continue their travels. Lying on cots in her big ballroom, which was made the sick chamber because of its coolness, they were regularly visited by the explorer John L. Stephens, now vice-president of the Panama Railroad Company, who was also fever ridden, and who used to say, "I have come to take my chill with you." Running up from Colon to New York on the mail steamer *Georgia*, Jessie was again attacked and grew worse; a gale which buffeted the ship till she had to be lashed to a sofa made her so desperately ill that she was later told that by all the laws of medicine she should have died. Frémont himself had meanwhile been seized with "Chagres fever," and was in bed. But at last they were safe home; they went immediately to the Irving House, and the press announced: "Mrs. Frémont has entirely recovered from her illness. The colonel has been indisposed for some time past with intermittent fever, but is now convalescent."

On September 9, 1850, California was admitted to the Union, and shortly afterward Frémont took his seat as one of her Senators.

Still half-ill, he was actually in the Senate only twenty-one working days. In this time he introduced eighteen measures, the principal ones being a bill to regulate the working of the mines in California; a bill to grant the State public lands for educational purposes; a bill to grant it six townships to found a university; a bill to give it land for asylums for the deaf, dumb, blind, and insane; and a bill to open a wagon-road across the continent. He meanwhile distinguished himself for his anti-slavery temper. He voted for the suppression of the slave-trade in the District of Columbia, and against a measure which provided a heavy prison-sentence for any one who should entice a slave to run away. During the session he came into collision, in none too creditable a way, with Senator Foote of Mississippi. In debate the half-tipsy Foote angered Frémont by charging that his bill to regulate the operation of the mines in California was drafted for his own private advantage. A hot altercation in the antechamber followed. Thereupon the Colonel sent Foote a letter demanding a retraction of his language, to be signed in the presence of witnesses, and penned also a challenge to a duel if he refused. Foote, though declining to sign the retraction, wrote Frémont to disclaim any intention of giving offense in his language; and this satisfied every one, including Benton, to whom the explorer referred the matter. Meanwhile, the young Senator's stern anti-slavery temper gave offense in California, and the Southern forces there began to rally to prevent his reëlection.

Living again at Benton's house in Washington, Jessie and he enjoyed the social life of the capital. Mayor Seaton has sketched him for us as he appeared at a dinner party, a man of "arresting dignity," but looking worn and thin. "His black hair, heavily streaked with gray, gave distinction to his weather-worn features. His eyes shone youthfully as he answered questions as to the possibilities of the coast under a railway project." Often silent, he watched with frank admiration his wife, talking and laughing with the sparkle of a care-free girl. "When Jessie caught his glance upon her, there was an exchange which I can only describe as a mental wink, a flash of eye, a fleeting smile, discreet flirtation throughout the long dinner." [14] Gradually he gained strength. But when the Mississippi and Pacific Railroad Convention met in Philadelphia in the spring of 1851, a convention to which he sent a long letter urging the route between the thirty-eighth and thirty-ninth parallels for the railroad, he was still confined to his room by "Chagres fever."

[14] Catherine Coffin Phillips, *Jessie Benton Frémont*, p. 171.

XXIV

Managing the Mariposas

FRÉMONT had now risen to a pinnacle where his opportunities seemed far greater than ever before. He commanded wealth; he had held political office and power; he possessed a reputation as the foremost explorer of the West. He was a busy man of affairs, supervising his estate, laboring for the cause of free-soil democracy in Washington and California, answering scientific inquiries, and keeping abreast of geographical advances. His ambitions were increasingly complex, for he hoped to be one of the statesmen of the new West and one of her business entrepreneurs as well as the pathmarker who mapped her highways. Five years were to pass before he was to be widely discussed as a presidential candidate. How fruitfully was he to spend them?

Thus far his life had been shaped largely by personal forces —by Poinsett, Nicollet, Benton, Jessie, Stockton; now there enters the drama a powerful and on the whole sinister impersonal force, the Mariposa estate. For the next fifteen years this ten-league grant, rich in gold and grazing land, was to dominate all too much of Frémont's activities. Promising him wealth and happiness, it was to bring him in the end little but trouble and disappointment. Seeming a beneficent gift of luck, it was destined before it vanished—vanished as suddenly as a rainbow bubble—to appear rather like some malignant stroke of Fate. It did more to govern the central part of his career, and in the large view to warp it, than any other element; for it led him from the scientific pursuits for which he had been trained into the alien world of business.

To give Mariposa its true significance it must thus be treated

not as a mere mining enterprise, but as one of the great controlling influences upon Frémont's career. Its business history
is a thorny and profitless maze. From the outset the estate
proved to be a perfect Pandora's box of complications. Its
boundaries were undetermined; it was difficult to obtain an
American title, for Congress in 1851 passed an act refusing
confirmation to any California titles without absolute written
proof, and the papers of the Mexican administration were
nailed up in various repositories; while the region abounded in
land-jumpers. The state witnessed a half-dozen years of partial
chaos in landholding, many settlers taking up unauthorized
abodes wherever they pleased, and defending them with shot-
guns. Frémont's Sonoran workers, with the first flood of other
miners, shortly exhausted the rich placer deposits in the Mariposa area. There remained not merely its vast possibilities in
grain and cattle-growing, but plain evidences of gold-bearing
quartz—Alexis Godey picked up the first gold-veined rock—
which would pay well, but would first require a heavy capital
investment in mining tools and ore-crushing machinery.[1] Study
of these possibilities filled the sanguine Frémont with an un-

---

[1] News of this find was given in the California correspondence of the
Trenton, New Jersey, *Daily True American*, November 13, 1849: "But by far
the most magnificent discovery is that recently made upon the rancho of
Col. Frémont, on the Mariposas River. It is nothing less than a vein of
gold in the solid rock—a bona fide mine, the first which has been found in
California. I saw some specimens which were in Col. Frémont's possession.
The stone is a reddish quartz, filled with rich veins of gold, and far sur-
passing the specimens brought from North Carolina and Georgia. Some stones
picked up on the top of the quartz strata, without particular selection, yielded
two ounces of gold to every twenty-five pounds. Col. Frémont informed me
that the vein had been traced for more than a mile. The thickness on the
surface is two feet, gradually widening as it descends, and showing larger
particles of gold. The dip downward is only about twenty feet, so that the
mine can be worked with little expense. These are the particulars first given
me, when the discovery was announced. Still more astonishing facts have
just come to light.
"A geologist sent out to examine the place arrived here [San Francisco]
last night. He reports having traced the vein a distance of two leagues, with
an average breadth of 150 feet. At one extremity of the mine he found large
quantities of native silver, which he calculates will fully pay the expenses
of setting up machinery and working it.... This discovery has made a great
sensation throughout the country...."

fortunate conviction that he could be a highly successful business-man.

Within a year he began to learn that the Mariposa was a will-of-the-wisp, beckoning him forward with promises of stupendous wealth, sometimes placing small gifts within his grasp, and yet always cheating him. In June, 1850, he authorized an agent named David Hoffman to act for him in London and to organize mining companies upon the basis of leases. At the same time, he made out some other leases to Thomas Denny Sargent, who proceeded to California, duly located them on the property, obtained surveys and other necessary papers, and then going to London in the early spring of 1851, disposed of them in Great Britain at a large profit. Senator Benton was struck by Sargent's enterprise, and having received a power-of-attorney from Frémont, agreed with Sargent that he should take over the whole tract for a million dollars. Sargent seems to have made his first payment, to have proceeded to England, hustled about there, convinced capitalists of the value of the property, and concluded arrangements for its resale at a handsome price. Meanwhile, Hoffman had concluded important business arrangements of his own in London, and was filled with consternation to learn that the area had suddenly been whisked from beneath his feet. He protested, while Frémont declared that he had never authorized a sale. It was a very pretty and complicated quarrel till the Colonel cut through it in the fall of 1852 by ordering a temporary suspension of all transactions with regard to Mariposa.[2]

It was high time that he did so, for he was by no means certain that the government would recognize his claim to the land, and a long course of litigation, which finally landed him in the Supreme Court, was looming up ahead. His claim was duly filed before the Federal commissioners in the opening days of 1852, and by the autumn of 1853 was being fought out with

[2] David Hoffman, *The Frémont Estate: An Address to the British Public.* See also the anonymous pamphlet of 1856, *Who is Frémont? By One who has Known Him Socially, Financially, and Politically.*

Attorney-General Caleb Cushing in the Federal District Court. Even if Frémont got the land, he might well be refused title to the minerals. But the explorer was still exuberantly confident of becoming a millionaire, and had embarked upon efforts to develop the property with money of his own, and funds of the San Francisco banking house of Palmer, Cook & Co. This house, which was also interested in the defense, seems to have taken a certain part of the estate as security, and to have cut this part up into shares which were sold to certain other capitalists.[3]

Frémont had the more time for Mariposa in that his senatorial career had been brief, and his ambitions to succeed himself had proved abortive. The needs of the estate and his desire to campaign for reëlection took him hurriedly back to California in the fall of 1850. In San Francisco, after a long search, he finally bought an ugly but comfortable domicile high on Stockton Street, overlooking the Plaza. Here Frémont found that the pro-slavery wing of the Democratic party had grown in strength. Had his health been good, he might have done more to rally the free-soil element. But in December he was taken ill, and, as Senator Benton said in Congress, was chained to his bed "by sciatica, rheumatism, neuralgia," paying the penalty of his past exposures. Jessie hurried out from the East to nurse him. The legislative balloting came on in February, 1851; more than one hundred and forty votes were taken, and he was decisively defeated, though no choice was made. Nearly a year later, Colonel John B. Weller, of the now dominant slavery faction, was elected in his stead.

Frémont would have liked nothing better than to continue in the area of state and national politics, but the situation was unfavorable to a man of his temperament. The population of California was still rising like an irresistible tide, and the voters were a rough, heterogeneous lot who responded readily to the arts of the demagogue. The census of 1850 gave the state

---

[3] Montgomery Blair was retained as Frémont's attorney; W. E. Smith, *The Francis Preston Blair Family in Politics,* II, pp. 53, 54.

122,000 people. That summer the tide of emigration was so great that 9,270 wagons passed Fort Laramie on the California and Oregon Trail, and 42,000 persons registered with the commandant.[4] In 1852, the torrent overflowed all bounds. Before the close of May more than 2,600 wagons, more than 26,000 cattle, and some 11,000 men, women, and children had reached Fort Kearny on the way to the Coast. On the principal trails, the road showed almost a continuous line of covered wagons. San Francisco had sprung up into a great sprawling city, with many miles of graded streets, ambitious blocks of business buildings, and flimsy residences which proved food for a series of conflagrations. The majority of the new-comers were rude and illiterate frontier folk, or urban adventurers. They mingled in city and mining-camp with Mexicans, Chileans, swarms of Europeans, men from the British penal colonies, and Chinese. The French Government had taken deliberate measures for sending over a large part of the *Garde Mobile,* a turbulent body which Louis Napoleon had at one time found useful, but which had proved too troublesome to keep in Paris. But the convicts and ne'er-do-wells from Botany Bay and Sydney, who "escaped" to California in shiploads, were the most vicious of all; and they gave the English immigrants in general a bad name.

Racial antagonisms were intense; while the resentment which the landless squatters felt against the great estate owners like Frémont was strong. Disorder seemed to increase steadily. The electorate was easily played upon by such adept politicians of southern sympathies as Gwin, Weller, and the unprincipled Governor John Bigler,[5] but it was instinctively hostile to such a man as Frémont.

To Mariposa and other business, therefore, Frémont gave most of 1851. Always restless, always inclined to speculation, he did not confine himself, as common sense dictated, to his estate. His most impetuous venture was a contract for supply-

[4] John Bach McMaster, *History of the People of the United States,* VIII, p. 58.

[5] Compare Cardinal Goodwin, *Establishment of State Government in California, passim.*

ing beef to the Indians. The overrunning of the foothills and valleys by miners had driven many of the savages from their old hunting grounds; and pressed by hunger, they commenced killing live stock belonging to the whites. The settlers retaliated. There seemed danger of a general Indian war, which would wipe out isolated miners and prospectors, and Federal commissioners were hastily sent to treat with the tribes. These commissioners adopted the wise principle that it was better to feed the Indians than to fight them; but when they sought for beef they found that the ranchers were trying to take advantage of the emergency by demanding exorbitant prices. Frémont happened to have cattle interests, and he offered to furnish some $180,000 worth of beef at the usual rates; an offer which the commissioners accepted as "the lowest and best yet made by any responsible man." [6] The commissioners gave him drafts upon the Treasury, but they had heavily overdrawn their credit, and he met a great deal of trouble in getting his money. Special legislation by Congress was ultimately necessary to compensate the explorer for what was not merely a fair but a public-spirited transaction.[7] He had other irons in the fire at the same time. Leaving Jessie in San Francisco, where the disorders were growing dangerous and were resulting in incendiarism, he spent much time in the saddle or at Mariposa.

The first great San Francisco fire of 1851, that of May 4th, which destroyed at least seven million dollars' worth of property,[8] cost Jessie—who had given birth to another son two weeks earlier, and was confined to her bed at the time—a night of feverish excitement, but that was all. The Frémont home on Stockton Street, near the Plaza, was high up on the hillside, and her windows looked down into the sea of flames. At one time, it was necessary to hang soaking-wet carpets over the sides of the house to counteract the fierce heat; boxes of legal papers and silverware were taken to a friend's house on Russian

---

[6] MS Memoirs, Bancroft Library.

[7] See full history of the matter in Senator Weller's speech, *Congressional Globe*, August 11, 1856; *34th Cong., 1st Sess.*, p. 2022.

[8] J. S. Hittell, *History of San Francisco*, p. 168.

Hill; while the hammock and blankets in which she was to be carried away, if necessary, were placed ready beside her bed. But friendly fire-fighters, scorched and wet, ran in from time to time to reassure her. The second fire, occurring late in June while Frémont was at the Mariposas, proved much more dangerous.

This conflagration started at ten o'clock on a Sunday morning, and it was soon clear that it would sweep away the Frémont residence. Jessie and her baby were taken to the home of a hospitable South Carolinian on a safe elevation not far away. Other refugees were gathered there. One of them was a young Frenchwoman who had been very ill, and who took a large chair by a window overlooking the advancing fire. "Her wild fevered gaze was fixed on her burning home," writes Jessie. "Suddenly, with a crazy laugh, she rose and offered me her seat—'C'est votre tour, Madame; your house goes next,' she said. And after we had made her lie down and let wet cloths be applied to the poor fevered head, I in my turn watched from that window the burning of my home." Suffering from the shock, Jessie was transferred to one of the few houses available, a lonesome bare place, where she could do little more than camp out. Here, however, she met an unexpected piece of good fortune. Frémont had invested in a considerable tract of land in the city, and had leased it to an industrious, cleanly colony of English people, who had erected there a brewery and a number of cottages. They now came to the rescue in dramatic fashion:[9]

A procession of our English tenants came to me carrying parcels and bundles, and leading small carts over the uneven sand drives. A middle-aged man and his wife led them and spoke for the others. When the fire began on Sunday, they said, they thought it might take the direction of our house; assuring themselves of this, they at once started in force to offer their services, but I had already gone. Then they proceeded to save everything; working with such cool method that mirrors, china, and glass, several hundred books, fur-

[9] Jessie Benton Frémont MSS, Bancroft Library.

niture, even kitchen utensils, and all our clothing, were saved in good condition. The motherly woman apologized for having laundered the soiled clothing, but, she said, "I thought you might be so put about with the changing, the clothes would have long to wait." Then the man put down on the table a smaller but heavy parcel tied in a big red silk handkerchief. "We knew the master was from home," he said, "and there was a young babbie in the house, and we thought money might come in handy, so we brought a quarter's rent in advance"; untying the heavy red bundle and showing the heaps of silver and some gold. That made me cry—it was all so kind, so unexpected, and from people who were kept chilled by public ill-will.

When Frémont returned from Mariposa, he saw the sun shining on many acres—more then ten blocks—of smoking ashes. Of his own home, only a single shattered chimney remained. The city hospital had been burned; so had the office of the *Alta California,* the Jenny Lind Theatre, where the miners were entertained by rough and ready farces, and the "old adobe" on the Plaza, the last relic of the village of Yerba Buena. He learned that Mrs. Frémont and the children were somewhere upon the hill near Grace Church—that was all his informants could tell him. Thousands were utterly homeless, shivering amid the chaparral and sand beside what fragments of their household possessions they had been able to save. Standing near the church, Frémont gazed about and identified Jessie's temporary habitation by a set of upper windows where white muslin curtains with pink ribbons were fluttering in the fresh morning air; for, like her father, she insisted upon thorough ventilation. When he heard what the English tenants had done, he sent at once to thank them. They had previously asked him to sell them their home sites, and he had refused; but now he told them that as a mark of gratitude he would have deeds of sale prepared at once, at a low valuation. Decades later, Jessie could "remember clearly the dawning surprise and happiness lighting up the large-featured heavy faces, the hearty words of gratitude, and the large grip of the very big hands as they thanked us."

Jessie's health had been affected by the ordeal of the two fires. She frequently woke at night to find herself groping at the window or the door, with the sound of fire bells haunting her ears. Both she and her husband disliked the rough society of the state, where lynch law was now in full ascendancy, and a vigilance committee had just been organized in San Francisco as a last desperate means of stopping the disorder and violence. Moreover, he was badly in need of capital to develop the Mariposa mines, and it was only in Europe that he could obtain the funds to buy machinery and erect ore mills. One evening in December, 1851, he suddenly asked Jessie, "How would you like a trip to Paris as a New Year's gift?" She uttered some incredulous words about a trip to the moon being equally nice. Thereupon he took from his wallet brightly colored steamer tickets for passage to Chagres and thence to France. To her ecstatic exclamation that it would be his first vacation, he replied that it would also be hers: "The first rest since you spoke those fateful words, 'whither thou goest, I will go.' " [10]

What impression the history, the monuments, and the society of Europe made upon Frémont, who loved a lonely mountainscape better than a royal dinner party, we do not know; but the alert and social Jessie was in her element. Her pen has given us an animated record of the delights of transatlantic travel. Even the discomforts were remembered later with pleasure. Missing the European steamer at Chagres, they went to New York, stayed four days (March 6 to 10, 1852) at the Irving Hotel, and took the Cunard side-wheel steamer *Africa* for Liverpool, the bracing cold of the North Atlantic driving away their touch of the Isthmus fever. The roomy, rolling old vessel, where they were quartered in the ladies' parlor, with the ship's library and an open fire all the way over, was delightful. In London rooms had been prepared for them at the Clarendon Hotel by the Marchioness of Wellesley, who had been one of the three beautiful Misses Caton of Maryland, and who had long known Jessie; while Abbott Lawrence, the Amer-

[10] Catherine Coffin Phillips, *Jessie Benton Frémont*, p. 178.

ican minister, and his daughter, exerted themselves from the first day to make the newcomers welcome, and arranged what Mrs. Frémont called a terrifying program.

Jessie, it is clear, found every hour of the foreign sojourn enchanting. In her pages we find a description of meetings with the Duke of Wellington, stooped and abstracted in his old age; of dinners and teas at the important London houses; of an evening with Sir Roderick Murchison, president of the Royal Geographical Society; and of her presentation to Queen Victoria, who made an "impression of womanly goodness combined with a look of power." From London they went on to Paris early in May. Here they met a grand seigneur, the Comte de la Garde, who was connected by marriage with the Bonaparte family, and who was captivated by Jessie's vivacity and interest in life. He introduced them to the best Parisian society, and his talk and personality gave them glimpses into the most romantic and highly colored pages of French history. Later, when he died, he bequeathed Jessie a precious collection, chosen from among his treasures, to illustrate the topics of which they had often chatted: autographs, paintings by Isabey, watercolors of Queen Hortense, and so on. Through his kindness, they were allotted places on the official tribune to view the grand military parade before the Prince-President, Louis Napoleon, at which the imperial eagles were restored to the French standards—a symbol that the end of the Republic was near.[11]

To both Frémont and Jessie, Paris seemed very homelike: to him because his father had been French, to her because the city was only a splendid amplification of the old French St. Louis with which she had been so familiar. She surrounded herself with French servants, two of whom came back with her to America, where they remained fifteen and twenty years respectively in the Frémont household. They took a whole house to themselves, Lady Dundonald's mansion in the Italian style on the Champs Elysées, between the Place de l'Étoile and Rond

[11] See Jessie Benton Frémont, *Souvenirs of My Time*, Chs. 14-21 inclusive.

Point, and kept the children at home, with a governess to teach them. They kept a brougham and pair with an Irish coachman, had ponies for the youngsters, and every luxury that heart could desire. They drove out to Versailles, Fontainebleau, and other points near Paris, staying overnight. They saw Rachel at the Théâtre Française, and went to the opera. Frémont spent a good deal of time in fencing and in long walks. He made numerous friends in the scientific world, obtained an introduction to Arago, and entertained lavishly. It is plain that the Mariposa estate was furnishing, in spite of all financial and legal tangles, a handsome revenue. Jessie relates a revealing incident of her husband. He was fascinated, she says, by a magnificent Cedar of Lebanon which shaded part of the lawn of the Lauriston Hotel near by; in all his camp life he had never seen anything like its great layered boughs. Under this spell, he "opened negotiations for the purchase of the hotel when we were told it was for sale."

From the Tuileries, thanks to the Comte de la Garde, came cards to every fête, ball, or other court occasion. Many of these affairs were dreams of splendor to the Americans. Once, for example, they went to the dansant given by the Prince-President at St. Cloud, and found the magnificent rooms, the endless mirrors, and the brilliantly dressed company a delightful sight. "Far below the steep hill was the Seine, and the Bois du Boulogne lay between the river and the city four or five miles away. A full moon was shining on this, and made a perfect picture as we sat by one of the great open windows." Louis Napoleon, short, fat, dull-eyed, and yet impressive, entered, followed by a train of ladies and gentlemen in gay uniforms and lace and silk dresses; walked through the parted lines of guests, and seated himself above the diplomatic corps; and Jessie, who loved the theatrical, drew a sharp breath of admiration.

As a double climax, the Frémonts witnessed, in the closing days of 1852, the official entrance of Louis Napoleon as Emperor, and, in the first days of 1853, the pomp and pageantry which accompanied his marriage to Eugénie de Montijo. Jessie's house, with its balcony overlooking the Champs Elysées, was crowded with American friends and acquaintances when the new-made Emperor rode bowing through the avenue, twisting his long mustaches, and apparently quite unafraid—"alone, no troops, not a single officer within forty feet of him." From a different balcony, commanding a view of the Tuileries, they saw all the blare and pomp of the imperial wedding: the grenadiers, Cent Gardes, and cavalry, emerging from the Grand Court and pouring like a river into the streets, where they made a compact military order with tens of thousands of brightly dressed people pressing behind; the military escort; the Marshal de Loestine, representing the First Empire, riding alone; and then the bride and groom in their glass coach, surmounted by a gold crown and swung like some great bonbonnière between the front and rear wheels. The Emperor and Empress sat beside each other on white satin seats, the former stiff and upright in brilliantly decorated uniform, with half-shut eyes, the latter as pale as some waxen image, and as rigidly still, like some figure in a painful dream. A far cry, all this, from the deserts and forests of the West, the crudity of the California mining-camps!

As "Mariposa business" helped take Frémont to Europe, so now it and other financial perplexities quickly summoned him home. His title to the estate was still uncertain. His claim upon the Treasury for $180,000 upon the Indian beef contract was still unsettled. As yet the government had not paid the bills which he had incurred for the California Battalion, and he had received a sharp reminder that he might be held personally liable for them. In London, early in April, 1852, as he was stepping into a carriage with Jessie to go to a dinner, he was arrested by a party of Bow Street officers, who were accompanied by an insolent clerk from a solicitor's firm. The four constables hurried him off to prison, and, despite his protests, he was kept there until next day, when George Peabody furnished the necessary bail. This arrest was for the nonpayment of four drafts, amounting to $19,500 and interest, which he had drawn as governor of California upon Mr. Buchanan as Secretary of State, for supplies furnished to the Battalion by one F. Huttman.[12] Buchanan could not pay these drafts when they were presented, for Congress had made no appropriation. Since the government could not be sued, the holders of the notes concluded that the shortest way to get their money was to take the position that Frémont had acted upon his own responsibility in California. An expensive lawsuit against him at once began; and seeing that it might be followed by others, for amounts far beyond his ability to pay, Frémont hastily appealed to his friend Senator Gwin to press in Congress an old bill for payment of the claims arising from the conquest of California.[13]

While these affairs required his presence in America, Jessie had her own family reasons for returning. Benton had written her from St. Louis, in March, 1852, that her only brother Randolph was dead. A sudden illness had seized him just as he was about to enter St. Louis University. "His disease had all the violence of cholera, though bilious," wrote the Senator,[14] "and quickly set his bowels on fire with inflammation. On the second day he became delirious, not from fever but agony, and with three lucid intervals towards the last day, knew little but the torment he suffered." Deeply attached to her brother, Jessie was for a time almost prostrated, and her eyes were weakened by her constant weeping. Finally, as a decisive reason for hurrying home, Frémont learned that an important piece of government exploration was about to be carried out. He immediately determined to share in it, and Arago himself helped him select his scientific instruments.

The Pacific railway enterprise had taken another long stride ahead. Congress, early in 1852, had ordered several routes to be explored to the Pacific, to afford a wide choice for the site;

[12] New York *Tribune*, July 9, 1853. Ultimately Congress by act of March 3, 1854, paid the interest on the debt and the cost of the judgment against Frémont, amounting in all to $48,814. But the original $15,000 borrowed by Frémont was charged against him until he should prove that he had spent this money in the public service. He apparently never made any effective effort to do so. H. H. Bancroft, *History of California*, V, p. 465*ff*.

[13] *Congressional Globe*, April 28, 1852; *34th Cong., 1st Sess.*, p. 1205*ff*.

[14] In Jessie Benton Frémont MSS, Bancroft Library.

and it had apparently been understood by Benton that Frémont should head one of the various parties. If this were so, the expectation was disappointed. Jefferson Davis, as Secretary of War, designated five different lines to be explored, and five different sets of men to do the work. One route, running along the forty-seventh parallel through the Dakota and Montana country, was assigned to Captain George B. McClellan and Isaac I. Stevens; one running through Salt Lake City and the Humboldt Valley, to Lieutenant E. J. Beckwith; one between the thirty-eighth and thirty-ninth parallels, to Captain John W. Gunnison; one along the thirty-fifth parallel, west of Fort Smith in Arkansas, to Lieutenant A. W. Whipple; and the one farthest south, running through El Paso and Yuma, to Captain John Pope and others. Frémont was passed over.

Unquestionably the explorer felt a grievance in the fact, and with some reason. His fourth expedition had been specifically designed to blaze a path for a railway between the thirty-seventh and thirty-eighth parallels, and he had given much publicity to his belief that he had found there the best possible route. He had written the Philadelphia railroad convention in 1850 his reasons for the preference: it was direct, was centrally situated, had marked advantages of wood, water, and soil, was healthy, ran through an area fitted for general habitation, and had a much milder climate than any route running farther north. Senator Benton had been the foremost advocate in America of the transcontinental railway. No officer of the army possessed so much practical experience of western exploration and surveying as Frémont; the name of none would carry so much weight in any official recommendation. But Jefferson Davis, a West Pointer who had been with the regular army till 1835 and had fought in it again during the Mexican War, felt that regular army officers were entitled to preference. Frémont could not even protest. But he was not to be easily thwarted in his ambition to be a pathmarker for steam transportation, as he had been for the wagon trains of the emigrants; and he prepared to set on foot an expedition of his own.

Jessie had given birth to a daughter, Anne Beverley, in Paris on February 1, 1853—a *petite Parisienne,* as the Comte said. They waited in France till mother and baby were able to travel, and then returned to Washington, where Jessie settled herself near her father. Frémont was busy with preparations for his western trip. For a time all went well. Then the heat of early summer affected the baby, and Jessie took her at once to the Francis Blair estate at Silver Springs, Maryland, just outside Washington. On July 12th, the child suddenly died in her arms. It was the second loss of the kind the family had sustained, and it helps explain the entry Jessie made in her family Bible after the list of births and deaths: "Care and sorrow and childbirth pain." Yet Frémont told Benton that she had shown more courage than he: "It was she who remained dry-eyed to comfort me, for I was unmanned over the cruelty of this bereavement. Her calm stoicism, so superior to mere resignation, soon shamed me into control." [15]

[15] Catherine Coffin Phillips, *op. cit.,* pp. 190, 191.

XXV

The Fifth Expedition

THE background of Frémont's fifth and last expedition was the now fully awakened rivalry of North and South over the route of the first transcontinental railroad. It was evident to every one acquainted with the West that the plains and mountains could be traversed by not merely one but numerous railways. But the nation was unlikely to give Federal aid to more than one at a time, and each section felt it important to prove that the most practicable and economical route lay westward from its own portals. Many Northerners were suspicious of the five surveys for which Congress had appropriated $150,000; they were not astonished when Secretary Jefferson Davis, after their completion, declared that the line along the thirty-second parallel—that is, the southernmost route—was clearly the best. It was to counteract the plans of the Southerners that Benton and other advocates of a central route encouraged Frémont, doubtless by financial assistance as well as applause, in his new expedition.[1]

Indeed, Benton believed that Southern interests had laid an elaborate plot to defeat a central railroad to the Pacific and build a line westward from Texas instead. In a letter to citizens

[1] As early as the spring of 1850 Benton's interest in a railroad to the Pacific was keen. He, Asa Whitney, and Robert J. Walker all had plans, and Benton obtained a good deal of newspaper publicity for his ideas. He proposed to build a railroad from St. Louis to San Francisco, with branches to the Columbia River, Salt Lake City, and Santa Fé; to apply the proceeds of public-land sales to the object; and to sell mortgage bonds in anticipation of this revenue. He wished the government to complete a wagon-road to the Pacific within a year, and a railroad within seven years. Like Frémont, he believed the line between the thirty-eighth and thirty-ninth parallels would furnish the best route. Indeed, he and Frémont were partners in supporting the consideration of this line. See New York *Tribune*, April 3, April 5, 1850.

of Green County, Missouri, early in the summer of 1853, he declared that the first plans "for a southern sectional route," had been devised six years earlier. A provision had been inserted in the treaty of peace with Mexico to make possible the construction of a road along the Gila, or within a marine league on either side. "With the design for the Gila road went the amputation of El Paso from New Mexico, and its surrender, with about 70,000 square miles of New Mexico, to Texas, all for the purpose of helping the Gila road." Now it was learned that the Gila route was impracticable, and Southern leaders were trying to find a new one. Benton was instrumental during the summer of 1853 in sending westward by the central route a party which included two active young men, Harris Heap and Lieutenant Edward F. Beale, and the aged Washington banker Riggs. Beyond doubt the Senator was one of the chief promoters of Frémont's expedition, which expected to cover the same route during the winter months. We find Benton writing in the *National Intelligencer* of September 6, 1853, on these parties:

I sent you two letters just received from Superintendent Beale and Mr. Harris Heap, and giving information of their having reached the Great Colorado of the West, and found the country good for a railway and for settlement all the way out to that river, which they reached in five days after crossing the divorce line of the waters... between the Atlantic and the Pacific, in the middle of that pass, Coo-che-topa, which Frémont went to find, which Leroux said was there, and which Beale's party had gone through. It is not merely a pass, but a valley between two mountains, with a distinct name of its own, Sah-wah-che Valley, some forty miles long, good for railways and settlements, and only wanting the hand of man to make it a perfect garden; and this in addition to the Valley of San Luis, which connects with it. So that problem is solved, at least so far as summer travel is concerned, and Frémont has gone out to solve it in *winter*....

These letters from Beale and Heap cover the only debatable ground on the Central Route. The whole route has now been seen (for Frémont knows the Grand River, and all beyond), and the passes traversed; and all found to be good for roads and settlements, and inviting the hand of the farmer to improve it. Nothing is now wanting but the *winter* exploration which Frémont has set out to give. He is not afraid of snows in the mountains where there are valleys and passes and wood.... He has been safe in his camp in a grove in a snowstorm which killed all animals on the prairies; witnessed the loss of about a thousand head of government oxen returning from New Mexico in 1848, while he, in the same snowstorm, sheltered by woods, lost not an animal, and his men amused themselves in hunting and killing buffalo.... He means to stand in the most elevated of these passes on the Central Route in January next. He will have with him Indians and mountainmen who are no more afraid of snow than himself.

The press told readers in July, 1853, that Frémont had arrived from England with the finest instruments that money could buy, and would do his utmost to demonstrate the superiority of the line crossing the Rockies at about the thirty-eighth parallel. "He proposes to start in November," remarked the St. Louis *Democrat,* "and thus to test the practicability of the route during the season of snows. This intelligence will be hailed with pleasure by the people of Missouri.... We understand that Colonel Frémont undertakes this survey without aid from the government, and if so, it gives him an additional claim to the gratitude of the whole country." The newspapers which carried this news also published an advertisement of a million dollar seven per cent bond issue which the Pacific Railroad of Missouri was selling. This company was already building from St. Louis to Independence, about two hundred and eighty miles, "on the line advocated by Colonel Benton as the central route to the Pacific"; it also proposed to construct a branch into southwestern Missouri, about three hundred miles. "Whichever route may be adopted for the national road," remarked the New York *Tribune,* "the Missouri company claims to be on the track."

The fifth expedition counted twenty-two members, ten being

Delaware Indians and two Mexicans. It included a topographer named Egloffstein, two other scientific assistants, and most interesting of all, an artist and daguerreotypist named Solomon N. Carvalho—the first official photographer ever attached to an exploring expedition.[2] Carvalho, who was of American birth despite his Portuguese name, had lived in Charleston in his early days, but was now owner of a daguerreotype studio in Baltimore. He had met Frémont in New York, and possessing no experience of life in the open, having never even saddled a horse, accepted the appointment on the spur of the moment, without consulting his family. It was the fascinating personality of the explorer which conquered him, he writes: "I know of no other man to whom I would have trusted my life under similar circumstances."[3] In thus hiring a photographer Frémont displayed no little enterprise; it was to be more than a year before the Englishman Roger Fenton joined the British forces in the Crimea as the first official war photographer. The daguerre process consisted essentially of exposing a highly polished silver plate to iodine vapor until the silver surface turned a bright golden yellow; the image from this exposed plate was then developed by subjecting it to the fumes from mercury heated in a saucer by a spirit lamp. Carvalho tells us that his friends asked how he could do all this on the summit of the Rockies, standing up to his waist in snow; but he successfully performed the feat. One W. H. Palmer joined the expedition as passenger. Preuss wished to go, but after his sufferings in 1849 his wife would not let him, and Jessie tells us that when he definitely saw that his glad free days in the open were over, he went into the woods near Washington and hanged himself.[4]

On the first part of this expedition Frémont was less a pathfinder than ever before. The route he had planned to travel

[2] See Charles Macnamara, The First Official Photographer, *Scientific Monthly*, January, 1936, XLII, pp. 68-74.
[3] S. N. Carvalho, *Incidents of Travel and Adventure in the Far West With Col. Frémont's Last Expedition*, pp. 17, 18.
[4] Jessie Benton Frémont MSS, Bancroft Library.

by Cochetopa Pass had just been covered not only by the
Beale-Heap party, but by one of the men appointed by Jefferson Davis, Captain Gunnison. The latter this summer went
up the Arkansas River, followed the Huerfano Valley, and
crossed the Cochetopa Pass into the arid basin of the Uncompahgre. In October, just as Frémont was about to set out,
Gunnison and seven of his men, including two who had been
on the 1848 expedition, R. H. Kern and Creutzfeldt, were
killed by Utes near Sevier Lake. But Frémont made no pretense to pathfinding. He had insisted ever since 1848 that the
trail he had then partially blazed along the thirty-eighth parallel offered the best railroad route, and he believed that the
Beale-Heap and Gunnison expeditions were simply proving his
point. He would still further prove it by doing in winter what
they did in summer.

The exploring party, which had no guide, was delayed in
starting by the sudden illness of Frémont, who wrote Jessie
that a wet saddle no longer made him a good pillow. He finally
joined the camp on the Saline Fork of the Kansas on October
31st, and found it uneasily watching a great prairie fire approaching from the east. That night the fire jumped the Kansas. The next day on starting their "only escape was through
the blazing grass; we dashed into it, Colonel Frémont at the
head . . . passed through the fiery ordeal unscathed; made that
day over fifteen miles, and camped that night on the dry
bed of a creek, beyond the reach of the devouring element." [5]
They crossed to the Arkansas and reached Bent's Fort on
November 30th. From this point they traveled up the Arkansas
and the Huerfano, finding the country hilly, well-watered, and
abounding in grass and pine. Of the latter part of this journey
Carvalho exuberantly exclaims: "If ever a railroad is built
through this valley, I suggest that an equestrian statue of Col.
J. C. Frémont be placed on the summit of Huerfano Butte;
his right hand pointing to California, the land he conquered."
On December 3rd they plunged into the mountains, and cross-

[5] Carvalho, *Incidents of Travel*, p. 51.

ing the divide between the Huerfano and the Rio Grande at Sand Hill or Williams Pass, proceeded to the Cochetopa Pass. This they surmounted on December 14th, finding only four inches of snow, and thus confirming Frémont's opinion that a railroad would be perfectly feasible.

From here they struck westward to the Uncompahgre River, and followed it, the Gunnison, and the Grand River till they arrived on the Green River in Utah. In part of this area he was again a true pathfinder; Dellenbaugh tells us that even on the War Department map of 1860 much of the region he traversed was a blank. Of the rest it is sufficient to say that his travels beyond the Green, through a difficult country of mountains and cañons, almost every league of it toilsome and dangerous, carried him across a great part of central Utah, and finally brought him out at the Mormon town of Parowan, in the southwest corner of the state, some sixty miles from the Nevada line. Long before they reached this isolated settlement, they were suffering terribly from want of food and proper clothing. They had to kill the animals for rations; the men lost heart and believed death was near; and at one time even Frémont's strength seemed utterly exhausted.

Carvalho's book on the expedition contains a vivid picture of Frémont as leader, and is warm in its tribute to his qualities of courage, endurance, and resourcefulness. Many of its pages illustrate the Colonel's incessant vigilance. In the after-midnight cold, when the sentries least expected it, he would suddenly appear, and the man who was caught napping had to expiate his offense by walking for a day or week while the others rode. Once his vigilance, when other watchers nodded, prevented a band of Cheyennes from stampeding the whole body of horses and mules, and thus leaving the expedition without transport, six hundred miles from the frontier, at the onset of bitter winter weather, with hostile Comanche, Pawnee, and Sioux Indians awaiting a chance to wipe them out. At every alarming incident the guards were doubled and guns examined; and any one who, like Carvalho on one occasion, let snow get into the barrel of his piece, was severely lectured.[6] Other pages in Carvalho's book illustrate Frémont's prudence and tact. He made it a strict rule never to give any Indian, in barter for food or horses, either firearms or ammunition. Once on the Grand River the camp was alarmed at supper by the approach of three-score mounted Utes, who, armed with rifles, bows, and knives, galloped at full speed upon the whites. Displaying their powderhorns and cartridges conspicuously, they demanded payment for a fat young horse which the party had recently killed for food, and for which they had already indemnified another band of savages. Frémont, as was his custom at such times, never showed himself, a fact which increased the respect of the savages for "the great Captain" and gave a mysterious impressiveness to the orders he issued from his tent.

In this instance Carvalho was much disturbed by the threatening demeanor of the Indians, but Frémont reassured him. He knew them thoroughly, he said; they were simply blustering and did not have powder enough to load a single rifle; "if they had any ammunition, they would have surrounded and massacred us, and stolen what they now demand and are parleying for." It proved true that their horns and cartridge-boxes were empty.

Carvalho makes it clear that the hardships and sufferings which rose in a seemingly interminable crescendo simply brought out Frémont's highest qualities. He never allowed himself or others to be discouraged. On one occasion when he felt himself collapsing, he simply pointed out a spot near by as an admirable situation for a camp, and ordered a stop there; the next morning he was able to go on, and he never mentioned his weakness to his subordinates. No matter how much he was suffering for want of food, no matter how intense the cold or stormy the weather, he kept up his astronomical observations, sometimes standing for hours in the deep snow taking his bearings. He never lost his temper; he never dropped his dignity or acted with excitement. Not once, amid vicissitudes

[6] *Ibid.*, pp. 89, 90.

which tried everybody's patience, and in the face of stupidly irritating mistakes by his men, did Frémont forget that he was a gentleman; not once was there an oath or a display of uncontrolled anger. He gave his orders calmly, and they were always obeyed. The starvation and cold would have rendered some of the party insubordinate had the men not been handled with great tact, but "in no instance was a slight request of his received with anything but the promptest obedience." So devoted were the Delaware Indians that they would have gone to certain death for him. He never asked an officer or man to undertake duties which he was not willing to share. And, says Carvalho: [7]

Although on the mountains and away from civilization, Col. Frémont's lodge was sacred from all and everything that was immodest, light, and trivial; each and all of us entertained the highest regard for him. The greatest etiquette and deference were always paid to him, although he never ostensibly required it. Yet his reserved and unexceptionable deportment demanded from us the same respect with which we were always treated, and which we ever took pleasure in reciprocating.

Only twice did Frémont betray in any fashion the strain under which he labored. In the worst days of starvation, he took his scanty meal of mule-gristle or horse-entrail soup alone in his tent. This he explained by saying that it brought back such vivid memories of the tragic experience of 1848-49 that he wished for solitude; but Carvalho thought that the actual reason was that he wished to allow his companions free speech during their meals. He knew that they would grumble over their hard fate, and to save his feelings from being hurt he retired to his lodge. Again, when the first horse was killed for food, Frémont called his men together and addressed them with evident emotion. After emphasizing the terrible necessities to which they were reduced, he recalled the suspicion that during his last expedition a party of men whom he sent out for succor

[7] *Ibid.*, pp. 133, 134.

had been guilty of eating one of their own number. He proposed that they should make a solemn compact that if they succumbed, they should die together like men, and he threatened to shoot the first person who hinted at cannibalism. It was a solemn and impressive sight, says Carvalho, to see this body of Americans, Indians, and Mexicans, on a snowy mountainside at night, the stars sparkling above in the cold sky, entering into their fervent agreement.

Evidently the idea of cannibalism preyed upon Frémont's mind as it did upon the hero of Joseph Conrad's *Falk*. Because, later, one or two disgruntled followers of Frémont spread malicious stories of his poor qualities as leader, Carvalho's testimony is important. We may pause here to note that it is supported by other men. A Captain Aram of Santa Clara, California, who had served with Frémont in the California Battalion, a little later, in a campaign speech of 1856, told an anecdote illustrative of his consideration for his men. He said:

On his march down the coast the supplies were furnished by a commissary named King, who, finding the stock of groceries running short, being enabled to procure a limited quantity along the route, concluded to use them only at the officers' mess. Frémont noticing some new articles on the table, inquired how they came there. Upon being informed, he immediately ordered a parade next morning. After the battalion was formed, Frémont ordered the commissary to give a history of the transaction, and his inquiry as to whether the rations had been distributed for the soldiers as well as officers being answered in the negative, he reprimanded Mr. King and informed him that upon a repetition of the offense he should be dismissed from the service.

To this testimony may be added that of Alexis Godey, who praised "his daring energy, his indomitable perseverance, and his goodness of heart": [8]

And now as to Frémont's private character, his tyranny, his arrogance, his exclusiveness, and others of like nature, as alleged against

[8] New York *Evening Post*, October 30, 1856.

him. No man who ever traveled with him but knows their falsity. Frémont, more than any other man I ever knew, possessed the respect and affection of his men; he ever lived on terms of familiarity with them. Yet never did commander possess more complete control. He ever partook of the same fare; underwent like hardships; rode when they rode—walked when they walked; and unhesitatingly exposed himself to every danger and privation.

In his private character he is a model; singularly temperate and abstemious in his habits, he never uses spirituous liquors; profane language is a stranger to his lips; and I never recollect to have heard, during my long intercourse with him, anything like blasphemy issue from his lips. I never knew him to have any difficulties with his men; disturbances were a stranger to his camp. He had a manner and a bearing toward his men which admitted of none of those petty altercations, or more serious occurrences, which are so common among parties beset with hardships and dangers, which are ever all-powerful to develop the most unfavorable features in the character of those composing them; and the truth of these things can be attested by all of the old companions of Frémont.

It was to Frémont's assiduity and skill that the expedition, when on its last legs, owed its final extrication. After one of his observations, apparently in Circle Valley, he told his associates that the Mormon hamlet Parowan, forty rods square, was just over the mountains in the Little Salt Lake Valley, and that he would reach it in three days.[9] The mountain ranges loomed tremendously ahead; the ascent was so steep and the snow so deep that the surviving animals could hardly be got up; and at the top of the first peaks the prospect seemed hopeless. "When I surveyed the distance," says Carvalho, "I saw nothing but continued ranges of the everlasting snow, and for the first time my heart failed me." But Frémont plunged con-

[9] Carvalho's account throws some light upon the endurance Frémont often showed in making his observations. "I selected a level spot on the snow, and prepared the artificial horizon. The thermometer indicated a very great degree of cold; and standing almost up to our middle in snow, Col. Frémont remained for hours making observations, first with one star, then with another, until the occultation took place. Our lantern was illuminated with a piece of sperm candle." *Incidents of Travel,* p. 129.

fidently onward; he took out his pocket compass, and pointing in a certain direction, began the descent. It led through a seemingly incomprehensible maze of defiles, slopes, cañons, and valleys. Thus they went on.

...and on the very day and hour previously indicated by Colonel Frémont, he conducted us to the small settlement of Parowan, which could not be distinguished two miles off, thus proving himself a most correct astronomer and geometrician. Here was no chance work—no guessing—for a deviation of one mile, either way, from the true course, would have plunged the whole party into certain destruction.

It was on February 8, 1854, that the four hundred people of Parowan welcomed Frémont's party, who had been for forty-eight hours without food of any kind. Every family took in one or several members. The kindness of these Mormons completely altered the explorer's views of the sect, and many years later he refused to introduce Kate Field in a hostile lecture in Los Angeles on the ground that "the Mormons saved me and mine from death by starvation in '54." One man, and one only, the assistant engineer Oliver Fuller of St. Louis, had died just before they reached safety.

Mrs. Frémont and her family always believed that she had a strange psychic revelation, precise to the day and hour, of her husband's emergence from the jaws of death.[10] She had been almost ill from anxiety during the last fortnight of the period of his perilous exposure. Then, she relates, on the very evening that he reached shelter her sister Susan and a young cousin came to spend the night with her. The fire needing fuel, she went to an adjoining room for some wood. As she stooped for it she felt a touch on her shoulder, and heard Frémont gaily whisper her name as he used to do when he meant to play some practical joke; and at once her heart grew light. Hurry-

[10] While Frémont states that he reached Parowan on the 8th, the *Deseret News* of March 16, 1854, contains a letter from J. C. L. Smith, who left Parowan on the 20th, saying that Frémont had arrived there on the 7th. This would overthrow Dellenbaugh's objections to the psychic communication story on the basis of time.

ing into the other room, she found Susie half-fainting from the sense of a mysterious presence. Whether some thought-transference had actually occurred or not, the incident completely revived Jessie's spirits.

Frémont left the hospitable Mormons on February 21, 1854. Two routes, he wrote later, suggested themselves for examination: one directly across the plateau between the thirty-seventh and thirty-eighth parallels, the other keeping south of the mountains, following for about two hundred miles the Virgin River, and thence running direct to the Tejon Pass at the head of the San Joaquin Valley. As the latter route had been examined by himself in 1844, he determined to take the more direct road. He struck west from the new Mormon settlement of Cedar City across the Escalante Desert into unknown territory; and passing the Utah boundary, crossed all of Nevada until his party met the California boundary at about the thirty-seventh parallel. West of this they found the Sierras blocked by deep snow. Frémont therefore turned southward, and crossed the range at the first favorable point, apparently a little south of Walker's Pass. The approach to the pass was so gradual and the terrain so smooth that he said later he could have set off in a buggy from a point fifteen miles east of the crest, and driven without difficulty to a point thirty-five miles west of it. Many of the party, indeed, would not believe that they had reached the summit.

On April 16, 1854, Frémont was in San Francisco, where the *Alta California* reported him "well, and so hearty that he is actually some fourteen pounds heavier than ever before." Declining a public dinner because he was eager to get back to the East, he was soon in New York again. Here he published in the press a long letter, setting forth the advantages of his easy central route to the Pacific. Though he called it central, actually its remoter section was a southwestern route. He declared against throwing a railroad across the high Sierras in the area later traversed by the Union Pacific-Central Pacific line, and in favor of "the low dry country, the long slope" to

the southward, not far from the line subsequently used by the
Santa Fé. The precise route which he advocated was never
used, though some of his information, given by Jessie to the
builders of the Santa Fé, was of value to them. Nor, unfortunately, did he find leisure to prepare a detailed account of
his expedition. The daguerre plates taken by Carvalho were
printed in the studio of the photographer Brady in Washington,
and Jessie tells us that almost all of them were "beautifully
clear." For a time Frémont planned to bring out the journals
of all his expeditions under the imprint of George Childs of
Philadelphia, as a companion-volume to the book of Elisha
Kent Kane's Arctic travels, published by the same house. But
first his business affairs and then his immersion in the Presidential campaign of 1856 forbade. The notes and plates alike
were placed in a warehouse, where long years later they were
destroyed by fire.

On the whole, the expedition was not much more fruitful
than that of 1848-49. Its principal result was simply to encourage the general idea of a transcontinental railroad; and
Frémont perhaps instinctively felt this when he penned the last
sentence of his newspaper letter.

It seems a treason against mankind and the spirit of progress which
marks the age to refuse to put this one completing link to our national prosperity and the civilization of the world. Europe still lies
between Asia and America; build this railroad and things will have
revolved about; America will lie between Asia and Europe—the
golden vein which runs through the history of the world will follow
the iron track to San Francisco.

XXVI

The Republican Nomination

WHILE Frémont had been dining in London and watching the pageantry of Versailles, while he was making his last invasion of the Rockies, while he was defending his property at Mariposa, the sectional antagonism of North and South had been rapidly rising. The Compromise of 1850 had proved but the briefest of truces. Before Clay was carried in 1852 to his grave at Lexington and Webster was laid by the sea at Marshfield, northern opposition to the new Fugitive Slave Act had excited a fierce southern resentment. The publication of *Uncle Tom's Cabin* converted hundreds of thousands to anti-slavery views. Extremists on both sides of the border, as the Pierce Administration proved subservient to the South, grew fiercer in their denunciation of each other. Then at the beginning of 1854 Douglas placed his Kansas-Nebraska Bill before an excited Congress, and a new and blacker storm began to arise. The intensity of the northern wrath over this repeal of the Missouri Compromise, opening the plains of Kansas to possible occupation by slaveholders, took Douglas and Pierce by surprise. From that moment the old Whig Party was doomed, and a new party dedicated to the exclusion of slavery from all the territories began to rise in its place. The bill passed Congress amid southern cheers and northern execration; and as Chase walked at dawn down the Capitol steps with the boom of exultant Democratic cannon in his ears, he truly said to Sumner, "They celebrate a present victory, but the echoes they awake shall never rest until slavery itself shall die."

The year 1855 opened with sectional tension at an alarming

pitch. The Fugitive Slave Act had now been proved impossible
of enforcement in many northern states; when the slave Burns
had been delivered to his master in Boston, it required the
force of the whole city police, the state militia, and the Federal
army and navy to carry him a few blocks through the aroused
populace. Men were organizing both North and South to gain
a secure grip upon Kansas. The first ebullition of violence in
that territory sent a tremor of foreboding throughout the
country. In the spring elections of 1855, some five thousand
boisterous pro-slavery Missourians, armed with revolvers,
bowie-knives, and guns, crowded over the boundary to vote.
Northern ministers were making pleas for money to equip
anti-slavery settlers with Sharp's rifles. Frémont had especial
reason to be aware of the rising passion of the day. In Missouri
the animosity had risen so high that his father-in-law Benton,
hated by many for his free-soil views, had been ejected in
1851 from the Senate seat he had so long and ably occupied.
But the indomitable old statesman refused to be silenced, and
promptly obtained a seat in the House. Benton was in fact one
of the men whom the crisis most deeply alarmed. He attacked
the Kansas-Nebraska Bill as a clumsy attempt to smuggle
slavery into the territories, and indeed throughout the whole
West up to the Canadian line. The year 1855 found him proclaiming on every side that the extension of slavery must be
opposed by all constitutional means; and even more fervently
proclaiming that the Union was in danger of dissolution, and
its friends must rally to its defense. Losing even his seat in
the House in the fall elections of 1854, he prepared to go on
the lecture platform to arouse the country to its danger. He
would be a new Peter the Hermit, he declared, and if the people
now called him mad, later they would admit that he had been
inspired. As the year 1855 piled the explosives higher in Kansas, other moderate leaders in both parties showed the same
anxiety.

The Frémonts in the spring of 1855 definitely gave up their
residence in Washington, where a succession of sorrows had

fallen upon Jessie's father. Mrs. Benton had died the previous September. On her last day she had asked Jessie to help her walk into the library, had gazed about the book-lined room, had fondly touched Benton's desk and chair, and then tottering back to her couch, had fallen into a sleep from which she did not awake. The following February, while Benton was at the Capitol and Jessie with her cousin Mrs. Preston, word came that the family home was on fire. Half the town hurried to watch, but the struggles of the firemen were useless; books, furniture, and papers, including the manuscript of the second volume of Benton's *Thirty Years' View*—which Jessie's older sister Eliza risked her life in trying to save—were lost. It was a severe shock to them all. President Pierce, who embraced Jessie and called her by her first name as in childhood days, asked the family to stay at the White House, but they declined. The rising political bitterness made Washington uncongenial to all of them. Jessie, who had borne another son, named Frank Preston, while the battle over the Kansas-Nebraska Bill was raging, has recorded her feeling: "Before my baby was a month old, the bitterness of the coming strife invaded even my guarded room. I felt the ground-swell—I felt I was no longer in my place—it was certainly too hard on Mr. Frémont, and as soon as I could be moved, New York became our city of refuge."

More squatter troubles at Mariposa again called Frémont to California; and while he was absent, Jessie took the children to spend the summer of 1855 at Siasconset, Nantucket. Here she was visited by Benton, who told her of his lecture-engagements in New York and Boston. Deeply depressed, he recalled John Quincy Adams's assertion in 1843: "I am satisfied slavery will not go down until it goes down in blood." By this time both great parties were looking anxiously to the campaign of 1856.

During the late summer or fall of 1855 the first clear intimation that he might be nominated for the Presidency came to Frémont from leaders of the Democratic Party. According to his daughter Elizabeth, her cousin William Preston, later Minister to Spain, brought the first proposals from that party. A writer in the Detroit *Tribune* the following year states that Frémont was about to sail for California in October, 1855, when John B. Floyd, recently governor of Virginia, came to offer the assistance of various Democratic leaders in obtaining the nomination, and that in two interviews the offer took explicit form. These two stories are not inharmonious. Floyd's wife had been Sally B. Preston of Virginia, a relative of William Preston and a member of Jessie's connection; and Floyd and Preston were doubtless working together. Their object was to have Frémont nominated as head of a Democratic-Know-Nothing combination. But Frémont in his manuscript *Memoirs* has told a fuller story.

He relates that in Washington he had become acquainted with Edward Carrington, a nephew of John B. Floyd and a relative of the Bentons, and through him was drawn into a number of discussions with southern leaders. That secret political order called the Native American or Know-Nothing Party was then rising to the height of its brief strength, having just swept Massachusetts and Delaware. Such leaders as Millard Fillmore and John B. Clayton thought that the new party might offer a strong haven from sectional strife. Frémont, impressed like many others by the disorderliness of the Irish in New York and other cities, felt some sympathy for its restrictionist aims. Though without prejudice against any nationality, he believed that America might be happier and better-governed if it granted citizenship less easily to a mass of ill-assimilated immigrants. His views interested those southerners who hoped for an alliance of the Native Americans and Democrats; and a group headed by John B. Floyd undertook to negotiate with him upon his possible nomination for the presidency. They wished an attractive and popular leader who was not connected in any way with the horrible Kansas struggle.

Finally, a conference lasting several days took place at the St. Nicholas Hotel in New York; at which place, writes Frémont, the southern agents offered to support him for the Democratic nomination if he would subscribe to stringent conditions. Frémont took to the conference Nathaniel P. Banks of Massachusetts, his friend and admirer since 1853, who held precisely his own political tenets; Banks was a former Democrat, who had been reëlected to Congress the previous fall as a Know-Nothing, but was now actually an ardent Free Soiler, and was soon to be the successful candidate of that group for Speaker. Both men objected vehemently to the proposal that Frémont should endorse the Kansas-Nebraska Act and Fugitive Slave Law, and Banks denounced these measures so violently that he broke up one conference. Jessie recalls that before her husband gave his final no, he came to Siasconset to consult her: [1]

One of them [the Democratic agents] said, "the Democratic party was sure to win, and no woman could refuse the Presidency." After tea Mr. Frémont said if I could walk as far as he wished me to with him to the Lighthouse Hill he had something to say to me without interruption. And so there and then he told me of the offered nomination, and of the conditions attached.

There was no shadow of doubt in our minds. At the foot of the bluff on which the lighthouse stood were the remains embedded in the sands of a ship, the seas washing into her ribs. Above, steady and brilliant, flashed out the recurring light. "It is the choice between a wreck of dishonor, or a kindly light that will go on its mission of doing good. You cannot give in to the execution of all the laws. [The fugitive slave law was specified.] And so his decision was made.

After Frémont had rebuffed the Democrats, certain leaders of the new Republican Party turned to him. Both Banks and Senator Henry Wilson of Massachusetts were intensely interested in the Republican organization, and they caught with enthusiasm at the suggestion that Frémont would make an ideal nominee. Joseph Palmer, head of Palmer, Cook & Co., was in the city in November, 1855, and at the Metropolitan Hotel

[1] Jessie Benton Frémont MSS, Bancroft Library.

conferred with Banks, Wilson, and Senator John P. Hale of
New Hampshire, doing his utmost to persuade them that Frémont was their best candidate. He advised the explorer to stay
and await developments. In consequence, instead of returning
to California, Frémont took up his residence in the city. We
find him writing Francis Lieber from 176 Second Avenue on
November 18th that he regretted missing the latter:

The day after your departure I arrived here with my family with
the intention of establishing ourselves for the winter. We have succeeded in doing this comfortably, and now in our temporary resting-
place have leisure to look around and inquire how it fares with our
friends and among the first of those who rise before us, is yourself.
With some little amusement I am about to combine a good deal of
labor in writing, and a kindred occupation naturally recalls you more
to my mind.

He asked for Lieber's views on public affairs.[2]

During the winter the movement to make Frémont the Republican candidate gathered strength as rapidly as the new
party itself. His boom fairly opened about Christmas, and
moved forward with a simultaneous rush in Washington, New
York, and Boston. At all three points Banks, later called by
Boutwell the discoverer of Frémont as a presidential candidate,
was the most active agent. Though engrossed during early
December in his Speakership fight, he took some days at
Christmas to work for his friend, visiting several cities. Carrying his message to influential newspapermen like John Bigelow
of the New York *Evening Post* and Charles Congdon of the
Boston *Atlas,* as well as politicians like ex-Representative
Charles W. Upham, later one of Frémont's campaign workers
and biographers, Banks told them that the free soil cause could
make no headway till they had a man as well as a platform,
and that Frémont was ideal; the others had been too active
partisans to run well. Bigelow, Congdon, and Upham were all
won over, and Bigelow began to convert his chief, William

[2] Lieber Papers, Huntington Library.

Cullen Bryant. Then Frémont's old friend Francis P. Blair, the veteran Washington journalist, and his son Frank P. Blair of St. Louis, took up the cause. The snowball was growing.[3]

At the famous conference at Blair's Silver Spring estate late in December, 1855, called to lay plans for a national anti-slavery party, Frémont's name was discussed. According to one newspaper, the members—Blair, Banks, Preston King, Chase, Sumner, and others—decided that he would be the most suitable candidate. And there is no doubt that another conference summoned by John Bigelow in New York in the first days of 1856, with the elder Blair, Edwin D. Morgan, and some lesser politicians present, determined to back Frémont to the limit. Early in the year a strong machine was being set up. Capable men were obtained as organizers—Isaac Sherman of New York, Israel D. Andrews of Massachusetts, Colonel Charles James of Wisconsin, and others. Bigelow reported: "Thurlow Weed says he is contented with Frémont, and if so, of course Seward is."

Before spring fairly opened, a strong current of Frémont sentiment was manifest among Republicans all over the North. First various Massachusetts newspapers, such as the Worcester *Spy*, influenced by Banks, Wilson, and John R. Andrew, came out for the explorer. The Blair organ in St. Louis, the *Democrat*, echoed the demand, and Bryant's *Evening Post* took up the cry. The Cleveland *Herald* pronounced for Frémont in March; and "Frémont is very popular in Ohio," wrote the Cleveland correspondent of the New York *Tribune* on April 3rd. The *Herald of Freedom*, organ of the Emigrant Aid Society, had published a laudatory article in January, and at

[3] On this subject a main source of material is the Frémont MSS in the Bancroft Library. But see also A. W. Crandall, *Early History of the Republican Party*; R. J. Bartlett, *John C. Frémont and the Republican Party*; W. E. Smith, *The Francis Preston Blair Family in Politics*, Vol. I; Roy F. Nichols, "Some Problems of the First Republican Campaign," *American Historical Review*, XXVIII, pp. 492ff.; and Fred Harvey Harrington, "Frémont and the Nomination of 1856," *American Historical Review*, XXIX, p. 921ff. Mr. Reinhard H. Luthin has kindly furnished me transcripts from the Seward Papers in Auburn, New York, and the Thurlow Weed Papers at Rochester University.

the beginning of April placed his name at its masthead: "Our Candidate: John C. Frémont." Meanwhile, on February 2nd, the day Banks was elected Speaker, Ben: Perley Poore wrote the Boston *Journal* that the Republicans would undoubtedly nominate the explorer. New York organizers, abetted by Thurlow Weed, were earnestly at work, and Isaac Sherman told Banks early in February that he considered it settled that both the Republicans and Barnburners—the free-soil Democrats— desired Frémont as their candidate. By the time of the Pittsburgh Convention (February 22nd to 23rd), which officially organized the Republican party, his lead was established. An interesting feature of his strength was the support of German newspapers and such German leaders as Philip Dorsheimer of Buffalo, who believed him the least anti-foreign of the Republican aspirants.

As the spring advanced the argument of his "availability" rapidly became irresistible. Many Eastern Republicans would have preferred Seward, Chase, or some other leader who, as Bryant put it, bore the scars of long warfare against slavery. But it seemed clear that none of these veterans could win. Seward and Chase had taken too extreme a stand upon the slavery issue, both demanding the abolition of slavery in the District of Columbia and the repeal of the Fugitive Slave Act; both, and especially Seward, were repugnant to the Native Americans. A third possibility was John McLean of Ohio, associate justice of the Supreme Court, who had many adherents in Pennsylvania, New Jersey, and Illinois—among them Abraham Lincoln. But he was an old man, past seventy, and an uninspiring, colorless figure. Dana of the *Tribune* called him "an old fogy," "a marrowless old lawyer," and the younger and more aggressive Republicans turned away from him. To this element Frémont seemed by far the most effective candidate. He was just forty-three; he had no embarrassing record on the slavery question; a romantic aura hung about his name, and his activity and daring made him seem just the leader to typify a crusading new party. Such was his strength that certain supporters of Millard Fillmore, after his nomination this spring by the pro-slavery Know-Nothings, considered deserting him to support Frémont.

During May the race narrowed to a contest between McLean and Frémont, with the latter almost certain of the prize. Seward had been definitely withdrawn by Thurlow Weed, who believed that he should wait until 1860 for his chance. Chase was unacceptable, for it was now evident that the cry of Abolitionism would cost him tens of thousands of votes in southern Indiana and Illinois. Samuel Bowles wrote that the Frémont movement in the West was "going like a prairie fire"; Greeley, though noncommittal, was arguing that the paramount consideration was the ability to draw votes—and this meant Frémont. A letter of sympathy from the explorer to the free-soil governor of Kansas, Charles Robinson, published early in April, impressed all northern free-soilers. According to the Chicago correspondent of the New York *Tribune*, he was more frequently spoken of in Illinois than any other man. "A sort of intrusive feeling pervades the people that he will be nominated and elected. The same sentiment is extending over Iowa and spreading into Wisconsin. He seems to combine more elements of strength than any man who has yet been named."

But one great threat still menaced Frémont's ambitions, a threat from an extraordinary quarter. The anti-slavery Know-Nothings, who had tentatively parted from the pro-slavery wing during 1855, constituted a strong party; one which many observers as late as the fall of 1855 thought stronger than the Republicans. They were still a powerful factor in the situation when, in February, 1856, they cut entirely loose from the pro-slavery or Fillmore Know-Nothings to set up a national party of their own. Leaders in this party had no intention of making an independent fight, for that would mean certain defeat; but they wished to join the Republicans on equal terms, not to be swallowed by them. They felt that they would gain more by fusion if they had their own national committee and nominating convention; and they called this convention for

June 12th, five days before the Republicans were to meet. It was evident that they hoped to use it to dictate the choice of a candidate for both parties! This impaled the followers of Frémont upon the horns of a dilemma. If the anti-slavery Know-Nothings nominated McLean or Stockton, and the Republicans ratified the nomination, all would be lost. If the Know-Nothings nominated McLean and the Republicans Frémont, two anti-slavery tickets would divide the vote and make victory impossible. But if the Know-Nothings nominated Frémont on June 12th, then this action would weaken him with foreign-born voters, and might defeat him in the Republican Convention or afterwards. "I cannot solve the problem," Isaac Sherman despairingly wrote Banks; "it is out of my reach." Greeley was also deeply worried. "Our *real* trouble is the K.N. convention on the 12th," he declared.

It was while faced with this dilemma that Frémont prepared a letter to one of his supporters, Governor Ford, which was held in reserve for possible use. It was a stiff refusal to accept the Know-Nothing nominations on terms that might embarrass the Republican party. He spoke out plainly against racial or national prejudices: [4]

The people throughout the free States, with extraordinary unanimity and enthusiasm, appear to be rising in a simultaneous effort upon a single and great issue, regardless of the minor questions of party policy which in quieter times have sundered the north and nullified its power. On all sides there is a generous disposition to rise above all political animosities and all prejudices of birth and religion. With the feelings which are actuating the body of the people at this moment I take pleasure in saying that I am thoroughly imbued. I am hostile to slavery upon principle and feeling. While I feel myself inflexible in the belief that it ought not to be interfered with where it exists under the shield of state sovereignty, I am as inflexibly opposed to its extension on this continent beyond its present limits. Animated with these views, confident of their success, and earnestly disposed to do battle persistently in their behalf,

[4] Copy in Bigelow MSS, New York Public Library.

and having but little active sympathy with secondary questions, which are not involved in the great issue, I am naturally identified with the cause represented by the great Republican Convention about to assemble in Philadelphia. I could not therefore accept unconditionally the candidateship of the American party, inasmuch as I would feel bound by the decisions of that party with which I am identified.

But the problem was solved without issuance of such a drastic letter. Great numbers of Frémont men descended upon the Native American Convention in Philadelphia as its delegates gathered in early June. Thurlow Weed was busy buttonholing delegates; so were Preston King, E. D. Morgan, and other shrewd politicians. Money flowed freely, and one participant said later that the Frémont men spent $30,000 to control the gathering. With this to assist, agreement was easy. Isaac Sherman had broached a shrewd plan—a plan that the Know-Nothings should nominate Banks for President and some good Whig for Vice-President; and that as soon as the Republican Convention nominated Frémont, Banks should resign in his favor.

This plan was duly carried out. On June 16th the Know-Nothings nominated Banks and William F. Johnston of North Carolina, though a rump bolted in order to name Commodore Stockton of New Jersey and Kenneth Raynor of North Carolina. Next day the Republican Convention opened, and on the nineteenth nominated Frémont and William L. Dayton of New Jersey. Some of the Know-Nothings were offended that not even their vice-presidential candidate had been accepted, and threatened to kick over the traces. But the explorer's managers were determined and adroit. They took a group of the hesitant Native Americans to New York to call on Frémont at his Ninth Street home, and these men came away satisfied. The candidate, whose above-quoted letter to Ford would utterly have ruined him with the Nativists, gave such assurances as were necessary to satisfy his guests on points of principle. Moreover, he or the other Republican leaders promised that Day-

ton would be withdrawn in favor of Johnston. Next day, the
20th, the requisite program was carried through by the Know-
Nothings. They let Banks withdraw, and substituted Frémont and Johnston. But as Johnston was persuaded to resign
in favor of Dayton, the final ticket of both parties was Frémont and Dayton. Such were the virtuous circumstances amid
which the Republican party, destined to so virtuous a career,
entered upon its first race.

* * *

Upon some details of this first Republican National Convention we may well pause. Its delegates, nearly a thousand
strong, met in the Musical Fund Hall of Philadelphia at
eleven o'clock on the morning of June 17, 1856. Certain characteristics were strongly stamped upon it. It was a sectional
gathering; only four slave states were represented, Delaware,
Maryland, Virginia, and Kentucky, and they sent but a handful of members. All the free states and the territories of Kansas, Nebraska, and Minnesota had sent delegates. It was also
a gathering in which the evangelical element—there were many
vociferous ministers present—and the radical anti-slavery element, led by Wilmot, Lovejoy, and Giddings, were prominent.
From the outset a camp-meeting fervor, a crusading enthusiasm
such as was hardly known again in American politics till the
Progressive Convention of 1912 in Chicago, marked the public
proceedings. Most of the delegates believed that a great movement for free men, free speech, and free thought was being
launched. They boasted that the moral elevation of the assemblage, its dignity and decorum, stood in bright contrast with
the rowdy bar-room atmosphere of the Democratic Convention which had just named Buchanan at Cincinnati.

One name was plainly in the ascendancy—Frémont. Before
the doors swung open, J. S. Pike wrote the *Tribune* that two
days of investigation had satisfied him that Frémont's nomination was inevitable. The New York delegation, ruled by Thur-

low Weed, was, he said, almost unanimously for the explorer; the majority of the Pennsylvania and New Jersey delegations were for McLean; Ohio's delegation was divided, some for Frémont, some for McLean, and most for Chase; a majority of the Illinois members were at least nominally for McLean; and the remainder of the country had generally chosen Frémont delegates. "The fact is not disguised," Pike concluded, "that as a general thing the outright, progressive-movement men are in favor of Frémont, while McLean is the candidate for the slow and hunkerish part of the convention. The general sentiment of all is conciliatory." But the "progressive" men were obviously in control, applauding every radical utterance and distributing such inflammatory literature as the House Committee Report on the assault of Brooks upon Sumner.[5]

The first important task was the platform. Edward D. Morgan called the Convention to order, and Robert Emmet of New York was made temporary chairman. With eighty-odd reporters scribbling like mad before him, and the delegates wild with enthusiasm, David Wilmot on the second morning read the platform. It was a brief document of nine "resolutions," which did not take ten minutes to recite. Each separate plank rang out like the report of a cannon and was followed by a salvo of applause. The denunciation of the Kansas atrocities was the signal for a tremendous demonstration. The band played and cheer followed cheer as Wilmot disclaimed that: "It is our fixed purpose to bring the perpetrators of these atrocious outrages, and their accomplices, to a sure and condign punishment hereafter." The platform upheld the Missouri Compromise, opposed the extension of slavery, demanded the admission of Kansas as a free state, denied the power of Congress or any local legislature to establish slavery within a territory, and declared that the Ostend Circular was "the highwayman's plea that 'might makes right.'" Mormon polygamy

[5] Upon the preference of the younger, more aggressive Republicans for Frémont see J. S. Pike, *First Blows of the Civil War*, p. 338.

and southern slavery were linked together as "twin relics of barbarism." [6]

On the third day came the balloting. Ex-Governor George W. Patterson of New Jersey formally withdrew the name of Seward; he was followed by Ex-Judge Rufus P. Spalding of Ohio, who by authority withdrew the name of McLean; and Thomas J. Mitchell of Ohio in the same way withdrew Chase. The convention, tense with excitement, expected Frémont's nomination to follow at once. Frank P. Blair, who had in his pocket a letter from Frémont authorizing him to do anything except permit the explorer to be named for Vice-President, felt that victory was within his grasp. At this moment, Thaddeus Stevens rose and begged for delay. One man only, he said, could carry Pennsylvania; that man, McLean, had been withdrawn; and it was necessary for the delegates from his state to consult on the situation. All the previous day Stevens, Wilmot, and other McLean men had done their best to make converts from the Frémont ranks, and had succeeded in winning over a number of Maine delegates. Now, during the recess, Stevens made a passionate appeal to the Pennsylvania delegation to stand fast for McLean; if Frémont were nominated, he told them, the Republicans would lose not only Pennsylvania but the whole election.

Stevens's effort was in vain, though immediately after the Convention reopened McLean was again put in nomination. An informal ballot at once showed that Frémont had 359 votes, McLean 196, Sumner 2, and Seward 1. David Wilmot then took the floor and made a plea for unanimity, after which the formal ballot resulted in Frémont's nomination with 529 votes against 37 for McLean. The usual scene of mass excitement ensued. The band blared forth, the floor and galleries were a sea of tossing hats and waving handkerchiefs, and as an American flag bearing Frémont's name was raised from the platform, and a broad pennant inscribed "John C. Frémont for President" was drawn the full width of the hall, the cheer-

[6] Charles W. Johnson, *First Three Republican National Conventions*, p. 35ff.

ing became deafening. Banners were flung from the windows, and applause from crowds in the streets mingled with that in the hall. "The enthusiasm is tremendous," Greeley wired his office while the demonstration still continued.

Then followed what Frémont thought the great error of the Convention—the nomination of W. L. Dayton for Vice-President. He had no personal objection to the man, but held that Simon Cameron should have been named instead, thus permitting a stronger fight against Buchanan in Pennsylvania. Frémont believed that Cameron would perhaps have received the nomination had not Francis P. Blair, whose antagonisms were always intense, sternly vetoed the suggestion. Thurlow Weed, who shared his view of Dayton, later placed the blame elsewhere. He wrote Cameron: [7] "The first, and as I still think fatal error, was in not taking a Vice-President in whose nomination the North Americans would have concurred cordially. The McLean men, aided by Greeley, threw us off the track."

* * *

The Republican press rallied to Frémont with unaffected liking and hope. Few editors knew much about him, but all that they did know seemed highly favorable. The *Tribune* declared that "having exhibited a singular force of character and a distinguished ability in every undertaking to which he applied himself," he had now been called to the difficult but glorious enterprise "of rescuing the government and the Union from the hands of a body of unprincipled politicians." Bryant asked what was the secret of his overwhelming popularity. "The times require in the chief magistrates of the nation an unshaken courage, perfect steadiness of purpose, and a ready command of resources. The times require a man who has something heroic in his character"; and the people believed that the Frémont who had so firmly surmounted western perils possessed these qualities. Raymond in the *Times* declared that the citi-

[7] Weed to Cameron, November 12, 1856, Cameron Papers, Library of Congress.

zens could not fail to elect him if they had "any admiration for high personal qualities, for perseverance, bravery, disinterested benevolence, generosity, heroism, for noble-mindedness, high attainments, and devotion to duty." The Frémont legend was approaching its rather absurd zenith. Republican writers and orators began to magnify the explorer into a figure

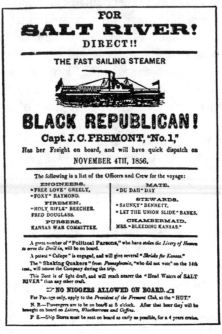

of heroic proportions, a combination of Lochinvar, Deerslayer, and William Pitt; and some newspapers even instituted a comparison between his achievements in his first forty years and the lesser feats of George Washington.

Frémont, waiting quietly at 56 Ninth Street, accepted his nomination in a serious spirit. Having been fairly certain of it, he had written Frank Blair several days earlier that he felt as men do who, after preliminary tremor of an earthquake,

are momentarily expecting the great shock. But my nerves seem to preserve their usual tranquillity, and I am well satisfied with myself.

From the anxious inquiries of friends for some days past it seems to have been expected that I should be ill, but I continue in rather better than ordinary health, which it will please you to know.

At once, friends crowded to congratulate him; he was overwhelmed with the usual mass of telegrams and letters; and, on June 25th, there was a great ratification meeting at the Tabernacle, with bands, speeches by Robert Emmet, Lyman Trumbull, and others, and an enthusiastic torch-light procession afterward up Broadway to the Colonel's home. Frémont spoke a few words, and Jessie was called forth to acknowledge a round of cheers. A fortnight later, on July 9th, his brief formal acceptance of the nomination was published. One passage, in which he declared against filibustering expeditions or aggressions upon the domain of other nations, attracted attention abroad and was warmly commended in London by *The Times*. But Americans were interested chiefly in his remarks upon slavery. He alined himself with the explicit declarations of the Republican platform:

Nothing is clearer in the history of our institutions than the design of the nation, in asserting its own independence and freedom, to avoid giving countenance to the extension of slavery. The influence of the small but compact and powerful class of men interested in slavery, who command one section of the country and wield a vast political control as a consequence in the other, is now directed to turn back the impulse of the Revolution and reverse its principles. The extension of slavery across the continent is the object of the power which now rules the government; and from this spirit have sprung those kindred wrongs of Kansas so truly portrayed in one of your resolutions, which prove that the elements of the most arbitrary governments have not been vanquished by the just theory of our own.

It would be out of place here to pledge myself to any particular policy that has been suggested to determine the sectional controversy engendered by political animosities, operating on a powerful class banded together by common interest. A practical remedy is the admission of Kansas into the Union as a free state. The South should, in my judgment, earnestly desire such a consummation. It would vindicate its good faith. It would correct the mistake of the repeal; and the North, having practically the benefit of the agreement between the two sections, would be satisfied and good feeling be restored.

With this acceptance—the first and last public utterance of any note by Frémont in the campaign—the battle of 1856 opened.

XXVII

The Campaign of 1856

ELEVATED thus suddenly to a conspicuous political pedestal, chosen by a powerful party as its leader in a great moral crusade, the unexperienced Frémont might have been pardoned some display of awkwardness, at least some tactical misstep. Fifteen years before he had been an obscure, impoverished army lieutenant, without resources or prospects. Now he was rich, famous, and admired, his name written large on the Golden West, the reputed conqueror of California, the dashing young marshal of a gallant cause. It illustrates his modesty and tact that his conduct was exemplary. Frémont had his faults, but lack of taste was never among them. The critical Gideon Welles, in a severe passage written some years after, did him the justice to remember that at this time his public demeanor was winning. "His bearing was very well so far as he appeared before the public. I saw that he was anxious to be elected but not offensively so; he was not obtrusive, but, on the contrary, reserved and retiring." [1] If his part in the campaign was open to criticism, it was on the ground that, with his public views and capacities still largely unknown, he kept too much in the background and made altogether too few statements. The nation was asked to accept this untrained man quite too completely on faith.

From the beginning of the campaign, Frémont and the other leaders had genuine hope of victory, which rapidly mounted as news of an increasing free-soil enthusiasm came in from many parts of the North and West. The strategic elements of the situation, as Greeley insisted, were simple. The Republicans

[1] Gideon Welles, *Diary,* II, p. 41.

were certain of 114 electoral votes—those of the New England
states, New York, Ohio, Michigan, Wisconsin, and Iowa. The
Democrats were certain of 108 electoral votes from the South
and the border states. The doubtful factors were Pennsylvania
with 27 electoral votes; Indiana with 13; Illinois with 11;
Maryland with 8; New Jersey with 7, and California with 4
—that is, 70 in all. Since 149 were sufficient to elect, the
Republicans needed only to carry Pennsylvania and Indiana,
or Pennsylvania and Illinois, to be victorious. Was this impossible? The best judges thought not.

Three tickets were in the field: Buchanan and Breckinridge
for the Democrats; Frémont and Dayton for the Republicans
and one section of Know-Nothings; and Millard Fillmore and
Donelson for the expiring Whigs and another section of Know-
Nothings. The great danger was that Fillmore would draw
enough votes from Frémont to defeat him; but, as the canvas
proceeded, the energy of the Republican organization surprised
even its members.

Throughout the North, indeed, the Republican campaign
awakened a fervor recalling the log-cabin campaign of 1840,
but possessing a moral character and a degree of statesman-
ship which the Harrison campaign had lacked. Mass meeting
followed mass meeting; torch-light procession, with red fire
and marching bands, followed torch-light procession. The nomination was immediately "ratified" by gatherings all over the
country. Then came a series of tremendous "rallies." Rock-
wood Hoar and Hannibal Hamlin spoke in Faneuil Hall;
Bryant, Franz Sigel, Friedrich Kapp, and Charles A. Dana
were heard in the Tabernacle in New York. Little preliminary
organization was needed in many parts of the North besides
that supplied by the existing Emigrant Aid Societies and other
agencies for the relief of Kansas, which already reached into
every county and almost every township. The gatherings
seemed to spring spontaneously from some pent-up popular
feeling. A Frémont demonstration of 25,000 people took place
at Massilon, Ohio, another of 30,000 at Kalamazoo, Michigan;

and a third of equal size at Beloit, Wisconsin, where the crowds cheered a procession six miles in length. Illinois was not behind her neighbors. Lincoln spoke to 10,000 at Princeton, and at Alton addressed an enormous concourse—some said 35,000 people—brought together by the State Fair; while at Jacksonville Lyman Trumbull reviewed a procession a mile and a quarter long. Perhaps most striking of all was the tremendous Frémont rally in Indianapolis in July, which attracted the most attention.

Here, while cannon roared all day, the procession took hours to pass a given point; a single delegation numbered almost 4,500 men; 50 blaring bands were in line; 25 marshals kept the ranks in order; uncounted gay floats rolled down the streets, the chief carrying 32 young women in white, one for each state, with a 33rd girl in black for bleeding Kansas; hundreds of banners and transparencies waved above the long line; and platoon after platoon of Germans, with their own flags, formed a special section of the pageant. At 5 different stands orators took turns exhorting the crowd to stand fast against slavery and polygamy, against border ruffians and Bully Brooks. That night a huge torch-light procession turned the streets into streams of fire, above which rose the voices of haranguing orators.

The West and North were rallying against slavery with a new ardor. An intense resentment had been aroused in the breasts of millions by the Kansas-Nebraska Act, and it was finding a sudden release in acclamation of Frémont and the Republican cause. Companies of Wide-Awakes, carrying torches and transparencies, sprang up everywhere. Fife and drum corps shrilled and rattled. Frémont glee clubs shook the village lyceum halls and opera houses. Long lines of gigs and wagons raised the dust on prairie roads as farming people streamed to Frémont picnics and rallies. A powerful array of Republican campaign speakers took the stump. In the East they included Banks, Chase, Greeley, Sumner, William M. Evarts, and John P. Hale, while even the aloof Emerson and the retiring Bryant made speeches. In the West, Schuyler Colfax of Indiana was active, Carl Schurz was busy addressing the Germans, and striplings like Whitelaw Reid were pressed into service. Lincoln, speaking ninety times in all, made some of the ablest addresses he had yet delivered. On every hand, newspapers which for years had been Whig or Democratic were turning to the new party.

Song, slogan, and picture lent their aid in the campaign. Banners were flung across village streets, emblazoned with such devices as "We Follow the Pathfinder"; "We Shall Be Redeemed From the Rule of Nigger Drivers"; "We Are Buck-Hunting"; or with a still bolder pun, "Jessie Bent-on Being Free." [2] The Democrats were taunted as Buchaneers. One slogan was repeated everywhere in Republican newspapers and on Republican posters: "Free Speech, Free Press, Free Soil, Free Men, Frémont and Victory." Jessie played only a slighter part in the campaign than her husband, and "Frémont and Jessie" seemed to constitute the Republican ticket rather than Frémont and Dayton. "We go for our country and Union, and for brave little Jessie forever," ran one ditty. A Philadelphia rally in June popularized a campaign song, chanted to the tune of "Camptown Races," which spread rapidly all over the North:

> There's an old gray horse whose name is Buck; Du da, du da,
> His dam was Folly and his sire Bad Luck; Du da, du da day.

> Chorus:—We're bound to work all night,
>   We're bound to work all day,
>   I'll bet my money on the Mustang Colt,
>   Will anybody bet on the Gray?

> The Mustang Colt is strong and young, Du da, du da,
> His wind is sound and his knees not sprung, Du da, du da day.
> The old gray horse when he tries to trot, Du da, du da,
> Goes round and round in the same old spot, Du da, du da day.
> The mustang goes a killing pace, Du da, du da,
> He's bound to win in the four mile race, Du da, du da day.

[2] New York *Evening Post*, September 1, 1856.

The most powerful Northern newspapers supported Frémont. In New York he had the loyal assistance of not only the *Tribune, Evening Post,* and *Times,* all possessing a national circulation, but also of James Gordon Bennett's *Herald,* which had long been Democratic and which four years later was panic-stricken in its desire to let the South have its way. The Philadelphia *North American,* edited by Morton McMichael, took the Republican side; so did the Chicago *Tribune* of Medill and Horace White. The German press did as valiant service as the German speakers, who included Philip Dorsheimer, Gustav Koerner, and Schurz. German songs were written, for one of which, by E. V. Scherb, the poet-editor Bryant paid a prize of $100:

> *Hurrah! Bald tönt der Jubelschrei!*
> *Kansas ist jetzt gerochen,*
> *Die Knechtschaft ist gebrochen,*
>   *Frei ist Amerika!*
> *Frémont der Siegeskräftige,*
> *Er hat den Feind bezwungen,*
> *Drum jauchzen alle Zungen;*
>   *Frémont! Victoria!*

Large lithographed portraits of Frémont, manufactured in New York and retailed at a dollar each, blazed forth in shop-windows and local headquarters. Two extended campaign biographies were prepared, one by John Bigelow, with the aid of Jessie Frémont, which Derby & Jackson of New York sold in huge quantities at a dollar, and one by Charles Wentworth Upham, published by Ticknor & Fields in Boston. The *Tribune* also issued an excellent pamphlet life by Greeley. All the larger newspapers made a special campaign price to summer subscribers. John G. Whittier celebrated Frémont's achievements in his poem, "The Pass of the Sierras," recalling the day when the explorer bade his men press on "and look from Winter's frozen throne on Summer's flowers and grass!" and urging him now to lead the nation into the promised land; while such minor poets as T. B. Read and the Cary sisters lent their pens. Above all, the women·of the North enlisted under Frémont's banner as never before in politics, while most of the Protestant clergy of the section boldly used the pulpit to urge his election.

The Democrats were sufficiently shrewd enough to take the offensive, and their tactics embraced two main sets of operations. Although the Republicans made no attack upon the private character of Buchanan except to insinuate that a bachelor ought not to be President, the Democrats leveled scurrilous charges against Frémont. Their main accusation, made with ceaseless iteration for its effect upon the Know-Nothing vote, was that Frémont was secretly a Catholic. As "proofs," they declared that in his first western expedition he had carved a cross upon Rock Independence; that he and Jessie Benton had been married by a Catholic priest; that he had sent a ward and relative, his niece Nina, to a Catholic school; and that his father was a French Catholic. The New York *Express* fortified these allegations by a half-dozen absurd stories. It declared that he had been seen crossing himself in the Catholic cathedral in Washington, that he had once told a West Point professor that he was a Catholic, and that over a hotel table he had avowed the doctrine of transubstantiation! Of course John Bigelow and others had no difficulty in proving that Frémont was a good Episcopalian. A committee of Protestant clergymen, including several professors at the Union Theological Seminary, called upon Frémont and received proofs that he worshiped at Grace Episcopal Church; that Mrs. Frémont, reared as a Presbyterian, had united with the Episcopal Church on her marriage with him; and that the children had been baptized as Episcopalians.[3]

Nevertheless, these charges did Frémont substantial harm. Schuyler Colfax wrote Bigelow at the end of August that of hundreds of letters from the Northwest, "scarcely any omits a reference to the fact that the Catholic story injures us ma-

---

[3] Bigelow MSS, New York Public Library; compare the campaign pamphlet, *Col. Frémont's Religion;* also the pamphlet *Republican's Outfit, 1856.*

FILLMORE AS A REPRESENTATIVE OF THE MODERATES

(From *American Caricatures Pertaining to the Civil War*, Brentano's, 1918)

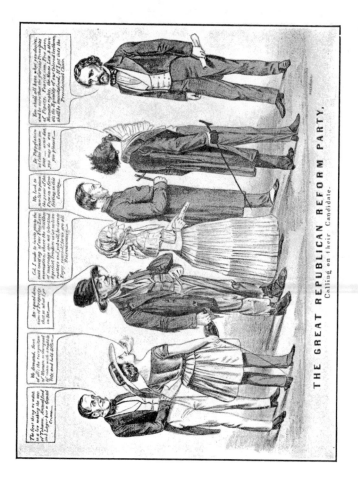

THE GREAT REPUBLICAN REFORM PARTY,

Calling on their Candidate.

THE LUNATIC FRINGE OF REPUBLICANISM

(From *American Caricatures Pertaining to the Civil War*, Brentano's, 1918)

terially, both in keeping men in the Fillmore ranks who ought to be with us, and in cooling many of our friends who fear from Colonel Frémont's silence and the cloud of rumors on the subject that there may be some truth in it." He added that unfortunately they made nothing on the other side, the Catholics being solidly against the Republicans.[4] So they were, chiefly because they believed the Know-Nothings to be behind Frémont; of nearly forty Catholic journals, not one in July was found on the Republican side.[5]

At the height of the campaign, some forty Republican leaders, meeting at the Astor House, discussed the charge with Frémont, and Thurlow Weed declared that he ought to make a public disavowal. This the candidate declined to do. He took the position that the main issue of the campaign was freedom, intellectual as well as physical, that under the Constitution no religious belief disqualified a man for office, and that he would not ask for a single vote if in so doing he had to appeal to the religious fanaticism which had long cursed certain nations of Europe. After the conference, he decided to consult James Gordon Bennett. "What are your convictions?" asked the editor, and Frémont told him. "Follow those convictions, Colonel, and I will sustain you," was the reply.

A multitude of other charges, many of them silly, were brought against the explorer. The most abstemious of men, he was accused of being a hard drinker. It was said that he had owned seventy-five slaves, whom he had hired to Colonel Brant of St. Louis. The fact was, of course, that both Frémont and Jessie had again and again declined to accept a single slave from their southern relatives, though often pressed to do so during their privations on the frontier; for both had an unconquerable aversion to slavery. The Democratic press made much of Frémont's financial perplexities. He had signed a note for $1,891, it said, due in a year, and when the brokers refused to discount it, had offered it to Horace Greeley at 2 per cent

[4] Bigelow MSS, August 29, 1856.
[5] New York *Tribune,* July 21, 1856.

a month. Greeley angrily rejoined that in the first place he was not a note-shaver, and in the second everybody knew he did not have $1,891! Stories were printed that Frémont was ineligible to the presidency, having been born abroad, and a man came forward who recalled the very house in Montreal in which he had first seen the light! Most painful of all to Frémont's friends, the Democrats seized upon the whole dark story of his mother and her Anna Karenina elopement with a man of her own age, and magnified its unpleasant aspect.

Much more nearly legitimate were the attacks directed against Frémont's military and financial transactions in California. During the previous session of Congress, a foundation for these assaults had been laid by Senators Thompson of New Jersey and Bigler of Pennsylvania, who in bitterly partisan speeches raked over all Frémont's campaigns and California contracts. At the same time, the Los Angeles *Star* charged the explorer with cruelty and rapacity in his treatment of the native Californians during and after the Bear Flag War. So far as his share in the American acquisition of the Coast went, the Republicans had a sweeping answer ready. They simply quoted the testimony of Buchanan himself, in the British judicial inquiry into the suits against Frémont in 1852, that "his services were very valuable; he bore a conspicuous part in the conquest of California, and in my opinion is better entitled to be called the conqueror of California than any other man." The answer to the charges of cruelty was equally decisive. At Los Angeles and San José many native Californians, led by Don Pio Pico, signed statements denying them completely and appealing for the election of Frémont.[6] Thomas O. Larkin, former American consul, testified that Frémont had lived in his house for weeks or months at a time, from 1850 to 1854. Seeing the explorer at this close range, he had found him "of reserved and distant manners, active and industrious in his official duties, anxious to finish the business on hand and before him and to be on the march to accomplish more"; never coarse or profane;

[6] New York *Evening Post*, October 29, 1856.

always "polite, kind, and courteous." Larkin concluded with an emphatic sentence: "I consider Mr. Frémont a just, correct, and moral man, abstemious, bold, and persevering."[7]

Nevertheless, in California especially, the history of Frémont's share in the Indian beef contract and his connection with Palmer, Cook & Co., financial agents of the state of California and city of San Francisco, who had defaulted owing those bodies $100,000, was so retold as to cost the explorer heavily. Actually, he had performed a public service in forestalling a threatened Indian war. But his handling of the contract, his protracted siege of Congress to obtain payment, and his negotiations with his creditors, were all interpreted in hostile manner. The San Francisco *Globe*, in a long and venomous article, reviewed these business affairs and also accused Frémont of complicity with Palmer, Cook & Co., in trying to swindle the public in exploiting the Mariposa mines. This article was an adroit tissue of lies. Frémont and his friends did everything in their power to disassociate his name from that of the discredited banking firm, making it clear that he had never been a partner or associate. But many Republicans on the coast feared that there was some basis of truth for the reports.

Dozens of "Bear Clubs" and similar organizations were founded in California to support Frémont—sixteen in San Francisco alone; six or seven newspapers vigorously defended him. Nevertheless, a good deal of the mud stuck. The San Francisco *Bulletin*, James King of William's paper, was friendly toward the Republican nominee. But it declared its firm conviction that "this disreputable firm has lost thousands of votes for Frémont in this state," and that it had injured him more than any other factor.[8]

The second main element in Democratic strategy lay in systematic use of the bogey of secession as a consequence of

[7] Letter to Alpheus Hardy, August 2, 1856; Larkin Papers, Bancroft Library.
[8] San Francisco *Morning Globe*, August 19, 1856; San Francisco *Bulletin*, November 5, December 2, 1856.

Frémont's election. Buchanan men declared that the Black Republicans, the party of "free soilers, Frémonters, free niggers, and freebooters," were the first sectional party in our history. Buchanan himself in his letter of acceptance recalled the warning of Washington against political organizations formed upon geographical lines. The Democratic platform repudiated "all sectional parties and platforms concerning domestic slavery," saying that they must eventuate in civil war and disunion. A multitude of patriotic men who disliked slavery as much as Frémont himself were converted to this point of view. One was Thomas Hart Benton, who with his usual high devotion to principle uncompromisingly opposed his son-in-law, and published an open letter attacking the proposed Frémont ticket in Missouri; the whole Republican movement, he said, was accentuating the hostility between the two sections. Denouncing any political party which tried to elect candidates from one part of the Union to rule over the whole of it, he asked if the people believed that the South would submit to such a President as Frémont? "We are treading," he said, "upon a volcano that is liable at any moment to burst forth and overwhelm the nation." [9]

Numerous Democratic newspapers, like the Washington *Union*, Richmond *Enquirer*, and Charleston *Mercury*, predicted disunion in emphatic terms if Frémont were elected. John Forsyth of Alabama wrote that "the South ought not to submit to it, and will not submit. The government of the United States will be at an end." Preston Brooks, the assailant of Sumner, fierily addressed a great mass meeting at Ninety-Six, South Carolina. "I believe the only hope of the South," he said, "is in dissolving the bonds which connect us with the government—in separating the living body from the dead carcass." If Frémont were actually chosen, he added, the news should be the signal for an instant southern march upon Washington, for it would be a patriotic duty to "lay the strong arm of Southern freemen upon the treasury and archives of the gov-

[9] New York *Tribune*, August 18, 1856.

ernment." [10] Senator Slidell asserted that if the Republicans triumphed, "the Union cannot and ought not to be preserved." Senator Mason declared that only one course would be open— "immediate, absolute, eternal separation." The editor of the Charleston *Mercury* believed that such an event "will be and ought to be the knell of the Union." When John Minor Botts defended the idea of an indissoluble Union, the Richmond *Enquirer* called him a traitor and threatened him with lynching. That the threat of secession was real is evident from a letter that a Southerner, T. Turner, wrote Hamilton Fish in September: [11]

I live farther South, see more and know more of Southern people than you do. Last evening was with Cobb of Ga. and Judge Stuart of Maryland—if I am wrong, they are wrong—they both emphatically declare, and with great calmness, that if Frémont is elected, secession follows fast as soon as they can receive the news. Cobb told me that Georgia has already taken the first step, in anticipation of this crisis, by the enactment of a law by the last Legislature empowering the Gov. to call a state convention, as soon as he might deem it necessary. I saw other Southern gentlemen—who talk precisely in the same way.

While many Republican newspapers and speakers affected to scoff, these secessionist utterances awakened a profound dread among conservative Northerners. Bryant's *Evening Post* felt it necessary to publish long editorials assuring the nation that Frémont was not a radical, and would not countenance Sumner in his denunciation of the South, or Seward in his insistence upon repeal of the Fugitive Slave Act. An impressive list of northern Whigs were so affected by the southern threats that they alined themselves with Buchanan, and appealed to the voters to take the same position. Rufus Choate, in a long public letter, well reasoned and well written, declared that it was the first duty of Whigs "to defeat and dissolve the new

[10] New York *Evening Post*, October 9, 1856.
[11] Fish MSS, Library of Congress.

geographical party," and that in these circumstances he would vote for Buchanan.[12] Webster's son Fletcher violently assailed the new party, and so did James B. Clay, son of Henry Clay. Such other old-time Whigs as Caleb Cushing, Robert Winthrop, and Amos A. Lawrence, all influential, took their stand by Choate to "prevent the madness of the times from working its maddest act." Meanwhile, Wendell Phillips gloried in the sectional nature of the new party, and asked why the North had never before dared to assert its sectional convictions.

It was one of the paradoxes of the campaign that while the South was thus fulminating against the "Black Republicans" for their hostility to slavery, the Abolitionists were assailing them for their tolerance of the institution. William Lloyd Garrison abused the Republican organization as feeble and indefinite, and sneered at the leaders for reassuring men of moderate views in order to poll a large vote at the election. An abolitionist ticket was placed in the field, with Gerrit Smith as its candidate, and its mouthpiece, the *Radical Abolitionist,* attacked Frémont in every issue as a leader who would compromise with a great evil.[13]

As the campaign drew toward its close, Frémont continued to play a rôle of dignified aloofness. He greeted the curious and for the most part friendly crowds of people who came to his Ninth Street home, made brief and perfunctory speeches to various delegations, and carried on a wide correspondence. He maintained his health by fencing every morning and taking long walks after dark, while in the middle of October he made a brief run into Vermont. The actual management of the campaign was in the hands of E. D. Morgan, Francis P. Blair, John Bigelow, Isaac Sherman (who took New York for his special province), a Charles James, and Thurlow Weed, men in whom Frémont had full confidence. Bigelow, James, and

[12] S. G. Brown, *Life of Rufus Choate,* p. 321; New York *Times,* August 15, 1856.
[13] W. P. and F. J. Garrison, *William Lloyd Garrison,* IV, p. 442ff.

Sherman made up a private committee which, together with Mrs. Frémont, handled the mail.

The most painful aspect of the campaign was the growing intensity of the personal and sectional animosity which accompanied it. A fair illustration of the vituperation which Southerners of the Rhett and Brooks type poured forth is furnished by a speech of Henry A. Wise in Richmond:

Frémont is nothing. (Cheers.) He is less than nothing in my estimation. (Enthusiastic cheering.) He is but a mere personification of Black Republicanism, the bearer of the black flag. (Cheers.) The question will not be, shall Frémont reign over you and me? but it will be, shall the black flag be erected, shall the higher law be executed by the President of the United States over the reign of the Constitution and the laws? Shall property be invaded with impunity? Yes, you will find hundreds that will say—they begin already to say—"O, wait, wait for some overt act!—wait for him to do some wrong!" Tell me, will any person entertaining feeling of self-respect, having the spirit and courage of a man, wait to prepare for war while its cloud is on the horizon until after the declaration of war is made?

Tell me, if the hoisting of the Black Republican flag in the hands of an adventurer, born illegitimately in a neighboring State, if not ill-begotten in this very city—tell me, if the hoisting of the black flag over you by a Frenchman's bastard, while the arms of civil war are already clashing, is not to be deemed an overt act and declaration of war?

One southern friend and relative after another, both of Frémont and his wife, now renounced them forever. From a former comrade, later a distinguished soldier and historian— Edward McCrady—with whom Frémont had grown up in Charleston, and for whom he had named a stream in the Far West, he received a note in explanation of the unauthorized publication of a private letter; and McCrady closed thus:[14]

Mrs. Johnson and myself keenly feel the gross outrage committed upon us, by this most unwarranted reference to our private. cor-

[14] Frémont, MS *Memoirs*, Bancroft Library.

respondence. After your course in reference to the Presidential election, any correspondence with you is painful to me, and nothing but the necessity of vindicating myself and family from a suspicion of such gross indelicacy as is implied in that reference, could have induced me again to address you.

The chief compensating feature of the campaign was the enthusiasm with which the youth, the womanhood, the clergy, the cultural and intellectual leaders of the North, united in what seemed to them a great moral crusade. The universities, with such spokesmen as Felton of Harvard and Silliman of Yale, were almost unanimously for Frémont. The literary leaders of New England and New York had actively espoused his candidacy—Emerson, Longfellow, Bryant, Whittier, Bayard Taylor, and even the venerable Washington Irving. One of George W. Curtis's campaign utterances, a felicitous address to the students of Wesleyan University in Connecticut, at once became a classic of American politics—"The Duty of the American Scholar." The religious press rallied under the leadership of Henry Ward Beecher, whose pen in the pages of the *Independent* was only less effective than Greeley's in the *Tribune*. On the Sunday preceding the election, most of the New England ministers preached and prayed for the defeat of Buchanan, and the pulpits of the Middle West poured forth a thousand pleas for the Republican cause.

The critical event of the early autumn was Pennsylvania's state election of October 14th, which was universally expected to show how her twenty-seven electoral votes would be cast. Both sides girded up their loins. Two state parties were in the field, one the Democratic and the other the Union, the latter supposedly comprising the Republicans, Whigs, and Native Americans. At the beginning of the battle, all Republican strategists had pointed to Pennsylvania as the crucial ground and urged that money be poured into it. Unfortunately, the party was straitened for funds, while its state organization was weak and defective. It was said later that the Democrats had spent nearly $500,000 in Pennsylvania, and it is certain that

John W. Forney and others came to New York, demanded large sums from merchants in the southern trade, and used the funds to subsidize not merely the Democratic but also the Native American party. August Belmont was reported to have given $50,000, and other Wall Street bankers and brokers $100,000 more. The Republicans loudly lamented their poverty. "When Frémont was nominated," Russell Errett wrote reproachfully from Pittsburgh to Salmon P. Chase, "our friends in New York, and Ohio, and everywhere, assured us that we could and should have whatever aid we needed, both in money and speakers, to carry the State; yet, so far ... we have failed to get either." "We Frémonters of this town," Greeley wrote from New York, "have not one dollar where the Fillmoreans and Buchanans have ten each, and we have Pennsylvania and New Jersey both on our shoulders. Each State is utterly miserable, so far as money is concerned." [15]

The Republicans placed a brigade of speakers in the field in the closing days of the fight, Charles A. Dana writing jubilantly, "I suppose there are about two hundred orators, great and small, now stumping Pennsylvania for Frémont"; but they included few men of national renown. The ablest campaigners were Robert Collyer, the great-hearted Yorkshire workingman and minister, whose rugged eloquence went straight to the hearts of the laborers, David Wilmot, and Hannibal Hamlin. State affection for Buchanan, as a favorite son,

[15] C. B. Going, *David Wilmot, Free Soiler*, p. 493; J. S. Pike, *First Blows of the Civil War*, p. 346. The Gideon Welles Papers in the Library of Congress contain several letters from Chairman E. D. Morgan to Welles on money matters. He writes September 30th: "It rained hard last night, and yet I succeeded in getting 38 to 40 pretty good men, and got subscribed $8,000. If it had been pleasant we would have got from $12,000 to $15,000, which we will get, but with more effort." On October 8th: "We are still at work for Pennsylvania. ... I have raised something near $15,000, and have appropriated it, since which under the arrangement with Ford he has turned up suddenly with a list of 15 or 18 persons in Pa. and drafts on Howard for $8,000." On October 22nd: "We have been and are now exerting ourselves to raise money for Pa. I authorized a draft on me yesterday for $8,000—and for $25,000 in event of Frémont's election. At Boston the true men meet at three o'clock today for the same purpose. At Philadelphia Mr. Lindley Smith, a merchant, is at the same thing."

counted for a great deal; the Republican press, outside of Philadelphia, counted for little. Moreover, the Union leadership was weak and divided. Simon Cameron wrote Thurlow Weed later: "From the first I saw little hopes of Pennsylvania. I saw the error committed in placing the movement in the hands of ignorant and conceited men. The Whigs of this State cannot control a campaign; and they would not permit Democrats to advise or help them." [16] But perhaps the decisive factor was the fear of the conservative, peace-loving "Pennsylvania Dutch" that Frémont's election would produce a costly upheaval, and their consequent decision to cling to the older parties.

Election day in Pennsylvania dawned with party feeling so intense that sober men were glad to find the weather raw and drizzling, for they feared a clash of turbulent crowds. The streets of Philadelphia that night were jammed with people eager to hear the news. Two days elapsed before it was certain that the Buchanan state ticket was elected, and a still longer period before it was known that its majority fell short of 3,000. A change of 1,500 votes would have given Frémont's Union party the victory. Yet this close result was decisive; it was at once seen that if the free-soil forces, uniting Whigs, Know-Nothings, and Republicans under one banner, could not carry Pennsylvania, the Republicans single-handed could not do so. The same day also witnessed elections in Ohio and Indiana, and although Ohio went Republican, Indiana proved safely Democratic. Buchanan's election thus seemed doubly sure. Young Rutherford B. Hayes expressed the opinion of a host of Republicans. "Before the October elections in Pennsylvania and Indiana," he wrote, "I was confident Colonel Frémont would be elected. But the disastrous results in those states indicate and will probably do much to produce his defeat. The majori-

---

[16] November 9, 1856, Weed Papers, University of Rochester. Cameron added that he believed that if he and Weed had met in July and laid complete plans for Pennsylvania they could have carried the state. Weed replied on the twelfth: "Our organization in your State was sadly neglected. We had feeble men in Philadelphia."

ties are small—very small—but they discourage our side." [17]

More than a fortnight before the final election, therefore, Republican leaders knew that they were virtually beaten. They still affected to look forward confidently to the result, but their hopes were gone. To the end of his life, Frémont believed that if his wishes had been followed in the selection of Simon Cameron as running mate, and an organization developed in Pennsylvania sufficient to prevent Democratic corruption of the voters, he would have carried the state in both October and November, and the resulting prestige of the Republicans would have swept Indiana or Illinois into line. This is doubtful, for even had Frémont won the state election, Buchanan's chances for carrying Pennsylvania in November would have remained good; the Whig supporters of Fillmore, who in Philadelphia outnumbered the Republicans three to one, would have voted almost *en masse* against Frémont. But it is interesting to note that Cameron believed that if he and Thurlow Weed had been able to organize the state fully in July, victory would have been certain.

The complete returns were just what the shrewder politicians expected. Of the thirty-one states, Buchanan carried nineteen, Frémont eleven, and Fillmore one; Buchanan had 174 electoral votes, Frémont 114, and Fillmore 8. No fewer than 1,341,264 votes were polled by Frémont, about a half-million fewer than those received by Buchanan, and a half-million more than those cast for Fillmore. New York was safely in the Frémont column, for his vote outside of the Democratic metropolis was prodigious; so were Ohio, Michigan, Wisconsin, and Iowa. The principal disappointments, aside from Pennsylvania, were Illinois and Indiana. A broad view of the election showed that the Republicans had been beaten by the Whig votes cast for Buchanan and Fillmore. Fillmore alone received the support of almost 900,000 Whigs and Native Americans, a third of them in the North; they were cast against a sectional party and to avert the threat of civil war, and not against Frémont.

[17] C. R. Williams, *Life of Rutherford B. Hayes*, I, pp. 105, 107.

Frémont took his defeat philosophically, and Mrs. Frémont accepted it with a surprising restraint of emotion. They had spent election night at headquarters, and then returned at dawn with old Francis P. Blair to their home for breakfast. When they spoke of the Missouri result Jessie remarked brightly: "Colonel Benton, I perceive, has the best of the family argument." Frémont smiled, but Blair's voice choked and tears rolled down his cheeks as he declared: "Tom Benton's stubborn stand cost us many a vote outside Missouri." At this Lilly, who had set her heart on the White House as a delightful place of residence, broke into loud weeping. Jessie forthwith sent her for a long walk, and as she rebuked the little girl Blair blew his nose and said contritely: "That will do for me too, Jessie Anne. Come, Colonel, let's go to headquarters." [18]

As they looked about after election day, the Republicans had much with which to console themselves. The Whig party was dead; it was now evident that Millard Fillmore's campaign represented its expiring throes, and that it would never again figure in a presidential campaign. Such northern Democrats as President Pierce, Lewis Cass, and John A. Dix, detested by many free-soilers because of their complaisance toward slavery, had been stingingly rebuked by their states; so had such New England Whigs as Choate and Caleb Cushing. In the brief space of six months the Republican party had succeeded in crystallizing public sentiment throughout the North and establishing itself in that section as the dominant party. The *Tribune* rejoiced that the future success of the Republicans seemed certain, the *Herald* proposed that Frémont should be at once renominated for the campaign of 1860, and, in the *Evening Post*, Bryant proclaimed that the tide was becoming irresistible:

In those States of the Union which have now given such large majorities for Frémont, pubic opinion, which till lately has been shuffling and undecided in regard to the slavery question, is now clear,

[18] I. T. Martin, *Recollections of Elizabeth Benton Frémont*, pp. 79, 80.

fixed, and resolute. If we look back to 1848, when we conducted a Presidential election on this very ground of opposition to the spread of slavery, we shall see that we have made immense strides towards the ascendancy which, if there be any grounds to hope for the perpetuity of free institutions, is yet to be ours. We were then comparatively weak, we are now strong; we then counted our thousands, we now count our millions; we could then point to our respectable minorities in a few States, we now point to State after State....The cause is not going back—it is going rapidly forward; the Free Soil party of 1848 is the nucleus of the Republican party of 1856; but with what accessions of numbers, of moral power, of influence, not merely in public assemblies, but at the domestic fireside!

For Frémont himself the outlook was of less roseate character. True, he had borne himself through a heated and abusive campaign with notable dignity and poise, and had emerged from it with no lessening of public esteem. The Republican party would have pursued a more courageous course had it nominated some veteran of the free-soil struggle, some man of greater public experience. But parties have to think of expediency; and the Republicans owed Frémont a good deal, for his gallant record and attractive personality had served them well in their first national campaign. Neither Chase nor McLean would have obtained more votes, and Seward would probably have polled fewer. At the same time, his political career was now plainly ended. He had neither the gifts nor training that a politician needs; he had failed to make any public utterances that impressed the country with his intellectual powers or force of character. He must turn back to private life—to the vexatious business affairs he had dropped the previous fall.

Historians of the period, almost without exception, have declared it fortunate that Frémont was not elected and that the United States did not have to face the possible ordeal of civil war under a head so inexperienced, so rash and impetuous, so brilliantly erratic. Assuming that secession would have followed a Republican victory, they are unquestionably right.

At no stage of his career did Frémont exhibit the qualities indispensable to the head of a nation racked by civil strife; he held in reserve none of these powers which Lincoln, coming to Washington in 1861 and seeming to many easterners totally incapable of meeting the crisis, possessed. Had there been no secession, Frémont might have made a far better President than Buchanan. He would have shown none of the feeble pliancy of that Executive, and while doing his best to conciliate the South, would have capitulated to it in no essential point. Frémont always believed that, had he been elected, the influence of his and Mrs. Frémont's large family connections in the South, and of Benton's name, would have done much to prevent for all time a resort to arms. During the campaign he had given attention to a plan, one which later commended itself to Lincoln, for the gradual abolition of slavery with Federal compensation, and had spent some time with Jeremiah S. Black, the able Pennsylvanian who became Attorney-General and Secretary of State under Buchanan, in discussing its details.[19] But the danger of secession was too real to be trifled with. It was well for the country that Frémont was not placed in the White House.

[19] Frémont, MS Memoirs, Bancroft Library.

XXVIII

New Mariposa Troubles

WITHIN eighteen months after Frémont's defeat for the presidency, the last heroic chapter in the career of Thomas Hart Benton—never more Roman than in the shadow of death—was written. In his departure the Frémonts lost a greater pillar of strength than they realized.

In the spring of 1857 Frémont went to California to look after his properties, while Jessie took the children, two of whom had been seriously ill, to Paris for change and rest. Her sister Susan had married Baron Gauldrée Boileau, formerly in the French legation in Washington; and as an accomplished pianiste, whom Rossini liked to have at his Sunday musicales, she had made herself a place in Paris society. She and the Comte de la Garde saw to it that Jessie was again widely entertained. A quaint little house was found at St. Germain-en-Laye, and the children were enjoying the forest, the donkey-ride, and the peasants when news came by a friend that Benton was seriously ill. He had written Jessie that he was troubled by a slight fistula, when actually he was painfully dying from cancer. She at once caught a steamer home, while at the same time Frémont returned from the West. During the winter of 1857-58 they occupied a furnished house in Washington near the venerable Senator, now thin, pallid, and in constant pain. He was laboring with iron determination upon his final literary task, the compilation of his *Digest of Congressional Debates;* and he resolutely kept up a show of good spirits even when he could gain sleep only by the use of opiates.

Though even yet they hardly realized how ill he was, the Frémonts would have liked to stay with him. But Mariposa dfficulties called the explorer back to the Coast, and in February Jessie left with him on the Panama route. Benton made a last grim effort of will to maintain a cheerful mien as they said good-by; and on the day they sailed took to his bed, never again to leave it.

Jessie records that during part of the outward voyage a dull, haunting depression gripped her, and that early in April she broke down completely, unable to eat or sleep and submerged in gloom. The attack departed as quickly as it had come, and at the Mariposas she wholly recovered her spirits. Here she was extremely busy fitting up her new home. She and Frémont bought household furnishings in San Francisco, took them by river steamboat to Sacramento and thence by wagon across the Sierra foothills into Bear Valley, and deposited them in the wooden cottage they were to occupy on a hillside above the little mining village. The bare, comfortless little house would have depressed a less resourceful woman, but Jessie soon made it cheerful. Enlisting a lanky Pennsylvanian named Biddle Boggs, she built a fireplace in the living-room, added a lean-to kitchen at the rear, covered the canvas partitions with bright wallpaper, and threw rugs and skins on the floor. Giving the cottage a gleaming coat of whitewash, she christened it the "White House," to Frémont's delight and the mystification of Boggs, who grumbled: "Anybody can *see* it's white!" But while she was lending the place its final touches, one day Frémont's lawyer and his wife rode out to the estate. Jessie relates what followed:

He left her sitting on her horse outside the gate, and I went to her to say some polite word. She surprised me by saying that she was glad to see me in colors, and cheerful again.

"Why not?" I answered. "I am very well now."

"O, so soon after your father's death—" Her husband sprang over the fence and seizing her bridle tore off with her heedless of bushes and every obstacle.

Mr. Frémont was by me at once. "Is my father dead?" I asked.

For answer he gathered me in his arms, and as I asked "When?" I saw his tears....

April the tenth the soul was freed.

When he was gone, Missouri, which had discharged him from Congress, realized that it had lost by far its greatest leader. Twenty-five thousand people viewed the body as it lay in state in St. Louis; on the day of the funeral the entire population of the region seemed to gather in the city; the cortège was two miles in length, and as it passed every head was bare. The border states and the Union, their darkest hour just ahead, lost much. But the Frémonts lost more; Benton's calm sagacity, his weight of judgment, had been invaluable, and the impetuous explorer and his enthusiastic wife were henceforth without them. Had Benton survived till 1861, Frémont's wartime task in Missouri would have been far easier.

The Frémonts made themselves at home on the Mariposa estate for what was to prove an exciting summer. Their cottage, three miles from the quartz mines and half a mile from the hamlet Bear Valley, had delightful surroundings; it stood in an oak-studded glade of the foothills with pleasant walks and views. The agent who had occupied it before them had left a good collection of English and French books. Their household numbered seven, for in addition to the parents, Lilly, and the two boys, it included an attractive English lad, Charles Douglas Fox, who wanted practical mining experience, and Frémont's niece Nina, a graceful, vivacious girl of nineteen. As frequent guests they had Frémont's business associate John Howard of Brooklyn, who had been an active and generous supporter in the campaign of 1856; his son; and a mining engineer named Dr. Festus Adelbery. All these up a lively group.

Indeed, for a brief period every prospect was hopeful—especially to Jessie, who knew nothing of business accounts and of squatter turbulence. Money seemed pouring in, for the ore-mills whose stamps filled the valley with a continuous clamor furnished a weekly revenue of $2,600 in the spring of 1858, and the output steadily increased; it was not so evident that money was also pouring out. The young people made free use of the stable, including the Colonel's own spirited mount. During the day the family read, wrote, and chatted indoors; but when the sun sank behind the western hills they would climb the slopes or gallop down the valleys. For the hottest weather a camp had been established atop a neighboring mountain, where the high air was always crisp, and whence they could look northeast over the wonderful panorama of the Yosemite Valley, the far-off silver falls, and the heights surrounding them. The Irish cook provided good food, and after dinner at night the whole group sang to the accompaniment of violin and guitar. Usually Frémont was at the estate, rising almost before dawn to ride off to the mines; sometimes, in company with his attorney and the elder Howard, he went to San Francisco or Monterey on business. As summer came on Jessie was told nothing of the excitement and danger gathering about them. In consequence, she was not alarmed when one morning she heard a heavy knock on the window of the beddoom she and Frémont used, and a voice announced:

"Colonel, the Hornitas League has jumped the Black Drift!"

"What does that mean?" she asked.

"Only mining work," Frémont answered. "You had best go to sleep again."

And in the refreshing coolness of the dawn she did sink back to sleep.

The Supreme Court, in a historic opinion written by Chief Justice Taney, and of great importance as a precedent on Mexican land grants, had duly confirmed Frémont's title to the Mariposa estates during 1855.[1] This decision followed a brilliant legal duel between Attorney-General Caleb Cushing for the government, and John J. Crittenden and Montgomery Blair for Frémont. Mr. Crittenden, we are told,

[1] Howard, *Supreme Court Reports,* XVII, p. 564*ff.*; Charles Warren, *History of the Supreme Court* (two-vol. ed.), II, p. 350.

brought into the argument not only legal acumen and research, but all the impassioned eloquence that has distinguished his most powerful efforts, whether in the Senate or before judicial forums, and was listened to with marked attention by a crowded audience of the beauty and intellect at present congregated in the city. We presume from all we have heard that the eloquent Kentuckian equaled, if he did not surpass, any previous effort, forensic or senatorial." [2]

But this victory had proved only the beginning of fresh difficulties.

On the basis of his Federal patent, the Colonel had requested the state authorities to measure off seventy square miles along both banks of the Merced River in a long, irregular strip. They quite properly refused, holding that in the interests of the public the grant must be compact; whereupon Frémont, who under the vague terms of the grant had a wide latitude of choice, caused his estate to be so defined as to include valuable mining claims theretofore in the possession of others. The length of this property was seventeen miles, and its width varied greatly. His action was perfectly legal—doubtless also perfectly equitable—but in the eyes of a good many miners it seemed unjust, and aroused their angry resentment. It would have been impossible for him to "locate" his estate in any fashion whatever without awakening the jealousy and illwill of men who had swarmed over that region for gold. The whole tract—on which Frémont ultimately found twenty-nine different gold-bearing veins—had been overrun by prospectors who had cut up its fields, chopped down its timber, and used its grass at will, leaving him the privilege of paying the taxes, which shortly reached sixteen thousand dollars a year. A suit at law was now brought against him by the Merced Mining Company, which operated one of the mines included in his new limits, and armed violence was threatened against him and his

[2] Washington *National Intelligencer*, February 26, 1855. Frémont's grant had originally been confirmed in December, 1852, by the Commissioners appointed to settle the private land claims in the State of California. The Attorney-General in September, 1853, filed an appeal; the District Court decided against Frémont; but now the Supreme Court sustained him.

property by irresponsible men, some of them under the Company's influence.

The news that the Hornitas League had seized the Black Drift meant that a body of aggrieved miners and hired thugs, variously estimated at from seventy-five to one hundred and twenty in number, had taken possession of one of Frémont's richest shafts. A recent decision by Chief Justice Terry of the State Supreme Court had interpreted the California law as giving all persons the right to enter and hold any "unoccupied" claim or mine. The Merced Company had bribed the night watchman of the Black Drift mine to leave his shaft open to them, and had at once entered and fortified it. Fortunately for Frémont, one of two neighboring shafts which the League wished to capture was occupied by six men still working there, so that the invaders could lay siege to them only at the entrance. All three mines opened high on the mountain side upon a small leveled plateau just large enough to enable the ox teams to take wagon-loads of ore from the shafts and turn them easily; it was reached only by a single narrow road cut into the face of the mountain. The rocky slope fell almost perpendicularly below this road sixteen hundred feet to a ravine opening to the Merced River. This plateau and slope were now the scene of a stubborn contest of armed forces. The six besieged miners entrenched themselves behind rocks, machinery, and powder kegs; the Hornitas League lay on its arms about them and devised plans to capture the whole property; while farther down the road Frémont's hastily rallied force of some twenty men tried to cut off the League from reinforcements. A single shot, fired by chance, might be the signal for a bloody affray.[3]

It is unnecessary to relate in detail the steps by which the attack was foiled. How the seventeen-year-old English boy, Douglas Fox, saddled Lilly Frémont's horse Ayah; how, knowing that all the roads and trails were guarded, he led it up a hidden mountain path and over the summit; how he dashed

[3] John R. Howard, *Remembrance of Things Past*, Ch. 9.

along the banks of the Merced into the town of Coultersville; how messengers were thence hurried off to Stockton, eighty miles distant; and how the Governor at once ordered five hundred militia to the Mariposas, promising to follow himself if necessary. The troops came in good season, for not a shot had been fired by the forces glowering at each other about the mines. Jessie's relief was enormous. She had been threatened with personal injury if the Leaguers captured her, and her servants had been instructed to shoot her rather than let her fall into their hands. One of the Hornitas leaders immediately deserted to Frémont's side, saying: "When I go gunning next time I'll make sure first if we are after wild duck or tame duck"; and thereafter such troubles as Frémont had with the Mariposa property were confined to the courts and counting rooms.

The Colonel now rapidly pushed forward the physical development of the estate. His works were of the most ambitious character. A storage dam was built on the Merced and gave them water power in place of the steam power which had been denuding the mountain sides; apparently this was the first power dam constructed in California. New and better ore-crushing apparatus—"the Benton Mills"—was installed on the river. With the aid of hundreds of Chinese workmen, a railroad more than three miles in length—the first railroad in the state —was built, winding along the steep slopes with connecting links of trestlework. Smelting works were erected in the village. Honest shopkeepers were brought in; a Viennese baker and an Italian restaurant keeper were installed to prepare food for the men who had no wives; and to maintain order, Frémont required that his employees must neither drink nor carry weapons. The village was as peaceful as a New England mill town.

It need not be said that Frémont was now, through his wealth and renown, one of the first citizens of California. The country was full of colonels; but when men spoke of "the Colonel," as Richard Henry Dana said, they meant Frémont.

When Horace Greeley visited the Pacific slope early in 1859 he spent some days with the Frémonts at Mariposa, and wrote a glowing letter to the *Tribune* upon the prosperity of the settlement and the orderliness and productiveness of the estate. Frémont told him that his aggregate liabilities from taxes, litigation, and the costs of development had mounted, when he returned to California in 1857, to at least $500,000. He had set to work resolved to extricate his great property. "In the spirit of that determination," wrote Greeley, "he has since lived and labored, rising with the lark and striving to obtain a complete knowledge and mastery of the entire business, taking more and more labor and responsibility upon his own shoulders as he felt able to bear them, until he is now manager, chief engineer, cashier, accountant, and at the head of every other department but law, for which he finds it necessary still to rely upon professional aid." The editor thought that his mines were at length becoming profitable. The steam mill near his home ran eight stamps a day and night to crush the ore, while his water mill on the Merced operated twelve stamps. The two, Greeley declared, "are producing gold at the rate of at least $250,000 per annum at an absolute cost, I am confident, of not more than $150,000." Always sanguine, Frémont was talking of a hundred stamps in constant operation before the close of 1860; and with that number, expected to clear at least $10,000 a week, which would soon relieve him of his burden of indebtedness.[4]

The editor was surprised by the luxury in which Jessie seemed to live, and inquiring how she managed to provide herself with beautifully ruffled muslin gowns and French cooking, ejaculated: "Well, you have executive faculty—my poor wife has none." He did not know that Jessie, with only three days' warning of Greeley's arrival, had cut up two well-worn cashmere dresses to make a new one, had turned some white jaconet undershirts into new frocks for Lilly and Nina, and

[4] Horace Greeley, *An Overland Journey from New York to San Francisco,* p. 316ff.

had cut down a linen dress-shirt of Frémont's for Charley. R. H. Dana, Jr., visiting them at about the same time, was charmed equally by the beauty of the spot and the attractiveness and comfort with which the house had been fitted up. He had been in California or off its coast, collecting the experiences described in *Two Years Before the Mast,* in 1835-36, and he and the explorer drew many contrasts between the past and the present. Dana told the Colonel he was "especially glad to have met you coming out of your mine on a mountain, and not in a parlor."

To escape the hot summer and withering dry air, in the spring of 1859 Jessie returned to San Francisco to find a delightful surprise which Frémont had made ready for her—a new home. She was entranced when she saw it: a little promontory, jutting into the channel entrance of San Francisco harbor directly opposite Alcatraz Island, and bearing the name "Black Point" from its thick covering of mountain laurel. Standing on this hundred-foot bluff, a sweeping glance embraced to the west the Golden Gate and the blue Pacific between its portals; far away over miles of water to the east the Contra Costa Mountains; and, beyond Alcatraz, more high hills. It had historic associations, for near by Frémont had rowed across the Bay and spiked the old brass Spanish guns. He was able to buy the twelve acres and house from the banker Mark Brumagin for $42,000. Once ensconced in the cottage here, isolated and yet within the city limits, Jessie found that all desire to return East left her. "At last," she wrote, "after many wanderings, many separations, and many strange experiences, we saw a home of congenial beauty and repose—a home which time would make a fortune to our children as holders of this little property; its thirteen acres were more dear to me than the many miles and mines of the Mariposa." Unfortunately, the title to the property was clouded, and during the Civil War the Government was to order the seizure of the whole peninsula for military purposes.

Black Point soon became the center of a small but congenial

group of friends. One was Thomas Starr King, the slight, eloquent Unitarian minister and patriot who a little later did so much to save California to the Union; he arrived from Boston in the spring of 1860, and was promptly writing east of dinners at Black Point with such other guests as Colonel Edward D. Baker, the new senator from Oregon. Another was Bret Harte, whose genius Jessie perceived in his newspaper writings before she knew his name. She insisted that the shy, proud, unhappy young journalist should visit her, and for more than a year he dined with the Frémonts every Sunday, bringing his manuscripts and listening to their praise and criticism. Mrs. Frémont encouraged him to send the *Atlantic Monthly* the sketch called *The Legend of Monte del Diablo,* and did him a still larger service when, through General Fitzhugh Beale, now head of the Coast Survey, she obtained him a government appointment. "I shall no longer disquiet myself," he wrote, "about changes in residence or anything else, for I believe that if I were cast upon a desert island, a savage would come to me next morning and hand me a three-cornered note to say that I had been appointed governor at Mrs. Frémont's request, at $2,400 a year." He always spoke of Jessie as his "fairy godmother." [5]

This free outdoor life in California, this management of one of the great American mines, would have suited Frémont's restless, adventurous, sanguine temperament precisely if only the estate had been more profitable. But even as gold-production increased, Mariposa ran into deeper difficulties. He was learning the truth of the Spanish proverb that "it takes a mine to work a mine." At a later date he computed the value of the whole output from 1850 to 1862 at about $3,000,000. But his

[5] C. H. Wendte, *Thomas Starr King,* p. 90*ff.*; Henry C. Merwin, *Life of Bret Harte,* pp. 34, 35. "Mrs. Frémont," writes Merwin, "was an extremely clever, kind-hearted woman, who assisted Bret Harte greatly by her advice and criticism, still more by her sympathy and encouragement. Bret Harte was always inclined to underrate his own powers, and to be despondent as to his literary future." Harte named Lilly Frémont's pony "Chiquita," after the mare in his poem of that name. Many letters which he wrote the Frémonts were later lost in a fire in New York.

ambitious works had cost large sums, and California interest rates were cruelly high—2 per cent a month or more, compounded monthly. Frémont's letters of 1858-60 indicate constant embarrassment. One written on June 6, 1858, from Bear Valley, reads: "Last week the sheriff attached all moneys, etc., which might be in my hands and belonging to or due from me to Mr. Hammett. Will you be kind enough to refer to the books so as to ascertain what is the condition of his account and transmit accordingly a statement to the sheriff at Mariposas by today's mail and oblige yours truly, J. C. Frémont." A series of letters in the spring of 1860 exhibit heavy pecuniary pressure. Dated at Black Point, they are addressed to the Bear Valley manager, Hopper: [6]

(June 2): As no boat leaves tomorrow I write to acknowledge yours of the 31st, and to say that I continue yet unwell. I hope by next mail to be able to write at length. Let Mr. Williams know that I will write to him next week. In regard to the men whose wages we wished to reduce at the mines, and Mr. Davenport's action in regard to them, I think that it will be well as much as possible to let it stand until I get back. I would very much regret any difficulty just now, and intend to rely upon your prudence and good judgment to see that none does take place....

(June 5): I am still quite unwell, with the usual feeling of mental indolence belonging to the condition, and came in only to get your letter. Dr. Raymond called on me at Black Point this morning with a letter from Mr. Charter, giving a statement of your conversation with him. Manage affairs along so as to keep everything quiet until I get back—meanwhile I will talk over the whole matter with Dr. Raymond. I have seen very little of him since I came here and he knows nothing whatever of my affairs. In regard to the mines, have a friendly conversation with Ketton and Davenport about the pay of the men and let it rest until I come back. I think you will find them disposed to do all that they can for our interest....

(June 13): I have finally succeeded in making arrangements for putting the estate, or rather its operations, upon a cash basis, but the large amount of money which would have been required under

---

[6] Copies furnished me from various private sources.

the operation of the new attachment law has obliged me to make these arrangements in a manner entirely different from what I had proposed when I left Bear Valley. But the great object, which is the uninterrupted carrying on of the works and the security and continuous improvement of the estate, will be quite as fully accomplished in this way. Mr. Park will be in Bear Valley on Saturday night or Thursday morning, and you should be there to meet him. He will give you all necessary information....

But despite the hopeful tone of this last letter, his mining operations continued to bring him heavy financial perplexities.

For the Republican nomination in 1860 Frémont was, of course, not seriously considered. An unsuccessful candidate for the Presidency is almost never named again; and Frémont had done nothing to improve his political standing, while other aspirants had come steadily forward. When Gideon Welles made inquiries of friends as to the complete dropping of Frémont, he heard various gossipy explanations which—recorded in the Welles papers—are of no value save as they indicate that John Bigelow had become extremely dubious of Frémont's stability, while the Blair family had grown actively critical. Old Francis P. Blair spoke of the explorer with positive dislike. The ground had been laid for the subsequent breach between the two men. Yet some talk of Frémont persisted till the very eve of the convention. The explorer thought it worth while to authorize a California friend to withdraw his name if presented, saying he would not stand against any man acceptable on general grounds, and as zealous as himself for building a Pacific railroad from the Middle West. Edward Bates of Missouri helped spread the news of this position among delegates to the convention.

Following Lincoln's election, Frémont late in 1860 received a visit from Senator Baker, who had been campaigning in the East and who brought him a strong intimation that he would be offered either a Cabinet position or one of the principal diplomatic posts. We know from other sources that Seward had suggested that he be made Secretary of War, while Lincoln had thought of him for Minister to France. At the moment his eternal "Mariposa business" had developed a new crisis. Needing funds for development and for discharging his debts, he had resolved to go to Europe, form a company, and sell enough shares for his purposes. He asked Baker to tell Lincoln that his hands were tied for the moment, while he would prefer, if civil war began, to take command of an army in the field. As state after state seceded, he and Starr King agreed that hostilities were inevitable. During the fall of 1860 careful data were assembled on the resources of Mariposa, and a series of costly photographs (now in the Bancroft Library) were taken of all the works. With this material, Frémont and his lawyer Frederick K. Billings sailed in January, 1861, for Europe. Jessie, who had suffered a bad carriage accident, was left behind, with instructions to join him in New York if he was given a military command; and affairs at Mariposa were placed in rough shape for a protracted absence. Little did either think that they would never again set foot on their famous estate as its owners.

Staying for a few days in New York in the middle of February, Frémont had a brief and cordial interview at the Astor House with Lincoln, who was on his way to Washington. He found the President-elect still outwardly strong in his hope that peace would be preserved, but all his own convictions were that fighting was inevitable. He wrote Jessie: "With the inflammatory press and inflammatory conversations on every hand, I am convinced that actual war is not far off." Sailing at once for France, he soon found that the threat of civil war made it impossible to raise money for Mariposa on any acceptable terms. He was still in Europe when news of the firing upon Fort Sumter reached him; and, having already written to Washington to offer his services, he was there notified that his abilities and experience had been recognized by appointment as one of the ranking Union generals. He at once sent word to Jessie to join him in the East. Doubtless he was proud and elated that he was to have a new opportunity to serve his country; certainly his wife was so, for she expressed her feelings with characteristic frankness in a letter to the estate-manager, Hopper:

Mr. Frémont has written to us to join him at once at New York, where he was to be about the 30th of May. We shall leave in the next steamer, the 21st. I wish it could have been on that of to-day, but we got our orders too late for that.

Mr. Frémont's last letters were to noon of May 10th, London. Mr. Billings was to remain, but Mr. Frémont was called to his old first love and duty, and I have not been so happy in years for him as now—

> What if the storm clouds blow?
> What if the green leaves fall?
> Better the crashing tempest's throe
> Than the army of worries
> That gnawed below.

An army of cares has been boring into our lives these few years past, and I thank heaven for this noble chance in a great cause, which has come to Mr. Frémont now. He promised me other and fuller letters before his leaving Europe, which was fixed for the 21st May. We leave certainly on the 21st, so that you will only have time to let me know this has reached you. I take your picture of Bear Valley cottage with us, and it will always remind me of the many times you helped to smooth worries away from Mr. Frémont. I am so glad I am going into an atmosphere where dollars and cents are not the first object. The noble and beautiful side of the nation is now apparent, and it will be a comfort to feel its influence.

XXIX

Civil War in the West

JULY of 1861 found Frémont commander of the Department of the West—the great military area comprising Illinois and all the states and territories between the Mississippi and the Rockies—with his headquarters in St. Louis.

A St. Louis how changed! Once the most hospitable and cordial of towns to all who bore the name Frémont or Benton, now it was a shuttered, sullen, and hostile city. The hot July sun beat down upon a river that stretched empty from shore to shore—the steamboats laid up at their wharves with fires out and crews gone. The streets were half deserted, with knots of unemployed men glowering resentfully at the soldiers who patrolled the corners, with curtains drawn in the shop windows, and with the wheels of the few vehicles echoing loudly against empty warehouses. Of the 160,000 people, a majority seemed definitely alined against the Union. Hardly an American flag was flying; but in its stead the secession banner hung over the buildings in which recruiting for the Confederate armies was being publicly carried on, while in the best residential sections the Stars and Bars were lavishly displayed. Army officers, intimidated and few in number, dared not venture far from the arsenal, the barracks, and the center of the city. At night bands of ruffians, armed or unarmed, marched through the streets hurrahing for Jeff Davis and the rebel cause. This was the disaffected town, the metropolis of a half-disaffected state, in which Frémont arrived from New York on the morning of July 25, 1861.[1]

---

[1] Jessie Benton Frémont, *Souvenirs of My Time,* p. 166*ff.*

The previous two months had been full of labor and anxiety. Overtaken in Europe by the news of war, and knowing how destitute of arms the government was, he had instantly dropped his private affairs and begun examining field-guns, rifles, and ammunition in both France and England. It was a characteristically impetuous enterprise, for he had no authority from the government, no certainty of a cent of money, and no knowledge even of how serious the war might be. But it was patriotic and timely. By the end of May, Confederate agents were on the ground, but no Federal emissary; and Frémont stepped into the breach. We find him writing from the Athenaeum Club in London on May 24th to Francis P. Blair.[2]

I had fully intended to sail for New York in the *Asia* to-morrow but under all the information that I can obtain I judge that a supply of efficient arms would be valuable to our cause just now and I have decided to remain a short time longer with the object of bringing them with me. I have succeeded in producing the control of funds sufficient to purchase three or four batteries of guns fully equipped for the field and perhaps 10,000 rifles. The guns will be of the most approved construction, and will be accompanied with carriages, shot, shell, etc. The difficulty was first, to obtain the means, and now that the means are obtained the difficulty is in having the guns cast, ammunition got ready, etc., within the few weeks that I can bring myself to remain over here. I shall have an answer from foundries and factories before night and if I get them in time will advise you. I trust that you have already offered my services to the President. If not, pray do so, and in either case explain to him the cause of my delay. I think that this delay is justifiable if it enables me to come prepared with an equipment of all arms and of the most efficient kind, sufficient to put a force of ten thousand men directly in the face of the enemy. Pray don't let these few weeks operate prejudicially to me. My great desire is to serve the country in the most direct and effective way that possibly I can. From all that I can see I judge that there will be need for our best services. The agents for the Seceders are very active here. The last steamer brought them an accession of credit, and they completed yesterday the purchase of

[2] Letter in my possession.

two screw steamers (one for £75,000) and are contracting for more. These steamers are to sail from Liverpool and are to endeavor to enter the port of Charleston. They are to be under English colors, are not to carry any contraband of war, and will probably be underwritten here. The former owners were yesterday endeavoring to obtain underwriters. I will try to let you know the names, captains, underwriters, when to sail, etc., etc. Meanwhile I will let Sanford (Belgium) who is here know of this, and also Mr. Adams, if I see him to-day. Mr. Sanford is an admirable representative, and Mr. Adams in this respect more than justifies his good old name.

Our minister to France hesitated to support him, but in England Charles Francis Adams had the courage to do so. In the end, Frémont contracted for $75,000 worth of cannon and shells in England, and for 10,000 rifles in France, to be shipped at his personal charge if necessary; and Adams boldly drew on the government to pay for them.[3] Then Frémont, notified that he had been appointed one of the first four major-generals authorized by Congress, had caught a fast ship, arrived in Boston on June 27th, and at once reported to the President in Washington.

He found the government eager for his services. He and Postmaster-General Montgomery Blair held several conferences with Lincoln upon the command to which he should be assigned; and he tells us that although the military authorities suggested eastern positions, he insisted upon the West. This suited the views of Montgomery Blair. For the command in Missouri, the Blair family would have preferred their favorite, Nathaniel Lyon, but the conservative Unionists of that state, led by Attorney-General Edward Bates, would not hear of him. Frémont made an admirable compromise. Early in July the Western Department was created, with the understanding that it should include not only the loyal prairie region, but the wavering state of Kentucky as soon as Frémont had raised and organized a sufficient force to descend the Mississippi. He

[3] J. B. McMaster, *United States During Lincoln's Administration*, p. 190; Frémont, MS. *Memoirs*.

immediately took up the task of creating an army—finding out what troops were available, how he could concentrate and drill them, and how he could get them armed and supplied.

Not one labor but a myriad; in these hot July days he had suddenly a million things to do. Frémont has been harshly criticized by Nicolay and Hay, chiefly upon the basis of statements which Montgomery Blair made after he became the General's enemy, for his delay in reaching St. Louis. But this criticism is unjustified. He stayed in the East just three weeks, and would have left sooner—in fact, would have left on July 16th or 17th—had he not been told that General Winfield Scott had further instructions for him. He remained principally because his Department was destitute of munitions of all kinds, and he could best procure them from New York and Washington. The troops being enlisted in Illinois, Iowa, Missouri, and other states were wretchedly supplied with blankets, shoes, tents, uniforms, and firearms. Governor Richard Yates of Illinois, who was in Washington, declared that their condition was a public scandal. After obtaining the personal intervention of President Lincoln, Frémont received an order for only 17,000 stands of arms from the government arsenals, the number later being reduced to 5,000. In desperation, he examined various supplies of arms in the hands of private owners, and was on the point of having 25,000 carbines sent to the West; but finding that they were not rifled, left the transaction uncompleted. The main object of the Administration at the moment was to equip the armies in Virginia, and it was difficult to interest the War Department in Missouri.

In these three weeks, Frémont was also assembling his aides and sketching the outlines of a plan of campaign. As chief of staff he appointed General Alexander S. Asboth, a Hungarian who had served with distinction under Kossuth in the great revolt of 1848-49 and who had come to the United States with his chief in 1851. Asboth was destined to do good service throughout the Civil War, to be brevetted a major-general, and to die minister to the Argentine. As chief topographical engineer Frémont appointed another Hungarian, Colonel John Fiala. From Cincinnati he summoned a lawyer of distinction, R. R. Corwine, to be judge-advocate of the Department. A multitude of other details had to be attended to. As for the plan of campaign, Frémont later told the Committee on the Conduct of the War that the government had given him none whatever. General discussions with Scott and others resulted in an understanding that the great object in view was the descent of the Mississippi, and that when his army was ready for this he was to let the President know. He himself devised a scheme whose main features were the clearance of all rebels from Missouri, and a movement down the Mississippi upon Memphis; and he tells us that he consulted Lincoln upon it: [4]

The President had gone carefully over with me the subject of my intended campaign, and this with the single desire to find out what was best to do and how to do it. This he did in the unpretentious and kindly manner which invited suggestion, and which with him was characteristic. When I took leave of him, he accompanied me down the stairs, coming out to the steps of the portico at the White House; I asked him then, if there was anything further in the way of instruction that he wished to say to me. "No," he replied, "I have given you *carte blanche;* you must use your own judgment and do the best you can. I doubt if the States will ever come back."

It was nine o'clock of the hot morning of July 25 when Frémont was ferried across to St. Louis, and, without pausing for rest, he called a staff meeting at noon.[5] He immediately began the most strenuous activity of his life. He rose at five in the morning and labored almost without intermission till twelve at night. The problems before him were staggering. The curtain had risen on the drama called "the hundred days in Missouri" —the drama which tested Frémont's strength and weakness as never before, and which fixed in the popular mind a cruelly unjust impression of his character and capacities.

[4] MS. *Memoirs,* Bancroft Library.
[5] New York *Tribune,* August 9, 1861.

He had arrived at a critical moment, with disaster looming just ahead and prompt action imperative. Missouri, with a population of slightly more than a million, was attached to the South by blood, tradition, a common history, and similar institutions. When the Confederacy was formed, a militant minority took the view, at first partly concealed, that the state must join her southern sisters. This group included the governor, Claiborne F. Jackson, the lieutenant-governor, both United States Senators, and a majority of the legislature, and it had powerful newspaper support.[6] Another group, for a time larger and stronger, believed that secession might ultimately be necessary, but that it should not be attempted until every hope of a peaceable adjustment of the difficulties between the North and the South had been destroyed. This group included ex-Governor Robert M. Stewart, Alexander W. Doniphan, Sterling Price, and some influential editors. The trend of events slowly forced an alliance between many of its members and the uncompromising secessionists, but the tact of the Union leaders saved a large part of this faction for the Federal cause. Beneath the American banner rallied, not merely many of the Lincoln Republicans of Missouri, who had cast only one-ninth of the ballots at the last election, but many of the followers of Douglas, Breckinridge, and Bell, who were too much attached to the Union to countenance its disruption.

The struggle thus far in Missouri had been, in its main outlines, a contest between the astute secessionist governor, Claiborne Jackson, and the courageous Frank P. Blair, Jr., who was the brains and backbone of the Union element. Blair converted the Republican Wide-Awakes into Union Clubs. Decisive measures by him and Captain (later General) Nathaniel Lyon, a Connecticut veteran of the Mexican War, saved the St. Louis arsenal from the rebels when they were about to seize it. An equally decisive movement enabled Lyon to strike the rebel militia—for Governor Jackson, issuing a proclamation of war, had called fifty thousand militia into service for the

[6] Thomas Snead, *The Fight for Missouri in 1851*, p. 53ff.

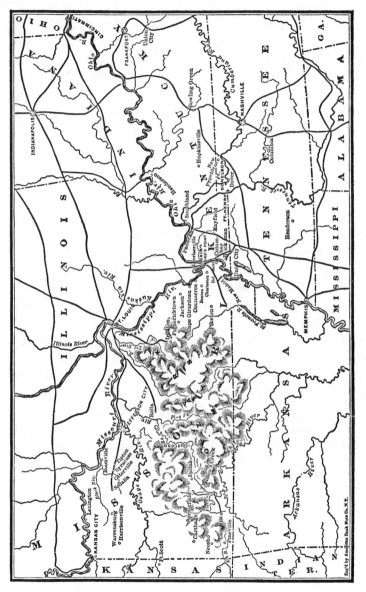

THE THEATER OF WAR IN THE WEST

Confederacy—at Booneville, a town on the Missouri River, and after a sharp engagement to put them to flight. The state capital at Jefferson City was meanwhile wrested from the Confederates. All this had occurred by June 17th, before Frémont' had even landed in Boston.

The Unionists in the state had the advantage of superior numbers, for a heavy majority of the population were loyal; but after the initial steps by Blair and Lyon, the Confederates had the advantage of superior boldness, energy, and quickness. A genuine danger existed that the quickly rallying rebels would sweep all lower Missouri, take possession of Cairo and southernmost Illinois, where secessionist sentiment was strong, carry Kentucky into the Confederacy, and make even southern Indiana, where later the Knights of the Golden Circle flourished, doubtful territory. If they succeeded in this, the war might be virtually lost for the North. Rebel camps were formed throughout a great part of Missouri, commissions were issued in a skeleton rebel army, and adventurous young men of pro-slavery sympathies flocked to the Confederate standard, delighted at the prospect of army life. Governor Jackson and General Sterling Price united their forces, collected from these camps, in a formidable little army of about thirty thousand in the southwestern corner of the state. At Carthage they soon came into collision with the Federal forces under Franz Sigel, and in a comparatively bloodless battle, defeated him and drove him back upon Springfield. In southeastern Missouri the Confederates under Pillow were gathering another force of about twenty thousand, while Hardee with five thousand was said to be marching on Ironton.

When Frémont took command, sharp fighting was about to commence. Jackson and Price, flushed with their little victory, elated by the news of Bull Run, and pleased by reinforcements from Arkansas and a constant accession of volunteers, were moving northward. They would soon have full control of a rich lead-bearing region. To face them and the other armies, Frémont (according to Colonel Chester Harding's later evidence before the Committee on the Conduct of the War) had only 15,943 men, scattered at nine points in Missouri, ill-equipped, ill-trained, and ill-organized. As he had Jessie write to Montgomery Blair, he found the enemy already occupying in force positions which he had intended holding against them; found himself without money, arms, or moral support; found that even St. Louis needed more men to keep its unruly elements quiet. Jessie herself soon sent Francis P. Blair's daughter a spirited picture of the situation: [7]

You say all we need is "Generals." That is simply and literally the whole provision made for the Dept. An arsenal without arms or ammunition—troops on paper, and a thoroughly prepared and united enemy. Thick and unremitting as mosquitoes. The telegraph in the enemy's hands and the worse for us as not being avowed enemies. In Ohio and all the way we met Western troops on their way to the Potomac—the western waters left to defend themselves as best they might.... The President is a Western man and not grown in red tape. If he knew the true defenseless condition of the West it would not remain so. I have begged Mr. Frémont to let me go on and tell him how things are here. But he says I'm tired with the sea voyage —that I shan't expose my health any more and that he can't do without me.

It's making bricks without straw out here and mere human power can't draw order out of chaos by force of will only.

The Union flag was upheld at Springfield in southwestern Missouri by Lyon, who had reached there July 13th with a combined force of Missouri and Kansas troops numbering between 7,000 and 8,000 men. But in spite of this strength, Lyon's position was highly perilous. He had no adequate line of communications at his rear. From St. Louis, three railways then radiated—one toward the west, terminating at Sedalia,

[7] W. E. Smith, *The Francis Preston Blair Family in Politics,* II, p. 59. Frémont in his own article on the situation later wrote that of 23,000 men of all arms, only some 15,000 were available, the remainder being three months' men. Most of his disposable force was being used by General John Pope in North Missouri to check rebellion there. R. U. Johnson and C. C. Buel, eds., *Battles and Leaders of the Civil War,* I, p. 278ff.

about three-fourths of the way across the state; one toward the southwest, ending at Rolla, scarcely halfway across the state; and the third toward the south, ending at Ironton, also hardly halfway across. Between Lyon's army and the nearest rail-head at Rolla, stretched 120 miles of broken country, with bad roads which any hard rain would make almost impassable. Provisions and supplies had failed to arrive as he had expected. Moreover, about half of his army consisted of the ninety-day men raised under President Lincoln's first proclamation, and their terms expired the middle of July. Many of these three-months volunteers would immediately reënlist for a longer term, and many would remain for the battle which seemed to be impending; but there was nevertheless much confusion, and the army was materially shrinking.[8]

If imminent danger threatened Lyon at Springfield, almost equally grave danger threatened the Federal forces at Cairo, the vital point at the junction of the Ohio and the Mississippi which must be used as a base for any advance into Kentucky. Major-General Leonidas Polk, commanding the Confederates at Memphis, made preparations early in July to lead his Tennessee contingent into Missouri for a campaign with a double objective. One column, under McCulloch, was to proceed against Lyon at Springfield; while the other was to march up the Mississippi under Generals Pillow and Hardee to cut off Lyon's retreat toward the East, was to take St. Louis if possible, and on its return was to enter Illinois and capture Cairo. This was too ambitious a program to be carried out. Nevertheless, about the time that Frémont arrived in St. Louis, Polk moved 6,000 troops up to New Madrid, where he reported that his force, with the German unionists of Missouri in front of them, were "full of enthusiasm and eager for the 'Dutch hunt.' " [9] It was rumored in Missouri and Illinois that a further advance by Polk's troops was imminent. The frightened Union

[8] See Nicolay and Hay, *Lincoln*, IV, Ch. 11, p. 23.
[9] *Official Records*, Series I, Vol. III, p. 617ff.; Nicolay and Hay, *Lincoln*, IV, p. 405.

commander at Cairo, General Prentiss, sent a series of urgent messages to Frémont, imploring him to send help to save this great strategic key to the Mississippi Valley. He wrote July 23rd: "Have but eight regiments here. Six of them are three-months men. Their time expires this week—are reorganizing now. I have neither tents nor wagons, and must hold Cairo and Bird's Point."

On the heels of this he informed Frémont that the rebels were about to capture Bird's Point, just across the Mississippi from Cairo, and that he had only two six-pounders ready to move. On July 29, 1861, he added another panicky appeal for aid:

On yesterday, three thousand rebels west of Bird's Point forty miles; three hundred at Madrid and three regiments from Union City ordered there; also troops from Randolph and Corinth. The number of organized rebels within fifty miles of me will exceed twelve thousand—that is, including Randolph troops ordered and not including several companies opposite in Kentucky.

On August 1st came another telegram imploring immediate help. Prentiss stated that the previous day General Pillow had been at New Madrid with 11,000 well-armed and well-drilled troops, two regiments of splendidly equipped cavalry, and 100 pieces of artillery; that 9,000 more men were moving to reinforce him; and that he had promised to place 20,000 troops in that vital corner of Missouri at once. On September 4th, Polk's troops did occupy the strategic post of Columbus, Kentucky.

Frémont thus had to answer the demands of two widely separated commanders, each menaced by strong Confederate armies; he had to take steps to pacify Missouri, where a ghastly guerrilla struggle was beginning to break out; he had to organize the raw volunteers who were trickling into St. Louis, and to make frantic efforts to find them food, uniforms, and arms; and he had to keep the city, with its large population of rebel sympathizers, under strict control. All this had to be done by a man who had never commanded forces of more than a few hundred, who had for years been engrossed in civilian pursuits, and who was new to the city, the post, and the problems about him. It had to be done with the most inadequate resources, under a War Department indifferent to the West. The situation would have taxed the capacity of abler men than Frémont.

His first decision was on the whole correct: to send word to Lyon at Springfield that he had best fall back on his base at Rolla, and to hurry reinforcements forward to Cairo. There was no particular reason for holding Springfield. It was not an important strategic point. There was, however, every reason for safeguarding Cairo, which was vital for the command of the Ohio and Mississippi. If Pillow really had the army credited to him, and if he could cross the Mississippi above Cairo and cut off Prentiss's force, the result might be a horrible disaster. Within a week after his arrival, Frémont, though burdened with other business, had chartered a fleet of eight steamboats, loaded them with soldiers and with artillery and stores which he had ordered from the East, and set off down the river.[10] He had labored like a slave to make this expedition of nearly 4,000 men ready. The night before it set out he retired at midnight, and was at his desk again at 4:30 A.M., where he remained till just before the departure of the flotilla at three o'clock in the afternoon.[11]

The trip, however, gave him not only the first rest he had enjoyed since he took up his command, but also the gratification of a wildly enthusiastic reception by the nervous little army under Prentiss. On five o'clock of an effulgent day, the sun turning the Mississippi into a broad path of gold, his flagship the *City of Alton* approached Cairo, and fired its eight-pounders as a signal. At once the guns on shore replied. For half an hour there was a perfect roar of artillery, the

10 St. Louis *Republican,* quoted in New York *Tribune,* August 9, 1861.
11 New York *Herald,* August 12, 1861.

echoes rolling away into the woods of Missouri and Kentucky. The banks of the two rivers were peppered with excited groups of soldiers. As the *City of Alton,* bedecked with evergreens and flags, churned in to the Cairo water-front, the wharves became black with uniformed men yelling "Frémont! Frémont!"; and when Prentiss led the General down the gang-plank and up to his headquarters at the St. Charles Hotel, the uproar was deafening. He had come in the nick of time. Prentiss's army was small, and much of it fast disintegrating; while in that swampy position, fever and dysentery were taking a heavy toll of it. Frémont had many of the sick transferred from the low ground to the breezy decks of his steamboats, and from that date made use of floating hospitals wherever he could.

Meanwhile, what of General Lyon? That commander was now in a mood which almost approached despair. He saw only retreat or ruin ahead of him. He must go back, he wrote Colonel Chester Harding at St. Louis, unless he received large reinforcements and supplies. "Our troops are badly clothed, poorly fed, and imperfectly supplied with tents. None of them have as yet been paid." [12] A little later he charged the Administration and General Scott with an inexcusable neglect of the West, and declared that they were allowing that section to become "the victim of imbecility or malice." Frémont had written to Montgomery Blair for "money and arms without delay and by the quickest conveyance," and Blair had replied from Washington on July 26th that "I find it impossible now to get any attention to Missouri or western matters from the authorities here. You will have to do the best you can and take all needful responsibility to defend and protect the people over whom you are specially set." [13] When Frémont opened his headquarters, three messengers were awaiting him from Lyon, all insisting that danger was imminent and that help must be sent him at once.

As it proved, there was a good fortnight in which help might

---

[12] Despatch of July 15, 1861, before Frémont's arrival.
[13] *Congressional Globe,* March 7, 1862; *37th Cong., 2d Sess.,* p. 1126.

have been despatched, and even a moderate force might have saved Lyon from defeat. But circumstances made it impossible for Frémont to furnish the required aid. It has been asserted that while he was taking 3,800 men to Cairo, he could also have sent several thousand by rail and wagon-road to Springfield, and so have saved the day. But, as a matter of fact, the troops were simply not available. Colonel Chester Harding later testified that while large numbers of volunteers were arriving in St. Louis in the first days of August, nearly all were unarmed, they were totally untrained and did not even know how to use a musket, and they were wholly without transport animals or wagons; and that regiment after regiment lay for days in the city without equipment, for the arsenals were empty. Having so few men, Frémont thought it unwise to divide his reinforcements. Above all, it can be urged in his defense that he expected Lyon to retreat, and issued orders with that definite end in view. As a matter of fact, he did on August 4th send two regiments marching toward Lyon's assistance, one from Booneville and the other from Leavenworth, Kansas—the only regiments available. He expected Lyon to retire to meet them. One of the messengers who reached him from Springfield, entreating him for "soldiers, soldiers, soldiers," told him that Lyon would fight at that town whether he got more troops or not; to which Frémont replied, "If he fights, it will be upon his own responsibility." [14]

By the beginning of August, the Confederate army under McCulloch numbered almost 13,000 men. It began its march toward Springfield, about fifty miles distant, on July 31st, and its approach filled Lyon with apprehension. He exaggerated its numbers, believing that almost 30,000 men opposed him, and even when he learned its true size, he realized that his plight was desperate. His own forces had by now shrunk to about 5,000 effective troops. If he remained stationary, he would be surrounded and captured; if he retreated from Springfield, he

[14] Snead, *Fight for Missouri*, p. 253; *Official Records*, Series I, Vol. III, p. 57ff.

would leave the southwestern section of Missouri, with its farm resources, lead-mines, and thousands of volunteers, to the enemy. He would have to traverse a rough country, and cross many difficult streams and ravines. To do this with some 5,400 disheartened men, his passage encumbered by four hundred army wagons, along roads blocked by crowds of refugees, would at best be a slow and painful operation. To do it with a powerful army hanging on his heels and a force of cavalry harrying his flanks might be dangerous.

Yet Lyon's duty was clear—it was to go back. A council of his officers three days before the battle showed that most of them believed a retreat proper and even imperative. The second in command was General John T. Schofield, who always declared that the fruitless sacrifice at Wilson's Creek was unnecessary and wholly unjustifiable. As he wrote long afterward, "our retreat to Rolla was open and perfectly safe, even if begun as late as the night of the ninth. A few days or a few weeks at most would have made us amply strong to defeat the enemy and drive him out of Missouri, without serious loss to ourselves." Schofield urged this opinion upon Lyon with vehemence. As for Frémont's orders, on August 6th he sent a letter to Lyon which reached the latter on the ninth; and although this letter has unfortunately been lost, we have two statements, corroborating one another, as to its contents. Both Schofield and Frémont tell us that it instructed Lyon that if he were not powerful enough to maintain his position at Springfield, he should fall back toward Rolla until he was met by reinforcements.[15] But Lyon was headstrong, he exaggerated the disaster to the loyal citizens of the region if he abandoned them to Confederate wrath, and he moved out to attack McCulloch's force of more than twice his numbers.

It was desperate, it was foolhardy, but it was sublime, and the news of that hopeless attack and its tragic result sent a thrill throughout the North. In the faint summer dawn of August 10th, Franz Sigel fell suddenly with 1,200 men upon the

[15] MS. *Memoirs;* John T. Schofield, *Forty-Six Years in the Army,* p. 40.

enemy's right flank, while simultaneously Lyon with 3,700 troops went into action against their left center. Sigel after some initial success was repulsed, but Lyon drove the enemy out of their camp, and then as the morning advanced threw back attack after attack by the Confederates, desperately trying to regain their positions. Within its limits, it was one of the fiercest encounters of the Civil War. The two main lines of battle, Federal and Confederate, were less than a thousand yards in length. Yet along this line almost every available company was brought into action. The Confederates would appear out of the billowing smoke in ranks three or four deep, one file lying down to fire, another kneeling, and one or two standing, and they sometimes pushed to within thirty or forty yards of the Union rifles and cannon before they were repulsed. Both Price and Lyon exhibited the greatest personal gallantry, Lyon receiving three wounds without going to the rear. At last a final heavy assault was made by the Confederates, and Lyon, leaping upon a horse and waving his hat in air, called to some fragments of reserves to close ranks and plunge into the mêlée. A part of the Second Kansas surged forward beside him, and as they met the Confederate line a ball pierced Lyon's breast. He fell from his horse and died almost instantly. A few minutes later, at half-past eleven in the morning, the chief surviving officers held a hasty council and gave the order to retreat.[16]

As graphic accounts of this battle of Wilson's Creek appeared in the northern press, and as Lyon's body with much pomp and public sorrow was taken from city to city to be buried at his New England home, the first loud criticism of Frémont arose. It was easy to say that he should have reinforced Lyon, and many said it. It was not so easy to say that Lyon should have retreated; nobody outside Missouri knew that Frémont had ordered him to do so unless he were certain of his safety, for Frémont never published his letter. Nobody knew how Cairo had been imploring Frémont for men, how in-

[16] *Official Records,* Series I, Vol. III, p. 62ff.

sistent President Lincoln had been that Cairo be safeguarded at all costs, and how limited were his forces in semi-hostile St. Louis. The consequence was that Frémont was attacked then and later for a catastrophe which it had been almost beyond his power to prevent. Later the Committee on the Conduct of the War reported that this first demand from Lyon had been pressed upon him so hastily, before he could measure his resources, "that even if he failed to do all that one under the circumstances might have done, still your committee can discover no cause of censure against him."

Once the criticism of Frémont was fairly loosed, it found much upon which to feed. No man on earth could have taken charge of the chaotic Department of the West, no general could have tried to bring well-prepared armies out of that confusion of unpreparedness, without committing blunders and making enemies. Frémont's blunders were peculiarly unhappy, and his enemies were soon a host.

His industry was unceasing, and within a few weeks he had to his credit an important list of achievements, to which his defenders were later able to point with warm praise. He policed the city, stopped the Confederate recruiting which had been openly conducted at the Berthold Mansion, and made life and property secure. He ordered General John Pope, another Mexican War veteran, to northern Missouri with instructions to organize local committees of safety and halt the guerrilla warfare being waged there by Confederate sympathizers. Since approximately ten thousand of the men under his command were three-months volunteers, and it was urgently necessary to keep them under arms while the raw recruits were being drilled, he personally guaranteed their pay if they would stay a fourth month. The morale of the officers showed immediate improvement following his arrival; tippling ceased, and the booksellers reported an unusual demand for Hardee's *Tactics* and Scott's *Tactics*.[17] He ordered a reorganization of the Reserve Corps in St. Louis, to be enlisted for the war, and to comprise infantry,

[17] New York *Herald*, August 12, 1861.

cavalry, and artillery units. In the first few days after assuming command he took possession of the Iron Mountain and the Pacific railroads, stationed small forces to protect them, garrisoned Ironton with a force under Colonel B. Gratz Brown, and took equal precautions for the safety of Cape Girardeau —these points being important for the defense of St. Louis.

Arms and money were still desperately needed; many of the soldiers had long been unpaid, and some volunteers as they arrived had to be set drilling with sticks, while even the trained men were armed with almost anything—some with smoothbores, some with rifled muskets, and some with nothing but sabers. As July closed, he appealed to the War Department agent in New York. The Adams Express Company, he wired, would bring by passenger train any arms directed to him; "send everything you have"; the arsenal was empty and "we must have arms—any arms, no matter what." At the same time he wrote directly to Lincoln, stating that he had found "nearly every county in an insurrectionary condition"; the enemy advancing in force from different points on the southern frontier; and besides the troops menacing Prentiss, 5,000 Tennesseans and Arkansas marching upon Ironton: [18]

I am sorely pressed for want of arms. I have arranged with Adams Express Company to bring me everything with speed, and will buy arms to-day in New York. Our troops have not been paid, and some regiments are in a state of mutiny, and the men whose term of service is expired generally refuse to enlist. I lost a fine regiment last night from inability to pay them a portion of the money due. This regiment had been intended to move on a critical post last night. The treasurer of the United States had here $300,000 entirely unappropriated. I applied to him yesterday for $100,000 for my paymaster-general, Andrews, but was refused. We have not an hour for delay. There are three courses open to us. One, to let the enemy possess himself of some of the strongest points in the state and threaten St. Louis, which is insurrectionary. Second, to force a loan

[18] *Official Records,* Series I, Vol. III, p. 416.

from secession banks here. Third, to use the money belonging to the government, which is in the treasury here. Of course I will neither lose the state nor permit the enemy a foot of advantage. I have infused energy and activity into the department, and there is a thorough good spirit in officers and men. This morning I will order the treasurer to deliver the money in his possession to Gen. Andrews, and will send a force to the treasury to take the money, and will direct such payments as the exigency requires. I will hazard everything for the defense of the department you have confided to me, and I trust to you for support.

Believing there was a shortage of both horses and arms in the United States, Frémont proposed to the Washington authorities that his former attorney F. P. Billings be allowed to buy the former in Canada, and that agents be hurried to France for the latter. The deficiency of arms was a terrible reality. But there were plenty of horses as near as Quincy, Illinois, at prices $30 a head lower than Frémont proposed to pay in Canada. The War Department forbade the Canadian purchases in a telegram which, because it was sent to a subordinate, aroused the General's anger.

Frémont's plan was to take the field with his army as soon as possible; and he reasoned that in order to hold St. Louis as his base he would either have to garrison it with a considerable force, or fortify it. As events turned out, St. Louis was soon perfectly safe. At the moment, however, his reasoning did not appear fallacious. He began digging a crescent-shaped line of intrenchments about the city, employing not the new recruits, who needed drilling and were in large part unfit for such heavy work in the August heat, but the laboring population of St. Louis. The city was full of turbulent men, their families in want, who presented a constant danger of riots; and government wages were an important factor in pacifying the community. In the same way, he planned to fortify Cape Girardeau, Ironton, Rolla, and Jefferson City, and thus enable small garrisons to hold the state tranquil.[19] Enlisting a confi-

[19] MS *Memoirs*, Bancroft Library.

dential agent or spy named Captain Charles D'Arnaud, the General sent him within the Confederate lines to prepare a correct map of the highways, bridges, and forts in Kentucky and western Tennessee, and to ascertain the probable movements of the enemy. D'Arnaud shortly returned with much of the desired information, and with useful maps showing the position of Fort Henry and Fort Donelson, then being constructed.

To expedite the transportation of troops, Frémont promptly took two steps of great importance. The railroads entering St. Louis had different terminals, some of them far from the river. The General had a union station built and fortified on the river bank, so that, upon a day's notice, 20,000 troops could be moved through the city from a point on one railway to a point on another. Troops arriving from Illinois could be ferried directly to the station with all their supplies, without need of wagons to haul them through the streets. It was a common-sense step. At the same time, Frémont began to organize a river service. He asked Governor O. P. Morton of Indiana, though ineffectually, for some regiments of men experienced in steamboating; and upon his own authority sent for a veteran river captain in St. Louis, Thomas Maxwell, and authorized him to organize a "marine corps" of pilots, engineers, mates, firemen, and sailors, three companies in all.[20] On the very day he crossed the Mississippi to take command, Frémont directed his chief of staff to find out what river boats were available for refitting as gunboats. Asboth and Fiala, as it happened, were familiar with the armed craft used by the Austrians upon the lower Danube. On August 24th Frémont ordered the construction of thirty-eight mortar-boats, and later of eight steam-tugs to move them, and the adaptation of two strongly built vessels as gunboats. The sides of all these craft were lined with iron. Work was pushed on them by torch-light all night long. Captain James B. Eads was frequently at headquarters, and the drawing of the plans was placed under his control.

[20] Sen. Exec. Doc. 412, 57th Cong., 1st Sess., p. 195ff.

Unfortunately, while Frémont was carrying through these constructive labors, he was making a series of errors, small in detail but large in the aggregate, which were destined to cost him dear. Reports reached the East that he was vain, capricious, and arrogant. It was complained that he had taken for headquarters an elegant private mansion at a rental of $6,000 a year; that the Hungarian and Garibaldian officers whom he had brought out as his personal staff wore gaudy uniforms and used fantastic titles; that he clattered through the streets with an ostentatious bodyguard; that he was so hedged about with sentinels that it was impossible to see him on business; that he issued commissions and gave out contracts in a shockingly irregular way; and that he and his assistants were preposterously extravagant. He was accused of surrounding himself with a knot of flatterers, and of ignoring able but plain-spoken men.[21]

In these charges there was a limited element of truth. Frémont's use of the splendid residence of Colonel J. B. Brant on Chouteau Avenue was entirely proper, for it enabled him to house under one roof the whole administrative activities of his Department. In a large second-floor room were desks for himself, his secretaries John R. Howard and William Dorsheimer, and Asboth and other staff officers. Large tables were placed in the room and covered with maps, diagrams, calculations of distances, and similar material prepared with care by Asboth. Downstairs were subordinate officers. The basement held a veritable arsenal, from which arms and ammunition were dealt out for emergency service. But Frémont guarded the approaches by so many sentries that men complained it was like capturing the Gorgon's head to fight their way in. General G. B. Farrar, who brought an important message from Springfield, declared that it took him three days to gain an audience with Frémont; that there were guards at the street corners, guards at the gate, guards at the outer door, guards at the

21 Nicolay and Hay, *Lincoln*, IV, p. 412.

office, and a whole regiment of troops in the adjacent bar-racks.[22]

The personnel and titles of Frémont's staff were certain to grate upon rough and practical westerners. He had brought with him not merely the Hungàrians named, and Major Charles Zagonyi, who organized a spirited cavalry battalion, but such Italians as Captain Antonio Cattanco, Captain Ajace Saccippi, and Lieutenant Dominica Occidone. Another officer was said to be a natural son of Lord Byron. Frémont actually seemed to prefer foreigners to Americans. On August 5th he wrote Francis Lieber: "Are there any experienced artillerists, officers or men, one or both, Germans, Prussian, or French, in New York, who can be gotten immediately and sent to me here without any loss of time? I am distressed for want of men to man my guns and the enemy is at our door." He had twenty-eight staff members, altogether too many. Some bore sonorous and absurd foreign names—"adletus to the chief of staff," "commander of the bodyguard," "musical director," and "military registrator and expeditor." Among the fifteen aides-de-camp were several politicians, who received no pay but served in order to exert their influence upon affairs. They included Owen Lovejoy, a portly, kindly, rhetorically eloquent gentleman, who sat in Congress for the Princeton district of Illinois, and who, embittered by the death of his brother Elijah many years before at the hands of an anti-Abolitionist mob, was warmly opposed to slavery; John A. Gurley, well known as an Abolitionist leader and a Representative from Ohio; and Representative John P. C. Shanks of Indiana, also of radical anti-slavery views. This trio was close to Frémont, as were young Howard and Dorsheimer, his immediate secretaries. Dorsheimer, a lawyer with a Harvard education, had ability, and later rose to be lieutenant-governor of New York, but his aristocratic elegance (he had a valet) amused many observers.

---

[22] Gustav Koerner, *Memoirs*, II, p. 170ff. The fact that Brant was a relative of Mrs. Frémont made the $5,000 rental seem suspicious to some; actually it was moderate.

FRÉMONT IN 1861

BUILDING GENERAL FRÉMONT'S BRIDGE ACROSS THE OSAGE

(From *Harper's Weekly*)

Gustav Koerner, a brilliant young German-American, served on the staff as the representative of Governor Yates of Illinois.[23]

Unfortunate in some members of his personal staff, Frémont was unfortunate also in several officers of the regular army whom he found already stationed in St. Louis. The most important, bustling, and unpopular was Major Justus McKinstry, the quartermaster-general, who had become provost-marshal of St. Louis when the city was placed under martial law. He owed his command there to Blair himself. Before Frémont arrived the quartermaster-general in Washington had given McKinstry broad powers in making purchases, instructing him that while economy was important, promptness and efficiency were more so. A tall, dashing fellow, with dark complexion, resolute features, and "an eye like Mars to threaten and command," he looked, especially when galloping about the streets, the *beau idéal* of a soldier. But he had always been disliked in the army, and as censor of the activities of the St. Louisians he was hated by the people. His refusal to let any one enter or leave the city without passes, his rule that nobody should be on the streets after 9 P.M., and his restrictions on the press, aroused bitter complaint. He turned against Blair; and one of Frémont's worst blunders was to permit him to suppress the St. Louis *Republican,* a Unionist newspaper published by Blair's friends and close to Blair's heart. Blair came to consider this appointee of his own the most tyrannical and corrupt of the General's subordinates.

Frémont cannot be exonerated from blame for the chaos, friction, and extravagance which arose; a commander with more practical vigor would have cut through many of the difficulties directly. He would have mastered affairs, instead of

---

[23] Ida M. Tarbell, *Abraham Lincoln,* II, Ch. 24. As page in the Frémont headquarters there served a lad named Francis Grierson, who had been born in England and reared in Illinois, and who was destined to become a noted mystic and essayist. His impressions, recorded in a chapter of *The Valley of Shadows: Recollections of the Lincoln Country,* have slender historical value but great literary charm. He was impressed, as a boy would be, by the pomp and parade surrounding the headquarters and the strangeness of the foreign officers.

letting them master him. The General lacked high executive ability; still more, he lacked judgment of men. To be sure, much of the irregularity in letting contracts, the general confusion, and the tactless exclusion of important visitors, arose from the fact that he was crushed under a mountain of labor. He had to conduct an enormous correspondence with governors of the states and territories in his Department, with Washington officials, with his scattered commands, and with private citizens. It was more than Dorsheimer, Howard, and the devoted Jessie could manage. His troops were strewn all over the West—part in Missouri, part in Kansas, part in Chicago, part in southern Illinois, and soon part in Paducah, Kentucky. Once he kept his telegraphers busy thirty-six hours without intermission. With the lesson of Bull Run before him, he had resolved not to move forward till he had organized his force and collected adequate supplies; and Washington, intent on the eastern armies, hindered rather than aided him. But these excuses cover only part of his failure. Gustav Koerner correctly wrote Lyman Trumbull on November 12, 1861: [24]

There was a great amount of labor performed day and night but there appeared to be no proper system or method. Some of his most intimate friends were undoubtedly cheating and circumventing him, I thought. He is no judge of men at all, it seems to me, and he can readily be imposed upon by plausible knavery. I think he is honest and honorable himself, but too impulsive and too impressionable.

Necessarily, he had to depute much business to subordinates, who sometimes managed it badly. Breezy western citizens, who thought that everybody, whether President, Senator, or General, should stop and give them a half hour's chat, were turned back by sentries with a curt "What's your business?" or, if they gained entry, found Frémont preoccupied and hurried. They went out denouncing him as aristocratic and cold, when he was only protecting his time. Frémont's green staff helped him to make mistakes, for neither Howard nor Dor-

[24] Trumbull Papers, Library of Congress.

sheimer knew the difference between a rascally contract hunter and a distinguished citizen of St. Louis, and sometimes admitted the former while debarring the latter. Their inexperience conspired with Frémont's own impatience of red tape to produce many irregularities. His unauthorized issuance of commissions became the despair of the War Department, while orders and requisitions were frequently signed without scrutiny. General Schofield tells us that he went repeatedly to Frémont for authority to have certain rifled guns in the St. Louis arsenal issued to his new artillery regiment; that he always received the authority, but before he got to the armory it was invariably countermanded by telegraph; and that finally he suggested to Frémont that he be sent East to procure fieldpieces and equipment. Frémont at once acquiesced, bade Schofield sit down and write the necessary order, and "signed it without reading." A well-known and able Missouri Congressman, John Phelps, came down the steps of the Brant House in high dudgeon, complaining that he could see nobody and get no business attended to. In many ways the Department of the West by mid-August, 1861, seemed in dire confusion.

Yet some were favorably impressed. John Hay, Lincoln's secretary, went to St. Louis late in August and for several days saw much of Frémont and Jessie. He thought the latter talked too much and too loudly. But Frémont "was quiet, earnest, industrious, imperious." Returning East, Hay wrote articles in two New York papers defending the General.

The increasing storm of criticism, made louder by prejudice and ignorance, and swelled by the clamor of selfish "patriots"—many of them Frank P. Blair's friends—who had been refused contracts for horses, beef, mules, or wagons, and who were highly disgruntled, dismayed Frémont. He winced under the attacks. A great deal of outright mendacity entered into them. An impartial Missouri observer, B. Rush Plumeley, later wrote Secretary Chase that he had taken the charges one by one and sifted them without regard to Frémont or Blair. "My dear friends, they are...lies." A friend of Blair, he added, had been the largest buyer of horses, and had supplied such miserable steeds that Frémont was compelled to issue an order that no more Missouri stock should be bought. The records of the War Department bear this out. They contain a number of Blair's brief notes to McKinstry. "Dear Major: If you buy any more horses, I wish you to give Jim Neal a fair chance. He is a personal friend of mine and a sound Union man." Again, "Dear Major: I shall be obliged to you if you can give Mr. Alec Peterson a contract for buying horses. He is a good friend of mine..." And to still another officer, "General Meigs: If you want horses in Missouri, I most cordially recommend Mr. Farrar to purchase them for you." It was Farrar who supplied the most defective animals. Frémont was fiercely criticized for a purchase of Hall's carbines to arm his half-defenseless troops, and since this purchase involved no less a person than young J. Pierpont Morgan, the accusations have been repeated and embroidered in numerous books. But a careful investigation has shown that the much-denounced transaction was really prudent and commendable.[25]

While the storm of attacks increased, the military situation in these first weeks after Lyon's defeat and the retreat of his shattered army to Rolla seemed full of the gravest peril. Union leaders believed that there were now 60,000 or 70,000 armed rebels in the state, of whom perhaps 40,000 were Missourians. Troops had suddenly appeared in great force from Arkansas, Tennessee, and other states, and with the benefit of comprehensive military plans matured by Leonidas Polk and others, had overrun half the state. Living on the country, they were seizing horses, grain, meat, clothing, and other supplies from Union citizens. Meanwhile, in central and northern Missouri the rebel guerrillas, recruited from the countrysides, were en-

[25] Koerner, *Memoirs*, II, p. 168; on Frank Blair's desire for contracts, W. E. Smith offers a fair treatment in *The Francis Preston Blair Family in Politics*, II, p. 67. McKinstry published a pamphlet defense of himself which contains a mass of material on contracts and corruption, and which is more severe upon Frank Blair than Frémont; *Vindication of Quartermaster-General McKinstry*. For this whole subject of wartime corruption see Appendix II.

gaging in appalling outrages. They were burning bridges, wrecking railway trains, cutting telegraphs, raiding farms, and falling in sudden force upon exposed Union units, only to scatter again in a hundred directions. Their warfare was driving the loyal population by thousands to take refuge, penniless, in Illinois, Iowa, and Kansas. There seemed danger that parts of the state would become a stark wilderness.[26] And nobody knew where Pillow and McCulloch would strike next.

Under these circumstances Frémont, believing some decisive stroke to be necessary, resolved suddenly upon a proclamation of military emancipation. In this step he was unquestionably urged forward by his immediate associates. Two parties had arisen among the loyal citizens of Missouri, the radical Union men or "charcoals," and the conservatives, or "claybanks." The former, who included most of the Germans, believed in aggressive, uncompromising action, while the latter advocated patience, conciliation, and caution. The latter were led by Frank Blair and provisional Governor Hamilton R. Gamble; it was the former who surrounded Frémont, and who, with the radical Lovejoy, Gurley, and Shanks among their spokesmen, had obtained a marked ascendancy over him. They held a decided conviction that the slaves of rebels ought to be forfeit. Secession, they reasoned, had destroyed all constitutional protections and safeguards which formerly shielded southern citizens; it was now perfectly legal to confiscate the property of men in arms, and slaves were of course property. Every report of outrage and destruction in peaceful Union counties, of depredations by bushwhackers and guerrilla gangs, was an argument for stern measures. Men were being killed and their homes wiped out. Should the Federal Government hesitate to free the slaves of miscreants responsible for such acts? To this view Mrs. Frémont was completely won over, and she added her arguments to those of Lovejoy and Gurley.

How long Frémont debated the question with himself and

[26] Compare *Official Records*, Series I, Vol. III, p. 417.

others, we do not know; but his wife tells us that at the end
he moved with his accustomed impetuosity: [27]

The State outside of the fortified points was becoming more and
more unsettled. The farmers would, when notified, join the camps
of the rebel commanders in great numbers, suddenly augmenting
their forces, and then, if the projected raid or attack was deferred,
would return again to their homes, reducing the force correspond-
ingly.

In this manner, however, it was impossible to foresee which point
would be threatened next, and failing sufficient troops to control
the State through force of arms, it became necessary to devise some
means to prevent this guerrilla warfare. The credit of the government was about used up, and it had so lost prestige through the
non-payment of its debts to the soldiers, and those who furnished
the supplies, that it was regarded with contempt by the Secessionists, and many Unionists came to doubt its power to compel. For
many days and nights the situation had been a most anxious one
for Gen. Frémont; with unfilled requisitions in Washington, commanders of troops demanding reinforcements where there were none
to give, troops clamoring for pay when there was no money.... He
determined to force the rebel sympathizers, who did not join the
rebel armies as soldiers, to remain at home, and to make them feel
that there was a penalty for rebellion, and for aiding those who
were in rebellion.

On the morning of the 30th of August, shortly after daybreak,
Mrs. Frémont found Gen. Frémont at his desk. He had sent for
Mr. Edward Davis, of Philadelphia, who arrived as she came. It
was sufficiently light to see plainly, and the General said, "I want
you two, but no others." Then in the dawn of the new day, he read
the Emancipation Order, that first gave freedom to the slaves of
rebels, and which he had thought out and written, in the hours
taken from his brief resting time.

The proclamation with which Frémont thus astonished the
nation declared that he found it necessary to thrust aside the
provisional governor and assume the administrative powers of
the disordered state; that all Missouri would thenceforth be

[27] MS *Memoirs*, Bancroft Library.

under martial law; that the lines of the Union Army should for the present extend from Leavenworth by way of Jefferson City, Rolla, and Ironton to Cape Girardeau on the Mississippi; that all persons found with arms in their hands north of these lines should be tried by court-martial, and if guilty, should be shot; and that "the property, real and personal, of all persons in the state of Missouri directly proven to have taken an active part with their enemies in the field is declared to be confiscated to the public use, and their slaves, if any they have, are hereby declared freemen." His intention was to penalize the disloyal slave-owners of northern and central Missouri who were organizing or supporting the guerrilla warfare of those regions. But his action had a far wider significance. The conflict had thus far been a war to preserve the Union, and no members of the Administration and no general had suggested any other object; Frémont's proclamation, if its principles were sustained and applied to other fields, would convert it into a war to liberate the slaves.

Already many radical-minded Northerners, including, of course, the Abolitionists, had demanded just this. Gerrit Smith, in an open letter of July 12th to Frémont's staff assistant, Owen Lovejoy, had said that the government did right to call for millions in money and hundreds of thousands of soldiers if they were really needed to put down the rebellion. "But why take a costly and weary way to put it down," he asked, "when a cheap and short one is at hand? Why choose crushing burdens of debt and immense human slaughter when both can be avoided? The liberation of slaves has obviously become one of the necessities and therefore one of the rights of the country. Let the President, in his capacity as commander of the army, proclaim such liberation and the war would end in thirty days." Moncure D. Conway was putting through the press a book, received enthusiastically by the newspapers and by radicals like Sumner, entitled *The Great Method of Peace*, which declared emancipation the master-key of victory. Announce it, he wrote, and "every Southerner would have to hurry

home to be his own home-guard and his own home-provisioner."
Even those who held no such illusions thought, as the *Tribune*
said, that it was "time to be in earnest; that handling traitors
with kid gloves is not the way to subdue them." [28]

Frémont's proclamation of August 30th, therefore, coming
at a moment of growing antagonism between radical and conservative Northerners, and his action immediately afterward
in setting up a commission to take evidence and in issuing deeds
of manumission to slaves, fell upon the country like a thunder-
bolt.

[28] New York *Tribune,* July 28, 1861 (for Gerrit Smith's letter); September
1, 1861.

XXX

Frémont *vs.* Blair and Lincoln

BEYOND question Frémont issued his proclamation simply as a war measure in Missouri, and with little if any thought of its effect outside that state. He has been accused by Nicolay and Hay of drafting it as an appeal to the support of the northern radicals, and as a last desperate attempt to regain the popularity which he had lost through Lyon's defeat. No foundation exists for this view, which is unjust in attributing to the impetuous General a measure of shrewd, scheming calculation which he never possessed. He planned the proclamation merely as a weapon against the guerrillas who were laying northern Missouri waste; he designed it, as he said, "to place in the hands of the military authorities the power to give instantaneous effect to existing laws, and to supply such deficiencies as the conditions of war demand." It was characteristic of him that he did not wait to consult the Administration on so momentous a step; had he paused to think of its effect outside turbulent Missouri, he would have done so. But he did not know how fiercely the radicals and Lincoln were already at odds over emancipation.

He was warned, as he read it to his wife and friend in that gray August dawn, that Washington would be hostile. "General," said Edward Davis, "Mr. Seward will never allow this. He intends to wear down the South by steady pressure, not by blows, and then make himself the arbitrator." "It is for the North to say what it will or will not allow," replied Frémont, "and whether it will arbitrate, or whether it will fight. The time has come for decisive action; this is a war measure, and as such I make it. I have been given full power to crush rebellion in this department, and I will bring the penalties of rebellion home to every man found striving against the Union." [1]

The reception met by the proclamation has been described by many historians, and it is sufficient to say that it aroused the enthusiasm of radical anti-slavery elements in the North as nothing had done since the firing on Fort Sumter. New England was jubilant. From all parts of the Middle West came reports that men were saying, "Now the Administration is in earnest," or "That looks like work!" In Lincoln's own state of Illinois the outburst of applause was such as to give the President genuine pain. The German-Americans rose *en masse* to this new and higher object which Frémont seemed to have given the war; recruiting increased by a sudden leap. The press of the North was almost a unit in commendation. In Chicago, the *Tribune;* in Washington the *National Intelligencer;* in Boston, the *Post;* and in New York, Raymond's *Times,* Horace Greeley's *Tribune,* and Bryant's *Evening Post* all praised the proclamation in high terms. Even James Gordon Bennett's *Herald,* lately on the side of the South, and the Chicago *Times,* which was at one time briefly suppressed as a copperhead organ, joined the chorus of approbation. [2] George Julian, an Indiana member of Congress, later wrote that "it stirred and united the people of the loyal States during the ten days of life allotted it by the Government far more than any other event of the war." Perhaps the most extraordinary fact was that Simon Cameron, the Secretary of War, who was at his home ill, thought it an admirable stroke, and telegraphing his congratulations to Frémont, returned to his desk ready to give it hearty endorsement. He was surprised to find that Lincoln was hostile. [3] Sumner was enthusiastic. From that moment, Frémont became more than a general—to millions, especially in New England and among the German and Yankee elements

[1] MS *Memoirs,* Bancroft Library.

[2] The Chase MSS, Library of Congress, contains a mass of approbatory letters; see Frank Moore, *Rebellion Record,* III, 33*ff.* for press comment.

[3] Cameron advocated arming Negro soldiers; *Diary of Edward Bates,* p. 203.

of the West, he became a symbol. His name represented the crusade for the extinction of slavery.

How Lincoln, with his usual calm sagacity, took a broader and wiser view; how with the necessity of conciliating the hesitant Kentuckians in mind, he patiently and kindly asked Frémont to modify his proclamation—this, too, is an old story. His letter of September 2nd to the General is worth quoting in full: [4]

MY DEAR SIR: Two points in your proclamation of August 30th give me some anxiety:

First: Should you shoot a man, according to the proclamation, the Confederates would very certainly shoot our best men in their hands in retaliation; and so, man for man, indefinitely. It is, therefore, my order that you allow no man to be shot under the proclamation without first having my approbation or consent.

Second. I think there is great danger that the closing paragraph, in relation to the confiscation of property and the liberating slaves of traitorous owners, will alarm our Southern Union friends and turn them against us; perhaps ruin our rather fair prospect for Kentucky. Allow me, therefore, to ask that you will, as of your own motion, modify that paragraph so as to conform to the first and fourth sections of the act of Congress entitled, 'An act of Congress entitled, "An act to confiscate property used for insurrectionary purposes," approved August 6, 1861, and a copy of which act I herewith send you.

This letter is written in a spirit of caution, and not of censure. I send it by special messenger, in order that it may certainly and speedily reach you.

This request for a modification Frémont foolishly refused. His eyes were bent wholly upon Missouri, without thought of the other border states, and he tells us in his unpublished *Memoirs* that the effect there was striking. "The Union people rejoiced openly. The class of sympathizers with the South became quiet and careful, finding that they must respect the laws

---

[4] Nicolay and Hay, *Lincoln*, IV, Ch. 24, give it and the circumstances.

of the land they lived in. To the rebels everywhere it was a blow. It affected not only their principles but their property." He wrote to Lincoln a stubborn explanation: [5]

Trusting to have your confidence, I have been leaving it to events themselves to show you whether or not I was shaping affairs here according to your ideas. The shortest communication between Washington and St. Louis generally involves two days, and the employment of two days in time of war goes largely toward success or disaster. I therefore went along according to my own judgment, leaving the result of my movements to justify me with you. And so in regard to my proclamation of the 30th. Between the rebel armies, the Provisional Government, and home traitors, I felt the position bad and saw danger. In the night I decided upon the proclamation and the form of it. I wrote it the next morning and printed it the same day. I did it without consultation or advice with any one, acting solely with my best judgment to serve the country and yourself, and perfectly willing to receive the amount of censure which should be thought due if I had made a false movement. This is as much a movement in the war as a battle, and in going into these I shall have to act according to my judgment of the ground before me, as I did on this occasion. If, upon reflection, your better judgment still decides that I am wrong in the article respecting the liberation of slaves, I have to ask that you will openly direct me to make the correction. The implied censure will be received as a soldier always should the reprimand of his chief. If I were to retract of my own accord, it would imply that I myself thought it wrong, and that I had acted without the reflection which the gravity of the point demanded. But I did not. I acted with full deliberation, and upon the certain conviction that it was a measure right and necessary, and I think so still. In regard to the other point of the proclamation to which you refer, I desire to say that I do not think the enemy can either misconstrue or urge anything against it, or undertake to make unusual retaliation. The shooting of men who will rise in arms against an army in the military occupation of a country is merely a necessary measure of defence, and entirely according to the usages of civilized warfare. The article does not at all refer to prisoners of war, and certainly

[5] *Official Records,* Series I, Vol. III, p. 477.

our enemies have no ground for requiring that we should waive in their benefit any of the ordinary advantages which the usages of war allow to us.

Already Frémont had been asked by the Confederate commander to explain his article upon the shooting of prisoners. On receipt of Frémont's despatch, Lincoln in a courteous letter made a public order:

Your answer, just received, expresses the preference on your part that I should make an open order for the modification, which I very cheerfully do. It is therefore ordered that the said clause of said proclamation be so modified, held, and construed as to conform to, and not to transcend, the provisions on the same subject contained in the act of Congress entitled, "An act to confiscate property used for insurrectionary purposes," approved August 6, 1861, and that said act be published at length, with this order.

The news was received by many in the North with gnashing of teeth. Judge George Hoadly of Cincinnati wrote that the prevalent sentiment in his city could be described only by the word "fury." [6] "How many times," asked James Russell Lowell, "are we to save Kentucky and lose our self-respect?"

This rebuke by the President in the sight of the nation was but the first of a series of disasters which befell Frémont. The next and the most catastrophic was an open estrangement between him and the powerful Blair family. The Blairs, as Lincoln later told some friends in a confidential chat, were a proud clan, with the spirit of a close corporation, and with a tendency to go in a headlong rush for any object. Related to the Bentons through the Preston family of Virginia, they and the Frémonts had long been close friends. The two sons, Montgomery and Frank, had gone to Missouri to have the benefit of Senator Benton's influence in practising law; while Jessie had spent much time with the "old gentleman," Francis P. Blair, on his attractive estate at Silver Spring, just across

[6] Chase MSS, Library of Congress.

the Maryland line, whither he had retired with his slaves, dogs, and books. To this place, with its groves and grottoes, she had brought her second baby daughter in 1853 to die. Lincoln later testified that he had appointed Frémont as western commander at the earnest solicitation of the Blairs, and that he was their "pet and protégé." There seemed every reason for complete harmony. Yet a swift and angry breach ensued—a breach which disrupted the Unionists of Missouri, and shook the whole Northwest.[7]

The reasons for this duel between Frémont and the Blairs, with political results that tormented the Lincoln Administration till the last year of the War, were complex. Temperamentally, the men were certain to clash. Frank Blair, who had taken the helm in Missouri, had gained thereby a national reputation. He was shrewd, direct, practical, and aggressive, and the erratic, impetuous, visionary traits of Frémont grated upon him. Both were hot-tempered and tenacious. Frank Blair expected to continue to be the directing force in Missouri affairs, while Frémont had no intention of letting anybody dominate them but himself. Already the Blair clan had shown what it would do with any commander who crossed its path in that state. A few months earlier, it had taken General William S. Harney in hand because he seemed slow and conservative, and had broken him with cruel despatch. Frank had pulled all the wires he could in Missouri; his brother the Postmaster-General, "the Pisistratus of his race," had exerted pressure at the capital; and Harney had been ignominiously removed. Now Frank desired to have his wishes treated as something like commands, and was chagrined when Frémont, with Jessie at his back, followed his own course. Missouri had shown promise of becoming a political enclave of the Blairs; it dismayed them to see Frémont taking steps which rallied the Germans at his back and looked like the erection of a possible machine of his own. Finally, Frank had many Missouri friends who, having helped

[7] For a vigorous sketch of Frank Blair, see G. W. Nichols, *Story of the Great March*, p. 97ff.

him "save" the state, thought they were entitled to the contracts which were being lavishly distributed; while Frémont had contract-hungry friends of his own—men whom Blair called "California vultures." [8]

For a time after Frémont's arrival, matters had gone with fair smoothness. Montgomery Blair supported him loyally in Washington. He encouraged the General in his expenditures, and criticized the Secretary of the Treasury for his parsimonious ways—"Chase," he wrote, "has more horror of seeing Treasury notes below par than of seeing soldiers killed." He talked with Lincoln about Frémont's needs, and criticized Lincoln, too—"he is of the Whig school, and that brings him naturally not only to incline to the feeble policy of the Whigs, but to give his confidence to such advisers." [9] Frank Blair was much at Frémont's headquarters, and asked and received not a few favors. Quite naturally, he requested consideration in contracts for his friends among the important merchants and manufacturers of St. Louis; and this consideration was cheerfully granted. But the time came when Frémont denied some of Blair's requests. In particular, he and McKinstry declined to grant two friends of Blair a contract to supply clothing and other equipment for forty thousand men—Frémont not believing he needed so much.[10] Frank believed in this and other contracts; he did not believe in others which Frémont was letting—some of them shown later to be full of fraud—to men whom he characterized as "obscene birds of prey." There was fault on both sides. When Frank wrote east, his father showed that he also had some grasping ideas. The old gentleman sent Frémont a decidedly irritated letter, in which he suggested "a copartnership in the West," and said that he and his sons would do everything in their power to aid the commander, if on his part he would

[8] W. E. Smith, *The Francis Preston Blair Family in Politics,* II, p. 67*ff.,* reaches my own conclusion that the principal basis of the Frémont-Blair quarrel lay in rival ambition for power and prestige. Missouri was not big enough for both men.

[9] Report, *Committee on Conduct of the War,* Part III, p. 115*ff.*

[10] Report, *Committee on Conduct of the War,* Part III, p. 178*ff.*; p. 202*ff.*

be obliging to them. Frank, he added, wanted a new military post.[11]

I shall expect you to exert your utmost influence to carry my points, and now to begin, I want to have Frank made a militia major-general for the State of Missouri. This, I presume, Gov. Gamble can do, and as Major-General Frost nipped his military honors in the bud, by turning traitor and absconding with Jackson, it would seem but a completion of what was gained in substituting Gamble for the abdicating governor, to make Frank, as the military man of the State, take the position deserted by Gen. Frost. Frank might have accepted a generalship, offered him by Lincoln, but he felt that he might be useful in Congress and hence declined a commission from that quarter which would have vacated his seat in the House. He has no commission now and acts only as colonel by the election of the regiment and courtesy of the army.

Frémont felt unable to grant this unblushing demand and said so. He tried to soften the refusal by writing the Blairs that Frank's regiment would amount to a brigade, but the rebuff stung them. Actually, he hoped that Frank Blair would accept a command in the East and so cease to complicate the Missouri situation. But the elder Blair continued to insist, by letters and telegrams, that Frémont yield to and coöperate with his son. He believed that Frank was on the high road to the Presidency, and was determined that nothing should check his son's promising career. Montgomery also thought that Frank was, as Gideon Welles records, "the greatest man in the country." All the ambitions and the wishes of the family were concentrated upon the young man. As Lincoln shrewdly put it, "Frank is their hope and pride." [12]

In so far as they were motivated by political ambitions and

[11] Frémont MSS, Bancroft Library.

[12] But Frémont did write Provisional-Governor Hamilton R. Gamble on August 18th requesting that as a special favor he "immediately commission with the rank of Brigadier-General the Honorable Frank P. Blair, now colonel of the 1st Missouri Volunteers." Gamble lacked power to do so. Gamble Papers; courtesy of Miss Marguerite Potter. For Welles on Frank Blair, see his *Diary*, III, p. 408.

a desire for personal favors, the Blairs appear to poor advantage in their attack on Frémont; but there was a better side. Frank Blair came honestly to believe that Frémont lacked the high military talents his position required. He thought that St. Louis was overwhelmingly loyal, and objected to the measures which Frémont and McKinstry took to police it under martial law. Later, he declared that Frémont's acts were "the offspring of timidity, seeking to prevent imaginary dangers by inspiring the terrors with which he himself was haunted." There was room for a sincere divergence of opinion upon this policing, and it is not easy to say which man was right. Most merchants were sympathetic with secession, and even after Frémont's work was done, the secessionist candidates for officers of the Chamber of Commerce and the Mercantile Library Association, two powerful organizations, were elected by heavy majorities.[13] Frémont's force of effective troops was much smaller than it appeared to be, and he knew that he might have to denude the city of men to answer some urgent call from the East or the West. On the whole, his precautions appear to have been justified.

Again, Blair condemned the fortification of St. Louis as another evidence of the same wasteful timidity, and as a step both useless and in its execution needlessly extravagant. These defensive works included ten forts, and the labor on them was prosecuted until the middle of October, when the War Department ordered them dropped. It is impossible to say that they were useless. There seemed genuine need in July and August, 1861, for protective measures of this character, and the precaution was probably wise. Washington was heavily fortified; General Ormsby Mitchel took great care in the summer of 1861 to fortify Cincinnati. But Blair was right as to the extrav-

[13] *Congressional Globe*, March 7, 1862. Frémont thought the Board of Police Commissioners for St. Louis, which had been appointed by ex-Governor Jackson, disloyal. He wrote Provisional-Governor Gamble on August 18th urging that they be dismissed, and suggesting men to take their place. Action should be taken without delay, he declared. But Gamble found himself without power to remove them except on formal complaint (Gamble Papers).

agance. Frémont, who should have assigned the work to army
engineers, gave it instead to a Californian named Beard, who
did it incompetently and made extortionate profits. A leading
army engineer later testified that if the War Department had
not interfered, the government would have lost $240,000 on
forts useless for defense.

The defeat and death of Lyon, a close friend, was a severe
shock to Frank Blair, and in itself raised a doubt in his mind
of Frémont's capacity. Lincoln tells us that at first he had
spoken of Frémont with high admiration and warm hopes for
the future. "But at last," said Lincoln, "the tone of Frank's
letter changed. It was a change from confidence to doubt and
uncertainty. They were pervaded with a tone of sincere sorrow
and of fear that Frémont would fail." General John M. Schofield states that the change in Frank's attitude was manifest
just after Lyon's defeat. Late in August, Schofield and Blair
called together upon Frémont at the Brant mansion: [14]

The general received me cordially, but, to my great surprise, no
questions were asked, nor any mention made, of the bloody field
from which I had just come, where Lyon had been killed. . . . I was
led at once to a large table on which maps were spread out, from
which the general proceeded to explain at length the plans of the
great campaign for which he was then preparing. Col. Blair had, I believe, already been initiated, but I listened attentively for a long
time, certainly more than an hour, to the elucidation of the project.
In general outline the plan proposed a march of the main army of
the West through southwestern Missouri and northwestern Arkansas
to the valley of the Arkansas River, and thence down that river to
the Mississippi. . . . As soon as the explanation was ended, Col. Blair
and I took our leave, making our exit through the same basement
door through which we had entered. We walked down the street
for some time in silence. Then Blair turned to me and said: "Well,
what do you think of him?" I replied, in words rather too strong
to repeat in print, to the effect that my opinion as to his wisdom
was the same as it always had been. Blair said: "I have been suspecting that for some time."

[14] J. M. Schofield, *Forty-six Years in the Army*, p. 48ff.

It was a family maxim that: "When the Blairs go in for a fight, they go in for a funeral." [15] So it was this time. The quarrel was heated enough when Frémont issued his emancipation proclamation. That made it worse, for the Blair family took the President's view that it was necessary to conciliate the people of the border states, and to refrain from direct attacks upon slavery. Frank Blair when aroused had all the dour fury of his Scotch Covenanter blood. His letters shortly stirred up a hornet's nest in Washington. On the other side, Mrs. Frémont came to her husband's aid with all the invincible tenacity and vigor she had inherited from her father. It was a duel to the death. When the smoke of battle cleared away, Frémont was a ruined man, and the political future of the Blairs was almost hopelessly compromised.

The public gained its first clear intimation of this quarrel early in September, when Lincoln despatched Postmaster-Blair and his brother-in-law, Quartermaster-General Meigs, to St. Louis to make a thorough inquiry and a report, and also to give Frémont friendly advice and admonition. They bore a letter from Lincoln to General David Hunter in Chicago. "General Frémont," wrote the President, "needs assistance which it is difficult to give him. He is losing the confidence of men near him, whose support any man in his position must have to be successful. His cardinal mistake is that he isolates himself, and allows nobody to see him; and by which he does not know what is going on in the very matter he is dealing with. He needs to have by his side a man of large experience. Will you not, for me, take that place?" [16] Montgomery Blair and Meigs arrived at St. Louis on September 12th. Their friends gave it out that their purpose was to look after the overland mails, but this deceived nobody. Popular gossip at once decided, said the St. Louis correspondent of the New York *Herald,* that the gov-

---

[15] Compare E. C. Kirkland, *The Peacemakers of 1864,* p. 145; A. G. Riddle, *Life of Benjamin Wade,* p. 287. It must be remembered, in interpreting Montgomery Blair's attitude toward such enemies of Frémont as General John Pope, that he himself had received a West Point training.

[16] Nicolay and Hay, *Lincoln,* IV, p. 413.

ernment was discontented "with the way General Frémont has expended money and made proclamations, while at the same time he does nothing in the way of getting the state into Federal possession." Frémont himself saw the handwriting on the wall, for he later wrote: [17]

Early in September, I began to feel the withdrawal of the confidence and support of the Administration. The visits of high officials charged with inquiry into the affairs of my department, and the simultaneous and sustained attacks of leading journals accumulated obstructions and disturbed my movements. In fact, my command virtually endured little over one month. But the measures which I had initiated had already taken enduring shape.

It was inevitable that Montgomery Blair, after talking with the embittered Frank and with others who were thoroughly prejudiced against Frémont, should come back with an unfavorable report. Deciding to his own satisfaction that the public welfare required Frémont's removal, on his return he recommended steps to this end.[18] Writing to Sumner, he declared that his brother was thoroughly aroused. Frank, he asserted, "cannot tolerate trifling in a great cause, and when he discovered that Frémont was a mere trifler, he was not to be reconciled to seeing the State overrun by pro-slavery myrmidons, by an empty proclamation threatening to deprive them of their negroes." Nothing could have been more unfair than to call Frémont "a mere trifler," and yet this was the impression the Blairs were vigorously attempting to diffuse both east and west.

At the same time the provisional governor of Missouri, Hamilton R. Gamble, who had been appointed by a state convention, was seeing Frémont on behalf of the President, and meeting none too cordial a reception. Lincoln had heard that Frémont as a radical Unionist and Gamble as a very conservative Unionist were not getting on well, and he sent Gamble a letter to show to the General. Their meeting took place at headquarters

---

[17] Frémont MSS, Bancroft Library; New York *Herald,* September 18, 1861.
[18] See *Report, Committee on the Conduct of the War,* Part III, p. 170.

on the fourteenth. According to Gamble's account, Frémont was very odd in manner, sitting silent and apparently distracted much of the time. But he made it clear that he did not believe that Gamble had coöperated properly with him, complaining that the governor had not made militia appointments which he desired, and had not dismissed various officers upon request. Gamble pointed out that he was bound by constitutional limitations. Next day Frémont sent the governor a note requesting another interview. Thereupon Gamble stayed in the city for two days before returning to the capital at Jefferson City; but on the first day Frémont failed to make an appointment, and on the second he failed to keep one that he himself had made! Gamble, according to his own story, waited half an hour in an anteroom, and then not being admitted, went away in disgust. Of all this he sent Lincoln a circumstantial though indirect report, which left it plain that he thought little of Frémont's capacity.[19]

Meanwhile, Mrs. Frémont, angry and overwrought, had embarked upon a course which made matters ten times worse for her husband. Aware of the fast-growing distrust in Washington, she resolved to strike at once and strike hard. She would go to Washington with a confidential letter from Frémont to Lincoln explaining the Western situation. She would seek a special interview with the President, defend her husband roundly, and denounce his accusers as they deserved. This was much the same hot-headed course which Benton had followed with Polk when a court-martial threatened Frémont. Doubtless the General knew that it would be better to keep the fiery Jessie at home, but she would suffer no restraint. On September 8th she set out, taking her English maid. After sitting for two nights and two days in the hot, overcrowded trains, at the close of the 10th she reached Washington, and drove to Willard's Hotel to meet some friends from New York.

[19] Gamble Papers; these were kindly searched for me by Miss Marguerite Potter. Gamble asked for arms for his state troops; Frémont promised them, but Gamble nevertheless wrote immediately afterward that he had no expectation of getting them.

Of her ensuing interview with Lincoln we have two accounts by the two participants. The President, in an informal conversation with some associates more than two years later, recorded by one of his secretaries, remarked:

> She sought an audience with me at midnight, and tasked me so violently with so many things, that I had to exercise all the awkward tact I have to avoid quarreling with her. She surprised me by asking why their enemy, Montgomery Blair, had been sent to Missouri. She more than once intimated that if General Frémont should decide to try conclusions with me, he could set up for himself.[20]

It is difficult to believe this last. Mrs. Frémont's story differs from Lincoln's in essential particulars. Her narrative is probably more accurate than Lincoln's casual conversation, some two years after the event, casually jotted down later by John Hay, for the interview must have been burned deep into her retentive memory. She writes: [21]

> I went for Gen. Frémont to Washington to give his letter into President Lincoln's hands—both of us doubted its reaching him in the usual way.
>
> I got in at the end of the day, tired, for I had travelled night and day from St. Louis in an ordinary car, and at once sent my card (from Willard's Hotel) with a written request to know when I might deliver the letter to the President.
>
> The messenger brought back a card on which was written, "Now, at once, A. Lincoln."
>
> It was nearly 9 P.M., the date September 10 [1861].
>
> As I had not been able to undress or lie down since leaving St. Louis I had intended taking a bath and going to bed at once. But I walked over immediately, just as I had been for two days and nights, in my dusty black mourning dress.
>
> Judge Edward Coles of New York city was with me.
>
> We were asked into the usual receiving room, the red room, next the large dining room. After some little waiting the President came in from that dining room by the farther door, leaving the door partly

---

[20] Nicolay and Hay, *Lincoln*, IV, p. 415.
[21] No date; Jessie Benton Frémont MSS, Bancroft Library.

open. As he crossed the room that door was still more widely set open.

I introduced Judge Coles, who then stepped into the deep doorway leading to the blue room—we were just by it—and there he remained walking to and fro, keeping in sight and hearing, just within the range of the doorway. For he was struck at once, as I was, by the President's manner, which was hard—and the first tones of his voice were repelling. Nor did he offer me a seat. He talked standing, and both voice and manner made the impression that I was to be got rid of briefly.

I often told over this interview to friends. It was clear to Judge Coles as to myself that the President's mind was made up against General Frémont—and decidedly against me. It would be too long to give you fuller detail. Briefly, in answer to his "Well?" I explained that the general wished so much to have his attention to the letter sent, that I had brought it to make sure it would reach him. He answered, not to that, but to the subject his own mind was upon, that *"It was a war for a great national idea, the Union, and that General Frémont should not have dragged the Negro into it— that he never would if he had consulted with Frank Blair. I sent Frank there to advise him."* The words italicized are exactly those of the President.

He first mentioned the Blairs, in this astonishing connection.

It was a *parti pris,* and as we walked back Judge Coles, who heard everything, said to me, "This ends Frémont's part in the war. Seward and Montgomery Blair will see to that, and Lincoln does not seem to see the injustice, the wrong of receiving secret reports against him made by a man authorized to do so, and as everyone knows, with his mind often clouded by drink and always governed by personal motives."

The President said he would send me his answer the next day.

The next day passed and nothing came from him. But Mr. Blair, Sr., came and told me many things. I had known him always and liked him, though Mr. Frémont did not. He was very angry with me for not letting Montgomery "manage things." He talked angrily and freely, as was natural to one who had grown up to defer to him, and in his excitement uncovered the intentions of the Administration regarding the protection of slavery.

That caused me to write note number two to the President. The originals of these must have been in possession oı the secretaries. I have the copies which I kept for Gen. Frémont. I confined my request to asking for the promised letter, and for copies of the charges against Mr. Frémont.

In the President's answer he says "not hearing from me," he had sent the answer by mail and declined to give letters without consent of owners. Yet he acted on them injuriously to the reputation of Gen. Frémont.

I did not risk a direct telegram to Gen. Frémont, but through my English maid I sent a cipher telegram in her name to an operator at headquarters, a man we could trust, and in that way the general was warned against being trapped into any steps aimed at by a show of "friendship" from Postmaster-General Blair. I returned immediately to St. Louis and found him working to "modify" and reshape the General's course—but he had been listened to only, and my arrival ended all attempts at concealing their real conduct. I did not speak to him then, or ever again.

In a later document, the unpublished part of the biographical *Memoir* of the explorer written by his wife and son, Mrs. Frémont adds some significant details to this brief narrative. She states that when she handed the President the General's letter, "he smiled with an expression that was not agreeable," and stood under the chandelier to read it. Meanwhile, trembling with fatigue, she sat down uninvited. When he had finished, the President told her that he had already written the General, and that he knew what the Administration wished done. To this she replied that Frémont thought it would be well if Mr. Lincoln explained personally his ideas and desires, for "the General feels he is at the great disadvantage of being perhaps opposed by people in whom you have every confidence." Lincoln was a little startled. "What do you mean? Persons of different views?" he inquired. Thereupon Mrs. Frémont began to talk about the difficulty of conquering by arms alone, and the necessity of appealing to the sentiment of England and other nations by a blow against slavery; expressing ideas that had certainly not been in Frémont's head when he issued his proclamation as an effort to intimidate the farmer-guerrillas of northern Missouri. Apparently nettled, the President remarked, "You are quite a female politician." He at once went on to speak vehemently of Frémont's mistake in converting a war for the Union into a war against slavery.

Mrs. Frémont also writes that when Francis P. Blair came to see her early the next day, he grew heated. "Well," he said, "who would have expected you to do such a thing as this, to come here and find fault with the President? Look what you have done for Frémont; you have made the President his enemy!" The old editor, saying that Montgomery would talk with Frémont "and bring him to his senses," gave her to understand that five days earlier Lincoln had received from Frank Blair a letter containing various charges against Frémont; and that it was because of this letter that the Postmaster-General had been sent to St. Louis to make an examination. As she has related, she asked Lincoln in "note number two" for a copy of these charges. The President's reply was brief:

It is not exactly correct, as you say you were told by the elder Mr. Blair, to say that I sent Postmaster-General Blair to St. Louis to examine into that department and report. Postmaster-General Blair did go, with my approbation, to see and converse with Gen. Frémont as a friend. I do not feel authorized to furnish you with copies of letters in my possession, without the consent of the writers. No impression has been made on my mind against the honor or integrity of General Frémont, and I now enter my protest against being understood as acting in any hostility towards him.

Taken together, Mrs. Frémont's display of temper in Washington and Montgomery Blair's highly prejudiced report concerning affairs in St. Louis unquestionably deepened the President's feeling that Frémont had been an unfortunate choice for the Western Department. Jessie, having done irreparable harm, turned back to St. Louis. Lincoln still showed patience with the General. But Mrs. Frémont had no patience with any one. Her burning resentment against the Blairs, her belief that they

had devised a conspiracy against her husband, made her anything but a calm and prudent assistant at headquarters. She
was no sooner back at the Brant Mansion than she inspired
another of Frémont's indiscreet steps.

This was nothing less than the arrest of Frank Blair, September 18th, on a charge of insubordination. Frémont telegraphed Cameron that "information of such positive character
has come to my knowledge, implicating Col. F. P. Blair, Jr.,
1st Missouri Volunteers, in insidious and dishonorable efforts
to bring my authority into contempt with the government, and
to undermine my influence as an officer, that I have ordered
him in arrest, and shall submit charges to you for his trial." [22]

The hatred between the two men was now so intense that
neither would listen to reason regarding the other. Blair sin-
cerely believed that Frémont was a confused, incompetent
trifler whose continued control would soon lose the whole state
to the Confederates. Frémont sincerely believed that Blair was
an ambitious scoundrel, frequently drunk, and always eager
to advance his own fortunes by any means whatever. He and
Mrs. Frémont make much in their manuscript *Memoirs* of the
clothing contract and similar matters; they believed Blair willing to wreck the Union cause to satisfy his private plans and
grudges. Mrs. Frémont, as Montgomery wrote a friend, was
mainly responsible for the arrest—it was "General Jessie's
doing." The Postmaster-General sent Frémont a sensible telegram, asking his brother's release, and concluding: "This is no
time for strife except with the enemies of the country." [23] But
for a time Blair refused to be released, demanding a trial at
which his charges could be sifted. Meanwhile, St. Louis was in
a furor of excitement over the affair, and the Unionist party
suffered.

For both Frémont and the Federal cause, the episode could
hardly have occurred at a more unhappy time; for once again
a heavy military blow was about to fall.

[22] MS *Memoirs,* Bancroft Library.
[23] W. E. Smith, *The Blair Family,* II, p. 77.

The military situation in the West had developed rapidly in early September, and had now reached a point where in one quarter it offered the brightest hopes, while in another it threatened a second heavy disaster. The hopeful quarter was the Mississippi River area near and below Cairo and Paducah. Two or three days before Mrs. Frémont set off for Washington, a new brigadier-general named Ulysses S. Grant marched into Paducah, at the mouth of the Tennessee River a short distance below Cairo, and took possession of this portal to a great waterway. He had acted in the nick of time, without orders from Frémont, for Leonidas Polk was about to seize the town. Frémont deserves credit, however, for having on August 28th placed Grant in command of southeastern Missouri and southern Illinois with headquarters at Cairo; the region where the great campaign to open up the Mississippi was certain to develop. He gave Grant written instructions to take possession of points threatened by the Confederates on the Missouri and Kentucky shores. In his manuscript *Memoirs* the explorer states that he chose Grant for this position, when men near him would have sent General John Pope, because he had discerned his unusual qualities:

I believed him to be a man of great activity and of promptness in obeying orders without question or hesitation. For that reason I gave General Grant this important command at this critical period. I did not then consider him a great general, for the qualities which led him to success had not had the opportunity for their development. I selected him for qualities I could not find combined in any other man, for General Grant was of unassuming character, not given to self-elation, of dogged persistence and of iron will.[24]

Grant had the able John A. Rawlins with him.

A great part of Frémont's troops were now disposed in this quarter, and he looked forward to a rapid advance down the river. The letter he sent to Lincoln by Mrs. Frémont was pri-

[24] MS *Memoirs*, Bancroft Library.

marily an outline of this plan, and shows a genuine comprehension of the strategic situation: [25]

I...ask your attention to the position of affairs in Kentucky. As
the rebel troops driven out from Missouri had invaded Kentucky
in considerable force, and by occupying Union City, Hickman, and
Columbus were preparing to seize Paducah and attack Cairo, I
judged it impossible, without losing important advantages, to defer
any longer a forward movement. For this purpose I have drawn
from the Missouri side a part of the force which had been stationed
at Bird's Point, Cairo, and Cape Girardeau, to Fort Holt and
Paducah, of which places we have taken possession. As the rebel
forces outnumber ours, and the counties of Kentucky, between the
Mississippi and Tennessee Rivers, as well as those along the latter
and the Cumberland, are strongly secessionist, it becomes impera-
tively necessary to have the cooperation of the loyal Union forces
under Generals Anderson and Nelson, as well as of those already
encamped opposite Louisville, under General Rousseau.

I have reinforced, yesterday, Paducah with two regiments, and
will continue to strengthen the position with men and artillery. As
soon as Gen. Smith, who commands there, is reinforced sufficiently
to enable him to spread his forces, he will have to take and hold
Mayfield and Lovelaceville, controlling in this way the mouths of
both the Tennessee and the Cumberland Rivers.

Meanwhile, General Grant would take possession of the entire
Cairo and Fulton Railroad, Piketown, New Madrid, and the shore
of the Mississippi opposite Hickman and Columbus. The foregoing
disposition having been affected, a combined attack will be made
upon Columbus, and if successful in that, upon Hickman, while
Rousseau and Nelson will move in concert by railroad to Nashville,
Tenn., occupying the State capital, and, with an adequate force,
New Providence.

The conclusion of this movement would be a combined advance
toward Memphis, on the Mississippi, as well as the Memphis & Ohio
Railroad, and I trust the result would be a glorious one to the
country.

[25] *Official Records*, Series I, Vol. III, p. 478.

In its main outlines this was a sensible plan, which did credit to Frémont. But while the prospects in this quarter looked bright, in northwest Missouri another defeat was imminent. Here Colonel James A. Mulligan, with the Chicago Irish Brigade and some Illinois and Missouri troops, had just taken up a position at Lexington, some 160 miles up the Missouri River. Reaching it on September 9th, he had hastily thrown up entrenchments. A Confederate army under Sterling Price immediately advanced upon him from southwestern Missouri, where the battle of Wilson's Creek had brought a large influx of Confederate volunteers. Mulligan appealed for reinforcements, and labored frenziedly in gathering munitions and forage. After preliminary skirmishing, on September 18th Price began his attack in force. His army far outnumbered the Federals, and the result was never in doubt. Though the Irish soldiers made a gallant defense, their water supply was finally cut off, and on September 21st they were compelled to surrender. It was an even more stinging reverse than the defeat of Lyon. With a loss of only twenty-five men killed, Price exultantly reported the capture of 3,500 men (including home guards), 7 guns, large quantities of munitions, and $100,000 worth of commissary stores. When men realized that a small army had been lost in the center of a supposedly Union State, a tremendous cry of indignation went up. For a week the fate of Lexington had been in the balance, and the press had reported every scene in the drama to an anxious nation.

The Missouri River, though low at that season, was open. It seemed feasible to send Federal troops up it by steamboat. Union detachments were stationed at various points in northern Missouri, some within short marching distance. Why, men demanded, did not Frémont hurry reinforcements to Lexington in time? Frank Blair's organ, the *Evening News,* carried an angry editorial on September 23rd. Mulligan, it declared, had been confident "that with forty thousand friendly Federal troops within a few days' march of him," he would be rescued. "But the heroic officer calculated too largely on the coöperation of the authorities at St. Louis." They, with their 40,000 men, their vast stores of munitions, their command of all the railroads and steamboats, had let a ragged, ill-armed, unpaid Confederate army march all the way from Springfield and bag an important town, an army, and invaluable supplies.

Certainly Frémont should never have sent Mulligan to his exposed position in Lexington without guarding against movements which might cut him off. Nevertheless, he was in part the victim of circumstances. His Department, far from having 40,000 men available, was desperately poor in properly trained troops. Schuyler Colfax, arriving in St. Louis on September 14th, when the whole city was excited by news that Price was advancing upon Lexington, hurried to Frémont and asked if he could not send rescuing troops. The General replied: "Mr. Colfax, I will tell you confidentially how many men we have in St. Louis, though I would not have it published on the streets for my life. The opinion in the city is that we have 20,000 men here, and this gives us strength. If it were known here what was the actual number, our enemies would be promptly informed." He rang for the muster-rolls. They showed that the city had but 6,800 men, home guards and all; and of this force there were only two full regiments, the remainder being fragmentary, undisciplined detachments of 200 to 600 men. Said Colfax: "This is not really enough for the proper defense of St. Louis; but even so, couldn't you spare some for the emergency?" He tells us that tears stood in Frémont's eyes as the General handed him two telegrams.

One from Secretary Cameron, dated September 14th, stated that the President had determined to call upon him for "five thousand well-armed infantry, to be sent here without a moment's delay." The other was from Winfield Scott of the same date. "Detach five thousand infantry from your department, to come here without delay," it ordered, "and report the number of troops that will be left with you. The President dictates." Colfax asked Frémont if he could not expostulate with the government. "No," said he, "that would be insubordination, with which I have already been unjustly charged. The capital must be again in danger, and must be saved, even if Missouri fall and I sacrifice myself." [26]

Frémont hurriedly telegraphed Governors Morton of Indiana and Dennison of Ohio for aid, but both replied that they were under orders to send all available troops to the East. He sent orders on September 13th and 14th to Generals Pope at Palmyra, Sturgis at Mexico, and Jefferson C. Davis at Jefferson City, to march troops at once to the relief of Lexington; this a full week before the capitulation. [27] Pope promised that by the 18th he would have two full regiments of infantry, a detachment of cavalry, and 4 pieces of artillery in the threatened town, and that by the 19th he would have 4,000 soldiers there. Yet none of them arrived. Jefferson C. Davis set out, but let his troops fire into each other in the darkness, and failed to reach his objective. Sturgis came within a few miles of the river opposite Lexington, and then hearing of Price's heavy forces (which rumor exaggerated to 35,000 men), and learning that he had seized the ferries, timidly retired, though if he had hurried on he might have saved the day. In a word, three commanders showed insufficient energy, and Frémont was left to shoulder the blame for their failures.

It was now a perfect storm of abuse that he faced, and only the fervent belief of great masses of northern haters of slavery in his ability and earnestness enabled him to continue his work. After the *Evening News* published its bitter editorial on the fall of Lexington, he suppressed it for a day and arrested Blair's friend Charles G. Ramsay, its proprietor—an indiscreet step, for which friendly Eastern newspapers properly criticized him. A malignant letter appeared in the *National Intelligencer*, asking why with his 60,000 splendidly equipped soldiers, "the very élite of the West," he did not drive the half-naked, ill-armed rebels out of the state. [28] So he now had 60,000 men!

---

[26] Colfax tells this in *Congressional Globe,* March 7, 1862, p. 1128.

[27] Frémont Order Book, Bancroft Library.

[28] See New York *Herald,* September 21, 1861.

This letter was reprinted all over the North. Signed "A Missourian," it bore sufficient resemblance to the *Evening News* editorial to indicate that Frank Blair inspired or wrote it. Despatches from Washington declared that the President and his Cabinet were "amazed" that Frémont had failed to relieve Mulligan.[29] Meanwhile, exaggerated stories of the extravagance in his Department passed from tongue to tongue. His enemies sneered at one of his orders for 500 tons of ice, and talked of the sherry cobblers which his officers expected to enjoy; the fact being that the ice was supplied on a requisition from the surgical staff for use in Western hospitals. He was accused of surrounding himself with a set of sharpers from California, and winking at their thievery. Worst of all, Frank Blair and others gave currency to the report that he was thinking of erecting a western military republic, similar to that which Sam Houston had set up in Texas. It was a ridiculous charge, but it found believers even in Washington. Lincoln's secretary Nicolay left a sealed envelope in his manuscripts endorsed "A private paper, Conversation with the President, October 2, 1861." The first sentence ran: "Frémont ready to rebel." It is safe to say that Frémont never entertained a disloyal thought in his life.[30]

On September 26th Frank Blair, who had now been released from arrest, filed formal charges against Frémont, which through Adjutant-General Lorenzo Thomas were laid before Lincoln. They included neglect of duty, disobedience of orders, conduct unbecoming an officer, extravagance and waste, and despotic and tyrannical conduct. Among the specific charges were Frémont's alleged failure to repair to St. Louis promptly; his neglect to reinforce Lyon and Mulligan; his suffering Brigadier-General Hurlburt, "a common drunkard," to continue in command; his refusal to see people who sought him

[29] New York *Herald, Tribune,* September 23, 24, 1861.
[30] Helen N. Nicolay, *Personal Traits of Abraham Lincoln.* See Ida M. Tarbell, *Lincoln,* II, Ch. 24, for Dr. Emil Preetorius's angry statement on this charge. A shrewd St. Louis observer, he pronounces Frémont "a patriot and a most unselfish man."

on urgent public business; his violation of Presidential orders in the emancipation proclamation; and his persistence in keeping disreputable.persons in his employ. It was a blanket indictment. Every one who knew the situation in Missouri was aware that it grossly misrepresented Frémont's conduct there; every one who knew Frank Blair was aware that all his statements demanded a liberal discounting. His fits of temper were always leading him into extravagant utterances and rash acts. The Blair papers reveal that on October 7th Frank Blair was writing his brother Montgomery in the following terms:[31]

I think God has made up his mind to ruin this nation, and that the only way to save it is to kick that pack of old women who compose the Cabinet into the sea. I never since I was born imagined that such a lot of poltroons and apes could be gathered together from the four quarters of the globe as Old Abe has succeeded in bringing together in his Cabinet, and I believe that the first duty of every patriot is to stop fighting Jeff Davis and turn in on our own Government and make something out of it with which to carry on the war against the traitors. Jeff Davis and his whole crew have not done us half the harm that has been inflicted upon the country by the cowardice, ignorance, and stupidity of Lincoln's Administration.

At a later date the nation learned more about Frank Blair's infirmities of temper; in 1868 his wild utterances cost the Democratic ticket of Seymour and Blair all its slender chances of victory. But at this time his name was still potent and his charges impressed the country. The New York *Times* under Henry J. Raymond took them up and called for Frémont's dismissal. The harried commander in St. Louis could now see how much his failure to conciliate the powerful Blair clan was costing him. Whether Frémont was right or Frank Blair was right on specific matters of fact was a minor question. The major consideration was that their quarrel was dividing the Unionists of Missouri into two glowering factions, and was going far

[31] Smith, *The Blair Family,* II, pp. 83, 84.

toward paralyzing all their activities in the war. Such a division could not long be tolerated. And no matter how much of the right was on Frémont's side, Lincoln could not forget that Montgomery Blair was in his Cabinet; he, who thought constantly of the wavering border, could never forget that the Blairs were the most powerful personal force in the Border States. He was still keenly resentful of the radical demand that he make the extinction of slavery a direct object of the war, and he knew Frémont was a radical hero.

XXXI

The End of the "Hundred Days"

THE first summer of the War was passing into autumn; McClellan was still drilling his Army of the Potomac, still sneering at the Administration in letters to his wife, still exaggerating the forces of the enemy; Secretary Cameron was rapidly losing the confidence of intelligent observers; and northerners looked back upon a series of defeats— Bull Run, Ball's Bluff, Wilson's Creek, Lexington—with scarcely a victory to counterbalance them. The uneasy nation was beginning to demand that the Administration give it commanders who would move forward and win victories. To this demand, McClellan was deaf; while Frémont, with a weaker and much more poorly equipped force, was necessarily keenly aware of it. Working night and day under a sword of Damocles, he knew that within a few weeks the thread which sustained it would probably break. He had but one hope. Before those weeks expired, he must win a victory which would restore his prestige and cause the Administration to stay its hand.

Frémont had realized this fact at once when Lexington fell. Reporting the disaster to Winfield Scot, he added, in an effort to forestall criticism: "I am taking the field myself, and hope to destroy the enemy, either before or after the junction of the forces under McCulloch. Please notify the President immediately." Scott replied that the President was glad to see him hastening to the scene of action; "his words are, 'he expects you to repair the disaster at Lexington without loss of time.'"

Sterling Price, with his booty and prisoners, was retreating from Lexington to join McCulloch's army in southwestern Missouri. Frémont at once reorganized his available troops in five divisions, and ordered the commanders, Pope, McKinstry, Hunter, Sigel, and Asboth, to concentrate at Springfield, still held by the enemy. It was easy to give the order, but for the commanders to obey was a different matter; for the divisions were without adequate transportation, rations, uniforms, or munitions for a campaign. Congresman Gurley was frenziedly writing Lincoln on October 1st that the lack of supplies was scandalous, and that if Frémont were not given men, money, and arms, even St. Louis might fall.

Although Lincoln had now virtually made up his mind to remove Frémont, with his usual patience he determined first to send Secretary Cameron, who had inclined to Frémont's side, to make a personal inquiry.[1] He gave Cameron authority to displace the General at once if he thought it expedient, but asked for careful action. The Secretary stopped in St. Louis, where he talked with the Blair-Gamble group, and received a vivid impression of the schism in the Union ranks. Near the middle of October he reached Frémont's new field headquarters at Tipton, Missouri. He found the camp in confusion, with the troops badly in need of arms, ammunition, and clothing. Evidently Cameron had made up his mind in St. Louis to remove Frémont, but he now—seeing the general's energy—changed it:

I had an interview with General Frémont [he wrote Lincoln on October 14th], and in conversation with him showed him an order for his removal. He is very much mortified, pained, and, I thought, humiliated. He made an earnest appeal to me, saying that he had come to Missouri, at the request of the government, to assume a very responsible command, and that when he reached this state he found himself without troops and without any preparations for an army; that he had exerted himself, as he believed, with great

[1] Attorney-General Edward Bates wrote his brother-in-law, Governor Gamble, on September 27th: "I thought (I wrote so to several of my friends at St. Louis) that Frémont would certainly be relieved, but this day I find that that result is not probable, therefore I am in deep trouble on account of our poor betrayed and sacrificed state.... General Frémont is not to be removed— at least until he has had a full opportunity to retrieve his fortunes, or to ruin our state utterly and endanger our cause."

energy, and now had around him a fine army, with everything to make success certain; that he was now in pursuit of his enemy, whom he believed were now within his reach; and that to recall him at this moment would not only destroy him, but render his whole expedition useless. In reply to this appeal, I told him that I would withhold the order until my return to Washington, giving him the interim to prove the reality of his hopes as to reaching and capturing the enemy, giving him to understand that, should he fail, he must give place to some other officer. He assured me that, should he fail, he would resign at once.[2]

Both Pope and Hunter gave Cameron a highly unfavorable opinion of Frémont's military capacity and acts, and both regarded the apparent plan of campaign with mystified astonishment. Nevertheless, Frémont was actively taking the field while McClellan, with every advantage of supplies and official support, was still drilling his army in Virginia. Cameron did well to refrain from dismissing a commander really eager to fight.

But from the moment he left St. Louis Frémont felt that he was between two enemies, the Confederates in front, his personal assailants in the rear. Frank Blair was continuing his attacks with increasing bitterness. Released from arrest at Montomery's request on September 24th, he had been stung to rage by rebukes from Frémont, who accused him of using his family position to lay deliberately false statements before the President. In submitting his formal charges against Frémont, Blair published a letter to Adjutant-General Lorenzo Thomas which answered this accusation in withering terms.[3] For this and his continued efforts to undermine the General, Frémont had him rearrested; and though this episode was soon terminated, it left him (as his biographer says) a raging lion. With Blair against him, with provisional-Governor Gamble against him, with several of his own generals against him, Frémont was in an agonizing position. Just before leaving St.

[2] Nicolay and Hay, *Lincoln*, IV, p. 430.
[3] Published in New York *Herald*, October 9, 1861.

Louis for the field he poured out his bitter emotions in a letter to a New York friend:[4]

I . . . send you this hurried note in the midst of the last arrangements before leaving.

We have to contend with an enemy having no posts to garrison and no lines of transportation to defend or guard, whose whole force can be turned at will to any one point, while we have from Leavenworth and from Fort Scott to Paducah to keep protected.

I wish to say to you that, though the position is difficult, I am competent to it, and also to meet the enemy in the field. I am not able at the same time to attend to the enemy at home. It is a shame to the country that an officer going to the field, his life in his hands, solely actuated by the desire to serve his country and win for himself its good opinions, with no other objects, should be destroyed by a system of concentrated attacks utterly without foundation. Charges are spoken of when there are none to be made. What is the object of the repetition of these falsehoods, except to familiarize the public mind to the idea that something is wrong? Already our credit, which was good, is shaken in consequence of the newspaper intimations of my being removed. Money is demanded by those furnishing supplies. To defend myself would require the time that is necessary to and belongs to my duty against the enemy. If permitted by the country, this state of things will not fail to bring on disorder. . . . My private character comes in only incidentally. I defend it because, naturally, his reputation is dear to any man; but only incidentally. This is the foundation of many of my acts, and will be if I stay here. Everything that hurts, impedes, or embarrasses the work entrusted to me I strike at without hesitation. I take the consequences. The worst that can happen to me is relief from great labor.

The advance toward southwestern Missouri in pursuit of Price's retreating army lurched forward as rapidly as unfavorable circumstances would allow. When Frémont and his staff

---

[4] Published in St. Louis *Democrat*, September 28, 1861. This journal, like the *Republic*, was as friendly to Frémont as the *Evening News* was hostile. But Frank Blair believed that Frémont had obtained their friendship by a mixture of threats and material inducements.

reached Jefferson City on September 27, 1861, they found a multitude of difficulties awaiting them at Camp Lilly, as the place had been named in honor of his daughter. A thousand wagons sent him from the East had proved to be made of rotten wood, and were breaking down everywhere on the roads and in the streets.[5] By October 7th, all the troops which Frémont had been able to collect were on the road for Tipton, one hundred sixty miles from St. Louis, where they again paused. Rations were scanty, and sometimes the men were on half their proper allowance of food. Large herds of cattle had to be collected by foraging parties and tons of corn brought in to be ground at Frémont's portable mills. The dearth of horses and vehicles continued, and the march, as one young aide said, was a continual "wait for the wagon."

Yet the obstacles were slowly overcome, and Frémont's hopes rose higher and higher. Writing to Jessie in St. Louis, he declared that his men would emulate the fine marches of the California Battalion. "The army is in the best of spirits, and before we get through I will show you a little California practise, that is, if we are not interrupted." Dreams of a spectacular achievement floated before his eyes. He would scatter Price's army and push rapidly on south. "My plan is New Orleans straight," he wrote, "Foote to join on the river below. I think it can be done gloriously, especially if secrecy can be kept.... It would precipitate the war forward and end it soon and victoriously." [6]

Mid-October found his steadily growing army under way for Warsaw on the Osage River, where the fleeing Price had burned the bridge behind him. Here a trained engineer, using men from the ranks, succeeded in stretching a pontoon bridge, eight hundred feet long, across the stream within thirty-six hours. Some of the lumber came from the demolition of old houses, but most of it was cut green in the neighboring woods. It was no sooner finished than the army was streaming forward again

[5] John R. Howard, *Remembrance of Things Past*, Ch. 19.
[6] Jessie Benton Frémont, *The Story of the Guard*, pp. 72*ff*., 85.

upon Springfield, the key to that section of the state and the city near which Lyon had met defeat two months earlier. The General had communicated his dream of a march down the Mississippi to his men, and the watchword went about: "New Orleans and home again by summer!" [7]

Frémont paid little heed to obstacles in this march, and where horses and wagons were lacking, sent off into the country about for them. He had established supply depots with about a million rations at Tipton and two million at Jefferson City; but he was enough of a frontiersman to know how to subsist in large part on the country and to meet problems as they arose. Food taken from loyal citizens was paid for in government orders; that taken from secessionists was simply confiscated.[8] Most of his division commanders showed the same spirit and coöperated zealously in the advance. The glaring exception was John Pope, whose unexpected failure to reinforce Mulligan at Lexington, after promising to do so, still rankled in Frémont's mind. "Pope," said Frank Blair later, out of intimate knowledge,[9] "is a braggart and a liar, with some courage, perhaps, but not much capacity." Rising in time to high command, he made an utter botch of his brief campaign against Lee. He had done well in stamping out the guerrilla warfare in northern Missouri, but he now showed nothing less than a spirit of insubordination.

When Frémont ordered him to join in the forward movement, Pope wrote Hunter that he was stupefied by the way in which the General ignored actual conditions. "There is not transportation enough," he declared, "to move this army one hundred yards." He complained that the troops had not been properly organized into brigades and divisions, and that he had no supply trains or cavalry. These statements were partly inaccurate, and showed a disposition to magnify every possible difficulty. The ragged, ill-armed, ill-supplied Confederates,

[7] *Ibid.*, pp. 45, 46.
[8] MS *Memoirs,* Bancroft Library.
[9] Welles, *Diary,* I, pp. 104, 119.

living on the country, found no difficulty in moving where they liked. Pope had caught the spirit of contempt for Frémont in certain St. Louis and Washington circles, and knew that powerful men would only too gladly support his recalcitrance. To Hunter, he wrote a few days later in a tone of sheer impudent scorn of his commander: [10]

I received your note yesterday morning and I am really sorry I could not come down to see you before I left Syracuse. I am anxious to know the result of the Secretary's visit and its object. Upon his action on the subject, in my judgment, rests the safety of this command from great suffering. If we attempt to go south of the Osage without supplies for at least a month, and without much better preparation for everything that exists now, I do not believe that one half of these troops will ever return alive. The winter is coming on us. The men of this division are without overcoats, their clothes in rags, and only one blanket apiece; no provision trains or depots organized, and, so far as I can see, no object in view.

I shall, however, move from here and occupy the point designated, with five regiments, being all I can get anything like transportation for. I can, perhaps, carry eight or ten days' rations for the five regiments by making very short marches....

Each division commander is left to himself. I don't know where to look for provisions short of St. Louis, or where for quartermaster or any other stores, short of the same place, neither do I know to whom I can apply for anything this side of St. Louis. I have written and telegraphed for 300,000 rations, as I intend to establish at Otterville a depot of provisions and of such stores as I can get for my own command. Altogether, this is the most remarkable campaign I ever saw, heard of, or read of.

Frémont was led by his scouts to believe that at a point a little beyond Springfield the Confederates would face about and give battle. We now know that this was actually their intention. Price wrote his superiors: [11]

[10] Copy in Frémont MSS, dated October 18, 1861; Compare *Official Records,* Series I, Vol. III, p. 527.

[11] *Official Records,* Series I, Vol. III, pp. 731, 732.

I am now falling back on Pineville, where General McCulloch and myself have concluded to make a stand. Should the Federal forces advance from Springfield for the purpose of attacking us, we will act on the defensive, depending on the rugged nature of the country to compensate for any inequality in numbers. Our position will be so chosen that we will be able to make our artillery effective....

McCulloch also wrote that he had agreed with Price to fight a battle in Missouri, although the combined Confederate armies amounted only to about seventeen thousand men, and he feared the outcome. Pineville is a county seat in the extreme southwestern corner of Missouri. But Pope, Hunter, and the Washington authorities, lacking Frémont's special information, felt almost certain that the Confederates would not pause until they were safe in the wilds of Arkansas, and that Frémont was conducting a wildgoose chase. To Pope, it seemed a criminal enterprise, and he wrote Hunter:[12]

When our forces have succeeded in reaching Neosho, or Arkansas itself, what is to be accomplished, or rather what does any sane man suppose will be the result? The prospect before us is appalling, and we seem to be led by madmen. Of course, Gen. Frémont and the men around him, whose official existence depends upon his not being superseded, are desperate. But should they be permitted to drag to destruction, or at least to great and unnecessary suffering, the 30,000 men of this army, for no other purpose than to save, if possible, their own official lives?

While Major Zagonyi and his so-called Frémont Bodyguard of picked cavalrymen, 150 strong, were delivering a victorious and memorable charge against the Confederate garrison at Springfield,[13] and while Frémont's army was pushing beyond that town, the sands of the President's patience were running out. He feared the loss of invaluable troops in the hills of

[12] Copy in Frémont MSS; Pope to Hunter, October 26, 1861.
[13] For accounts of this spirited affair see Moore, *Rebellion Record*, III, pp. 235-239. Zagonyi had three companies, while the garrison numbered 2,000 men. Zagonyi wrote that he had never seen such bravery as his cavalry showed: "Their war cry, 'Frémont and the Union,' broke forth like thunder."

BRILLIANT CHARGE OF GENERAL FRÉMONT'S BODYGUARD THROUGH THE TOWN OF SPRINGFIELD, MISSOURI, ON OCTOBER 24, 1861

(From *Harper's Weekly*)

GENERAL FRÉMONT'S ARMY ON THE MARCH THROUGH SOUTHWESTERN MISSOURI

(From *Harper's Weekly*)

Arkansas. Adjutant-General Lorenzo Thomas had gone to St. Louis with Cameron and made an inspection of his own; and upon his return he published a report caustically arraigning Frémont for incompetence, extravagance, and irregularity.[14] Thomas had moved exclusively in the Blair circle in Missouri and formed his conclusions there. He declared, naturally enough, that in the opinion of many observers Frémont "is more fond of the pomp than of the realities of the war—that his mind is incapable of fixed attention or strong concentration—that by his mismanagement of affairs since his arrival in Missouri, the State has almost been lost—and that if he is continued in command the worst results may be anticipated." This conclusion he supported by a series of hearsay allegations. Obviously, none but a prejudiced witness would talk about the state being lost when order was wholly restored and the last important Confederate force was scurrying for Arkansas. It was widely known that Thomas disliked Frémont, that he had opposed Frémont's appointment, and that from the beginning he had spoken abusively of Frémont.[15] It was also obvious that his allegations, when analyzed, contained little specific evidence. He reported that there had been irregularities in the pay department, and that the chief paymaster complained of improper orders; that the quartermaster in St. Louis instanced confused and irregular requisitions; and that many people were suspicious of the contracts Frémont had let. While all this was true, irregularities and fraudulent contracts marked every stage of the initial war effort East and West, from Cameron's office down; the country could better condone them than excessive caution and inactivity. Of such evidence as a court of law would admit Thomas offered little. Nevertheless, as a general impression his report was damaging.

And, unfortunately for Frémont, Thomas by no means stood alone. General Hunter had categorically told Cameron that he

---

[14] *Official Records,* Series I, Vol. III, p. 540*ff.;* New York *Tribune,* October 30, 1861.
[15] Jessie Benton Frémont, *Story of the Guard,* pp. 86, 87.

did not think Frémont fit for the command. Lincoln had hoped that Frémont would make Hunter his adviser and guide; but the two had not got on—Hunter underrated Frémont, and Frémont, thinking that Hunter wished to harass him, detached him for a comparatively unimportant field command. Brigadier-General S. R. Curtis of St. Louis expressed the same conclusion. "In my judgment," he wrote the President, "General Frémont lacks the intelligence, the experience, and the sagacity necessary to his command." [16]

At the same time Elihu B. Washburne, who visited St. Louis at the head of a Congressional subcommittee upon government contracts, wrote members of the Administration that "such robbery, fraud, extravagance, peculation as have developed in Frémont's department can hardly be conceived of." He spoke of a "horde of pirates" ruining the credit of the government.[17] His phraseology was exaggerated; he had accepted without independent investigation the stories of the Blair circle and of some disappointed contractors; moreover, he was an economical Yankee (later known in Congress as a Treasury Watchdog) who had not yet grasped the fact that it is impossible to wage war without a lavish expenditure. All Frémont's contracts for fortification, supplies, foodstuffs, arms, steamboats, and so on, totaled only about twelve million dollars. At the moment, however, Washburne's voice carried great weight. Moreover, even men cordially disposed toward Frémont joined the chorus of criticism. Gustav Koerner wrote his wife that the confusion was preposterous and that he might resign at any time. The evidence for the essential features of the indictment against the General seemed overwhelming.

It was a bizarre situation. It was bizarre in that the commander of the West, while thus denounced as incompetent by

[16] Nicolay and Hay, *Lincoln*, IV, Ch. 24. A friend of Governor Gamble's in Washington, Charles Gibson, also preferred charges against Frémont to the President; Gibson to Gamble, September 27, 1861 (Gamble Papers).

[17] See his letter to Chase, October 31, 1861 (Chase MSS). Gideon Welles states that Washburne had the reputation of being the meanest man in the House; *Diary*, I, p. 234.

a vigorous group in Missouri and by the Administration's best observers, was regarded with admiring devotion by his army, applauded by most Unionists of the state, and looked upon as a hero by nearly all the radicals of the North. It was bizarre in that Frémont, exalted one hour by his expectation of crushing Price's army and turning triumphantly against the Confederates on the Mississippi, was depressed the next by Pope's and Hunter's insubordination and the fear of a sudden removal. His letters to Jessie show a feverish alternation of hope and despair. Just as he had the West well in hand, he felt that he was being stabbed in the back. "I assure you I am getting pretty well tired of being badgered in this way," he wrote, with an express threat of resignation.[18] To drop his load would be a relief, he added; but he could not think calmly of the scoundrels who were throwing away brave lives and imperiling the war to gratify their base ambitions.

To Lincoln it appeared that a change was imperative. Yet even at the last he acted with characteristic forbearance. Attorney-General Bates's diary shows that as late as October 22nd the Cabinet hesitated, with Seward, Chase, and Cameron all for delay, and the President in "painful and mortifying doubt." On October 24th, Lincoln wrote an order relieving Frémont from his command, which was to be given to General Hunter; and he despatched it by a personal friend to General Curtis in St. Louis:

Dear Sir [he wrote Curtis], On receipt of this, with the accompanying enclosures, you will take safe, certain, and suitable measures to have the enclosure addressed to Major-General Frémont delivered to him with all reasonable dispatch, subject to these conditions only, that if, when General Frémont shall be reached by the messenger—yourself or anyone sent by you—he shall then have, in personal command, fought and won a battle, or shall then be in the immediate presence of the enemy in expectation of a battle, it is not to be delivered, but held for further orders. After, and not

[18] Jessie Benton Frémont, *The Story of the Guard*, p. 174*ff*.

till after, the delivery to General Frémont, let the inclosure addressed to General Hunter be delivered to him.

Under these circumstances, the final scene of the "hundred days" was played out. Frémont's army on November 2nd was encamped just beyond Springfield, with all dispositions made for an immediate advance and battle; for on information furnished him by Generals Sigel and Asboth, division commanders, he learned that the advance guard of the enemy was on Wilson's Creek, nine miles distant. The spirit of the troops was high. With nearly all of them the commander was enormously popular, and they were convinced that a victory was at hand. He was serenaded and cheered at every opportunity. The official messenger with the order of dismissal entered the camp by stratagem, and after much difficulty in gaining an audience was taken at nightfall before Frémont.

The general [he tells us], was sitting at the end of quite a long table facing the door by which I entered. I never can forget the appearance of the man as he sat there, with his piercing eye and his hair parted in the middle. I ripped from my coat lining the document, which had been sewed in there, and handed the same to him, which he nervously took and opened. He glanced at the superscription, and then at the signature at the bottom, not looking at the contents. A frown came over his brow, and he slammed the papers down on the table and said, "Sir, how did you get admission into my lines?"[19]

Frémont had lost his command—lost it under circumstances of the most humiliating character. Many of his officers were dismissed with him, without pay, on the ground that their commissions had been irregularly issued. But the sting of the blow was largely taken away by the outburst of feeling which it produced in his army and all over the North.

The intelligence, spreading like a prairie fire through the camps at Springfield, aroused indescribable indignation and

[19] Tarbell, *Lincoln*, II, Ch. 24. Frémont writes: "The order had been hurried forward by General Hunter, who superseded me." *Battles and Leaders*, I, p. 287.

excitement.[20] Officers by the dozen declared they would resign at once. Many companies threw down their arms, saying they would fight under nobody but Frémont. Impromptu mass-meetings were held in every tented street. The General had to spend much of the evening expostulating with officers and men and urging them to stick by their posts. The German soldiers talked loudly of resisting General Hunter when he came to assume command, and Frémont felt impelled to issue strict orders that there should be no insubordination and no demonstration when he left. Finally the troops quieted down, but their spirit was gone. "It would be impossible to exaggerate the gloom which pervaded our camps," wrote the New York *Herald's* correspondent of the scene the next morning, "and nothing but General Frémont's urgent endeavors prevented it from ripening into general mutiny." Hunter was delayed in arriving to assume the command. Every one believed still that the enemy was close in front, and that but for this change of command a decisive success might have been achieved. Finally, toward evening of November 3rd, Frémont promised the officers who thronged his quarters that if Hunter did not arrive, he would lead the army to the attack next morning.

There ensued one of the strangest scenes of the war. "I never saw anything at all approaching the excitement this announcement created," wrote an observer.[21] Officers ran from the headquarters shouting the news. Men threw their hats in air. Wave after wave of cheering arose, spreading from camp to camp and growing more remote as distant regiments heard the news. Band after band began to play, and soon twelve of them were massed in front of the General's tent, serenading him simultaneously. The universal depression changed to exultant joy, and everybody prepared to start for the battle-field at daylight. A battle might soon have taken place, for McCulloch really did await the attack. He later reported to the Confederate gov-

[20] New York *Herald*, Springfield correspondence, November 3, 4, 1861.
[21] *Ibid.*, November 8, 1861.

ernment that he intended to turn and fight, the ground to be selected by Price and himself.

But unfortunately for the soldiers' hopes, at ten that night Hunter arrived. Frémont handed over the command, and prepared to leave the next day. The generals spent two hours in conference, and Frémont outlined his plan of battle. But Hunter had received strict orders from Lincoln that he was not to continue a risky pursuit of the elusive Confederates. "You are not likely to overtake Price," wrote Lincoln, "and are in danger of making too long a line from your own base of supplies and reinforcements." The President clearly implied his condemnation of what he supposed to be Frémont's general strategy: "While, as stated in the beginning of the letter, a large discretion must be and is left with yourself, I feel sure that an indefinite pursuit of Price, or an attempt by this long and circuitous route to reach Memphis, will be exhaustive beyond endurance, and will end in the loss of the whole force engaged in it."

In St. Louis, the news of Frémont's arrival produced the same shock of excitement and anger, followed by the same general gloom. Citizens put their flags at half mast or draped them with black. Soldiers dashed their arms to the cobblestones in the streets, declaring that they were through with the war. The local authorities were fearful, as on an earlier occasion when a false rumor of Frémont's dismissal had been published, that a mob would lynch Frank Blair and his associates, and the angriest threats were heard against Blair's life. When Frémont arrived in the city on November 8th he was met by a tumultuous assemblage, which welcomed him with bands of music, and cheering vociferously, surrounded his headquarters. A committee of German-Americans read a complimentary address, and handed him a set of resolutions, declaring that "we recognize in John C. Frémont the embodiment of our patriotic feeling and political faith," that "he has performed his arduous and responsible tasks with all possible energy and honesty," and that they believed that "a wise Providence may have reserved him for a still wider sphere of action in future times." [22] Jessie, who had denounced the treatment of her husband, left to organize and lead his army without money or the moral aid of the government, as "treason," was with him to lend her comfort and voice a resentment which he never publicly expressed.

Unquestionably, Lincoln did wisely in removing Frémont. The antagonisms he had aroused would alone have made his continuance in command impossible. Nevertheless, a great body of observers in Missouri believed then and always that he had acted, not merely with high patriotism, but with sagacity and efficiency. Many members of his command defended both his integrity and devotion. One of his soldiers, George E. Waring, Jr., later eminent as a civic leader in New York, records in his autobiography: "He was the life and the soul of his army, and it was cruelly wronged in his removal." The views of his adherents are well expressed in a letter which W. G. Eliot, later president of Washington University, a close and shrewd observer of Missouri events, had written Secretary Chase late in October: [23]

I can easily understand that to unfriendly eyes Gen. Frémont may have laid himself open to censure in many particulars. There has been at times a degree of military demonstration, a seeming tendency to extravagant parade, a boldness in taking responsibility even at the risk of exceeding his authority, that has surprised and alarmed the semi-loyal. Even some hearty Unionists have doubted his wisdom and desired a greater degree of conciliation and caution. But we must consider the extreme difficulty of his position. Many things which would be wrong in time of peace, are right and wise in time of war, and promptness of action is sometimes better than

[22] *Appleton's Annual Cyclopaedia,* 1861, p. 494.

[23] Frémont MSS. Eliot (of the same family as the president of Harvard) was a bold opponent of slavery, an active assistant of Lyon and Blair in the opening days of the war, and one of the leaders in the Western Sanitary Commission—the appointment of which by Frémont was an important and valuable act. It has been said of him (*Appleton's Cyclopaedia of Biography,* II, 325) that "he was engaged in all sorts of public and philanthropic enterprises, and has probably done more for the advancement of St. Louis and all the Southwest than any other man that has ever lived in that section." His judgment demands respect.

caution and refusal to take responsibility. It should be remembered that Frémont assumed command at a time of the greatest difficulty, just after the Manassas disaster, when the Union cause was at the lowest ebb. He found St. Louis terribly demoralized. The Secessionists were in ecstasies, and had little doubt of speedy success. One of them openly said to me that "there was a bullet moulded for every Yankee Abolitionist in St. Louis." Many of our wealthiest men openly declared themselves for the South. At one of the most conspicuous corners of the city, Fifth and Pine Streets, in the well-known Berthold mansion, the Confederate headquarters were established, with the Confederate flag conspicuously flying, and recruits were openly enlisted for the Confederate cause. The city authorities did not dare to interfere. There was not a United States flag to be seen anywhere, and Union men spoke with bated breath. The city was not secure from insurrection or the State from secession.

Now without going into details, at the end of two or three weeks after Frémont's arrival, everything was changed. The Union flag went up and the Confederate flag came down. The secession headquarters were closed, and troops of Union soldiers from Iowa and Illinois and Missouri poured into the city attracted by the prestige of Frémont's name. The bold demonstration of strength created strength. The prompt declaration of martial law throughout the State, by many denounced as an extreme measure, held in check the disloyal tendencies, and in a short time gave a totally new aspect to affairs. By erection of earthworks around the city, employment at high wages was given to two or three thousand discontented laborers, all of whom were required to take the oath of allegiance, thus controlling effectually the most unruly part of the population.

The general result is that the city is now safe from attack or insurrection. The defences around it are equal to an army of 20,000 men for resisting an attacking force, and for the control of the city itself. I do not know that they were strictly necessary from a military point of view, but the moral effect has been great, and if any unexpected reverses should occur, they will be of great use. So long as the city is held, the pacification of the State is only a question of time. St. Louis may be now regarded as a thoroughly loyal city. The thought of secession is getting to be absurd. Such is now the public sentiment of the better classes and the final settlement seems sure.

I do not claim that the whole credit of this great change belongs to Frémont, but he has been the responsible leader, and as the blame of every disaster is laid upon him, he should have a measurable share of the praise for what is good. A commander-in-chief is properly judged by the general effect of his administration, rather than by the special incidents of progress. He is sorely blamed for not sending reinforcements to General Lyon, but I doubt if he could have done so consistently with his more imperative duties in the occupation of Cairo and Bird's Point, which were sharply threatened by the Confederate forces. The official documents will show.

I have almost no personal acquaintance with Gen. Frémont, and have nothing to lose or gain through him, except as a loyal citizen of Missouri. I am pleading not for him, but for the cause he represents. He is now at the head of an enthusiastic army, almost in the presence of the enemy. It would not only be unjust and unfair but unwise, to supersede him until a battle is fought.

But outside Missouri a great number of Frémont's adherents cared little about defending the details of his military administration. He had become a symbol. To a multitude in the North and the West his name stood for the radical demand that the abolition of slavery be made an object of the war. If the modification of his proclamation had caused a storm, his removal now aroused a perfect hurricane of wrath. The very threat of it had checked recruiting in Ohio and other states. Many felt implicit confidence in him, and no attack by Frank Blair or Lorenzo Thomas could shake it. In Cincinnati a great county mass meeting had cheered his proclamation "with the wildest outburst of continued applause that was ever witnessed" there, "screaming, yelling, stamping, whooping, throwing hats, and embracing each other." [24] In New England men had agreed with Garrison's *Liberator,* which greeted it with a *"Laus Deo,"* as "the beginning of the end." Ben Wade had written Frémont in the middle of October that "all your enemies have yet been able

[24] Chase MSS, September 15th, to October 1st, contain many letters defending Frémont and picturing the popular anger over his treatment.

to do has not in the least shaken the unbounded confidence which the people have ever had in you, and we all hope you will persevere in the course you have thus far pursued. No greater misfortune could befall the country than that you should retire at this period." [25] Now that the blow had fallen thousands were embittered and angry. Whittier wrote:

> Thy error, Frémont, simply was to act
> A brave man's part, without the statesman's tact,
> And, taking counsel but of common sense,
> To strike at cause as well as consequence.
>   O, never yet since Roland wound his horn
> At Roncesvalles, has a blast been blown
> Far-heard, wide-echoing, startling as thine own,
> Heard from the van of Freedom's hope forlorn!

Secretary Chase's confidential agent in St. Louis had informed him at the first ill-founded report of Frémont's removal that "if the President had emptied the arsenals of the government into the camps of the rebels, he could not have so effectively strengthened them." His agent in Pittsburgh wrote him that some capitalists there were so enraged that they would not put a cent into government securities:

Is it known to the Administration [demanded the editor of the Cincinnati *Gazette* in a letter to Chase], that the West is threatened with a revolution? Could you have been among the people yesterday, and witnessed the excitement; could you have seen sober citizens pulling from their walls and trampling under foot the portrait of the President; and could you hear today the expressions of all classes of men, of all political parties, you would, I think, feel as I feel, and as every sincere friend of the government must feel, alarmed.

Professor C. E. Stowe of Andover, Massachusetts, wrote in the same terms: "I wish you could hear the voices of surprise, indignation, disgust and contempt which now everywhere find

25 Frémont MSS, Bancroft Library.

utterance at the removal of Frémont. The feeling is frightfully earnest." Few believed that the reports of Meigs, Cameron, and Thomas were fair. "The thing," declared Simeon Nash of Gallipolis, Ohio, "has been done in a way to destroy public confidence in its honesty." Another correspondent wrote Chase that he had just returned from a tour as far west as Iowa, and that "I never have seen such excitement, such deep indignant feeling everywhere I have travelled." [26]

"Where are you," demanded Thaddeus Stevens of his fellow-radicals in Congress, "that you let the hounds run down your friend Frémont?" Stevens was a formidable political figure, and he did not stand alone. A mass meeting at Cooper Institute on November 27, 1861, listened to an oration by Charles Sumner warmly laudatory of Frémont, and—with Schuyler Colfax, David Dudley Field, Charles King, William M. Evarts, and other distinguished men on the platform—adopted resolutions indorsing his doctrine upon the emancipation of the slaves of rebels. Henry Ward Beecher asked the General to come to Plymouth Church one Sunday morning, and in his sermon harshly condemned Daniel Webster as a statesman who had timidly compromised with slavery. "He died, and is dead," said Beecher. "But," turning to Frémont, "your name will live and be remembered by a nation of freemen."

If from the voice of his contemporaries Frémont could derive much comfort, he could feel a little later that he had been publicly vindicated. The Committee on the Conduct of the War, after an elaborate investigation, reported in the spring of 1863 that he was not to blame for the failure to reinforce Lyon or Mulligan; that he had acted with energy and promptness; that various of his measures, such as the building of gunboats, had been of the highest value; and that his administration of the Western Department "was eminently characterized by earnestness, ability, and the most unquestionable loyalty." Its members, Ben Wade, Zachariah Chandler, John Covode, and George W. Julian, were politically sympathetic toward Frémont, yet

[26] Chase MSS, especially November 4, 5, 6, 1861.

their verdict carried weight. In Congress, his record was enthusiastically defended by Schuyler Colfax, Roscoe Conkling, and others, though Colfax regarded himself as a family friend of the Blairs.

The consensus of historical opinion has been less kind. James Ford Rhodes, John Fiske, and Nicolay and Hay have all agreed that Frémont's record shows that he was poorly fitted for the command which he took. In this judgment they are unquestionably right. He was deficient in ability to organize the complex and multifarious activities of his Department, his estimate of men was highly faulty, he showed a signal lack of tact, and his characteristic impulsiveness led him into a cardinal and fatal error—the emancipation proclamation, which he should never have issued without consulting the President. A man with genuine military genius would have managed to save Mulligan, and possibly Lyon as well; Frémont showed no spark of that rare quality. A leader with more address and adaptability would never have estranged Blair and his supporters so completely and quickly as Frémont did. He admitted to the Committee on the Conduct of the War that he had done much war business "a little loosely"; that a great deal in the Department "was not consistent with strict military propriety, a great deal." He never learned to coördinate his forces properly, and in his military plans, as in all else, he remained something of a dreamer—prone, as General Curtis said, to "dash at a shadow."

But this is not all the story, and most historians have done less than justice to Frémont. His earnestness, zeal, and patriotism were above question. He labored with almost superhuman energy, and gave his best talents to the cause. The difficulties of his position, tossed as he suddenly was into a Department without organization, money, arms, or stores, without anything but raw recruits, asked not merely to raise and use armies but to equip them, left to shift largely for himself by an Administration intent upon the eastern front, and compelled to deal with sedition at home as well as organized enemies in the field, can hardly be exaggerated. They would have tried the capacities of the ablest men. Grant himself might have failed. With all his shortcomings, Frémont in three months did bring an army into being, did virtually clear Missouri of the enemy, did order gunboats, tugs, and motor-boats, and take other practical measures important for the future, and did help to place in Kentucky a force and a commander, the then unknown Grant, who were destined to win the first real victories of the War.[27]

[27] For a generous estimate of Frémont's constructive services in Missouri, see William Wood, *Captains of the Civil War* (Yale Chronicles of America), p. 119. See also T. Harry Williams, "Frémont and the Politicians," *Journal of the American Military History Foundation*, II, No. 4. Ben Wade wrote Charles A. Dana, a few days after Frémont concluded his testimony before the Committee on the Conduct of the War, a remarkable letter, in which he bitterly asserted that the general was the innocent victim of a wicked plot, and that "no public man since Admiral Byng...has suffered so unjustly as General Frémont." Dana Papers, Library of Congress, February 3, 1862.

XXXII

The Mountain Department

WHEN Frémont left the army at Springfield and with the Zagonyi Guard and his personal staff as escort set out for the railhead at Rolla, his associates were struck by his gaiety; as he cantered along, he laughed and chatted like a schoolboy set free for a holiday. These high spirits remained with him in St. Louis. He busied himself for a fortnight collecting documentary evidence upon the transactions of the Western Department, to be used in his defense. He continued to suffer various humiliations. Not merely was the Zagonyi Guard mustered out without pay, quarters, or rations, on the ground that at Springfield they had expressed disloyal sentiments, but all his contracts had been suspended, and officers were now sent from Washington to determine whether the bills he had incurred should be paid. Yet his aides tell us that the Brant mansion resounded with vivacity and humor. The General, wrote one in his diary, was "absolutely on the rampage with fun and fire. Our table is about the jolliest, most sociable, most enjoyable spot of its kind that I have experienced." [1]

Underneath this buoyancy, however, lay a smoldering sense of injustice; and from this moment Frémont was a confirmed opponent of the Administration. He shared the belief of many Republicans that its military, political, and diplomatic policies were inept and inefficient. His papers show that, feeling he had been grossly wronged, he was convinced that part of the Administration—especially the Blair element—had acted under the influence of selfish and malignant motives. Why had it failed

[1] John R. Howard, MS Diary, November 16, 1861.

to supply him with funds and munitions? Why, at the moment when Mulligan was reported in danger and every man was needed at Paducah, had it stripped his command of 5,000 well-armed troops, not revoking the order till the harm was done? Why had Secretary Cameron and General Thomas left him in command when they thought he was stuck fast in the mud at Tipton, but removed him when he had extricated himself and was about to defeat Price or drive him from the state?

Jessie's wrath exceeded his own. Her indignation was so intense that for a time it led her to believe that Frémont was the victim of a traitorous conspiracy on the part of the Blairs. Throughout the hundred days, her anxieties and labors had matched those of her husband. In a curious scrap of autobiography, she tells us that when Frémont was in pursuit of Price a well-known St. Louis merchant, Thornton Grimsley, had come and told her that confidential information of the Union movements was being treacherously smuggled to Price's headquarters, and that the enemy was thus aware that neither Hunter's nor Pope's divisions would join Frémont's army. Mrs. Frémont, in a frenzy of anxiety, hurried a trusted Negro off with the news to her husband. She was oppressed all day by fears of some frightful disaster. That night at dinner her cousin, Mrs. Brant, remarked: "We have had such a rain to-day that I can't understand why your hair is all dusty." Nobody thought more of the subject; but the next morning her English maid began combing the hair, and stopped suddenly with tears in her eyes. "It had been a chestnut brown," writes Mrs. Frémont, "but now every hair was marked with an alternating white patch about an inch apart, giving an odd look of mottled gray to the whole." [2] At this time she was only thirty-six.

If this indicates the emotional stress under which she had labored, another autobiographical fragment indicates how sternly she nursed her wrath. Returning to New York, the Frémonts stayed for a time at the Astor House, where they

[2] Jessie Benton Frémont MSS, Bancroft Library.

received much attention from radical Senators and Congressmen; they then took apartments on Fourth Avenue, and shortly went to Washington, so that Frémont might aid the investigation into the Western Department. Early in 1862 they were invited to the famous party of February 5th at the White House, the last really brilliant social occasion till the war ended. Many members of Washington society refused; a friend told Jessie that Mrs. Lincoln had shown her eighty declinations, among them one by Senator Wade, who wrote upon the card: "Are the President and Mrs. Lincoln aware that there is a civil war? If they are not, Mr. and Mrs. Wade are, and for that reason decline to participate in feasting and dancing." But the President sent a messenger to say that he especially desired Frémont to be present, and they joined the five hundred guests. The morning before the ball Dorothea Dix told Jessie that she had just left the White House, where Lincoln was deeply perturbed by the illness of his son Willie:[3]

The President spoke of the ball, and wanted to stop it, but it came off. The only alteration made was that there was no dancing. It was announced officially that on account of the illness in the house there would be no dancing; but the Marine Band at the foot of the steps filled the house with music while the boy lay dying above. A sadder face than that of the President I have rarely seen. He was receiving at the large door of the East Room, speaking to the people as they came, but feeling so deeply that he spoke of what he felt and thought, instead of welcoming the guests. To Gen. Frémont he at once said that his son was very ill and that he feared for the result. On seeing his sad face and grieved appearance, the feeling with which we had gone gave way to pity, and after expressing our hopes for the lad's recovery we passed on to make our respects to the President's wife. The ball was becoming a ghastly failure....

The political feeling of the country was represented there that night by strangers, members of Congress, and persons brought down

[3] *Ibid.* Willie, who had taken a cold which turned into fever, died February 20th. The doctor had said before the party that there was as yet no reason for alarm, and Jessie's account is characteristically overdrawn.

to Washington by the business of the war. Uniforms and ladies' evening dress gave their brightness, but almost angry feeling for and against emancipation, and for a quick sharp conduct of the war, found its expression there that night. The President was so sad, so bowed down by the thought of the coming loss of his son, that it seemed to depress the company, and they shifted around until the larger portion had congregated on the other side of the East Room, where Gen. Frémont was standing. The whole talk was on the necessary peremptory pursuit of the war to make the South realize that it could not maintain slavery under the protection of the North.

So many criticized the conduct of the war and...there was so much feeling of sorrow that Gen. Frémont's policy of emancipation was not to be carried out, that it became embarrassing, and we left. I had hardly got my wraps on before we were recalled by Mr. Sumner, who came with a message from the President saying that he wanted us to return, that he specially wanted Gen. Frémont. It seemed the President had found that Gen. McClellan and Gen. Frémont had never met....

As we crossed the long East Room, the President came ferward to meet the General; took him by the arm leading him to Gen. McClellan who was at the upper end of the room, and introduced them to each other, then introducing Mrs. McClellan and myself. We bowed, but as each seemed to wait for the other, neither of us spoke a single word. One look showed me she was dressed in the Secession colors. A band of scarlet velvet crossed her white dress from shoulder to waist, and in her hair were three feathers of scarlet and white. If this was intentional, it was unpardonable in the wife of the commander-in-chief of the Union armies, and yet it seemed impossible to have been quite an accident. After a few minutes' talk between the President, Gen. McClellan, and Gen. Frémont, we left.

At this moment the pressure for Frémont's reappointment to a military command was becoming irresistible. Many radicals and many even of the moderate German-Americans were implacable in their anger over his treatment. When early in 1862 Frémont had appeared before the Committee on the Conduct of the War, reports had reached the public that it was "staggered" by the ease with which he disproved every accusation. In March he gave the press the full text of his defense, including numerous documents. The *Tribune,* publishing it complete in an extra sheet, seized the occasion for a long and belligerent editorial defending his record and declaring that no other commander had been pursued with such unjust malevolence. A great part of the press both East and West took his side. There ensued an immediate explosion in Congress. Frank Blair, on March 7th, made a vitriolic speech attacking Frémont's Missouri record, and the Congressional radicals rushed to the fray. The leading address in Frémont's behalf, delivered by Schuyler Colfax, was a masterly presentation of his case. Lincoln saw that it was best to yield to the storm, and give Frémont another opportunity in the field.

The general was immediately assigned to head the newly created Mountain Department, which comprised western Virginia (where Rosecrans had commanded), eastern Kentucky, and a part of Tennessee. Proceeding with his wife and two children to Wheeling, Frémont there relieved Rosecrans on March 29, 1862. He took his own staff, many of them young Germans, Hungarians, and Frenchmen, whose foreign tongues—as in St. Louis—created a prejudice against him. His first headquarters were at the McLure Hotel in Wheeling, where Jessie placed herself in an anteroom and did her utmost to protect his time. Assuring important callers that he was so busy with his plan of campaign that his moments were gold, she turned them over to staff members and yet made no enemies. The general devoted himself entirely to military affairs, leaving all orders touching civil policy and the relations of Unionists and Confederate sympathizers to his Judge-Advocate, Corwine, and to Governor Francis H. Pierpont of West Virginia.[4] He knew that much was expected of him in the field. Though his force was small, amounting to about twenty-five thousand men on paper, and actually to much less, and though it was badly equipped, his Department represented a pet idea of the President's.

[4] C. H. Ambler, *Francis H. Pierpont,* pp. 144-147.

Lincoln believed it feasible to march from western Virginia over the mountains into East Tennessee and seize the railroad at Knoxville, rescuing the Unionists of that region. This would have been impossible even for a much larger force. As Jacob D. Cox has written in *Battles and Leaders*, extensive operations across the Alleghenies from east or west were impracticable, because a wilderness a hundred miles wide, traversed by few and wretched roads, rendered it impossible to supply troops from depots on either side. The country was so wild that it did not afford even forage for mules. Yet Frémont was put in a position where he had to promise to attempt the feat.

A month after he took command, he departed for the military frontier; his plan being to march into the Shenandoah Valley, and then (as he had arranged with Lincoln) move to break the Virginia & Tennessee Railroad. Unfortunately, Lincoln's whole disposition of forces in this region was at fault, and in the next few months Stonewall Jackson made a spectacular demonstration of the fact at the expense of the three generals opposing him. These were N. P. Banks, who had a small army at Strasburg in the Shenandoah—9,000 men at the time of Jackson's raid; Frémont, with about 15,000 troops at different points in the Shenandoah; and McDowell, who was at Fredericksburg charged especially with the defense of Washington, but who at the critical moment despatched 20,000 men up the valley to help bag Jackson. These three forces should have been under the command of a single general. Instead, the only central command was that which Lincoln and Stanton themselves, acting on telegraphic advices to Washington, undertook to furnish.

The story of Jackson's brilliant and spectacular Valley campaign against the three generals has often been told, and needs no rehearsal in detail.[5] He had some 17,000 effective men, and the armies brought against him outnumbered his troops by at least two to one. Yet by daring rapidity of movement, by the

[5] J. G. Ropes, *Story of the Civil War*, II, p. 115*ff.;* James Ford Rhodes, *History of the United States*, IV, p. 13*ff.*

ability to appear at unexpected points and to dodge pursuit, Jackson managed to strike blow after blow, to defeat or evade each opposing commander, and, after throwing Washington into a panic, to return to a safe position with rich spoils and thousands of prisoners. Meanwhile, he had prevented McDowell's 40,000 men from joining the Union army before Richmond. He whipped Schenck at the village called McDowell, overwhelmed Banks at Winchester and drove him across the Potomac in wild disorder, eluded Frémont, who was checked at Cross Keys by Ewell, crushed two brigades under Tyler at Port Republic, and got safely away; all this between May 19 and June 10, 1862. James Ford Rhodes places the blame for this chiefly on Lincoln. Issuing orders by telegraph, he devised a plan that "was too complicated to succeed," and that Lee himself would never have risked.

Frémont in this campaign has been accused of showing a lack of energy. If he and McDowell had met at Strasburg on May 30th they could possibly have cut off Jackson's retreat, but Frémont did not get there even by the thirty-first, when he could do no more than strike at Jackson's rear. Moreover, he was ordered by Lincoln at an earlier stage of the campaign to march to Harrisonburg, and instead turned up at Moorfield. For all this, he is censured, at least by implication, by the historian Rhodes.[6] But the censure is hardly deserved. When Lincoln early in June sent Carl Schurz to the scene to make a confidential report, Schurz exonerated the commander upon both heads. "It is a fact which admits of no doubt," he wrote the President, "that when you ordered Gen. Frémont to march from Franklin to Harrisonburg, it was absolutely impossible to carry out the order. The army was in a starving condition, and literally unable to fight. ... Thus it seems to have been necessary to move back to Moorfield, in order to meet the supply trains." He added that the troops had proceeded by forced

[6] Rhodes, *op. cit.*, IV, p. 15ff. Frémont himself wrote later that Cross Keys "was not indecisive. I was engaged with General Jackson for eight days with constant sharp skirmishing driving his force before me, I with an inferior force, he burning bridges and culverts to delay us." Frémont MSS, Bancroft Library.

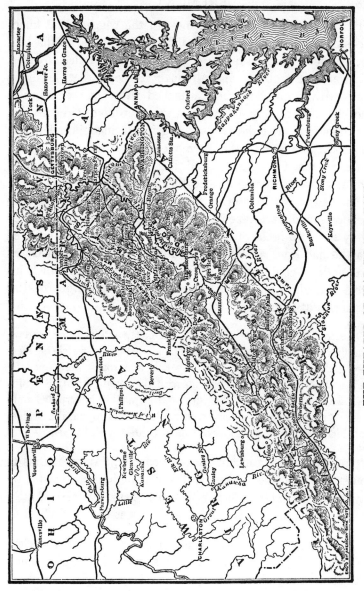

THE THEATER OF WAR IN THE EAST

marches to Strasburg, leaving most of the baggage and knap-
sacks behind. "The march was difficult, and owing to the lack
of provisions, very hard on the men. The army failed to arrest
Jackson at Strasburg, and although it seems that Jackson's
rear guard might have been attacked with more promptness
and vigor, yet it is undoubtedly a very fortunate circumstance
that Gen. Frémont did not succeed in placing himself across
Jackson's line of retreat." Frémont had at most 10,000 men,
"in a wretched condition," and Jackson's larger army would
almost certainly have defeated the ill-conditioned force.

As Schurz wrote later, a highly resolute, self-reliant commander would have taken the risk of this defeat and strained
every nerve to be at Strasburg on time; yet Frémont believed
that he had done all that was humanly possible. He declared
that nothing could have excelled the devotion with which his
tired, ill-clad, ill-fed troops pursued Jackson's rear-guard after
the action at Strasburg:

> The road was strewn with arms, blankets, and clothing, thrown
> away in their [the rebels'] haste, or abandoned by their pickets where
> they had been surprised, and the woods and roads were lined by
> their stragglers, unable to keep up with the rapid retreat. For nine
> days we kept in sight of the enemy—the pursuit interrupted only
> by the streams where the enemy succeeded in destroying the bridges
> for which our advance was in continual contest with his rear.[7]

After Cross Keys, Lincoln telegraphed him, "Many thanks to
yourself, officers, and men for the gallant battle of last Sunday"; and he later added, in another message: "You fought
Jackson alone and worsted him"—which was not precisely true.

Schurz had heard much of Frémont, and studied the General with curiosity. He found him a man of "elegant build,
muscular, and elastic, dark hair and beard slightly streaked
with gray, a broad forehead, a keen eye, fine regular features."

---

[7] For Frémont's letter see New York *Tribune*, February 12, 1863; compare
Col. G. R. F. Henderson, *Stonewall Jackson and the American Civil War*, I,
Ch. 11.

He praised his air of refinement, his easy and unaffected manners, and his low, gentle tone of voice, which carried a suggestion of reticence. "The whole personality," he concluded, "appeared rather attractive—and yet, one did not feel quite sure." In his report to Lincoln, Schurz included a sage word of political warning: [8]

This morning I found General Frémont in a somewhat irritated frame of mind, and I must confess I understand it. The government has plenty of provisions, and our soldiers die of hunger; plenty of shoes, and they go barefooted; plenty of horses, and we are hardly able to move. I would entreat you let it not be said that this army is more neglected than any other. It would appear that it is willfully so, and you know how this will be interpreted. The task this army has before it is an important one, and it ought to have the means to fulfill it.

But Lincoln had been too thoroughly imbued by the Blairs' prejudices to trust Frémont, and under any circumstances the General's services would have been brief. In the middle of June, Frémont asked the President to increase his force, promising that if it were augmented to 35,000 men, the strength originally promised him, he would capture Staunton, seize the Richmond-Newbern Railroad, and prevent the enemy from using western Virginia as a rich granary. The correspondence which ensued reveals Lincoln's deep-seated distrust for his commander. Frémont had been courteous in reminding the President of his promise of a larger army. "I now ask from the President the fulfillment of this understanding," he wrote, "and ask it only because, under the conditions of war, I should be able to render good and immediate service." But the President telegraphed a reply next day which showed not a little asperity:

Your dispatch of yesterday, reminding me of a supposed understanding that I would furnish you a corps of 35,000 men, and

[8] Compare Carl Schurz, *Reminiscences*, II, 343-346.

reminding me of the "fulfillment of this understanding," is received I am ready to come to a fair settlement of accounts with you on the fulfillment of understandings.

Early in March last, when I assigned you to the command of the Mountain Department, I did tell you I would give you all the force I could, and that I hoped to make it reach 35,000. You at the same time told me that within a reasonable time you would seize the railroad at or east of Knoxville, Tenn., if you could. There was then in the department a force supposed to be 25,000, the exact number as well known to you as to me. After looking about two or three days, you called and distinctly told me, that if I would add the Blenker Division to the force already in the department, you would undertake the job. The Blenker Division contained 10,000, and at the expense of great dissatisfaction to Gen. McClellan I took it from his army and gave it to you. My promise was literally fulfilled. I have given you all I could, and I have given you very nearly, if not quite, 35,000.

Now for yours: On the 23d of May, largely over two months afterward, you were at Franklin, Va., not within three hundred miles of Knoxville, nor within eighty miles of any part of the railroad east of it, and not moving forward but telegraphing here that you could not move for lack of everything. Now, do not misunderstand me. I do not say you have not done all you could. I presume you met unexpected difficulties; and I beg you to believe that as surely as you have done your best, so have I. I have not the power now to fill up your corps to 35,000. I am only asking of you to stand cautiously on the defensive; get your force in order, and give such protection as you can to the valley of the Shenandoah and to Western Virginia.

Have you received the orders and will you act upon them?

Lincoln's despatch showed all too clearly that he was unconvinced of Frémont's military capacity and ready to find fault with his acts. As a matter of fact, its criticism was hardly fair. Military critics have agreed that Lincoln's plan for the capture of Knoxville was romantic and highly impracticable. Blenker's division, which was to raise Frémont's army to 35,000, was not ordered to him until the beginning of April

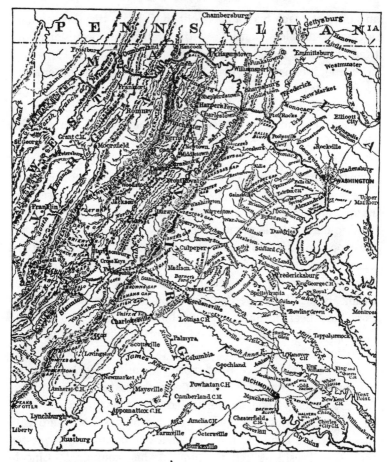

SCENE OF JACKSON'S SHENANDOAH CAMPAIGN

and did not reach his Department until May 5th, then coming
in ragged, shoeless, tentless, without sufficient provisions, and
tired. Frémont could not argue with the President. He sent a
brief and submissive reply, saying simply that the orders had
been received, and that he would of course act upon them, as
he was already acting. But he read between the lines of the
message its full significance, and it played its part in his
almost immediate decision to withdraw.

For this decision the President furnished before the end of
June what Frémont regarded as sufficient reason. Lincoln,
wisely but belatedly, consolidated the forces of Frémont,
Banks, and McDowell into one army, to be called the Army
of Virginia, and placed it under the command of John Pope,
the troops of the Mountain Department being constituted the
First Corps under Frémont's command. Since his removal in
Missouri, Frémont detested Pope only less than he detested
Frank Blair. They were avowed enemies. He believed that
Pope had been disloyal and insubordinate, and had tried to
encompass his defeat. He could not bring himself to hold any
intercourse with the man. It would perhaps have been wiser—
it would certainly have been more patriotic—had he sunk his
personal resentment and stuck doggedly to his work until, as
was inevitable, Pope demonstrated his utter incapacity. But
such a course did not square with his or Jessie's pride, with
their sensitive conception of personal honor; and he requested
that the President relieve him of his command. Lincoln
promptly did so, turning the corps over to Sigel. Before the
summer ended, Pope had sustained one of the worst defeats
of the war at the second battle of Bull Run.

All these events naturally increased the antagonism between
Frémont and the Administration. Lincoln was more convinced
than ever that Frémont was intractable and unsafe. He regarded the explorer as a troublesome man providentially
shelved. Frémont, chafing for action, but unwilling to surrender
his dignity, was convinced that he had been the victim of a
new indignity, and that he could never expect justice from

Lincoln or the Blairs. He returned to New York, taking his personal staff with him, in an embittered frame of mind. For a time he kept his peace. He was still one of the high officers of the Army, and he had hopes that some conjunction of circumstances might recall him to the field. His radical friends and the radical press were vociferous in urging his claims; Mrs. Frémont pulled whatever wires she could reach. Among others, she approached Hannibal Hamlin. "What can I do?" the Vice-President wrote her. "The slow and unsatisfactory movements of the Government do not meet my approbation, and that is known, and of course I am not consulted at all, nor do I think there is much disposition in any quarter to regard any counsel I may give much if at all." Still, he tried. Others tried, with equal lack of success. At one time they seemed likely to succeed. In the first weeks of 1863 a highly important command was arranged expressly for Frémont by Stanton. Both the command and his designation to it received the approbation of the President; but the post was finally given to another officer. Frémont continued to draw pay, but used it, as he publicly announced, to relieve wartime distress. Watching Lincoln's policies with increasing disapproval, he looked forward to the time when he might cross swords with his enemies—and that time was soon to come.

XXXIII

The Defeat of the Blairs

THE year 1864 opened with storm-clouds billowing thickly about the Lincoln Administration, and Frémont watching the omens of trouble with keen interest. Discontent was rife in every quarter—in the Cabinet, in Congress, in the country at large; and everywhere it was breeding political machinations against the President. In these plots, Frémont had no mind to play an active rôle. He had turned at once to his private business pursuits and was willing to lose himself completely in them. But he fully realized that to hundreds of thousands of voters his name still possessed a magical ring.

A new Congress had convened the previous December, and had promptly shown that it was under the domination of radicals who were thoroughly unfriendly to the Administration. Lincoln's candidate for the speakership had been decisively defeated—defeated by the brilliant Indianian, Frémont's warm defender, Schuyler Colfax. The important committees had been filled by men who opposed Lincoln's conservative policy. In the Senate, Charles Sumner, icy, solemn, and pontifical, felt a personal cordiality for Lincoln, but sternly deplored his official course. Zachariah Chandler, a rough backwoods type of politician, blunt and ruthless, took the same attitude. He, like Lyman Trumbull, the irrepressible Illinoisan, John P. Hale, a supercritical, nagging New Englander, and that domineering egotist, Benjamin F. Wade, was a member of the Committee on the Conduct of the War. Wade as chairman had made this body a thorn in Lincoln's side. Its final report on April 3, 1864, was a resounding blast in favor of a more vigorous prosecution of the conflict. Then a new joint committee of the same name was organized, and with much the same personnel resumed the attack on the President.

In the House, the foremost place among Lincoln's opponents was taken by the bitter, narrow, patriotic Thaddeus Stevens, now aged and bowed by disease, but unrelenting as ever. Beside him stood the dashing and comparatively youthful Henry Winter Davis of Maryland, who disputed control over that state with the Blair dynasty. Another who shared their views was George W. Julian of Indiana, who had been disgusted by Lincoln's slowness in proclaiming emancipation. He would never have proclaimed it, Julian believed, if he had not feared that Congress would refuse to vote supplies unless the war were placed upon a definite anti-slavery basis.[1] Lincoln in his December message had proposed to Congress a moderate and tolerant plan for reconstructing the lost states, and the radicals had lost no time in preparing to knife it. Thaddeus Stevens had exploded a little earlier that he was "tired of hearing damned Republican cowards talk about the Constitution," and that the North should give the rebels "reconstruction on such terms as would end treason forever." Now Henry Winter Davis brought forward a bill which was intended to destroy Lincoln's reconstruction scheme and furnish a harsher system in its stead. The hostility of all these men toward Lincoln's renomination was open and bitter. Young James A. Garfield, who had fought at Shiloh and had just entered Congress from the Ashtabula district of Ohio, wrote that "we hope we may not be compelled to push Lincoln four years more."

If Congress seemed alive with discontent and opposition, the Cabinet was even more savagely divided. Stanton, a man compounded of disagreeable qualities, jealousy, arbitrariness, ambition, and ill temper, and yet laborious, enormously energetic, a vast organizing force, a thorough patriot, seemed at times to hold Lincoln in utter contempt. He had called him

[1] Julian, *Political Recollections*, p. 227.

a gorilla and talked of his "painful imbecility."[2] At other
times, his loyalty and admiration appeared perfect. Salmon P.
Chase was at work day and night laying mines, stringing wires,
and planning to make himself President in the stead of the
Illinois lawyer whose powers he distrusted and whose aims he
thought inadequate. After some initial coyness, his candidacy
was perfectly open, and Lincoln had to tolerate it. Wade and
Winter Davis gave him their support, while various Congressional radicals and prominent citizens formed a committee—
the Republican National Executive Committee—under Senator Samuel C. Pomeroy of Kansas to push his candidacy.
From this body shortly came a vigorous pronunciamento, declaring that if the anti-slavery principle was to triumph, if
the war was to be vigorously prosecuted and the country made
safe, the voters should rally to elect Chase instead of Lincoln.[3] Chase clubs began to spring up over the North. Meanwhile, other members of the Cabinet were hopelessly antago-
nistic to each other.

The principal cause of the Cabinet antagonisms was evident to every observer—the Blairs. The Postmaster-General,
Montgomery Blair, had early become a storm center. Like his
father and brother, he basked in Lincoln's favor, which the
whole family repaid with warm-hearted devotion to the President; but other leaders regarded the tall, angular Missourian
with dislike. His talk of solving the slavery question by measures of colonization and compensation enraged the radicals.
When emancipation was proposed, the emancipation for which
Sumner and Greeley, Wade and Beecher were calling, he had
stubbornly opposed it to the last. He declared it inexpedient and
would have postponed it even when Lincoln decided to issue
his proclamation. Upon the reconstruction issue, the radicals
thought him equally perverse. The whole Blair family was for
treating the South mildly and kindly, and restoring its rights
promptly. Montgomery Blair loosed a tremendous broadside

---

[2] Morgan Dix, *John A. Dix*, II, p. 19.
[3] *Annual Cyclopaedia* (1864), p. 783; Nicolay and Hay, *Lincoln*, VIII, p. 319.

against the men who stood for "amalgamation, equality, and fraternity" with the Negro race.[4] To the old Abolitionists and to all who, like Zachariah Chandler and Thaddeus Stevens, thought that the Negroes should be treated as friends and the rebels as enemies, the Blairs had become anathema.

Commanding the President's support, Montgomery Blair might have seemed in a position to hold his Cabinet portfolio without making enemies in the President's official family. Instead, he quickly surrounded himself with feuds and antagonisms, which by 1864 had become dangerous in their intensity. He and Seward felt nothing but dislike for each other. The elder Blair had by some strange process of reasoning associated Seward and Frémont as allies, and regarded them as twin agents of the Abolitionist cause, an opinion which he took no pains to conceal. Montgomery Blair believed that Seward had tried deliberately to provoke the clash between the North and the South, and made reckless and unfounded charges to that effect.[5] As for Attorney-General Edward Bates, the Blairs had systematically undermined and opposed him in Missouri politics, and he well knew it. The peppery Stanton and the intriguing Montgomery Blair did not get on at all. Montgomery, recalling Stanton's record as a member of Buchanan's Cabinet, doubted his loyalty and zeal in the Union cause, while the two were utterly incompatible in temperament. Stanton was never a man to repress his private hatreds, and he struck out at the Blairs by having some of their Maryland relatives arrested on the charge that they had smuggled supplies of medicine over to the Confederates.[6] When it came to Chase, of course, Blair's enmity was still more open.

Outside official circles, there seemed—to the superficial observer—many evidences of popular chilliness toward Lincoln. The correspondence of Chase and Lyman Trumbull is filled with letters from bitter-enders who resented the President's

---

[4] Kirkland, *The Peacemakers of 1864*, p. 185.

[5] T. K. Lothrop, *William Henry Seward*, p. 123.

[6] Kirkland, *op. cit.*, p. 187.

seemingly tepid policy. The northern pulpit was largely un-friendly. The strongest church magazine, Henry Ward Beecher's *Independent,* declared that: "Great statesmen are few in any country, but few as they are we must make diligent search to find one for the next presidency." Of course, the Democratic newspapers were shrill in abuse; James Gordon Bennett's *Herald,* which the President himself read for its unrivaled war news, lashed the Administration unmercifully. But part of the Republican press was not much less hostile. Greeley's *Tribune* declared that Lincoln's nomination would at once awaken "the fear that the disasters, the burdens, the debts, and the hopes deferred will be revived." Utterances of similar purport could be found in William Cullen Bryant's dignified *Evening Post.* Both Bryant and Greeley believed that the nomination of a Republican candidate for the Presidency should be deferred until the close of the summer of 1864, in order that the people might know whether the overthrow of the Rebellion was in sight, or its speedy termination was out of the question. If the battles of July and August showed that it was impossible to crush the Rebellion at once, then another and better leader than Lincoln could be called to the helm. But some editors were for rejecting Lincoln out of hand. The youthful Whitelaw Reid of the Cincinnati *Gazette* declared that the President was ready to "surrender the cause of human freedom to the masters of slave plantations." [7]

It was inevitable that much of the opposition to Lincoln should crystallize about the name of Frémont. He was sin-cerely indifferent to any movement of the sort. Giving up all hope of military employment, he had plunged with his usual enthusiasm into a new business field—railroad building. The newspapers had suggested that if he was not to be allowed a command, he might be appointed military governor of North Carolina or one of the other reconquered states. The great task in these states, said the *Tribune,* was to organize the eman-

[7] New York *Tribune,* June 6, 1864, and subsequent issues; for Reid see Wil-liam E. Dodd, *Century Magazine,* Vol. 114, p. 48.

cipated slaves: "The first condition for the success of such an effort is to win their confidence. We cannot do it by sending them a general whom they do not know. But Frémont's name has been a watchword in every cabin since 1856, and will be heard at once as a war-cry by the slaves waiting to rally under the Union flag." Lincoln, however, refused to heed such suggestions. When George Julian called at the White House to urge a post for the explorer, the President replied that he was willing, but that he did not know where to place him. The situation, he said, reminded him of the old man who advised his son to take a wife, to which the son replied, "Whose wife shall I take?" There were important positions in sight, but they could be reached only by removals which he did not care to make.

A somewhat different answer was given to a deputation which, including Senator Henry Wilson, Wendell Phillips, Moncure D. Conway, and Oakes Ames, came to the President to discuss the governorship of North Carolina. Some one suggested Frémont, and Lincoln tolerantly indicated why he thought the proposal bad. "I have great respect for Gen. Frémont and his abilities," said the President slowly, "but the fact is that the pioneer in any movement is not generally the best man to carry that movement to a successful issue. It was so in old times, wasn't it?" he continued with a smile. "Moses began the emancipation of the Jews, but didn't take Israel to the Promised Land after all." The truth was that Lincoln could not have appointed Frémont without offending his conservative supporters, and he did not think it necessary to act.

While Chase was coming brazenly into the open in his pursuit of the nomination, while Thaddeus Stevens was expressing the sagacious view that Ben Butler would make a much better President than Lincoln, and while Greeley was declaring in the *Tribune* that Chase, Frémont, Butler, and Grant ought all to be considered, the explorer had immersed himself in railway operations. His enthusiasm for the development of the great trans-Mississippi region was as fresh as ever. The action of

Congress in richly endowing a Pacific railroad stirred his imagination. Commanding large funds on the credit of Mariposa, having a name valuable to any enterprise, and personally familiar with western topography, he felt that this offered an ideal field for his energies. In June, 1863, the New York press announced with applause that he had put his hand to the helm. Capitalists had been reluctant, with the war raging, to undertake new lines across the plains. But now Frémont had come forward with Samuel Hallett, widely known, as the *Tribune* said editorially, "in moneyed circles as a man of large financial experience, combined with an energy and indomitable will to which all obstacles are made to succumb." [8] They intended to build a line through the state of Kansas—what was later known as the Kansas Pacific—connecting on the east with the Missouri River terminals; and for this purpose, took over a paper railway called the Leavenworth, Pawnee, & Western. A new directorate was chosen, and Frémont elected president. In a few weeks he was advertising from his Beaver Street offices for bids to deliver 4,000 tons of iron rails at Leavenworth or Kansas City.

But if he would willingly have kept aloof from politics, an increasing number of radicals were insistent that he be drafted for service in 1864. Many German-Americans and Abolitionists preferred him above all other candidates; while, as the weeks passed, supporters began to drift in from other camps. Butler's name aroused more derision than enthusiasm. The Chase candidacy, blazing brilliantly in the political heavens in February, came down like a rocket-stick in March. Pomeroy's circular in behalf of the Secretary of the Treasury aroused wide comment. But on February 22nd, the Republican National Committee, sitting in Washington, virtually came out for the renomination of Lincoln, and called the Republican Convention to sit for that purpose at Baltimore in June. More decisively, on March 5th, the Republican caucus of the Ohio Legislature refused to endorse Chase as a "favorite son," which meant

[8] New York *Tribune,* June 4, 1863.

that Ohio was for Lincoln. Chase reluctantly and ungracefully withdrew, though his desire to see Lincoln supplanted was as strong as ever; and many of his adherents turned toward Frémont.

The first token of the way the wind was veering appeared on March 19th, when radical and old-school Abolitionists of New York came together at Cooper Union in an earnest "Frémont meeting," of which Frémont knew nothing in advance. The men in charge were for the most part obscure. Under the blazing gas jets in Room 20 the erudite Friedrich Kapp declaimed, with a marked accent, upon the need for a change of government. A Mr. Whipple gained the floor, and launched into personal abuse of Lincoln. He had himself seen, he said, the bad effects of liquor and the evil influence of slavery. A platform calling for "vigorous, consistent, concentrated prosecution of the war" was read amid cheers. Then there was a stir at the door, a sudden clapping of hands, and everybody arose as the loose, ill-clad figure of Greeley shuffled in. The editor's remarks, as reported by his own journal, were confused, but he squeakily made three facts clear. First, that he thought it would have been well to postpone all nominations and campaigning until people could see what Grant would do in the summer campaigns; second, that he advocated a single term for Presidents; and third, that while he expected to support the regular nominee of the Republican Convention, he believed that "the people of New York were in favor of putting down the rebellion and its cause, and sustaining Freedom, and he believed that John C. Frémont would carry out such views."[9]

As luck would have it, at this moment Frank Blair executed a stroke which aroused the radicals to a new pitch of anger. The current seemed to be setting against the President. Pennsylvania, Massachusetts, and New York were apparently hostile to him. All Frank Blair's innate recklessness and pugnacity came to the surface. As major-general he had no right to hold civil office, but he had made an arrangement by which

[9] New York *Tribune*, March 20, 1864.

he had surrendered his commission temporarily and Lincoln placed it in a secret drawer, to be restored upon demand. By this adroit if illegal maneuver, Frank was able to return to Congress. In January, he had begun to make war upon Secretary Chase by calling for an investigation of certain Treasury regulations. Now, on April 23, he suddenly arose in his place and made the most sensational and ferocious speech which Congress had heard in years. He accused Chase of public and private corruption; he declared that he had squandered public funds, wrung from a hard-pressed people, to advance his candidacy; and he charged that he had used hundreds of Treasury agents to build up his machine. To support this tirade, he read a letter from a New York financier, which spoke of reports afloat that Chase had given his son-in-law, Governor Sprague, a permit to buy cotton at the South by which the latter would probably make two million dollars.[10]

This vicious and ill-considered attack created an uproar among the radical leaders and editors, and increased the resentment with which they viewed the Administration. The New York *Tribune* declared that it had left a more painful impression than any other utterance in the House in years. Chase denounced the speech as an "outrageous calumny." The special car in which he left Washington that day for Baltimore fairly "trembled with his rage." [11] There seems no question that Lincoln was much annoyed by Blair's indiscretion. The man had kicked over another beehive, he said; and for a time he hesitated to restore Blair to his military command, though he had already given the needed instructions. But the radicals naturally believed that Lincoln had done something to instigate Blair's onslaught, and that he had taken satisfaction in it. After this event, Chase and Montgomery Blair glared daggers at each other whenever they met in the Cabinet room.

But Chase was out of the running for the presidency, and it was now evident to everybody that Lincoln would be nom-

---

[10] *Congressional Globe*, 38th Cong., 1st Sess., Part II, p. 1831ff.
[11] A. G. Riddle, *Recollections of War Times*, pp. 267, 268.

inated at Baltimore at the beginning of June. It was by no means so clear that he would be successful in November. James A. Garfield wrote despondingly: "Lincoln will be nominated and a copperhead will be elected. Not a dozen men in Congress think otherwise." Chase grumbled to the governor of Ohio: "The Convention will not be regarded as a Union Convention, but simply as a Blair-Lincoln Convention, by a great body of citizens whose support is essential to success." But even to have the President again placed at the head of the Republican party was a bitter dose to many of the extremists, and they turned to the idea of a third ticket. It might be used to obtain the withdrawal of Lincoln from the race; it could certainly be used to increase the chances of his ultimate defeat. On May 4, 1864, a group of radical Republicans who were known to favor the choice of Frémont sent out an invitation to a mass convention in Cleveland, to meet May 31st for the purpose of forestalling the action of the regular Republicans. The signers did not constitute an impressive group. Representing only eleven states, they included no names more distinguished than those of B. Gratz Brown, Friedrich Kapp, Emil Preetorius, and James Redpath. However, their call was shortly reinforced by one emanating from a number of minor state officials in New York, and one sent out by a considerable number of Abolitionists.[12]

Frémont's papers do not indicate that he was excited by the prospect for another nomination for the presidency, or that he had any illusions as to the chances for his election; indeed, it appears that he was by no means certain of consenting. His papers do show that he was urged to take a receptive position by such men as Governors Andrew and Curtin, and David Dudley Field. The coming convention was derided by William Lloyd Garrison. "General Frémont, as yet," he wrote, "has not shown a single state, a single county, a single town or hamlet in his support. Who represents him from Massachusetts, on the call for the Cleveland Convention? Two men,

[12] *Annual Cyclopaedia*, 1865, p. 783ff.

both non-voters, I believe, and neither of them has a particle of political influence." [13] But men like Wendell Phillips and Schuyler Colfax, women like Elizabeth Cady Stanton, were for Frémont, and when the Convention actually met, it had a good press. Even the Democratic journals, for selfish reasons, spoke well of it.

It opened formally on May 31, 1864, in Cosmopolitan Hall in Cleveland, with ex-Governor William F. Johnston of Pennsylvania calling the motley body of about four hundred Radicals, Germans, and War Democrats to order. Many of the delegates had no credentials, though they represented various political organizations. Sixteen states had sent members. For the most part everything went like clockwork. Frémont was nominated by acclamation, General John Cochrane of New York was named for Vice-President, though many had supposed that the honor would go to B. Gratz Brown, and a platform was adopted which expressed radical ideas from beginning to end. It called for uncompromising prosecution of the war, the constitutional prohibition of slavery, free speech and a free press, ,and a one-term presidency; for leaving reconstruction exclusively to Congress, and for the confiscation of rebel lands to be divided among active soldiers and sailors. Frémont promptly accepted the honor, declaring that "today we have in this country the abuses of a military dictation without its unity of action and vigor of execution"; but he dissented from the plank upon the confiscation of rebel property.

For the moment, his nomination was regarded in Administration circles with comparative indifference. Lincoln, upon hearing of the proceedings, opened his Bible at the twenty-second chapter of I Samuel and read aloud: "And everyone that was in distress, and everyone that was in debt, and everyone that was discontented gathered themselves unto him; and he became a captain over them: and there were with him about four hundred men." As June began, in fact, everything seemed going well for the President. Sherman was pressing forward

[13] New York *Evening Post,* June 3, 1864.

upon Atlanta; Grant was facing Lee on the Chickahominy, and the nation's trust in Grant was enormous. It had been made emphatically clear that the Republican rank and file wanted Lincoln. As Bryant put it: "In the first place, he is popular with the plain people, who believe him honest, with the rich people, who believe him safe, with the soldiers, who believe him their friend, and with religious people, who believe him to have been specially raised up for this crisis; and in the second place, because many of the thieving and corrupt scoundrels of the political mews, who know the fact of his popularity, have eagerly attached themselves to the car of his success." [14] Lincoln had the votes, and nobody else had. The Baltimore Convention witnessed a spontaneous outburst of enthusiasm for the President. The delegates, trying again and again to burst through parliamentary forms, nominated him amid deafening cheers and cries of "God bless him!"

But the week of Lincoln's triumph was a week of humiliation for the Blairs. They had made enemies on every hand who were now gathering to crush them. The first blow fell upon the head of the much-hated Frank Blair. His diatribe against Chase had prompted Thaddeus Stevens to introduce in the House a resolution asking the President to explain just how Frank had been able to be a major-general and a member of Congress at the same time. The House responded by passing a resolution which declared that Blair had never possessed a legal right to his seat as Representative, and another asserting that any officer of the United States Army who had severed his connection with it by written resignation or by service in Congress must have a second appointment, in the manner required by the Constitution, before he could resume his sword. [15] This was a stinging rebuke, but worse was to come. For three years denunciation and dislike of the Blairs in Missouri, their special political barony, had been growing. Men there looked back upon Frank Blair's acts in 1861 and decided that he had

---

[14] New York *Evening Post,* June 3, 1864.
[15] *Congressional Globe,* 38th Cong., 1st Sess., Pt. II, p. 1854*ff.*; Pt. IV, p. 3389*ff.*

been a marplot and a curse. In the spring of 1864, this opposition had come to a head, and the radicals, meeting in State Convention, had sent an implacably anti-Blair delegation to Baltimore. Another gathering sent a set of delegates friendly to Blair.

Which delegation should be admitted? On June 8th, this question came before the Baltimore Convention, and Preston King of the committee on credentials read a report excluding the Blairites. The Convention rocked with joy, and all proceedings were suspended while the tide of applause rose and ebbed. Then the report was put to a vote. State after state cast votes for its approval, until Maryland and Delaware were reached, and they voted "aye" too! Once more the Convention broke into thunderous applause, which still echoed around the hall when it was announced that the anti-Blair delegates had been seated by a vote of 440 to 4.[16] In effect, the Republican Party served notice upon Lincoln that it had no use for the "Blair malcontents." This notice was underlined when, at the instance of the Missouri delegates, a resolution was passed declaring for the reorganization of the Cabinet—which meant that Montgomery Blair should go.

If in early June the skies had seemed bright for Lincoln, in July and August they grew overcast again. The losses at Cold Harbor and the Wilderness, when the people at last realized them, had a stunning effect. Heavy fighting by Grant in front of Petersburg ended in a checkmate. The hospitals were choked with wounded, and the Army of the Potomac was exhausted. The spectacular raid of General Early at the beginning of July brought Washington within an inch of capture—so close that the Navy Department hastily prepared a vessel to carry the President down the Potomac. The Treasury was empty, and greenbacks fell during part of the summer to forty cents on the dollar. Gloom was general throughout the North, and it found an inevitable outlet in dissatisfaction with Lincoln. The elder Blair, in something like a panic, employed the closing

[16] New York *Tribune;* New York *Evening Post,* June 9, 1864.

days of July in visiting various leaders in New York City—
Bryant, Greeley, James Gordon Bennett, and McClellan, now
about to be made the Democratic candidate—and pleading
with them to support Lincoln, or at least to refrain from opposing him. He and Montgomery even hoped that they could
influence McClellan to decline the Democratic nomination, but
in this they utterly failed. On August 5th the Administration
sustained a new blow—for that day appeared the bitter manifesto of Ben Wade and Henry Winter Davis against Lincoln's
reconstruction policy. Greeley wrote Lincoln on August 9th
that if the election were held next day, the Democrats would
sweep New York and Pennsylvania by one hundred thousand
majority; while near the middle of that month Thurlow Weed,
one of the most sagacious of practical politicians, told the
President that his reëlection was an impossibility.[17]

This sudden and steady drop of the Republican barometer
produced an equally sudden change in the Administration's
attitude toward Frémont. It was seen that his candidacy might
be disastrous. His followers were intensely in earnest, and a
great part of the German press had rallied to his side. He
would poll a large vote, and would poll it in states likely to
be close. The ticket was considered strong, for Cochrane was
a War Democrat of radical views—a former congressman, a
brigadier-general till his health failed, and an early advocate
of the policy of calling the emancipated slaves to arms. It was
recalled by political wiseacres that a third party in 1844, the
Abolitionists under Birney, had beaten Clay for the Presidency,
and that another third party in 1848, the Free Soilers under
Van Buren, had beaten Cass. Some Bostonians of prominence
were so alarmed by the outlook that they published a letter
proposing that both Frémont and Lincoln withdraw in favor
of a compromise candidate, and to this Frémont returned a

[17] New York *Sun* in late June and early July, 1889, published a series of letters in reply to Nicolay and Hay's *Lincoln,* showing that the Frémont movement was a very serious matter, and placed the Lincoln ticket in actual jeopardy.
By mid-June, twenty-six German-language papers had come out for Frémont,
New York *Herald,* June 15, 1864.

somewhat inconclusive but generally favorable reply. A movement was begun to use the Frémont party as a nucleus for the nomination of Grant, with the object of forcing Lincoln out of the field.

With affairs in this posture, Frémont soon learned that a number of practical politicians were holding consultations with Lincoln upon the best means of strengthening his presidential prospects. The participants included Elihu Washburne, Senator Harlan of Iowa, James M. Edmunds of the Union League, and most active of all, Zachariah Chandler. Much alarmed by the Wade-Davis manifesto, Chandler first bent his efforts to conciliate these redoubtable leaders. He, Cameron, and Wade in the stormy days before the war had made a triple alliance to take up each other's quarrels if insulted by any Southern Senator; and as a result of this early friendship, Chandler could appeal to Wade—like himself a quick-tempered, rough-spoken, aggressive man—with some confidence. Their interview at Wade's home near Ashtabula is described by David H. Jerome of Detroit, who was present, as "rather titanic." Wade finally demanded as his ultimatum the withdrawal from the Cabinet of Montgomery Blair, whom he thought at heart a Democrat. Chandler then went directly to the President, and—according to two different authorities, both good—obtained Lincoln's pledge that if the negotiations he had undertaken proved successful, Blair would be retired. Then visiting Henry Winter Davis in Baltimore, Chandler easily persuaded him to promise party loyalty on the same condition made by Wade. His next problem was to obtain the withdrawal of the Frémont-Cochrane ticket. In a letter written long afterward, he said that he deemed this of vital importance, and procured the consent of Lincoln and the chairmen of both the National and Congressional Committees for his negotiations.[18]

[18] On this subject I have drawn my material from the Frémont MSS; Chase MSS; Charles Moore's letter in the *Century Magazine,* July, 1895, based on conversations with David H. Jerome and others; the diaries of Edward Bates, Gideon Welles, and Orville H. Browning; Donnal V. Smith, *Chase and Civil War Politics;* W. E. Smith, *The Blair Family;* and Charles R. Wilson, "New Light on the Lincoln-Blair-Frémont 'Bargain' of 1864," *American Historical Review,*

Going to New York, Chandler established headquarters at the Astor House. Assisted by George Wilkes, a capable war correspondent, he approached Frémont, who divided his time between Nahant and New York, and several interviews followed in the office of Frémont's attorney and political adviser, David Dudley Field. Field prepared the way by telling the general that while the war had plainly not been conducted with sufficient energy and ability, the assurances of a change in Administration policy were so full that he thought it best for him to do what he could for party unity. Chandler then made his appeal. Lincoln would not withdraw, he said, and yet he would certainly be defeated by McClellan if Frémont remained in the field. He was empowered, he went on, to say that if Frémont would step out, he would immediately be given active service in a high command, while those who had persecuted him (meaning the Blairs) would be placed where they could do him no further harm. Frémont wrote to friends for advice. Wendell Phillips urged him to stay in the field; Whittier paid him a special visit at Nahant to ask him to withdraw. One reply he had from Nathaniel P. Sawyer of Pittsburgh, dated September 13th, throws light on the negotiations: [19]

Your esteemed favor of the 7th reached me yesterday.... In reply, if you have assurance of Mr. Blair's immediate removal and also Mr. Stanton's and the assurance that Mr. Seward will not be reappointed, my advice is that you withdraw as soon as practicable in favor of Lincoln and Johnson.

Something tells me that Lincoln will never fill a second term. If I am right, Johnson will be the President, a man who I have loved since Sixty-one. I have no doubt he will do you and your friends justice. There is no man living I would sooner see President.

It will be time enough after the election to consider the propriety of accepting a position. For the present I would advise you to

---

XXIX, p. 71ff. The subject is intricate, but the evidence that Frémont was offered a bargain and rejected it is to my mind conclusive.

[19] This extraordinary letter, whose author seems to have anticipated Lincoln's assassination, is in the Andrew Johnson Papers, Library of Congress, Vol. 48.

entertain no proposition. I have perfect confidence in Horace Greeley and have no doubt he will be able to carry out any promises he may or has made.

If you withdraw, Gov. Johnston and myself will support Lincoln and Johnson....

It is evident from this that Chandler was trying to strike a bargain with Frémont. The promise that Blair would be retired was but a minor part of this bargain—that promise had already been made to Wade and Davis, and the retirement would occur no matter what Frémont did; but the promise of an active position was important. Some evidence exists that Frémont had temporarily considered withdrawing in favor of McClellan, a purpose which would heighten the eagerness of Lincoln's friends to buy his friendship. But the general, after due consideration, indignantly declined the proffered inducements. For this we have two pieces of evidence. One is a statement he left in his manuscripts. Offered "patronage to my friends and disfavor to my enemies," he writes, "I refused both. My only consideration was the welfare of the Republican party." The other evidence is a telegram which Col. R. B. Marcy sent from St. Louis to McClellan at this very time. He had learned from Frémont's friend Justus McKinstry, he telegraphed, that Chase and Henry Wilson had approached the explorer with the promise of a Cabinet position and of the dismissal of both Blairs "if he would withdraw and advocate" Lincoln. Frémont had replied that this was "an insult." [20]

The tone of Frémont's letter of withdrawal, published September 22nd, is further evidence that he had rejected a bargain as dishonorable. Had he made a dicker, he would have treated Lincoln gently. Instead, his language was harsh. "In respect to Mr. Lincoln," he declared, "... I consider that his Administration has been politically, militarily, and financially a failure, and that its necessary continuance is a cause of regret for the country." He withdrew not because he approved of Lin-

[20] McClellan MSS, September 22, 1864; compare William Starr Myers, *General George Brinton McClellan*, p. 448.

THE F. P. BLAIR FAMILY IN POLITICS

F. P. BLAIR, JR.   F. P. BLAIR, SR.   MONTGOMERY BLAIR

(From W. E. Smith, *The Francis Preston Blair Family in Politics,*
by courtesy of The Macmillan Company)

BUST OF FRÉMONT FROM THE ORIGINAL BY AUSTIN JAMES

(Courtesy of Catherine Coffin Phillips)

coln's policies, he wrote, but because McClellan had declared in effect for the restoration of the Union with slavery, and the Democrats must therefore at all costs be defeated. While between the two parties no man of liberal convictions could hesitate, he believed that Lincoln's reëlection was simply the lesser of two evils.

But if Frémont was above a bargain, Wade and Davis were equal to it. Now that Frank Blair had been humiliated, it was the turn of the Postmaster-General. He had lately increased the number of his bitter enemies. When Early's troops made their raid north of Washington, they burned Montgomery Blair's beautiful home, Falkland, at Silver Spring. A friend expressed sympathy, and Blair burst out with the bitter remark: "Nothing better could be expected while politicians and cowards have the conduct of military affairs." Halleck heard of this and wrote a letter about it to Stanton, which Stanton angrily laid before the President. In consequence, Stanton and Blair ceased to speak. But Montgomery was now disliked in every quarter. He had been barred from the Union League; a radical committee including George S. Boutwell and John Covode had lately demanded his dismissal; Henry Wilson wrote Lincoln that his retention would cost tens of thousands of votes. Men spoke of the Blairs as "a nest of Maryland serpents." On September 22nd, Chandler, accompanied by David H. Jerome, later governor of Michigan, had a private interview with Lincoln. He announced the complete success of his labors; he had gotten Frémont out of the race, though not by the means he had expected. That afternoon the Washington papers contained Frémont's card of withdrawal, and next day Lincoln asked for and received the resignation of Montgomery Blair, to take effect at once.

It was an unexpected stroke. Montgomery, joining his associates Bates and Welles as they emerged from a Cabinet meeting at the White House, took their breath away by coolly remarking: "I suppose you are both aware that my head is decapitated—that I am no longer a member of the Cabinet."

As Welles gasped, Blair took Lincoln's letter from his pocket and read it aloud. Couched in cordial terms, it reminded him that he had frequently stated that he was willing to leave the Cabinet when the President thought it best, and informed him that the time had arrived. Both Welles and Blair agreed that Frémont was not the moving cause. Welles muttered something about Chase; but, "Oh," said Blair, "there is no doubt Seward was accessory to this, instigated and stimulated by Weed." Such was the fraternal spirit in the Cabinet! None of the three thought of Zach Chandler as the principal agent.

Jessie tells us that she had thoroughly approved of Frémont's refusal of a field-command or Cabinet office as part of the proposed bargain; "with a feeling of joy akin to ecstasy I heard his decision to remain in private life." Though his withdrawal might have been phrased more generously, it effected its purpose. With a united party behind him, Lincoln received a majority of nearly a half million votes at the polls. Long afterward, in 1889, Jessie wrote the poet Whittier to thank him again for helping Frémont to reach the right decision: [21]

Among the words I remember from you are: "There is a time to do and a time to stand aside." I never forget your saying this to me at our Nahant cottage in 1864 when you had come to say them to Mr. Frémont. Wendell Phillips, who saw the *do* more clearly than the *stand aside*, insisted I had dreamed your visit. "Whittier goes nowhere. He never visits. His health does not let him," and laughing arguments against your wise and necessary view of what the time demanded of Mr. Frémont—to renounce self for the good of the greater number. Do you not remember it too? It was a deciding word, coming from you.

[21] Catherine Coffin Phillips, *Jessie Benton Frémont*, pp. 271, 272.

XXXIV

A Financial Debacle

THE virtual ending of Frémont's public career left him free to turn his attention to private affairs, and opened one of the strangest chapters of his career. It is a chapter marked by dramatic incident and tragic climax. When the war began, Frémont was a multimillionaire; a dozen years later, he was so nearly penniless that but for a few loyal friends he and Mrs. Frémont would hardly have known where they could lay their heads or obtain their next meal.

On the morning of December 13, 1864, a large and curious crowd surged into the Manhattan courtroom in which Judge Mason was presiding over Part Three of the State Supreme Court. The famous trial of ex-Mayor George Opdyke against Thurlow Weed for an alleged libel was about to begin. Every newspaper had sent its reporters to write columns of matter. The ablest lawyers of the city were enlisted, William M. Evarts and Edwards Pierrepont appearing for Weed, and David Dudley Field and former Judge Emott for Opdyke. In later years, men looked back upon the trial as heralding the disclosures of graft in national and city affairs which have made the Reconstruction period seem so shameful in our history. The principal charges published by Weed were that Opdyke had defrauded the city in claims growing from the destruction of a gun factory in the draft riots, had made illicit profits in war contracts, and had despoiled Frémont of much of his California property.[1]

---

[1] This trial is fully treated, with verbatim testimony, in a pamphlet published by the American News Company: "New York Supreme Court: The Great Libel Case of George Opdyke vs. Thurlow Weed, 1865."

From the intricate testimony which occupied the next fort-night, it is possible to piece together a story which would have made a fitting theme for one of Balzac's novels of business life. Evarts struck the dominant note of the tale when he said, in summing up: "The one phrase on everybody's lips is 'poor Frémont!'" It is a story of the Mariposa estate, 44,386 acres, from which many millions had been taken in placer gold and 3 million dollars in quartz gold, and which was valued on a production basis at 10 million dollars; of Frémont as the owner of this estate, unworldly, a rash enthusiast, quite uninformed upon the sharp practices of a shady era of business; of his trust in Opdyke, a slippery speculator long known as hungry for money and political preferment; of his confidence in David Dudley Field, an astute lawyer later identified with some of the most outrageous operations of Jim Fisk and Jay Gould, and the counsel of Tweed; of his faith in a financier well named Ketchum—Morris Ketchum—and others of similar stripe. He was among friends, said Evarts sarcastically; "and he may thank God that he did not fall among thieves"—at which the courtroom laughed. It is a story of the Mariposa estate involved, while Frémont was commanding in Missouri and West Virginia, in heavy debts for litigation and the expense of development—debts that bore 2 or even $2\frac{1}{2}$ per cent interest a month, in some instances compounding; of the manipulation of the estate by Opdyke, Ketchum, Hoey, and others, always to their own benefit; of a fee of $200,000 charged by Field; and of attempts, legal but barefaced, to deprive the owner of his just rights and revenues.

Frémont himself took the stand, his hair grizzled, his face, according to the reporters, showing a touch of genius and poetry, his eyes still lit by a deep smouldering blaze.[2] He had a natural reluctance to accuse old associates and expose himself as a victimized man. When, on cross-examination, he was asked whether a harsh advantage had been taken of him by his "friends," he stammered slowly: "I—I—I think not." When

[2] New York *Herald; World; Tribune;* December 14 and later issues, 1864.

Field himself asked if the gentlemen named did not fairly and honorably execute their agreement, the General answered: "You will remember, Mr. Field, there were controversies which were adjusted that grew out of our different interpretations of the agreements." The indignation of the spectators was especially aroused by the testimony regarding one transaction. It was shown that Frémont had been induced to transfer $2,500,000 of his stock in the Mariposa estate to Ketchum by proxies so that Ketchum, acting as his deputy, could control it. But when Frémont wished to recover some of his proxies, he was told that he had signed a document which amounted to a deed of trust, and he had to commence a suit to get his shares back. On the settlement of the suit, his opponents offered to give him 2 million dollars of the stock if he would sell them the remaining $500,000 at 25 cents on the dollar, though it was then rated at 50 cents on the market. "His hand was in the lion's mouth," as Edwards Pierrepont put it, "and he got out the best he could. He made this sacrifice of $125,000."

Family papers show that Frémont had gone to Europe in 1861, with his lawyer, Frederick Billings, in the hope of selling an interest in the estate, or at least procuring a favorable loan to pay its debts; and that he had talked with the Rothschilds and the Paris bankers without avail. They show that the debts at the beginning of 1862 or thereabouts were estimated at a total of $1,250,000, but actually came very close to $2,250,000, and that interest charges were about $13,000 monthly. Tormented by anxiety, the General was eager to shift the growing burden from his shoulders. At this time he held a five-eighths interest in the estate, Billings one-eighth, A. A. Selover of California one-eighth, and Trenor W. Park, who had advanced a large sum against the debts, the remaining eighth. It became imperative to raise money and stop the drain of interest-payments. Frémont was finally forced into a very bad bargain. As a result of complicated negotiations in New York, in June, 1863, a company was formed with 100,000 shares of stock, of $100 par value each. Of these 12,500 each went to Billings, Selover, and a creditor named Parker; while 25,000 were turned over to three men who engaged to pay off the debts, Ketchum, Hoey, and Opdyke. This nominally left 37,500 shares to Frémont. But he paid 2,000 (of par value $200,000!) to Field for legal services; and he placed 25,000 in the hands of Ketchum, who represented that he needed power to vote them to insure control for the New York group. They were to be held in trust until the bonds for clearing off the debts were repaid, and then returned to Frémont. Meanwhile, the explorer kept only 8,500 shares in his own hands. As we have seen, the task of getting Ketchum, Hoey, and Opdyke to disgorge the other 25,000 proved anything but easy.

Writing long after the event,[3] Mrs. Frémont asserted that if her husband had not carried through this desperate and costly transaction when he did, "those interested in accumulating the indebtedness on the property, and so depriving him of the estate, would have succeeded." As it was, she added, in every way feasible by litigation they tried to hamper the actions of the company and, if possible, obtain control of parts of its property. She and her husband believed that the sweeping away of the costly dam which he had built across the Merced River was attributable to the treachery of an agent who deliberately neglected to open the sluice-gates in flood time. Legal expenses ran up to a total of $600,000! There is no doubt that he did well to get out of the mess when he could, and with what money he could. He had not the cold, calculating business sagacity which was needed to rescue Mariposa from the ravenous sharks circling about it. Judge Pierrepont told the jury (which incidentally refused to convict Thurlow Weed of libeling Opdyke) that "this genius of a man once worth $10,000,000 and more" would testify that it had almost all "been stripped away from him, and he has but little left."

[3] MS. *Memoirs*, Bancroft Library. Trenor W. Park, who played the part of a rapacious creditor in the affair, was later the principal promoter of the Emma Mine, and induced General Schenck to discredit himself by lending his name to the mine promotion while Minister to England.

This was not quite true. When he sold his shares, he was still a rich man. But he had only a fragment of his once-great fortune.

It would have been well if, recognizing that the ruthless hurly-burly of business in the seventies was no place for him, Frémont had invested his money in safe securities and devoted himself to some professional pursuit. But such a course was alien to his temperament. He was too active, ardent, and imaginative. Always some great object, wealth or fame or power, floated just before his outstretched hands. The great spaces of the West still called to him for conquest. His dream of leadership in opening the gates upon their vast resources still burned in his brain, and it led him into an inevitable field. As the war closed, construction gangs began racing westward across the plains and eastwards across the Sierras to join the two sections of the first transcontinental railroad, the Central Pacific-Union Pacific. Plans were already on foot for the Northern Pacific, which soon enlisted Jay Cooke. Frémont had devoted two expeditions to exploring for a south-central or southwestern route, and it was natural for him to turn eagerly to various projects for railroads in that quarter.

With characteristic impetuosity, he hastened to throw not a quarter, not a half, but all his money into these enterprises. His first step was to purchase the franchise and property of the infant Kansas Pacific and begin its construction; then he bought the Missouri Pacific, and induced Congress to rename it the Atlantic & Pacific, extend its line, and give it a large land-grant. But his interest in these lines soon became subordinate to another undertaking, and he surrendered his holdings in both of them. This other undertaking was built about the Memphis & El Paso, of which he bought control, shortly becoming president. He writes in his manuscript *Memoirs:*

The Memphis & El Paso had a large segregated grant of lands from Texas, in no wise connected with the [Federal] Government. I procured from the Texas Legislature a large grant of lands, which was all in the interest of the Memphis & El Paso, which was planned to run from the harbor of Norfolk to San Diego and San Francisco, and its extended name was the Transcontinental, and I had acquired for it franchises in South California, Arizona, and Arkansas. An interest had been bought by me in the Memphis & Little Rock Railroad, and arrangements were being made with the intervening lines.

This is correct. The unbuilt Memphis & El Paso, chartered in 1856 by Texas, had received from the State promises of about 18,200,000 acres in all, a small principality. Frémont believed that with this line as a beginning he could bring into existence a mighty system from Memphis through to San Diego. Before him floated the vision of finally extending his southern transcontinental to the Atlantic at Norfolk—that vision which Collis T. Huntington ultimately realized.[4]

With this object in view, Frémont and other heads of the Memphis & El Paso in 1867-68 offered two bond issues totaling 10 million dollars. He acquired franchises in several States and Territories, bought lands for terminals at San Diego, and made tentative arrangements with a projected western line called the San Diego & Fort Yuma Railroad. While it built east from San Diego to the Gila, the Memphis & El Paso would build southwest through Arkansas, Texas, and the Territories to a junction at Yuma. What could be simpler? General Rosecrans and Sedgwick inaugurated work on the San Diego & Fort Yuma in September, 1869, when it was announced that sufficient funds were in hand to build to the Gila.[5] Frémont expected his bond issues to carry his own line forward rapidly, and while fifty miles of Texas track were being graded and the first locomotives ordered, he placed surveyors at work in the mountain passes of New Mexico.

In planning this southern transcontinental, he asked for no Federal land-grant; he believed that the Texas grant was sufficient. He did go to Congress for a right of way through the

[4] Frémont's railroad ventures are somewhat fully and very harshly analyzed in Cardinal Goodwin, *John Charles Frémont*, Ch. 13. The transcontinental venture, which had a separate existence from the Memphis & El Paso, was called the Memphis, El Paso, & Pacific Railroad.

[5] New York *Herald*, September 16, 1869.

Territories, and the House passed the necessary measure in February, 1869, by a vote of 121 to 41. The bill then went to the Senate, where Oliver P. Morton and Roscoe Conkling pressed it earnestly, but Howard of Michigan was instrumental in strangling it. This misfortune precipitated a wordy battle between Greeley's New York *Tribune*, which had been praising Frémont's enterprise in the highest terms, and Senator Howard. The *Tribune* not only declared Howard's motives selfish, but hinted that they might be corrupt. He was chairman of the committee on the Pacific Railroad. One transcontinental had been built with a large Federal subsidy; at least two more must be added, with various branches: "There are always crowds in the lobby of either House raving for more subsidies." Indeed, said the *Tribune*, only President Grant's intervention had prevented a steal at the previous session. Now came Frémont offering to build a transcontinental line without costing the nation a cent—threatening to spoil the subsidy business; and Howard, holding a position "in which a corrupt man may make a great deal of money," hampered his undertaking by quibbles and sharp manœuvers. When Howard explained that he had threatened a filibuster against the bill because he questioned the continued validity of the Texas land grant, the *Tribune* pooh-poohed his excuse, remarking that if any such doubts existed they were for the financiers of the road, not for Congress, to consider.[6]

That summer of 1869 witnessed efforts, much more strenuous than discreet, to float the bonds of the Memphis & El Paso in France. They were fairly successful; a total of $5,343,000 worth of securities was sold in Europe, almost wholly to French investors. But of this the French agents of the road, after the custom of the time, paid only three-fifths into the company treasury, taking two-fifths for their trouble. The money came in slowly and irregularly, much of it being used in France to buy rolling-stock and rails; obligations at

---

[6] For the controversy between the *Tribune* and Howard, see its issues for August 5, 11, and 17, 1869.

home meanwhile rose steadily. Moreover, unexpected physical obstacles were met; a freshet blocked the channels of the Red River and steamboats could not come within fifty miles of the point where construction had begun. The cost of grading the first seventy miles far exceeded the early estimates. Nevertheless, Frémont's faith in his road remained undiminished. So did that of the *Tribune*. Senator Howard's Pacific Railroad Committee early in 1870 showed fresh hostility, for on April 22nd a subcommittee reported that it believed the road had forfeited its land-grant by tardiness in construction. The *Tribune* scolded this report vigorously while praising Frémont's undertaking anew. Greeley was always a staunch friend: [7]

The proposition of a railroad on the 32d parallel of latitude has been before the public in various shapes for twenty years, and yet the enterprise is still struggling desperately for existence. Then Texas was the only State of the Gulf region, to whose prosperity the completion of the road is of almost vital importance, which gave it the least encouragement. Louisiana was cold because New Orleans was passed by, and Arkansas offended because Memphis was aimed at. But so earnest was Texas in its desire to see the road built that its several legislatures under rebel and loyal rule affirmed and reaffirmed the grant of lands made to the road in 1856. California on the Pacific Coast was desirous of making the port of San Diego the western terminus of the line, chartered and aided the partial construction of another line. The Texas route is the Memphis & El Paso line; the California route is usually called the San Diego & Fort Yuma Railroad. Of the former more than fifty miles are graded, and twenty-three miles laid with rails. Of the latter we know only that work is in progress. Without doubt the two lines have more of finished work, larger land grants, and better prospects of being eventually completed than any other Southern Pacific Rrd. These two roads are under the control of Gen. John C. Frémont; and he has asked Congress to consolidate, charter, and aid them under the title of the "Southern Transcontinental Railway.

[7] New York *Tribune,* May 25, 1870.

The Senate Committee on the Pacific Railroad has not only reported adversely to this consolidation, but has proposed to authorize an entirely new line, to be called the Texas Pacific Railroad, with branches and connections; and the bill makes large land grants....

Frémont's enterprise, while ambitious, was not more grandiose than many others in the Gilded Age, and the methods by which he tried to finance his scheme were merely typical of these flush and optimistic years. In view of the apparent security which 18,200,000 acres (10,240 for each mile built) offered, they were not reckless.[8] Compared with Jay Cooke's methods of booming the Northern Pacific or "banana belt" route they were conservative; compared with the operations of the Credit Mobilier in building the Union Pacific, they were decidedly decent. They differed little from the financial arrangements made for dozens of other lines which went bankrupt in or before 1873. To be sure, the Memphis & El Paso actually laid down only short stretches of track, and only three locomotives were placed on them, but the land grants were, as the press agents wrote, "an empire in themselves." However, high construction costs, the ebbing flow of French money, Senator Howard's doubts as to the land-grant, and other factors all sapped the credit of the company. In midsummer of 1870 the blow fell. The road failed to meet payments, mortgage-holders applied for a receivership, and the Federal courts appointed John A. C. Gray to take possession of the property.

To Frémont this meant ruin—ruin utter and irretrievable. His Kansas Pacific enterprise had already shaken his position, for after paying $200,000 for this road and investing large sums in construction, he had lost it all. Now his remaining money was gone. Family tradition describes the blow as paralyzing in its completeness.

Throughout these years of railroad-planning, the General's household had lived on a lavish though hardly ostentatious scale; he was a millionaire, and he had dwelt like one. During

[8] *Commercial and Financial Chronicle,* August 9, 1873.

the war he had bought a commodious brownstone mansion at what is now 21 West 19th Street, between Fifth and Sixth Avenues. This was a fashionable part of town, and his neighbors included Theodore Roosevelt, Sr., and (for a time) Senator John Sherman. Early in the sixties he had also bought a comfortable summer home on the Hudson, "the old Webb place," some two miles north of Tarrytown—later a part of John D. Rockefeller's estate. Here, amid more than a hundred acres of lawn and woodland, he had a fine house of rough gray stone, commanding a view of the broad Tappan Zee. Both houses afforded every comfort—a good cuisine, presided over by a French chef, well-drilled servants, flowers, music, and handsome furniture. Frémont, keeping a spirited horse, rode much in Central Park with Colonel Zagonyi and others, while his daughter Lilly drove a pair of Kentucky thoroughbreds. The children had tutors, and Lilly in especial became an excellent linguist. Mrs. Frémont, interested in many charities, gave to them with a generous hand.

At all times Frémont's personal tastes were simple, and in some ways he maintained a Spartan existence even when his wealth seemed greatest. He ate astonishingly little, never touched spirits, and drank wine—a glass of claret or Matrai —only when he was tired. He did not smoke, saying that he had taken warning from his men on his expeditions, who seemed to suffer as much from the deprivation of tobacco as of food. He dressed plainly. He used to say that he preferred "old garments, old books, old friends." His library was large, filling from floor to ceiling, in these years, all sides of a room twenty by thirty feet; indeed, after Humboldt's death in 1859 he had purchased the books of the great geographer. Here were also other volumes in beautiful bindings, including a set of the Audubon which had so fascinated Jessie as a child in the Congressional Library. His own room held a special set of cases covering the art of war from the earliest time to his own day. But books and horses were his chief indulgences. He belonged to no clubs, costly or otherwise; he cared little for the theater and nothing for elaborate social entertainments; and he liked to go to bed by ten or earlier, rising at the glimmer of dawn. The household was hospitable, for nothing pleased Frémont more than having friends about him. At the estate on the Hudson—which Mrs. Frémont christened by the local Indian name Pocaho—guests were usually present, and in town an extra plate was always laid at dinner for the chance comer. But balls, receptions, and large dinner-parties were avoided. The general liked better a good fencing-match, a long country walk, or a quiet chat with some congenial friend like N. P. Banks, Thurlow Weed, or John Sherman. A young woman, Nellie Haskell, who lived with them for a time at Pocaho has described his routine:

The general was often away in the West on his railroad business, but when home he usually read quietly or took evening walks with Mrs. Frémont or long rides through the woods and along the post-roads with the boys, Lil, and myself. He loved to listen to what he called home-made music. He went occasionally to the theatre when Mrs. Frémont asked him, which was seldom, because she knew he preferred to play chess or chat with the neighbors, the Phelpses, Schuylers, Aspinwalls, or Beechers, who dropped in often. As to formal dinners, he attended them only when Mrs. Frémont said: "You really must go this time." She attended many such functions when he was West on business, going to Washington for dinners and musicales. She was present at Mrs. Grant's first White House reception....But when Mr. Frémont was at home, she tried to have only the sort of guests in the house agreeable to him.

In these years he and Mrs. Frémont spent much time and money in travel. In 1869 they visited France, Germany, Austria, and Scandinavia, the General combining pleasure with a certain amount of business; and they left two of the children in Dresden for schooling. As a railway president, he was in Washington, Texas, or California—everywhere that affairs called him. Both he and Jessie were personages, and they moved with dignity. The summer of 1868 they visited St. Louis to witness the unveiling of a statue of Thomas Hart Benton. In Mrs. Frémont the event awakened the deepest emotion. A holiday crowd of 40,000 filled the park, and thousands of school-children carrying roses were massed about the pedestal. A band played in the hot afternoon sun. As Jessie pulled the cord and the white drapery fell away the children threw their flowers at the base of the statue; an outgoing train to San Francisco halted and saluted with whistle and waving flags; and she gazed through a mist of tears at the bronze image of her father, facing westward, with the words carved below: "There Is The East. There Lies the Road to India." To both Frémont and Jessie, movement, action, and the sense of important pursuits were the breath of life; and Jessie in especial delighted to live with a certain largeness and splendor.

Now the spacious, luxurious days were suddenly gone forever. There was no money for travel, for tutors, or for servants. The Nineteenth Street home and the much dearer Pocaho on the Hudson were both swept away. Even prized personal belongings had to be sold. Bierstadt's painting of the Golden Gate with the sun setting behind it was bought by a friend for $4,000, just what Frémont had paid for it. The library, portraits, and mementoes of California, Washington, and Paris in large part disappeared. Land which had been held in California in the name of Mrs. Frémont and the children was sold with the rest. For a brief period the two could not even live together, Mrs. Frémont going into the country to take refuge in one friendly household, and Frémont staying at another in the city. It was a chilling plunge from wealth to penury.

It could not be said that Frémont had fared better than other investors in the Memphis & El Paso, for he was the last man in the world to use his inside knowledge to escape scot-free from the crash which ruined others. Yet about his name there instantly collected the atmosphere of a scandal. The reason for this lay in the means used to sell the Memphis & El Paso bonds in France. Frémont, with his usual poor judgment of men, had been unfortunate in his agent. The French consul-general in New York, Frémont's brother-in-law Gauldrée Boileau, had introduced to him a M. Henri Probst, whom he endorsed as a well-known businessman in Paris. Probst had in fact been connected with the French Government in supplying the troops engaged in the Mexican occupation; Frémont liked the man, and at his instance the executive board appointed him agent in France. It was agreed that for the first series of bonds issued 60 per cent of the face value was to be paid to the Company, 34 per cent was to be given to the banking house selling the bonds, and 6 per cent was to go to the agent.[9] Probst, after associating with himself a prominent French railway engineer, Antoine Lissignol, to lend an appearance of technical strength to the enterprise, arranged with the great brokerage house of Paradis et Cie. to float the bonds. This house made harsh stipulations, requiring that all possible materials be purchased in France or Belgium; and one reason why the road shortly failed was that contracts for 100 engines and 45,000 tons of rails, costing 14,000,000 francs, were let in France.

Going from New York to Paris late in 1867, Probst had concluded this arrangement with Paradis et Cie. during the latter part of 1868; and either Probst or Paradis et Cie. then indulged in a series of remarkable misrepresentations. A fullpage advertisement in *La Liberté* of May 15, 1869, is typical of the extravagant claims made for the enterprise. This described the company as the "Transcontinental Memphis Pacific," and pictured its line as running from Baltimore, Norfolk, and Charleston, the three Eastern termini, westward through Chattanooga, Memphis, Arkansas, Texas, and the Territories to San Diego. The roads from the Eastern seaports to Memphis were spoken of as "that part of the transcontinental railroad which is finished and in operation," while it was stated that the section from Memphis to Little Rock was in working order and the line from Little Rock to the Red River was being

---

[9] *Commercial and Financial Chronicle*, September 4, 1875; Frémont, MS *Memoirs*.

"pressed forward actively." Part of the advertisement reads like some dream of Tartarin of Tarascon. "Entering the territory of New Mexico," it declared, "the Transcontiental meets the great commercial route from Guaymas and the interior of Mexico at Santa Fé. It will, for the future, suppress the dangerous marches of caravans from Santa Fé to San Francisco, New Orleans, and St. Louis. It then reaches California, after receiving at Arizona City the traffic of the great River Colorado." [10]

This was bad enough; but there were still worse misrepresentations. In *La Liberté* and other newspapers the brokers stated that "the company with the approbation of Congress has fused itself with the lines constructed and at present working from Memphis to Chattanooga, Chattanooga to Washington and Baltimore, Chattanooga to Norfolk, and Washington to Norfolk through Richmond." They also declared that the Federal Government had subsidized the Memphis & El Paso as it had the Union Pacific. "Besides the grants of land," ran the advertisements, though there were no congressional grants, "the Federal Government has voted a guarante of interest of six per cent in favor of the ordinary construction bonds." Of course this was preposterous. The American minister, Elihu Washburne, promptly sent copies of the advertisements and the placards which were stuck up over Paris to the secretary of state, suggesting that he investigate and take remedial action. He was the more ready to act because ever since his visit to St. Louis in 1861, and his formulation then of charges which the Committee on the Conduct of the War declared unfounded, he had keenly disliked Frémont. By this time, fifteen million francs' worth of the bonds had been sold.

Of these falsehoods circulated in Paris, Frémont knew nothing till later. "At the time the misstatement was made," he writes, "I was in Washington asking Congress for the right of

---

[10] A full history of the Memphis, El Paso & Pacific, and of the methods used to sell the bonds in France, is given in *Senate Misc. Doc.* 121, 41st Cong., 2d Sess.; this contains more than a hundred pages of data and testimony.

way for this road through the Territories to the Pacific. This fact was widely known—spoken of in the newspapers in editorials and otherwise; and a telegram from Paradis et Cie. to any banker in New York would have corrected an error which the face of the bonds should have suggested." The bonds declared explicitly that they were based upon lands granted by the State of Texas, and in no way indicated any connection with the Federal Government. No doubt some of the material for the glowing account of the "Transcontinental" as a system running from Norfolk to California was drawn from the hopes and imaginings of Frémont and his associates, who believed in the line. But even the mildest representations of the French agents were made without his authority or knowledge, on their own responsibility.[11]

Reaching Paris in the summer of 1869, Frémont published a letter in an influential French journal in which he tried to set the public right on the main facts as to the bonds. "It is completely false," he wrote, "that we have ever declared that our mortgage bonds enjoy a Federal guarantee of six per cent interest." On the contrary, he declared, the security for the bonds was the mortgage placed upon the state land-grant.[12] In a supplementary statement published on September 27th he added that the company was pressing Congress for a Federal charter, the result of which would be a new land subsidy from the states which had not disposed of their public domain, and the recognition of the line as a postal and military railroad. His optimism unquestionably operated, like Jay Cooke's optimism about the Northern Pacific just before its collapse, like the optimism of many an enterpreneur, to lead investors into a highly speculative enterprise. He should have been more indignant, explicit, and thorough in contradicting the lies cir-

---

[11] Fremont's full statement in self-defense on the sale of the bonds, in the form of a letter to Senator Howard, is published *Senate Misc. Doc.* 96, 41st Cong., 2d. Sess. It is complete and explicit, filling nine pages. It contains no date, but was apparently written about March 25, 1870. One feature is Frémont's sharp attack on Washburne.

[12] *La Phare de la Loire,* September 18, 1869.

culated by Probst. He should also have included a warning
that some question had recently arisen as to the continued
validity of the Texan land-grant. But his sanguine temperament conspired with his desire not to injure the bonds un-
necessarily.

The bankruptcy of the Memphis & El Paso caused an indignant outcry in France and a feeling of dismay among right-
thinking Americans. For some time the press devoted much
space to the affair. Three years later such failures were to become commonplace. But the post-war boom still endured, and
many Americans were anxious to determine who was blameworthy for these losses. They agreed with Senator Howard's
emphatic statement that "a more stupendous fraud never was
committed or attempted upon a friendly people," and that
"it is one which, if the work of Americans, should make every
American blush." They turned back to the published report
of April 22nd upon the railroad, with its mass of testimony by
Frémont, Corwine, and others upon the operations of the company.

Senator Howard, who compiled this report and who had
shown a hostile attitude to Frémont from the beginning, now
told the Senate that while he could not hold him "personally
responsible" for the misrepresentations, he did not "think Gen.
Frémont's skirts are clear in reference to these transactions."
Many Representatives and not a few Senators were ready to
defend Frémont. In debate half a dozen champions challenged
Howard's statement with asperity.[13] Sumner declared that it
was highly unjust, for there was no evidence of privity on the
part of the explorer. Lyman Trumbull of Illinois, James Nye
of Nevada, and Simon Cameron of Pennsylvania all took the
same side. Trumbull demonstrated that Howard's statement
represented only his individual judgment, that it was based
chiefly on one-sided French and American newspaper reports,
and that a majority of the subcommittee had dissented from it.
He also made the valid point that the French themselves were

[13] For this debate see *Congressional Globe,* June 20-23, 1870.

largely blameworthy for their losses—that they had no excuse for not learning the truth:

Sir, he [Howard] brings no fact against Frémont that I have heard. He brings charges against the Memphis & El Paso Railroad; he complains that its bonds were puffed up. I understand that a single party in France was the purchaser of those bonds, and afterwards put them upon the market in Paris, and he had various publications inserted in the papers in order to sell them for as much as he could get. Is General Frémont responsible for that?... The bond itself shows what its security is; and the Senator will hardly make the Senate or the country believe that capitalists do not look to see what security the bond is issued on. Capitalists understood this thing quite as well as the Senator from Michigan did. They knew what they were buying.

Nevertheless, the episode left an unhappy blemish upon Frémont's reputation. It is evident that he had acted with entire honesty in the matter, but it is also certain that he had shown a lamentable lack of discretion and care. It was his business, in the conscientious discharge of his duties, to scrutinize the advertisements of his company's bonds in all markets, to insist upon fair statements, and to caution his agents against exaggeration. His fault was of omission, not commission, but it was nevertheless real. When he learned of the false statements he should have been more emphatic in denying them. We cannot believe that a man of his sense of honor consented to an improper act, but he did not sufficiently guard against such acts by others. Once more his precipitancy and lack of circumspection betrayed him.

Irate Frenchmen came to America and filed affidavits demanding his arrest; French bondholders commenced suits in New York against him and his associates. The Paris office of the Memphis & El Paso was closed by the authorities, and all books and papers were seized. Criminal proceedings were begun against the men supposed to be responsible for selling bonds under false pretenses, including Frémont. After a thorough official examination, lasting more than two years, his name was removed from the list of those accused; but just before the trial commenced it was suddenly restored. Later he was told that this was at the instance of our minister, Elihu Washburne, whom he had attacked in his published defense. He was given inadequate time to appear before the *juge d'instruction*—only ten days after the summons was served in New York; he had scanty funds for travel or for hiring counsel, and in his absence was condemned for failing to reply. Though his French counsel, M. Allou, was in the courtroom, in accordance with French law the judge refused to hear him. The publicity given to this condemnation left a totally unjust impression.

Some years later, in closing his work as Federal receiver for the Memphis & El Paso, John A. C. Gray wrote the General on the subject. "I deem it fair to say," he stated, "that throughout the long and careful scrutiny which I have made into the affairs of the company, I have found no proof that would sustain the charges brought against you regarding the fraudulent sale of the company's bonds in France." Gray's testimony is the more important in that he was an attorney of marked distinction. The Marquis de Chambrun, who represented the French bondholders in America, gave the same testimony. He also wrote for Frémont a letter explaining the condemnation in Paris. "The judgment pronounced against you," he said, "was nothing more than a judgment by default resting upon the *prima facie* case submitted to the tribunal of *police correctionale* by the judicial officer or officers who had directed the preliminary investigation. Under this state of affairs no defense could be offered in your behalf." He added that these ex parte proceedings were an absolute nullity in the eyes of American law, were in direct conflict with the safeguards of personal liberty in the American constitution, and "are now void in France." [14]

---

[14] The letters of Gray and Chambrun are in the Frémont MSS. Gray went on to say: "The misrepresentations under which the bonds were sold to the

As the wreck of the Memphis & El Paso was cleared up, and the Texas Pacific Railroad took over its debts and assets, Frémont beyond doubt felt that his honor remained unblemished; that his motives and aims had always been of the highest character. Jessie shared this conviction. "It is an inextricable mass," she told a friend, "out of which I can glean only an impression of millions of dollars of railroad bonds floated abroad which brought profit only to the agent, advertisements published abroad that misrepresented the whole railroad picture, of which Mr. Frémont knew nothing.... He has had no part in any dishonest transaction. Certain of that, I am strong for whatever is to come." But he had little left but his self-respect. His career as a financier was as decisively ended as his career as an explorer. The demonstration that he was unfitted for business affairs was so complete that no acceptable employment was open to him. He was past sixty; he had three dependent children; he was almost penniless. All the courage that he had shown in facing the snow-choked Sierras and the storm of wartime obloquy in St. Louis was needed again; all of it and more.

public, were made by parties in Paris to whom the entire issue of bonds had been sold by the Company, and my examinations fail to show any proof that these misrepresentations were made with your authority."

XXXV

Poverty and Labor

IN this family crisis, it was Mrs. Frémont who, with characteristic vigor, came to the rescue. "I am like a deeply built ship," she used to say; "I drive best under a stormy wind." She had already discovered that she could earn money with her pen. During the Civil War she had set herself, with a frenzy of energy, to write the history of Zagonyi's brave troopers who made the charge at Springfield; and within ten days, according to family tradition, had produced the spirited little book called *The Story of the Guard*, the profits of which she devoted to the Sanitary Commission. Now, while the family went to live first on Madison Avenue, far uptown at Seventy-second Street, and then scraped together its resources to rent a cottage on what was called "the Esplanade" on the waterfront of Staten Island, she became a breadwinner.

Spurred on by the illness of her younger son, who was threatened with tuberculosis, and who must—the physician said—be sent to a dry high climate, she approached Robert Bonner of the New York *Ledger*. He offered her $100 each for a series of articles. Doubtless he thought it would be months before they were all completed, but she went home, sat down at her desk, and for days labored almost incessantly, hardly pausing for food or rest. When they were all done, she took them to the Ledger office and demanded payment in a lump sum to meet her son's needs. At once she began contributing to other magazines. In the fifteen years between 1875 and 1890, she produced article after article, story after story. She contributed tales for children to the *Wide Awake*, popular essays to the *Ledger*, historical sketches to *Harper's* and the *Century*. Some of this magazine work was made over into books: *A Year of American Travel,* dealing with California and Panama in the gold-rush days; *Far West Sketches,* concerned chiefly with Mariposa life; *The Will and the Way Stories* for juveniles; and most important of all, in 1887, the *Souvenirs of My Time,* an episodic review, brightly written, of her eventful life from the Bodisco wedding to the last tour of Europe.

Frémont was one of the incorporators of the Texas Pacific, which took over the wreck of the Memphis & El Paso, and till March, 1878, when the receivership was terminated, he was largely occupied in helping adjust the affairs of his dead railroad enterprise. For his labors, he received only a slender compensation. He hence had reason to be glad when, in 1878, upon the intercession of Zachariah Chandler and other old friends, he received from President Hayes the appointment as territorial governor of Arizona. The salary was but $2,000 a year, yet that sum meant much to the General. So, too, did the opportunity to revisit the wild West, and to see his surviving friends, including Alexis Godey, who traveled with him from San Francisco to Los Angeles.[1] There was still a halo of legend about Frémont's head, and his journey along the transcontinental line was a modest ovation. In Chicago and Omaha, he was offered banquets; in San Francisco the Pioneer Association of California gave him a reception; in many smaller towns, the stations were crowded with people eager to see him once more; and the friendly demonstrations continued through lower California to the end of the railroad at Yuma. Thence he had a "camping-out journey," as Mrs. Frémont called it, to Prescott, the territorial capital.

Frémont enjoyed such administrative opportunities as the post offered, and busied himself with recommendations regarding mining development, railway building, and irrigation by storage reservoirs. With his characteristic liking for large projects, he raised also the question of using the Colorado River to flood the depressed region above the head of the Gulf of

[1] I. T. Martin, *Recollections of Elizabeth Benton Frémont,* p. 136.

California known later as the Salton Sink, where a great inland sea could easily be recreated. The climate and vegetation of Arizona, he believed, might be essentially affected for the better. There was a congenial if narrow social life at Prescott, where a number of army officers were stationed. He delighted in the return to an outdoor life, and was capable of being in the saddle for twelve hours at a stretch. He thought nothing of riding eighty miles in two days. But poverty remained a sore burden even in the distant Southwest, where house rent was ninety dollars a month and provisions were atrociously high. It is an eloquent fact that although Mrs. Frémont and her daughter knew that the wonders of the Grand Canyon were at hand, it was a financial impossibility to visit them. After a time the high altitude of Prescott told so heavily on Jessie's health that she returned to a small house on Staten Island, and there continued writing stories and essays.

In 1883, hopeful of reëstablishing himself in the business life of New York, Frémont resigned and joined Jessie on Staten Island. On the day of his arrival Mrs. Frémont wrote a friend: "There is only one piece of news in the world to-day, the General is here. He tells me I am beautiful, but I tell him the truth. He looks young, rested, and as handsome as that day in '41 when I saw him swinging down the avenue in his new uniform." [2] One undertaking which floated elusively before him was a plan for enlisting the Barings and other English capitalists in the development by irrigation of the rich Imperial Valley in California. While in Arizona he had become interested, in association with Judge Edward Silent, in various mining enterprises, notably in the rich copper area now known as the Verde—enterprises which ultimately made Judge Silent rich. He was as eager and hopeful as ever. He believed that fortune always lay just ahead. But of actual monetary returns, there was pitifully little.

These trying years brought into relief some of the best qualities of Frémont and his wife. They did not conceal their strait-

[2] Catherine Coffin Phillips, *Jessie Benton Frémont*, p. 305.

ened lot. Newspaper reporters who visited their cottage for a "story" exclaimed over their evident poverty.[3] Yet they made the most of their few paintings, their bric-a-brac, their books, and the many trophies of Frémont's work as an explorer and soldier—the presentation swords he had received from the people at Charleston, the Germans of St. Louis, and Captain Cathcart; his foreign medals; the flag he had unfurled from the Wind River Peak, and the campaign banners of '56. Their pride permitted not the slightest recognition, by word or gesture, that they had fallen in fortune, or the slightest intimation of regret. In dignity of bearing, Mrs. Frémont was as much the *grande dame* as ever; her husband was the same grave, reserved, courteous gentleman, a little quieter as the years passed, but with the same piercing eye. Their devotion was, as always, beautiful to see. Observers who were much with them have said that they seemed never to need to discuss a question to reach the same conclusion; they intuitively knew each other's wishes and mental processes. They appeared to have some strange spiritual bond, such as that which Mrs. Frémont suggested when she described for the Psychical Research Society the telepathic message which she believed she had received, after long days of emotional prostration, of Frémont's safety at Parowan in 1854.[4]

Both of them struggled valiantly to make the best of their position. The two sons were educated at the Naval Academy and the Military Academy. Constant but unavailing efforts were made to obtain from the Government some compensation for the house and land seized at Black Point, near San Francisco, in 1863, for the erection of a fort; compensation which should have been made without hesitation, and which would have rescued them from all their difficulties. Mrs. Frémont wrote with unresting pen. In 1886, her husband also turned to literary labors. The *Personal Memoirs* of General Grant were then being read with intense interest, and the explorer was

[3] Compare Leander Richardson in Boston *Herald*, August 14, 1884.
[4] Described also in *Far West Sketches*, pp. 29-41.

seized by the idea that his own reminiscences would be of considerable value. Going to Washington, the Frémonts took a house for a year so that he could have access to official papers and reports, and set to work. A newspaper writer has given us a picture of them at their labors:[5]

The Frémonts live in a commodious house that overlooks the wooded grounds of the British Legation, the trees of Nineteenth Street, and the shrubbery of Dupont Circle. The family at present here consists of the General and Mrs. Frémont and their daughter. The two sons are married. One is in the navy, the other lives in Montana. The workroom is on the second floor of the house.... There is a bay window in the east end of the room, on the right of which is placed the General's table, surmounted by a tall set of pigeonholes, where letters, notes, and papers are kept. On the other side of the window is placed Mrs. Frémont's table, a large plain affair, covered with green leather. The General dictates and Mrs. Frémont writes down each word of the story as it falls from his lips. The family group is, however, not yet complete. In the alcove is placed a typewriter, and with it Miss Frémont transforms her mother's manuscript into neat, legible print. Here they all work together...all day long. The rule of the house is to rise at seven, take a cup of tea and a roll, and begin at eight, and continue until twelve, when breakfast is taken. At one o'clock they resume work and forge ahead until six, when the stop for the day and for dinner is made. In the evening the copy is sent out, and in the morning the proof-sheets are received from the printer. Gen. Frémont is now seventy-four years old, but looks scarce sixty. His hair, short beard, and moustache are white, but his brown eyes are clear and bright as stars, and his complexion has the ruddy, healthy glow of childhood.

To find a publisher was not easy, but at last Belford, Clarke & Co. of Chicago and New York entered into a contract. The first of the two volumes, a ponderous 650-page work, appeared in 1887 under the title of *Memoirs of My Life: A Retrospect of Fifty Years*, with a sketch of the life of Benton written by

[5] New York *Evening Post*, September 7, 1886, quoting the Washington *Star*.

Jessie. Based largely upon the reports of the exploring expeditions, much of which was reprinted almost verbatim, the first volume came down only to the capitulation of Couenga in 1847. Its full detail proved wearisome to general readers. Some of the numerous plates, from paintings and drawings based upon the daguerreotypes made by Carvalho in the fourth expedition, were admirable, but others were weak. The price of the book, ranging from $5.75 to $12.50 according to binding, was too high for ordinary purchasers. As a result it was a commercial failure, and the second volume was never published. For all his labors on the *Memoirs* Frémont received almost nothing. He spoke occasionally in public, as when in 1884 he campaigned in Michigan for Blaine, but he never lectured for pay. There were still times when the wolf howled very near the door.

At last a sudden crisis arose, Frémont's health seemed to break under the strain of writing, and late in 1887 he was seized with so severe an attack of bronchitis that his physician declared he must be taken at once to a warmer climate.[6] There was no money. In desperation—doubtless also in humiliation—Mrs. Frémont went to her old friend, the eminent railway builder Collis P. Huntington, who was all concern. "It must be California," he said; "you should have my private car, but it is already lent." That night he came in person to bring tickets, letters to officials of different railways, and a generous sum for expenses. Frémont was reluctant and almost angry, but Mrs. Frémont insisted. So did Huntington, who tactfully remarked: "You forget our road goes over your buried campfires and climbs many a grade you jogged over on a mule; I think we rather owe you this." A day later they were in a Pullman, running out of the stormy December weather into the bright sunshine of Kentucky:

It had been a trial to see the General's sad, unsmiling face [wrote Mrs. Frémont afterward], but toward evening he beckoned me across to his section, and holding my hand said, "You were right to come.

[6] I have received much material on this period of family life from the late Major Frank P. Frémont.

I feel better already." Whereupon I cried heartily. Instantly a young conductor was beside me with words of genuine compassion. "O, it is not that," I said, "I am so happy, the General says he feels better." "We all know who you are," the tender-hearted man said, "but we respected General Frémont's wish for silence."

This was the beginning of the end, though Frémont's long rest in California—they settled in a cottage on Oak Street in Los Angeles—seemed to restore his health. He returned to New York in 1889 to look after what he still proudly called his business affairs, leaving Mrs. Frémont on the Pacific Coast and writing to her daily. He had high hopes that he would yet induce Congress to make a proper payment for the Black Point property. Moreover, he had been deeply touched and gratified when his friends (prompted, it must be confessed, by Jessie) set on foot a movement to have him restored to the Army as a major-general, and placed on the retired list with pay, and he now gave them every assistance that was proper. He had outlived most of his enemies—the Blairs, Elihu Washburne, and others—and all the ill feeling of the past. Public sentiment supported the measure, and in April, 1890, Congress, "in view of the services to his country rendered by John C. Frémont, now of New York, as explorer, administrator, and soldier," duly made the appointment. It secured to him, for the first time in more than fifteen years, an adequate income, $6,000 annually, and enabled him to look forward to his last days in peace.[7]

His relief and pleasure, his friends in New York have said, were childlike. He proposed to go back as quickly as possible to Los Angeles, and there make his permanent home. Early in July, 1890, he wrote Mrs. Frémont that he would set off the following week and spoke of "living out our years together in a content most absolute." He had become involved with Josiah Royce in a controversy over his rôle in the conquest of Cali-

[7] Jessie, who believed the government owed them more than $40,000 for the Black Point property, declared with her usual spirit that this allowance was "small payment on account," and "sadly delayed" at that.

fornia, and wished to complete an article for the *Century Magazine*. But he had less strength than he or his sons, with whom he had spent much time in Washington, supposed.

The end came as a direct result of a kindly act. On a hot July Sunday, he made a pilgrimage to the grave of a little boy friend in Brooklyn. The English mother had obtained from him a promise that he would lay flowers there in memory of the child's birthday, and he kept the promise. That night occurred a sudden fall in temperature, and his boarding-house bed had insufficient coverings. Frémont had been overheated and fatigued, and was seized with a violent chill. His physician and close friend, Dr. William J. Morton, was called, and immediately upon arriving telegraphed up the Hudson to Ossining for the only son in reach, John C. Frémont, Jr. When the latter arrived, it was evident that peritonitis had set in, and that in a man seventy-seven years old it could only terminate fatally. Within a few hours it was all over. There was little time to warn Jessie. A telegram had gone to her from Charley: "Father is ill." Three hours later came another: "Father is dead." But the suddenness was perhaps best. "The end came painlessly," wrote the son to his sister Elizabeth, in words which recall Kent's exclamation over the dead Lear, "and without knowledge to him. It was blessedly quick and easy, and as I looked at him lying there so still and peaceful I questioned whether I was not heartless, for I could find no sorrow or pity for him at all, but a feeling of relief that his life was over. And how thankful I am that the last few months were made more peaceful and happier for him." The date was July 13th. He added: "Of what the effect is going to be on mother, I don't dare think. And when I do think, I doubt whether the cruelest result would not be the kindest. They lived in each other so that I don't think there is any life for the one left."

It was a characteristic end for a life full of misfortune— almost alone in a cheerless Manhattan boarding-house, with no friends near, and with Jessie three thousand miles away; his hope of their comfortable days together, all financial anxiety at last removed, never to be realized. Doubtless he knew, as his life ebbed away, that his wife would be plunged back again into utter poverty. When he was placed in his coffin—he had instructed that it be a plain pine box, and that he be buried in an ordinary black suit, not his uniform—his son took a miniature of Jessie as she had been in the days of her youth, and the telegram that was her last message to him, and folded them in one of his crossed hands. It was the end of the romance that had begun in Washington in the bright autumn days of 1840.

* * *

Mrs. Frémont was destined to outlive her husband by a dozen years, residing constantly with her daughter in Los Angeles. The death of the General, who had received only two months' pay since his restoration to the army lists, left her in sorely straitened circumstances; but her friends and admirers came at once to her aid. Within a few months, in the latter part of 1890, she was presented with a handsome cottage in the newer part of Los Angeles. At the same time, Congress, spurred on by exaggerated press stories that she was in actual destitution, passed a bill giving her the ordinary pension of $2,000 allowed to widows of major-generals. Her future was thus secure. For many years, she was one of the prominent figures of Los Angeles, deferred to on all public occasions. When President McKinley and John Hay visited the city in 1901, one of their first acts was to drive to Mrs. Frémont's home to pay her their respects. "My goodness, John," Mrs. Frémont said with a twinkle to the portly Secretary of State, whom she recalled as a slender stripling in the White House in Lincoln's time, "how you have grown!" She was then confined to her chair, and on December 27, 1902, she died.

They are buried together at Piermont on the Hudson, near the brink of a bluff looking out over the broad Tappan Zee to the old home, Pocaho, where they spent some of their happiest years together. Over their grave, the state of New York in 1906 erected a dignified monument, with bronze flag, sword, and a medallion head of the explorer against a granite stone, and on it are recorded his many achievements and titles. He would have chosen for himself a shorter, simpler inscription—perhaps the sentence in which Buchanan declared that to him more than any other belonged the credit for the conquest of California. Some of his friends would have chosen the line of Whittier—"Frémont, who struck the first brave blow for liberty." But the most fitting epitaph, recalling his happiest achievements, and his most remarkable services to the nation, is furnished by the words of Jessie Benton Frémont—"from the ashes of his campfires have sprung cities."

XXXVI

Character and Fame

IN this varied and energetic career, so full both of achievement and frustration, there is much which appears psychologically puzzling. The fact that to many of Frémont's contemporaries his personality seemed alien and impenetrable helps to explain why his aims and motives were frequently misjudged, and his acts aroused such violent antagonism. He made ardent friends who loved him (some of them) just this side of idolatry; he made enemies who found no condemnation too harsh. Many who attempted to measure him in a detached way formed, after long study, an impression that he was a genius *manqué,* a distinguished and valuable man who just fell short of being effectively great. Josiah Royce, not the friendliest of observers, wrote that the most transient personal intercourse with this romantic and fascinating figure left a sense of a peculiarly hidden and baffling character. "The charming and courtly manner, the deep and thoughtful eyes, the gracious and self-possessed bearing, as of a consciously great man at rest, awaiting his chance to announce his deep purpose and to do his decisive deed—all these things perplexed one who had any occasion to observe, as some did, that the deep purpose seemed always to have remained in reserve, and that there had been some reason in his life why the decisive deed had never been done." Other men, like Schurz, felt strongly attracted to him at first sight, and yet retained, in a sense of some subtle deficiency combined with great capacities, an unwillingness to give him their complete confidence.

Yet Frémont's character and mind are essentially simple and clear, and both his talents and limitations are susceptible of as close analysis as those of most men of reserved temperament. He has sometimes been described as a showy and pretentious personality. Nothing could be further from the truth. All his closest associates testify that the outstanding qualities of his character were sincerity and simplicity. For ostentation—despite certain appearances to the contrary when in 1861 he tried to impress his strength upon hostile St. Louisans—he not only had no taste, but a decided distaste. He dressed with the utmost plainness. He avoided public appearances, and would go far to avoid a reception or civic dinner. He disliked public speaking, and it required a strong attachment to a man or cause to induce him, as in his brief tour for Blaine, to appear before an audience. He was simple in all his private habits: he liked plain food, gave a plain hospitality, and found his chief amusements in horseback riding and walking. In Mrs. Frémont's tastes there was always a strong element of liking for the dramatic, but of this Frémont himself showed not a trace.

Frémont's habits and impulses were essentially restless and kinetic. His friends noted that, beneath his quietness and dignity, he was always active, always moving, always concerned with action rather than thought. In his leisure at Pocaho he was incessantly busy outdoors. Though he had a large library, especially strong in military works and exploration, he was seldom observed sitting with a book in his hand. His friends remember him eagerly mastering one of the high-wheeled bicycles just coming into vogue, going on long botanical excursions, and overseeing the gardens and stables. He was extremely fond of dogs and horses. The years in which he furiously organized the mining activities at Mariposa, building flumes, stamp-mills, and roads, were as congenial to him as the years of outdoor exploration. Rather strangely, he had little aptitude for mechanical contrivance; as one of his family expressed it, he was "not a putterer." But he loved activities in the open and had little taste for study; in his later years, when master of his time, he retired early that he might be outdoors with the dawn. Yet there was no nervousness in this; when he was induced to take his seat in the circle indoors, his restlessness abruptly left him, and his dignified immobility, his perfect quiescence, with never an unnecessary gesture or motion, impressed all who saw him.

His social needs were fully met by a family life which was singularly attractive in its warmth and devotion, and in which he displayed the knightliest side of his character. It is significant that he not merely refrained from joining any clubs, but that he took no part in the activities of such bodies as the Grand Army of the Republic, in which he might have been a prominent figure; he was honored by the Royal Geographical Society, but joined no American scientific body. His circle of friends was limited, for his love of home life and his native reserve kept him from making new acquaintances readily. Yet with the men and women whom he knew best his reserve gave way to animation and even fun. His son writes that there was—

A sharp division between the two sides of his character; the questing side, which was expressed in his explorations, and the human side, which was companionable, cheerful, and with a tendency to gaiety accounted for by his French forbears. He heartily enjoyed a joke or a bright story, so long as it was keen and clean. Though in no sense pharisaical, he instinctively avoided the unclean, both physical and moral; and with all this, he was intensely human and understanding. One trait, or it might be said fault, was an indifference to what the general public might think, so long as he was sure that his action was right. Appearances are sometimes more important than facts, and I am sure that it was this indifference which has left him to a certain extent a misunderstood figure. Perhaps a sentence I remember may explain what I mean more clearly. One day when I was commenting upon the injustice of the government toward him in a certain case, he checked me by saying: "No! The United States and its government are all right. The fault lies in the fact that the conscience of the people is delegated to the members of Congress, and a delegated conscience never functions."

Frémont's primary talent was as an explorer; and just as he was rarely fortunate in the circumstances which threw him as a youth so quickly and effectively into the field of exploration, so he was unfortunate that later circumstances cut him off from all achievement therein. He was only rarely a "Pathfinder"; for the most part he was a Pathmarker. At times, particularly in his explorations of the Great Basin, he really made a new area known to the world. But in general he traveled over trails which had been found before by trappers, hunters, and traders, and through regions that were at least partially known to frontiersmen. His distinction lay in the scientific equipment he brought to the task of surveying, observing, and describing these trails and regions. For his period he was an excellent topographer, surveyor, and mathematician, and a good amateur geologist and botanist. For zoölogy, which was less important, he showed slighter aptitude. It would be hard to overemphasize the zeal and conscientiousness which he gave to the work of mapping his routes, collecting specimens, noting geographical and topographical facts, and at night taking his observations of the stars. He had a true scientist's reverence for his calling. Few distinctions pleased him so much as his medal from the Royal Geographical Society, and he spoke warmly of that body as his "alma mater"; while he took pride in naming one of his rivers after Alexander von Humboldt. "I am given by myself," he wrote, "the honor of being the first to place his great name on the map of this continent."

As an explorer he showed qualities of precision, industry, and resourcefulness that are quite incompatible with the conception of a flashy, unstable nature, a man of meretricious parts. His expeditions had no picnic aspect. For every member they were full of toil, hardship, hunger, fatigue, and peril; for Frémont they were full of constant and heavy responsibility. The romance of the western explorer's life, like that of most adventurous callings, largely vanishes on close examination; as the British soldier said of trench service, it was damned dirty, damned uncomfortable, and damned dangerous. To rise in the chill gray dawn; to tramp all day, twenty-five or thirty miles, over rough country; to eat half-raw, inadequate food and drink dirty water; to enforce discipline at every step; to be responsible for every animal, every piece of equipment, every life; to remain awake even to midnight in the harshest weather, after benumbing toil, in order to take astronomical observations; to sit up later still with cramped fingers noting the day's results; to rouse himself to see that watches were duly kept—such was Frémont's lot. It was his lot to frighten cowards out of his expedition before it got into the wilderness; to rise to sudden emergencies—now to replace the broken glass of the barometer without any glass, now to cross a rushing torrent without boats or material to make them; to hearten his men in undertakings that made even Indians quail, as in the winter passage of the Sierras; to be first on his feet in a surprise attack, as when the Klamath Indians struck. No poseur could have lasted ten days on these expeditions. The explorer deserved Kit Carson's heartfelt tribute of 1856:

> I was with Frémont from 1842 to 1847. The hardships through which we passed, I find it impossible to describe, and the credit which he deserves I am incapable to do him justice in writing.... I have heard that he is enormously rich. I wish to God that he may be worth ten times as much more. All that he has or may ever receive, he deserves. I can never forget his treatment of me while in his employ and how cheerfully he suffered with his men when undergoing the severest of hardships.

Two contrasting traits are evident in Frémont the wanderer and explorer. He brought to his labors an enthusiasm which had in it more than a touch of poetry. The grandeur of the West became a passion with him. When he speaks of valley flowers "in brilliant bloom," of some lake "set like a gem in the mountains," of a camp where "the rocks lit up with the glow of our fires made a night-picture of very wild beauty," of Mount Hood rising "like a rose-colored mass of snow," he is recording an emotion that touched his innermost being. After the hardest day's march, he could write of some strange landscape that "the interest of the scene soon dissipated fatigue."

To many this poetic enthusiasm over the fresh beauties of the West will seem the most attractive element in Frémont's character. The other trait is represented by his skill as an organizer, his iron discipline, and his fierce contempt for cowardice or shirking. The poet gave way to the martinet when it came to mounting guard against Indians, protecting camp equipment, barring liquor, or demanding the intensest exertions in Nevada deserts or Sierra snows. Himself uncomplaining and indomitable, he could not forgive the quitter. There is an undertone of scathing contempt, in his letter to Mrs. Frémont after the calamitous expedition of 1848-49, describing how one man gave up. "Proue laid down in the trail and froze to death. In a sunshiny day, and having with him means to make a fire, he threw his blankets down in the trail and laid there till he froze to death."

To the end of his life Frémont retained his ardent enthusiasm for wild nature in all its aspects. He read nothing with so much interest as accounts of travel in uncharted lands, from the penetration of tropical Africa to polar expeditions. He never hunted or fished, and taught his children not to take animal life except under necessity.

Out-of-doors was life to him [writes his son], indoors, a place sheltered from the elements. Stormy weather appealed to him as well as fair. Trees were to him sacred, and he would not let them be cut down on our property, unless dead or dying; then he would do the cutting himself. Flowers especially appealed to him; being a botanist, he took a double interest in them. Travelling with him through the mountains of Arizona on horseback, when he was governor, I have noticed he would guide his horse so as to avoid crushing a flower or ant-hill; all life had a significance for him. Once we were climbing in the mountains near Innsbruck, and I came across a snake. Boylike, I started to kill it, but he would not permit it. "No, let it go! It has not harmed you and probably enjoys life," he said, adding: "Besides, any Indian knows that to kill a snake causelessly will bring rain and a wet camp."

The two salient faults in Frémont's composition, as the fore-going chapters amply illustrate, were his impulsiveness or rash-ness, and his weak judgment of men and of critical situations. The two faults were closely allied. A greater endowment of caution or practical sagacity would have saved him from expul-sion at college; it would have withheld him from descending the dangerous Platte cañon with his instruments and records in a frail boat; it would have prevented the unnecessary clash with Castro on his first entrance into California. His midwinter crossing of the Sierras was an act of reckless impetuosity, in which he brilliantly succeeded because of favorable weather and the aid of two of the best frontiersmen of the time, Carson and Fitzpatrick. His attempted midwinter crossing of the San Juan and other mountains in 1848-49 was another impetuous act, which this time ended in irretrievable disaster. If Carson had been with him here when the storms smote him with irre-sistible force, he would have urged Frémont to make camp, gather wood, put up shelters for the men and animals, weather the storm, and at its termination go back instead of forward. A different decision on Frémont's part would have saved hu-man lives. But his most unfortunate display of imperfect judg-ment was in St. Louis in 1861. He surrounded himself with poorly selected men; he treated tactlessly men and forces re-quiring careful conciliation; he disregarded the wise and kindly efforts of Lincoln to counsel him. It is but a partial excuse to say that his judgment, with all its defects, was in many respects better than the judgment shown by Cameron, the Blairs, and others in Washington.

Our statement as to his deficiencies requires a certain elab-oration. Lack of judgment frequently means lack of general ability; but not so with Frémont, who had extreme quickness of mind and some very brilliant abilities. It sometimes means lack of foresight, a tendency to live too narrowly in the pres-ent; but Frémont if anything lived too much in the future. With him it meant a disproportion between his ardent imagina-tion, and his mediocre grasp of practical means to achieve the

goal he so vividly saw—to measure the hard, practical, intermediary steps separating him from it. He was a man who
dreamed dreams and saw visions. They fired his heart and
carried him, always intense and dynamic, into well-intentioned
action. They were such dreams as others might have brought to
practical fruition. His dream, when commander of the Department of the West in Missouri in 1861, of marching through
Arkansas to Memphis, living on the country as he went—it was
such a dream as Sherman realized in his march to the sea. His
dream of throwing a railroad from Little Rock or New Orleans
to the Pacific—it was the dream that the builders of the Santa
Fé and Southern Pacific made reality. But once transported
outside his true scientific vocation into the hard world of clashing human interests, he lacked the shrewdness, the grasp of
human nature, the insight into ways and means, to give his
grandiose plans effect. Without the imagination, he would have
been a more useful though a far less striking man. If fate had
gifted him with strong practical grasp as well as soaring imagination, he might have been one of the dominant figures of his
time. He was not a rudderless ship, but a ship whose swelling
sails made its rudder seem feeble.

The result was a career that was never quite tragic, never
quite victorious, but often midway between the two as he played
out an elaborate drama of frustration. Again and again he
was placed in situations where he seemed on the eve of some
great triumph, his wife watching with elation by his side. Again
and again the promised triumph turned into sorry futility, and
the indomitable Jessie steeled herself once more to meet disaster with queenly dignity. He might have scored a resounding
success in 1853 in finding a practicable winter route for a railway through the Sangre de Cristo range—but he lost his men
and some starved to death. He might have carried Pennsylvania
and the Presidency in 1856—but the election left him no happier a figure than many another defeated candidate. He might
by rapid marches and masterly maneuvering have swept Mis-

souri and Arkansas free of Confederates; but a subordinate was thrown back at Wilson's Creek, and a rash defiance of Lincoln's wishes brought about his removal. He might have made a fortune from the Mariposa grant—but financial harpies snatched it from his hands. He seemed about to become a commanding figure in the railroad world; but the result of all his effort was heavy financial loss and the discredit of a French indictment. "It was as if a character of pure poetry," writes Royce, "some Jaques or some lesser Round Table Knight, had escaped from romanceland and were wandering about amongst live men on the Earth. Always his promises and gifts would vanish, as by the stroke of an enchanter's wand, when men stooped to pick them." His career remained thus frustrated to the end—to the time when the leader who had come so close to the Presidency was glad to accept a territorial governorship, and when he gained his long-sought retirement pay in the Army only to die before he could collect it.

In studying this strange career we can readily understand why it excited the harsh censure of many observers. Frémont seemed after 1850 to seek easy success in a world where true success almost always comes hard. His great achievement for the American nation, his geographical work, followed upon ten years of severe practical training under the ablest masters; it was well earned by that and additional years of peril and effort in the field. The Frémont of the first three expeditions every one must admire. But by 1850 the tide of events had moved so rapidly that his geographical vocation was gone; and like Othello, he knew not where to turn. He sought the laurels of the Presidency without the stern practical preparation which men like Lincoln gave themselves during half a lifetime of political labor. He sought the glory of a Civil War general, never having commanded five hundred men, without that protracted and often bitter training which men like Grant and Lee had received in military academy, camp, and field. He sought the rewards of a railroad-builder without passing through that grim business tuition which Cornelius Vanderbilt and Collis P.

Huntington had gained long before they constructed their first short railroad line. Frémont tried too often to reap where other men had sown, and it was not surprising that he met with scathing condemnation from critical onlookers.

Yet the fault was not all his own. His associates, and the American people as a whole, bear no little responsibility for his failures. The people after 1847 created a legend, and this legendary Frémont bore as remote a relation to the real man as the legendary Grant in 1870 bore to the real President. Nor can we altogether regret the many vicissitudes of this half-frustrated, half-successful career. Although the legend has been dissipated, Frémont, himself a man of imagination, must appeal poignantly to the imagination of successive generations. If he was not always heroic in defeat, he was unfailingly picturesque; and because picturesqueness has an ineffaceable charm, we cannot but deal leniently with the figure who offers it.

His greatest definite contribution to American life was his geographical work—his careful mapping of old paths, his discovery of some new ones, his revelation of the true character of what he was first to call the Great Basin, his share in dispelling the myth of a wide desert in the Platte country, and his encouragement to well-planned emigration. The maps on which he and Preuss collaborated and the reports which he wrote with Jessie's assistance were models of their kind. But we must not think of Frémont's services in purely definite and practical terms. His life is memorable partly because it so strikingly illustrates the possibilities of adventurous action in the wide American scene. Where is a career with more of contrast, of vicissitude, of wide-ranging effort, of varied participation in national life? His name evokes a series of scenes which appeal irresistibly to the imagination: the great untamed West in the era of the buffalo herds and roving Indian, of Kit Carson and Johann Sutter; the clash of Mexicans and Americans over the imperial domain stretching from the Rio Grande to Shasta; the excited rush of Forty-Niners to the gold fields; the idealistic crusade for freedom which gave birth to the Republican

Party; the anguished years of civil conflict, with armies grappling in Missouri and the Shenandoah Valley; the desperate political intrigues of 1864, and the railway building and financial speculation of the Gilded Era. His name evokes, too, the fragrance of one of the truest love stories in American history. To have lived so daringly and completely, to have written so many pages fascinating in their dash and color, to have touched so many important events, makes him a contributor not only to the history but to the romance of America.

XXXVII

Some New Light on Frémont

Ancestry and Birth

Two bits of evidence indicate that Charles Frémon was an excellent French teacher. Samuel Mordecai, in "Richmond in Bygone Days: Being Reminiscences of an Oldtime Citizen" (1856), states that early in the century a large brick building on Carey Street was occupied by Haller's Academy, a private school. Haller was a Swiss or German of a little learning and a good deal of address and pretension. But "he also had judgment enough to enable him to select good teachers. Among these was Mons. Frémont, the father of Col. Frémont, of Pacific and warlike celebrity." The civil engineer R. B. Osborne, in his life of Moncure Robinson, privately printed in 1889 and later republished in the *William and Mary College Quarterly* for 1921, writes that Robinson, by studying under Frémon at William and Mary, gained a "remarkably perfect" knowledge of French.

Frémont's birthplace in Savannah is preserved and still shown to visitors. It is a two-story and basement house, rectangular, of solid brick construction, with a door and a full-length French window on the first floor, two windows on the second.

The Third Expedition and the Bear Flag War

The New York *Herald* gave a good deal of attention to the start of Frémont's Third Expedition. It carried a front-page article and map on October 19, 1845, followed by articles on October 26 and November 2 of that year. While these contain no new information, they indicate that Frémont already had a certain renown. Another article on November 11, 1846, dealt with the explorer's travels in Upper California.

The question of the exact tenor of Archibald Gillespie's message to Frémont remains unresolved. We might assume that it contained nothing that was not in the instructions which Gillespie carried to Sloat and Larkin, bidding them pursue a policy conciliatory to the Californians, but for one fact: Why, if that were true, should Gillespie push on posthaste hundreds of miles to the north, through dangerous Indian country, to overtake Frémont homeward bound to the Atlantic Coast? Actually, the instructions sent Commodore Sloat were two-headed. One part required him to treat the native Californians with great friendliness. The other part ran: "If you ascertain with certainty that Mexico has declared war against the United States, you will at once possess yourself of the port of Saint [*sic*] Francisco, and block and occupy such other ports as your force may permit." Sloat had five warships. The text of the letter to Larkin is known only from a copy sent by ship around Cape Horn; Gillespie, before landing in Mexico, committed it to memory and destroyed it. Of Frémont, Gillespie later testified that he had been instructed by Secretary of State Buchanan to "confer" with him, and "make known my instructions." These again were two-headed. One part told Frémont "it was the wish of the Government to conciliate the feelings of the people of California, and encourage a friendship towards the United States." The other part, said Gillespie, called upon him "to watch over the interests of the United States, and counteract the influence of any foreign agents who might be in the country with objects prejudicial to the United States."

Obviously, when Gillespie began to "confer" with Frémont, he might emphasize the conciliatory side of the instructions—a side not pertinent if Frémont continued to travel east. Or he might emphasize the Government's desire that Frémont watch over American interests and counteract foreign machinations—a side very pertinent if Frémont turned back. And then there were oral messages from Benton and others.

A dim ray of light is thrown on the subject by a letter of Benton's in the Buchanan Papers in the Pennsylvania Historical Society. Senator Lewis Cass on February 17, 1848, wrote Buchanan that the Senate Military Committee were investigating the origins of the military operations in California against the Mexican authorities before the news of war; that they had examined Gillespie; and that if no state reason existed to the contrary, they would like to see a copy of the instructions. Buchanan evidently consulted Benton. The Missouri Senator wrote back February 18, 1848:

I do not think it necessary, nor desirable, to publish the instructions, nor in fact, any part of them. The depositions of Frémont and Gillespie are brief and general, and only go to the general point of observing and counteracting foreign designs in California and conciliating the people towards ourselves. No authority for hostilities is claimed under them; and as they stand, they only showed the natural and proper desire of the government to frustrate the prejudicial designs of foreigners in Cal.—which designs were found to be far more dangerous than known of here and requiring a remedy of a much stronger kind than the govt. contemplated; and fortunately, we have the full proof now here to show the danger of the designs which were then on foot, and the necessity for the strong remedy which was applied.

For the downright Benton, this has an evasive ring. We now know that the British had no "designs" on California. Yet the matter cannot be dismissed with that statement.

When Secretary Buchanan wrote his message of October 17, 1845, to Consul Larkin, and when Gillespie left Washington the next month, relations between Britain and America were gravely strained by the Oregon issue. Polk had declared in his inaugural message that the United States had good title to all Oregon. Withdrawing previous offers of compromise, in December, 1845, he called for ending the joint occupation. When the following April he gave notice of this termination, the two powers were at an impasse. War between them was possible, and to many seemed probable. One reason why the Mexicans attacked Taylor's troops was that they expected Anglo-American hostilities. Earlier, in 1844, an influential body of native Californians had asked Alexander Forbes, the British agent in the province, whether they could obtain a British protectorate. The British Foreign Office wrote Forbes (December 31, 1844) that Britain would not assent to this, for it would be a breach of faith. But it added: "Great Britain would view with much dissatisfaction the establishment of a protectual power over California by any other foreign state." Sir George Seymour, who commanded the British warships on the Pacific coast, asked the Admiralty in March, 1846, for an increased force.

Thus Gillespie might well have got the impression in Washington, in Mexico, and in Monterey that a British threat was real and powerful. Not until June 15, 1846, was the memorable treaty settling the Oregon question signed in Washington— some five weeks after Frémont turned back from Klamath Lake. In 1848, when Benton wrote Buchanan, the impression of a British threat still lingered in many quarters. Indeed, Buchanan in a letter to T. Miller as late as January 15, 1866, speaks of the acquisition of California to keep it from Great Britain (Buchanan Papers, Pennsylvania Historical Society). It is certain that the State Department late in 1845 and early in 1846 feared action by the British as soon as they heard (1) that California had declared its independence of Mexico, or (2) that war between the United States and Mexico had begun; such action being perhaps a mere recognition of California's independence, in line with the Foreign Office's letter to Forbes. Had Gillespie emphasized the importance of Frémont's being on the scene "to watch over the interests of the United States, and counteract the influence of any foreign agents," this might account for the explorer's turning back. Pressure from American settlers would account for his ensuing activities.

The Court Martial

That the events leading up to Frémont's court martial contained much that was discreditable alike to Frémont, Kearny, and the Administration (whose orders led to a conflict of authority), is plain. But Benton, Jessie, and Frémont never wavered in their conviction that the verdict was a gross injustice to the explorer. After it was rendered Secretary Buchanan urged the young officer to resume his command. On March 7, 1848, Frémont replied from the Benton residence (Buchanan Papers, Pennsylvania Historical Society):

I have to make you many thanks for the kind interest which you have manifested in my behalf, and would take great pleasure in conforming my conduct to your opinion, if it were possible. But it is not possible. I *feel* the sentence of the court martial against me to be unjust; and while that feeling remains I can never, by any act or word whatever, even by the remotest implication, admit, or seem to admit, its justice.

One of the main results of the court martial was to confirm the hostility of West Point graduates to Frémont. They resented his rapid rise to fame, his strong political support first from Poinsett and later from Benton, and his position as a brilliant amateur in military affairs. This hostility had been patent in California before and after his arrest by Kearny; it was plainly manifested, according to the press, by officers at his trial. It would cost Frémont dear in the Civil War. Other Civil War generals, like Jacob D. Cox and John A. McClernand, complained bitterly of the jealousy, arrogance, and clannishness of West Pointers in dealing with high volunteer officers. From John Pope and others Frémont was destined to suffer much.

Frémont later (September 4, 1856) wrote T. S. King, editor of the San Francisco *Bulletin*: "From the day when my connection with the army was dissolved, I have considered my life consecrated to the construction of this Pacific [rail] road."

The Fourth Exploring Expedition, 1848–49

That devoted member of the expedition, Micajah McGehee —according to Stark Young's article, "Cousin Micajah," in the *Saturday Evening Post*, April 13, 1935—was "shy and silent, taller than medium, with fine hair of a golden brown, and a fine white skin." When graduated from the University of Virginia he did not go home, for he was in love with the girl his brother courted, and did not wish to complicate affairs. So he joined Frémont to see the West. His father owned the Bowling Green plantations in Mississippi.

McGehee wrote in his MS Journal that the object of Frémont's expedition "was to finish his exploration of California and the Rocky Mountains, particularly of the Great Interior Basin, of which so little had hitherto been known. It was considered a vast, barren desert, inhabited by savage tribes, and rarely entered by trappers. He wished also to discover a direct practicable traveling route, and, if possible, railway route, from the Mississippi Valley to the Pacific on the 38th degree of latitude." St. Louis lies between the 38th and 39th degrees. It is evident from various sources that Frémont confided a good deal in McGehee.

On this disastrous fourth expedition, Benton wrote in the *National Intelligencer* of November 8, 1853, Frémont was turned out of his right path by his guide. Some of the reasons for believing that Old Bill Williams misled the party are stated in the text. Additional evidence to that effect is furnished by the letter of one of the most intelligent members of the party, Edward M. Kern, dated Taos, New Mexico, February 11, 1849, to A. Robidoux, published in the St. Joseph *Gazette* and reprinted in the *Missouri Statesman* of April 27, 1849. It ran:

My dear Robidoux:

I arrived at this place last evening from Rio Colorado, from about as hard a trip and as total destruction of an expedition as possible.

As rumors will reach you I thought it would be as well to give you some little correct information on the subject, though my time will scarcely allow of anything like detail.

As far as Bent's we met with no obstacle or loss and everything bade fair to give us a tolerable pleasant trip, considering the season. Our animals were in good condition; and procuring corn at Hard Scrabble for the worst part of the road, we calculated passing the mountains with success. Old Bill was with us as a guide, and that of course gave confidence, supposing none so capable as he to carry us through. Leaving Hard Scrabble, we continued up its creek into the mountains. As we advanced the snow increased. Crossing the first range we fell upon the waters of the Wappanah [Huerfano], passing through the mountains to the Del Norte by your old wagon road— the snow still increasing.

We continued a couple of days on the Del Norte, and then turned up what Williams called your pass on to the Compadne [Uncompahgre?]. In this he was evidently mistaken, for a worse road I never saw. If you ever got over it with wagons, I should like to have seen the operation. We went on up the canon, our animals failing and the snow deepening every step we took, bidding fair, as it subsequently turned out, to defeat our crossing. On the 15th of December we attempted to cross what we supposed to be the dividing ridge between the St. Johns [San Juan] and the waters of the Del Norte, but were driven back by the storm. The next day we returned to it again, and were successful enough to get on the other side to a small clump of pines. We unpacked our animals on a bare point and drove them to the hill top in hopes of their finding sufficiency of food for a day, as the snow had drifted from it in places. From this hill they never came again; the storm continuing, and having no shelter, they perished.

Camp then commenced making portages, in hopes of reaching the river. This you may suppose was a severe undertaking in the cold, and no positive hopes ahead of reaching any place, even should we have been able to get out our effects. By hard labor we worked our way gradually down. On the 26th, King was sent ahead with Old Bill to Abaque to bring us relief, while we were to continue down. On the 11th of January, he not arriving, the Colonel became anxious and started with his mess and Godey in hopes of meeting the relief party. Our provisions had given out, and we were living on parfleshes and tug ropes. Already Proulx had perished from hunger and exposure.

On the 16th, all having reached the river, we made our little packs of bedding and with our rifles started for—God only knows where. Here commenced our greatest suffering. The company had for its head Vincut Hatter [Vincent Haler], about as contemptible and cowardly a fellow as ever walked: his own lack of courage quickly diffused itself among the men—so you may suppose how things went on. Probably up to the 27th we had lost nine men. Our mess and another had made our final camp. A dead wolf was all we had to sustain life among nine men. I had closed all my affairs and felt that a day or two more would end my troubles, when, about noon on the 28th, we heard a shout, and Godey entered camp. Here ended our troubles. From him we learned the fate of King's party who had been found by him on the way down on the 16th. Poor King had died from exhaustion somewhere on the 9th; and the rest were in a miserable condition—frozen and partly crazed. They had given up all hopes of returning to us with relief.

Thus has ended the expedition—commenced, so far as outfit was concerned, under as flattering prospects as ever one started. The loss in dollars has mounted to over 10,000—in life 10.—My brothers and myself will winter somewhere in this vicinity, and return home early in the spring, when I shall pay you a visit at your pleasant town of San Jose.

Adios,

NED KERN

This letter apparently convicts Old Bill Williams of completely mistaking the pass up which he turned the expedition.

The Fifth Exploring Expedition, 1853–54

Intended to support the demand of St. Louis interests for full consideration of a Pacific railway route lying somewhere near the 38th or 39th parallel, this expedition deliberately tried a winter journey. Frémont had told Benton after returning from California in 1850 as Senator that only two sections of this Central Route remained to be explored. One extended from the head of the Rio Grande across the valley of the Upper

Colorado; the other from Las Vegas de Santa Clara west to the Sierra passes. He felt confident that a good roadway and good land for settlement existed in both areas.

Benton in a letter published by the *National Intelligencer,* October 13, 1853, declared that the recent journey of Harris Heap and Major Edward F. Beale had proved Frémont correct with respect to the first section. As for the second section, Benton believed that a still more recent crossing by an emigrant party which included the Rev. J. W. Brier had again proved Frémont right. Brier's party, after leaving Salt Lake, made use of a Mormon "way bill of a new and better route to California." This led from a point on the Old Spanish Trail about seventy-five miles southwest of Little Salt Lake, called "The Divide," to Owen's Lake, Walker's Pass through the Sierra, and Tulare Valley. Brier estimated the entire distance from "The Divide" to Walker's Pass as about three hundred and fifty miles, and found the pass itself easy, with no snow in January.

Benton, continuing to beat the St. Louis drum for the Central Route, sent a new letter to the *National Intelligencer* of November 8, 1853. A Virginia emigrant had just written him from Fort Massachusetts (a small post established the previous year in the San Luis Valley, at the foot of Blanca Peak, to protect settlers on the upper Rio Grande from the Ute Indians), praising the Beale-Heap route. This emigrant had found the country for seven hundred miles from the Missouri frontier largely rich and beautiful, and the San Luis Valley—which lies in present-day southern Colorado—very attractive. "In short," wrote Benton, "I now feel emboldened to repeat what Frémont has often told me, that in the central part of the Rocky Mountains covering the Three Parks, the headwaters of the South Platte, the Arkansas, and the Del Norte, and the headwaters of the East Fork of the Great Colorado of the West, and about halfway between them, there is good country enough to make a mountain State double the size of all the Swiss cantons put together, and presenting everything grand and beautiful to be found in Switzerland, without the drawbacks of glaciers and avalanches, and consequently without its cold." Benton is writing of what is now south central Colorado, the area roughly bounded by Aspen, Leadville, Colorado Springs, Pueblo, and Telluride, with Frémont County at its heart.

Frémont meanwhile was toiling westward. He wrote Benton, November 25, 1853, from "Big Timber" on the upper Arkansas, about the site of present-day La Junta, Colorado, that the expedition had made successful progress and had found large beds of coal:

I am determined to carry the enterprise through to the end, contending with the winter and every obstacle, prudently and cautiously, but never giving way. I have presents to conciliate the Indians, and our vigilance will prevent attacks. Our movement now will be a struggle with the winter. We have December and January, the mountains and the strength of the winter before us, and shall move slowly, but do good work. The astronomical, barometrical, and topographical work all go on well. After surmounting some difficulties with our *daguerre* (which it required skill to do), it has been eminently successful, and we are producing a line of pictures of exquisite beauty which will admirably illustrate the country. We hope to get through in two months, and to make a complete winter exploration of the route.

The news of Frémont's emergence at Parowan, completely across the Colorado and Utah mountains and near the Nevada boundary, and of his subsequent arrival in San Francisco, reached the East by way of the Isthmus and New Orleans. It included the absurd statement that Frémont, on reaching San Francisco, had been accompanied "with only twenty men, the greater part of them having deserted after leaving the Colorado." This elicited from Benton an irate letter to the *National Intelligencer*, with some sharp animadversions on West Point hostility to the explorer, and on the frequency of desertion in the regular army. He scored the "Telegraphic" or telegram which brought this San Francisco news from New Orleans:

I have to remark upon this Telegraphic that, like all the first reports given out about Col. Frémont, it is disparaging to him; and, like all such disparaging accounts is false to the extent of the disparagement. This is so upon its face. It says he arrived in California with *"only"* twenty men. Very well: that much is true. He set out with only twenty from Paroan; and, as he went through a wilderness, he had no chance to get more. He set out from the United States last fall with "only" twenty-one men, and one of them died after he reached the valley of the Paroan, which leaves "only" twenty.

Now for the *deserters*. The Telegraphic says *"the greater part of his men deserted after crossing the Colorado."* This is false. Frémont was not educated at West Point, and his men—whether Americans, Germans, Irish, French, Indian, mulatto, or black—do not desert him. They die by him, but never *"desert."* As for this particular story of "desertion," it is as ignorant as false. Frémont and his twenty men were seen by Babbitt after they had crossed the Upper Colorado at Paroan, nearly two hundred miles west of the Colorado; and Frémont wrote letters home (which were published) showing that his entire company (21) had all arrived there—one to fall dead from his saddle.

The Telegraphic is probably true in this, that Col. Frémont had arrived in California the 16th of April. He left the Mormon settlements of the Little Salt Lake and the Santa Clara meadows [Parowan is near Little Salt Lake] about the 20th of February to explore a new route (in that part of its course) for the CENTRAL ROAD, and would be occupied some two months in this new exploration. It is probable, therefore, that he had got through by the 16th of April. We rely upon that much of the Telegraphic to be true; but repulse the *"desertion"* part of the story as false, and as an aspersion upon Frémont from which the conduct of his men in all time past should exempt him. No man ever deserted from him. His men die with him, as for him; but never desert. He was not educated at West Point. And if any person wishes to know why the United States army has been in a state (nearly) of dissolution for some years past they have only to read a brief letter from Mr. Mason to me, printed in the *Thirty Years' View*, at page 182, at the beginning of the chapter headed "MILITARY ACADEMY."

Frémont sat down in Parowan on February 9, 1854, to write Jessie and Benton. He reported that the winter had been exceedingly severe; in that valley the severest since it was settled. But when he found only four inches of snow on the Cochetopa Pass in Colorado, even among the pines and in the shade of rock walls, he decided that the expedition had successfully proved its point. "I congratulate you on this verification of your judgment, and the good prospect it holds out of final success in carrying this road by the central line." He spoke of the large supplies of coal, iron, and timber near at hand in present-day Colorado. "In making my expedition to this point I save nearly a parallel of latitude, shortening the usual distance from Green River to this point by over a hundred miles." He expected to blaze a new line from Parowan to the Tejon Passes in the Sierra, and into the head of the Joaquin Valley; passes "through which in 1850 I drove from two to three thousand head of cattle that I delivered to the Indian Commissioners. I shall make what speed I can, going light, and abandoning the more elaborate survey of my previous time. . . ."

A good deal of publicity attended Frémont's emergence from this winter journey. C. L. Smith of Parowan wrote the *Deseret News* of Salt Lake City an account of the arrival. Frémont, he added, "was sanguine in his opinion that he had found the best route for the great national railway." On the explorer's arrival in San Francisco the *Alta California* carried a long news story, reprinted in the *National Intelligencer* of May 26, 1854. Other newspaper accounts could easily be found.

Frémont himself published in the *National Intelligencer* of June 15, 1854, a full statement, of perhaps 3,000 words, on his journey (see also the New York *Herald* of the same date). He was sure that his explorations contradicted the Southern leaders who insisted that winter snow and storms made a central railroad impracticable. He wrote of the central chain of the Rockies in what is now southern Colorado, just beyond San Luis Valley:

Across these wooded heights—wooded and grass-covered up to and over their rounded summits—to the Coo-che-to-pe pass, the line followed an open easy wagon way, such as is usual to a rolling country. On the high summit lands were forests of coniferous trees, and the snow in the pass was four inches deep. This was on the 14th of December. A day earlier our horses' feet would not have touched snow in the crossing. Up to this point we had enjoyed clear and dry pleasant weather. Our journey had been all along on dry ground; and travelling slowly along waiting for the winter there had been abundant leisure for becoming acquainted with the country. The open character of the country, joined to good information, indicated the existence of other passes about the head of the Sah-watch. This it was desirable to verify, and especially to examine a neighboring and lower pass connecting more directly with the Arkansas valley, known as the Poow-che.

But the winter had now set in over all the mountain regions. . . . We were moving in fogs and clouds, through a region wholly unknown to us, and without guides; and were therefore obliged to content ourselves with the examination of a single line, and the ascertainment of the winter condition of the country over which it passed; which was in fact the main object of our expedition.

Our progress in this mountainous region was necessarily slow, and during ten days which it occupied us to pass through about one hundred miles of the mountainous country bordering on the eastern side of the Upper Colorado valley the greatest depth of the snow was, among the pines and aspens on the ridges, about two and a half feet, and in the valleys about six inches. The atmosphere is too cold and dry for much snow, and the valleys, protected by mountains, are comparatively free from it, and warm. We here found villages of Utah Indians in their wintering ground, in little valleys along the foot of the higher mountains, and bordering the more open country of the Colorado valley. Snow was here (December 25) only a few inches deep—the grass generally appearing above it, and there being none under trees and on southern hillsides.

The horses of the *Utahs* were living on the range, and, notwithstanding that they were used in hunting, were in excellent condition. One which we had occasion to kill for food had on it about two inches of fat, being in as good order as any buffalo we had killed in

November on the eastern plains. Over this valley country—about one hundred and fifty miles across—the Indians informed us that snow falls only a few inches in depth; such as we saw it at the time.

In present-day Utah the Frémont river, with the town of Frémont on its headwaters, empties into the Colorado. Frémont described the southerly reaches of the Wasatch and connecting ranges, which again he thought no impediment to easy railroad operation:

They lie between the Colorado valley and the Great Basin, and at their western base are established the Mormon settlements of Parowan and Cedar City. They are what are called fertile mountains, abundant in water, wood, and grass, and fertile valleys, offering inducements to settlement and facilities for making a road. These mountains are a great storehouse of materials—timber, iron, coal— which would be of indispensable use in the construction and maintenance of the road, and are solid foundations to build up the future prosperity of the rapidly increasing Utah State.

Salt is abundant on the eastern border mountains, as the Sierra de Sal, being named from it. In the ranges lying behind the Mormon settlements, among the mountains through which the line passes, are accumulated a great wealth of iron and coal and extensive forests of heavy timber. These forests are the largest I am acquainted with in the Rocky Mountains, being, in some places, twenty miles in depth of continuous forest; the general growth lofty and large, frequently over three feet in diameter, and sometimes reaching five feet, the red spruce and yellow pine predominating. At the actual southern extremity of the Mormon settlements, consisting of the two enclosed towns of Parowan and Cedar City near to which our line passed, a coal mine has been opened for about eighty yards, and iron works already established. Iron here accumulates in extraordinary masses, in some parts accumulated into mountains, which comb out in crests of solid iron thirty feet thick and a hundred yards long.

In the interest of St. Louis and its central route, Frémont was exaggerating the resources a bit. He closed by praising the advantages of Walker's two passes and the Tejon Pass in the southern Sierra over those farther north. "The low dry country and the long slope, in contradistinction to the high country and short sudden descent and heavy snows of the passes behind the bay of San Francisco, are among the considerations which suggest themselves in favor of the route by the head of the San Joaquin."

Railroads from the east today ascend the Arkansas River on Frémont's route past Pueblo and Canon City, one line crossing the Rockies just above the Sangre de Cristo Range near Salida, and thence running down the Gunnison River (mainly between the 38th and 39th parallels) to the Colorado River and the Utah boundary, whence it pushes on west and northwest to Provo and Salt Lake City. No railway crosses southern Utah to any point near Parowan; but a line does run down from Provo and Nephi a little west of Parowan, and on into Nevada. Had it not been for the Civil War, Frémont's route might have received more consideration for a central railroad. The Union Pacific-Central Pacific line built with government aid was not preferable from an engineering standpoint; the main reason for its selection was that it better suited Chicago and the Northwest.

The Mariposa Estate

Some additional details on Frémont's close escape from losing this estate in 1851–52 are supplied by a letter which Edwin A. Post, a New York attorney, sent the New York *Courier and Enquirer* early in 1852 (reprinted in *National Intelligencer*, February 21, 1852). This shows that in July, 1851, Frémont's agent, Eugene Flandin, made a sale of the Mariposa estate to T. Denny Sargent of Washington, subject to Frémont's ratification. In October, Frémont sent Benton a power of attorney to give this ratification; and on January 31, 1852, Benton completed the sale. G. Harris Heap then sailed from New York in the *Empire City* in February to take possession of the estate for Sargent, while Sargent left the same month for London to obtain funds to finance the development of the mines. In cancelling this sale Frémont was no doubt aided by the Federal suit against his title.

When early in 1852 one Dr. John B. Trask of California attacked Frémont on the ground that he had allowed exaggerated representations of the value of the gold veins on his estate, the explorer wrote the assayer, John L. Moffat, a German geologist, S. C. Wass, and a mining expert, Frederick Goodell, all of San Francisco, for written opinions. The answers were highly favorable. "I have twice visited the Mariposa vein," stated Moffat on January 15, 1852, "in March and July last. In both instances, I judge from what I saw and what I learned, that it was producing then, and had averaged for several months, forty dollars per ton, worked with close mortars and shaking tables. With better amalgamators, I am of opinion twice that amount could have been saved from the same ore." Goodell wrote on the same date: "The veins upon your property in the Mariposa and Agua Frio districts are numerous, and rich in gold; and I am confident that large results can be realized by a judicious outlay of capital and the use of heavy and well-constructed machinery." This correspondence, and an editorial in the *Alta California* defending Frémont, are published in the *National Intelligencer* of February 24, 1852.

The great extent and irregular bootlike shape of Frémont's estate, covering some of the richest mineral lands in Mariposa County, resulted in inconvenience to many settlers, some of whom alleged real grievances. Details of the way in which the owner, supported by Governor J. B. Weller, maintained his Mariposa rights against the Merced Mining Company, may be found in the interesting two-column narrative of Bear Valley troubles in the New York *Weekly Tribune* of August 14, 1858, and in a shorter article in the *National Intelligencer* of August 21, 1858, taken from the Boston *Transcript*. Someone interested in the reputation of California for law and order sent the *Intelligencer* of November 3, 1857, a paper on Frémont's return to his estate. After remarking that vigilante troubles had given the State a bad name, the anonymous writer continued:

All have heard of the numerous settlers on the Frémont estate (the Mariposas), and of the violent language and conduct of some of the intruders, so conducting themselves as to pass for all—holding public meetings, adopting resolutions, charging the Supreme Court with bribery when they heard that it had confirmed Frémont's grant, burning Chief Justice Taney in effigy, binding themselves to stand together to resist the decision, and menacing Frémont himself if he came upon the place. Well, after three years' absence he returns to California, lands at San Francisco, and without accompaniment of force proceeds directly to the Mariposas, to the heart of the estate, and arrives at the town of Mariposas, 3,000 souls, and which is the seat of justice for the county. There are 16,000 settlers on the estate, and not one molested him! On the contrary, all received him kindly, and with the deference due to a proprietor; many asking for leases, or purchase of parts; and all wishing him to take charge of the property, and make it more productive by conducting streams of water through it.

Frémont made his return to Mariposa more welcome by bringing some capital and the promise of much more. During his European sojourn and the campaign of 1856 Bear Valley operations had become confused and inefficient. He paid judgments against his property reaching nearly $18,000, hired men, imported machinery, and planned the construction of two canals, the Merced and the Frémont.

The Mariposa difficulties had the effect of stirring up in California much ill-founded criticism and belittlement of the explorer. The Mariposa *Gazette* of December 3, 1858, in an editorial copied by the Sacramento *Union* of December 7, declared that "he is and has been the subject of more bitter personal enmity and abuse than any man we ever heard of. So far as we know, there is no reason for it, and for the benefit of all concerned, it should stop until it fully appears that he *is* the autocratical swindler, scoundrel, and rascal that it seems the heart's desire of some men to make out." Feeling over the Mariposa boundaries perhaps helps to explain a letter which Henry A. Wise, naval officer and author of *Los Gringos,* wrote his father-in-law, Edward Everett, from Washington, February 1, 1851. Describing a Congressional debate on a California land title bill in which Benton had pertinaciously defended the claims of Frémont, he added: "We who knew the latter gentleman on the field of his California exploits, regarded him as a very unscrupulous character. I would at the same time, however, award him the real merit he has hardly won in his scientific explorations, and admiration for the indomitable energy, perseverance, and skill with which he accomplished them." (Everett Papers, Massachusetts Historical Society.)

The Blairs and the Frémonts

After Thomas Hart Benton's death on April 10, 1858, Francis P. Blair, Sr., sent Jessie at Mariposa a paternal letter of affection and sympathy. She replied in May, thanking him and his daughter Elizabeth for their kind messages. She had known her father was dying when she left the East, but he had forbidden her to stay. She was thankful that his period of extreme suffering had been short and that no cloud had dimmed his great mind:

I had a letter from Father the day I left New York. In it he tells me I ought to go—that it is not right for a family to be divided. It was a hard choice—one that left lasting regret for whichever was set aside but it is done and I am more than justified in being here when I see how much I do to keep Mr. Frémont where his interests require—the children too are so strong and well here and so entirely free from any influence but our own. . . .

Mr. Frémont has a great deal to do—for the present lawsuits carry him occasionally to San Francisco, but a few weeks more will give order and then he enters regularly on his writing—it is quite impossible until he is through these interruptions. With all he finds more time to take care of me than ever in all the time we have been together, and when I remember that my father's last days were untroubled about me and my children because he could rely on Mr. Frémont's care for us, it gives a new value to my home here and a new reason for making it every way pleasant to Mr. Frémont.

She described the scenery near their house, and a mountain excursion on which Frémont had hurried them away from a bear they heard growling in the brush. They had killed rattlesnakes near their door:

But snakes and sounds of grizzly bears do not follow us indoors where everything looks as secure and peaceful as at Silver Spring. When the cool evenings come now we shall sit around a fire of oak and pine. . . . This range back of us and nearest the Sierra was named years ago for Father and the tallest peak is Mt. Bullion. On its summit a bonfire had been prepared by Mr. Frémont's friends (there are more friendly than unfriendly here) and it was lit the evening of our arrival. It was Friday the 16 April. At the same time he was laid in the ground at St. Louis his mountain was a blazing beacon of welcome to us. You know how fond Father was of the classics and classical comparisons. It seems to me he would have liked to hear me—his favorite scholar—tell him what thought links itself with that day—how as the old Greeks sculptured a jet of flame on the tomb to typify the soul purified and ascending so that great flame rising from the mountain of gold rock is to me an image of his great heart and mind freed from the clay and rising to the great Master. . . .

We had a last talk together the Sunday of his birthday. When he saw my heart too full he changed the topic for he evidently dreaded excitement or emotion. But he knew he would not see me again and I did not know the end was so soon, but I saw his changed face and evident pain and his voice was like a death knell while he was telling me of his will and his motives in making it. Mr. Frémont will be steady and faithful to his trust as Trustee and so must Montgomery and Mr. Lee. . . .

This letter in the Blair-Lee Papers at Princeton University is accompanied by a note from Montgomery Blair, August 8, 1858, to his sister Elizabeth Blair Lee:

The old gentleman asked me to take the enclosed letter out of his desk this morning and send it to you and tell you he would write you soon. By the by he seems a good deal out with Jessie. She has not written to him for a long time and now that she does write there is merely a tedious description of her camp—no reference to his heart out pouring, wishing her to make his home her home, consider him her father etc. etc. He does not say much about it but I think he is hurt by her proceedings and rather inclined not to give himself so much concern about her in future. But I have no doubt she will come to presently and greet him affectionately and then his big heart will forget all this.

Later, Montgomery Blair, as one executor of the Benton estate, received a complaining letter from Baron Gauldrée Boileau, one of Benton's sons-in-law; and he concluded that Jessie Frémont, who had expressed keen disappointment over the condition of the estate, was equally discontented. "I do not know how such expectations were created," he wrote his sister Elizabeth of the hopes of the Benton children for a larger inheritance (July 22, 1859; Blair-Lee Papers). Relations between the Blairs and Frémonts were thus under a certain strain even before 1861.

Frémont's Operations in Missouri, 1861

To a remarkable extent the accounts of Frémont's Missouri command have followed the narrative of Nicolay and Hay, subsequent authors failing to give the subject fresh research. This has resulted in an endless repetition of certain misinterpretations and misstatements. The older history by the Comte de Paris is fairer, more accurate, and more penetrating than that of Lincoln's biographers. Frémont's worst errors were political: his proclamation freeing the slaves of Missourians who aided the enemy, and his final agreement with the Confederate leader Price for a joint prohibition of the formation of partisan bands. These political blunders and his quarrel with Frank P. Blair, Jr., fully justified Lincoln in removing him. His military career, however, offers a more complicated, difficult, and creditable story than most writers have supposed. A careful book devoted to all its ramifications is much needed.

It seems anomalous that the Confederates in Missouri were

able to concentrate their forces more efficiently than the Unionists, and to strike two heavy blows, the defeat of Lyon at Springfield and the capture of Mulligan's little force at Lexington, before Frémont could prepare a counterstroke. The explanation lies partly in the fact that Missouri was an exposed salient of the North, partly in the superior strength of secessionist sympathizers outside St. Louis, and partly in the length of the Northern lines in that region. From southern Kansas, Arkansas, Tennessee, and Kentucky, all contiguous, the Confederates could pour forces into Missouri. The Missouri River tier of counties across the State was heavily slaveholding and secessionist in sentiment. Frémont had to hold the Missouri River from Kansas City to its mouth, the capital at Jefferson City, the railhead at Rolla, and the Mississippi as far as Cairo. He was essentially on the defensive; the Confederates could mass against any point, while he had to maintain his grip everywhere. His most vital positions were Cairo, Jefferson City, and St. Louis; to lose any one of them would be a disaster indeed. All were held.

Among secondary reasons for the Federal reverses in Missouri were shortage of weapons; the persistent preoccupation of Washington with the Virginia theater, and its readiness to deprive the West of troops to strengthen McClellan—who made no use of them in 1861; the inexperience of Frémont and other commanders in handling large bodies of men; the rashness of Lyon; the violent quarrel between Frank P. Blair, Jr., and Frémont; and the practical insubordination of General John Pope and General Samuel D. Sturgis.

The want of arms was lamentable. Before leaving Washington, Frémont had received an order for 7,000 stand, but it was at once countermanded; he then got a new order for 5,000 to be delivered from the St. Louis arsenal, but on reaching the West discovered it no longer afforded more than 1,300 arms. His total force when he arrived in St. Louis on July 25 was nominally 25,000, but was actually only about 15,000 when the departing three months' men were deducted. Of these about 7,000 had no weapons at all; indeed, Governor Richard Yates of Illinois had told Frémont in Washington that Illinois troops were largely defenseless (Committee on the Conduct of the War, III, 44, 45). "We must have arms—any arms, no matter what," Frémont telegraphed Major P. V. Hagner, in charge of War Department purchasing, on July 29. No response came. To meet the deficiency and arm incoming volunteers he made emergency purchases, including 25,000 Austrian muskets for the quality of which his Hungarian chief of staff, A. S. Asboth, vouched. Nevertheless, the shortage continued all summer and fall, his troops using "all kinds of arms" when they had any. Three officers who examined the weapons of John A. McClernand's regiments at Cairo shortly reported that his queer mélange included Prussian muskets, English Tower muskets, French minie rifles, three patterns of American muskets, and English contract muskets made by Lacy & Co. Only a trifle over half his force was armed at all, reported McClernand on September 30, "and they with dangerous and insufficient weapons, and without a supply of available ammunition." (McClernand Papers, Illinois State Historical Library.)

Lyon's rash precipitancy was the cause of his own defeat. Southwestern Missouri being largely Unionist in sentiment, he had pushed down to Springfield, in the Ozark country, to sustain the loyal inhabitants. But this was too far. His movement entailed a dangerous stretching of Union lines, a wide scattering of Federal units in his rear, and a risk of being overwhelmed by superior forces. On July 27, Lyon asked Frémont for reinforcements—"a few regiments." (Committee on the Conduct of the War, III, 96.) That same day (when Frémont had been in St. Louis only forty-eight hours) 10,000 Confederates were concentrating at Warsaw just to the southwest, and he needed an additional regiment. On the 28th, General B. M. Prentiss telegraphed that more than 12,000 organized Confederates were within fifty miles of Cairo, while he had but 6,350 men at Cairo and Bird's Point to meet them. On August 1, a telegram from Colonel C. C. Marsh in southeastern Missouri announced that G. J. Pillow had been at New Madrid the previous day with 11,000 well-armed Confederates, including cavalry and artillery, while 9,000 more troops were coming up to assist him. In these circumstances sound strategy required a retreat by Lyon, and the reinforcement of Cairo, capture of which would have imperilled a wide area in Kentucky, Missouri, and southern Illinois (Committee on the Conduct of the War, III, 96–99).

Frémont hastily reinforced both Cairo and Cape Girardeau. Meanwhile, ordering various units to Lyon's aid, he instructed that general, if not strong enough to hold his position, to fall back toward the railhead at Rolla until met by these detachments. On August 9, Lyon wrote from Springfield that he was "at present unable to determine whether I shall be able to maintain my ground or be forced to retire." Retreat, though difficult, would have been feasible, and his shrewd adjutant-general John M. Schofield urged it. But stung by being superseded in the chief command, Lyon probably thought that retirement would discredit him (a West Pointer) and strengthen Frémont; he attacked with disastrous results. Colonel John M. Palmer of Illinois, stationed at Rolla, wrote his wife on August 15 that the Union forces were winning until "Gen. Lyon made the terrible mistake of ordering Col. Totten's artillery to open on Sigel's command who had changed positions without his knowledge. They fired upon Sigel and killed many of his men and scattered his prisoners." Like Schofield, Palmer thought Lyon's attack a deplorable blunder in the first place. "The truth is that the battle of Wilson's Creek was a folly which the gallant death of Gen. Lyon does not atone for." (Schofield, *Forty-six Years in the Army;* Frémont, MS Memoirs; Palmer Papers, Illinois State Historical Library.)

Early August found a majority of the ninety-day troops first called out by Lincoln, and especially the foreign-born elements, leaving the service. "The new levies," Frémont wrote Montgomery Blair, "are literally the rawest ever got together." (August 9, 1861; Committee on the Conduct of the War, III,

119.) Nearly all the recruits sent to St. Louis from various parts of the Northwest were unarmed, and all lacked transport. One regiment after another lay for days in the city without weapons, ammunition, accoutrements, or wagons. As in Washington, soldiers patronized the grog shops heavily and disgusted residents by their rowdy behavior. "It is a rehearsal of the state of affairs in Washington before the fight at Manassas," exclaimed Frank Blair (Frank to Montgomery Blair, St. Louis, September 1, 1861; Blair-Lee Papers). Some officers were outrageously unfit. More than half the six Illinois regiments at Cairo, Gustave Koerner reported to Lyman Trumbull, would ultimately re-enlist, but never under their former colonels. Governor Yates's thirteen new regiments, he predicted, "will be officered in the usual way by incompetent men." (July 29, 1861, to Lyman Trumbull; Trumbull Papers, Library of Congress.) One Illinois brigadier-general whom Frémont had to use in northern Missouri, Stephen A. Hurlbut, was grossly intemperate; before joining his command, testified the editor, Joseph Medill, he was drunk every day in Chicago (Medill, July 13, 1861, to Trumbull; Trumbull Papers).

To help drill what he called his "unmanageable mob" of raw recruits, Frémont asked Washington to authorize him to collect veteran soldiers throughout the Northwest, and use them as a framework to form an army. Receiving permission, he brought to the field a considerable number of such drillmasters. He also created a special infantry unit, the Benton Cadets, which he expected to make a school for infantry officers; and he intended to make his so-called Frémont Bodyguard (an unfortunate name for what was a very efficient cavalry unit) a school for cavalry officers. He came nearer the idea of officers' training camps than anyone else in this early period of the war.

His energy also did much to give the troops a partial supply of arms. The statement of Frank P. Blair that it was impossible to get the Administration to give any attention to Western needs (Frank, as head of the House Military Committee, knew the facts) was for a time literally true. Frémont's contracts later came under fire. But it appears that the Austrian arms which he bought were quite serviceable, became excellent when rifled, and cost but $11.50 each when finally ready. His purchase of 5,000 breech-loading Hall carbines at $22.50 each, an emergency order which at a later period was given much publicity because J. P. Morgan was involved in it, was also defensible, the government's own commissioners pronouncing the price entirely fair. Some field artillery was supplied by a Cincinnati firm at the same price for which it had made guns for the State of Indiana. The Frémont Hussars, under Major George E. Waring, bought some 500 horses under special contract, while nearly 6,000 more were purchased in the open market. Both East and West, in 1861, intolerable confusion and waste, and much corruption, accompanied the purchase of arms, munitions, and stores; but the waste was chiefly attributable to frenzied haste and War Department inefficiency, while corruption never touched Frémont's skirts (37th Cong., 2d Sess, House Exec. Doc. No. 94, and House Report No. 2; Gordon Wasson, *The Hall Carbine Affair*; Committee on the Conduct of the War, III; Anon., *Vindication of Quartermaster General McKinstry*).

In the opinion of shrewd observers, one main cause of confusion, shortages, and excessive costs in the Western Department lay in the failure of the national government to provide adequate funds. When the time of the three months' men expired, Frémont kept many of them only by a personal guarantee of their fourth month's pay. He had to buy large quantities of material on credit. Colonel I. C. Woods told the Committee on the Conduct of the War that for every dollar of unnecessary cost arising from collusion among contractors or suppliers, ten dollars were lost for want of ready money. As soon as the Western Department had to use credit, control over prices passed into the hands of banks, brokers, speculators, and moneyed merchants, the intermediary links between the army and its sources. In buying mules, the government lost heavily because it did not furnish money for proper corrals, feed, shoeing, and attendance in St. Louis; in buying wagons, because it supplied no money for repairs. Treasury policy was responsible. "Chase," Montgomery Blair explained to Frémont on August 24, "has more horror of seeing Treasury notes below par than of seeing soldiers killed, and, therefore, has held back too soon. . . . It is better to get ready to beat the enemy by selling stocks at fifty per cent discount than wait to negotiate [stocks] and lose a battle." (Committee on the Conduct of the War, III, 115 ff., 222 ff.; Frémont Papers.)

John Pope, one of the West Pointers who gave Frémont the most trouble, burst out August 22, 1861, in a letter to V. B. Horton, in the following violent denunciation of the Lincoln Administration (Civil War MSS, New-York Historical Society):

They [the Illinois troops] find themselves neglected, abandoned and humiliated by the President they have themselves put into the White House, and they have resolved to endure it no longer. A deputation reached Washington yesterday representing the State authorities and the military which will force upon Mr. Lincoln either an open rupture or a redress of their wrongs. They warned him that neither Banks nor Hunter will be suffered to take command of Illinois troops and that if it is attempted the whole of the Illinois forces will march back into the State and have no more to do with the war.

We are certainly cursed with rulers in this country and especially at such a time. This Administration will do in a different manner what Jeff Davis is doing directly. I mean that by neglect, corruption and outrage, the States of the West will be driven to group together and act without reference to the authority of the General Government. You would be surprised to find how prevalent this idea is today and unless some change is made in Washington I fear we shall see before long Illinois, Iowa, and perhaps Indiana carrying on this war in defiance of any authority or control from Washington.

Frémont's staff came under much captious criticism. Actually it was an able staff. When first appointed he was allowed only three officers, but the Act of August 5, 1861, permitted major-generals to nominate for presidential appointment as many aides as they needed. General Orders No. 15, dated headquarters St. Louis, September 20, 1861, announced a sensible list. Chief of staff was Brigadier-General A. Asboth. General John A. Dix wrote the elder Blair on September 23 that he voted with Jessie on the question of Asboth. "I think him a very able man as an engineer and he is certainly very intelligent on general subjects." (Blair-Lee Papers.) Frémont's military secretary was Colonel John H. Eaton, later noted for his work with the freedmen. Among the others were Brigadier-General Justus McKinstry as assistant quartermaster-general, and Colonel John T. Fiala as chief topographical engineer. George E. Waring thought highly of the staff. "Frémont," he wrote Frederick Law Olmsted on October 31, 1861, "is hampered in every way, but he has good heart of it, and does more than could be expected under the circumstances. Asboth is a good engineer and plans well. Fortunately General Albert, his confidential adviser, is a man of excellent executive ability, and our Division is consequently in excellent condition for a fight." (Olmsted Papers, Library of Congress.) The most dubious element in the staff were several politicians, notably Representative Owen Lovejoy, who were probably forced on Frémont.

The origins of the quarrel between Frémont and Frank P. Blair, Jr., were complex. Frémont, General Justus McKinstry, Colonel I. C. Woods, and others declared that it began when McKinstry refused to make a $750,000 contract with two of Blair's friends, one Gurney of Chicago and ex-Mayor How of St. Louis, after Blair had strongly pressed the matter (Committee on the Conduct of the War, III, 202). Frémont also emphasized the elder Blair's arrogant demand that Frank be given an appointment which was outside Frémont's power—"I shall expect you to exert your utmost influence to carry my points, and now, to begin, I want to have Frank made a militia major-general for the State of Missouri." (This Blair letter is in the Frémont Papers at the University of California.) Frank, for his part, declared that he became convinced of Frémont's in-

competence (as Schofield and John H. Eaton also declared).
On both sides this oversimplifies the dispute. The two men were
temperamentally incompatible. Frank was shrewd, direct, prac-
tical, aggressive, and imperious; Frémont was erratic, impetuous, and imaginative. Both were proud and hot-tempered.
Frank, now recognized nationally as the principal savior of the
Union cause in the State, expected to continue to dominate
Missouri; Frémont had no intention of letting his own authority
be weakened. In dealing with the lukewarm General Harney,
Frank had shown how quickly, using his father and brother in
Washington, he could break an opponent. Returning to Missouri in August from Congress, he expected to have his wishes
treated as commands, and was irritated by the independent
course of Frémont and Jessie. Motives on both sides were
mixed. But essentially both men were ambitious for power and
prestige; each became jealously suspicious of the other; and in
the confused Missouri situation, with radical and conservative
parties already forming, "charcoals" and "claybanks," it was
easy for each to misconstrue the other's actions.

Frémont's proclamation announcing that the property of
Missourians actively aiding the Confederacy would be confiscated, and their slaves, if any, freed, was in part a military
measure designed to help stamp out the horrible guerrilla warfare then raging; in part a declaration that he stood with the
radicals or "charcoals." To what extent it was encouraged by
Lovejoy, who on July 8 had offered in Congress a resolution forbidding Union soldiers to halt or return fugitive slaves, we do
not know. To what extent it was the product of sheer impetuosity—the impetuosity of a harried, overworked general who sat
up all night worrying over guerrilla outrages, worrying over
demands for troops, arms, and wagons when he had none to
give, worrying over the clamor of soldiers for pay when money
was lacking, worrying over the problem of keeping rebellious
counties in check once he concentrated his army to march
against Price—we can only guess. It was a cardinal blunder.
Confiscation was a subject for Congress, and emancipation Lin-

coln rightly regarded as a question for himself. Perhaps Frémont did not realize how his action would reverberate through
the country.

That proclamation at once made a new enemy for Frémont
in the Administration. Attorney-General Bates, who hated all
the Blairs as a set of "tricky politicians" (*Diary*, 291), but
who stood with the conservatives in Missouri, now turned violently against the general. "I have demanded the recall of
General Frémont—possibly with too much emphasis, and too
often repeated," he wrote J. O. Brodhead of Missouri on September 28 (Brodhead Papers, Missouri Historical Society).
Of course the radicals in Washington vigorously defended the
proclamation. William Pitt Fessenden of Maine wrote that it
had electrified the country as a statesmanlike stroke. Ben
Wade, when Lincoln overruled it, burst out angrily to Zack
Chandler that the President was universally condemned and
execrated in the North. "I have no doubt that he has done more
injury to the cause of the Union, receding from the stand taken
by Frémont, than McDowell did by retreating from Bull Run."
Lincoln's sagacious friend, Orville H. Browning, himself far
from a radical, and later in Andrew Johnson's Cabinet, sent
the President on September 30, 1861, a letter warmly defending
the general. He wrote (Browning Papers, Illinois State Historical Library) from his home in Quincy, Illinois:

My acquaintance with him has been very limited, and I have had
no personal feeling in the matter. If he was honestly and faithfully
doing his duty, justice to him and regard for the country alike required that he should be sustained.

There was much complaint and clamor against him, and as I am
not quick to take up evil report I went twice to St. Louis to see and
learn for myself all that I could. It is very probable he has made
some mistakes, but in the main he seemed to be taking his measures
wisely and well. Many of the charges against him appeared to me
frivolous, and I do not know of anyone who could take his position
and do better amid the surrounding difficulties, and was confident
his removal at the time and under the circumstances would be dam-

aging both to the administration and the cause. Hence I wrote you, as I thought it my duty to do, certainly not intending any impertinent interference with executive duties, or expecting what I said to have any greater scope than friendly suggestion.

His proclamation in my opinion embodies a true and important principle which the government cannot afford to abandon, and with your permission, and with all deference to your opinions so clearly stated, I will venture a few suggestions in regard to it.

It is very important that the law which governs the case should be certainly and clearly understood, but either you have greatly misunderstood it, or I have. According to my understanding of it, it does not deal with the relations between the government and its citizens at all. It does not deal with citizens, but public enemies. It does not touch a legislative function, but only declares a pre-existing law, and denounces consequences which that law has already attached to given acts, and which would follow as well without the proclamation as with it. It was neither based on the act of Congress of August 6th nor in collision with it, but had reference to a totally different class of cases, provided for long ago by the political law of nations. . . .

It . . . rests upon the well ascertained and universally acknowledged principles of international law as its foundation.

But the power of the Blairs and of Bates, with their free access to Lincoln, far outweighed that of Browning, Wade, and Chandler. When Frank's formal charges against Frémont came, Montgomery Blair took them to the White House and read them to the President. Frémont's family later believed that the three Blairs, plotting the general's fall, enlisted General David Hunter and Adjutant-General Lorenzo Thomas for the purpose. Frémont had seven large boxes, full of wartime letters and documents, which were destroyed in a fire in the Morrell Warehouse in New York in 1877. "If you could have seen the statements of prominent men of that era, their conversations with Lincoln and others high in authority," Major Frank Frémont wrote the author in 1927, "you would know that the above combination was not to examine, but to determine on the best way to get rid of Frémont without implicating Lincoln." Much more credible is the statement of George E. Waring, writing from Missouri to Frederick Law Olmsted, October 31, 1861, that several regular army officers, notably John Pope and David Hunter, deliberately acted against Frémont through jealousy.

Frémont always believed that Brigadier-General John Pope, given orders a week before the fall of Lexington to march to its relief, could have done so but for his desire to injure his commander. Pope's capacity for negligence later proved extraordinary. When in 1862 he was removed from command of the Army of the Potomac, McClellan hailed this as "retributive justice." (W. S. Myers, *McClellan*, 351.) This boastful officer held peculiar political ideas, believing that Illinois should maintain a State army, and use it to gain a dominant position in the nation. He had written Senator Lyman Trumbull, July 6, 1861 (Trumbull Papers):

Illinois, if properly cared for, occupies today a most peculiar and commanding position in this country. On the one side Missouri has as much as she can do to take care of herself, while Iowa, Minnesota, and Wisconsin have had their troops drawn off for service eastward. On the other hand, Ohio and Indiana have been depleted of their volunteers for service in Western Virginia. Illinois so far stands nearly intact with a powerful force of nearly 20,000 men in the field.

If this force can be kept together and properly officered and commanded, upon Illinois will devolve largely the reconquest of the Valley of the Mississippi. Where she moves, with such a force, she will of necessity stand first—and hers will be the voice which controls the warlike operations in this valley.

If we can be kept together we shall constitute two-thirds of any army sent south from this region and our position and influence will dominate in any settlement of affairs west of the Alleghenys. To secure this vital object to our State I have been working from the beginning for some *head* to our troops, even if it be a wooden one— some commander who shall be a citizen and native of this State, and who shall move to the execution of any great military operation with the concentrated forces of Illinois.

For this reason also I have objected whenever I could exercise any influence to the separation of any isolated regiments from our troops. I deem this object vital to our military reputation and efficiency, and I appeal to you to interfere against the system which is now demoralizing us—frittering away our strength—subjecting our volunteers to the most obscure and odious service—and absolutely destroying the identity of the State. We want a military commander of our own troops, who shall have full authority in this State.

Although we have force enough on foot for two Major Generals and at least four Brigadiers, only two Brigadiers have been appointed and neither of them has been assigned to duty. Give us a Major General and one of our own people, to whom the welfare and reputation of our State are dear, and who can enable us to move with the whole military force of Illinois.

I feel deeply on the subject. . . .

Pope believed that *he* should be the major-general of the dominating Illinois army. He was perhaps just as lukewarm in Frémont's service as Fitz-John Porter later proved to be in John Pope's. He at any rate escaped the court-martial that befell Porter; but Frémont felt so strongly that he declined to serve under Pope in the Virginia theater.

Samuel D. Sturgis was also accused by Frémont of insubordination. Ordered to march from Mexico, Mo., to the relief of Lexington, he approached the town, heard rumors of Price's superior force, and hastily retired. Grave as the charge is, we have reason for crediting it. Sturgis, though a Northerner by birth, had strong social sympathy for Southerners. "He has been accustomed, we are assured," said the New York *Tribune* editorially on June 30, 1862, "to protest that the only gentlemen in the country are those of the South, and that when he died he intended to have his body carried to the South and buried there." When Senator Zack Chandler of Michigan criticized McClellan, Sturgis got considerable publicity by calling the radical leader "a liar, scoundrel, and coward." As a West Pointer and a strong Democrat, Sturgis had reasons for wishing to see Frémont fail.

At Second Manassas, Sturgis distinguished himself by a display of malevolence toward his commander, John Pope, whom he hated as McClellan's successor. As that terrible battle closed, Pope and his defeated troops found themselves on Sunday, August 31, moving under a drizzling rain back into the entrenchments built at Centreville the year before by the Confederates after Bull Run. The terrible toils and sufferings of the campaign had ended in futility; the death and maiming of hosts of northern soldiers had all been in vain. As darkness fell, Sturgis, with his reserve division, reported to Pope's headquarters. According to Franz Sigel, the commanding general called out to him in the despairing voice of a man for whom the game is lost: "Too late, Sammy, too late!" And Sturgis harshly replied: "Damn it, didn't I tell you that all that was necessary for you to hang yourself was to give you plenty of rope?" (Jacob Picard, MS Life of Franz Sigel.)

Sturgis was one of the men with whose conduct at the battle of Fredericksburg General Ambrose E. Burnside was dissatisfied; and on January 23, 1863, in General Order No. 8, which Lincoln did not approve and which therefore remained ineffective, Burnside included Sturgis among a group of officers relieved from duty because they "can be of no further service to this army." (*Battles and Leaders*, III, 216.) The evidence shows that when Sturgis served a commander he liked, such as McClellan at Antietam, he fought well; but under a commander he disliked, he fought badly or not at all.

The condition of the Union forces in Missouri by October was one of real and rising efficiency. Frémont concentrated a large command at Jefferson City, which he and his staff reached September 27. Though a thousand rotten wagons sent him from the East broke down, by October 7 all his troops were on the march to Tipton. Supply depots were established at Jefferson City (two million rations) and Tipton (one million), but the general expected to subsist largely on the country, paying loyal citizens and confiscating from the disloyal. He intended to move with great rapidity to the Arkansas line.

Sterling Price, with booty and prisoners, had quickly retreated from Lexington to join Ben McCulloch's forces in

southwestern Missouri. Taken together, they would have but
about 17,000 men, and Frémont believed that by bringing them
to battle in that area he could crush them. He had written
Winfield Scott just after Lexington that he hoped to crush
Price either before or after his junction with McCulloch. His
five divisions under Pope, Sigel, McKinstry, Hunter, and
Asboth were directed to concentrate at Springfield, and all but
one of the five commanders gave energetic cooperation. The
exception was Pope, whose letters show a spirit approaching
insubordination. Even after the main force reached Springfield
in southwestern Missouri, the lagging Pope was convinced that
the march was preposterous. "The prospect before us is appalling, and we seem to be led by madmen," he wrote Hunter on
October 26, 1861. The fact was, however, that Frémont's
troops were in high spirits, enthusiastically loyal to their general, eager for battle, and expectant of victory. Many in St.
Louis held the same faith. The journalist, John F. Hume, in
his reminiscences (*The Abolitionist,* 1905), declares that if
Frémont had been permitted to hold his Western command a
little longer, he would have scored a brilliant military success.

That was also strongly the opinion of the St. Louis educator
William T. Harris, who defended Frémont's military record at
every point. (Kurt F. Leidecker, *Yankee Teacher: The Life of
William Torrey Harris,* 201–204.)

It is a fact, though one denied or ignored in most histories,
that the Confederate forces were ready to give battle. Price
wrote Albert Sidney Johnston on November 7 that although
Frémont's estimated force of 35,000 to 40,000 men, with 100
guns, far outnumbered his army, he and McCulloch had agreed
to make a stand at Pineville, trusting to the rugged country to
compensate for their inadequate numbers. Price actually could
not retreat farther than the Arkansas line, because his troops
would not fight outside Missouri. The two generals, McCulloch
states in his report on the campaign, dated December 22, 1861,
met midway between their forces; "where it was agreed upon
by all the Mo. Genls that we should await an attack from the

enemy, the ground to be selected by Genl Price and myself."
(Price in *Official Records*, I, III, 732; McCulloch's report in
Missouri Historical Review, 1932, p. 354 ff.)

Both Confederate leaders were disheartened by the bad state
of their commands. "Our combined forces cannot cope with
them (the Federals) in numbers," declared Price to the governor of Arkansas. "Men, men are now what we want. . . ."
His Missourians, he informed Jefferson Davis, were half-fed,
half-clothed, half-armed. McCulloch, speaking contemptuously
of the Missouri militia as undisciplined, officered largely by
politicians, and ill-equipped, states that the Arkansas men got
on badly with them—"but little cordiality of feeling between
the two armies." (*Official Records*, I, III, 731–734.) Nearly
5,000 Missourians, their time up, were ready to disband. It is
evident that Frémont risked far less than Washington supposed
by his advance toward Arkansas. He might have cleared all
Missouri of the enemy, and by a battle at Pineville have won
the victory that early the next year was won at Pea Ridge near
by. But on November 2, Frémont, to the wrath of his troops,
was relieved.

President Lincoln, in his assignment of the command to
Hunter, had left future operations to the judgment of that
commander, but had stated his opinion that the best plan would
be to give up the pursuit, divide the main army into two corps,
post one at Sedalia and the other at Rolla, and drill and equip
the men. Hunter consulted his subordinates. McKinstry,
Asboth, and Sigel were for advancing; Pope was noncommittal
(Committee on the Conduct of the War, III, 240). Hunter
turned back. Sigel later called this decision "an outrage without parallel in history." As soon as the retreat of Hunter and
Pope became known, he wrote, the Union people of southwestern Missouri were struck with terror and despair. Within a
radius of more than fifty miles, abandoning all nonportable
property, they flocked into the Union lines at Springfield. Then,
as the Federal forces retreated from Springfield, the woebegone, impoverished mass of fugitives, including nearly every

family in the city who had sympathized with the national cause, took to the roads with the troops—refugees and beggars, without shelter, clothing, or adequate food.

A friend of Sam Ward's, writing from St. Louis, November 25, similarly declared that Hunter's retreat had plunged Missouri into a sorry mess. Price and McCulloch were rapidly reoccupying the country they had evacuated; they could threaten Rolla, Jefferson City, and Leavenworth as they had done after Wilson's Creek; they could lay waste the country up to the Union encampments (S. L. M. Barlow Papers, Columbia University). Sigel believed that if the Union army which Hunter took from Frémont had thrust hard at the enemy at Cassville and Pineville, it might have won a great victory and completely liberated the State. As it was, the Confederates had their will of southwestern Missouri for months.

Thus the Missouri chapter of the war in 1861 remained a dreary series of blunders to the end. For the miscalculations, errors, and failures blame has to be widely distributed. The War Department was blameworthy for failing to supply arms, and the Treasury, money, to the West. McClellan was blameworthy for detaching an important part of Frémont's force, at a critical moment, to meet an entirely imaginary threat in Virginia. Frémont and Frank Blair were censurable for quarreling so violently and for thinking almost as much of their private feud as of defeating the enemy. Francis P. Blair, Sr., and Montgomery Blair were at fault for throwing themselves so headlong into Frank's duel. John Pope was to blame for a disaffected spirit which approached insubordination. Hunter could be criticized for his eagerness to replace Frémont, and his hurried reversal of Frémont's orders—he knowing well that a victory with Frémont's army would have gone far toward showing that the replacement was a mistake. The patient, generous Lincoln appears better than anyone else in this unhappy scene. He did his best to inform himself upon the tangled situation in that distant area, and acted with sagacity upon the facts as he saw them.

Senator Ben Wade of Ohio went too far when he told Charles
A. Dana, February 3, 1862: "No public man, since Admiral
Byng was sacrificed by a weak and wicked administration to
appease the wrath of an indignant people, has suffered so unjustly as General Frémont. His persecution will prove the
darkest page in our history." (Dana Papers, Library of Congress.) But Greeley had some warrant for writing his wife,
October 27, 1861, that Frémont had accomplished *something*
with eight or ten million dollars, whereas McClellan had done
nothing with ten times the sum. And Senator James W. Grimes
of Iowa, who had not wanted to see Frémont appointed, decided, after a minute scrutiny of his record in Missouri, that
he was guiltless of the main allegations against him, and the
victim of "a regular conspiracy to destroy his influence in the
country and with the army." (William Salter, *Life of Grimes*,
152–156.)

Frémont's Withdrawal from the Presidential Campaign, 1864

For the history given in Chapter XXXIII, two corroborative
pieces of evidence have been unearthed. One is a long-forgotten
letter by David H. Jerome, a close associate of Senator Zachariah Chandler, in the New York *Nation*, September 26, 1889;
the other a manuscript letter of Montgomery Blair's to John
A. C. Gray of New York, December 12, 1864, of which the
late Henry G. Gray sent the author a copy.

Jerome's explicit statement supports the account in this book
at every point. It asserts that Ben Wade, when approached by
Zach Chandler early in September, 1864, agreed to desist from
his opposition to Lincoln and support the President, if only his
colleague in assailing Lincoln's Reconstruction plans, Henry
Winter Davis of Maryland, should be satisfied. Chandler then
approached Congressman Davis, who agreed to rally to the
Republican standard on one condition—that his personal enemy
and political antagonist, Montgomery Blair, should be dismissed from the Cabinet. Chandler went to Lincoln. He
assented. Thereupon Chandler journeyed to New York, accom-

panied by Jerome, to open negotiations with Frémont and his associates. The two made their headquarters at the Astor House; they were efficiently aided by George Wilkes, editor of *The Spirit of the Times*; and they prevailed upon the Frémont group to agree to the general's withdrawal, without condition or reward.

"At one time during the negotiations," writes Jerome, "Mr. Bryant of the *Evening Post,* feeling the necessity of harmony, and fearing that the opposition to Mr. Lincoln in certain quarters might prove disastrous to his reelection, had in type an editorial for his paper advising Mr. Lincoln's withdrawal, and a united Republican support of Gen. Frémont or some other available candidate; but, by the vigorous assurances of Senator Chandler that harmony could better be reached in the support of Mr. Lincoln, the editorial was withheld from publication."

The night after they had made the arrangement with Frémont's friends, Senator Chandler and David H. Jerome went to Washington, arriving in the morning. They at once called at the White House, where they were "anxiously and eagerly received by the President." When Chandler had announced the result of his negotiations, "Mr. Lincoln at once fulfilled his part by addressing a note to Mr. Blair asking his resignation (which was promptly tendered), thereby closing the dangerous breach, and making certain his reelection."

It is clear from this explicit letter, which Jerome writes is based on both his personal recollection and the authority of Senator Chandler, that Frémont made no bargain and asked no price. It was Henry Winter Davis, reinforced by Ben Wade, who demanded Montgomery Blair's head.

This conclusion is reinforced by Montgomery Blair's remarkable letter of 1864 to his friend Gray. Blair, licking his wounds and nursing his wrath, was eager for a bit of revenge upon Secretary Stanton. He wrote:

Mr. Sumner told me on Friday last that Senator Chandler had told him that I had been removed in consequence of his reporting to

Lincoln a conversation between himself and Gen'l Frémont, the purport of which was that Frémont agreed to withdraw in the event of my removal.

I have two reasons for discrediting this so far as it relates to Frémont. The first is your statement to me. Second, W. O. Bartlett, who has always had a kindness to Frémont, met me and told me that Frémont denied having made any such proposition directly or indirectly. My impression is that it was a suggestion of Stanton acted on by Chandler who has been very intimate with Stanton for some time. I wish you could see Frémont and report the matter to him and see what he says about it. If it is false, I would like you to get him to write you a letter denying it as broadly as the facts will admit of his doing. Frémont owes nothing to Stanton and he is aware of that I presume and would not be unwilling to see him bite the dust. Having got his revenge on me through Stanton he may now be willing to have Stanton come to grief also.

I don't know that I can fix the lie on Stanton, but I shall bring it pretty near when I get it fixed on Chandler. I want you to show Frémont's letter to Old Abe when you come on and tell him the whole story.

To this discreditable epistle Montgomery Blair appended the form of the letter which he wished Frémont to sign! Of course he was mistaken in thinking Stanton the prime mover; mistaken also in thinking that Chandler was not concerned. But his letter brings in two witnesses, John A. C. Gray and W. O. Bartlett, to add their testimony that Frémont never stooped to bargain with Lincoln in this matter.

Frémont and His Retired Pay

Our last glimpse of Frémont, in a letter to John A. C. Gray, February 27, 1889, is as a petitioner in Washington for his pay as a retired major-general of the army. "I find good will here," he wrote, "and plenty of it, but I am afraid that we are too near the end of the session. I could not get away from New York until yesterday afternoon. Senator Palmer's carriage met me at the station here and I am staying with them. I went with him to the Capitol this morning and we saw some members of the Committee on Rules. All are friendly except Reed of Maine, who says he will interpose no obstruction. But the difficulty is in the mass of business which interferes to prevent the Rules Committee from discriminating in favor of any particular bill. I think I shall know positively tomorrow." The morrow brought postponement. It was not for more than a year, within a few months of his death, that he was placed on the retired list with pay.

Frémont's Children

JESSIE BENTON FRÉMONT'S Bible lists the births and deaths of her children. The roster is as follows: Elizabeth Benton Frémont, born Washington, November 13, 1842; Benton Frémont, born Washington, July 24, 1848; John Charles Frémont, born in California, April 19, 1851; Anne Beverley Frémont, born Paris, February 1, 1853; Frank Preston Frémont, born Washington, May 17, 1854. Benton Frémont died on the Missouri River, October 6, 1848—his being the grave that lay between Jessie and General Kearny; Anne Beverley Frémont died at Silver Spring, Maryland, July 12, 1853. Below the list Jessie wrote: "Care and sorrow and childbirth pain."

Corruption in St. Louis, 1861

AT THE OUTBREAK of the Civil War few men foresaw the wide scope or prolonged duration of the conflict. Lincoln appointed to the Secretaryship of War a politician, Simon Cameron, who was quite incompetent for the proper discharge of his duties. The result was that, amid general confusion, months passed before the government in Washington appreciated the necessity for setting up a central purchasing agency for ordnance stores, and months more elapsed before order began to appear in government buying. Immediately after the firing on Fort Sumter volunteer military units sprang up all over the North under state and city auspices. Union Defense Committees sprang up alongside them. The state and local governments and these Defense Committees began frantically buying arms, clothing, and other equipment. In an ill-stocked market, they drove prices sky-high.

Not until July was far advanced did the highly competent Chief of Ordnance, James W. Ripley, delegate Major P. V. Hagner to take charge of War Department purchases from private contractors in New York. Hagner was a blunt, sharp-spoken, conscientious military man, impatient with the inefficiency and chicanery about him, and so stubborn in his business dealings that, as he himself later testified, other buyers often took arms away from him by topping his price. When he reached New York on July 13, 1861, he found a scene of wild confusion. States, cities, Defense Committees, generals, colonels, and speculators were bidding frantically against each other and the Federal Government. The market was plagued with middlemen and profiteers. Men who had no arms were struggling to land government contracts at high figures, hoping afterwards to make a profitable arrangement with some manufacturer. The confusion spread to Europe; it was said that five northern agents took the same boat to England and were soon bidding against each other there! The same confusion spread to St. Louis.

In St. Louis the principal purchaser was Justus McKinstry. He had been assigned to that city as quartermaster by Secretary of War Floyd; removed by Secretary Holt; and replaced by Secretary Cameron long before Frémont arrived. Frank and Montgomery Blair were responsible for his reappointment, the latter going personally to Cameron to obtain it.[1] Before Frémont reached St. Louis, McKinstry had practically been given *carte blanche* in purchases by the authorities in Washington. E. S. Sibley, Acting Quartermaster-General, wrote him early in June: "You are authorized without reference to this office, under his direction [the commanding general's] to procure such means of transportation as he may deem neces-

[1] House Exec. Doc. No. 94, 37th Cong., 2d Sess., p. 15.

sary, practising a sound economy in making your purchases, and if the exigency is not immediate or pressing, conforming to the law or regulations in relation to the manner of making purchases or contracts for supplies."

On June 25th the newly appointed Quartermaster-General Meigs wrote again: "The department approves your course, ... but desires that while economy is right, there be no room left for charging the failure of any military movement upon a want of promptness and efficiency in the quartermaster's department."[2] McKinstry was shortly brought under great pressure by Frank P. Blair to award contracts and make purchases from a long list of Blair's friends and political supporters.[3] Meanwhile Frémont himself, earnestly trying to find supplies for ill-clothed, ill-mounted, and totally unarmed troops, made purchases on his own responsibility with greater regard to speed than economy. Some were very indiscreet; none was dishonest.

The most famous was the Hall carbine purchase, given much publicity because it involved J. P. Morgan, Sr. Frémont knew when he returned home to America of the appalling shortage of arms. He spent much of early July in New York trying to obtain guns, and did order 23,000 stand which were never delivered to him.[4] When he reached St. Louis he found his recruits defenseless. On July 29th he telegraphed Hagner: "We must have arms—any arms, no matter what." But Hagner replied that after Bull Run the government had ordered all arms diverted to the Potomac! The 23,000 stand Frémont had bought went there. From that moment Frémont in desperation bought arms wherever he could find them. On August 5th an eastern arms dealer named Simon Stevens telegraphed Frémont that he had "five thousand Hall's rifles, cast-steel carbines, breech-loading, new, at $22, government standard, fifty-eight," and invited an order.[5] Frémont had used Hall's carbine on

[2] See pamphlet, *Vindication of Quartermaster-General McKinstry*, p. 12.
[3] See appendix to the *Vindication*.
[4] *Battles and Leaders*, I, p. 278, 279.
[5] War Department records.

one of his western expeditions and liked it. Stevens's telegram seemed manna from heaven. On August 6th he telegraphed that he would take the 5,000 pieces, and wanted them by express, not by freight. For them he promised to pay the $22 demanded. Before the end of August, 2,500 of the carbines had been shipped to Frémont, and the second 2,500 were all in St. Louis by Sunday, September 15th. When Frémont bought them he did not know that they had recently been sold by the incompetent and confused War Department itself to a man named Eastman, who had in turn let Stevens (financed in part by J. P. Morgan, Sr., have them. How could Frémont know it? The government's sale of these pieces, thoroughly good though slightly outmoded, was a piece of the grossest idiocy.

This transaction was subsequently inquired into by a number of government bodies. A select committee of Congress reported on the subject December 17, 1861.[6] It cleared Frémont, saying that he had acted unwisely but probably "under some misapprehension as to the nature of the purchase of the arms." It estimated that the pieces were really worth $12.50 each. Early in 1862 Stanton created a special Commission on Ordnance Claims and Contracts. In June, 1862, this body held that $65,228 was a fair price for the carbines and should be paid. Later still, in the Court of Claims, it was decided that Frémont had acted with full legal right and no impropriety in buying the arms.[7] Those who declared he had acted illegally were thus confuted.

Whether he paid too much for the carbines is a matter on which judgments might well differ. Government records showed that while he was paying $22 for newly rifled carbines (pieces that had cost the government $17.50 when new and been rifled subsequently), the Ordnance Bureau in Washington was paying $35 for Sharp's carbines, $32.50 for Smith's, and $35

---

[6] House Report No. 2, 37th Cong., 2d Sess.

[7] Stevens vs. U.S., Cases Decided in the Court of Claims, December term, 1866, Vol. 2, pp. 95-103.

for Burnside's.[8] The Bureau bought 10,000 of Smith's pieces at $32.50 on August 27, 1861, and 7,500 of Burnside's at $35 the same day. Yet it did not need arms so badly, and did not have to have them in such a hurry, as Frémont.

Beyond doubt there was great waste and some corruption in St. Louis, as in Washington and New York, in connection with arms purchases; but none of the corruption was Frémont's, and the waste was largely attributable to the War Department's own inefficiency.

APPENDIX III

The Writings of John Charles Frémont, with Related Material

A REPORT on the Exploration of the Country Lying between the Missouri River and the Rocky Mountains on the Line of the Kansas and Great Platte Rivers, by J. C. Frémont, of the Corps of Topographical Engineers. 27th Congress, Third Session, Senate Document 243. Washington, 1843. Pp. 207.

Report of the Exploring Expedition to the Rocky Mountains in the Year 1842, and to Oregon and North California in the Years 1843–44, by Brevet Captain J. C. Frémont. . . . under the Orders of Colonel J. J. Abert, Chief of the Topographical Bureau. 28th Congress, Second Session, House Executive Document 166. Washington: Blair & Rives, Printers, 1845. Pp. 583, maps.

The Same. 28th Congress, Second Session, Senate Executive Document 174. Washington: Gales & Seaton, Printers, 1845.

(Both editions of the Report contain scientific materials by John Torrey on botany, and James Hall on geology and organic remains. The Senate edition only contains the astronomical and meteorological observations. Other editions of the Report are those of H. Polkinhorn, Washington, 1845; D. Appleton, New York, 1845; G. S. Appleton, Philadelphia, 1846; and Hurst & Company, New York, 1885.)

Charges and Specifications and Findings and Sentence of a General Court Martial in the Case of Lieutenant Colonel John C. Frémont. U.S. War Department General Orders No. 7, February 17, 1848. Washington, 1848. Pp. 28.

Defence of Lieutenant Colonel J. C. Frémont, Before the Military Court Martial, Washington, January, 1848. Washington (?), 1848. Pp. 78.

Message of the President of the United States Communicating the Proceedings of the Court Martial in the Trial of Lieutenant Colonel Frémont. 30th Congress, First Session, Senate Executive Document 33. Washington (?), 1848. Pp. 447.

Geographical Memoir upon Upper California, in Illustration of his Map of Oregon and California: Addressed to the Senate of the United States, by John C. Frémont. Washington: Wendell & Van Benthuysen, Printers, 1848. Pp. 67, with folding map.

Oregon and California. The Exploring Expedition to the Rocky Mountains, Oregon, and California, by Brevet Colonel J. C. Frémont, to which is added a Description of the Physical Geography of California, with Recent Notices of the Gold Region from the Latest and Most Authentic Sources. Buffalo: G. H. Derby & Company, 1849, 1851. Pp. 456.

Central Railroad Route to the Pacific. Letter of J. C. Frémont to the Editors of the *National Intelligencer*, Communicating Some General Results of a Recent Winter Expedition Across the Rocky Mountains, for a Survey of a Route to the Pacific. 33rd Congress, Second Session, House Misc. Doc. 8. 33rd Congress, First Session, Senate Misc. Doc. 67. Washington, 1854. Pp. 7.

The Mariposas Estate. Papers by J. D. Whitney, J. Adelberg, Frederic Claudet, and T. W. Park, Showing the Condition and Resources of the Estate. Preface by J. C. Frémont, Frederick Billings. London: Whittingham & Wilkins, 1861. Pp. 63, with folding map.

Memoirs of My Life, by John Charles Frémont. Including in the Narrative Five Journeys of Western Exploration during the Years 1842, 1843–44, 1845–46–47, 1848–49, 1853–54. Together with a sketch of the life of Senator Benton in connection with western expansion, by Jessie Benton Frémont. A retrospect of fifty years covering the most eventful periods of modern American history. With maps and colored plates. Volume I. Chicago and New York: Belford, Clarke & Company, 1887. Pp. 655 + xix, with maps, in part folding.

BIBLIOGRAPHICAL NOTE

The first three books written upon Frémont were campaign biographies. John Bigelow's *Life of John Charles Frémont* (1856) is a hasty compilation of about five hundred rather dull pages, eulogistic throughout. It, however, contains some documents of permanent value, including Commodore Stockton's report on his Pacific Coast operations, Frémont's defense before his court-martial, his letter from Taos in January, 1849, the Frémont-Wilkes correspondence, and his letter to the *National Intelligencer* on his expedition of 1854. S. M. Smucker issued *The Life of Colonel J. C. Frémont* in 1856. Charles Wentworth Upham's *Life, Explorations, and Public Services of John Charles Frémont* (1856), is a brief, clear, undistinguished compilation, also eulogistic. Two later volumes have been published. As a scientific and critical account of Frémont's explorations, Frederick S. Dellenbaugh's *Frémont and '49* (1914) is invaluable. The author is well acquainted with most of the country traversed. He identifies localities, furnishes information on topography, climate, and Indians, corrects many of Frémont's minor observations, explains others and presents a wealth of maps and pictures. The book, which virtually closes with 1850, is sympathetic. It contains a valuable bibliography. Cardinal L. Goodwin's *John Charles Frémont, An Explanation of his Career* (1930) is a brief and studiously hostile estimate.

Frémont's own *Memoirs of My Life* (1886) is based directly upon his reports, and chapters four to eleven inclusive add little to them. The first three chapters contain a rapid account of his education, early adventures, and work with Nicollet. The last four chapters deal, often sketchily yet with evident sincerity, with the events of 1845-46 in California up to the Capitulation of Couenga. The government published for Frémont in 1845 his *Report of the Exploring Expedition to the Rocky Mountains in the year 1842, and to Oregon and North California in the years 1843-44* (Senate Doc. 174, 28th Congress, 2d Session). It also published in 1848 his *Geographical Memoir upon Upper California, in Illustration of his Map of Oregon and California* (Senate Doc. 148, 30th Congress, 1st Session). Numerous commercial editions of Frémont's reports for 1842-45 were issued by publishers in the United States, England, Ireland, and Germany. References in the text are to the edition of George H. Derby & Company, *The Exploring Expedition to the Rocky Mountains, Oregon, and California* (1849), used because a copy furnished by the Frémont family contained certain corrections in Frémont's hand. This contains also the official report of Colonel Richard B. Mason on the gold regions.

Catherine Coffin Phillips has written an excellent biography of *Jessie Benton Frémont, A Woman Who Made History* (1935). All Jessie's own books, while highly readable, must be used with care, for she wrote rapidly and with an eye to dramatic effect. The most valuable are *The Story of the Guard* (1863), *A Year of American Travel* (1877), *Souvenirs of My Time* (1887), and *Far West Sketches* (1890). *The Recollections of Elizabeth Benton Frémont* (1912) compiled by E. T. Martin, have material of interest upon the years at Mariposa and at Prescott. A fairly full list of magazine publications by Jessie Benton Frémont is given in Mrs. Phillips's biography, pp. 350-352.

The Frémont manuscripts used by the author in preparing this volume were supplied him by Major Frank P. Frémont and other heirs, and were later sent by the author (with collateral material) to the Bancroft Library at the University of California. They fall into four groups: (1) a few letters of Thomas Hart Benton to his daughters; (2) a body of letters and autobiographical writings by Jessie Frémont; (3) a number of letters and memoranda by Frémont himself; and (4) the manuscript of perhaps 100,000 words to which I have referred as MS *Memoirs*. This was written chiefly by Mrs. Frémont, with some assistance from Major Frank P. Frémont upon the military chapters. In part, these memoirs were composed with General Frémont's direct assistance and supervision, and among his papers are a number of loose sheets dealing with moot points in his career. It is greatly to be regretted that these *MS Memoirs* are not more complete, and that the first volume of the published *Memoirs* did not meet with a sufficient sale to justify the issuance of the second.

The author has also made extensive use of manuscript material from other sources. The courtesy of Professors Herbert I. Priestley and Herbert E. Bolton enabled him to obtain much that was valuable from the Bancroft Library. The more important narratives by American settlers and others thus used are the *Narrative of John C. Frémont's Expedition in California in 1845-46, and Subsequent Events in California Down to 1853,* by Thomas S. Martin, one of Frémont's men (Cal. MSS. D. 122); the *Statement of William F. Swasey* (Cal. MSS. D. 200); the recollections of John Fowler of Napa County upon *The Bear Flag Revolt in California, 1846* (Cal. MSS. D. 83); and *California in 1846,* as related by William Hargrave, of Napa. The letters and reports of Thomas O. Larkin in the State Department in Washington were used, and Mr. R. L. Underhill of Berkeley kindly allowed the author to see his excellent manuscript life of Larkin. The author also saw the Larkin Papers in the Bancroft Library and obtained some copies. The long-lost papers of Edward Kern, recovered and now kept in the Huntington Library in San Marino, California, have been reprinted as the *Fort Sutter Papers* in a small edition edited by Seymour Dunbar; I have consulted the originals at the Huntington Library. In New York I have used the John Bigelow papers and Bigelow's unpublished diary. In the Library of Congress I have used the Welles MSS, the John Sherman MSS, the Washburne MSS, the Chase MSS, and other papers. The Gamble Papers in the Missouri Historical Society have kindly been searched for me by Miss Marguerite Potter.

Lists of printed books upon Frémont and the many events he touched are easily available. In my original two volumes on Frémont I included an eight-page bibliography. Good bibliographies may also be found in Mrs. Phillips's *Jessie Benton Frémont* and in Cardinal L. Goodwin's *Frémont;* while there is an excellent list of titles on the trans-Mississippi in E. W. Gilbert's *The Exploration of Western America, 1800-1850* (1933). H. R. Wagner's *The Plains and the Rockies: A Bibliography of Original Narratives of Travel and Adventure, 1800-1865* (1921), is, of course, invaluable.

INDEX

(1)